Kalīlah and Dimnah: Fables of Virtue and Vice

Letter from the General Editor

The Library of Arabic Literature makes available Arabic editions and English translations of significant works of Arabic literature, with an emphasis on the seventh to nineteenth centuries. The Library of Arabic Literature thus includes texts from the pre-Islamic era to the cusp of the modern period, and encompasses a wide range of genres, including poetry, poetics, fiction, religion, philosophy, law, science, travel writing, history, and historiography.

Books in the series are edited and translated by internationally recognized scholars. They are published as hardcovers in parallel-text format with Arabic and English on facing pages, as English-only paperbacks, and as downloadable Arabic editions. For some texts, the series also publishes separate scholarly editions with full critical apparatus.

The Library encourages scholars to produce authoritative Arabic editions, accompanied by modern, lucid English translations, with the ultimate goal of introducing Arabic's rich literary heritage to a general audience of readers as well as to scholars and students.

The publications of the Library of Arabic Literature are generously supported by Tamkeen under the NYU Abu Dhabi Research Institute Award G1003 and are published by NYU Press.

Philip F. Kennedy
General Editor, Library of Arabic Literature

كتاب كليلة ودمنة

عبد الله بن المقفّع

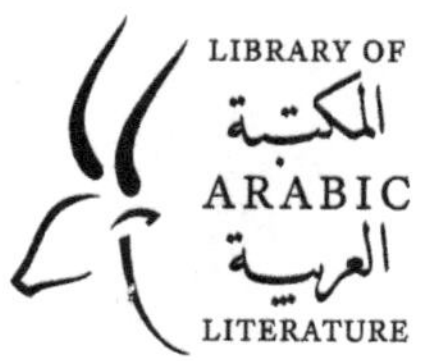

Kalīlah and Dimnah

Fables of Virtue and Vice

IBN AL-MUQAFFAʿ

Edited by
MICHAEL FISHBEIN

Translated by
MICHAEL FISHBEIN and JAMES E. MONTGOMERY

Volume editors
BEATRICE GRUENDLER
JAMES E. MONTGOMERY

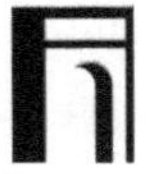

NEW YORK UNIVERSITY PRESS
New York

NEW YORK UNIVERSITY PRESS
New York

Library of Congress Cataloging-in-Publication Data

Names: Ibn al-Muqaffaʿ, -approximately 760 translator. | Fishbein, Michael, editor translator. | Montgomery, James E. (James Edward), 1962- translator.
Title: Kalīlah wa-Dimnah : fables of virtue and vice / Ibn al-Muqaffaʿ ; edited by Michael Fishbein ; translated by Michael Fishbein and James E. Montgomery = [Kitāb Kalīlah wa-Dimnah / ʿAbd Allāh ibn al-Muqaffaʿ].
Other titles: [Kitāb Kalīlah wa-Dimnah] | Kalīlah wa-Dimnah. English.
Description: New York : New York University Press, 2021. | Includes bibliographical references and index. | English translation and Arabic original text on facing pages.
Identifiers: LCCN 2021014622 | ISBN 9781479806539 (cloth) | ISBN 9781479806546 (ebook) | ISBN 9781479806560 (ebook)
Classification: LCC PJ7741.B5 E5 2021 | DDC 892.7/334--dc23
LC record available at https://lccn.loc.gov/2021014622

New York University Press books are printed on acid-free paper, and their binding materials are chosen for strength and durability.

Series design by Titus Nemeth.

Typeset in Tasmeem, using DecoType Naskh and Emiri.

Typesetting and digitization by Stuart Brown.

Manufactured in the United States of America
c10 9 8 7 6 5 4 3 2 1

Table of Contents

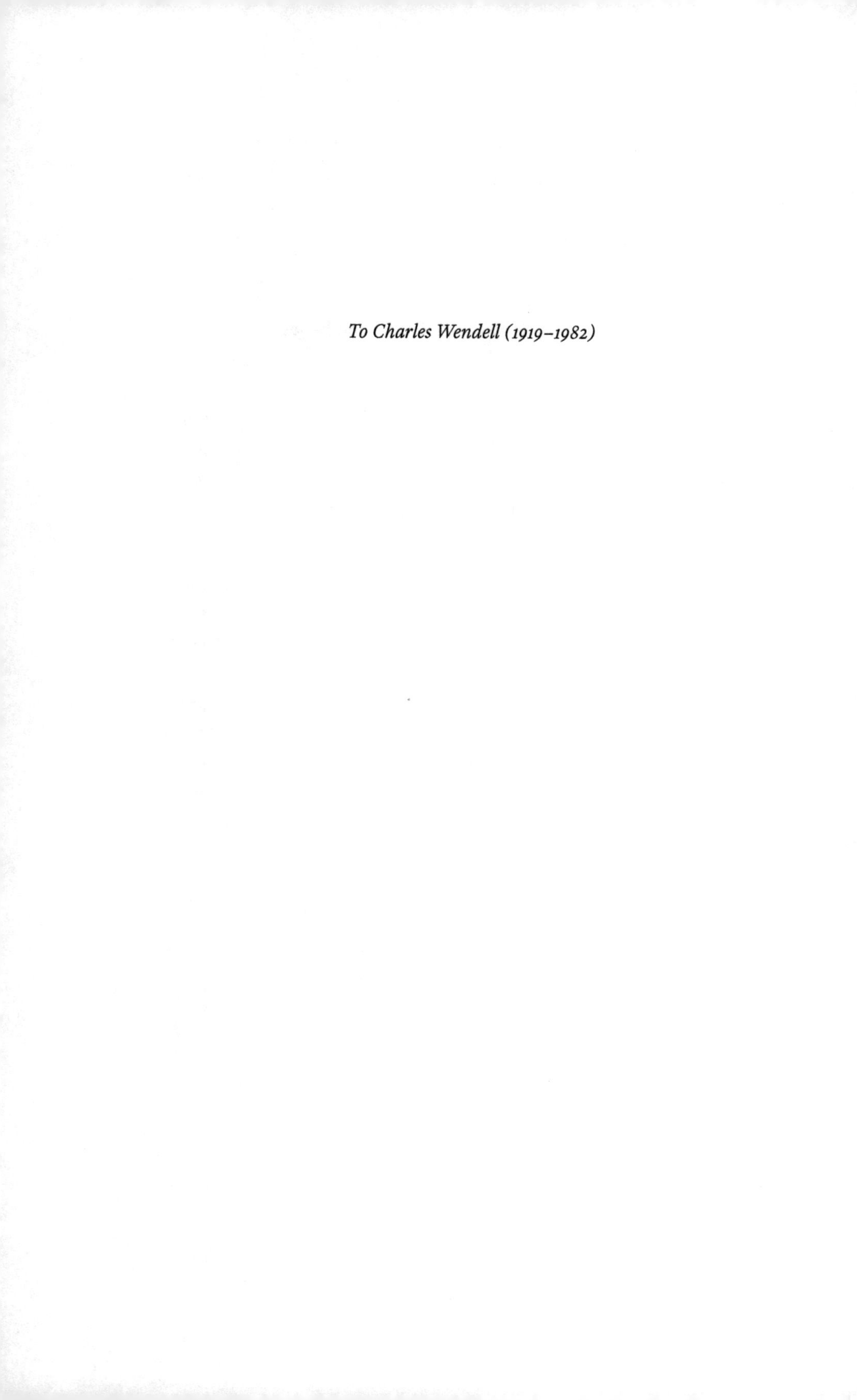

To Charles Wendell (1919–1982)

Acknowledgments

I owe an immense debt of gratitude to the late Charles Wendell (1919–82) of the University of California, Santa Barbara, who first drew my attention to the significance and beauty of *Kalīlah and Dimnah*, at a time when I was beginning my study of Arabic. Professor Wendell was in the process of preparing a translation of the work, based on ʿAzzām's text, at the time of his untimely death; sadly, his translation, left incomplete, never saw the light of day. Next, I wish to thank my teachers and colleagues at the University of California, Los Angeles (UCLA), and at the American University in Cairo. In particular, I'd like to thank Claude Audebert, who enthusiastically imparted to her students at UCLA the skills necessary to appreciate the beauty of Arabic literature. Anyone working today on the text of *Kalīlah and Dimnah* owes a tremendous debt of gratitude to Beatrice Gruendler of the Freie Universität Berlin, the director of the project Anonym-Classic, devoted to collecting and studying all the surviving texts of *Kalīlah and Dimnah*. Professor Gruendler and her associates have been constantly helpful in giving me access to the results of their research and in guiding the present edition and translation. James Montgomery of Cambridge University has been so constant a help with stylistic matters in English and with difficulties in the Arabic that I have asked him to accept the honor of being listed as co-translator. The staff of the Library of Arabic Literature, headed by editorial director Chip Rossetti, assistant editor Lucie M. Taylor, and digital production manager Stuart Brown, have shown constant understanding in tolerating my frequent requests for more time. Copious thanks are due to all those in the production staff of the Library of Arabic Literature, who worked so hard to make this volume a pleasure to read.

Michael Fishbein
Los Angeles, California

James Montgomery would like to thank Michael Fishbein for so generously acknowledging his contribution to the translation; Beatrice Gruendler for her vital interventions in the genesis of the project; the anonymous reviewer for many improvements to the book, especially the felicity of the English; Keith Miller for his copyediting panache; Stuart Brown for producing yet another glorious book; and Chip Rossetti and Lucie Taylor, without whose skill and dedication the Library of Arabic Literature could not function.

James E. Montgomery
Cambridge

Introduction

Ibn al-Muqaffaʿ: His Life and Works

Ibn al-Muqaffaʿ, who lived from about 102/720 to 139/757, was an author and translator of exceptional ability and broad interests who played a crucial role in mediating between the civilization of Sasanian Iran (AD 224–662) and the Islamic world of his day.[1] He was born in the Iranian province of Fārs into a wealthy Iranian family that had adapted to Arab and Muslim rule. Originally named Rōzbih, he took the name ʿAbdallāh upon his conversion to Islam, which must have occurred sometime after the Abbasid revolution in 132/749, his twenty-ninth year. He received a thorough education in the languages of two cultures: Persian and Arabic. The names of his Arabic teachers have been preserved, along with the fact that one was of Bedouin origin—the Bedouins were considered to speak the purest and most eloquent Arabic. The many translations from Middle Persian (Pahlavi) attributed to him testify to his mastery of the Iranian historical and literary tradition; his surviving Arabic works testify to his mastery of the Arabic language and to his broad intellectual interests, which included history, religion, political theory, law, philosophy, and literature.

His father, Dādūyah, a tax collector under the late Umayyads, acquired the surname al-Muqaffaʿ ("having a shriveled limb; cripple") as the result of being subjected to torture for misappropriation; hence ʿAbdallāh's surname, Ibn al-Muqaffaʿ ("Son of the Cripple"). Ibn al-Muqaffaʿ at first followed in his father's footsteps and served the Umayyad governors of Fārs and Kirmān provinces. After the overthrow of the Umayyads—the first Abbasid caliph, Abū l-ʿAbbās (surnamed al-Saffāḥ), came to power in 132/749—Ibn al-Muqaffaʿ attached himself to the service of the new caliph's uncle, ʿĪsā ibn ʿAlī ibn ʿAbdallāh ibn ʿAbbās, whom he served as *kātib*, or private secretary. It was a powerful political connection. One of ʿĪsā's brothers, ʿAbdallāh ibn ʿAlī, was the commander responsible for the defeat of the last Umayyad caliph, Marwān II, and for the elimination of much of the Umayyad family. Another of ʿĪsā's brothers, Sulaymān ibn ʿAlī, became governor of Basra, and it was there that Ibn al-Muqaffaʿ spent most of his life, in what was a center of intellectual ferment in the Arab-Islamic world until the founding of Baghdad in 145/762.

Few of Ibn al-Muqaffaʿ's works have survived. Some have been lost completely; others have survived only as excerpted or adapted by later authors.[2] The latter is the case with his translations from Pahlavi: works such as *The Book of Kings* (*Khwadāynāmag*), a royal chronicle; *The Book of Rules* (*Āyīnnāmah*), a picture of the customs of the Sasanian court; and *The Book of the Crown* (*Kitāb al-Tāj*), about the lives of the rulers of Iran, Anūsharwān in particular.[3] These works indicate that his translation of the collection of stories we know as *Kalīlah and Dimnah* was part of a larger interest in the cultural and historical heritage of Iran, not an isolated fascination with a single literary work.

Beyond its significance as a monument of Persian literary culture, *Kalīlah and Dimnah* may have been of interest to Ibn al-Muqaffaʿ for more specific reasons. One of his other surviving works, *The Great Book of Conduct* (*Kitāb al-Adab al-kabīr*),[4] resembles *Kalīlah and Dimnah* in purpose, if not in method: a section addressed to a prince offers advice about the skills, moral qualities, and conduct required in a successful ruler; a subsequent section describes the skills, moral qualities, and conduct appropriate to a ruler's minister or adviser; the final section deals with the value of friendship and proper relations between friends. Another surviving work, the *Epistle on the Caliph's Entourage* (*Risālah fī l-Ṣaḥābah*), gives practical advice to a ruler—apparently the second Abbasid caliph, al-Manṣūr (r. 136–58/754–75)—about the proper management of a variety of issues. The work also discusses more theoretical questions, particularly the nature and limits of caliphal authority in the context of the developing system of Islamic law.[5]

The relation between these two didactic works and *Kalīlah and Dimnah* is evident. Although the stories of *Kalīlah and Dimnah* are, on the surface, entertaining narratives, their underlying purpose, as Ibn al-Muqaffaʿ emphasizes in his Preface (Chapter 2 in this edition), is didactic: to inculcate certain skills and virtues, and warn against certain vices. The original Indian collection from which the Middle Persian book was assembled was explicitly addressed to the sons of a king, to teach them the skills needed for the proper governance of the state. The stories display the benefits of judiciousness (*ḥilm*) and careful examination of the facts (*tathabbut*) before acting; they warn against rash action. They stress the role of the good counselor, warn against incompetent or malicious counselors, and highlight the danger of rivalries among courtiers. Many of the animals who populate the book are, in effect, ministers giving advice to rulers, friends giving advice to friends, or wives giving advice to husbands. The book contains many set pieces in which successive advisers debate policy by giving competing advice to a ruler: the speeches offered by the advisers in Chapter 7 ("The Crows and the Owls") serve as an example. Other stories illustrate the importance of alliances for a common goal, even between former enemies, along with the limitations of such ad hoc alliances (for example, Chapter 10, "The Cat and the Rat").

Other aspects of the work that might have attracted Ibn al-Muqaffaʿ's interest were personal, religious, and philosophical. We have already mentioned his relatively late conversion from Zoroastrianism to Islam. Many readers of *Kalīlah and Dimnah* have interpreted the biography of Barzawayh,[6] the physician who procured and translated the text of *Kalīlah and Dimnah* for Anūsharwān (his autobiography appears here as Chapter 3, "The Chapter of Barzawayh the Physician"), as having been "enriched" by Ibn al-Muqaffaʿ to give a hint of his own religious development, particularly as regards a certain skepticism about all religious traditions, thus making the Persian physician a kind of alter ego for Ibn al-Muqaffaʿ. But given the disappearance of the Middle Persian text, such speculation, however attractive, cannot be proven.

The anecdotes transmitted in the works of Arabic historians and biographers focus on Ibn al-Muqaffaʿ's mastery of the Arabic language, including correcting others' mistakes, his generosity, his elegant lifestyle, his meticulousness in matters of food and cleanliness, and his wit. The latter, unfortunately, may have hastened his demise, as he is said to have ridiculed in scurrilous verses the very man who by an ironic turn of fate subsequently replaced his patron's brother, Sulaymān ibn ʿAlī, as governor of Basra and carried out Ibn al-Muqaffaʿ's execution.

One might have thought that Ibn al-Muqaffaʿ's close connection to the caliphal family would have protected him. The opposite turned out to be the case. Ibn al-Muqaffaʿ fell victim to a conflict within the ruling family. Upon the death of the first Abbasid caliph, al-Saffāḥ, in 136/754, ʿAbdallāh ibn ʿAlī, the brother of Ibn al-Muqaffaʿ's patron, refused to acknowledge the succession of his nephew al-Manṣūr and claimed the caliphate for himself. ʿAbdallāh ibn ʿAlī was defeated in 137/754 and fled to Basra, hoping to be protected by his brothers from the wrath of the new caliph. The situation was precarious: although al-Manṣūr seemed reluctant to take action against his rebellious uncle, in the absence of a formal safe-conduct (an *amān*) there was danger that al-Manṣūr might change his mind at any moment. ʿAbdallāh's brothers, ʿĪsā (who was Ibn al-Muqaffaʿ's patron) and Sulaymān, decided to obtain a formal promise of safety for their brother from al-Manṣūr, and commissioned Ibn al-Muqaffaʿ to draft it. Ibn al-Muqaffaʿ, who could hardly refuse, performed the task only too well. To ensure ʿAbdallāh's safety, he included a warning that if al-Manṣūr should in any way harm his uncle:

> Everything that he owns in the way of slaves, clothes, goods, vessels, beasts of burden, and [his] landed property . . . will be [taken as] alms for the poor . . . . Each slave or concubine that he owns . . . will be freed . . . . Each of his wives will be divorced three times, irrevocably . . . . Muslims as a generality will . . . be completely freed from the oath of allegiance incumbent upon them to him, and relieved of the oaths regarding it.[7]

The caliph was to sign the document with his own hand. Al-Manṣūr was enraged. He secretly ordered the newly appointed governor of Basra to do away with the writer who had caused him such offense. Despite the pleas of his brothers, this was done. Ibn al-Muqaffaʿ was invited into the new governor's palace. He never emerged. According to one account, his limbs were severed one by one and thrown into an oven, and what remained of his body was incinerated.[8] Such was the untimely end of the translator–adapter of *Kalīlah and Dimnah* and, although the transmission of the text has been so faulty that we cannot recover with certainty the exact words of Ibn al-Muqaffaʿ, his achievement deserves full recognition.

The Odyssey of *Kalīlah and Dimnah*

As Ibn al-Muqaffaʿ explains in his Preface to *Kalīlah and Dimnah*:

> This book is a work of parables and stories composed by the people of India, who sought to incorporate into it the most eloquent speech they could find in the style they preferred. In order to make their intentions comprehensible, scholars of every nation and tongue have employed a variety of devices and means when presenting their arguments. One device was to put eloquent and elegant language into the mouths of animals and birds. This enabled them to accomplish a number of things: they found a way to speak indirectly and to

> communicate through implication. Because such a book combined entertainment with wisdom, the wise would study it for its wisdom, and the simple for its value as entertainment. (§2.1)

Many of the stories derived from a collection of fables composed originally in Sanskrit, sometime between the second century BC and the third century AD. Because the collection was organized into five books, each focusing on a particular theme, it was entitled *Five Discourses,* or *Panchatantra.*

In the middle of the sixth century AD, the work came to the attention of the ruler of Sasanian Iran, Khusraw I Anūsharwān (r. AD 531–79), or of figures at his court who were interested in Indian learning, and it was adapted into Middle Persian (Pahlavi). The process by which the book made its way from India to Persia is narrated in the first chapter of the present volume: "How Anūsharwān Sent Barzawayh to India." In Sasanian Iran, additional Indian stories translated from the *Mahābhārata* and elsewhere were added, and the composite work came to be known as *Kalīlah and Dimnah,* after the main characters who appear in its opening chapter. This Middle Persian work of translation and adaptation has not survived in its original language.

Sometime before the Islamic conquest of Iran, the Middle Persian *Kalīlah and Dimnah* was translated into Syriac, one of the languages of the Christians residing in the Persian Empire, and that translation survived in a single manuscript; it was edited and published in the nineteenth century, but is now lost. In the second/eighth century, the Middle Persian text came to the attention of Ibn al-Muqaffaʿ, who translated it into Arabic prose. This version became popular, inspiring many adaptations into both Arabic verse and prose, new Persian adaptations and versifications, and a later Syriac translation (from the Arabic this time, not from the Persian). Eventually the book made its way westward: in Islamic Spain it was translated into Old Castilian; other translations were made into Hebrew (from which it was translated into Latin) and Middle Greek. Each of these translations was made independently from different forms of the text. Later, the work was translated into German (from Latin), Ottoman Turkish (from Persian), and other languages. Regrettably, Ibn al-Muqaffaʿ's translation has not come down to us intact. Of the many surviving manuscripts of the Arabic *Kalīlah and Dimnah,* most are relatively late in date. They present a great diversity of versions.

The first printed edition of *Kalīlah and Dimnah* was published by Sylvestre de Sacy in Paris in 1819. He assembled a composite Arabic text based on a relatively late manuscript in the Royal Library in Paris, supplemented by additions and emendations based on other manuscripts available to him.[9] Earlier manuscripts have since become available. In 1905, Louis Cheikho published a critical edition of the work, based on a manuscript from Dayr al-Shīr, Lebanon, dated 739/1339. Later, ʿAbd al-Wahhāb ʿAzzām used the earliest known dated manuscript—an Aya Sofya manuscript dated 618/1221—as the basis of his 1941 Cairo edition. Early though this manuscript may be, it dates from more than four and a half centuries after the author's death. Another early manuscript, its text as yet unpublished, is located in the Royal Library in Rabat, Morocco, and can be dated on the basis of its illustrations to the second part of the thirteenth century (between 663/1265 and 679/1280).[10]

The discrepancies between these texts demonstrate that by the time of the earliest surviving manuscripts, *Kalīlah and Dimnah* had ceased to have a single authoritative text.[11] Even earlier evidence can be gleaned from quotations from *Kalīlah and Dimnah* in older Arabic works, such as *ʿUyūn al-akhbār* by Ibn Qutaybah (d. 276/889) and an entire work composed by a certain Muḥammad ibn Ḥusayn al-Yamanī (d. 400/1009) purporting to show that anything of value in Ibn al-Muqaffaʿ's translation was anticipated by Arabic authors.[12] Yet even these early citations differ among themselves.

Surviving manuscripts of *Kalīlah and Dimnah* diverge so widely that it is impossible to recover the text as it issued from the pen of Ibn al-Muqaffaʿ. It is not simply a problem of the usual copyists' mistakes, omissions, and misunderstandings; such things can be identified and corrected. The surviving manuscripts, even the earliest, differ so significantly in wording and content that one must conclude that the text has come down to us in differing recensions. Even worse, all of these recensions, or "continua," show clear evidence of adaptation and cross-copying.[13]

The connoisseurs of Arabic literature who oversaw the copying of *Kalīlah and Dimnah* for their own or their patrons' libraries, or for general circulation, felt free to adapt the text to their own interests and literary tastes or to those of their patrons and audiences. Passages were sometimes omitted, sometimes expanded; the flexibility of Arabic syntax was exploited to rephrase a given passage in a variety of ways. Sometimes the literary register of the language was highlighted by using learned vocabulary and complex syntax, and sometimes the vocabulary and syntax were simplified or bent toward a more colloquial register.

Certain philosophical or religious ideas were emphasized or downplayed, and the role of certain characters was changed.[14]

Several factors contributed to the freedom with which the text was handled. First, *Kalīlah and Dimnah* is a work of secular literature. Unlike the primary religious texts of Islam, such as the Qur'an and the Hadith (the sayings of the Prophet), which had to be copied verbatim or transmitted orally according to strict scholarly standards because of their theological and legal importance, literary works did not necessarily benefit from the same meticulousness. Books that formed part of the scholarly curriculum in Islamic schools were typically studied by students under the supervision of a professor, who ensured that the students' copies of the text were accurate—but *Kalīlah and Dimnah* never formed part of the scholarly curriculum. Collections of poetry were protected from change by their meter: changes would destroy the rhythm and would be obvious. The ornate style of rhyming prose known as *saj*ʿ also enjoyed a certain degree of protection due to its complex, intentionally inimitable style; works in relatively straightforward prose, such as *Kalīlah and Dimnah*, were not so protected. Finally, a work known to be a translation from a foreign language did not enjoy the prestige of original Arabic works.[15]

The Indian Sources of *Kalīlah and Dimnah*

The ultimate source of most, but not all, of the book Ibn al-Muqaffaʿ introduced to Arabic readers was a collection of Sanskrit fables known as the *Panchatantra*, or *Five Discourses*, as it was organized into five books.[16] The collection was intended to be a kind of "mirror for princes," teaching worldly wisdom to rulers. Each of the five books contained a main narrative illustrating a unifying theme, and each enclosed many related subordinate stories or parables. The actors in most of the stories, especially in the first three sections of the collection, are anthropomorphized animals, who combine aspects of their animal nature with human abilities of speech and reasoning, human virtues and vices, and human resourcefulness and cleverness in dealing with life's vicissitudes.

There is an ingenious weaving of stories within stories within stories: animals cite fables to each other in order to promote or discourage a course of action and, more generally, to illustrate instances of wise behavior and to warn each other against unwise behavior. Although the stories were narrated in Sanskrit prose, the wise sayings cited by their characters were in verse, a feature not preserved in the Arabic versions.

The frame story of the *Panchatantra* presents the entire work as narrated by a Brahmin sage commissioned by a king to teach his three unwise sons the principles of good conduct in this world: conduct that would lead to the princes' personal welfare and to the good order of the state. This frame story does not survive intact in the Arabic; it is replaced by a conversation between a king and a philosopher, with no elaboration of the motive for the conversation. In the Arabic edition presented here, teachings about the wise conduct of life in this world are set against a larger framework of Islamic ethics connecting conduct in this world with reward or punishment in the hereafter. The behavior of many of the characters may be, as Franklin Edgerton described it, "Machiavellian," but the overall world of the Arabic *Kalīlah and Dimnah* is moral and Islamic in coloring.

Each of the five major chapters of the *Panchatantra*, with their corresponding chapters in *Kalīlah and Dimnah*, illustrates the application of cleverness, resourcefulness, or foresight to a particular situation. The following are the five main *Panchatantra* stories (the translations are Edgerton's) and the corresponding stories in this edition:

1. "The Separation of Friends, or, The Lion and the Bull," corresponding to "The Lion and the Ox" (Chapter 4).
2. "The Winning of Friends, or, The Dove, Crow, Mouse, Tortoise, and Deer," corresponding to "The Ring Dove" (Chapter 6).
3. "War and Peace, or, The Crows and the Owls," corresponding to "The Crows and the Owls" (Chapter 7).
4. "The Loss of One's Gettings, or, The Ape and the Crocodile," corresponding to "The Turtle and the Monkey" (Chapter 8).
5. "Hasty Action, or, The Brahmin and the Mongoose," corresponding to "The Holy Man and the Mongoose" (Chapter 9).

The Middle Persian Version

Because the Middle Persian text from which Ibn al-Muqaffaʿ translated has not survived, we have only indirect evidence about the changes to the original Sanskrit collection that took place before Ibn al-Muqaffaʿ translated the text into Arabic. The prefatory material explaining the circumstances under which the

Indian work made its way to Sasanian Iran, along with the autobiography of the physician who brought the work to Iran (Chapters 1 and 3 of the present edition), almost certainly derive from Middle Persian materials, but it is not clear whether these prefatory chapters formed part of the Middle Persian *Kalīlah and Dimnah* or were attached to the book by Ibn al-Muqaffaʿ from other Middle Persian sources. There are two versions of the first preface, a longer and a shorter. Manuscript London Or. 4044 presents only the longer version. It relates how the physician Barzawayh, on orders from the ruler Anūsharwān, journeyed to India; how, through the good offices of an Indian scholar whom he befriended (the theme of friendship thus forms an important element even in this introduction), he surreptitiously obtained a copy of a book kept under lock and key in the royal library; and how he transcribed it, translated it into Persian, and brought it back to Anūsharwān. Anūsharwān is said to have rewarded Barzawayh by commanding that his biography (Chapter 3 of the present translation) be attached to the book.[17] (These introductory chapters do not form part of the Old Syriac translation, but no conclusion can be drawn from their absence, as the sole manuscript of the Old Syriac translation has lost its initial pages.)

A further departure from the *Panchatantra* in Ibn al-Muqaffaʿ's translation is the addition of stories from other Indian sources. Eight chapters of the present book can be so identified. Three of them (Chapters 10, 11, and 12 of the present text) came from Book 12 of the *Mahābhārata*, a section in which the sage Bhīṣma uses parables to instruct King Yudhiṣṭhira in the proper behavior (*dharma*) of a wise king; the remaining five (Chapters 13, 14, 15, 16, and 17) are of unknown provenance. In this case, the Old Syriac translation, made from Middle Persian sometime before Ibn al-Muqaffaʿ's Arabic translation, provides evidence that some of these additional stories were already part of the Middle Persian book.[18] Chapters 10, 11, 12, and 13 do occur in the Old Syriac, indicating that they were part of the Middle Persian *Kalīlah and Dimnah*. That leaves four chapters (14–17). The Syriac translator may have omitted them, or the surviving text of the Old Syriac may have lost its concluding chapters, or Ibn al-Muqaffaʿ may have taken them from other Persian translations from Sanskrit and added them himself to the Arabic *Kalīlah and Dimnah*. There is evidence from Ibn al-Muqaffaʿ's treatment of Middle Persian historical materials that he regularly combined material from several sources.[19] A reasonable hypothesis is that Ibn al-Muqaffaʿ supplemented his translation of an existing Middle Persian text with other Indian materials that he judged appropriate.

The added stories differ in construction from the *Panchatantra*-derived chapters: Although Chapters 10, 11, 12, and 16 have animals as their protagonists, they contain few embedded stories, and those that do occur (two in Chapter 13 and one in Chapter 17) are short and narrated by human beings, unlike the embedded stories in the *Panchatantra*-derived chapters, which are narrated by animals to animals. Chapters 13, 14, 15, and 17 have human protagonists. Even where there are animal actors, as in "The Mendicant and the Goldsmith" (Chapter 14), they carry out their roles in the human world. Thus, it is something of a misnomer to call *Kalīlah and Dimnah* as a whole a book of animal fables.

Ibn al-Muqaffaʿ's Additions

Two chapters can be attributed to Ibn al-Muqaffaʿ with confidence. Chapter 2 is a preface explicitly addressed to the Arabic reader. It presents the book as a serious work, stressing the benefits to be derived by a careful reading and warning against treating the book as mere entertainment. Another addition, Chapter 5, "The Investigation of Dimnah," records the subsequent trial and punishment of the crafty jackal Dimnah for his treachery; no such denouement exists in the *Panchatantra*, and it appears to have been absent from the Middle Persian as well, as the Old Syriac shows no trace of it. In Chapter 4, "The Lion and the Ox," Dimnah has tricked his master, the lion, into murdering Dimnah's rival, the ox Shanzabah, and, at the end of the chapter, apparently has succeeded to the ox's position at court. The story in the *Panchatantra* ends at this point. In the chapter added by Ibn al-Muqaffaʿ, Dimnah's treachery is uncovered, the lion's mother persuades her son to order a trial, and Dimnah is convicted and executed, despite his eloquent orations in his own defense. The chapter gives a sense of closure absent from the Sanskrit and presumably from the Middle Persian, where Dimnah, far from being punished for his duplicity, succeeds to his unfortunate rival's position and, we imagine, lives happily ever after. Although Cheikho postulated a Middle Persian source for the chapter, it seems more likely that it was written by Ibn al-Muqaffaʿ. Inasmuch as it does not form part of the Old Syriac translation, and many of Dimnah's arguments in his own defense echo themes in Islamic theology current in Ibn al-Muqaffaʿ's time—for example, the roles of predestination and human autonomy, the relation between physical endowments and moral qualities, and the duty of self-defense against unjust accusations—the likelihood is that even if there was a Middle Persian source for the chapter, Ibn al-Muqaffaʿ considerably adapted and expanded its text. Brockelmann's attribution of it to Ibn al-Muqaffaʿ is more likely.[20]

The Frame Story

Another change that presumably had already taken place in the Middle Persian from which Ibn al-Muqaffaʿ translated was the reworking of the *Panchatantra*'s overall frame story of a king commissioning a famous Brahmin sage to instruct the king's three sons. Instead, each chapter in the Arabic *Kalīlah and Dimnah* begins with a brief, formulaic conversation between a king, Dabshalim, and a philosopher, Baydabā.[21] No motive, other than the king's curiosity and desire for enlightenment, is given to explain the circumstances triggering these conversations. At the beginning of each chapter following the first, the king signals his comprehension of the moral of the previous chapter's story, and proposes a new subject for the philosopher to illustrate.

The introductory story of "The Lion and the Ox" may not serve as a frame for the later stories, but it does provide an ingenious transition between the world of human beings with its variety of characters (wise father, indolent sons, and one diligent son) and the world of animals with its own variety of characters. In the Arabic, the story of the merchant and his sons serves as an introduction only for the chapter of "The Lion and the Ox"; it does not serve as an overall frame for the successive stories, or even as a frame for the first story. The merchant and his sons do not reappear, either at the end of "The Lion and the Ox" or in the subsequent stories. This contrasts with the *Panchatantra*, where the overall frame story provides continuity: at the beginning of each "book," the sage instructing the king's sons proposes an enigmatic verse to serve as introduction to a new tale. The sons ask for an explanation, and the sage begins to relate the tale.

There was a later attempt in Arabic to explain the circumstances behind the story of Dabshalim and Baydabā. An otherwise unknown author, Bahnūd ibn Saḥwān (also known as ʿAlī ibn al-Shāh al-Fārisī) composed a preface that appears in some manuscripts (de Sacy included it in his edition). It explains that Dabshalim, the king who appears in conversation with the philosopher Baydabā in the bridge passages of Ibn al-Muqaffaʿ's work, ruled India in the wake of Alexander the Great's conquests. At first he ruled justly, but then he became a tyrant who needed to be reformed. To avoid the dangers of direct confrontation, the learned men of the kingdom decided to proceed indirectly. One of their number,

Baydabā, composed a series of fables to turn Dabshalim from his evil ways without incurring his wrath. The ruse succeeded: Dabshalim repented and Baydabā was rewarded.

Clever as this may be, there is no evidence in the *Panchatantra* or in *Kalīlah and Dimnah* itself that Dabshalim, the ruler to whom these fables are told, was a tyrant who needed to be restrained from wrongdoing or that his interlocutor, Baydabā, used fables because direct speech would endanger his life. Quite the opposite: in the surviving text, Dabshalim himself proposes the themes and Baydabā complies with his requests.

Barzawayh's Autobiography

Chapter 3, "The Chapter of Barzawayh the Physician," contains Barzawayh's autobiography. Although some scholars have attributed its composition to Ibn al-Muqaffaʿ, Theodor Nöldeke, who produced a separate edition and translation of it, argued convincingly that its origin as a composition in Middle Persian is historically plausible and that it contains material that would not have been available to Ibn al-Muqaffaʿ. This, however, does not rule out the possibility that Ibn al-Muqaffaʿ added material of his own, expanding on Barzawayh's religious ideas in the context of his own religious outlook. The chapter records Barzawayh's upbringing, his reasons for choosing medicine as a career, his devotion to his profession, his consciousness of the limitations of medicine, his increasingly ascetic religious outlook, and his agnosticism vis-à-vis existing religious traditions. Barzawayh distances himself from any existing religious community, having explored them all and found them wanting. It is this aspect that some readers have seen as having been highlighted or added in toto by Ibn al-Muqaffaʿ as a reflection of his own religious opinions.

It is tempting to read Ibn al-Muqaffaʿ into Barzawayh's biography, but this is speculative. We have little firm evidence about Ibn al-Muqaffaʿ's religious beliefs or the sincerity of his conversion to Islam. An anecdote in Ibn Khallikān's biography to the effect that Ibn al-Muqaffaʿ continued to recite Zoroastrian prayers on the eve of his formal conversion might be interpreted not as evidence of insincerity, but as evidence of a strongly religious personality, perhaps one likely to be as assiduous in observance of the rituals of Islam as he had been in the observance of those of his former religion. Ibn Khallikān cites a statement by the essayist al-Jāḥiẓ (d. 255/868–69) that Ibn al-Muqaffaʿ, along with the notoriously dissolute poets Muṭīʿ ibn Iyās and Yaḥyā ibn Ziyād, was suspected of heresy (*zandaqah*). Ibn Khallikān also cites a statement attributed to al-Manṣūr's successor, the caliph al-Mahdī (r. 158–69/775–85): "Never have I encountered a book of heresy whose source was not Ibn al-Muqaffaʿ." The contemptuous words that Ibn Khallikān attributes to Sufyān ibn Muʿāwiyah, the governor who oversaw the execution ("I have no qualms about rending you limb from limb, because you are a heretic [*zindīq*] and have corrupted the people"), express the governor's long-held animus against his victim, but can hardly be taken as evidence of Ibn al-Muqaffaʿ's real opinions.[22] Some modern commentators, such as Brockelmann, have seen Ibn al-Muqaffaʿ as highlighting Barzawayh's religious skepticism; others, such as Gabrieli, are less certain, given that certain currents of religious skepticism were already active in Anūsharwān's Iran.[23]

The Morality of *Kalīlah and Dimnah*

Franklin Edgerton initially characterized the moral world of the *Panchatantra* as follows: "Most of the stories remain true to the keynote of the book, its Machiavellian character; they are generally unmoral, and at times positively immoral, in the political lessons they inculcate."[24] Later in the same volume, he qualified this judgment:

> The Pañcatantra, like other books of the sort, often presents discordant views, evidently with intent; it arranges joint debates between characters in the stories. Thus it happens that at least one story occurs in it (Evil-wit and Honest-wit, I. 13)[25] which teaches, and is obviously meant to teach, the distinctly non-Machiavellian lesson that "honesty is the best policy." . . . It is embedded in a long moral lecture read by the virtuous jackal Karaṭaka to the tricky Damanaka, in which he reproves him for his villainy, assuring him that he will live to repent it, in spite of its apparent success.[26]

This balanced assessment applies all the more to *Kalīlah and Dimnah*, especially in the recension here presented, with its distinctly Islamic overtones. Although the virtues the stories illustrate tend to be practical worldly skills, faithfulness, truthfulness, and trust receive their share of praise. Some of the stories celebrate successful friendships (Chapter 6, "The Ring Dove") or the overcoming of difficulties (Chapter 15, "The King's Son and His Companions");

characters who are scheming, ambitious, and unscrupulous are presented as dangers to be avoided; ill-considered or impulsive actions are shown to have unsavory consequences (Chapter 9, "The Holy Man and the Mongoose").

If the dangers of life in this world are illustrated, this hardly amounts to a glorification of immoral behavior; rather, it is a frequent Islamic theme: the instability of this world, as contrasted with the permanence of the reward promised by God to the righteous. We are warned that friendships can succumb to the machinations of unscrupulous rivals (Chapter 4, "The Lion and the Ox"); alliances made for a specific end cannot be relied on once that end is achieved (Chapter 10, "The Cat and the Rat," with its decidedly unromantic ending: "I'll be your friend from a distance"); grievances are set aside, but suspicion persists (Chapter 12, "The Lion and the Jackal"). This world (*al-dunyā,* to use the Arabic term) is one of intrigues (Dimnah and his rival, the ox Shanzabah), innate antagonisms (owls and crows, cats and mice), and irreconcilable motives (in Chapter 8, "The Turtle and the Monkey," the turtle must decide between loyalty to his friend, the monkey, and loyalty to his wife, who has tricked him into believing that the only remedy for her disease is a monkey's heart). But for all these dark touches, evil never triumphs, except in embedded stories meant to be taken as a warning against thoughtless behavior.

A major theme of *Kalīlah and Dimnah* is a ruler's need for good counselors, of which there are many examples in the book. However, there are many warnings about the dangers lying in wait for anyone who would speak honest advice to power. One wonders whether Ibn al-Muqaffaʿ saw the dangers of his own position as a client of the caliphal family reflected in passages such as the following:

> "If this is your plan [that is, to enter the lion's service]," said Kalīlah, "I must warn you about the dangers of associating with rulers. Scholars say there are three things that only fools attempt and from which few escape unscathed: associating with rulers, trusting women with secrets, and drinking poison as an experiment. Scholars have likened a ruler to a steep, rugged mountain where all sorts of pleasant fruit grow, but which is home to lions, leopards, and every kind of ferocious beast—the ascent may be difficult, but staying there is harder yet." (§4.13)

Or consider the following speech by the ox Shanzabah, upon being told by Dimnah (falsely) that the lion intends to make a meal of him:

> Can anyone serve a ruler and remain in his good graces? How right the one who said that rulers, in their scant loyalty to companions and abandonment of those they no longer need, are like a whore with her customers: when one leaves, another takes his place! (§4.65)

Or consider the pious jackal of Chapter 12 ("The Lion and the Jackal"), voicing his reluctance to serve at a lion's court:

> Only two sorts of people can associate with rulers and do their bidding . . . and I'm neither. The two sorts are an unscrupulous flatterer who gets what he wants through scheming and ensures his own safety through flattery, and a pitiful fool whom no one envies. Rarely do things turn out well for the person who would associate with a ruler on terms of truthfulness, sincerity, and modesty, untinged by flattery, for the ruler's foes and friends will join forces against him in envy, enmity, and deceit. The ruler's friends will compete with him for rank and envy him for it; the ruler's enemies will hate him for his good advice and service to the ruler. When both groups join forces against him, he is likely to perish, God forbid (§12.8).

Islamic Elements in the London Or. 4044 Redaction of *Kalīlah and Dimnah*

As might be expected of a text translated into Arabic in early Abbasid times and subjected afterward to a complex process of transmission and adaptation even before the earliest surviving Arabic manuscripts were produced, the text of London Or. 4044 shows certain features that testify to the Islamic milieu in which it was produced and to the religious culture and philosophical interests of successive author-copyists and of the audiences for which they produced their texts. These features are subtle: there has been no wholesale rewriting such as one finds in the later Syriac version, with its explicit quotations from the Bible, or in various Arabic and Persian retellings that introduce quotations from the Qur'an, the Hadith, and even Arabic poetry. But Islamic overtones of various kinds are in fact present. First, there are turns of phrase that impart an Islamic patina to the work. In addition to the frequent contrast between the transitory, present world (*al-dunyā*) and the permanent afterlife (*al-ākhirah*), God is often referred to as *Allāh taʿālā* (God the exalted) or *Allāh subḥānahu wa-taʿālā* (God, glorified and exalted). One occasionally encounters predictions about the future qualified by the phrase *in shā' Allāh* (if God so wills)—such as in §9.2 and §13.28. The latter example is particularly striking, spoken as it is by a female dove telling her mate that his plan to store grain to tide them over the dry season will succeed, "God willing." Even the animals speak a language with Islamic overtones!

Closely related are the formulaic phrases addressed to rulers, examples of courtly etiquette not to be taken as having particularly deep religious or philosophical import. For example, when Queen Īrākht, at the prompting of the wise counselor Baylār, seeks to comfort the king, who has been terrified by his ominous dreams and by the frightful rites the Brahmins enjoin upon him to avert disaster, she begins by saying, "Do not be sad, blessed king. May God lengthen your life and grant you lasting joy" (§13.14). Later in the same chapter, the wise counselor, Baylār, begins an address to the same king with similar words: "May God grant Your Majesty long life, preserve you in health, and increase your judiciousness and nobility" (§13.76).

Sometimes the language reflects deeper Islamic religious and philosophical themes. This redaction frequently emphasizes the doctrine that the ultimate agent in all human actions is God; human beings (and the animal actors in the fables) accomplish what they accomplish only with the help of God. In "The Cat and the Rat," the rat explains to the cat, "Each of us, with God's help, will be the cause of the other's salvation" (§10.5). In "King Haylār and His Minister Baylār," the malicious Brahmins explain that the catastrophes foreshadowed by the king's dreams can be averted only through a series of killings and bloody rites, after which "God will avert whatever He wishes" (§13.4). This emphasis on God's role contrasts with the Old Syriac version, which antedates the Arabic, where the rites themselves appear to be effective *ex opere operato*; no divine intervention is mentioned. Later in the same chapter, King Haylār attributes his escape from the clutches of the Brahmins first to God and second to the good judgment of the queen: "If God in His mercy hadn't restrained me through the advice of Īrākht, the best and most blessed of women, I should have perished, caused death, and lost all I have in this world and the next" (§13.19).

The combination of God's help and individual efforts sometimes leads to rather strange juxtapositions. For example, in "The Monkey and the Turtle," the monkey, shocked to learn that the turtle wants to extract his heart to use as medicine to cure his sick wife, exclaims, "The only thing to be done is to seek help from God and to use my own cunning" (§8.11). In "The Cat and the Rat," the rat, seeing himself surrounded on all sides by danger, exclaims, "I am surrounded by troubles . . . all in league to spoil my joy over the cat's distress. I see no recourse for me but to rely on God, and to use my intelligence and ingenuity" (§10.3). Something similar happens in "The Lion and the Jackal," where the pious jackal initially agrees to serve as the lion's adviser only if the lion promises not to believe any slanders circulated against him by envious courtiers: "Should one of them, be it with his own lips or through someone else, mention to the king something intended to turn the king against me, the king will not act hastily against me, but will investigate and examine what has been brought to his attention and then do what God shows him to be best" (§12.10). In "The Trial of Dimnah," we meet a physician "who prospered because of the providential [that is, divinely decreed] cures that occurred at his hands through his treatments and drugs" (§5.29). In "The Owls and the Crows," the wise counselor tells the king of the crows: "I hope God will set in motion some good that will bring swift relief. Those in dire straits have often achieved through cunning what they could never have achieved in a contest of strength" (§7.20). Is it God's intervention, or is it cunning? Or are cunning and deception gifts imparted by God?

Finally, there is evidence in this redaction of a philosophical interest in the relations between individual volition and God's determination of events through His lordship over destiny and fortune (*al-qaḍā' wa-l-qadar*). In the world of *Kalīlah and Dimnah*, this divinely determined aspect of events operates through secondary causes (*ʿilal*, singular *ʿillah*). To naïve minds, these secondary causes appear to control the course of events; however, enlightened minds understand the role of divine providence in all things. Leaving aside the three introductory chapters, the first extended philosophical meditation on the subject occurs early in "The Lion and the Ox." The rich merchant's oldest son, heeding his father's warning about the need to pursue a gainful profession, loads an oxcart with merchandise and sets out for a land called Sūraqān to trade. On the way, one of the oxen, Shanzabah, sinks into a quagmire and, when extricated, is so exhausted that the son leaves him behind, instructing his assistant to wait for the ox to recover and then bring him to the city. However, the assistant tires, abandons Shanzabah, and tells his master that the ox has died. Shanzabah makes his way to a grassy meadow, where his bellowing eventually comes to the attention of the lion into whose court he will soon be introduced by Dimnah, thus setting the stage for the first story. We are told, however, that while Shanzabah, having been rescued from quagmire, stayed in the meadow, he was

> fearful that some inevitable misfortune might yet befall him—as happened, for example, to a man who, they say, was cutting hay when a wolf attacked him. Only when the wolf was near did the man notice and flee in terror toward a village on the bank of a river. When he reached the river, he found the bridge in ruins. With the wolf catching up, he said to himself, "What shall I do? The wolf is right behind me, the river is deep, the bridge is in ruins, and I can't swim. The safest thing is to entrust my life to the water." So he jumped in. The villagers saw him and pulled him out just as he was about to drown. Back among the villagers, as he leaned against a wall and began to tell them what had happened, the wall collapsed and killed him. (§4.3)

Even the occasional satirical touches in this recension have an Islamic coloring. In the story of the partridge, the rabbit, and the pious cat (§§7.15–17), embedded in "The Owls and the Crows," a partridge and a rabbit lay claim to the same hollow as their home. The partridge suggests that they take their claims for arbitration to a pious cat:

> "By the riverbank near us," said the partridge, "lives a cat who is an invalid. He fasts endlessly, prays night and day, harms no one, spills no blood, and is content to live on grass. If you like, we can go to him for arbitration and abide by his decision." (§7.15)

The cat, alas, turns out to be a hypocrite, but one skilled in the external observances of Islamic prayer. As soon as he sees the two potential victims approaching, he stands up on his hind legs in the posture of prayer. Then, having asked them to come closer, he being hard of hearing in his old age, he delivers a short sermon with Qurʾanic overtones:

> "Before pronouncing judgment, I'll start by giving you some good advice," he said. "I charge you to fear God and seek nothing but the truth: the seeker of truth prospers, even if the judgment goes against him; but the seeker of falsehood loses, even if the judgment goes in his favor. The only things an inhabitant of this world takes with him from his earthly existence are neither money nor friends, but the good works he has done. A wise man should seek what endures and will bring him benefit tomorrow, and abandon everything else."

> As he talked, they became more and more at ease with him and came closer and closer, until finally he pounced, grabbed them, and killed them both. (§7.17)

What stands out in this recension is how thoroughly and skillfully the Islamic elements, be they matters of vocabulary, turns of phrase, or more complex Islamic religious and philosophical arguments, are integrated into the dramatic structure of *Kalīlah and Dimnah*. Part of the pleasure for the reader lies in detecting these elements and in noting how ingeniously these sophisticated religious and philosophical ideas have been introduced into a dramatic situation or into the speech of animals.

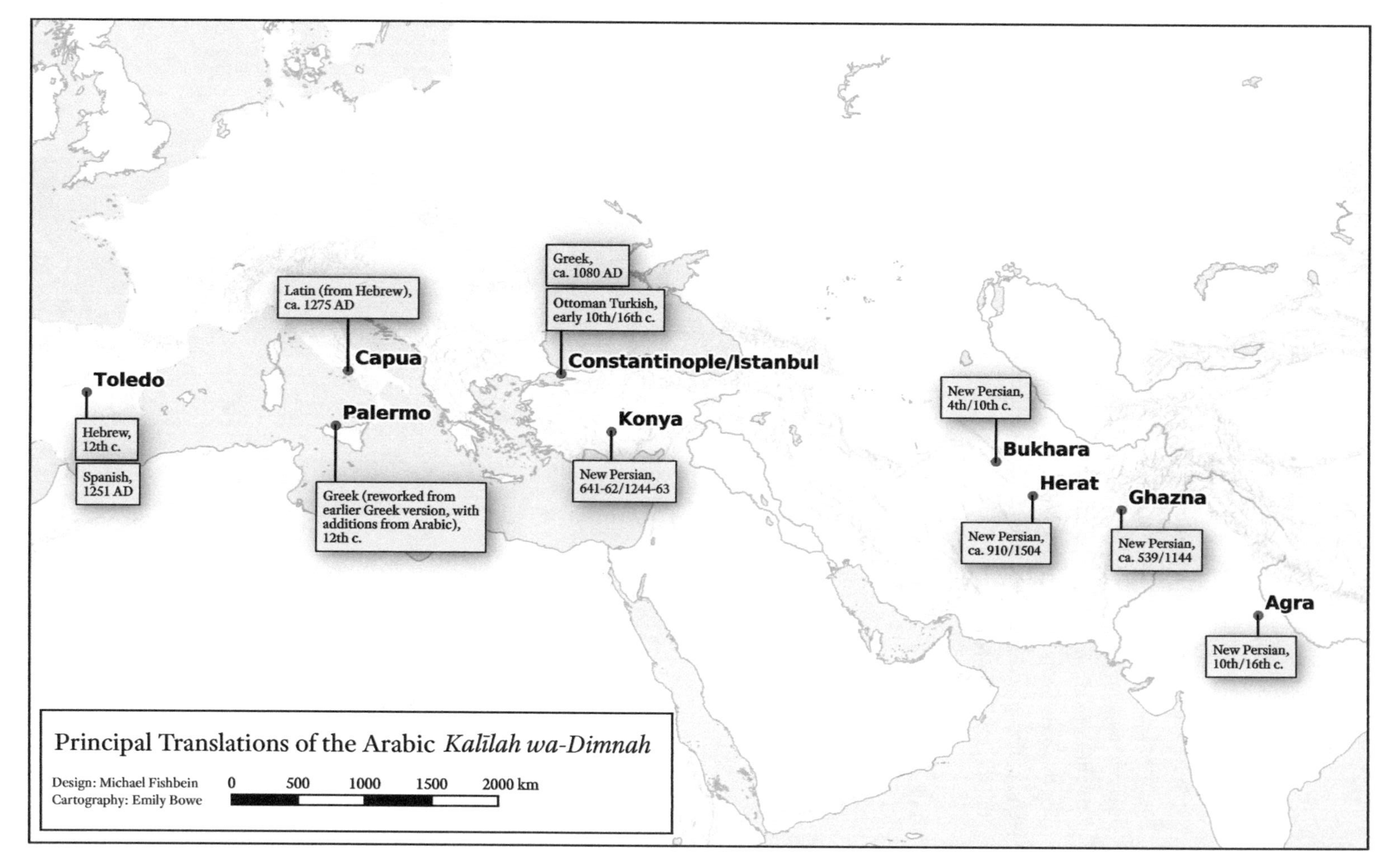
Toledo
Hebrew, 12th c.
Spanish, 1251 AD
Capua
Latin (from Hebrew), ca. 1275 AD
Palermo
Greek (reworked from earlier Greek version, with additions from Arabic), 12th c.
Constantinople/Istanbul
Greek, ca. 1080 AD
Ottoman Turkish, early 10th/16th c.
Konya
New Persian, 641-62/1244-63
Bukhara
New Persian, 4th/10th c.
Herat
New Persian, ca. 910/1504
Ghazna
New Persian, ca. 539/1144
Agra
New Persian, 10th/16th c.
Principal Translations of the Arabic *Kalīlah wa-Dimnah*
Design: Michael Fishbein
Cartography: Emily Bowe
0
500
1000
1500
2000 km

Note on the Text

The Arabic Edition

Given the divergence of the earliest manuscripts, any attempt to produce a composite text would result in an amalgamation of divergent textual families with little claim to authenticity. A sentence or paragraph in one style might well be followed by a sentence or paragraph in a completely different style. Even using a complete early text, as Cheikho did, is somewhat arbitrary because of the many emendations needed.

We have chosen to use a previously unedited manuscript as the base text for this edition, emending only when absolutely necessary. British Library Or. 4044 is undated but appears to have been copied relatively late (in the ninth/fifteenth century). A digital file of it was kindly provided by the AnonymClassic project. It is relatively complete, missing only about five folios in the first chapter and one or two folios at the very end, and without too many signs of intentional condensing or omission of passages.[27] It is carefully written by a copyist with a good knowledge of Classical Arabic. It also contains many skillfully executed illustrations, some in the margins, others filling an entire page.

Whenever there was a lacuna or defective reading, recourse was made to other manuscripts and printed editions, in the first instance Or. 8751 (dated 799/1396),[28] notably for the few missing pages of text. When Or. 8751 was not able to help with a lacuna or reading, we consulted another early manuscript: Royal Library of Morocco (Rabat) 3655, which can be dated on the basis of its illustrations to the second part of the thirteenth century (between 663/1265 and 679/1280).[29] A full copy of the Rabat manuscript's text, made in Egypt in 1175/1761, is now located in Paris (Bibliothèque Nationale, Arabe 3475), and can be accessed digitally.[30] Cheikho's edition has also been consulted, as well as an early manuscript at the Bibliothèque Nationale, Arabe 3466, which dates from 854/1450, and which was the main source of de Sacy's edition.[31] We refer in the footnotes to the base manuscript, Or. 4044, as (الأصل). When a reading is adopted from Or. 8751, we mention only that manuscript (ل٢), without indicating whether that reading is present in other manuscripts and editions; if we had to resort to Rabat 3655, we also mention only it (ر). If we have had to look elsewhere, the footnote reflects our reliance on every other manuscript and edition consulted. The notes thus respect the hierarchy:

1. Or. 4044—base manuscript
2. Or. 8751
3. Rabat 3655
4. All other manuscripts and editions

In editing Arabic manuscripts produced relatively late, the question of normalization inevitably arises: whether to normalize the text to the standard modern orthography and grammatical norms of Classical Arabic, whether to reproduce the text exactly as in the manuscript (including obvious errors by the copyist, lacunae, and missing dots differentiating otherwise identical letters), or to compromise. The latter has been the course taken here. We think it can be justified. Unlike works intended for a relatively uneducated audience or for oral performance—one thinks of the *Thousand and One Nights* (*Alf laylah wa-laylah*)—*Kalīlah wa-Dimnah*, with its ethical and philosophical discourses, is not written in colloquial Arabic. Other early manuscripts of the work testify to the care with which such illustrated manuscripts, intended for wealthy consumers, were copied. The richly illustrated MS Rabat 3655, for example, is completely vocalized, including the classical case endings, and several of the Paris manuscripts also include vocalization according to classical rules. Although vocalization is rare in MS Or. 4044, the departures from Classical Arabic norms are rare and to be expected in recensions produced in what has been termed the Middle Arabic period by copyists whose spoken language had already developed naturally into something intermediate between the classical language and the modern vernaculars. Such departures as occur have been indicated in the textual apparatus, so that the reading of the manuscript can be recovered.[32] The colophons at the end of each chapter have been preserved as in the manuscript. Although they may have been inserted by the copyist, they sometimes do not agree exactly with the title of the chapter and sometimes add information.

According to Library of Arabic Literature norms, added punctuation has been restricted to a minimum: periods have been added where needed for clarity, but no commas, question marks, or other modern devices have been used.

Note on the Text

The text has been separated into numbered sections for ease of reference and for synchronizing the Arabic text and its English translation.

The English Translation

The translation aims at a natural style. No attempt has been made to adhere exactly to the syntax of the Arabic or always to translate a given Arabic word by the same English word, as the result would produce a mechanical effect and hide the wide range of meanings of a given Arabic word. In dialogue, the aim has been to produce exchanges at once dramatic and expressive. The more philosophical speeches and orations have been rendered in a more formal English. For convenience, titles for some of the embedded tales have been added in the margin of the translation, although these are not in the manuscript. In these and other matters of style, the translator gratefully acknowledges that his inclination to prefer literalness over liveliness has been curbed by the efforts of his co-translator James Montgomery, whose mastery of English style matches his mastery of Arabic.

Manuscripts

الأصل London, British Library, Or. 4044.

ل٢ London, British Library, Or. 8751.

ر Rabat, Royal Library of Morocco (Bibliothèque Nationale du Royaume du Maroc), 3655.

پ٣٤٦٦ Paris, Bibliothèque Nationale, Arabe 3466.

پ٣٤٧٥ Paris, Bibliothèque Nationale, Arabe 3475.

Printed Editions

ج Guidi. *Studii sul testo arabo del Libro di Calila e Dimna*. In the case of Ignazio Guidi's work, which includes extensive citations from manuscripts located in Italy, the general siglum ج (G) has been used, followed by a slash and the designator of the particular manuscript: for example, ج/ف (G/F) for Guidi's manuscript F (Florence, Bibliotheca Palatina Medicea 95).

د De Sacy. *Calila et Dimna: Ou fables de Bidpai en Arabe*.

س Schulthess. *Kalīla und Dimna: Syrisch und Deutsch.*

ش Cheikho. *La version arabe de Kalîlah et Dimnah.* Where Cheikho cites two different manuscripts, these are identified as ش/١ and ش/٢.

ع ʿAzzām. *Kalīlah wa-Dimnah.*

ي Al-Yamanī. *Kitāb Muḍāhāt amthāl kitāb Kalīlah wa-Dimnah bi-mā ashbahahā min ashʿār al-ʿArab.*

Notes to the Introduction

1 For further details about the life of Ibn al-Muqaffaʿ, see Gabrieli, "Ibn al-Muḳaffaʿ"; Sourdel, "La biographie d'Ibn al-Muqaffaʿ d'après les sources anciennes"; and Kristó-Nagy, *La pensée d'Ibn al-Muqaffaʿ*.

2 For a summary of Ibn al-Muqaffaʿ's works, see Latham, "Ibn al-Muqaffaʿ and Early Abbasid Prose," 53–77; and Kristó-Nagy, *La pensée d'Ibn al-Muqaffaʿ*, 81–107.

3 On these works and the nature of Ibn al-Muqaffaʿ's translations, see Hämeen-Anttila, *Khwadāynāmag: The Middle Persian Book of Kings*, 89–99, 106, 128–30.

4 The word translated as "conduct," *adab*, is perhaps to be read in the plural, *ādāb*. It originally meant something like "training, special skill," but soon came to mean "cultivation, general culture, education." See Hämeen-Anttila, *Adab (a) Arabic, Early Developments.*

5 For an account of the *Risālah fī l-Ṣaḥābah*, see Lowry, "The First Islamic Legal Theory: Ibn al-Muqaffaʿ on Interpretation, Authority, and the Structure of the Law."

6 So vocalized in the manuscript. Also read as Burzawayh or Burzōe.

7 Text from Marsham and Robinson, "The Safe-Conduct for the Abbasid ʿAbd Allāh b. ʿAlī," 256.

8 See Ibn Khallikān, *Wafayāt al-aʿyān*, 2:151–55.

9 For a description of the manuscripts de Sacy used for his edition, see *Calila et Dimna*, 57–64. His base text (1483A) is now catalogued by the Bibliothèque Nationale de France as Arabe 3465 and can be accessed online.

10 See the description of Rabat 3655 by Khouloud Khalfallah on the AnonymClassic website: http://www.geschkult.fu-berlin.de/en/e/kalila-wa-dimna/topics/Digital-Reconstruction.html. Many of its leaves are damaged or missing. A full copy of its text made in Egypt in 1175/1761 survives, now located in Paris (Bibliothèque nationale, Arabe 3475). Unfortunately, the copyist appears to have worked quickly and not very carefully, as is evident from a comparison of the copy with the surviving parts of the Rabat manuscript. Other early manuscripts are Riyadh King Faysal Center 2536 and Cambridge Corpus Christi College Parker Library 578, both fourteenth century. A comparison of the earliest texts for one chapter ("The Cat and the Rat") can be accessed on the website of AnonymClassic: http://www.geschkult.fu-berlin.de/en/e/kalila-wa-dimna/index.html.

11 The instability of the text of *Kalīlah and Dimnah* was recognized by scholars very early. In 1873, Ignazio Guidi documented it in a study of manuscripts of the work accessible to

him in Italy. See Guidi, *Studii sul testo arabo del Libro di Calila e Dimna*. The situation as of 1924 was summarized by Martin Sprengling in his seminal article "Kalîla Studies. I."

12 Al-Yamanī, *Kitāb Muḍāhāt amthāl kitāb Kalīlah wa-Dimnah bi-mā ashbahahā min ashʿār al-ʿArab* (*How the Parables of Kalīlah and Dimnah Imitate Their Analogs in the Poetry of the Arabs*). Another early reference to *Kalīlah and Dimnah* can be found in the *Taʾrīkh* (*History*) of the third-/ninth-century historian al-Yaʿqūbī (d. 292/905), ed. Leiden, 1:97–99; trans., 2:351–52. Al-Yaʿqūbī lists ten of the chapters, with their titles, but does not mention Ibn al-Muqaffaʿ as translator.

13 The AnonymClassic project has classified the surviving manuscripts into two large groups or "continua," based on the presence and sequence of small units of the text. For a detailed description of the method and its provisional results, see Gruendler, "An Interim Report on the Editorial and Analytical Work of the AnonymClassic Project."

14 See Gruendler, "Les versions de *Kalīla wa-Dimna*: Une transmission et une circulation mouvantes."

15 On the tension between the native Arabic tradition and foreign, mostly Persian, cultural imports, see the article by S. Enderwitz, "al-Shuʿūbiyya," in *EI2*. For one major third-/ninth-century Arab author's view of the Persians, see Ibn Qutaybah, *The Excellence of the Arabs*, 1–103.

16 The *Panchatantra* underwent as many mutations in transmission in India as Ibn al-Muqaffaʿ's *Kalīlah and Dimnah* underwent in Arabic. See Edgerton, *The Panchatantra Reconstructed: An Attempt to Establish the Lost Original Sanskrit Text of the Most Famous of Indian Story-Collections on the Basis of the Principal Extant Versions*. Edgerton also discusses the relationship between the *Panchatantra* and the Middle Persian version translated by Ibn al-Muqaffaʿ; see *The Panchatantra Reconstructed*, 2:40–47. The earlier work of Johannes Hertel, *Tantrākhyāyika: Die älteste Fassung des Pañcatantra*, is still valuable, although many of his conclusions are contested by Edgerton.

17 Curiously, in Chapter 1 of the present text, Anūsharwān instructs his minister Buzurgmihr to prepare this biography; Chapter 3, however, is an autobiography narrated in the first person by Barzawayh. Various explanations have been proposed for the discrepancy.

18 Brockelmann dates it to around 570; see his article "Kalīla wa-Dimna." The Old Syriac also contains a chapter, "Mihrayār, King of the Mice," not found in London Or. 4044. As no Indian source for it has been found, it was probably an original composition in Middle Persian. See Nöldeke, "Die Erzählung vom Mäusekönig und seinen Ministern."

19 Hämeen-Anttila, *Khwadāynāmag: The Middle Persian Book of Kings*, discusses what can be determined about Ibn al-Muqaffaʿ's manner of dealing with his Middle Persian historical sources, and his conclusions can with caution be extended to apply to *Kalīlah and Dimnah*; see especially p. 130.

20 See Cheikho, *La version arabe de Kalîlah et Dimnah*, 49 (notes); Brockelmann, "Kalīla wa-Dimna."

21 The name was sometimes transliterated as Bidpai, and the whole collection has also come to be known as *Bidpai's Fables*.

22 Ibn Khallikān, *Wafayāt al-aʿyān*, 2:151–53.

23 See Brockelmann, "Kalīla wa-Dimna"; Gabrieli, "Ibn al-Muḳaffaʿ"; and Kristó-Nagy, *La pensée d'Ibn al-Muqaffaʿ*, 113–25.

24 Edgerton, *The Panchatantra Reconstructed*, 2:5.

25 In this translation, the story of the swindler and the simpleton (§§4.102–8).

26 Edgerton, *The Panchatantra Reconstructed*, 2:186–87.

27 Chapter 5 ("The Investigation of Dimnah") shows some signs of having been shortened, as does Chapter 14, "The Mendicant and the Goldsmith," with the clear motive of avoiding certain religiously suspect allusions to superstition and magic.

28 See the description in François de Blois, *Burzōy's Voyage to India and the Origin of the Book of Kalīlah wa Dimnah*, 66.

29 At some point, the manuscript lost leaves and was rebound with some disturbance to the order of folios. Khouloud Khalfallah, working with the AnonymClassic project, has reordered the pages digitally and has kindly provided access to the resulting reconstruction for this edition.

30 http://gallica.bnf.fr/ark:/12148/btv1b84539771.

31 http://gallica.bnf.fr/ark:/12148/btv1b10329769c.

32 The textual apparatus omits normalizations that affect only orthography, not grammar or syntax. For example, words containing *hamzah* have been written according to modern practice (the manuscript rarely employs the sign for *hamzah*); verbal and nominal forms ending in -*ū* (the manuscript invariably follows them with the otiose *alif al-wiqāyah*) have also been normalized. The copyist of Or. 4044 frequently omits the diacritical points that distinguish several Arabic letters from each other; these points have been supplied in the text, but a textual note has been added recording the exact reading of the manuscript when different possible readings of such an unpointed ductus could affect the meaning.

كتاب كليلة ودمنة

Kalīlah and Dimnah

بعثة أنوشروان بَرْزَوَيْه إلى بلاد الهند لانتساخ كليلة ودمنة

١٫١ أمّا بعد فإنّ الله تبارك وتعالى خلق خلقه برحمته وقوّاهم على عبادته بفضله ورزقهم ما يقدرون به على صلاح معايشهم في الدنيا وما يدركون به[1] استنقاذهم من العذاب في الآخرة. وأفضل ما رزقهم ومنّ عليهم به العقل الذي هو القوّة لجميع الأشياء ولا يقدر أحد من أهل الدنيا وطالب الآخرة المجتهد في الدنيا الذي ينجّي روحه من الأهوال على صلاح معيشته ولا ازدياد فضل ولا عمل إلّا به في الدنيا والآخرة فإنّ المجتهد في العمل لا يأمن من هولها ولا يقدر على إنفاذ العمل إلّا بالعقل لأنّ العقل سبب كلّ خير ومفتاح كلّ رغبة وليس لأحد غنى عن العقل.

٢٫١ والعقل مكتسب بالتجارب وهو غريزته مكنونة[2] في الإنسان ككمون النار في العود فإنّ النار طبعها في العود لكنّها[3] لا تخرج إلّا بالهزّ ولا تُرى حتّى يقدحها قادح فتلظى وتحرق. وطبيعة العقل كمين في الإنسان يظهره الأدب وتقوّيه التجارب فإذا استحكم كان أولى بالتجارب والمقوّي لكلّ أدب الجالب لكلّ المنافع والدافع لكلّ المضارّ فلا شيء أفضل ولا أحسن للإنسان من العقل إذا أُعين بالأدب وقوّته التجربة فمن منّ عليه خالقه بالعقل وأعان هو على نفسه[4] بالمثابرة على الأدب والحرص عليه سعد جدّه وأدرك في الدنيا أمله وفي الآخرة أفضل النصيب وأجزل الأجر وأعلى المنازل. والعقل هو المقوّي للدولة والمثبّت للمملكة والمشرّف للملك فالملوك والسوقة لا تصلح إلّا عليه وعلى تدبيره.

٣٫١ وقد رزق الله ملكنا أنورشروان سعيد الجدّ من العقل أفضل الرزق ومن الأنصباء أجزلها وأعانه على ما رُزق من ذلك بحسن[5] الأدب والبحث عن العلم

---

١ كذا ش، ع؛ ساقطة من الأصل. ٢ الأصل: مكتوبة. ٣ الأصل: لأنّها. ٤ فمن منّ... نفسه: كذا ل٢؛ الأصل: رزق على الأدب والعقل ومُنّ عليه به وساعدته نفسه. ٥ كذا ل٢؛ الأصل: بحسب.

How Anūsharwān Sent Barzawayh to India to Transcribe *Kalīlah and Dimnah*

God, who is blessed and exalted, created His creatures through His mercy, 1.1
and in His beneficence gave them strength to serve Him. He provided them with the means to live prosperous lives in this world and to save themselves from punishment in the next. The most excellent gift that God bestowed is the intellect. It is the faculty appropriate to all things. Only by means of the intellect can a dweller in this world who aspires to the hereafter—by striving here to save his soul from the terrors of what comes next—live a prosperous life, increase his merit, and perform deeds that are appropriate for both worlds. Only by means of the intellect can those who strive to do good act effectively and be safe from fear of punishment in the afterlife; for the intellect is the means to every good and the key to every desire—none can dispense with it.

Acquired through experience, the intellect is a faculty hidden within a 1.2
person, like fire latent in wood; the nature of fire is in the wood, but it only emerges by rubbing: it remains invisible until it is struck by something else, whereupon it ignites and burns. Similarly, the nature of the intellect is latent in a person: it is made manifest through education, and strengthened by experience. When it is strong, it is best at managing experiences and tempering behavior. It secures every benefit and repels every evil. Nothing, then, is better or more excellent for a person than the intellect, when it is supported by education and strengthened by experience. Someone who is endowed by his Creator with intellect and who bolsters himself by diligently pursuing education will enjoy good fortune and fulfill his hopes in this world; and in the next world he will attain the most excellent lot, procure the greatest reward, and reach the most exalted station. What is more, intellect bolsters the state, upholds the realm, and ennobles the king. Only through it and under its guidance do both kings and commoners prosper.

God has bestowed on our fortunate king, Anūsharwān, the most excel- 1.3
lent intellect and amplest fortune. He has also blessed him with a fine

والتفتيش بجميع الفلسفة والاستقصاء عمّا غاب والتحرّي للصواب ممّا ظهر فبلغ في ذلك ما لم يبلغه ملك قطّ ممّا مضى من الملوك قبله. وكان ممّا تيقّن عن العلم ويبحث عنه أنّه بلغه عن كتاب من كتب فلاسفة الهند عند ملوكهم وعلمائهم نفيس مخزون عندهم وهو أصل كلّ أدب ورأس كلّ علم والدليل على كلّ منفعة ومفتاح لطلب الآخرة والعمل للنجاة والمقوّي والمعين لما يحتاج إليه الملوك لتدبير ملكهم وأدب للسوقة لما يرضون به ملكهم ويصلحون به معايشهم وهو كتاب كليلة ودمنة.

٤،١ فلمّا تيقّن ما بلغه عن ذلك الكتاب وعمّا فيه من المنافع من تقوية العقل والأدب لم يطمئنّ ولم يسكن دون استفادته والنظر فيه وكان رجلاً عاقلاً أديباً فسأل أهل مملكته أن يطلبوا في جميع مملكته رجلاً عاقلاً أديباً عارفاً عالماً بلسان الفارسيّة والهنديّة كاتباً بهما جميعاً حريصاً على العلم مجتهداً في استكمال الأدب مثابراً على النظر والتفتيش لكتب الفلسفة فيؤتى به فطلبوا الرجل حتّى أصابوه ثمّ أتوا به وكان رجلاً شابّاً جميلاً ذا حسب كامل العقل والأدب صناعته التي[١] يُعرف بها الطبّ وكان ماهراً بالفارسيّة والهنديّة اسمه برزويه بن أزدهر.

٥،١ فلمّا دخل على الملك سجد ثمّ قام مكفّراً[٢] فقال له الملك يا برزويه قد تخيّرتك لما بلغني عنك من فضل علمك وعقلك وحسن أدبك وحرصك على طلب العلم حيث كان وأنّه قد بلغني عن كتاب بالهند.

وقصّ عليه قصّته وأخبره بما بلغه عن ذلك الكتاب وحبّه[٣] لاستفادته ورغبته فيه وقال له تجهّز فإنّي مسرّحك إلى أرض الهند فالطف بعقلك وحسن أدبك لاستخراج ذلك الكتاب من خزائنهم ومن قبل كلّ علمائهم وفقهائهم وحكمائهم تامّاً مكتوباً بالفارسيّة فتستفيده أنت وتفيدنا إيّاه من الكتب التي عندهم التي ليست في خزائننا ولا في مملكتنا واحمل معك من المال ما أحببت وإن أنت أنفدت ما معك من المال فاكتب إليّ حتّى أمدّك من المال وعجّل ذلك ولا تقصّرنّ في طلب علم وإن أكثرت فيه النفقة فإنّ جميع ما في خزائننا مبذول لك فيما أنفقته في طلب العلم.

١ كذا ل٢؛ الأصل: الذي. ٢ كذا ل٢؛ الأصل: مفكّراً. ٣ الأصل: وحثه.

education, a thirst for knowledge, an extensive knowledge of philosophy, an inquisitiveness about the unknown, and a keenness for the truth of things. In these he has attained what no king before him ever has. During his quest for learning, he heard about a book by India's philosophers, one so prized by that country's kings and scholars that it was kept under guard in their royal libraries. This book was the foundation of all education, the pinnacle of every science, the guide to every benefit, and the key to salvation in the hereafter. It supported and aided kings in all the ways they needed in order to properly administer their realms, and it educated the common people in the ways to please their king and to improve their lives. This work was *The Book of Kalīlah and Dimnah.*

When the king got confirmation of what he had heard about this book and its usefulness in educating and fortifying the intellect, he could not rest until he had acquired it and examined it. Being a man of intelligence and education, he also asked the people of his kingdom to search the realm for a learned man, intelligent, educated, literate in both Persian and Sanskrit, eager for knowledge, devoted to perfecting his education, and diligent in examining and explicating works of philosophy. Such a man was brought to the king: a handsome youth, highly accomplished, and perfect in intellect and education. He was a renowned physician, proficient in Persian and Sanskrit. His name was Barzawayh the son of Azdahar.[1] 1.4

When Barzawayh came before the king, he prostrated, then stood with head bowed. "Barzawayh," said the king, "I have selected you because I have been told of your superior learning and intellect, your fine education, and your eagerness to pursue knowledge wherever it may be found, and because I have received word about a particular book in India." 1.5

The king then told him the story, reported what he had heard about the book, and expressed a strong desire to obtain a copy. "Prepare to travel, for I am sending you to India. Use your intelligence and astuteness to extract the book from their libraries and get it away from their scholars, jurists, and sages. Transcribe it into Persian in its entirety, for your benefit and for ours, as there is no copy of this book in any of our libraries or anywhere in the kingdom.[2] Take as much money as you wish. If it runs out, send word and I will supply you with more. Hurry, and spare no effort in your pursuit of knowledge. Whatever the expense, everything in our treasury is at your disposal to cover your expenses in the pursuit of knowledge."

وأمر الملك المنجّمين فوضعوا له زايرجة[١] وتخيّروا له يوماً يسير فيه وساعة صالحة ووقتاً جيّداً وحمل معه من المال خمسة وعشرين جراباً في كلّ جراب عشرة آلاف مثقال.

٦،١ فخرج برزويه والمال معه وسار مجدّاً في السير يقطع الليل مع النهار فلمّا قدم برزويه بلاد الهند ونزلها طاف بباب الملك وتخلّل مجالس الأشراف والسوقة وسأل عن قرابة الملك والأرداف والعلماء والفلاسفة فجعل يغشاهم في منازلهم ويلقاهم بالتحيّة والمساءلة عن باب الملك وخبّرهم أنّه رجل غريب قدم بلادهم لطلب العلم والأدب وأنّه محتاج إلى معونتهم على ما طلب من ذلك وسألهم الإرشاد له في حاله والدعاء له ببلوغ آماله مع شدّة كتمانه لما له قدم ودفنه له وكنايته له عنه فلم يزل في ذلك زماناً طويلاً يري علماءهم أنّه يتأدّب ما هو به ماهر ويتعلّم من العلم ما هو به عالم ويفتّش في السرّ عن بغيته وحاجته.

٧،١ واتّخذ لطول مقامه أصدقاء كثيرة من الهند من الأشراف والسوقة ومن العلماء والفقهاء في كلّ صناعة واختار من أصدقائه واحداً فجعله صاحب سرّه ومشورته لما ظهر له من فضل أدبه وحسن علمه وجودة فهمه وكان هو مشاوره الذي إليه يستريح في جميع ما يهجم عليه من الأمور إلّا أنّه كان يكتمه الأمر الواحد الذي هو بغيته فكان يبلوه ويجرّبه باللطف وينظر هل يراه في طول مقامه موضعاً أن يطلعه على سرّه فلم يزل يبحث عن ذات نفسه حتّى وثق به وعرف أنّه لما استودعه من السرّ موضع[٢] ولما طلب منه محتمل[٣] وفيما يسأل مشفّع[٤] وفيما استعين به عليه مجتهد[٥] فازداد له إلطافاً وكان إلى ذلك اليوم الذي رجا فيه أن يكون قد ظفر بحاجته قد أعظم النفقة مع طول الغيبة في إلطاف الإخوان ومجالستهم على الطعام والشراب لطلب الثقات منهم لحاجته والبلوغ إلى بغيته فلم يطمئنّ إلى أحد ممّن آخى إلّا إلى صديقه ذلك الذي ذكرنا.

١ الأصل: ريازجة. ٢ الأصل: موضعًا. ٣ الأصل: محتملاً. ٤ الأصل: مشفعًا. ٥ الأصل: مجتهدًا.

The king commanded the astrologers to draw up a horoscope and select a day of departure, an auspicious hour, and a precise time. Barzawayh took twenty-five saddlebags of money with him, each containing ten thousand dinars.[3]

Barzawayh departed with the money and traveled quickly, day and night. 1.6
Once he reached India and had settled, he acquainted himself with the court and mingled in gatherings of nobles and commoners. He inquired about the king's favorites and assistants, and about the scholars and philosophers. He began paying his respects by visiting them in their homes, and would inquire about the court. He told them that he was a stranger who had come to their land to pursue knowledge and education, and that he needed their assistance in his quest. He asked for their guidance and prayers, but carefully concealed the goal of his journey, hiding any mention of it, and only alluding to it indirectly. Thus he continued for a long time, leading the scholars to believe that he was sharpening skills he already possessed and furthering his knowledge of subjects he already knew, but all the while he was surreptitiously inquiring about the object of his quest.

In the course of his long stay, he made many Indian friends—nobles, com- 1.7
moners, scholars, and masters of every trade. He made one friend his confidant and adviser, on account of his refinement, exceptional learning, and superior understanding. He sought his advice and felt at ease with him in every circumstance, and kept only the object of his quest concealed from him. He subtly probed and tested him, to determine whether he should be the one to whom he entrusted his secret during his stay there. He continued to examine his character and eventually came to trust him, realizing that he was indeed the right person to entrust with his secret, and that he would shoulder the burden of his request and assist him diligently in what he sought. So he treated him with more and more kindness. Given the length of his stay, by the time he hoped to achieve his purpose, he had incurred considerable expenses, entertaining people, and dining and drinking with them, in order to learn who was trustworthy and able to assist him in his objective. Of all his acquaintances, he felt at ease only with this one friend.

١،٨ وكان ممّا تكلّم به برزويه لصديقه ذلك وما ردّ عليه بعد أن فتّش برزويه بعقله حتّى وثق به واطمأنّ إليه أن قال له وهما خاليان يا أخي ما أريد أن أكتمك من أمري شيئاً أكثر ممّا كتمتك ولا أسترعنك أمري واعلم أنّي لأمرما جئت إلى أرض الهند وهو غير ما ترى ممّا يظهر منّي والعاقل يكتفي من الرجل[١] بالعلامات من نظره وإشارته بيده[٢] *فيعلم سرّ نفسه وما يضمر عليه قلبه.

١،٩ فقال له الهنديّ إنّي وإن لم أكن بدأتك وأخبرتك بما له جئت وإيّاه طلبت وأنّك تكتم أمرًا تطلبه وأنت مظهر غيره فإنّه لم يكن عنّي يخفى ولكن لرغبتي في إخائك كرهت أن أواجهك بأنّه قد ظهر لي ما تكتم فإنّه قد استبان لي ما أنت فيه وما[٣] تخفيه عنّي فأمّا إذا افتتحت[٤] الكلام فأنا مخبرك عن نفسك ومظهر لك سريرة أمرك ومعلمك حالك التي[٥] قدمت لها فإنّك قدمت بلادنا لتسلبنا علومنا النفيسة وكنوزنا الرفيعة فتذهب بها إلى بلادك لتسرّ بها ملككم فكان قدومك بالمكر ومصادقتك بالخديعة ولكنّي لمّا رأيت صبرك ومواظبتك على طلب حاجتك وتحفّظك في أن تسقط في الكلام في طول مكثك عندنا بشيء ليُستدلّ به على سريرة أمرك ازددت رغبة في عقلك وأحببت إخاءك فلا أعلم أنّي رأيت رجلاً أحسن منك أدباً ولا أصبر[٦] على طلب حاجة ولا أكتم لسرّ منك ولا أحسن خلقاً ولا سيّما في بلاد غربة ومملكة غير مملكتك وعند قوم لم تكن تعرف شيمهم وأمرهم.

١،١٠ واعلم أنّ عقل الرجل يستبين في ثماني[٧] خصال الأولى الرفق واللطف والثانية أن يعرف الرجل نفسه فيحفظها والثالثة الطاعة للملوك وتحرّي ما يرضيهم والرابعة معرفة الرجل موضع سرّه كيف ينبغي أن يطلع عليه صديقه والخامسة أن يكون على أبواب الملوك أديباً جميلاً ملق اللسان والسادسة أن يكون لسرّه وسرّ غيره حافظاً والسابعة أن يكون على لسانه قادرًا[٨] فلا يلفظ من الكلام إلّا ما قد روّى فيه وقدّره والثامنة أن يكون إذا كان في المحفل لم يجب إلّا عن ما يُسأل عنه ولم يظهر

١ والعاقل يكتفي من الرجل: كذا ل٢؛ الأصل: والرجل يكتفي من العاقل. ٢ هنا تبدأ فجوة في الأصل طولها عدّة صفحات وما أثبتنا فيما يلي من ل٢. ٣ فيه وما: كذا ش؛ ل٢: عليه وفيه ما. ٤ إذ افتتحت: ل٢: إذا فتحت. ٥ ل٢: الذي. ٦ كذا ش؛ ل٢: صبرًا. ٧ ل٢: ثمان. ٨ كذا ش؛ ل٢: واردًا.

After Barzawayh had sufficiently appraised his friend's intellect to trust him, he said to him one day when they were alone, "My friend, I don't want to hide from you any more than I already have, or keep you in the dark about me. I want you to know that I've come to India for a purpose, and it isn't what it appears to be. I know that a man of intelligence needs only certain signs—a look, a gesture—to know the secrets of another man's mind and his innermost thoughts."[4] 1.8

"None of this was hidden from me," said the Indian, "even though I haven't broached the subject of why you're here and what it is you're after, or mentioned that you're concealing the real object of your search by pretending it's something else. I wanted to treat you as a brother, so I was reluctant to confront you with my sense that you were hiding something. Now your secret designs are clear. Since you have spoken first, I will tell you about yourself, your secret mission, and why you've come. You've come to our country to rob us of our priceless knowledge and prized treasures, and take them back to your country to satisfy your king. Your presence here is a deception, and your friendliness trickery. But when I saw your patience throughout your stay, your dogged pursuit of your goal, and your care not to utter a single word that might hint at your secret, my admiration for your intellect grew, and I wanted to become your friend. Never have I seen anyone of more refinement, of greater resolve in pursuit of a goal, better able to keep something secret, or of finer character, especially in a foreign land among people whose nature and disposition are unfamiliar to you. 1.9

"A man's intelligence reveals itself in eight ways—first, in his kindness and graciousness; second, in knowing his soul's inclinations and safeguarding his tongue; third, in his obedience to kings and endeavoring to please them; fourth, in knowing to whom he can confide a secret and how to go about revealing it to a friend; fifth, in decorous comportment, elegant behavior, and sweet speech at court; sixth, in keeping his own secrets and those of others; seventh, in controlling his tongue and not saying anything without careful consideration and deliberation; and eighth, in answering at gatherings only what he has been asked and revealing nothing he will regret. Anyone who unites these qualities will attract good fortune and profit, and avoid misfortune and loss, and they all are clearly discernible in you and apparent to me. 1.10

من الأمر ما يندم عليه فمن اجتمعت فيه هذه الخصال كان هو الذي يدعو إلى نفسه الخير والربح والمجتنب للشرّ والخسران وهذه الخصال كلّها بيّنة ظاهرة فيك فالله يحفظك ويمتّعني بمودّتك ومن اجتمعت فيه هذه الخصال الثماني[١] كلّها شُفع في طلبه وأُسعف بحاجته ولكنّ حاجتك التي تطلب قد أرعبتني وأدخلت عليّ الوحشة والخشية فنسأل الله السلامة.

١١،١ ثمّ إنّ برزويه لمّا أن عرف أنّ الهنديّ علم أنّ مصادقته إيّاه كانت مكرًا وحيلاً لطلب حاجته وإنزال ذلك منه على اختلاس وسلب ولم يزجره ولم ينتهره وردّه عليه ردًّا ليّنًا وثق بقضاء حاجته وقال للهنديّ إنّي كنت قد هيّأت أعلامًا كثيرة ووضعت أصولاً وشعّبت شعوبًا وأنشأت لها غصونًا وأطرافًا أكفيت أنت عمّا كنت عليه فعرفتَ باليسير الكثير قسم الله لك في العقل والأدب فكفيتني مؤونة الكلام وحزت الجواب باليسير من القول بالإسعاف بالحاجة كما قد بدا لي منك فإنّ الكلام إذا انتهى إلى العلماء والسرّ[٢] إذا استُودع اللبيب الحافظ ثبت وبلغ غاية أمل صاحبه قويًّا ثابتًا كثبات القصر الذي أُحكم أساسه بالصخور وكالنخلة الراسية في الأرض وكالجبل الذي لا تزعزعه الرياح ولا تزلزله.

١٢،١ قال الهنديّ لا شيء أفضل من المودّة فمن كانت له مودّة في نفسه[٣] كان أهلاً أن يخلطه الرجل بنفسه ولا يدّخر شيئًا عنده ورأس الأدب حفظ السرّ لأنّ السرّ إذا تكلّم به لسانان صار إلى ثلاثة فإذا صار إلى ثلاثة شاع في الناس حتّى لا يستطيع صاحبه أن يجحده كالغيم[٤] الذي إذا كان متقطّعًا[٥] فقال أحدهم إنّ هذا غيم متقطّع لم يكذّبه أحد على ذلك بل يصدّقه كلّ من يراه متقطّعًا وأمّا أنا فقد اشتدّ سروري وابتهاجي بمودّتك وخلطتك وهذا الأمر الذي تطلبه فهو شيء غير منكتم ولا بدّ من أن يفشو في المجالس فإذا فشا وعلن هلكت نفسي هلاكًا لا أقدر على التخلّص منه بالفداء بمال وإن كثر لأنّ ملكنا فظّ غليظ يعاقب على الطفيف فكيف على مثل هذا.

١ ل٢: الثانية. ٢ إذا انتهى . . . والسرّ: كذا ش؛ ل٢: قد انتهى إلى من العلماء إنّ. ٣ فمن . . . نفسه: كذا ش؛ ساقطة من ل٢. ٤ كذا ش؛ ل٢: كالغنم. ٥ كذا ش؛ ل٢: منقطعًا (٣ مرّات).

God keep you and enable me to enjoy your friendship! Anyone in whom these eight qualities are found deserves assistance in his quest and in reaching his objective. But what you are seeking frightens me and fills me with anxiety and trepidation. We beseech God to keep us safe."

Barzawayh felt confident about accomplishing his mission when he dis- 1.11
covered that the Indian had answered him gently, without rebuke or chiding, even though the Indian had realized that Barzawayh's friendship with him was motivated by deception and cunning in pursuit of his objective and saw him as someone intent on plunder and theft. Barzawayh replied, "It turns out that I won't need to rely on the many types of learning in which I am proficient, the premises I've established, the ramifications I've detected, the branches and details I've devised—you've already divined a great deal about my intentions and discerned much on the basis of the slightest evidence. By your God-given intellect and discernment, you've spared me the trouble of arguing. I have received a response in a few words that apparently you will assist me in my mission. When a scholar learns a secret, when it is confided to a person of intelligence and discretion, he stands firm and fulfills all the hopes of the confider of the secret, as strong as a castle with a stone foundation, as a palm tree with deep roots, or as a mountain that winds cannot unsettle or shake."

"Nothing is better than love," responded the Indian. "Whoever has 1.12
love in his mind deserves to have a friend who shares his mind with him and doesn't hold back his thoughts. Good conduct begins with the keeping of secrets; when a secret is shared by two, it makes its way to three, and when it does, it becomes such common knowledge that its keeper will be unable to disavow it, like clouds when they are scattered—no one doubts that they are scattered, and anyone saying so will be believed by everyone who sees that they are. For my part, I am exceedingly happy and delighted with your friendship and company. What you seek, however, cannot remain concealed; it will inevitably leak out wherever people assemble, and when it becomes public, my life will be in such peril that no ransom, however great, could save it. Our king is harsh and severe. He punishes the slightest offense. Imagine what he will do in a case like this!"

قال برزويه إنّ العلماء قد مدحت الصديق إذا كتم سرّ صديقه وهذا الأمر الذي قدمت له إيّاك اعتمدت به وإليك أفشيته ومنك أرجو نجاحه وهو أمر جسيم وخطره عندي عظيم وأنا واثق بعقلك ولطفك وحسن تأنّيك وحيلتك في إدراكي ما أمّلت منه على يديك وبيمنك وإن مسّك في ذلك مشقّة من خشية وأنا أعلم أنك آمن من قبلي أن أطلع عليه أحداً ولكنّك تتّقي أهل بلادك المطيفين بالملك أن يشيعوا ذلك وأرجو أن لا يشيع لأنّي ظاعن وأنت مقيم وما أقمت فليس بيننا ثالث وإذا رحلت عنك أمنت نفسك أن تفشيه[١] عليك. ١٣،١

فشفعه الهنديّ لمّا سمع مقالته وأعطاه حاجته من الكتب فلمّا وقع برزويه في تفسير الكتب ونسخها أقام على ذلك زماناً طويلاً عظمت فيه مؤونته ونفقته وأنصب فيه[٢] بدنه وسهر[٣] فيه ليله ودأب[٤] فيه نهاره على خوف من نفسه فلمّا فرغ من ذلك الكتاب وغيره من الكتب وأحكمها كتب إلى أنوشروان يعلمه بما لقي من النصب والروع وأنّه قد فرغ من حاجته التي وجّهه فيها وغيرها ممّا يعلم أنّ الملك يحتاج إليه من علوم الهند وكتبها وأنّه يحمل إلى الملك ما حصل قِبَله منها. ١٤،١

فلمّا انتهى الكتاب إلى أنوشروان وقرأه وعلم أنّه قد فرغ من حاجته فرح فرحاً شديداً ثمّ تخوّف معاجلة المقادير أن تنغّص[٥] سروره بما استفاد له برزويه فعاجل ذلك وأمر بالكتاب إلى برزويه يسأله تعجيل القدوم وأن يبسط أمله بما جُدّد له من حسن رأي الملك فيه فإنّه مفضّله ومتّخذه وزيراً ووجّه بالكتاب مع بعض ثقاته على البريد وأمره أن يسير في غير الجادّة حذر أن يُوجد فيفشو ما كان أسرّ فيذهب كلّ ما كان عمل ضلالاً. ١٥،١

فلمّا انتهى الرسول إلى برزويه دفع الكتاب إليه سرّاً فلمّا قرأه تجهّز وبرح مكانه وسار حتّى قدم على أنوشروان فأُخبر بقدومه[٦] فأمر بإدخاله عليه فلمّا رأى ما به من الشحوب والنصب والضرر رقّ له وقال أبشر أيّها العبد الصالح فستأكل حلاوة ١٦،١

---

١ كذا ش؛ ل٢: يفشيها. ٢ كذا ش؛ ل٢: في. ٣ كذا ش؛ ل٢: وأسهر. ٤ كذا ش؛ ل٢: وذاب. ٥ كذا ش؛ ل٢: ينغّصه. ٦ أن يسير . . . بقدومه: كذا ش؛ ساقطة من ل٢.

Barzawayh replied, "Scholars have praised the friend who keeps a friend's secret. I rely on you in the matter that has brought me here. I've revealed it to you, and hope it will succeed because of you. It is serious business and I know the danger is great, but I trust your acumen, discretion, caution, and resourcefulness in devising a way for me to realize my hopes through your efforts and with your good fortune and blessing, even if you are troubled by fear. I know you aren't afraid that I'll tell anyone about it; you fear that your compatriots who surround the king might discover the secret. But I don't expect it to be leaked, since I am leaving and you are staying. For as long as I am here, there will be no third party; and when I leave, you need have no fear that you will reveal it to your own detriment." 1.13

At these words, the Indian granted his request and gave him the books he wanted. Barzawayh went to work interpreting and copying them. The task took so long that his provisions and expenses mounted. He wore himself out, staying up at night and working all day, fearing all the while for his life. When he was satisfied with the job he had done with the book, and with other books besides, he wrote to Anūsharwān that despite fatigue and fear he had completed the book he had been sent to get, along with other books of Indian science that he knew the king would need, and would convey to the king everything he had acquired. 1.14

Anūsharwān rejoiced when he read the letter and knew that Barzawayh had indeed accomplished his mission. Fearing, however, that fortune might intervene and frustrate his joy by depriving him of what Barzawayh had obtained, he immediately ordered a letter to be written commanding Barzawayh to come home without delay. He wrote that Barzawayh could expect to be handsomely rewarded as a result of the king's renewed esteem; that as the king's favorite he would be appointed vizier. The king dispatched the letter with a trusted courier. He ordered him not to take the main highway, lest he be intercepted and the secret be divulged, in which case all his efforts would come to naught. 1.15

When the messenger reached Barzawayh, he delivered the letter in secret. Barzawayh read it, packed his bags, and left immediately for Anūsharwān's court. As soon as Anūsharwān learned of his arrival, he ordered that he be brought into his presence. When he saw how pale, fatigued, and exhausted 1.16

ثمرة نصيحتك فقرّ عيناً فقد استوجبت شكرًا من جميع الرعيّة وعظيم المكافأة منّا. وأمره أن يريح نفسه وبدنه سبعة أيّام ثمّ يأتيه من بعد ذلك ففعل برزويه.

فلمّا كان اليوم الثامن دعا به وأمر أن تحضر العظماء والأشراف فلمّا اجتمعوا ١٧،١
وعنده برزويه أمر بإحضار الكتب التي قدم بها فُفُتحت وقرأها على رؤوس الأشهاد فلمّا سمعوا ما فيها من العلوم والآداب والعقل والأعاجيب التي حكوها على ألسنة الحيوان والطير ورأوا أعاجيبه فرحوا بذلك فرحًا شديدًا وشكروا الله جلّ وعزّ على ذلك وعلى ما منّ به عليهم على يدي برزويه ثمّ إنّهم دعوا لبرزويه وأحسنوا الثناء عليه في إنصابه بدنه واحتياله في استخراجها وإفادتهم إيّاها.

ثمّ إنّ الملك أمر أن تُفتح لبرزويه خزائن الجوهر والذهب الأحمر والفضّة والكسوة ١٨،١
وأقسم عليه الملك إلّا دخل فأخذ ما أحبّ منها. فسجد برزويه للملك وقال أكرم الله الملك كرامة يجمع له بها شرف الدنيا والآخرة وأحسن جزاءه فقد أغناني الله بحسن رأي الملك عن جميع عروض الدنيا بما وهب الله لي على يديك أيّها الملك العظيم الخطر الكريم الخلق السعيد الجدّ فلا حاجة لي إلى المال ولكن لسروري بموافقة الملك واتّباعي مسرّته آخذ من كسوة تختًا من طراز قوهستان[1] أتجمّل به في خدمة الملك وعلى بابه.

فأخذه وذهب به إلى منزله ليفاخر به من بباب الملك من أهل بيته وخاصّته ١٩،١
ثمّ قال أصلح الله الملك وأكرمه إنّ الإنسان إذا كان ذا عقل وأدب فأُكرم وأُعطي وأُحسن إليه وجب عليه أن يشكر ذلك وإن كان قد استوجبه قبل أن يُعطاه فأنا للملك شاكر أسأل الله أن يديم له السرور والغبطة في جميع الأمور ولي أعزّ الله الملك حاجة هي أعظم الحوائج عندي وأكملها لديّ وأجزلها قدرًا عندي بعد رضى الملك فإن رأى الملك أن يسعفني بحاجتي ويعطيني سؤلي فإنّها يسيرة على الملك عظيمة القدر والموقع عندي.

١ كذا ش؛ ساقطة من ل٢.

Barzawayh was, he took pity and said, "Rejoice, faithful servant; you shall soon taste the sweet fruit of your devotion. Be glad, for you have earned the gratitude of the entire nation as well as a great reward from us." He commanded Barzawayh to rest mind and body for seven days, and then return, which Barzawayh did.

On the eighth day, the king summoned Barzawayh and commanded all the high officials and nobles to attend. When they had all assembled, the king commanded that the books Barzawayh had brought from India be fetched. The books were opened and their contents read before the audience. When they heard the contents—the learning, culture, intelligence, and marvels the Indians had recounted via the tongues of animals and birds—they rejoiced and thanked God for what He had bestowed on them through Barzawayh. They invoked God's blessing on him and showered him with praise for his painstaking efforts to acquire the books and bring them. 1.17

The king commanded that the storerooms of jewels, gold, silver, and garments be opened, and entreated Barzawayh to take whatever he wished. Barzawayh prostrated himself before the king, invoked God's blessing on him, and said, "May God in His generosity grant the king honor in this world and the next, and reward him with the greatest reward. By the king's approval, God has freed me of need for the goods of this world by means of what He has bestowed on me at your hands, O great, generous, and fortunate king. I have no need for wealth. Nevertheless, because complying with the king's wishes and doing what pleases him gives me joy, I will take a garment of Qūhistān weave to wear while serving the king and at court." 1.18

Barzawayh agreed to take the garment home, if only to impress the royal family and the courtiers. He then said, "May God prosper the king and grant him honor! When a person of intelligence and cultivation is honored, given gifts, and treated with favor, it behooves him to be thankful, no matter how much he may deserve it. In gratitude to the king, I pray that God will grant him lasting joy and happiness in all things. But I have one wish—may God increase the king's might—which, to my mind, is the greatest, most perfect, and loftiest thing I could hope for after the king's approval. If the king sees fit, it will be easy for him to grant my request, but it will be something of great value and importance to me." 1.19

٢٠،١ قال أنوشروان سل تُعط[١] ما أحببت واشفع تُشفع بها وتُكرم فإنّ جزاءك عندي عظيم ولو سألت الشركة في الملك لم تخيّب طلبتك فكيف سوى ذلك فقل فإنّ جميع ما تسأل مبذول لك وحبّاً وكرامة.

٢١،١ قال برزويه أكرم الله الملك وأحسن عني جزاءه لست أمنّ على الملك بنصبي وعنائي له بل له الفضل عليّ بما عرّضني له وأشركني في هذه الفائدة ولكن بكرم الملك وفضل رأيه كافأني وأحسن إليّ فليعظّم المنّة على عبده باستتمام النعمة[٢] إليه وإلى أهل بيته ويشرّفه بأن يأمر بزرجمهر بن البختكان ويعزم عليه أن يجهد نفسه في وضعه باباً يذكر فيه أمري وحالي ويبالغ[٣] في ذلك بأحسن الكلام وأزين الذكر وأحسن التأليف ويأمر بذلك الباب إذا فرغ منه أن يضعه بين تلك الأبواب التي[٤] في الكتاب ليحيي به ذكري ما حييت في الدنيا وبعد وفاتي فإنّه إن فعل ذلك فقد شرّفني وأهل بيتي إلى آخر الأبد ما دام هذا الكتاب[٥] منشوراً في الدنيا يُقرأ.

٢٢،١ فلمّا سمع الملك وعلماؤه وعظماؤه مقالة برزويه عجبوا من عقله وممّا سما إليه رأيه وما طلب من الشرف الدائم في الدنيا فقال الملك لبرزويه نعم وكرامة أنت أهل أن تُشفع في طلبتك فما أيسر ما سألت في جنب ما تستوجب وإن كان عندك عظيم الخطر.

٢٣،١ فأرسل الملك إلى بزرجمهر من ساعته فلمّا دخل عليه قال له[٦] *يا بزرجمهر قد عرفت مناصحة برزويه لنا وتحرّيه لمرضاتنا وركوبه الهول والخوف فيما ينفعنا وإنضائه بدنه فيما سرّنا وما أتى إلينا من المعروف وأصبنا على يديه من العلم والحكمة وما عرضنا عليه من تعوّضه لما كان منه من خزائننا من الأموال واللطف فلم يقبل منّا شيئاً من ذلك وكان حاجته إلينا وإليه منّا أمراً يسيراً يرى أنّه الجزاء والكرامة وهو كذا وكذا فأنا أحبّ أن تشفعني في ذلك وأنّه بطلبتي فإنّه ممّا يسرّني وتجتهد وإن احتملت فيه مشقّة وهو أن تكتب باباً مشاكلاً لتلك الأبواب التي في ذلك الكتاب وتذكر فيه فضل

١ كذا ش؛ ل٢: تعطى. ٢ كذا ش؛ ساقطة من ل٢. ٣ كذا ش؛ ل٢: ويتابع. ٤ كذا ش؛ ل٢: الذي. ٥ كذا ش؛ ساقطة من ل٢. ٦ هنا تنبهي الفجوة وننقل بقيّة الباب من الأصل.

"Ask and you shall be given whatever you desire," said Anūsharwān. "Plead and your plea will be granted most generously, for we deem you worthy of a great reward. Even if you ask to be made co-ruler, we will not deny your request—let alone anything else. Speak! Everything you ask will be given freely and generously." 1.20

"May God honor the king and reward him well on my behalf," said Barzawayh. "I cannot reproach the king for my fatigue and trouble; on the contrary, he deserves my thanks for having compensated me and for allowing me to share in this benefit. The king's generosity and good opinion are the best compensation. May he then magnify his favor toward his servant and perfect his favor to him and to his family by commanding and enjoining Buzurgmihr the son of Bukhtigān to employ his talents to compose a chapter about my life and character. Let Buzurgmihr deploy his choicest language, his most elegant words, and his best style. May the king command that this chapter, when completed, be placed with the book's other chapters, to keep the memory of me alive as long as I am in the world and after my death. Should the king do this, he will have honored me and my family for as long as this book continues to circulate and be read in this world." 1.21

When the king, along with his scholars and officials, heard Barzawayh's words, they were pleased by his reasoning, high-mindedness, and desire for enduring honor in this world. "Gladly and with pleasure!" replied the king. "Your request deserves to be granted. It may seem momentous to you, yet how small it is compared to what you deserve!" 1.22

The king immediately sent for Buzurgmihr and said to him,[5] "Buzurgmihr, you know Barzawayh's devotion to us: how he strove to please us, exposed himself to perils and dangers for our benefit, and wearied himself to make us happy. You know the favor he has done us and the knowledge and wisdom we have gained through him. You know that we offered him wealth and gifts from our treasuries, but he accepted none of this. What he desires of us and for himself is something very small, something he sees as a reward and an honor." The king then explained Barzawayh's request. "I want you to assist me in this matter, for I request it and it will bring me joy. I want you to exert yourself, however difficult it may be, and to write a chapter to 1.23

برزويه وكيف كان أوّل أمره وشأنه وتنسبه فيه إلى نسبه وحسبه وإلى صناعته وأدبه وترفّعه من ذلك إلى بعثنا إيّاه إلى الهند في حاجتنا وما أفادنا من هنالك وشرّفناه به وفضّلناه وكيف كانت حال برزويه بعد قدومه من الهند بأفضل ما تجد من المدح في الكلام وبالغ في ذلك أفضل المبالغة واجتهد فيه اجتهاداً يسرّ برزويه ويسرّني ويسرّ جميع أهل المملكة ويسرّك خاصّة لطلبك العلم وحبّك أهله وأنا أرى لك أن تجتهد في أن يكون ذلك الباب الذي تضعه أفضل تلك الأبواب كلّها فإنّك أسعد الناس بذلك لأنّه لا يُقرأ ولا يُذكر برزويه إلّا كنت شريكاً[1] في ذلك الذكر والثناء واجعل ذلك الباب أوّل تلك الأبواب فإذا أنت فرغت من ذلك الباب ووضعته موضعه فآذنّي حتّى أجمع أهل المملكة وتقرأ على رؤوس الناس ليظهر لهم من حلمك وعلمك واجتهادك في مسرّتنا ما قد خفي عليهم.

٢٤،١ فلمّا سمع برزويه مقالة الملك والذي عظم خطره عنده ومنزلته منه خرّ ساجداً وقال أدام الله لك أيّها الملك السرور والفرح وقرّة العين ورزقك في الدنيا الشرف الذي تفوق به جميع المخلوقين وفي الآخرة أفضل المنازل مع الصالحين المستوجبين جنّات النعيم.

٢٥،١ فخرج بزرجمهر من عند الملك فأخذ في وضع ذلك الباب الذي أمره به الملك ووصف أمر برزويه من أوّل ما دفعه أبوه في التعليم إلى أن بعثه الملك إلى الهند وجاء بذلك الكتاب بأحسن ما يقدر عليه من الوصف بما قد كان عرف من أدب برزويه وسيرته وما ظهر[2] للناس منه من استحقاره للدنيا وزهادته فيها ورغبته في الآخرة وإلى ما تصير إليه نفسه في المعاد فلم يترك من أخلاق برزويه وصناعته شيئاً إلّا بيّنه بأحسن ما يقدر عليه في ذلك الكتاب بتأليف ونسق محكم ثمّ أعلم الملك بفراغه وأنّه قد وضعه في أوّل ذلك الكتاب.

٢٦،١ فجمع الملك الناس من العظماء والأشراف والعامّة فدخلوا عليه ودعا بزرجمهر بالكتاب بمحضر من برزويه فأمر بقراءته على رؤوس الناس فقام بزرجمهر ففتح

١ الأصل: شريك. ٢ وما ظهر: كذا ش؛ الأصل: وظهر.

go with the other chapters of the book, one that mentions Barzawayh's virtues, his early life, his distinguished lineage, his profession, his education, and his eminence, including how we sent him to India on our mission; the boons he brought back for us, for which we have honored and distinguished him; and the state he was in upon his return from India. Use the most laudatory language you can find. Spare no effort, so that you bring joy to Barzawayh, to me, and to the entire kingdom. It will bring joy to you, in particular, because of your love of learning and of scholars. You will be the most fortunate of people, for whenever the book is read and Barzawayh is mentioned, you will share in Barzawayh's fame and acclaim. Make it the first chapter of the book. Let me know when you have finished it and placed it where it belongs, so I can assemble the most important people in the kingdom and you can read it to them. In this way, the full extent of your judiciousness, learning, and effort to please us will become visible to them."

When Buzurgmihr heard the king's words and the great importance he 1.24
attached to the project, he bowed low and said, "Your Majesty, may God make your joy, gladness, and happiness endure! May He grant you in this world honor exceeding that of all creatures, and in the hereafter the best of dwellings with the righteous who merit the Gardens of Bliss."

Buzurgmihr left the king's presence and began composing the chapter the 1.25
king had commanded. He described Barzawayh's life from the time his father sent him to be educated[6] until the time the king sent him to India, and he returned with the book. In this chapter, he described as best he could what he knew about Barzawayh's education and way of life, his manifest contempt for the world, his asceticism, his desire for the hereafter, and what his soul longed for in its ultimate destination. He omitted nothing concerning Barzawayh's character and profession, all in his best style and manner of composition. Then he informed the king that he had completed the chapter and had placed it at the beginning of the book.

The king assembled high officials, nobles, and common folk. He sum- 1.26
moned Buzurgmihr to bring the book and—in Barzawayh's presence—commanded that it be read aloud to the people. Buzurgmihr stood up, opened the book, and read "The Chapter of Barzawayh" to the people. The king and all the people rejoiced at Buzurgmihr's intelligence and learning,

الكتّاب وقرأ باب برزويه على رؤوس الناس ففرح الملك وجميع الناس بما أُوتي بزرجمهر من العقل والعلم وبما اجتهد فيه من مدحه برزويه من غير تكذيب منه وادّعاء باطل وأثنى عليه الملك وجميع الأشراف وشكروا له ذلك ومدحوه أفضل المدح فأمر له الملك بجائزة عظيمة من المال والحليّ والثياب فلم يأخذ من ذلك شيئاً إلّا الكسوة فإنّه قبضها فكان يتجمّل بها ويفخر بها على نظرائه لأنّها كانت من كسوة الملوك خاصّة وشكر له برزويه وقبّل يده ورأسه وأقبل على الملك فقال أدام الله لك أيّها الملك الكرامة والجمال فقد أكرمتني بما أمرت به بزرجمهر في هذا الكتاب.

تمّت بعثة أنوشروان برزويه إلى أرض الهند وما كان من أمره.

and at the effort he had expended to praise Barzawayh without engaging in fabrication or specious claims. The king and all the nobles commended him, thanked him, and praised him in the highest terms. The king bestowed a splendid reward of money, jewels, and clothing, but Buzurgmihr accepted only one garment. He donned it to impress his colleagues, as it was a garment such as the king himself might wear. Barzawayh thanked him, kissed his head and hand, and then turned to the king and said, "Your Majesty, may God make your honor and beauty endure, for you have honored me by what you have commanded Buzurgmihr to write in this book."

Here ends the Account of How Anūsharwān Sent Barzawayh to India and What Happened to Him.

كتاب كليلة ودمنة

١،٢ وهو ممّا وضعت أهل الهند من الأمثال والأحاديث التي[١] التمسوا[٢] أن يدخلوا فيها أبلغ ما وجدوا من الكلام في النحو الذي أرادوا ولم تزل العلماء من كلّ أمّة وأهل كلّ لسان يلتمسون أن يُعقل عنهم ويحتالون لذلك بصنوف الحيل ويبتغون في إخراج ما عندهم من العلل حتّى كان من تلك العلل وضع بليغ الكلام ومنمّقه على أفواه البهائم والطير فاجتمع لهم بذلك خلال أمّا هم فوجدوا منصرفًا[٣] في القول وشعابًا[٤] يأخذون فيها ولهوًا وحكمة فاحتمله الحكماء لحكمته والسخفاء للهوه والمتعلّمون من الأحداث وغيرهم فنشطوا لعلمه وخفّ عليهم حفظه فإذا احتنك الحدث واجتمع له العلم وتدبّر[٥] ما كان حفظ ممّا صار مقيّدًا مزبورًا في صدره وهو لا يدري ما هو عرف أنّه قد ظفر من ذلك بكنوز عظام فكان كالرجل الذي يدرك حين يدرك فيجد آباءه قد حفروا كنوزًا من الذهب والفضّة واعتقدوا له عقدًا استغنى بها عن استعمال السعي والطلب. ولم يكن لمّا أن كثرت فروع كلّ صنف منها حتّى لا يستكمل منها شيء بدّ من أن تكثر العلل التي تجري عليها أقاويل العلماء فمن قرأ هذا الكتاب فليعرف الوجه الذي وُضع عليه فإنّه إن لم يعرف ذلك لم يدرِ إلى أيّ غاية يجري فيه وأيّ شيء جنى منه.

٢،٢ فأوّل ما ينبغي لمن طلب هذا الكتاب أن يبتدئ بجودة[٦] قراءته والتثبّت وأن لا تكون غايته منه بلوغ آخره ولكنّ الوقوع على معانيه ومعرفته بما يقرأ منه والتفكّر فيه فإنّه من كان همّه منه بلوغ آخره لا الإحكام لما يقرأ فليس ينتفع بقراءته ولا يستفيد منه شيئًا فإنّه من أصاب شيئًا فطمحت عيناه إلى جمعه ولم يأخذ منه ما صفا[٧]

---

١ الأصل: الذي. ٢ كذا ش/١، ع؛ الأصل: التمسوه. ٣ الأصل: مصرفا. ٤ كذا ع وهامش ش؛ الأصل: وصوبًا. ٥ كذا ش؛ الأصل: تدبر. ٦ بجودة قراءته: كذا ع؛ الأصل: وحوده وقراته. ٧ ولم يأخذ... صفا: كذا ل٢؛ ساقطة من الأصل.

The Book of Kalīlah and Dimnah[7]

This book is a work of parables and stories composed by the people of India, who sought to incorporate into it the most eloquent speech they could find in the style they preferred. In order to make their intentions comprehensible, scholars of every nation and tongue have employed a variety of devices and means when presenting their arguments. One device was to put eloquent and elegant language into the mouths of animals and birds. This enabled them to accomplish a number of things: they found a way to speak indirectly and to communicate through implication.[8] Because such a book combined entertainment with wisdom, the wise would study it for its wisdom, and the simple for its value as entertainment; young pupils and others would be delighted to read it and it would be easy for them to memorize. When the young person reached maturity and grew in knowledge, he would ponder what he had memorized—as it had been recorded and inscribed in his heart without his knowing its true nature—and would come to realize that he had acquired a great treasure. He would be like someone who, on coming of age, discovers that his parents had unearthed treasures of gold and silver, and had established a bequest for him, freeing him from the need to toil and seek a living. As each type of learning has many branches and nothing can encompass them all, therefore the means that scholars use to express them also need to be numerous. The reader thus needs to know the method used to compose the book, otherwise he will not comprehend its intention or realize what can be gained from it. 2.1

The Man Who Found a Treasure but Could Not Keep It

The first requirement for anyone studying this book is to begin with a careful, deliberate reading: the objective should not be to get to the end of the book, but to uncover its meanings and to understand and reflect on what is being read. No one will benefit from the book if his sole concern is to reach its end without thoroughly understanding what he is reading. The person who finds something and rushes to get it all at once, without stopping 2.2

الأوّل فالأوّل فهو خليق ألّا يصيب منه إلّا كما أصاب الرجل الذي أصاب الكنز ولم يحفظه. حديث الرجل الذي أصاب الكنز بلغني أنّه وجد في بعض الصحارى كنزًا فلمّا فتحه ونظر إليه رأى شيئًا عظيمًا لا عهد له بمثله فقال في نفسه إن أخذت في نقل ما هاهنا قليلًا قليلًا جعلت لنفسي شغلًا طويلًا ولم أحرز منه في الأيّام إلّا يسيرًا ولكنّي أستأجر رجالًا ينقلونه[1] إلى منزلي. ففعل ذلك وجاب[2] الرجال فجعل يحمل كلّ رجل منهم ما أطاق لينطلقوا به زعم إلى منزله فلم يزل دائبًا في ذلك حتّى فرغ منه واستنفده ثمّ انطلق إلى منزله بعد الفراغ فلم يجد منه في منزله شيئًا ووجد كلّ رجل منهم قد حاز ما حمل لنفسه فلم يكن له[3] منه إلّا العناء في استخراجه.

٣،٢ فكذلك الرجل ليس ينبغي له أن يجاوز شيئًا إلى غيره حتّى يحكمه ويتثبّت فيه ولا يطلب الآخر حتّى يحكم الأوّل فإذا تثبّت في قراءته وأحكمه فعليه بالفهم لما يقرأ والمعرفة له حتّى يضع كلّ شيء موضعه وينسبه إلى معناه ولا يعرض في نفسه إن قد أحكم القراءة وعرف ظاهر القول فقد فرغ ممّا ينبغي أن يعرف منه ولكن يعرف أنّ له باطنًا لم يعرفه فإذا لم يعرف ذلك لم ينتفع بما ظهر له منه كما لو أنّ رجلًا أتى بجوز صحاح في قشره لم ينتفع به حتّى يكسّره ويستخرج ما فيه.

٤،٢ وعليه أن يعلم أنّ له خبيئًا وأن يلتمس علم ذلك ولا يكون مثل الرجل صاحب الصحيفة الصفراء بلغني أنّه طلب شيئًا من علم الفصاحة فأتى صديقًا له ومعه صحيفة صفراء فسأله أن يكتب له أصل العربيّة في تلك الصحيفة فكتب له شيئًا من ذلك فأخذ الرجل الصحيفة فانطلق بها إلى منزله وجعل يقرأها وهو لا يدري ما معنى الذي يقرأه إلّا أنّه يقرأ الذي يرى في الصحيفة وجعل يقعد مع القوم وهو يظنّ أنّه[4] قد أحكم ما في الصحيفة فتكلّم بكلمة أخطأ فيها فقال له بعض من عنده من القوم لحنت أيّها الرجل. فقال ألحن والصحيفة الصفراء في منزلي.

---

١ الأصل: ينقلوا. ٢ الأصل: وحاب. ٣ كذا ش، ع، پ٣٤٧٥؛ ساقطة من الأصل. ٤ الأصل: أن.

to understand it bit by bit, is likely to suffer the fate of the man who discovered a treasure but couldn't hold on to it. This man, I was told, found a treasure chest in a desert. When he opened it and looked inside, he saw that it was greater than anything he had ever seen, and said to himself, "It will take a long time to carry it away little by little—even a small amount will take me days. I will hire men to bring it all to my house." And that is what he did. He brought the men, and each picked up what he could carry, heading—as the man supposed—to his house. When the job was done and the hoard had been removed, the man went home, where he found nothing. He realized that everyone he had hired had made off with whatever he could carry. All the man had to show for it was the trouble he'd taken to extract the treasure.

Similarly, you shouldn't pass from one thing to the next until you thoroughly understand the first thing; don't try to get to the end before you know the beginning. Once you are able to read this book properly, you must understand what you are reading and familiarize yourself with it, so that you can put each thing in its proper place and connect it with its meaning. You must not assume that if you have read the book through and know its outward sense, you are done with what you need to know. You must realize that the book has an inner meaning still to be learned and that you will not benefit from the outward sense until you become acquainted with the inner meaning—just as unshelled nuts bring no benefit until you crack them and extract their kernels. 2.3

The Man Who Thought He Had Mastered the Rules of Good Arabic

The book has a hidden sense that the reader must seek to know. He must not be like the man in the story, who, I've been told, in order to acquire proficiency in the art of eloquence went to a friend with a clean page and asked him to write down the rules of good Arabic. The friend did so and the man took the page home and read it, but he didn't know the meaning of what he was reading—he was only reading the words on the page. Thinking he had mastered the contents, he took a seat among a group of experts. When he spoke and made a mistake, one of the men said, "Sir, you have made a grammatical error." "How can I speak ungrammatically," he replied, "when I have my page at home?" 2.4

فالمرء حقيق أن يطلب العلم فإذا وجد حاجته وفهم[١] وعرف وبلغ غايته انتفع[٢] بما عرف وتأدّب بما رأى فيه من الأدب فإنّه يقال في أمرين لا ينبغي لأحد أن يستكثر منهما كثيرًا العقل والتزوّد للآخرة. ويقال أيضاً في أمرين يحتاج إليهما كلّ من يحتاج إلى الحياة الأدب الصالح والمال الكثير. ويقال الأدب يجلو العقل كما يجلو الودك ظلمة النار ويزيدها ضوءًا والأدب يرفع منزلة صاحبه كما ترتفع الكرة يضربها الرجل الشديد. ٥،٢

ومثل[٣] من علم ولم يستعمل علمه[٤] ولم ينتفع به كالرجل الذي مثله مثل حديث الرجل والسارق زعموا أنّ رجلاً دخل بيته سارق ليلاً وهو في منزله فاستيقظ صاحب المنزل وقال لأسكتنّ حتّى أنظر ما يصنع ولأدعنّه حتّى إذا فرغ ممّا يأخذ قمت إليه فنغّصته وكدّرته عليه. فسكت وهو على فراشه وجعل السارق يطوف[٥] بالبيت ويتردّد حتّي غلب على الرجل النوم فنام ووافق ذلك فراغ السارق ممّا أراد من جمع متاع البيت فانطلق واستيقظ الرجل بعد ذهاب السارق فلم ير في بيته شيئًا فأقبل يلوم نفسه ويعاتبها أنّ علمه لم ينفعه شيئًا إذ لم يستعمله. ٦،٢

فالعلم لا يتمّ لامرئ إلّا بالعمل والعلم هو الشجرة والعمل هو الثمرة وإنّما يطلب الرجل العلم لينتفع به وإذا لم ينتفع به فليس له أن يطلبه كمثل رجل لو قيل له أنّ رجلاً كان عارفًا بطريق مخوف ثمّ ركبه فأصابه فيه مكروه لتُعجّب من جهله ولعلّ غيره أن يركب من الأمور ما يعرف منه القبح والدناءة وسوء العاقبة فهو بذلك منه أشدّ استيقانًا من ذلك الرجل الذي ركب بجهله وحمله على ذلك هواه أو كالمريض العالم الذي يعرف ثقيل الطعام وخفيفه ثمّ يحمله الشهوة والشره على أكل الثقيل منه فأقلّ الناس عذرًا في ارتكاب قبيح من قد عرف قبحه وأقلّهم عذرًا في ترك الأعمال الحسنة من قد عرف فضلها وما فيها من المنفعة وليس يُعذر أحد بالخطا كما أنّه لو أنّ رجلين أحدهما بصير والآخر أعمى وقعا في بئر فهلكا جميعاً ولم ينجّ[٦] البصير من الهلكة أنّه ٧،٢

١ الأصل: فهم. ٢ الأصل: وانتفع. ٣ الأصل: من استعمله و. ٤ كذا ل٢: ساقطة من الأصل. ٥ كذا ل٢؛ ساقطة من الأصل. ٦ الأصل: ينجوا.

We ought to seek knowledge. When we have found what we seek—when we have understood it, become acquainted with it, and have reached our goal—we should derive benefit from what we have learned and be guided by the education we have acquired. It is said that there are two things we can never have too much of: intelligence, and provisioning for the hereafter. It is also said that there are two things required by all who would live a full life: sound education and great wealth. Education, they say, makes intelligence apparent in the way that grease increases the brightness of a dim flame. It raises the station of its possessor just as a poloball struck by a strong man soars through the air. 2.5

A man who has acquired knowledge but hasn't put it to good use is like the man in the following story. Once, they say, a burglar entered a man's house at night. The man woke up and said to himself, "I'll keep quiet and see what he does. I'll leave him be, and when he's done taking things I'll get up, stop him, and spoil his fun." So he kept quiet in his bed as the burglar began prowling around the house. Finally, just as the burglar finished gathering everything he wanted and left, the man grew drowsy and fell asleep. He woke up after the burglar had gone and, finding the house empty, began to chide and berate himself. He realized that because he hadn't used his knowledge, he hadn't benefited from it at all. 2.6

The Man Who Neglected to Put His Knowledge to Use

Only through actions can knowledge be perfected. Knowledge is the tree; actions are the fruit. A man seeks knowledge only to benefit from it; if he doesn't benefit from it, he has no reason to seek it. You would marvel at the ignorance of a man who was told that a road was known to be dangerous yet followed it and came to grief. And the person who does what he knows to be low and vile, with bad consequences besides, may be even more certain of what he is doing than the man who puts himself at risk out of ignorance and caprice. You might compare him to a sick man who knows the difference between heavy and light food, yet is led by appetite and gluttony to eat food that is heavy. There is little excuse for committing vile deeds when we know they are vile, and little excuse for failing to do praiseworthy deeds when we know their merits and benefits. Neither mistake can be excused. It is as if two 2.7

وقع في البئر وهو يبصرها وكلاهما بمنزلة واحدة في الهلكة غير أنّ البصير[١] عند العقلاء أقلّ عذرًا.

٨،٢ فمن كان يطلب العلم ليعلّمه غيره وليُعرف به فإنّما هو مثل عين الماء التي ينتفع الناس بمائها وليس لها من تلك المنفعة شيء فقد ينبغي لمن يطلب العلم أن يبدأ فيعظ به نفسه ثمّ عليه[٢] بعد ذلك أن يُقبسه غيره فإنّ ثلاثًا ينبغي لصاحب الدنيا أن يقتبسها ويُقبسها منها العلم ومنها المال ومنها اتّخاذ المعروف.

٩،٢ وقد قيل إنّه لا ينبغي لطالب أمر أن يطلب الأمر إلّا بعد معرفته بفضله فإنّه يُعدّ جاهلاً من طلب أمرًا أعنى نفسه فيه وليس له منه منفعة وقد نرى أنّ بعض من يقرأ هذا الكتاب ممّن يفعل ذلك فاحذر أن تكون منهم[٣] فإذا أنت كالأعمى الذي عيّر الأعور بعوره.

١٠،٢ وينبغي لمن له عقل ألّا يطلب أمرًا فيه على صاحبه مضرّة يطلب بذلك صلاح نفسه فإنّ الغادر مأخوذ ومن فعل ذلك كان خليقًا أن يصيبه ما أصاب الرجل التاجر وشريكه الذي نذكره حديث الرجل وصاحبه صاحبي السمسم. بلغنا أنّه كان رجلاً يبيع السمسم وكان له شريك وكان سمسمهما في بيت واحد غير أنّ الذي لكلّ واحد منهما على حدته. فأحبّ أحدهما أن يذهب بالذي لشريكه من السمسم فجعل له علامة إذا جاء الليل ليأخذه فأخذ رداءه فغطّى به سمسم شريكه ثمّ انطلق إلى صديق له فأخبره بالذي همّ به من ذلك وسأله أن يعينه فأبى صديقه ذلك حتّى جعل له نصف ما يأخذ منه ثمّ إنّ شريك التاجر دخل إلى البيت فرأى سمسمه مغطّى برداء شريكه فظنّ أنّه غطّاه له من التراب والدوابّ فقال في نفسه لقد أحسن شريكي في تغطية سمسمي وإشفاقه عليّ وسمسمه[٤] أحقّ أن يغطّى بردائه. فحوّل الرداء على سمسم صاحبه فلمّا كان من الليل جاء التاجر والرجل معه فدخلا البيت وهو مظلم فجعل يلتمس ويجسّ حتّى وقعت يده على المغطّى من السمسم وهو يرى أنّه كما غطّاه وأنّه سمسم صاحبه فأخذ نصفه وأعطى صاحبه النصف الآخر فلمّا

١ كذا ل٢؛ الأصل: الاعمى. ٢ الأصل: علمه. ٣ الأصل: منهما. ٤ كذا ع، پ٣٤٧٥: الأصل: سمسمه.

men, one sighted and one blind, were to fall into a well and perish. The ability to see did not save the man who could see, for both are in the same predicament in terms of dying. But to the intelligent mind, the man with full use of his sight has less of an excuse.

Those who seek knowledge only to impart it to others or to acquire fame are like a spring from whose waters people benefit, but that gets no benefit itself. The seeker of knowledge should first use his knowledge to counsel himself; then he should impart it to others. There are three things in this world a man should acquire for himself and impart to others: knowledge, wealth, and a desire to do good. **2.8**

It has been said that you should not seek a thing until you know its value. To exhaust yourself in seeking something that will not bring you any benefit must be deemed ignorant. We know that some readers of this book are guilty of this. Beware of being one of them; don't be like the blind man who reproached the one-eyed man for being blind in one eye. **2.9**

The Sesame Merchant Who Tried to Cheat His Partner

No one with any intelligence should try to benefit himself by harming his companion, for treachery never goes unpunished. The treacherous are likely to suffer the fate of the sesame merchant and his partner in the story. Once, we are told, there was a sesame merchant who had a partner. They kept their sesame in one room, but each man kept his stock separate. One of them decided to make off with his partner's sesame. As a way to identify it when he came to take it at night, he covered his partner's sesame with his coat. Then he went to a friend, told him his plan, and asked for his help. The friend refused until he was promised half of the take. Meanwhile, the merchant's partner went to the storeroom and saw his share of the sesame covered with his partner's coat. Thinking that the partner had covered it to protect it from dust and vermin, he said to himself, "How nice of my partner to cover my sesame and be concerned about it!—but it's more fitting for his sesame to be covered with his coat." So he moved the coat over to his partner's sesame. Once night fell, the merchant and his accomplice arrived. They entered the dark room, and the man groped about until his hand touched the covered sesame. Thinking it was his friend's stock, he took half of it and gave his accomplice the other half. The next morning, when the merchant and his partner entered the room, the partner saw that it was his sesame that **2.10**

أصبح جاء هو وشريكه فدخلا البيت فلمّا رأى أنّ الذاهب هو الذي له خشي[١] أن يذكر شيئاً فيكون ما فيه من العار أشدّ عليه من ذهاب السمسم.

١١،٢ فالواجب على من طلب أمرًا أن يكون له فيه غاية ينتهي إليها فإنّه من جرى إلى غير غاية أوشك أن تقوم به دابّته وهو حقيق أن لا يحدّث نفسه بما لا يعنيه أو يطلب ما لا يوجد وما لا يصيبه أحد من قبله ولا ييأس ممّا يكون أن يوجد ويكون لأخراه مؤثرًا على دنياه فإنّه من قلّ تعلّقه بدنياه[٢] قلّت مساءته عند فراقها وينبغي أن لا ييأس من أن يصير ذلك إليه وإن قسا قلبه فإنّه يقال في أمرين يجملان بكلّ أحد النسك والمال وأيضاً مثل ذلك مثل النار المؤجّجة التي ليس من شيء يُقذف فيها إلّا أكلته ونقلته إليها موافقاً.

١٢،٢ وربّما أصاب الرجل الشيء وهو غير راجٍ له كما أصاب الرجل الذي بلغني أنّه كانت به حاجة شديدة وفاقة وعري فشكا ذلك إلى معارفه وطلب إليهم ثوبًا يلبسه مثل الرجل والسارق فأعياه ذلك فالتمس ذلك بجهده فلم يصب شيئاً فلمّا أيس من ذلك رجع إلى منزله فلمّا كان الليل إذا هو بسارق قد دخل عليه في منزله فقال الرجل في نفسه ليس في منزلي شيء يستطيع هذا السارق أن يسرقه فليصنع ما شاء وليجتهد جهده. ثمّ إنّ السارق طاف في البيت فلم يجد شيئاً يأخذه فغاظه ذلك وقال في نفسه ما أرى هاهنا شيئاً فما أحبّ أن يكون عنائي باطلاً. فانطلق إلى خابية فيها شيء من برّ فقال في نفسه ما أجد بدًّا من أخذ هذا الزاد فإنّي لم أجد غيره. فبسط ملحفة كانت عليه وصبّ من ذلك البرّ فلمّا أبصر الرجل البرّ قد صبّه لينطلق به قال ليس على هذا صبر يذهب ويجتمع عليّ أمران الجوع والعري ولا يجتمعان إلّا أهلكا. فصاح بالسارق فهرب من بين يديه فترك الملحفة فأخذها صاحب المنزل فلبسها وأعاد البرّ مكانه.

١٣،٢ وليس لأحد أن ييأس من أن ينال أجرًا ولا[٣] يطلب ما لا يُنال وليس ينبغي له أيضاً أن يتّكل على هذا المثل فيدع الطلب ولا يدع جهدًا في الطلب على معرفة

---

١ الأصل: وخشي. ٢ تعلّقه بـ: كذا ع، پ٣٤٧٥؛ الأصل: تقلبه فى. ٣ كذا ع؛ الأصل: ان.

was gone, but was afraid to say anything, lest the disgrace be worse than the loss of the sesame.

To seek you must have a goal to reach. An endless journey is only going to exhaust your mount. You should not set your mind on something that doesn't concern you, or seek what doesn't exist or what no one before you has been able to find; but you shouldn't despair of finding what can be found. You should give your life in the next world precedence over life in this world; the less attached you are to life in this world, the less distressed you will be when you must leave it. You shouldn't despair of success, even though your heart is troubled. Two things, it has been said, are an adornment for everyone: piety and wealth. An analogy for this is provided by the blazing fire: it consumes everything thrown into it and converts it into a substance compatible with itself. 2.11

The Poor Man Who Received an Unexpected Boon from a Thief

Sometimes you obtain what you never hoped to obtain, as happened to the man in the following story. Once, I've been told, there was a man who was destitute and naked. He lamented this to his acquaintances and begged for something to wear. He begged and begged, exhausting himself in the process, but got nothing and returned home in despair. That night, noticing that a thief had slipped into the house, he said to himself, "There's nothing in my house for this thief to steal. Let him do what he wants and waste his energy." The thief prowled about but found nothing to take. Exasperated, the thief said to himself, "I don't see anything here, but I don't want my hard work to have been in vain." He approached a large jar of wheat and said to himself, "Since I've found nothing else, I'll just take these provisions." So he spread out his coat and poured some of the wheat onto it. When the man saw him pour out the wheat to make off with it, he thought, "This is too much to bear. If this fellow takes my wheat, hunger and nakedness will join forces. To fall victim to both at one and the same time is sure death." So he shouted at the thief, who fled, leaving his coat behind. The man kept the coat, put it on, and returned the wheat to the jar. 2.12

You shouldn't despair of obtaining a reward, nor should you seek something unobtainable, but you also shouldn't rely on this example and cease to seek knowledge or make no effort to find it. Favor and sustenance sometimes come to the person who isn't seeking them, and are withheld from someone who is; however, if you consider the matter, you'll find that those who 2.13

فإنّ الفضل والرزق يأتيان من لا يطلبهما ويمتنعان ممّن يطلب ولكن إذا نظر في ذلك وجد من طلب وأصاب أكثر ممّن أصاب بغير طلب فلم يكن[1] حقيقاً أن يقتدي بذلك الواحد لكنّه ينبغي أن يقتدي بالكثير الذين طلبوا فأصابوا.

١٤،٢ ويحقّ عليه أن يكثر المقايسة وينتفع بالتجارب فإذا أصابه الشيء فيه مضرّة عليه حذره[2] وأشباهه وقاس بعضه ببعض حتّى يحذر الشيء بما لقي في غيره فإنّه إن لم يحذر إلّا التي لقي بعينها لم يحكم التجارب في جميع أموره ولم يزل يأتيه شيء لم يكن أتاه بعينه وينبغي مع ذلك أن يحذر ما يصيب غيره من الضرّ حتّى يسلم هو أن يأتيه مثله ولا يكون مثله مثل الحمامة التي تؤخذ فراخها فتُذبح وترى ذلك في عشّها ولا يمنعها أن تقيم مكانها حتّى تؤخذ هي فتُذبح.

١٥،٢ وينبغي له مع ذلك أن يكون للأمور عنده حدّ لا يجوزه ولا يقصر عنه فإن جاوز الحدّ كان كمن قصر عنه لأنهما خالفا الحدّ جميعاً.

١٦،٢ وينبغي أن يعلم أنّ كلّ إنسان ساعٍ فمن كان سعيه لآخرته فحياته له ومن كان لآخرته ودنياه فحياته له وعليه وإن كان سعيه لدنياه خاصّة فحياته عليه. ويقال في ثلاثة أشياء يحقّ على صاحب الدنيا إصلاحها والابتذال[3] لنفسه فيها أمر دنياه وأمر معيشته وأمر ما بينه وبين الناس. وقد قيل في أمور ثلاثة[4] من كانت فيه لم يستقم له أمره منها التواني ومنها التضييع للفرص ومنها التصديق لكلّ مخبر وربّ رجل خُبّر بالشيء لا يقبله عقله ولا يعرف استقامته فيصدّق به ومن يفعل ذلك ثلاثة رجل يصدّق به لما جرّب من تصديق غيره ممّن دأبه ذلك ورجل يصدّق به لهواه في الأمر الذي يُخبر به[5] فالعاقل لا يزال لهواه متّهماً[6] وينبغي له أن لا يقبل من أحد وإن كان صدوقاً للأصدقاء وينبغي له أن لا يتمادى في الخطأ ولا يتوانى في النظر فيها وينبغي له إن التبس عليه أمره أن لا يلج في شيء منه ولا يقدم عليه قبل أن يستيقن بالصواب منه فيكون كالرجل الذي يجور عن الطريق فيسير كما هو بالجور

---

١ فإنّ الفضل . . . فلم يكن: كذا ع؛ الأصل: فان المضل والررق ياتيان من يطلبهما ويمسعان ممن يطلب الفاضات من عير طلب فاصاب اكثرممن طلب فلكن. ٢ كذا ع؛ ساقطة من الأصل. ٣ الأصل: ابتذال. ٤ الأصل: ستّة. ٥ ورجل يصدّق . . . يُخبر به: كذا ع؛ ساقطة من الأصل. ٦ لهواه متّهمًا: كذا ش/٢؛ الأصل: هواه مسميا.

seek and find outnumber those who find without seeking. Therefore, don't emulate the few who find without seeking; rather, emulate the majority who seek and find.

Make it your practice to compare one thing with another and benefit from your experience. Be wary of things that harm you and of things that resemble them. Compare one thing with another, so as to beware of one thing as a result of your experience with something else. The person who guards only against things he has already encountered has not made experience the arbiter of his affairs; he will continue to be exposed to things he has never actually encountered. Guard against the things that harm others, lest you suffer the same. Don't be like the dove who sees her nestlings snatched and slaughtered, but stays put until she herself is snatched and slaughtered in turn. 2.14

Everything should have a measure that you neither exceed nor fall short of; to exceed a measure is like falling short of it, inasmuch as both miss the mark. 2.15

Know that every man is striving for something. If he strives only for the sake of the hereafter, his life will be accounted to his credit; if he strives for the sake of both this world and the hereafter, his life will be accounted partly to his credit and partly as a loss; and if he strives only for the sake of this world, his life will be accounted as a loss. It is said that in this world we should work as hard as we can to set three things right: our life in this world, our means of livelihood, and our relations with others. It is said that our affairs will not go well if we are discovered to have three[9] things: laziness, missing opportunities, and believing every informant. Sometimes we are told something unacceptable to our reason, the soundness of which we do not recognize, but we believe it anyway. Three kinds of people do this.[10] Sometimes a person believes a thing because he sees someone else believing it and it is his habit to follow him. Sometimes a person believes a thing out of a desire to believe the thing he is told. An intelligent person is always suspicious of his desires: he shouldn't accept what anyone says, even if that person is truthful to his friends, nor should he persist in an error or hesitate to examine what he has been told. When he is uncertain, he should not undertake a thing or embark on it until the right way becomes apparent, lest he be like a man who strays from the road and gets more and more lost: 2.16

وعلى الاعوجاج ولا يزداد في المسير بعدًا إلّا ازداد في الطريق بعدًا أوكان كالرجل يدخل في عينه القذى فلا يزال يدلكها ويحكّها حتّى يعلوها البياض فتذهب وعلى العاقل أن يأخذ بالحزم ويعلم أن الجزاء كائن ومن[١] أتى إلى صاحبه مثل ما لو أتي عليه فشقّ عليه فقد ظلم.

فمن قرأ هذا الكتاب فليقتد بما فيه من هذا الباب وليبدأ به فإنّي أرجو أن يزيده ١٧،٢
بصرًا بما قرأ ومعرفة وإن عرفه اكتفى واستغنى عن غيره وإن لم يعرفه لم ينتفع به.

ولمّا رأينا أهل فارس قد نشروه وأخرجوه من الهنديّة إلى الفارسيّة ألحقوا ١٨،٢
فيه باب برزويه الفارسيّ المتطبّب فلم يذكروا فيه ما ذكرنا من هذا فرأينا إذا فسّرناه وأخرجناه من الفارسيّة إلى العربيّة أن نلحق فيه بابًا من العربيّة يكون له أساس فيه أمر هذا الكتاب لمن أراد قراءته واقتباس العلم منه.

---

١ الأصل: وما.

the farther he travels, the farther he strays from the road. Nor should he be like a man who rubs a mote of dust in his eye until a white film develops over the eye and destroys it. The intelligent person acts resolutely and knows that there will be a reward. Doing to a comrade something that would distress you if it were done to you is to act unjustly.

Let the reader take what is in this chapter as a model to guide him. Let him begin with it, for it will, I hope, increase his insight and his understanding of what he reads. Once he is acquainted with it, it will suffice and he will need nothing else; otherwise, he will not profit from the book. 2.17

When I saw that the Persians, in disseminating and translating this book from Sanskrit into Persian, had added the Chapter of Barzawayh the Physician, but made no mention of any of the things we've just discussed, I decided that when I translated it from Persian into Arabic I would add a chapter, one that would serve as a foundation for understanding the book for all who decide to read it and gain knowledge from it. 2.18

باب بَرْزَوَيْه المتطبّب

١.٣ قال برزويه رئيس أطبّاء[١] فارس وهو الذي تولّى انتساخ هذا الكتاب وترجمته من بلاد الهند إنّ أبي كان من المقاتلة وكانت أمّي من بنات الزمازمة وكان من عظم كرامتي على ربّي أنّي كنت أكرم ولد أبويّ عليهما فأسلماني الى تعلّم الطبّ حين[٢] بلغت سبع سنين فلمّا بلغت إلى عشر سنين وعرفت الطبّ وفضله شكرت لأبويّ رأيهما[٣] كان في ذلك ورغبت في تعلّمه وحرصت عليه حتّى إذا شددت ما وثقت به واتّمنت[٤] نفسي على مداومة المرضى وهممت بذلك آمرت نفسي وخيّرتها بين الأمور الأربعة التي إيّاها يطلب الناس وإليها يجرون فقلت أيّ هذه الخلال ينبغي لمثلي في مثل عملي أن يطلب وأيّها أحرى إن هو ابتغاه أن يدرك حاجته منها المال أم اللذّات أم الذكر أم أجر الآخرة فوجدت الطبّ[٥] محمودًا عند العقلاء كلّهم ولم أجده مذمومًا عند أحد من أهل الملل والأديان وأصبت في كتب الطبّ أنّ أفضل الأطبّاء من واظب على طبّه لا يبتغي بذلك إلّا أجر الآخرة وثواب العاقبة فرأيت أن أواظب على الطبّ ابتغاء أجر الآخرة ولا أبتغي بذلك ثمنًا فأكون كالتاجر الخاسر الذي باع ياقوتة كان مصيبًا في ثمنها غنى الدهر بخرزة لا تساوي شيئًا مع أنّي وجدت[٦] في كتب الطبّ أنّ الطبيب المبتغي بطبّه أجر الآخرة لا ينقص ذلك من حظّه في الدنيا شيئًا وأنّ مثله مثل الحرّاث الذي إنّما يثير الأرض ويعمرها[٧] ابتغاء[٨] الزرع لا ابتغاء العشب ثمّ هي لا محالة نابت فيها من ألوان العشب.

٢.٣ فحينئذ أقبلت على مداواة المرضى رجاء أجر الآخرة فلم أدع مريضًا أرجو له البرء ولا آخر لا أرجو[٩] له البرء إلّا أنّي أطمع له في خفّة وجعه وما[١٠] به من الأذى إلّا

---

١ كذا ش، ع؛ ساقطة من الأصل. ٢ كذا ل٢؛ الأصل: حتى. ٣ كذا ل٢؛ الأصل: حرابهما. ٤ الأصل: واتميب. ٥ الأصل: الطلب. ٦ كذا ل٢؛ الأصل: دكرت. ٧ كذا ر؛ الأصل: ويمنعها. ٨ الأصل: لابتغاء. ٩ ولا آخر لا أرجو: كذا ل٢؛ الأصل: ولا من اترحوا. ١٠ الأصل: ومما.

The Chapter of Barzawayh the Physician[11]

Barzawayh, the chief physician of Persia, who copied out and translated this book of Indian provenance, related: My father belonged to the military, and my mother to a family of Zoroastrian clergy. A mark of God's great favor toward me was that I was my parents' favorite child and that when I reached the age of seven, they sent me to study medicine.[12] When I reached the age of ten and had become better acquainted with medicine and its merits, I thanked my parents for their decision and was eager to study it further. I applied myself and acquired enough confidence to trust myself attending to the sick, and was about to begin my practice, but then I stopped to consider. I asked myself to choose among the four goals for which men strive. Which of these four, I asked, should someone of my profession seek? Which, when pursued, is most likely to give satisfaction: wealth, pleasure, fame, or reward in the hereafter? Medicine, I found, was praised by all who possess intelligence and was censured by no religious community. I read in medical texts that the best physician was the one who practiced his craft solely for heavenly reward, so I decided to seek heavenly reward through medical practice and demand no other payment. I didn't want to be like the unfortunate merchant who, for a worthless bead, traded a ruby that would have made his fortune forever. I also read in the medical texts that the physician who through his craft seeks reward in the hereafter is not precluded from achieving success in this world. He is like a farmer who plows and cultivates his land to grow crops, rather than grass; yet inevitably the land produces various kinds of grass, too. 3.1

I therefore set out to treat the sick with my hopes fixed on reward in the hereafter. I never abandoned a patient whom I hoped to cure or, if that proved impossible, whose pain and suffering I hoped to alleviate, without 3.2

بلغت في مداواته فمن قدرت على القيام عليه قمت عليه ومن لم أقدر على القيام عليه وصفت له وأمرته ونهيته وأعطيته ما يحتاج إليه من الدواء ولم أرد من أحد فعلت به أجرًا ولا مكافأة رجاء أجر الآخرة ولم أغبط من نظرائي من هو مثلي في العلم وفوقي من المال والجاه[١] إلّا بصلاح نيّة وحسن سريرة في الناس قولاً وعملاً وكنت أورّع نفسي إن هي نازعتني أن تغبط أولئك وتتمنّى مثل منازلهم وآبى لها إلّا الخصومة[٢] وأقول لها يا نفس ألا تعرفين[٣] نفعك من ضرّك ألا تنتهين عن تمنّي ما لم ينله أحد إلّا قلّ متاعه وكثر عناؤه فيه[٤] وخباله عليه واشتدّت خسرته عند فراقه وعظمت التبعة منه عليه بعده.

٣،٣ يا نفس أما تذكرين ما بعد هذه الدار فينسيك ما تشرهين إليه من هذه الدار ألا ترغبين عن مشاركة الفجرة الجهّال في حبّ هذه الصاحبة الفانية البائدة التي من كان في يده شيء منها فليس له وليس يبقى عليه والتي لا يألفها إلّا المغترّون الغافلون. انصرفي عن هذا السفه والمزحة[٥] وأقبلي بقوّتك وقدرتك وما تملكين على تقديم الخير والأجر ما استطعت وإيّاك والتسويف والتواني وتعلّمي أنّ هذا الجسد رخو ذو آفات[٦] وأنّه مملوء أخلاطًا فاسدة وقذرة وتجمعها أربعة أخلاط متغالبة متعادية تعمدهنّ الحياة والحياة إلى نفاد كالصنم المنفصلة أعضاؤه ثمّ إذا ارتُكبت تلك الأعضاء ووُضعت في مواضعها جمعها مسمار واحد يمسك بعضها على بعض فإذا أُخذ المسمار تساقطت الأوصال.

٤،٣ ويا نفس لا تغترّي بصحبة أحبّائك وأخلّائك ولا تحرصي على ذلك وأقلّي الحرص فإنّ صحبتهم على ما فيها من السرور والبهجة كثيرة الأذى والمؤذيات[٧] مختومة تحت ذلك بعاقبة الفراق فمثلهم مثل المغرفة التي تستعملها في سخونة المرق أيّام صحّتها فإذا انكسرت صارت[٨] عاقبة أمرها خسرًا وتُحرق بالنار.

---

١ كذا ل٢؛ الأصل: والجده. ٢ وآبى...الخصومة: كذا ع؛ الأصل: ولا اابالها الا باالخصومه. ٣ كذا ل٢؛ الأصل: تعرفى. ٤ عناؤه فيه: كذا ر؛ الأصل: عناه عنه. ٥ الأصل: والمرينه. ٦ رخو ذو آفات: كذا ر؛ الأصل: هدا الحسد رحر وافات. ٧ الأصل: والموذنان. ٨ كذا ل٢؛ الأصل: صار.

treating him to the best of my ability. If possible, I attended to him personally; if I couldn't, I diagnosed, instructed, and dispensed medicine. Hoping for reward in the next world, I demanded no fee or remuneration from any patient. I envied none of my colleagues who equaled me in knowledge but surpassed me in wealth and prestige, except for the righteous intentions and kindheartedness they displayed in word and deed. I restrained my soul whenever it incited me to envy such men and to desire a similar social standing. "Soul," I said, "can't you distinguish gain from loss? Will you not stop yearning for something the acquisition of which brings little enjoyment and great trouble and confusion, the loss of which brings great anguish, and the consequences of which after death are grievous?

"Soul, will you give no thought to what comes next, after this place? 3.3
Doesn't that make you forget the things you crave in this world? Will you not abstain from sharing the love that ignorant sinners feel for this fleeting and transient companion, where nothing you possess belongs to you or remains with you, loved only by the deluded and the heedless? Turn from this foolishness and levity, and strive with all your strength, energy, and wherewithal to lay up for yourself future blessings and reward. Beware of procrastination and indifference. Know that this fragile body is prey to infirmities; that it is filled with impure, corruptible mixtures bound together by four mutually antagonistic humors, all sustained by life; and that life will end. The body is like an idol made up of separate parts held together by a single nail: if the nail is removed, the parts will collapse.

"Soul, don't be beguiled by the companionship of friends and loved ones, 3.4
and don't yearn for it too strongly; though their companionship brings joy and happiness, it also brings much suffering and pain, and ultimately ends in parting. It is like a wooden ladle, which can be used in a heated pot for as long as it lasts, but which ends up being tossed into the fire as soon as it breaks.

٣.٥ ويا نفس لا يحملنّك أهلك وأقاربك على جمع ما تهلكين في جمعه تريدين بذلك رضاهم فإذا أنت كالدخنة الطيّبة التي تُحرق ويستلذّ بعرفها وتحرّقها الناس ولا تغترّي بالغنى والمنزلة التي تبطر أهلها فإنّ صاحب ذلك لا يبصر صغر ما يستعظم حتّى يفارقه فتكوني فيه كشعر الرأس الذي يكرمه صاحبه ويخدمه ما دام على الرأس فإذا فارق رأسه قذّره وفرّ منه ودومي على مداواة المرضى ولا يعتاقك[1] أن تقولي الطبّ مؤونة شديدة والناس بها وبمنافع الطبّ وفضله جهّال ولكن اعتبري علم ذلك برجل يفرج عن رجل كربة تحلّ به ويستنقذه منها حتّى يعود بعدها إلى ما كان عليه من الرَوْح والصحّة ما أخلقه بعظيم الأجر وحسن الثواب فإذا كان الذي يفعل هذا برجل[2] واحد يرجى ذلك له[3] فكيف[4] بالطبيب الذي يأتيه العدّة الله أعلم بها ابتغاء الأجر فيصيرون بعد الأوجاع والأسقام الحائلة بينهم وبين الدنيا ولذّاتها ونعيمها وطعامها وشرابها وأزواجها وأولادها إلى أحسن ممّا كانوا يكونون عليه من حال دنياهم إنّ هذا لخليق أن يعظم رجاؤه ويثق[5] بحسن الثواب على علمه.

٣.٦ ويا نفس لا تبعّدنّ عليك الآخرة الدائمة وتميلي إلى العاجلة الفانية فتكوني في تعجيل الحقير الذليل وبيع الكثير باليسير كالتاجر الذي زعموا أنّه كان له بيت مملوء من الخوخ فقال إن بعته وزنًا طال بيعه وطال عليّ فباعه مجازفة بأخسّ الثمن.

٣.٧ فلمّا خاصمت نفسي بهذا[6] وحذّرتها به وبصّرتها إيّاه لم تجد منه محيصًا ولا عنه مذهبًا فاعترفت وأقرّت ولهت عمّا كانت تنزع إليه وتسمو نحوه وترغب فيه فأقمت على مداواة المرضى ابتغاء أجر الآخرة ولم يمنعني ذلك أن أصبت من الدنيا حظًّا جسيمًا ونصيبًا عظيمًا من الملوك والأكفاء والإخوان قبل أن آتي الهند وبعد رجوعي مهنا فوق ما كنت له أهلاً.

٣.٨ ثمّ نظرت في الطبّ فوجدت الطبيب لا يستطيع أن يداوي المريض من مرضه مداومة تذهب عنه داءه فلا يعود إليه ذلك الداء وغيره من الأدواء التي هي مثله

١ الأصل: نعا نك. ٢ كذا ل٢؛ الأصل: الرجل. ٣ يرجى ذلك له: الأصل: يرحى له فى دلك. ٤ كذا ش، ع، پ٣٤٦٦؛ الأصل: وكيف. ٥ كذا ر؛ الأصل: ويوثق به. ٦ كذا ر، ش، ع، ل٢؛ ساقطة من الأصل.

"Soul, don't let the desire to please your family and relatives lead you to 3.5
destroy yourself by acquiring possessions. Don't be like a stick of incense that burns up while others enjoy its fragrance. Don't be beguiled by wealth and rank that lead people to insolence, not seeing the insignificance of the things they prize until they're gone, lest you be like hair on the head: cared for as long as it is there, but discarded as refuse once it is gone. Treat the sick diligently. Don't become discouraged and say that medicine demands great labor or that people are ignorant of its benefits and value. Consider that to relieve one person's distress, and rescue him so that he returns to his former state of comfort and ease, deserves the greatest reward and finest recompense. If doing this for a single person deserves such credit, then what about the physician who, in search of reward, treats ever so many patients—people who, after suffering pains and ailments that prevented them from enjoying the world and its pleasures—food, drink, spouses, and children—become even healthier than they were before? Surely such a physician should harbor great hopes and be certain of a fine reward for his knowledge.

"Soul, don't think that the everlasting world of the hereafter is far off. 3.6
Don't be so inclined to the transitory world of the here and now that in your haste to make a paltry profit, exchanging much for little, you become like the merchant, who, they say, had a roomful of peaches and said, 'It'll take too long to sell them by weight!'—so he sold them in bulk for a pittance."

When I had disputed with my soul, cautioned it, and gotten it to see this, 3.7
it could find no escape; it conceded, agreed, and turned away from its former desires. I made it my practice to treat the sick for the sake of a reward in the hereafter. This did not, however, prevent me from amassing a sizable fortune, even more than I deserved, from kings, friends, and colleagues, both before I went to India and after my return.

But when I thought about medicine, I realized that no physician could 3.8
treat a patient with a drug that eliminated the disease so thoroughly that it, or a similar disease, or an even more serious one, would never recur. I didn't see how I could regard something as a cure, when there was no guarantee the same disease wouldn't recur or a worse one develop. On the other hand, I found that work focused on the hereafter offered a deliverance such that a

أو أشدّ منه فلم أدر كيف أعدّ البرء برءًا والداء لا يؤمَن عوده أو اعتراء ما[١] هو أشدّ منه ووجدت عمل الآخرة هو الذي يسلّم من الأدواء حتّى يبرأ صاحبه برءًا يأمن بعده الأدواء كلّها واستخففت بالطبّ وأردت الدين.

فلمّا أن وقع ذلك في نفسي اشتبه عليّ أمر الدين أمّا كتب الطبّ فلم أجد فيها لشيء من الأديان ذكرًا يدلّني على أهداها[٢] وأصوبها وأمّا الأديان فالملل كثيرة مختلفة وليس منها شيء إلّا وهو عليه ثلاثة أصناف قوم ورثوا دينهم عن آبائهم وآخرون أُكرهوا عليها خائفين وآخرون يبتغون بها الدنيا ولذّاتها ومنازلها ومعيشتها وكلّهم يزعم أنّه على صواب وهدى وأنّ من خالفهم على خطأ وضلالة والاختلاف بينهم في امر الخالق والخلق ومبتدأ الأمر ومنتهاه وما سوى ذلك شديد وكلّ[٣] على صاحبه رادّ وله عدوّ وعائب فرأيت أن أضع علم كلّ أهل ملّة ورؤسائهم فأنظر فيما يصفون ويعرضون لعلّي أعرف بذلك الحقّ من الباطل فأختار الحقّ منه وألزمه على ثقة ويقين غير مصدّق بما لا أعرف ولا قابل ما لا أعقل ففعلت ذلك وسألت ولم أجد من أولئك أحدًا يزيدني على مدح دينه وذمّ دين من خالفه فاستبان لي أنّهم بالهوى يحتجّون ويتكلّمون بغير العدل ولم أجد عند أحد منهم صفة تكون عدلاً وصدقًا يعرفه ذو العقل ويرضى به. ٩،٣

فلمّا رأيت ذلك لم أجد إلى متابعة[٤] أحد منهم سبيلاً وعرفت أنّي إن أصدّق منهم أحدًا بما لا أعلم أكن كالمصدّق المخدوع الذي ذهب يسرق حتّى جاء على ظهر بيت رجل من الأغنياء ليلاً ومعه أصحاب له فاستيقظ صاحب المنزل بوطئهم وأحسّ بهم[٥] فعرف أنّه لن يعلو فوق البيت تلك الساعة إلّا مريب فنبّه امرأته وقال لها رويدًا إنّي لأحسّ اللصوص قد علوا بيتنا فأنا متناوم لك فأيقظيني بصوت يسمعه مَن فوق البيت واسأليني وقولي أيّها الرجل أخبرني عن أموالك هذه الكثيرة وكنوزك من أين جمعتها. فإذا أبيت عليك فألحي على السؤال. ١٠،٣

١ اعتراء ما: كذا ع؛ ر: يعتري؛ الأصل: اعنراضه. ٢ كذا ش، ع، ر؛ الأصل: مداها. ٣ كذا ش، ع، ر؛ الأصل: وكان.
٤ كذا ل٢؛ ساقطة من الأصل. ٥ كذا ل٢؛ الأصل: منهم.

person would obtain a cure that removed his fear of all diseases. My esteem for medicine accordingly diminished and I turned to religion.

When this occurred to me, I was unclear about the subject of religion. 3.9
In no medical books did I find any discussion that could lead me to the religion that was truest and offered the best guidance. Religious communities were many and diverse, and their adherents fell into three groups: those who inherited their religion from their forefathers, those who had been forced by fear to adopt their religion, and those who sought worldly pleasures, status, and prosperity through their religion. Each group claimed that their religion provided true guidance and that all who thought otherwise were in error. They differed greatly about the Creator and creation, the beginning and the end of things, and other matters. Each rejected the other and denounced its adherents as enemies. I therefore decided to examine the doctrines espoused by every religious community and its leaders, and look into what they prescribed and what they prohibited. In this way, I hoped to distinguish truth from falsehood, and then choose the truth and cling to it with confidence and certainty, rather than believing in something I didn't know or accepting something I couldn't understand. I did this and conducted inquiries, but I found that no one went beyond praising his own religion and disparaging the religion of those who disagreed with him. It became clear to me that their responses and arguments were arbitrary and tendentious. In none of them did I find any mark of impartiality and truth that could be recognized and accepted by a reasonable person.

This being so, I realized that it was impossible for me to follow any of 3.10
them. I saw that if I agreed with any of them on something about which I had no knowledge, I would be like the credulous dupe who went to commit a burglary. He and his companions climbed onto the roof of a rich man's house at night. The householder heard their footsteps, woke up, and sensed their presence. Realizing that no honest man would be on the roof at that hour, he roused his wife and whispered to her, "I think thieves have climbed onto our house. I'll pretend to be asleep. You wake me up in a voice loud enough to be heard by someone on the roof, and ask, 'Master of the house, won't you tell me where you got all your riches and treasures?' When I refuse, keep badgering me with questions."

The Credulous Burglar

ففعلت المرأة ذلك وسألته كما أمرها به وسمع اللصوص عند ذلك فقال الرجل أيّتها المرأة قد ساقك القدر إلى رزق واسع كثير فكلي واشربي واسكتي ولا تسأليني عمّا لو أخبرتك به لم آمن أن يسمعه سامع فيكون في ذلك ما أكره وتكرهين.

قالت المرأة أخبرني أيّها الرجل فلعمري ما بقربنا أحد يسمع كلامنا.

قال فإنّي أخبرك أنّي لم أجمع هذه الأموال والكنوز إلّا من السرقة.

قالت فكيف كنت جمعت كلّ هذه الأموال والكنوز من السرقة وأنت في أنفس الناس عدل مرضيّ لا يتّهمك أحد من الناس.

قال ذلك لعلم أصبته في أمر السرقة فكان الأمر أيسر وأرفق من أن يتّهمني فيه أحد ويرتاب بي.

قالت فكيف كان ذلك.

قال كنت أذهب في الليلة المقمرة ومعي أصحابي حتّى أعلو ظهر البيت الذي أريد أن أسرق أهله فأنتهي إلى الكوّة التي يدخل منها ضوء القمر فأرقي بهذه الرقية شولم شولم سبع مرّات ثمّ أعتنق الضوء الذي دخل البيت من الكوّة فأهبط فلا يحسّ بوقوعي أحد ثمّ أقوم في أصل الضوء فأعيد الرقية سبع مرّات فلا يبقى في البيت مال ولا علق إلّا بدا لي وأمكنني منه أن أتناوله فآخذ من ذلك ما أحببت ثمّ أعتنق الضوء فأرقي بالكلمة سبع مرّات فأصير إلى أصحابي وأحمّلهم ما معي ثمّ ننسلّ.

فلمّا سمع اللصوص هذه الكلمة الصفة فرحوا فرحاً شديداً وقالوا لقد ظفرنا من ١١،٣
هذا البيت بما[1] هو خير لنا من المال الذي نحن مصيبوه منه أصبنا منه علماً أذهب الله به[2] عنّا الخوف وأمنّا به السلطان. فأطالوا المكث حتّى إذا ظنّوا أنّ صاحب البيت وامرأته قد ناما[3] وظنّوا في أنفسهم صدق ذلك تقدّم رئيسهم إلى مدخل الضوء من الكوّة فقال شولم شولم سبع مرّات ثمّ اعتنق الضوء لينزل به إلى البيت فوقع في البيت منكّساً فوثب إليه الرجل فضربه حتّى أثخنه ثمّ قال له من أنت.

قال أنا المصدّق المخدوع وهذه ثمرة التصديق بالباطل.

---

١ كذا ل٢؛ الأصل: ما. ٢ كذا ل٢؛ ساقطة من الأصل. ٣ كذا ل٢؛ الأصل: ناموا.

The wife posed the question as instructed, and the thieves listened in. "Woman," said the husband, "destiny has led you to great prosperity, so eat, drink, and hold your tongue! Don't ask me to reveal anything that might be overheard and have unpleasant consequences for you and me both."

But the wife insisted: "Tell me, husband! By God, there's nobody here to hear our conversation!"

And he responded, "If you really want to know, I accumulated this wealth and these treasures by stealing."

"How could that be," she asked, "when everyone thinks you're honest and upstanding—a man no one mistrusts?"

"That," he said, "is because I became so adept at thievery and went about it with such ease and skillfulness that I was above suspicion."

"How so?" she asked.

"I would go out with my friends on a moonlit night," he replied, "climb onto the roof of the house I wanted to rob, and find the skylight through which the moonlight shone into the house. Then I would recite the charm '*Shawlam, shawlam*' seven times, wrap my arms around a moonbeam, and slide down—my landing would escape detection. Next, I would stand at the base of the moonbeam and repeat the charm seven times; any money or valuables in the house would become visible, and I would take whatever I wanted. Then I would grab hold of the moonbeam, repeat the charm seven times, return to my friends, get them to carry all I had seized, and we would slip away."

When the thieves heard this description, they rejoiced: "This is even 3.11
better than the money we were going to get from this house: we now have knowledge whereby God has banished our fears and rendered us safe from the authorities." They waited until they thought the man and his wife had gone back to sleep. Thinking that what they had heard was true, their leader went to the skylight, said, "*Shawlam, shawlam*" seven times, threw his arms around a moonbeam to lower himself into the house, and fell head over heels. The owner of the house jumped on him and gave him a thrashing. "Who are you?" he asked.

"I am a credulous dupe," answered the man, "and this is what comes of believing nonsense."

فلمّا تخوّفت من التصديق بما لا آمن أن يورّطني في مهلكة عدت للبحث عن الأديان والتماس العذر فيها فلم أجد ممّن كلّمت بتصديق في جواب ما سألت عنه ولا فيما أريده شيئاً نحو ما في عقلي أن أصدّق به وأن أتّبعه فقلت أمّا إذا لم أجد ثقة آخذ بها فإنّ الرأي أن ألزم دين آبائي الذي وجدتهم عليه. فلمّا ذهبت ألتمس العذر لنفسي في ذلك لم أجد إلى ذلك سبيلاً ولا في الثبوت على دين الآباء عذراً وقلت إن كان هذا عذراً فالساحر الذي وجد أباه ساحراً في عذر مع أشباه ذلك ممّا لا يحتمله الكلام وذكرت قول رجل كان فاحش الأكل إذا أكل فعيب بذلك عليه فقال هكذا كان يأكل آبائي وأجدادي. ١٢،٣

فلمّا لم أجد إلى الثبوت على دين الآباء سبيلاً ولا فيه عذراً أردت التفرّغ للعودة إلى البحث عن الأديان وللمسألة عنها والنظر فيها فعرض لي قرب الأجل وسرعة انقطاع الدنيا وفكّرت في ذلك وقلت أمّا أنا فلا أدري لعلّ فراقي للدنيا يكون أوشك من تقليبي كفّي وقد كنت أعمل أعمالاً أرجو أن تكون من صالح الأعمال فلعلّ تردّدي فيما أتردّد فيه وتحويلي فيما أريد البحث عنه يشغلني عن خير كثير أعمله ويكون أجلي دون بلوغ ما ألتمس منه ولعلّي في تردّدي وتجوالي[1] يصيبني مثل ما أصاب الرجل الذي زعموا أنّه علق امرأة ذات بعل وأنّ المرأة حفرت له من بيتها إلى الطريق سرباً وجعلت المفتاح عند حُبّ[2] الماء تخوّفاً من أن يفجأها الزوج وهو عندها حتّى إذا كان ذات يوم والرجل عندها علمت أنّ بعلها بالباب فقالت للرجل عجّل واخرج من السرب الذي عند الحبّ. ١٣،٣

فانطلق الرجل إلى ذلك المكان فوافق الحبّ قد رُفع من ذلك الموضع فانصرف إلى المرأة فقال قد انتهيت إلى السرب فإذا الحبّ الذي ذكرت ليس ثمّ.

فقالت أيّها الأحمق وما تصنع بالحبّ أو هل سمّيت الحبّ إلّا لتستدلّ به على السرب.

فقال لم تكوني حقيقة إذ لم يكن عند السرب حبّ أن تذكري الحبّ لي فتغلطيني.

---

١ كذا ش، پ٣٤٦٦؛ الأصل: حائرًا إلى أن. ٢ كذا ر؛ الأصل: جبّ.

Wary of believing something that might have perilous consequences, I went back to investigating the various religions, seeking to justify adherence to any one of them. But from no one I questioned did I receive any answers that my reason found worthy of belief or adherence. So I said to myself, "If I can find no one I can trust, the sensible thing is to adhere to the religion of my fathers." But try as I might, I could find no justification for doing so. By this reasoning, I realized, the sorcerer who discovers his father is a sorcerer is justified in following his example—clearly a specious argument. I was reminded of the glutton who, when rebuked, excused himself by saying that his father and grandfather were gluttons. 3.12

The Perplexed Lover

Finding it impossible to adhere to the religion of my fathers or to justify doing so, I wanted to devote more time to religious investigations and inquiries, but it occurred to me how near my end might be and how swiftly earthly life ceases. For all I knew, my departure from the world might come faster than the flick of a wrist. I planned to perform what I hoped were good deeds, but perhaps my hesitation, my querying, and my prospecting would keep me from performing those very deeds, and perhaps my time might come before I found what I was seeking. Through my indecision and vacillation, I might suffer the fate of the man who, they say, fell in love with a married woman. She dug him a tunnel from her house to the street and put the key by the water jar, for fear they might be surprised by her husband. One day, while she and her lover were together, word came that her husband was at the door, so she said to the man, "Hurry and leave through the tunnel by the water jar!" 3.13

The man rushed to the place, but found that the jar had been moved. So he came back to the woman and said, "I got to the tunnel, but the jar you mentioned isn't there."

"Fool!" said the woman. "Why are you worrying about the jar? I only mentioned it to help you find the way to the tunnel."

"Since there's no jar by the tunnel," he replied, "you shouldn't have mentioned it and gotten me so confused."

فقالت ويحك انج ودع الحمق والتردّد.

فقال كيف أذهب مع ما خلّطت عليّ.

فلم تزل تلك حالته حتّى دخل ربّ البيت فأخذ الخائن وأوجعه ضربًا ثمّ دفعه إلى السلطان.

١٤،٣ فلمّا خفت من التردّد والتجوال رأيت أن لا أتعرّض لما[١] خفت من ذلك وأن أقتصر على كلّ عمل تشهد الأنفس على أنّه برّ وتوافق عليه الأديان فكففت يدي عن القتل والضرب والغصب والسرقة والخيانة وحصّنت فرجي من النساء وحفظت لساني عن الكذب ومن كلّ كلام فيه ضرّ لأحد وكفّفت من أذى الناس والخناية والبهتان والغيبة والسخر والتمست لعلّي أن لا أتمنّى لأحد سوءًا ولا أكذّب بالبعث والقيامة والثواب والعقاب وزايلت الأشرار بقلبي ولزمت الصلحاء والأخيار فرأيت العلم[٢] ليس كمثله صاحب ولا قرين ورأيت مكسبه إذا وفّق الله يسيرًا ووجدت خيره على صاحبه أبرّ من الآباء والأمّهات ووجدته لا ينقص إذا أنفق منه صاحبه بل يزداد على الإنفاق ووجدته لا يخلق على الاستعمال والابتذال بل يزداد جدّة ووجدته لا خوف عليه من السلطان أن يسلبه[٣] ولا من شيء من الآفات أن يغيّره ولا من الماء ولا من النار ولا من الغارة[٤] ولا من اللصوص ولا من شيء من الهوامّ.

١٥،٣ ووجدت الرجل الذي يزهد في الصلاح وعاقبته[٥] ويلهيه عن ذلك قليل ما هو فيه من[٦] حلاوة الدنيا إنّما مثله فيما أنفق فيه أيّامه[٧] فيما يلهيه عمّا يفعله مثل تاجر زعموا أنّه كان له جوهر كثير ثمين فاستأجر لثقبه وعمله رجلًا بمائة دينار ليومه فانطلق به إلى بيته فلمّا قعد رأى في ناحية البيت صنجًا موضوعًا فقال التاجر لصاحبه هل تضرب بالصنج.

قال نعم.

قال فدونك.

١ الأصل: ما. ٢ ل٢: الصلاح. ٣ أن يسلبه: كذا ر؛ الأصل: إن سلبه. ٤ كذا ر؛ الأصل: الفارة. ٥ في الصلاح وعاقبته: كذا ل٢؛ الأصل: دو علم ى صلاح عاقبته. ٦ كذا ل٢؛ ساقطة من الأصل. ٧ كذا ش، ع؛ الأصل: ايام.

"Good grief!" she cried. "Save yourself! Enough of this foolishness and hesitation."

"But how can I leave," he said, "when you've gotten me so confused?"

So he carried on until the master of the house arrived, gave the wretch a thrashing, and handed him over to the authorities.

Anxious about indecision and vacillation, I decided not to expose myself 3.14
to the risk I feared. I decided to limit myself to deeds universally regarded as righteous and on which all religions concur. I avoided murder, assault, extortion, theft, and treachery. I kept myself chaste with respect to women. I guarded my tongue from lies and hurtful speech. I refrained from insult, obscenity, falsehood, slander, and ridicule. I strove never to wish anyone ill. I would not deny belief in the resurrection and reckoning, the reward and punishment. I avoided evildoers and associated with righteous and virtuous people. I saw that no friend or companion compares to knowledge, and that—with God's help and assistance—acquiring it is easy. I discovered that it has more affection for and devotion to those who possess it than his own parents. I came to see that dispensing it does not diminish it, but that instead it increases when dispensed. I found that, in spite of constant use and wear, it is always replenished. And I saw that one needn't fear that it will be confiscated by rulers, or damaged by disasters, floods, fire, invasions, thieves, or vermin.

The man who shuns righteousness and its reward and is distracted from 3.15
it by a taste of the world's sweetness has spent his days, I realized, like the merchant in the following story. Once, they say, a merchant who possessed many valuable jewels hired a man for a hundred dinars a day to bore holes in the jewels and prepare them.[13] He brought the man to his house. When the man sat down, he saw a harp lying in a corner of the room. "Can you play the harp?" the merchant asked.

The Merchant and the Musician

"Yes," replied the man.

"Go ahead!" said the merchant.

فتناول الرجل الصنج وكان به ماهرًا فلم يزل يسمعه ضربًا حسنًا وصوتًا شجيًا حتّى أمسى ولهي التاجر عن سفط جوهره وأقبل على الصوت واللهو.

فلمّا أمسى قال الرجل للتاجر زن لي أجرة يومي.

قال أوعملت شيئًا فتأخذ به أجرًا.

قال نعم عملت ما أمرتني به أن أعمل.

فأوفاه مائة دينار وبقي جوهره غير مثقوب.

فلم أزدد في أمر الدنيا وشهواتها نظرًا إلّا ازددت فيها زهادة[1] فرأيت أن أعتصم ٣،١٦
بالتألّه والنسك ورأيت النسك هو الذي[2] يمهّد للمعاد كما يمهّد للولد أبواه ورأيته كالجُنّة الحريزة في دفع الشرّ الباقي الدائم ورأيته هو الباب المفتوح إلى الجنّة ذات النعيم والخلد المقيم ووجدت الناسك قد فكّر فعلته السكينة وسكن فتواضع وقنع فاستغنى ورضي فلم يهتمّ وخلع الدنيا فنجا من الشرور ورفض الشهوات فصار طاهرًا وانفرد فكفي الأحزان فأمن الندامة ولم يخف الناس ولم يخافوه ولم يذنب فسلم ولم أزدد في النسك نظرًا إلّا ازددت فيه رغبة حتّى هممت أن أكون بين أهله.

ثمّ[3] تخوّفت أن لا أصبر على عيش النسّاك وأن تضرّ بي[4] العادة التي بها رُبّيت ٣،١٧
وغُذيت ممّا لم آمن أن أكون قد خلعت الدنيا وأخذت بالنسك أن أضعف عن ذلك فأكون قد رفضت أعمالًا ممّا أرجو عائدتها كنت أعملها قبل ذلك فيكون مثلي في ذلك مثل الكلب الذي مرّ[5] بنهر وفي فيه ضلع فرأى ظلّ الضلع في الماء فأهوى له ليأخذه فألقى ما في فيه ولم يدرك ما كان أمل من الضلع الذي رآه في الماء. فهبت النسك هيبة شديدة وخفت من نفسي الضجر وقلّة الصبر عليه وأردت الثبوت على حالتي التي كنت عليها.

ثمّ بدا لي أن أقيس بين ما أخاف أن لا أصبر عليه من الأذى والضيق في ٣،١٨
النسك وبين الذي يصيب صاحب الدنيا من البلاء فيها وكان بيّنًا عندي أنّه ليس

١ فيها زهادة: كذا ر؛ الأصل: فيه (بين السطرين علامة تدلّ على سقوط كلمة). ٢ ورأيت...هو الذي: كذا پ ٣٤٧٥؛ ساقطة من الأصل. ٣ كذا ل٢؛ الأصل: و. ٤ تضرّ بي: كذا ش؛ الأصل: نصربى. ٥ كذا ر؛ ساقطة من الأصل.

So the man picked it up and skillfully played one beautiful, plaintive air after another until the evening. The merchant forgot all about his jewels and was completely absorbed by the music.

When evening came, the man said to the merchant, "Pay me my day's wages."

And the merchant replied, "Have you done anything to be paid for?"

"Yes," said the man, "I did what you ordered me to do."

So the merchant paid him a hundred dinars, and his jewels remained unworked.

The more I considered the world and its desires, the more I was moved to 3.16
renounce them. I resolved to cling to acts of devotion and asceticism. I realized that asceticism smooths the path to one's ultimate state just as parents smooth the path for their child. I recognized it as a shield sure to ward off persistent evil, and as the gate that opens to the garden of bliss. I found that the ascetic, after meditating, is enveloped in tranquility; in his calmness, he becomes humble; in his contentment, he is free of want; in his satisfaction, he experiences no anxiety. He has cast off the world, and has escaped from its evils; he has rejected cravings, and has become pure; he is spared sorrows, and is safe from regret; he inspires no fear, so men do not fear him; he commits no transgressions, so is in no danger. The longer I considered the ascetic life, the more I was drawn to it, to the point that I was on the verge of living among its devotees.

Then I grew fearful that I might not be able to endure the life of an ascetic; 3.17
that I might be hindered by the habits I had been raised and nurtured on. I was afraid that if I renounced the world and embraced asceticism, I might be too weak to sustain it; and that, having renounced the work I had formerly pursued in hope of a good return, I would be like the dog who passed by a river with a bone in his mouth and, seeing its reflection in the water, jumped in to grab it, losing what he had in his mouth and not getting what he coveted. Thus, although I had great respect for the ascetic life, I feared that my soul might become distressed and impatient. So I decided to remain as I was.

It then occurred to me to weigh the suffering and privation of the ascetic 3.18
life, which I feared I might be too weak to sustain, against the troubles that assail a man in this world, and it became clear to me that there are no worldly

من شهوات الدنيا ولذّاتها شيء إلّا وهو متحوّل أذى ومورث حزنًا فالدنيا كالماء المالح الذي لا يزداد منه صاحبه شربًا إلّا ازداد عطشًا وكالعظم يصيبه الكلب ويصيب فيه ريح اللحم[١] فيطلب ذلك اللحم حتّى يدمي فاه[٢] ثمّ لا يزداد له طلبًا إلّا ازداد لفيه إدماء أو كالحدأة التي تظفر ببضعة لحم فتجتمع عليها الطير فلا تزال في تقلّب وهرب حتّى تلفظ ما معها وقد عنيت وتعبت وكالكوزة من العسل في أسفلها سمّ[٣] فللذائق منها حلاوة عاجلة وله في أسفلها موت ذعاف[٤] وكأحلام النائم التي تفرحه في المنام فإذا استيقظ انقطع الفرح وكالبرق الذي يضيء قليلًا ويُفقد ويبقى راجيه في الظلام مقيمًا وكدودة الإبريسم التي لا تزداد للإبريسم على نفسها لفًّا إلّا ازدادت من الخروج بعدًا.

١٩.٣ فلمّا فكّرت في هذه الأحوال والأمور راجعت رأيي في اختيار النسك والمسابقة إليه ثمّ خاصمت نفسي فقلت لا يجوز لي أن أفرّ من الدنيا إلى النسك إذا فكّرت في شرورها ثمّ أفرّ من النسك إلى الدنيا إذا تذكّرت ما فيه[٥] من الضيق فلا أزال في تصرّف لا أبرم رأيًا ولا أعزم على أمر فصرت كقضاء قاضي مرو الذي استمع من أوّل الخصمين[٦] فقضى على الآخر ثمّ إذا استمع من الآخر قضى على الأوّل.

٢٠.٣ فنظرت في الذي يكابده الناسك من أذى النسك وضيقه فقلت ما أصغر هذه المشقّة وأقلّها في جنب رَوح الأبد وراحته. ونظرت فيما تشره إليه النفس من لذّة الدنيا فقلت ما أمرّ هذا وما أوخمه وقد يدفع إلى عذاب الأبد وهوانه. فقلت كيف لا يستحلي الرجل مرارة قليلة تعقبه حلاوة طويلة وكيف لا تمرّ عليه حلاوة قليلة تورثه مرارة دائمة.

٢١.٣ وقلت لو أنّ رجلًا عُرض عليه أن يعيش مائة سنة لا يأتي عليه من ذلك يوم إلّا بُضع فيه بضعًا ثمّ أحيي[٧] وأعيد لمثل ذلك من الغد غير أنّه شُرط له أنّه إذا استوفى[٨] السنين المائة نجا من كلّ ألم وأذى فصار إلى الأمن والسرور كان حقيقًا أن لا يرى تلك السنين المائة شيئًا فكيف يأبى الصبر على أيّام قلائل يعيشها[٩] في النسك

---

١ ريح اللحم: كذا ل٢؛ الأصل: ادنى لحم. ٢ كذا ل٢؛ الأصل: فيه. ٣ وكالكوز . . . سمّ: كذا ع؛ الأصل: كالكمه السم فى العسل فى اسفلها. ٤ كذا ل٢؛ الأصل: زعاق. ٥ كذا ل٢؛ الأصل: فيها. ٦ كذا ل٢؛ الأصل: الخصماء. ٧ كذا ل٢؛ الأصل: اخر. ٨ كذا ل٢؛ الأصل: استوفاه. ٩ كذا ر؛ ساقطة من الأصل.

cravings or pleasures that do not turn into suffering and cause sorrow. The world is like salt water: the more you drink, the thirstier you become. It is like a bone picked up by a dog: he smells meat and gnaws at the bone until his mouth bleeds—the more he gnaws, the more it bleeds. It is like a kite that snatches a scrap of meat: other birds mob and harass her until, exhausted, she flees and drops it. It is like a jar of honey with poison at the bottom: your first taste is sweet, but death lurks below. It is like a dream that brings the sleeper joy but vanishes as soon as he wakes. It is like lightning that flashes for a moment and disappears, leaving in darkness the person who hopes for rain. It is like the silkworm: the more silk it wraps around itself, the more difficult it is for it to find a way out.

As I pondered these things, I again considered my decision about the ascetic life and striving to attain it. I debated with myself, saying, "It isn't right to flee from the world to asceticism whenever I ponder the world's evils, and from asceticism to the world whenever I consider the hardship asceticism involves—always shifting, without ever making a decision or resolving on a course of action, like the judge of Marw, who listened to the first litigant and ruled against his opponent, then listened to the opponent and ruled against the litigant." 3.19

I reflected on the annoyance and privation that the ascetic endures and said to myself, "How small and insignificant a hardship, compared to the rest and repose of eternity!" And I reflected on the worldly pleasures for which the soul hungers and said to myself, "How bitter and noxious they are, leading as they do toward eternal punishment and humiliation! Why not regard as sweet the brief bitterness that brings lasting sweetness in its wake? Why not regard as bitter the brief sweetness that brings a legacy of lasting bitterness?" 3.20

I thought, if a man were offered a hundred years of being cut to pieces every day, revived, then suffering the same again the next day, with the promise that when the hundred years were over he would escape all suffering and attain peace and happiness, he would be right to consider those years as nothing. How can one refuse to endure a few days of asceticism and a bit 3.21

وأذى قليلاً يصير إليه وليست الدنيا كلّها أذى وبلاء وعذاباً أوليس[١] الإنسان إذاً يتقلّب في ذلك من حين يبدو جنيناً إلى حين يستوفي أيّامه في البلاء فإنّا[٢] نجد في كتب الطبّ[٣] أنّ الماء الذي يُقدّر منه الولد السويّ إذا هو وقع في رحم المرأة اختلط بمائها ودمها وخثر[٤] وغلظ ثمّ أنّ الريح تمخض ذلك الماء والدم حتّى تتركه[٥] كماء الجبن ثمّ يصير كالرائب الغليظ ثمّ تُقسم أعضاؤه لأوان أيّامه فإذا كانت بنتاً فوجهها قبل بطن أمّها وإن كان ذكراً فوجهه قبل ظهر أمّه وقد تمّت خلقته لستّين ليلة منقبض في المشيمة كأنّه في صرّة وهو يتنفّس تنفّساً شاقّاً عليه وليس له عضو إلّا أنّه كأنّه مقموط بقماط فوقه حرّ[٦] البطن وثقله وتحته ما تحته من الظلمات والضيق وهو منوط بمعاء من سرّته إلى سرّة أمّه وبتلك السرّة[٧] يمصّ ويعيش من طعام أمّه وشرابها ويداه على وجنتيه وذقنه على ركبتيه فهو بهذه المنزلة في الغمّ والظلمات والضيق إلى يوم ولاده فإذا كان أوّل ذلك سُلّطت[٨] الريح على رحم أمّه وقوي على التحرّك فيصوّب رأسه قبل المخرج ويسنّيه للخروج فيجد في ضيق المخرج[٩] ما يجد صاحب الدهق من عصره.

٢٢،٣ فإذا وقع على الأرض فأصابته ريح أو مسّته يد وجد لذلك من الألم ما يجد الإنسان الذي قد سُلخ جلده ثمّ هو في ألوان العذاب إذا جاع فليس به استطعام وإذا عطش فليس به استسقاء وإذا وجع فليس به استغاثة مع ما[١٠] يلقى من الرفع والوضع واللفّ[١١] والحلّ والدهن والمسح فإذا نام على ظهره فليس يستطيع تقلّباً وأصنافاً من العذاب ما دام رضيعاً.

٢٣،٣ فإذا أفلت من عذاب الرضاع أخذ بعذاب الأدب والحمية والأوجاع والأسقام فإذا أدرك فالهمّ بالمال والأهل والولد والتعب الشره[١٢] والحرص وبمخاطرة الطلب والسعي وفي كلّ هذا تتقلّب معه أعداؤه الأربعة المرّة والبلغم والدم والسوداء والريح

---

١ كذا ر؛ الأصل: وليس. ٢ كذا ل٢؛ الأصل: فاىما. ٣ كتب الطبّ: كذا ل٢؛ الأصل: الكتب كب الطب. ٤ كذا ل٢؛ الأصل: وحبر. ٥ كذا ر؛ الأصل: يبرد. ٦ كذا ل٢؛ الأصل: حدا. ٧ وبتلك السرّة: كذا ر؛ الأصل: وبلك الصره.
٨ كذا ل٢؛ الأصل: مد لطب علىه. ٩ كذا ر؛ ساقطة من الأصل. ١٠ مع ما: كذا ع؛ ل٢: معا؛ الأصل: معيا.
١١ كذا ش، ع؛ ساقطة من الأصل. ١٢ كذا ل٢؛ الأصل: والشده.

of discomfort, when the world is nothing but suffering, affliction, and torment? Isn't man buffeted by affliction from the moment he's conceived till the end of his days? Medical books tell us that when the fluid destined to become a fully formed infant enters the womb, it mingles with a woman's fluid and blood; it curdles and thickens, and the wind churns the water and blood until they become like the fluid from which cheese is made.[14] Then it thickens like curds, and the infant's organs take shape at the proper time. If it is a girl, it faces its mother's belly; if male, its mother's back. After sixty nights, its formation is complete. It lies constricted within the caul as if bound in a sack, breathing with difficulty, as if every one of its members were in fetters. Above it lie the heat and weight of the stomach, and below it lie darkness and constriction. It is connected by a cord from its navel to its mother's navel, by which it lives and draws on her food and drink. Its hands are on its cheeks, its chin on its legs. It remains in this state of distress, darkness, and constriction until the day it is to be born. When that process begins, the element of wind is given power over the mother's womb and the infant becomes strong enough to move. It turns its head toward the outlet, and because of its narrowness it experiences what a man held in the stocks experiences when they are tightened.

When the infant arrives on earth and feels the wind or the stroke of a 3.22
hand, it feels pain like the flaying of skin. From then on, it suffers in all sorts of ways: it hungers, but cannot ask for food; thirsts, but cannot ask for drink; feels pain, but cannot ask for help. Add to this the experience of being picked up and put down, swaddled and unswaddled, anointed and wiped clean. If the infant falls asleep on its back, it cannot turn over—not to mention all sorts of other torments that continue while it is a nursling.

Having escaped the torment of being a nursling, the child begins the tor- 3.23
ment of discipline, purges, pains, and sicknesses. When he comes of age, there are worries about money, family, and children, along with fatigue, greed, covetousness, and the risks of buying and selling. In all this, his four enemies—gall, phlegm, blood, and black bile—are in a state of commotion

والسمّ المميت والحيّات اللادغة ومع ذلك خوف السباع والناس وخوف الحرّ والبرد والأمطار والرياح ثمّ ألوان عذاب الهرم لمن بلغه فلو أنّ الإنسان لم يخف من هذه الأمور شيئاً وقد كان شُرط له فوثق بالسلامة منها كان حقيقاً أن يتفكّر في الساعة التي يحضره فيها الموت ويفارق فيها الدنيا فيتذكّر ما هو نازل به تلك الساعة من فراق الأهل والأحبّة والأقارب وكلّ مضنون به وكلّ مرغوب فيه من الدنيا والإشراف على الهول العظيم المعضل[1] بعد الموت وأن يقدّر أنّه ضعيف وأمره واهٍ إذا هو لم يعدّ لذلك ولم يحتلّ له جهد حيله ولم يتأهّب لنجاته قبل حلوله ولم يرفض ما يشغله ويلهيه من شهوات الدنيا وغرورها من الاستعداد لما هو لاقيه.

ثمّ لا سيّما في هذا الزمان البالي الشبيه بالصُبابة والكدر فإنّا نرى الدهر مدبراً ٢٤،٣
بكلّ مكان حتّى كأنّ الفضل قد ودّع أهله فأصبح مفقوداً ما كان عزيزاً فقده[2] وموجوداً ما هو ضارّ وجوده وكأنّ الخير أصبح ذابلاً[3] والشرّ ناضراً[4] وكأنّ الغيّ أقبل[5] ضاحكاً وأدبر الرشد باكياً وكأنّ العدل أصبح غائراً[6] والجور عالياً وكأنّ العلم أصبح مدفوناً والجهل منشوراً وكأنّ الودّ أصبح مقطوعاً والبغض والحقد[7] موصولاً وكأنّ الخنا أصبح مستيقظاً والحياء نائماً وكأنّ الكذب أصبح غضّاً مثمراً والصدق ناحلاً يابساً[8] وكأنّ اتّباع الهوى وإضاعة الحكم أصبح بالحكّام موكّلاً وأصبح المظلوم بالخسف مقرّاً والظالم لنفسه مستطيلاً وكأنّ الحرص أصبح فاغراً فاه من كلّ جهة يتلقّف ما قرب منه وما بعد وكأنّ الرضى أصبح مجهولاً وكأنّ الأشرار أصبحوا يسامون السماء وأصبح الأخيار يريدون انخفاضاً في الأرض وأصبحت المروءة مقذوفاً بها من أعلى شرف في أسفل سفل وأصبحت الدناءة مكرّمة وأصبح السلطان منتقلاً من أهل الفضل إلى أهل النقص وكأنّ الدنيا أصبحت جذلة مسرورة مرحة تقول قد غيّبت الخيرات وأظهرت السيّئات.

---

١ كذا ر؛ الأصل: المعطل. ٢ كذا ل٢؛ الأصل: انفده. ٣ كذا ر؛ الأصل: رابلا. ٤ كذا ر؛ الأصل: بصيرًا. ٥ كذا ل٢؛ الأصل: اصبح. ٦ الأصل: عاىرا. ٧ والحقد: الأصل: والحقد أصبح. ٨ الأصل: باىسا.

within him, as well as wind; add to this deadly poisons, venomous snakes, and the fear inspired by men and by wild beasts; and he must also fear heat, cold, rain, and wind. Then come the pains of old age, for those who reach it. Even if he has no fear of these things and is guaranteed safety from them, he has to meditate on the moment of death, when he will bid the world farewell. He should meditate on what will descend on him at that moment: separation from family, loved ones, and kin, and from all that we cling to and desire in the world, and the impending terror to come after death. He would be deemed feeble and negligent if he did not make diligent provision and prepare in advance for its sudden appearance and reject the lusts and beguilements of this world that divert him and distract him from preparing for what he must face.

This is especially true in this decayed age, which resembles nothing so 3.24
much as dregs and mud. We see Time everywhere turn its back, so that it is as if Virtue had bidden its people farewell. Gone are the things whose loss we lament; present are the things whose presence is noxious. It is as if Good were wilting and Evil flourishing; as if Error were advancing in laughter, Integrity retreating in tears; as if Justice had set, Injustice risen; as if Knowledge had been buried, Ignorance resurrected; as if Love had been disinherited, Hatred and Resentment rewarded; as if Obscenity were awake, Shame fast asleep; as if Lying were fresh and fecund, Truth withered and dry; as if Capriciousness and Misrule had been given authority over rulers; as if the Oppressed had been cast deep into the earth, and the Tyrant had raised his head in exaltation; as if Greed, its maw agape in all directions, were devouring everything near and far, and Contentment had become unknown; as if the Ignorant were lifting their heads to the heavens, while the Pious and Good were sinking into the bowels of the earth. Virtue has been hurled from the loftiest height into the lowest abyss, Villainy is revered, and Authority has passed from people of merit to people of mediocrity. It is as if This World were proclaiming in joy and delight, "I have caused Good to disappear and made Evil manifest."

٢٥،٣ فلمّا فكّرت في الدنيا وأمورها وأنّ هذا الإنسان هو أشرف الخلق وأفضله فيها ثمّ هو على منزلته لا يتقلّب إلّا في الشرّ ولا يوصف إلّا به عرفت أنّه ليس من أحد له أدنى عقل إلّا وهو يعقل هذا ثمّ لا يحتال لنفسه ولا يعمل لنجاتها ولا يطلب الخلاص لها فعجبت من ذلك كلّه ونظرت فإذا هو لا يمنعه من ذلك إلّا لذّة حقيرة يسيرة من الشمّ والطعم والسمع والبصر واللمس لعلّه[1] يصيب منها طفيفاً أو يتمنّى منها اللطيف الذي لا يوصف قلّة وإلى سرعة انقطاع وامّحاق فذلك الذي يشغله عن الاهتمام بأمر نفسه وطلب النجاة.

٢٦،٣ فالتمست مثلاً فإذا مثله مثل رجل ألجأه خوف إلى بئر فتدلّى فيها وتعلّق بغصنين نابتين على شفيرها ووقعت رجلاه على شيء عمدهما فنظر إلى موضع رجليه فإذا هما على أربع حيّات قد أطلعن رؤوسهنّ من أجحرتهنّ ونظر إلى أسفل البئر فإذا هو بتنّين يبلع الناس فاغر فاه نحوه ورفع بصره فإذا في أصل[2] الغصنين جرذان أحدهما أبيض والآخر أسود يقرضان الغصنين لا يفتران فبينما هو بالنظر في ذلك والاهتمام لنفسه وابتغاء الحيلة لها إذ نظر فإذا قريب منه نحل قد صنعت شيئاً من عسل فتطعّم منه فشغل قلبه عن أن يتفكّر في شيء من أمر ما هو بسبيله ويلتمس حيلة ينجو بها[3] ولم يذكر أنّ رجليه على أربع حيّات لا يدري متى تهيج به إحداهنّ ولم يذكر أنّ الجرذين دائبان في قطع الغصنين وأنّهما إذا قطعاهما وقع في البئر فلم يزل لاهياً غافلاً[4] حتّى هلك.

٢٧،٣ فشبّهت البئر بالدنيا[5] المملوءة آفات[6] وشروراً ومخاوف وشبّهت الأفاعي بالطبائع الأربع فمتى ما هاج به منها شيء فهو كحمة الأفاعي والسمّ المميت وشبّهت بالغصنين الحياة وشبّهت بالجرذ الأسود الليل والجرذ الأبيض النهار وشبّهت بقرضهما الغصنين دائبين دور الليل والنهار في فناء الأيّام والآجال[7]

---

١ كذا ل٢؛ الأصل: ولعله. ٢ كذا ر؛ ساقطة من الأصل. ٣ حيلة . . . بها: كذا پ٣٤٧٥؛ ساقطة من الأصل.
٤ كذا ل٢؛ الأصل: وغافلاً. ٥ كذا ل٢؛ الأصل: الدنيا. ٦ كذا ل٢؛ الأصل: اثامًا (غير واضح). ٧ وشبّهت بقرضهما . . . والآجال: كذا پ٣٤٧٥؛ الأصل: وبعرصهما العصنين داسن ومنه الليل والنهار ى فنا الايام والامال.

When I considered the world and its affairs and how man, its noblest and most excellent creature, wallows in evil despite his station, so that evil becomes his main characteristic, I realized that anyone with the least intelligence could comprehend this and make provision for his soul, work for its deliverance, and seek its safety, and I was utterly amazed. I pondered and perceived that the only thing standing in the way of achieving this was a paltry bit of pleasure that comes from the senses—smell, taste, hearing, sight, and touch—the chance of obtaining something pleasant or hoping to gain a trifle of indescribable slightness soon to be cut short and wiped away. That is what distracts man from attending to his soul and seeking deliverance. 3.25

I have tried to find an analogy for this. It is like a man driven by fear to take refuge in a well. He lowers himself into it and clings to two branches on its edge.[15] His feet find something to support them. He looks down, and behold—his feet rest on four snakes that have thrust their heads out of their nests. He looks at the bottom of the well, and behold—a man-eating dragon with its mouth agape. He looks up, and behold—at the base of the branches are two rats, one white, the other black, gnawing away tirelessly. While he ponders his situation and tries to find a way to save himself, he sees some bees nearby that have made a bit of honey; he tastes it, and it distracts him from thinking about his situation and finding a way to escape. He forgets that his feet rest on four snakes—any of which, for all he knows, might attack him at any moment—and that the two rats are busily eating away at the branches, and that when they are cut he will fall into the well. And thus he continues, blissfully heedless, until he perishes. 3.26

The Man in the Well

I liken the well to the world, filled as it is with plagues, evils, perils, and dangers. I liken the snakes to the four humors, any of which, when excited, is like snake venom and deadly poison. I liken the two branches to life: the black rat to night and the white rat to day. I liken their constant gnawing at the branches to the cycle of night and day that consumes one's allotted time. I liken the dragon to destiny, from which there is no escape. I liken the honey 3.27

وشبّهت بالتنّين المصير الذي لا بدّ منه وشبّهت العسل بهذه الحلاوة القليلة التي يصيب الإنسان فتشغله عن نفسه وتنسيه أمره وتلهيه عن شأنه وتصدّه عن سبيل نجاته.

٢٨،٣ فصار أمري إلى الرضى بحالي وإصلاح ما استطعت أن أصلح من عملي لعلّي أصادف فيما أمامي زمانًا أصيب فيه دليلاً على هداي وسلطانًا على نفسي وأعوانًا على أمري فأقمت على هذه الحالة وانصرفت من الهند إلى بلادي وانتسخت من كتبها[١] كتبًا منها هذا الكتاب.

[١] من كتبها: كذا ل٢؛ الأصل: منها.

to the scant sweetness a human being receives that distracts him from his soul, making him forget his condition, diverting him from his welfare, and turning him from the path of deliverance.

In the end, I found contentment with my situation and with performing my work to the best of my ability,[16] hoping to find in future days a guide to lead me aright, a ruler over my soul, and aides to help me in my affairs.[17] I remained in this state and returned home from India, having transcribed a number of their books, including this one. **3.28**

باب الأسـد والثور

وهو مثل الرجلين المتحابين يقطع بينهما الغدّار الكذوب بنميمته

قال دبشلم ملك الهند لبيدبا[1] الفيلسوف رأس فلاسفته اضرب لي مثل الرجلين المتحابين يقطع بينهما الكذوب الخائن ويحملهما على العداوة والشنآن. ١،٤

قال بيدبا الفيلسوف إذا ابتلي الرجلان بدخول الكذوب الخؤون بينهما تقاطعا وتدابرا وتفاسد ما بينهما.

ومن أمثال ذلك أنّه كان بأرض دستنابد تاجر مكثر وله بنون فلمّا أدركوا شرعوا في مال أبيهم ولم يحترفوا حرفة يكتسبون بها مالاً فلامهم أبوهم ووعظهم وكان ممّا قال لهم يا بَنيّ إنّ صاحب الدنيا يطلب ثلاثة أمور لن تُدرك إلّا بأربعة أشياء. أمّا الثلاثة التي يطلب فالسعة في المعيشة والمنزلة في الناس والزاد إلى الآخرة. وأمّا الأربعة التي يحتاج إليها في إدراك هذه الثلاثة فاكتساب المال من أحسن وجوهه ثمّ حسن القيام على ما اكتسب والتثمير له ثمّ إنفاقه فيما يصلح المعيشة ويرضي به الله تعالى والأهل والإخوان ويعود في الآخرة نفعه عليه فمن أضاع شيئاً من هذه الخلال الأربع لم يدرك ما أراد فإنّه إن لم يكتسب لم يكن له مال يعيش به وإن كان هو ذا مال وذا اكتساب ولم يحسن القيام عليه أوشك أن يفنى ويبقى بغير مال. وإن هو أنفقه ولم يثمّره لم تمنعه قلّة الإنفاق من سرعة النفاد[2] كالكحل الذي لا يؤخذ منه إلّا مثل الغبار ثمّ هو مع ذلك سريع فناؤه. وإن كانت نفقته في غير مواضع الحقوق كان بمنزلة الفقير الذي لا مال له ثمّ لم ينفعه ذلك من تلاف المال للمقادير والعلل كالمكان الذي لا تزال تنصبّ فيه المياه فإنّه إن لم يكن له مخرج ومغيض يخرج منه الماء بقدر الذي يدخل انبجس وسال من نواحي كثيرة وربّما انبثق البثق العظيم فذهب الماء ضياعاً. ٢،٤

---

١ كذا ش، ع؛ الأصل: لبيدبا (وتكتب أحياناً: بيدنا). ٢ كذا ل٢؛ الأصل: النفاق.

The Lion and the Ox

A parable about two friends driven apart by the slander of a treacherous liar.

King Dabshalim of India said to Baydabā, his chief philosopher, "Tell me a parable about two friends driven apart by a treacherous liar who incited them to enmity and hatred." 4.1

And Baydabā the Philosopher said, "When two friends fall victim to a treacherous liar who comes between them, they part company, turn their backs on each other, and sever relations. Here is a story to illustrate this."

In the land of Dastanābad there lived a rich merchant and his sons. When 4.2
they came of age, his sons proceeded to squander their patrimony and pursued no gainful professions. Their father admonished them, saying, among other things, "My sons, a man in this world seeks three things, which can be obtained by only four means. The three things are: an ample livelihood, honor among men, and provision for the hereafter. The four means needed to obtain these three things are: acquiring wealth honestly; managing it well, once acquired; making it bear fruit; and spending it to enhance one's life, to please God, one's family, and friends, and to benefit oneself in the hereafter. If you neglect any of these four, you won't attain your desires. If you don't acquire, you'll have nothing to live on. If you acquire, but manage your wealth badly, it will soon disappear and you'll be left with nothing. If you spend it without investing it to bear fruit, it will be depleted quickly, however little you spend. It will be like kohl: you might only use a speck of it, but it disappears quickly. If you don't spend it where it ought to be spent, you'll be no better than a pauper; yet even this will not prevent your wealth from vanishing, be it by fate or by accident. It is like a cistern full of water: if more water pours in and there is no outlet to release the flow, the water will find a way to seep out, or it may even burst out all at once and everything will be lost."

٣،٤ ثمّ إنّ بني التاجر اتّعظوا وأخذوا بأمر أبيهم فانطلق أحدهم متوجّهاً نحو أرض يقال لها سورقان فمرّ في طريقه على مكان فيه وحل شديد ومعه عجلة يجرّها ثوران أحدهما يُسمّى شنزبة[1] والآخر نندبة[2] فوحل شنزبة في ذلك المكان فعالجه الرجل وأعوانه حتّى استخرجه بعد ما بلغه الجهد وخلّف التاجر عنده رجلاً وأمره أن يقوم عليه أيّاماً فإذا رآه قد صلح أتبعه فلمّا كان من الغد برم الرجل بمكانه فترك الثور ولحق بالرجل فأخبره أنّ ثوره قد مات. ثمّ إنّ الثور انبعث من مكانه فلم يزل يدبّ حتّى انتهى إلى مرج مخصب كثير العشب فدخل في موضع خوف أن يصيبه في ذلك المكان من العراض الذي لم يكن ليخطئه مثل ذلك فإنّهم زعموا أنّ رجلاً كان يجزّ حشيشاً فاغتاله ذئب ليأكله فلم يفطن له حتّى دنا منه فلمّا رآه اشتدّ وجله منه وخرج هارباً نحو قرية على شاطئ نهر فلمّا انتهى إلى النهر وجد عليه قنطرة منكسرة ورهقه الذئب فقال في نفسه كيف أصنع وهذا الذئب يتلوني والنهر عميق والقنطرة منكسرة وأنا لا أحسن السباحة غير أنّ أحرز الأشياء أن ألجئ نفسي إلى الماء. فوقع فيه فرآه أهل القرية فأرسلوا إليه من استخرجه بعد أن أشرف على العطب فأتاهم فاستند إلى حائط وجعل يحدّثهم إذ انهدم عليه الحائط فقتله.

٤،٤ ثمّ إنّ شنزبة لم يلبث أن عبل وسمن وبطن فرفع صوته بالخوار وقربه أسد هو ملك تلك الناحية ومعه سباع كثيرة من الذئاب والدببة وبنات آوى والثعالب وسائر السباع وكان مزهوّاً مكتفياً برأيه ورأيه غير كافٍ وإنّ الأسد لمّا سمع الخوار خوار الثور ولم يكن رأى ثوراً قطّ ولا سمع خواره رعب وكره أن يفطن لذلك جنده فأقام مكانه.

٥،٤ وكان ممّن معه ابنا آوى يدعى أحدهما كليلة والآخر دمنة وكلاهما ذو دهاء وأدب وكان دمنة أشرّهما نفساً وأبعدهما همّة وأقلّهما رضى بحاله ولم يكن الأسد عرفهما. فقال دمنة لكليلة ما ترى يا أخي شأن الأسد مقيماً بمكان واحد لا يبرح ولا يتنشّط.

---

١ كذا د، ع، هامش ش؛ الأصل: شنربه. ٢ كذا ع؛ الأصل: بيدنه.

The merchant's sons took their father's advice to heart. The eldest set out for a land called Sūraqān to trade. On the way, he came to a place that was very muddy. He had a cart with him, drawn by two oxen: Shanzabah and Nandabah. Shanzabah sank into the mud. With the help of his assistants, the man managed to extricate him, but Shanzabah was exhausted. So the merchant's son left behind a man who was under orders to watch over the ox for a few days; when the man saw that Shanzabah had recovered, he was to bring him and catch up. But the next morning the man, tired of waiting, abandoned the ox, caught up with the merchant, and told him that the ox had died. The ox, for its part, set off and plodded on until he came to a grassy meadow, where he stayed, fearful that some inevitable misfortune might yet befall him—as happened, for example, to a man who, they say, was cutting hay when a wolf attacked him. Only when the wolf was near did the man notice and flee in terror toward a village on the bank of a river. When he reached the river, he found the bridge in ruins. With the wolf catching up, he said to himself, "What shall I do? The wolf is right behind me, the river is deep, the bridge is in ruins, and I can't swim. The safest thing is to entrust my life to the water." So he jumped in. The villagers saw him and pulled him out just as he was about to drown. Back among the villagers, as he leaned against a wall and began to tell them what had happened, the wall collapsed and killed him. 4.3

The Man Who Escaped from the Wolf

Shanzabah soon grew fat and flourishing, and, with his belly full of food, he began bellowing loudly. Nearby there lived a lion. As king of that region, he had an entourage of many wild animals: wolves, bears, jackals, foxes, and so forth. He was proud and given to relying only on his own judgment, which was far from perfect. When he heard the ox bellowing—he had never seen an ox or heard one bellow—he grew frightened, but not wanting his soldiers to notice, did not leave his place. 4.4

Among the animals in his entourage were two jackals, one named Kalīlah, the other Dimnah. Each was clever and intelligent, but of the two Dimnah was greedier, more ambitious, and less contented. The lion had not yet made their acquaintance. Dimnah asked Kalīlah, "Brother, what do you think is wrong with the lion? Why is he staying put, not stirring or showing his usual liveliness?" 4.5

فقال كليلة بل ما شأنك وشأن المسألة عمّا ليس من شأنك أمّا نحن فحالنا حال صدق ونحن على باب ملكنا واجدون ممّا نأكل ولسنا من أهل المرتبة التي تتناول كلام الملوك وينظرون في أمورهم ويفحصون عمّا غاب عنهم منهم فاسكت عن هذا واعلم أنّ من تكلّف من الفعل والقول ما ليس من شأنه أصابه ما أصاب القرد.

قال دمنة وكيف كان ذلك.

٦،٤ قال كليلة زعموا أنّ قردًا رأى نجّارًا يشقّ[١] خشبة على وتدين راكبًا عليها[٢] كلّما شقّ منها ذراعًا أدخل فيها وتدًا فشبهه بالسوار ثمّ إنّ النجّار قام لبعض حاجته فانطلق القرد يتكلّف ما ليس من صنعته ولا من شأنه فركب الخشبة وجعل ظهره قبل مشقّ الخشبة ووجهه قبل الوتد فتدلّت خصيتاه في ذلك الشقّ ونزع الوتد فلمّا نزعه لجّت خصيتاه في مشقّ الخشبة حين انضمّت فخرّ مغشيًّا عليه وكان أشدّ من ذلك ما لقي من النجّار من الضرب.

٧،٤ قال دمنة قد سمعت مثلك وفهمت ما ذكرت ولكن اعلم أنّه ليس من يدنو من الملوك إنّما يدنو لبطنه فإنّ البطون تُحشى بكلّ مكان[٣] ولكنّ من تقرّب من الملوك قد يلتمس الرفعة والمنزلة ليسرّ به الصديق ويسمو به على العدوّ فأمّا أدنى الناس الذين يرضون بالقليل ويفرحون به فمثلهم كمثل الكلب الذي يصيب عظمًا يابسًا فيفرح به فأمّا أهل المروءة والفضل فلا يغنيهم القليل ولا يرضون به دون أن تسمو همّتهم إلى ما هو أعظم ممّا يستحقّون كالأسد الذي يفترس الأرنب فإذا رأى العير ترك الأرنب وطلب العير. ألا ترى أنّ الكلب يبصبص بذنبه حتّى تلقى له الكسرة فيقنع بها وأنّ الفيل المغتلم لمعرفته بقوّته وفضله إذا قُدّم له علفه مكرّمًا لا يأكله حتّى يُمسح ويُتملّق له فمن عاش ما عاش غير خامل المنزلة ذا فضل على نفسه وأصحابه فهو وإن قلّ عمره طويل العمر ومن كان عيشه في وحدة وضنك وقلّة خير على نفسه وعلى الناس فهو وإن طال عمره قصير العمر فإنّه يقال إنّ أشرّ الناس من طال عمره في ضرّ وشدّة وقد يقال يُعدّ من البقر والغنم من لم يكن همّه إلّا بطنه.

---

١ كذا ر؛ الأصل: فشقّ. ٢ كذا ل٢؛ الأصل: عليهما. ٣ الأصل: ما كان.

"Why are you asking?" replied Kalīlah. "It's none of your business. Our situation here is good; here at the king's gate we find enough to eat. We're not the sort of people who converse with kings, discuss their affairs, and inquire into unknown matters. Enough of this! Anyone who interferes in things that are none of his business will suffer the same fate as the monkey."

"And what was that?" asked Dimnah.

And Kalīlah told the following tale: A monkey, so they say, once saw a carpenter splitting a log using two wedges, straddling it like a knight on horseback. Whenever he split a cubit's length, he would drive in a wedge, sitting astride the log like a rider on a mount. At one point, the carpenter got up to relieve himself, and the monkey dashed over to try his hand at something that was none of his business. He straddled the log, with his back toward the split and his face toward the wedge,[18] with his testicles dangling in the split, and pulled out the wedge. When the wedge came out, the log closed with his testicles deep in the split. He fell over in a faint, and the beating he received from the carpenter was worse still. 4.6

The Monkey and the Carpenter

"I see what you're driving at," replied Dimnah. "But people who approach kings don't do it only to fill their stomachs. Stomachs can be filled anywhere. People who approach kings seek eminence: a position that enables them to gladden their friends and rise above their enemies. The lowest sort of people, content with a pittance, are like the dog that rejoices at finding a dry bone. People of valor and merit aren't satisfied with little, or content with a pittance; their ambition aspires to what they deserve—like the lion who catches a hare, but as soon as he sees a wild ass, drops the hare and pursues the ass. Haven't you seen that a dog will wag his tail until he is thrown a crust, but a full-grown elephant, conscious of his strength and worth, won't eat even the best fodder until he is stroked and coaxed? Anyone who does not live in obscurity, a credit to himself and to his friends, lives a long life, however short his years. Anyone who lives life in solitude and scarcity, of little use to himself or others, lives a short life, however long his years. The worst lot, they say, is a long life lived in scarcity and distress. They also say that anyone interested only in his stomach is no different from cattle and sheep." 4.7

٨،٤ قال كليلة قد فهمت ما قلت فراجع عقلك ورَهْ في أمرك واعلم أنّ لكلّ امرئ منزلة وقدرًا فإذا كان في منزلته متماسك الحال[١] كان حقيقًا أن يقنع ويرضى وليس لنا من المنزلة ما نسخط به حالنا التي نحن عليها.

قال دمنة إنّ المنازل متنازعة مشتركة فذو المروءة ترفعه مروءته من المنزلة الوضيعة إلى المنزلة الرفيعة ومن لا مروءة له فقد يحطّ نفسه من المنزلة الرفيعة إلى المنزلة الوضيعة والارتفاع من أدنى المنازل إلى أعلاها عسير ذو مؤونة والانحطاط منها إلى الضعة هيّن مثل الحجر الثقيل الذي رفعه من الأرض إلى العاتق عسير وطرحه من العاتق إلى الأرض يسير فنحن أحقّ أن[٢] نروم ما فوقنا من المنازل ونلتمس ذلك بمروءتنا فلا نقيم على مرتبتنا ونحن نستطيع الارتفاع إلى أسنى منها.

٩،٤ قال كليلة وما الذي أجمع عليه رأيك.

قال دمنة أريد أن أتعرّض للأسد عند هذه الفرصة فإنّ الأسد ضعيف الرأي وإنّه وجنده قد التبس عليه معرفة هذا الصوت ولعلّي على هذه الحال أدنو من الأسد بالنصيحة له فأصيب عنده مكانًا وجاهًا.

قال كليلة وما يدريك أنّ الأسد التبس عليه أمره.

قال دمنة أعرف ذلك بالرأي والحدس فإنّ الرجل ذا الرأي يعرف حال صاحبه وباطن أمره ممّا يظهر له من هيئته ونظره وصنعته حتّى ربّما عرف ذلك بدلّه وشكله.

١٠،٤ قال كليلة كيف ترجو المنزلة عند الأسد وأنت لم تصحب سلطانًا وليس لك علم بخدمتهم وأدبهم.

قال دمنة إنّ الرجل الشديد يروز الحمل الثقيل فإن استقلّه[٣] حمله ولا يعتنف على الشديد حمل ولا المقبل عمل فلا يضرّ العاقل غربة ولا يمتنع من اللّين الجانب[٤] المتواضع أحد.

١١،٤ قال كليلة إنّ الملك لا يتوخّى[٥] بكرامته أفضل من بحضرته مروءة ولكنّه يؤثر بذلك الأدنى فالأدنى ويقال إنّ مثل السلطان في ذلك مثل الكرم الذي لا يتعلّق بأكرم

١ متماسك الحال: كذا ل٢؛ الأصل: متماسك في الحال. ٢ أحقّ أن: كذا ر؛ الأصل: أخوان. ٣ الأصل: اعقله.
٤ الأصل: لجانب. ٥ كذا ر؛ الأصل: يواحى.

"I understand what you're saying," replied Kalīlah. "But think it over and consider your situation. Everyone has his place and measure. A person ought to be content and satisfied if he can hold his own. Our position is not so bad as to make us despise our present circumstances." 4.8

"Positions," replied Dimnah, "can be contested and shared.[19] The industrious person's industry raises him from a lowly to a lofty place, but the person who lacks industriousness lowers himself from a lofty to a lowly place. It is difficult and taxing to rise from the depths to the heights, but easy to fall from a height. It is like a heavy stone: hard to lift onto your shoulder, but easy to drop. So we ought to aspire to a higher place, seeking it through our industry, and not stay where we are when we can rise higher."

"What have you decided to do?" 4.9

"I intend to present myself to the lion straightaway. He's indecisive, and he and his soldiers are at a loss. I may be able to offer him good advice while he is in this state, and gain honor and glory in his eyes."

"What makes you think the lion is at a loss?"

"I know it by insight and by inference. A perceptive person can tell his companion's inward disposition from his visible demeanor and actions, and can infer it from his behavior and appearance."

"How do you hope to gain a place at the lion's court, when you've never 4.10
rubbed shoulders with rulers and know nothing about how to serve them or behave in their presence?"

"A strong person is equal to a heavy burden: if he can pick it up, he can carry it. No burden is too difficult for the strong, no work too arduous for the bold. An unfamiliar place poses no challenge for a person of intelligence, and no one can resist the blandishments of a person who pretends to be humble."

"A ruler doesn't bestow favor on the best of his courtiers; he honors them 4.11
according to their closeness. They say that in this respect a ruler is like a grapevine, which clings not to the noblest but to the closest tree, just as

شجرة ولكن يتعلّق بأدناه منه وكذلك النساء بأدنى الرجال فكيف ترجو المنزلة عند الأسد ولست تدنو منه.

قال دمنة لقد فهمت مقالتك وأنت صادق ولكن اعلم أنّ الذين هم بقرب السلطان قد كانوا وليست تلك منزلتهم ثمّ قربوا منهم بعد البعد وبلغوا المنازل فأنا ملتمس بلوغ المنزلة من الأسد بجهدي وقد كان يقال لا يواظب على باب السلطان أحد فيلقي عنه الأنفة ويحتمل الأذى ويكظم الغيظ ويرفق بالناس إلّا خلص إلى حاجته من السلطان.

١٢،٤ قال كليلة هبك قد وصلت إلى الأسد فما رفقك الذي ترجو أن تنال المنزلة به عنده.

قال دمنة لو قد لزمته عرفت أخلاقه وحططت في هواه ثمّ رفقت بمتابعته وقلّة الخلاف عليه فإذا أراد أمرًا هو في نفسي صواب زيّنته له وبصّرته فضله وشجّعته عليه حتّى يزداد بذلك سرورًا وإذا أراد أمرًا أخاف عليه ضرّه وشينه بصّرته بما فيه من الضرّ والشين فإنّي أرجو أن يزداد لي الأسد بذلك حبًّا ويرى منّي[1] ما لم ير من غيري فإنّ الرجل الأريب الرفيق ربّما أبطل الحقّ وحقّق الباطل كالمصوّر الماهر الذي يصوّر في الجدار تصاوير كأنّها خارجة من الجدار وليست خارجة وأخرى كأنّها داخلة وليست بداخلة فإذا أبصر الأسد فضلي وعرف ما عندي كان هو الذي يلتمس بقربي إكرامي.

١٣،٤ قال كليلة أمّا إذا كان هذا رأيك فإنّي أحذّرك السلطان فإنّ في صحبة السلطان خطر وقد قالت العلماء في أمور ثلاثة لا يجترئ عليها إلّا أهوج ولا يسلم منها إلّا قليل منها صحبة السلطان ومنها ائتمان النساء على الأسرار ومنها شرب السمّ للتجربة وإنّما شبّه العلماء السلطان بالجبل الصعب الوعر المسلك الذي فيه الثمار الطيّبة وهو معدن الأسود والنمور وكلّ سبع مخوف ضارٍ فالارتقاء إليه شديد والمقام فيه أشدّ.

[1] ويرى منّي: كذا ر؛ ساقطة من الأصل.

women cling to the closest man. How do you expect to gain a place at the lion's court, when you've never been close to him?"

"I understand what you're saying, and you're right. But you must realize that those close to the ruler at present weren't always so: they had been distant from him and then became close to him and acquired standing. I, too, will make every effort to acquire standing with the lion. They say that no one can fail to obtain what he wants from the ruler if he perseveres at the ruler's gate, swallows his pride, bears insults, controls his anger, and treats important people with skill."

"I understand. But let's assume you've gained access to the lion: what is 4.12
this 'skill' you hope to use to gain a place at his court?"

"Once I'm close to the lion, I'll get to know his character. I'll defer to his wishes, humor him, and rarely disagree with him. When he wants something I think is right, I'll praise it, extol its benefits, and encourage him, so his delight with it increases. If he wants something I fear may bring harm and disgrace, I'll make him see the harm and disgrace in it. I hope that in this way the lion will become more and more fond of me and see in me what he sees in no one else. If you're cunning and skillful enough, you can turn truth into falsehood and falsehood into truth—like an accomplished artist who paints a wall with designs that seem to jut out from the wall, though they don't in reality, and designs that appear to recede, though they don't in reality. Once the lion recognizes my merits and knows what I have to offer, he'll be all the more eager to honor me and keep me close."

"If this is your plan," said Kalīlah, "I must warn you about the dangers of 4.13
associating with rulers. Scholars say there are three things that only fools attempt and from which few escape unscathed: associating with rulers, trusting women with secrets, and drinking poison as an experiment. Scholars have likened a ruler to a steep, rugged mountain where all sorts of pleasant fruit grow, but which is home to lions, leopards, and every kind of ferocious beast—the ascent may be difficult, but staying there is harder yet."

قال دمنة قد صدقت فيما وصفت غير أنّه من لم يركب[١] الأهوال لم ينل الرغائب ومن ترك الأمر الذي لعلّه أن يبلغ فيه حاجته هيبة له ومخافة لما لعلّه يتوقّاه فليس جسيماً أمره وقد قيل في أعمال ثلاثة لا يستطيع أحد بلوغها إلّا بمعرفة وارتفاع همّة وعظم خطر منها عمل السلطان ومنها تجارة البحر ومنها مشاجرة العدوّ وقد قالت العلماء في الرجل الفاضل المروءة إنّه لا ينبغي له أن يُرى إلّا في مكانين ولا يليق به غيرهما إمّا مع الملوك مكرّماً وإمّا مع النسّاك متبتّلاً كالفيل الذي بهاؤه وجماله في مكانين إمّا في البرّيّة وحشيّاً وإمّا مع الملوك مركباً.

قال كليلة خار الله لك فيما عزمت.

ثمّ إنّ دمنة انطلق حتّى وصل إلى الأسد فسلّم عليه فقال الأسد لجلسائه من ١٤،٤
هذا. قالوا هذا فلان بن فلان. قال كنت أعرف أباه فدعا به ثمّ قال أين كنت تكون.

قال لم أزل بباب الملك مرابطاً رجاء أن يحضر أمر أعين الملك فيه برأيي ونفسي فإنّ باب الملك تكثر فيه الأمور التي ربّما احتيج فيها إلى من لا يؤبَه له وليس يصغر أمره عن أن يكون عنده بعض المنافع على قدره فإنّ العود المنبوذ في الأرض ربّما انتفع به المنتفع فيحكّ به أذنه عند الحاجة إليه والحيوان الذي يعرف الضرّ والنفع أحرى أن يُنتفع به.

فلمّا سمع الأسد كلامه أعجبه فظنّ أنّ عنده من الخيرات نصيحة ورأياً فأقبل ١٥،٤
على قربائه فقال لهم إنّ الرجل ذا العلم والمروءة ليكون غامض الأمر خامل المنزلة فتأبى مروءته إلّا أن تستبين وتُعرف كالشعلة من النار التي يضعها صاحبها وتأبى إلّا ارتفاعاً.

فلمّا عرف دمنة أنّ الأسد قد أُعجب به قال إنّ رعيّة الملك ومن يحضر بابه ١٦،٤
أحقّاء أن يعرّفوا الملك ما عندهم من علم أو مروءة ويبذلوا له الرأي والنصيحة فإنّ الملك لا يعرفهم ولا ينزلهم منازلهم دون أن يعرفهم بحالاتهم كالزرع المدفون في الأرض من الحنطة والشعير لا يستطيع أحد أن يعرفه وينزله منزلته حتّى يكون هو

[١] كذا ر؛ الأصل: يركب.

"That may be true," said Dimnah, "but without risk there is no reward. If we abandon a promising enterprise out of timidity or fear of the consequences, we shall never attain greatness. Three things, they say, can be accomplished only with knowledge, lofty ambition, and great danger: serving a ruler, sailing the seas as a merchant, and fighting an enemy. They also say that there are only two places where a man of great valor should be found: as an honored companion of kings or as a hermit in the company of ascetics—just like the elephant, whose majesty and beauty belong in only two places: either roaming free in the forest, or as a mount for kings."

"May God grant you success in your decision!"

So Dimnah set out, and when he arrived he greeted the lion. "Who is 4.14
this?" inquired the lion of his courtiers. They told him Dimnah's name and the name of his father, and the lion said, "I used to know his father." He told Dimnah to approach, then asked, "Where have you been living?"

"In readiness at the king's gate," Dimnah replied, "waiting for some matter to arise in which I could assist the king with my counsel and my services. There are many occasions when the assistance of someone who seems insignificant may be needed. No one, however lowly or insignificant, is without some use. A twig thrown on the ground can be used to scratch an itchy ear. A creature that knows the difference between gain and loss is even more likely to be of use."

The lion liked what he heard. Thinking that Dimnah might be blessed 4.15
with good judgment and the ability to give sound advice, he turned to his courtiers and said, "Someone of intelligence and virtue may be of low station and obscure origin, yet his virtue will shine forth and be recognized, like a torch whose flame rises even if it is pointed downward."

When Dimnah saw that the lion was pleased, he said, "The king's subjects 4.16
and courtiers have a duty to acquaint him with whatever knowledge and virtue they possess and offer him their opinion and advice. Only in this way can the king know them and assign them to the positions they merit. They are like seeds of wheat or barley buried in the ground: no one can determine what kind they are until they sprout. Those attending the ruler should

الذي يخرج ويظهر. وحقّ على من حضر السلطان أن يطلعه على ما عنده من
المنفعة والأدب ومن الحقّ على السلطان أن يبلّغ كلّ امرئ مرتبته على قدر رأيه
ونصيحته وما[1] يجد عنده من المنفعة والرأي والأدب.

فإنّه قد كان يقال شيآن لا ينبغي لأحد وإن كان ملكاً أن يضع شيئاً منهما ١٧،٤
غير موضعه ولا أن يزيله[2] عن منزلته أحدهما حلية الرجل والآخر حلية الرأس فإنّه
يُعَدّ جاهلاً من عقد على رأسه حلية رجليه وعلى رجليه حلية رأسه. ومن ضبّب
الياقوت واللؤلؤ بالرصاص فليس ذلك ينقص الياقوت واللؤلؤ ولكنّه يجهّل من يفعل
ذلك ولذلك يقال لا تصاحبنّ صاحباً لا يعرف ليمينه من شماله موضعهما.

وإنّما يستخرج ما عند الرجال ولاتهم وما عند الجند قادتهم وما في الدين من ١٨،٤
تأويل علماؤه وقد قيل في أشياء ثلاثة فضل ما بينها متفاوت وإن كان يجمعها اسم
واحد[3] فضل المقاتل على المقاتل والفيل على الفيل والعالم على العالم. فإنّ كثرة الأعوان
إذا لم يكونوا خبيرين مضرّة بالعمل فإنّ العمل ليس فائدته كثيرة بكثرة الأعوان ولكن
بصالح الأعوان ومثل ذلك كالرجل الذي يحمل الحجر الثقيل فيثقل[4] به نفسه ولا يجد
به ثمناً والذي يحمل الياقوت لا يثقل عليه حمله وهو يجد به حاجته. والعمل الذي
يُحتاج فيه إلى الجذع لا يجديه القصب وإن كثر. والوالي حقيق أن لا يحقر مروءة
يجدها عند رجل صغير المنزلة فإنّ الصغير ربّما عظم كالعصب يؤخذ من الميتة فإذا
عُملت به القوس أُكرم فقبض عليه الملك واحتاج إليه في لهوه وبأسه.

وأحبّ دمنة أن ينال[5] من كرامة الأسد ما ناله والقوم يعلمون أنّ ذلك ليس ١٩،٤
بمعرفة بأبيه فقط ولكنّه لرأي دمنة ومروءته فقال إنّ السلطان لا يقرّب الرجال
على قرب آبائهم ولا يبعدهم لبعدهم ولكنّه ينزلهم على قدر كلّ امرئ منهم ما ينتفع
به فإنّه لا أحد أقرب إلى الرجل من جسده فمن جسده ما يدوى عليه حتّى يداويه
ولا يدفع ذلك عنه إلّا الدواء الذي يأتيه من بعد والجرذ في البيت مجاور ولكنّه لمّا
كان ضارّاً نفي والبازي وحشيّ غريب ولكنّه لمّا كانت منه منافع اقتُني واتّخذ وأُكرم.

١ كذا ر؛ الأصل: ومن. ٢ كذا ر؛ الأصل: ىرىل. ٣ وإن... واحد: كذا ل٢؛ ساقطة من الأصل. ٤ الأصل: فىمل. ٥ الأصل: ساله.

inform him of their usefulness and skills, and the ruler should assign each to his proper place, both according to that person's opinion and advice, and according to the usefulness and skills the ruler discerns in him.

"They say there are two things that no one, not even a king, should put 4.17
in the wrong place or remove from where they belong: an ornament fashioned for the feet and an ornament fashioned for the head. Someone who puts a foot ornament on his head or a head ornament on his feet will be taken for a fool; someone who sets rubies and pearls in lead doesn't diminish their value, but he demonstrates his ignorance. They also say: Never take as your companion someone who doesn't know where to put his right foot and where to put his left.

"Only a ruler can know a man's true potential, only a general can know 4.18
a soldier's, and only a jurist can interpret religious law. Three things, they say, differ greatly in excellence though they are called the same thing: one soldier and another, one elephant and another, and one scholar and another. Many inexperienced helpers harm an enterprise: success depends on good helpers, not on their number. It is like a man who weighs himself down by carrying a heavy stone and gets nothing for it, while another carries a ruby that doesn't weigh him down and gets what he wants for it. Reeds, however many, are useless for a task that requires a beam. A ruler shouldn't despise anyone's virtues, however lowly, for something small can turn out to be of great importance, such as a sinew from a corpse used in a bow, which is then treated with dignity when brandished by a king in sport and war."

Dimnah wanted the courtiers to know that any honor he received from 4.19
the lion had not been conferred on him because the lion had known his father, but because of Dimnah's own intelligence and merit, so he said, "A ruler doesn't bring men near or keep them at a distance because of the respective positions of their fathers; he employs them according to the benefits each can bring. Nothing is closer to a man than his body, but sometimes part of it falls ill and only a medicine brought from afar can dispel the illness. The rat lives as a neighbor in the house, but when he causes damage he is driven out. The goshawk may be wild and from a distant land, but people acquire it, keep it, and treat it with honor because of its usefulness."

فلمّا فرغ دمنة من مقالته ازداد الأسد به عجباً وأحسن عليه الردّ فكان ممّا قال لجلسائه أن قال ينبغي للسلطان أن لا يلحّ في تضييع حقّ ذي الحقّ ووضع منزلة ذي المروءة وأن يستدرك الوالي ما مضى من تفريطه في ذلك ولا يغرّه أن يرى من صاحبه المفعول ذلك به رضى وإقراراً فإنّ الناس في ذلك رجلان رجل أصل طباعه الشراسة فهو كالحيّة التي إن وطئها الواطئ فلم تلدغه لم يكن جديراً أن يغرّه ذلك فيعود لوطئها ورجل أصل طباعه السهولة فهو كالصندل البارد الذي إذا أُفرط في حكّه عاد حارّاً مؤذيا. ٢٠،٤

ثمّ إنّ دمنة لمّا استأنس بالأسد وخلا به قال إنّي رأيت الملك أقام منذ زمان في منزل واحد لا يبرح منه فلم ذلك. ٢١،٤

قال الأسد نعم وكره أن يعلم دمنة منه جبناً فقال لم يكن ذلك لبأس.

فبينما هو كذلك إذ خار شنزبه خواراً شديداً فهيّج ذلك الأسد على أن[1] يخبر دمنة بما في نفسه فقال هذا الصوت الذي تسمع لا أدري ما هو غير أنّه خليق أن يكون الجثّة على قدر الصوت والشدّة على قدر الجثّة فإن كان كذلك فليس مكاننا هذا بمكان.

قال دمنة هل راب الملك شيء غير هذا الصوت.

قال الأسد لم يكن غير ذلك.

قال دمنة فليس الملك بحقيق أن يبلغ هذا الصوت منه إلى أن يدع مكانه لذلك فإنّه يقال إنّ السِكْر الضعيف آفته الماء وإنّ السرّ آفته صلف المستودع والمودّة آفتها النميمة والقلب الجبان آفته أن يستنفره[2] الصوت الشديد والجلبة وفي بعض الأمثال دليل وبيان أنّه ليس كلّ الأصوات تُهاب. ٢٢،٤

قال الأسد فما ذلك المثل.

قال دمنة زعموا أنّ ثعلباً أتى على أجمة فيها طبل ملقًى إلى جانب الشجرة فهبّت الريح فجعلت قضبان الشجرة تقرع الطبل فيصوّت صوتاً شديداً فسمع الثعلب ذلك الصوت فتوجّه نحوه حتّى انتهى إلى الطبل فلمّا رآه ضخماً ورأى صوته شديداً طمع ٢٣،٤

---

[1] كذا ل٢؛ ساقطة من الأصل. [2] الأصل: تستتره.

When Dimnah finished his speech, the lion was even more pleased. Replying graciously, he said to his companions, "A ruler shouldn't deprive a deserving person of his due or lower the rank of a person of merit, and he should remedy any past negligence. He shouldn't be fooled by an aggrieved party's apparent acquiescence and acceptance. In this regard, people are of two kinds. Some are ill-tempered by nature, like a snake: if someone steps on it and it doesn't bite him, he shouldn't be foolish enough to step on it again. Others are easygoing by nature, like cool sandalwood; and yet, if rubbed too much, it becomes hot and noxious." 4.20

When Dimnah felt confident that he had secured the lion's favor, he said, when he was alone with him, "I've noticed that the king has stayed put in one place for some time and hasn't moved. Why is that?" 4.21

"That's true," said the lion. But not wanting Dimnah to learn of his cowardice, he added, "But there's nothing wrong."

Just as the lion was saying this, Shanzabah gave a loud bellow, startling the lion into revealing his state of mind to Dimnah: "That sound you hear, I don't know what it is, but the voice must be matched by the body, and the body be matched by its strength. If that's the case, we can't stay here."

"Has anything besides the voice troubled the king?" asked Dimnah.

"Nothing else," replied the lion.

And Dimnah said, "This sound shouldn't distress the king and make him abandon his home. As they say, water is the ruin of a weak dam, a leaky vessel the ruin of a secret, slander the ruin of friendship, and fright caused by a loud noise and commotion the ruin of a cowardly heart. There is a story that clearly demonstrates that not all noises are to be feared." 4.22

"What story is that?" asked the lion.

The Fox and the Drum

And Dimnah told the following tale: A fox, they say, once came to a forest where a drum lay by a tree. When the wind blew, the tree's branches would strike the drum, producing a loud noise. The fox heard the sound and headed toward it. When he approached the drum and saw how big it was and how 4.23

نفسه بكثرة الشحم فعالجه أشدّ العلاج حتّى شقّه فلمّا وجده مجوّفًا قال ما أدري لعلّ أفسل الأشياء أعظمها جثّة وأشدّها صوتًا.

وإنّما ضربت لك هذا المثل رجاء أن يكون هذا الصوت الذي تزعزعت منه لو قد انتهينا إليه لوجدناه أيسر ممّا في نفوسنا فإن شاء الملك فليبعثني نحو هذا الصوت وليقم مكانه حتّى أرجع إليه ببيان ما يريد أن يعلم من أمره. فوافق ذلك الأسد وانطلق دمنة قبل المكان الذي فيه شنزبة.

٢٤،٤ فلمّا فصل دمنة من عند الأسد فكّر الأسد في أمره فندم على إرسال دمنة حين أرسله وقال في نفسه ما أصبت في ائتماني دمنة على ما ائتمنته عليه فإنّ الرجل الذي يحضر باب السلطان إذا كان قد أطيلت جفوته من غير جرم أو كان مبغيًا عليه أو كان معروفًا بالحرص والشره أو كان قد أصابه ضرّ وضيق فلم يُنعش أو كان قد اجترم جرمًا فهو يخاف العقوبة أو كان شريرًا لا يحبّ الخير أو كان قد حيل بينه وبين ما كان في يده من سلطان أو مال أو كان ولّي عملاً ففُرّق عليه أو نُقص منه أو شورك بينه وبين أحد أو قد كان اجترم جرمًا مع نظرائه فعفي عنهم فعوقب أو عوقبوا جميعًا فبُلغ منه في العقوبة ما لم يُبلغ منهم أو كان قد أبلى بلاء في نظرائه ففُضّلوا عليه في الجزاء أو كان له عدوّ مشاجر ونظير ففُضّل عليه في المنزلة والجاه أو قد كان غير موثوق به في الدين أو قد كان يرجو في شيء ممّا يضرّ السلطان نفعًا أو يخاف في شيء ممّا ينفعه ضرًّا أو قد كان لعدوّ السلطان مؤاخيًا فليس السلطان بحقيق أن يعجّل[1] بالاسترسال إليه والثقة به والائتمان له. فإنّ دمنة داهٍ أريب وكان ببابي مطروحًا مجفوًّا فلعلّه احتمل بذلك ضغنًا ولعلّ ذلك سيحمله على أن يخونني ويبغيني سؤًا[2] ولعلّه يصادف صاحب الصوت أقوى منّي وأفضل سلطانًا فيرغب فيما عنده فيميل معه عليّ ويدلّه على عورتي.

٢٥،٤ فلم يزل الأسد يتفكّر في ذلك حتّى استخفّه من مكانه وجعل يمشي ويتقدّم وينظر إلى الطريق حتّى رُفع له[3] دمنة مقبلاً فلمّا رأى أنّه قد أقبل وحده وليس معه

---

١ كذا ر؛ الأصل: يحعل. ٢ ويبغيني سؤًا: كذا ر؛ الأصل: وسعى فى سواى. ٣ رُفع له: كذا ر؛ الأصل: رجع اله.

loud the sound, he went to work on it, splitting it open in anticipation of a hearty meal. But when he discovered it was hollow, he said, "For all I know, the lowliest things have the biggest bodies and the loudest voices."

"I've told you this story because I expect that if we get to the source of this sound you find so disturbing, we shall find it to be less than we imagine. If the king wishes, he can send me to investigate, and stay here until I report back with information about the sound." The lion agreed, and Dimnah set off to find Shanzabah.

After Dimnah's departure, the lion thought things over and regretted 4.24
having sent him to investigate. "I was wrong to trust Dimnah with such a mission. No ruler should hasten to befriend, trust, or confide in anyone who has stood waiting at the king's gate and long been treated coldly for no offence; or who has been harassed; or who is notorious for his greed and covetousness; or who has suffered misfortune or deprivation without amends; or who has committed a crime and fears punishment; or who is wicked and no lover of the good; or who has been barred from some authority or stripped of some property that he possessed; or who has held an office that was divided, reduced, or shared with someone else; or who has offended along with his peers, but who was punished when they were pardoned, or who were all punished, but he most severely of all; or who has proved his valor as well as his peers, but they received a greater reward; or who has a hostile, quarrelsome rival promoted over him; or who cannot be trusted in matters of religion; or who has sought to benefit personally from something harmful to his ruler; or who fears harm to himself from something beneficial to his ruler; or who has been friendly with the ruler's enemy. Dimnah is clever and shrewd. He has been left to languish at my gate and may bear me a grudge that could lead him to betray me and seek to harm me. If he finds that the owner of the voice is stronger and preferable to me as ruler, he may find his prospects brighter and go over to his side and point out my weaknesses."

The lion pondered these things. Eventually he became so upset that he 4.25
rose from his place and began pacing back and forth, watching the road.

أحد[١] اطمأنّت نفسه ورجع إلى مكانه إرادة أن لا يظنّ دمنة أنّ شيئاً استخفّه عن مكانه فلمّا انتهى دمنة إلى الأسد قال له ما صنعت وما رأيت.

قال دمنة رأيت ثوراً وهو صاحب هذا الصوت الذي سمعت.

قال الأسد فما قوّته وشدّته.

قال دمنة لا شوكة له ولم أر له عزّاً أستدلّ به على قوّته فدنوت منه وحاورته محاورة الأكفاء فلم يستطع[٢] لي شيئاً من القوّة والشدّة.

قال الأسد لا يغرّنّك ذلك منه ولا تضعنّ ذلك منه على الضعف فإنّ الريح الشديدة لا تحطّم الحشيش ولكنّها تحطّم غليظ الخشب والشجر وكذلك الصناديد إنّما يصمد بعضهم بعضاً.

قال دمنة لا يهابنّ الملك منه شيئاً ولا يكبر أمره في نفسه فأنا آتيه به إن شاء الملك حتّى يكون له عبداً سامعاً مطيعاً.

ففرح الأسد بقوله وقال فدونك إذاً.

٢٦،٤ ثمّ إنّ دمنة انطلق إلى الثور فقال له غير هائب ولا متتعتع إنّ الأسد أرسلني إليك لآتيه بك وأمرني إن أنت عجّلت الإقبال إليه طائعاً أن أؤمّنك[٣] على ما سلف من ذنبك في التأخّر عن الأسد وتركك لقاءه وإن أنت تلكّأت أن أسرع الرجوع إليه فأخبره بذلك.

قال شنزبة ومن هذا الأسد الذي أرسلك إليّ وأين مكانه.

قال دمنة هو ملك السباع وهو بموضع كذا ومعه سباع كثير.

فرعب شنزبة من ذكر الأسد والسباع وقال لدمنة إن أنت جعلت لي الأمان أقبلت معك.

فأعطاه دمنة ما وثق به ثمّ أقبلا جميعاً حتّى دخلا على الأسد فأحسن الأسد مساءلة[٤] شنزبة وقال له متى قدمت هذه البلاد وما أقدمكها. فقصّ شنزبة على الأسد قصّته.

١ أحد: كذا ش؛ ساقطة من الأصل. ٢ كذا ر؛ الأصل: يسطلع. ٣ كذا ر؛ الأصل: امنك. ٤ الأصل: مسائله.

At last he caught sight of Dimnah approaching. When he saw that Dimnah was alone, he relaxed and made his way back, not wanting Dimnah to think that anything had prompted him to move. When Dimnah arrived, the lion asked, "How did it go and what did you see?"

"I saw an ox. His is the voice you heard."

"How strong and powerful is he?"

"Not strong at all!" replied Dimnah. "I saw no haughtiness that would indicate strength. I went up to him and addressed him as an equal. He wasn't strong enough or powerful enough to do anything to me."

"Don't let that fool you!" said the lion. "Don't attribute it to weakness! A strong wind doesn't uproot grass; it uproots mighty trees. Great warriors only challenge one another."

"The king should have no fear of him," said Dimnah, "nor exaggerate his importance. If the king wishes, I will bring him here to become Your Majesty's willing and obedient servant."

"Do it!" said the lion, delighted by Dimnah's words.

So Dimnah returned to the ox and said, with no fear or hesitation, "The 4.26
lion has sent me to bring you to him. He has commanded me to say that if you come to him promptly and obediently, I am to promise you immunity for your past misconduct in lagging behind and failing to present yourself to him. If you delay, I am to hurry back and inform him accordingly."

"And who," asked Shanzabah, "is this lion who sent you to me? Where does he live?"

"He is the King of the Beasts," replied Dimnah. "He dwells nearby and has many fierce animals with him."

Frightened by the mention of the lion and the beasts, Shanzabah said, "I'll go with you if you guarantee my safety."

So Dimnah allayed his fears and they set out together. When they came before the lion, he asked Shanzabah politely, "When did you come to this land? What brought you here?" And Shanzabah told the lion his story.

فقال له الأسد الزمني فإنّي مكرمك ومحسن إليك. فدعا له شنزبة وأثنى عليه ٢٧،٤
وأقام معه ثمّ إنّ الأسد قرّب شنزبة وألطفه وأكرمه وآنس منه رأياً وعقلاً وائتمنه
على أسراره وشاوره في أموره وكان لا تزيده الأيّام إلّا عجباً به ورغبة فيه وتقريباً له
حتّى حسده أصحابه منزلته عنده.

فلمّا رأى دمنة أنّ الأسد قد اختصّ الثور وفضّله عليه وعلى غيره من خاصّة ٢٨،٤
أصحابه وجعله صاحب خلوته وسمره وحديثه ولهوه وأنيسه في مشورته حسد
الثور حسداً شديداً وبلغ منه أمره كلّ مبلغ فشكا ذلك إلى أخيه كليلة وقال ألا
تعجب لعجز رأيي وصنيعي بنفسي ونظري في منفعة الأسد وإغفالي نفع نفسي
وضرّها حيث جلبت إلى الأسد ثوراً غلبني[١] على منزلتي منه.

قال كليلة أصابك إذاً ما أصاب الناسك.

قال دمنة وكيف كان ذلك.

قال كليلة زعموا أنّ ناسكاً أصاب من بعض الملوك كسوة فاخرة فبصر به لصّ ٢٩،٤
فرغب في الثياب وطمع أن يذهب بها واحتال الحيل لسرقها فانطلق إلى الناسك
وقال أريد أن أصحبك فأتعلّم منك وآخذ عنك. فأذن له في صحبته فصحبه[٢] متشبّهاً
بالنسّاك رفقاً بالناسك وأحسن الخدمة حتّى إذا اطمأنّ إليه ووثق به ظفر من
الناسك بغفلة فاحتمل تلك الثياب فذهب بها.

فلمّا فقد الناسك الثياب والرجل علم أنّه صاحبها فطلب مكانه حتّى توجّه في ٣٠،٤
طلبه قبل مدينة من المدائن فمرّ في بعض طريقه على وعلين ينتطحان فطال انتطاحهما
حتّى سالت منهما الدماء وجاء ثعلب يلغ الدم فبينما هو مكبّ يلغ في الدم إذ التفت
عليه الوعلان بانتطاحهما وهو غافل فقتلاه.

ومضى الناسك حتّى انتهى إلى المدينة ممسياً ولم يجد مأوًى إلّا بيت امرأة ٣١،٤
صاحبة بغيّ فنزل عليها وكانت للمرأة جارية تؤاجرها وكانت الجارية قد عشقت
رجلاً فهي لا تريد غيره وأضرّ بتلك المرأة بما تأخذ من أجرة جاريتها فاضطغنت

---

١ كذا ر؛ الأصل: علبه. ٢ كذا ل٢؛ ساقطة من الأصل.

"Stay with me," said the lion. "I will be generous and treat you well." Shanzabah invoked blessings upon the lion, praised him, and remained with him. The lion brought him into his inner circle, treating him with kindness and honor. Because he saw that Shanzabah had good judgment and intelligence, he trusted him with his secrets and consulted him in his affairs. Time only increased his admiration and esteem, and he drew Shanzabah closer and closer—so much so that Shanzabah's companions became envious of his closeness to the lion. 4.27

Dimnah was consumed with envy when he saw that the lion favored the ox over him and the other courtiers; had allowed the ox private access to him, as well as to his evening conversations and entertainments; and relied on him for advice. He became so upset that he complained to his brother, Kalīlah, "Aren't you amazed at my foolishness, at what I've done to myself, how I only considered the lion's gain, overlooking my own gain and loss by bringing him an ox who has ousted me from my place?" 4.28

"You've suffered the same fate as the ascetic," responded Kalīlah.

"And what was that?"

The Ascetic and the Thievish Disciple

And Kalīlah told the following tale: An ascetic, so they say, once received a splendid garment from a king. A thief noticed the garment and wanted it. Hoping to make off with it, he devised a way to steal it. He went to the ascetic and said, "I want to become your disciple, learn from you, and acquire some of your erudition." The ascetic agreed. The thief became his disciple and looked the part. He was courteous and served his master well. Once the master was comfortable with him and trusted him, the thief caught the ascetic off guard and made off with the garment. 4.29

The Fox and the Wild Goats

With both man and garment missing, the ascetic realized that the disciple must be the culprit. He searched his usual haunts, and then headed for the city in pursuit. On the way, he came across two wild goats that kept butting each other until they drew blood. A fox came to lap up the blood, and while he was busy lapping, the goats turned on him and butted him to death. 4.30

The Woman Who Kept Prostitutes

The ascetic continued on his way and arrived at the city. It was late in the evening, and the only lodging he could find was the house of a woman who kept prostitutes, so he stayed there. The woman had a maidservant, whom she used to hire out, but the girl had become so enamored of one man that 4.31

بذلك على الرجل صديق الجارية الذي عشقته جاريتها فاحتالت لقتله وأتاها صديق الجارية ليلة صادفها الناسك فسقته من الخمر صرفًا حتّى غلبت الرجل عيناه فنام ونامت الجارية معه فلمّا استُثقلا نوماً عمدت المرأة إلى سمّ قد كانت هيّأته فجعلته في قصبة لتنفخه في دبر الرجل فوضعت القصبة في دبره وفاها على القصبة فبدرتها ريح خرجت من الرجل فطار ذلك السمّ في حلق المرأة فوقعت ميّتة وذلك بعين الناسك.

٣٢،٤ ثمّ أصبح الناسك غادياً في طلب منزل غير ذلك فأضافه[١] رجل إسكاف وقال لامرأته انظري هذا الناسك فأكرميه وأحسني القيام عليه فإنّه قد دعاني بعض أصحاب الشراب لمنادمته. فانطلق الإسكاف وكانت امرأته قد علقت رجلاً وكان الرسول فيما بينهما امرأة حجّام فأرسلت امرأة الإسكاف إلى امرأة الحجّام وأمرتها أن تأتي خليلها فتأمره يأتيها فإنّ زوجها عند أصحاب له في الشراب وإنّه لا يرجع إلّا سكران ممسياً. فأقبل خليلها عند العشاء حتّى قعد على الباب ينتظر امرأة الإسكاف.

٣٣،٤ وانصرف الإسكاف إلى بيته حين أمسى وهو نشوان فلمّا رأى خليل امرأته هنالك ارتاب فغضب ودخل البيت وأخذ امرأته وأوجعها ضرباً ثمّ أوثقها إلى سارية في البيت فلمّا هدأت العيون جاءتها امرأة الحجّام فقالت قد طال قعود الرجل فماذا ترين.

قالت أما ترين ما بي فإن شئت أحسنت فيما بيني وبينك فحللتني[٢] وأربطتك مكاني ساعة ثمّ أنطلق إلى خليلي ثمّ أسرع الرجعة إليك.

قالت امرأة الحجّام فإنّي فاعلة ذلك. فحلّتها وصارت مكانها فاستيقظ الإسكاف قبل أن ترجع امرأته فناداها ودعاها باسمها فلم تجبه امرأة الحجّام مخافة أن يعرف صوتها فدعاها وسبّها مراراً فلم تجبه فازداد الإسكاف غيظاً حتّى قام إليها بسكّين فجدع أنفها ثمّ قال خذي هذا والحقي خليلك.

---

١ كذا ل٢؛ الأصل: فاصابه. ٢ الأصل: فحليتى.

she didn't want to go with anyone else. Faced with the loss of the girl's earnings, the woman developed a grudge against the lover and devised a plan to kill him, on the very night the ascetic became a guest. She plied the lover with undiluted wine until he passed out and fell asleep with the girl beside him. When both were sound asleep, she took some poison she had prepared and put it into a hollow reed in order to blow it into the man's posterior. She put one end of the reed into his posterior and the other end into her mouth, but before she could do anything, a puff of wind from the man's posterior drove the poison back into her throat and she fell down dead. The ascetic saw everything.

The ascetic set out early the next morning to find somewhere else to lodge. 4.32

The Shoemaker's Wife and the Barber's Wife

He was taken in by a shoemaker, who told his wife, "Watch over this ascetic; be generous to him and take good care of him. One of my close friends has invited me to a party." The shoemaker then departed. Now, the shoemaker's wife had a lover. Their go-between was a barber's wife.[20] The shoemaker's wife sent the barber's wife a message, asking her to go to the lover and tell him to come, as the shoemaker was out drinking with his friends and wouldn't be back until late, and would be drunk to boot. The lover arrived at dusk and sat by the gate waiting for the shoemaker's wife.

Late that evening, the shoemaker returned home drunk. He became sus- 4.33
picious and flew into a rage when he saw his wife's lover. He went into the house, grabbed his wife, beat her, and tied her to a post in the bedroom. When everyone was fast asleep, the barber's wife came over to her and said, "Your lover has been sitting by the door a long time! What do you plan to do?"

"Don't you see the state I'm in?" she replied. "If you'd be so kind as to untie me, I'll tie you up in my place for an hour, go to my lover, and come back as quickly as I can."

The barber's wife agreed, and she untied the shoemaker's wife and took her place. But the shoemaker awoke before his wife returned. He called out her name but the barber's wife, afraid he might recognize her voice, didn't reply. He called her and upbraided her repeatedly; still she made no reply. He got angrier and angrier, until he went at her with a knife and cut off her nose, saying, "Take this and go join your lover!"

فلمّا جاءت امرأة الإسكاف ورأت صاحبتها مجدوعة الأنف وزوجها نائم حلّتها وأوثقت نفسها مكانها وأخذت الأخرى امرأة الحجّام أنفها وانقلبت إلى بيتها وكان كلّ ذلك بعين الناسك وسمعه.

٣٤،٤ ثمّ إنّ امرأة الإسكاف رفعت صوتها تدعو ربّها وتتضرّع[١] إليه وتبكي وتبتهل وتدعو إلى زوجها وتقول اللّهمّ إن كان زوجي ظلمني فأعد إليّ أنفي صحيحًا. ثمّ نادت الإسكاف أيّها الظالم الفاجر قم فانظر إلى عملك وتغيير ربّك عليك ورحمته إيّاي قد أعاد أنفي صحيحًا. قال الإسكاف ما هذا الكلام يا ساحرة. ثمّ قام وأوقد نارًا فلمّا نظر إلى أنفها صحيحًا تاب من الذنب إلى ربّه واعتذر إليها وسألها أن ترضى عليه.

٣٥،٤ فلمّا أتت امرأة الحجّام إلى بيتها قلبت الحيل وقالت ما عذري عند زوجي وعند غيره من الناس في جدع أنفي. فلمّا كان السحر استيقظ الحجّام وقال لامرأته ائتيني بمتاعي فإنّي أريد أن أدلج إلى بعض الأشراف. فلم تأته المرأة من متاعه بشيء[٢] إلّا بموسى فقال له هلمّ متاعي كلّه. فعادت المرأة بتلك الموسى فغضب الحجّام فرماها بالموسى[٣] فرمت المرأة بنفسها إلى الأرض وولولت[٤] وقالت أنفي أنفي. فلم تزل تصيح وتنادي حتّى جاءها أقرباؤها فأخذوا زوجها فانطلقوا به إلى القاضي. فقال القاضي للحجّام ما حملك على جدع أنف امرأتك. فلم يجد حجّة يحتجّ بها فأمر القاضي بالحجّام أن يعاقب.

فلمّا قُدّم للعقوبة وافاه الناسك فتقدّم إلى القاضي فقال لا يشتبهنّ عليك إنّ اللصّ ليس هو سرقني وإنّ الثعلب ليس الوعلان قتلاه وإنّ المرأة ليس السمّ قتلها وإنّ امرأة الحجّام ليس زوجها جدع أنفها بل نحن جميعًا فعلنا ذلك بأنفسنا. فسأل القاضي الناسك عن تفسير ذلك فأخبره الخبر.

٣٦،٤ قال دمنة قد سمعت هذا المثل وهو شبيه بأمري لعمري ما ضرّ بي سوى نفسي ولكن ما الحيلة.

١ الأصل: وتضرع. ٢ الأصل: شيئًا. ٣ فغضب . . . بالموسى: كذا ر؛ ساقطة من الأصل. ٤ كذا ش، ع؛ الأصل: وولت.

When the shoemaker's wife came back and found her friend mutilated and her husband asleep, she released her friend and tied herself up in her place. The barber's wife picked up her nose and returned home. The ascetic saw and heard everything.

The shoemaker's wife raised her voice to God in prayer, beseeching 4.34
Him, weeping, and calling to her husband: "If my husband has treated me unjustly, give me back my nose, whole as it was!" Then she called out to her husband: "Get up, you evildoer! See how God has undone your work and has had mercy on me. He has given me back my nose, just as it was." The shoemaker exclaimed, "What is all this talk, you witch?" He got up and lit a lamp, and when he looked at his wife and saw that her nose was whole, he repented to God and apologized to his wife, asking her to forgive him.

Back home, the barber's wife turned over every conceivable scheme in 4.35
her mind. "What explanation can I present to my husband and to people for the loss of my nose?" Her husband awoke at dawn and called out to her: "Bring me my things! I want to pay a visit to an important customer." But the only thing she brought him was his razor. "My whole kit!" he repeated, but again she brought just the razor. The barber flew into a rage and hurled the razor at her, whereupon she threw herself to the ground, wailing, "My nose, my nose!" And she kept on shouting and crying out until her kinsmen came and hauled her husband off to the judge, who asked the barber, "What led you to cut off your wife's nose?" He had no argument to offer in his defense, so the judge ordered that he be punished.

Just as the barber was being led to his punishment, the ascetic arrived, and approached the judge. "There isn't any doubt about it!" the ascetic said. "It wasn't the thief who robbed me, it wasn't the wild goats who killed the fox, it wasn't the poison that killed the woman, and it wasn't the barber who cut off his wife's nose—we all did it to ourselves!" The judge asked the ascetic to explain, which he did.

Dimnah said, "I understand the story, and it does resemble my situation. 4.36
Indeed, no one has harmed me but myself. But what's to be done now?"

قال كليلة أخبرني أنت عن رأيك في ذلك.

قال دمنة إنّي لست ألتمس اليوم أن تزداد منزلتي فوق ما كنت ولكن ألتمس أن أعود إلى منزلتي التي كنت عليها فإنّ خلالاً ثلاثًا العاقل حقيق بالنظر فيها والاحتيال لها بجهده منها النظر فيما مضى من الضرّ والنفع وأن يحترس من الضرّ الذي أصابه فيما سلف لئلاّ يعود إليه ويلتمس النفع الذي مضى ويحتال لمعاودته. ومنها النظر فيما هو مقيم فيه من المنافع والمضارّ والاستباق لما ينفع والهرب ممّا يضرّ. ومنها النظر في مستقبل ما يرجو من مقبل النفع وما يتخوّف من مقبل الضرّ فيستقيم[1] ما يرجو ويتوقّى ما يخاف بجهده. وإنّي لمّا[2] نظرت في الأمر الذي أرجو أن تعود به منزلتي التي غُلبت عليها لم أجد لذلك دواء إلّا الاحتيال لأكل العشب حتّى يفارق الثور الحياة فإنّه إن فارق الأسد عادت إليّ منزلتي ولعلّ ذلك يكون خيرًا للأسد فإنّ إفراط الأسد للثور خليق أن يشينه ويطعن عليه عامّة قرابته.

قال كليلة ما أرى على الأسد من رأيه في الثور ومكانه ومنزلته عنده شينًا ولا ضرًّا. ٣٧،٤

قال دمنة بلى إنّما يؤتى السلطان من قبل ستّة أشياء الحرمان والفتنة والهوى والفظاظة والزمان والخرق فأمّا الحرمان فإنّه يُحرم الأعوان والنصحاء والساسة من أهل الرأي والنجدة والأمانة ويفقد بعض من[3] هو كذلك وأمّا الفتنة فهو تحارب الناس الناس ووقوع[4] الحرب بينهم وأمّا الهوى فالإغرام بالنساء وبالحديث وبالشراب وبالصيد وما أشبه ذلك وأمّا الفظاظة فإفراط الشدّة حتّى يجمح اللسان بالشتم واليد بالبطش في غير موضعهما وأمّا الزمان فهو ما يصيب الناس من السنين والموت والغرق ونقص الثمرات وأشباه ذلك وأمّا الخرق فإعمال الشدّة في موضع اللين واللين في موضع الشدّة وإنّ الأسد قد أُغرم بالثور إغرامًا شديدًا فهو الذي ذكرت أنّه خليق أن يضرّه ويشينه.

١ الأصل: فيستيم. ٢ كذا ر؛ ساقطة من الأصل. ٣ كذا ر؛ الأصل: ما. ٤ الأصل: ووقع.

"Tell me what *you* think."

"For the time being, I'm not seeking a higher place than before; I only want to regain what I had. There are three things a prudent man must take into account and work out how to deal with. He must consider past losses and gains, guarding against the recurrence of past losses and seeking ways to repeat past gains. Next, he must consider present gains and losses, striving with all his might for what results in profits and avoiding anything that results in losses. Finally, he must consider future gains he hopes for and future losses he fears, in order to obtain what he hopes for and guard against what he fears. When I consider how to recover the position that was wrested from me, the only remedy I can find is to scheme against this grass eater until the ox breathes no more. Once he has left the lion, not only do I regain my position, but it may also be better for the lion, as his excessive devotion to the ox is likely to disgrace him and spark resentment in most of his courtiers."

"But," said Kalīlah, "I see no disgrace or harm in how the lion views the ox 4.37
or in the favored position he enjoys."

"Not so!" replied Dimnah. "Six things can destroy a ruler: privation, sedition, self-indulgence, brutality, the adversity of fate, and folly. Privation is the loss or dismissal of aides, advisers, and administrators who possess good judgment, courage, and trustworthiness. Sedition is civil war and the outbreak of fighting among the people. Self-indulgence is infatuation with women, conversation, drinking, hunting, or anything of that sort. Brutality is excessive harshness, the tongue quick to revile, the hand quick to strike at the wrong time. The adversity of fate includes disasters such as famine, plague, flooding, poor harvests, and the like. Folly is resorting to harshness when leniency is required, and leniency when harshness is required. The lion has become too fond of the ox, and that, as I said, is likely to harm and disgrace him."

٤،٣٨ قال كليلة وكيف تطيق الثور وهو أشدّ منك بأساً[١] وأكرم على الأسد وأكثر أصدقاء وأعواناً.

قال دمنة لا تنظر إلى صغري فإنّ الأمور ليست تجري على القوّة والضعف فكم من صغير ضعيف قد بلغ بدهائه ورأيه وحيله ما يعجز عنه كثير من الأقوياء والأشدّاء ألم يبلغك أنّ غراباً احتال على الأسود حتّى قتله.

قال كليلة وكيف كان ذلك.

٤،٣٩ قال دمنة زعموا أنّ غراباً كان له وكر في شجرة في جبل وكان قربه جحر فيه أسود فكان إذا فرّخ الغراب ذهب الأسود إلى وكره فأخذ فراخه فأكلها فلمّا فعل ذلك مرّات وبلغ من الغراب كلّ مبلغ شكا ذلك إلى صديق له من بنات آوى فقال أردت أن أستأمرك في شيء هممت به إن أنت واطأتني عليه.

قال وما ذلك.

قال أريد أن آتي الأسود وهو نائم فأنقر عينيه لعلّي أفقأهما.

قال ابن آوى بئست[٢] الحيلة هذه والتمس حيلة تظفر بها من الأسود في غير الهلاك لنفسك بغير مخاطرة وإيّاك أن يكون مثلك مثل المكّاء الذي أراد قتل السرطان فقتل نفسه.

قال الغراب وكيف كان ذلك.

٤،٤٠ قال ابن آوى كان المكّاء معشعشاً في أجمة مخصبة كثيرة السمك فعاش هنالك ما عاش ثمّ هرم[٣] فلم يستطع صيداً فأصابه جهد وجوع فالتمس الحيل فقعد متحزّناً ذات يوم فرآه السرطان من بعيد فلمّا رأى حاله وعرف الحزن فيه دنا منه وقال إنّي أراك قد علتك كآبة.

قال المكّاء وكيف لا تعلوني كآبة وإنّما كانت[٤] معيشتي إلى اليوم أنّي كنت أصيد ممّا هاهنا في اليوم سمكة أو سمكتين فكنت أعيش بذلك وكان ذلك لا ينقص السمك شيئاً وإنّي رأيت اليوم صيّادين أتيا هذا المكان فقال أحدهما لصاحبه أرى هاهنا

[١] كذا ل٢؛ الأصل: رأياً. [٢] كذا ر؛ الأصل: ليست. [٣] كذا ل٢؛ الأصل: هرب. [٤] كذا ل٢؛ الأصل: كان.

“But how can you overcome the ox when he’s stronger than you, is shown more honor by the lion, and can count on more friends and supporters?” 4.38

“Pay no attention to my size. Things aren’t always decided by strength and weakness. Many a small, weak creature has accomplished by cleverness, intelligence, and cunning what many strong, powerful creatures were unable to achieve. Haven’t you heard how a crow outwitted the cobra and killed him?”

“How did that come about?”

The Crow Who Outwitted a Cobra

And Dimnah told the following tale: A crow, so they say, had a nest in a tree on a mountain, not far from a cobra’s den.[21] Whenever the crow had chicks, the cobra went to the nest and ate them. When the cobra had done this many times, the distressed crow complained to a friend of his, a jackal: “I’ve decided to ask you about something I intend to do, to see whether you agree with me about it.” 4.39

“What is it?” asked the jackal.

“I intend to go to the cobra while he’s asleep and peck out his eyes.”

“That’s not a good plan,” replied the jackal. “Find a way to defeat the snake without risking your life. Beware lest you suffer the fate of the heron[22] who wanted to kill the crab but ended up killing himself.”

“How did that come about?” asked the crow.

The Heron Who Would Kill a Crab but Killed Himself

And the jackal told the following tale: A heron built his nest beside a pond teeming with fish. He lived there for a time, but then grew old and could no longer fish. Weary and hungry, he looked for ways to cope with the situation. One day he sat himself down and made a show of sadness. From afar, a crab saw the state he was in and how sad he was, so he approached and said, “I see that you’re very dejected.” 4.40

“How could it be otherwise?” replied the heron. “Up to now, I’ve sustained myself by catching one or two fish every day. It was enough for me to live on, and it didn’t decrease the fish population. But today I saw two fishermen come by, and one said to the other, ‘I think there are lots of

سمكاً كثيراً أفلا نصيدهنّ. فقال صاحبه إنّي قد عرفت فيما أمامنا مكاناً فيه سمك والرأي أن نبدأ بما ثمّ فإذا فرغنا منه انصرفنا إلى ما هاهنا. وقد علمت أنّهما لو قد فرغا ممّا توجّها إليه انصرفا إلينا فلم يدعا في هذه الأجمة سمكة إلّا صاداها فإذا كان ذلك فهو يضرّني.[١]

٤١،٤ فانطلق السرطان إلى جماعة السمك فأخبرهنّ الخبر فأقبلن إلى المكّاء فاستشرنه وقلن إنّا أتيناك لتشير علينا فإنّ ذا العقل لا يدع استشارة عدوّه ذي الرأي في الأمر الذي يشركه في ضرّه ونفعه وأنت ذو الرأي ولك في بقائنا صلاح فأشر علينا.

فقال أمّا مكابرة[٢] الصيّاد وقتاله فلا نطيقه ولا أعلم حيلة إلّا أنّي قد علمت بمكان غدير كثير الماء طيّب وفيه قصب وخصب فإن استطعتنّ التحوّل[٣] إلى ذلك المكان ففيه صلاحكنّ وخصبكنّ.

قلن فمن يمنّ علينا بهذا غيرك.

قال إنّي أفعل.

٤٢،٤ ثمّ إنّ المكّاء كان يحمل في كلّ يوم سمكتين فينطلق بهما إلى بعض التلال فيأكلهما ولا يشعر بذلك بقيّتهنّ.

حتّى إذا كان ذات يوم جاءه السرطان فقال إنّي قد أشفقت من مكاني هذا فاذهب بي إلى ذلك الماء.

فحمل السرطان وجاء مشرفاً جاعلاً له حصّة يومه حتّى إذا دنا من التلّ الذي كان يأكل عليه السمك نظر السرطان فرأى عظام السمك مجموعة هنالك فعرف أنّ المكّاء صاحبها وأنّه يريد به مثلها فقال في نفسه إذا لقي الملاقي عدوّه في المواطن التي يعلم أنّه هالك فيها إن قاتل أو لم يقاتل فهو حقيق أن يقاتل كرماً وحفاظاً. فأهوى بكلبتيه إلى عنق المكّاء فعصره عصرة وقع منها إلى الأرض ووقع السرطان معه فمات المكّاء ورجع السرطان إلى السمك فأخبرهنّ.

---

١ ل٢: موتي. ٢ كذا ر؛ الأصل: مكادة. ٣ كذا ش؛ ساقطة من الأصل.

fish here. Why don't we catch them?' His companion said, 'I know a place with fish farther on. I think we should begin there; when we finish there, we can come back here.' I know that when they finish there, they'll come back and catch every single fish in this pond; if this happens, it will be the end of me."

The crab went to the community of fishes and informed them. They in 4.41
turn went to the heron to seek his advice. "We've come for your advice," they said. "An intelligent person doesn't fail to ask his enemy for advice, if the latter has good judgment and both stand to lose or gain in the affair. Your judgment is good, and our survival is to your advantage, so give us your advice."

"I don't think we can take on the fishermen and fight them," said the heron. "The only solution I can think of is a nice pond I've discovered with plenty of water, reeds, and vegetation. If you move there, you'll thrive and prosper."

"Who but you can do us that favor?" they asked.

"I will," he said.

So each day the heron would pick up two fish and carry them off to a hill, 4.42
where he ate them. The rest of the fish had no idea what was happening.

Then one day the crab came to the heron and said, "I, too, am worried about staying here. Take me to that pond."

The heron picked up the crab, planning to make him his meal for the day; but when he came to the hill where he would eat the fish, the crab looked down and saw piles of fish bones. Realizing that the heron was the offender and that he intended for him the same fate as the fish, he said to himself, "When you meet your enemy in a place where you know you'll die whether you fight or not, fight to save your honor." So he gripped the heron's neck with his pincers and squeezed so hard that the heron fell to the ground, taking the crab down with him. The heron died, but not the crab, who went back to the fish and told them what had happened.

فقال ابن آوى وإنّما ضربت لك هذا المثل لتعلم أنّ بعض[1] الحيل مهلكة للمحتال ولكنّي أدلّك على أمر إن قدرت عليه كان فيه هلاك الأسود. ٤٣،٤

قال وما ذلك.

قال تنطلق محلّقاً فتنظر لعلّك تظفر بحلي من حليّ النساء نفيس عندهنّ فتختطفها ثمّ تطير قريباً فلا تبرح واقعاً وطائراً حيث لا تفوت العيون ويطلبك الناس حتّى تنتهي بالحلي إلى جحر الأسود فترمي بها عنده فإذا انتهى الناس إلى الحلي أخذوا حليهم وأراحوك من الأسود.

فانطلق الغراب محلّقاً يبتغي حلياً فوجد امرأة على ظهر بيت قد وضعت ثيابها وحليها وهي تغتسل فاختطف من حليها عقداً فلم يزل يطير به تارة ويقع أخرى حيث يُنظر إليه حتّى انتهى بالعقد إلى جحر الأسود والقوم ينظرون فرمى به عنده فلمّا أتوه وجدوا الأسود عنده فقتلوه وأخذوا عقدهم. ٤٤،٤

قال دمنة وإنّما ضربت لك هذا المثل لتعلم أنّ الحيلة تجزي ما لا تجزي القوّة. ٤٥،٤

قال كليلة إنّ الثور لو لم يجمع[2] مع شدّته رأياً كان ذلك ولكنّه مع شدّته ذو رأي وعقل فماذا تستطيع له.

قال دمنة إنّ الثور كما ذكرت في قوّته وشدّته ورأيه ولكنّه بي مغترّ وإليّ آمن وأنا خليق أن أصرعه كما صرع مرّة أرنب أسداً.

قال كليلة وكيف كان ذلك.

قال دمنة زعموا أنّ أسداً كان في أرض كثيرة الماء والخصب والعشب وكان ما بتلك الأرض من الوحوش في سعة من الماء والمرعى إلّا أنّ ذلك لم يكن ينفعها من خوف الأسد فائتمرت تلك الوحوش واجتمعت إلى الأسد وقالت إنّك لا تصيب منّا الدابّة في اليوم إلّا بعد نصب وتعب وقد رأينا رأياً لنا ولك فيه راحة فإن أنت أمّنتنا ولم تخفنا فلك علينا دابّة في كلّ يوم نرسل بها إليك عند غدائك. ٤٦،٤

[1] كذا ل٢؛ ساقطة في الأصل. [2] كذا ر؛ الأصل: محتمع.

The jackal said, "I've told you this tale to teach you that some schemes are fatal to the schemer. But I'll show you how you can bring about the cobra's death." 4.43

"How?" he asked.

"Fly off and see if you can get hold of a valuable piece of women's jewelry. Snatch it and fly away in short bursts. Fly, then land, then take off again, so the people chasing you can keep you in their sights. When you reach the cobra's den, drop the jewelry there. When the people get there, they'll retrieve the jewelry and rid you of the cobra."

So the crow flew off and circled the sky looking for jewelry. He found a woman on a rooftop who had taken off her clothes and jewelry to bathe. He snatched a necklace and flew away, alighting from time to time so that he could be seen. When he reached the cobra's den, he dropped the necklace in full view of the people following him. They went to fetch the necklace and discovered the cobra there. They killed it and took their necklace. 4.44

Dimnah said to Kalīlah, "I've told you this tale to demonstrate that ingenuity can accomplish what force cannot." 4.45

"That would be so," replied Kalīlah, "if the ox didn't possess good judgment as well as strength, but he has good judgment and intelligence in addition to strength. How will you deal with that?"

"The ox, as you say, may be strong, powerful, and intelligent, but he's not on his guard against me and has no fear of me, so I'm likely to vanquish him, just as a rabbit once vanquished a lion."

"And how did he vanquish him?"

The Rabbit Who Vanquished a Lion

And Dimnah told the following tale: Once, they say, there lived a lion in a well-watered, fertile, grassy land. The animals there were surrounded by streams and pastures, but couldn't enjoy these blessings because of their fear of the lion. So they conferred among themselves, then went to the lion and said, "Every day you wear yourself out trying to catch one of us. We have an idea that will make things easier for you and for us. If you guarantee our safety and stop terrifying us, we promise to provide an animal every day and send it to you for your lunch." 4.46

فرضي الأسد بذلك وصالحهم عليه وأقمن على ذلك زمانًا وإنّ السباع كنّ يقترعن في كلّ يوم فمن أصابته القرعة منهنّ أرسلن به إلى الأسد مع بعض السباع يبلّغه ذلك حتّى يأكله.

٤،٤٧ ثمّ إنّ أرنبًا أصابتها[١] القرعة فقالت لهنّ إن أنتنّ رفقتنّ بي فلا يضرّكنّ لعلّي أريحكنّ من الأسد.

فقلن لها وما الذي تكلّفيننا من الرفق.

قالت هينًا من الأمر تأمرن الذي ينطلق بي إلى الأسد ثمّ لا يتبعني لعلّي أبطئ على الأسد بعض الإبطاء حتّى يتأخّر غداؤه ثمّ يتأخّر منّي وأتقدّم وحدي.

٤،٤٨ فقلن لك ذلك فانطلقت الأرنب متباطئة حتّى جاوزت الساعة التي كان الأسد يأكل فيها ثمّ أقبلت تدبّ وحدها رويدًا وقد جاع الأسد حين أبطأ غداؤه فغضب وقام عن مربضه يتمشّى وينظر فلمّا رأى الأرنب قال من أين جئت وأين الوحوش.

قالت إنّي رسول الوحوش بعثني إليك بأرنب معي فلمّا أن كنت ممّا هاهنا قريبًا لقيني أسد فانتزعها منّي فقال أنا أولى بهذه الأرض ووحشها.[٢] فقلت له إنّ هذا غداء الملك أرسلت به الوحوش إليه فلا تغضبنّه. فسبّك وشتمك وأقبلت مسرعة إليك لأوذنك بذلك.

٤،٤٩ فغضب الأسد فقال انطلقي معي فأريني هذا الأسد. فانطلقت الأرنب بالأسد إلى جبّ ذي ماء صافٍ غمر فقالت هذا مكان الأسد وأنا أفرق منه إلّا أن تحملني في حضنك حتّى أريكه. فاحتضنها الأسد فقالت له الأرنب أشرف على الجبّ وانظر الأسد. فأشرف فأبصر خياله وخيال الأرنب في حضنه في الماء فلمّا نظر خياله وخيال الأرنب وثب في الجبّ ليقاتله فغرق في الجبّ وفلتت الأرنب.

---

١ كذا ل٢؛ الأصل: أصابه. ٢ ووحشها: الأصل: ووحشها قالت.

The lion agreed. He made peace with them on these terms, and they honored their end of the bargain for a time. They drew lots every day and sent the unfortunate animal to the lion to be eaten, accompanied by an escort.

One day, a rabbit drew the short straw and she said to the others, "If 4.47
you do me a favor—it won't harm you at all—I may be able to rid you of the lion."

"What sort of favor?" they asked.

"Very simple," she said. "Command my escort not to hurry me along; I'll take my time, and the lion's lunch will arrive late. Also, tell my escort to lag behind, so I arrive alone."

"Agreed," they said, and the rabbit set off, taking her time. When it was 4.48
past the lion's lunchtime, she approached at her leisure. The lion, hungry and angry because his lunch was late, had risen to his feet and was pacing back and forth. When he saw the rabbit, he said, "Where have you come from? And where are the animals?"[23]

"I am the animals' messenger," she replied. "They dispatched me with a rabbit, but when I was close, a lion turned up and snatched her away, saying, 'I have a better claim to this land and its animals!' 'But this is the king's lunch!' I said. 'The animals have sent it to him. Don't make him angry!' But he cursed and reviled you. I've come as quickly as I could to bring you this information."

The lion grew angry. "Come with me," he said, "and show me this lion." 4.49
So she took him to a deep well filled with clear water. "This," she said, "is the lion's lair. I'm afraid of him, but if you hold me in your arms I'll show him to you." So he held her in his arms. "Look down into the well," she said, "and you'll see the lion." He looked down and caught sight of his own reflection and the reflection of the rabbit in his arms. When he saw his and the rabbit's reflection, he leapt into the well and drowned, and the rabbit escaped.

قال كليلة إن أنت قدرت على هلاك الثور في شيء ليس على الأسد منه مضرّة فشأنك فإنّ[1] مكان الثور قد أضرّ بي وبك وبغيرنا من الجند وإن أنت لم تستطع ذلك إلّا بما ينقص الأسد فلا تشترينّ ذلك بذلك[2] فإنّه غدر منّي ومنك ولؤم. ٥٠،٤

ثمّ إنّ دمنة ترك الدخول على الأسد أيّاماً ثمّ أتاه على حال خلوة منه فأراه التحرّز. ٥١،٤

فقال له الأسد ما حبسك منذ زمان لم أرك أخير.

قال دمنة ليكن[3] خير.

قال الأسد هل حدث شيء.

قال دمنة نعم حدث ما لم يكن الملك يريده ولا أنا.

قال الأسد وما ذلك.

قال دمنة إنّه ما كان من الكلام يكرهه سامعه ثمّ يتشجّع عليه قائله فهو خرق من قائله إلّا أن يثق بعقل المقول له ذلك فإنّه إذا كان المقول له عاقلاً احتمل ذلك واستمعه لأنّه ربّما عطب فيما بيّن ذلك غير أنّ القائل[4] يحتمل ما يتخوّف من عاقبته بما فيه من أداء ما لزمه من حقّ ذي الحقّ وأنت أيّها الملك ذو فضيلة في الرأي والأناة فأنا[5] متشجّع لثقتي بفضلك على أن أخبرك بما انتهى إليه علمي وإن ظننت أنّك له كاره واثق بأنّك تعرف نصحي لك وإيثاري إيّاك على نفسي وإنّه ليعرض لي أنّك غير مصدّق بما أنا مخبرك به ولكنّي إذا تذكّرت أنّ أنفسنا معاشر السباع معلّقة بنفسك لم أجد بدّاً من قضاء الحقّ الذي يلزمني لك أن أبلغه إليك وإن أنت لم تسألني أو خفت أن لا تقبل منّي فإنّه من كتم السلطان نصيحته والأطبّاء مرضه والإخوان رأيه فقد خان نفسه. ٥٢،٤

قال الأسد وما ذاك. ٥٣،٤

قال دمنة حدّثني المصدّق المؤتمن عندي أنّ شنزبة خلا برؤوس جندك وقال لهم قد عجمت الأسد وبلوت رأيه وقوّته ومكيدته فاستبان لي في ذلك كلّه ضعف

١ كذا ل٢؛ الأصل: ان. ٢ فلا . . . بذلك: كذا ل٢؛ الأصل: فلا تشتر بذلك. ٣ الأصل: لكن. ٤ الأصل: العاقل.
٥ كذا ر؛ ساقطة من الأصل.

Kalīlah said, "If you can destroy the ox without harming the lion, go ahead and do it; his position has harmed me and you, as well as members of the army. But if you can't do it without harming the lion, don't do one at the expense of the other: that would be both betrayal and villainy." 4.50

Dimnah avoided the lion for a few days; then, with a show of cautious reserve, he turned up when the lion was alone. 4.51

"What's kept you away?" asked the lion. "I haven't seen you for a long time. Is everything all right?"

"I wish!"

"Has something happened?"

"Yes. Something neither of us wanted, Your Majesty."

"What is it?"

Dimnah replied, "A speaker who dares to deliver an unwelcome message is acting foolishly unless he trusts the intelligence of the person he is addressing. The person addressed, if intelligent, will tolerate the message and listen to it because it might alert him to a potential disaster. The speaker will bear with any frightful consequences for the sake of fulfilling a duty incumbent upon him. Trusting in Your Majesty's excellent judgment and patience, I dare to inform you of something that has come to my knowledge. Unwelcome as it may be, I am confident that you know my devotion to you and how I put your welfare ahead of mine. You might not believe what I'm about to tell you; nonetheless, when I call to mind how our lives as animals are bound up with your life, I can do no less than fulfill my duty to inform you, even though you haven't asked it of me and even though I fear you might not be pleased. To withhold advice from your ruler, conceal illness from your physicians, or withhold an opinion from your brethren is to betray yourself." 4.52

"What is it?" asked the lion. 4.53

"A reliable source has informed me that Shanzabah met secretly with your chief officers and said to them, 'I've gotten to know the lion and put his judgment, strength, and shrewdness to the test. As a result, it's clear to me that he is weak and lacks judgment, and that he and I are bound to have a falling

وعجز رأي وهو كائن لي وله شأن. فإنّي لمّا بلغني هذا عرفت أنّ شنزبة هذا خؤون غدّار وعرفت أنّك تكرم شنزبة الكرامة كلّها وجعلته نظير نفسك حتّى دعاه إلى ما ظهر منه من الخيانة وسوء الرأي وأنّ نفسه تطلّعت إلى أنّك لو زلت عن مكانك صار له ملكك وهو لا يدع جهداً في الاحتيال لك وله عقل ورأي وإخوان وأعوان وكان يقال إذا عرف الملك[1] من الرجل أنّه قد تساوى به في الرأي والمنزلة والهيئة والمال والتبع فليصرعه[2] فإنّه إن لم يفعل ذلك كان هو المصروع.

وأنت أيها الملك أعلم بالأمور وأبلغ فيها رأياً وأنا أرى أن تحتال للأمر قبل تفاقمه ولا تنتظر به وقوعه فلا تأمن أن يفوتك حتّى لا تستدركه فإنّه قد كان يقال إنّ الرجال ثلاثة حازم وكيّس وعاجز فأحد الحازمين من إذا نزل به البلاء لم يدهش ولم يذهب قلبه شعاعاً فلم يعيَ برأيه وحيلته ومكيدته التي بها يرجو لها المخرج وأحزم من هذا المتقدّم ذو العدّة الذي يعرف الأمر قبل وقوعه فيعظمه إعظامه ويحتال له حيلته حتّى كأنّه قد لزمه فيحسم الداء قبل أن يبتلى به ويدفع الأمر قبل وقوعه وأمّا العاجز فهو في تردّد وتمنّي أمانيّ حتّى يهلك ومثل ذلك مثل السمكات الثلاث. ٥٤،٤

قال الأسد وكيف كان مثلهنّ.

قال دمنة زعموا أنّ غديراً كان فيه ثلاث سمكات عظام كيّسة وحازمة وعاجزة فكان ذلك المكان بنجوة من الأرض لا يكاد يقربها الناس فلمّا كان ذات يوم مرّ صيّادان على ذلك الغدير مجتازين فأبصرا السمكات الثلاث فتواعدا على أن يرجعا إليه بشبكتهما فيصيدا السمكات اللواتي رأيا فيه في الماء وأنّ السمكة التي كانت أحزم لمّا رأتهما ارتابت وتخوّفت فلم تعرّج أن خرجت من المكان الذي كان الماء يدخل فيه إلى الغدير من النهر وأمّا السمكة الكيّسة التي كانت دون الأولى في العقل ثبتت مكانها وأخّرت الحيلة حتّى كان بعد ذلك وجاء الصيّادان فرأتهما وعرفت ما يريدان ووجدتهما قد سدّا ذلك المخرج فقالت قد فرّطت وهذه عاقبة التفريط فكيف الحيلة على هذه الحال فقلّ ما تنجح حيلة العجلة والإرهاق ولكنّ العاقل ٥٥،٤

[1] عرف الملك: كذا ل٢؛ الأصل: عرف الرجل الملك. [2] كذا ر؛ ساقطة من الأصل.

out.' When I heard this, I realized that Shanzabah was a deceitful traitor. You've honored him in every way and have made him your equal—this has finally incited him to this clear treachery and malice. He hopes that your kingdom will become his once you're out of the way, and he's sparing no effort in scheming against you. He has intelligence, good judgment, friends, and accomplices. They say that a king should strike down anyone he discovers who rivals him in rank, appearance, wealth, and followers; otherwise, he'll be the one who is overthrown.

"Your Majesty is experienced in worldly affairs and a good judge of them. 4.54
I advise you to deal with the matter before it reaches a crisis. Don't wait for it to happen, lest it escape your control and cause irreparable damage. They say there are three kinds of people: prudent, quick-witted, and feckless. One kind of prudent person isn't confounded when trouble comes. He isn't thrown into confusion; he doesn't falter in his judgment, resourcefulness, and ingenuity—he hopes thereby to find a way out of trouble. Even more prudent is the person who is ahead of events and is prepared, who foresees an event before it happens, sizes it up, and looks for the means to deal with it as if it were already upon him. He stops the disease before it strikes and wards off trouble before it happens. The feckless person, on the other hand, hesitates and entertains vain hopes until he perishes. The story of the three fishes is an example of this."

"What happened to them?" asked the lion.

And Dimnah told the following tale: They say there was a pond where 4.55
three big fishes lived: one quick-witted, one prudent, and one feckless. The *The Three Fishes*
pond was on a highland that was hardly ever visited. One day, however, two fishermen passed by, saw the three fishes, and decided to return with their net and catch them. At the sight of the fishermen, the most prudent of the three fishes became apprehensive and fearful: she immediately left the pond by following its outlet to the river. The quick-witted fish, less intelligent, put off devising anything until the fishermen returned. At the sight of them, she realized what they intended to do, but discovered that they had blocked the outlet. "I was careless," she said, "and this is the result. Now that I've been so careless, how can I save myself? Desperate last-minute schemes rarely succeed! But someone with intelligence doesn't despair or give up looking

لا يقنط من منافع الرأي ولا يأسى على حال ولا يدع الرأي. ثمّ إنّها تماوتت فجعلت تطفو على الماء منقلبة على ظهرها فأخذها الصيّاد بحسبان الميّتة فوضعها على الأرض بين الغدير والنهر فوثبت في النهر فنجت من الصيّاد وأمّا العاجزة فلم تزل في إقبال وإدبار حتّى صيدت.

٥٦،٤ قال الأسد قد فهمت ما قلت ولكن لا أظنّ الثور يغشّني ويبغي لي الغوائل مع حسن بلائي عنده وكيف يفعل ذلك ولم يرمني سوءًا قطّ.

قال دمنة إنّه لا يحمله على ذلك إلّا أنّه لم يرمنك سوءًا قطّ ولم تدع خيرًا إلّا صنعته به ولا مرتبة إلّا أبلغته إيّاها ولم تبق مرتبة يسمو إليها إلّا مرتبتك فإنّ اللئيم العاجز[1] لا يزال ناصحًا نافعًا حتّى يرتفع إلى المنزلة التي ليس لها بأهل فإذا بلغها منّته نفسه ورغب عمّا هو عليه فعاد نصحه غشًّا ومنافعه خيانة وضرًّا والتمس ما فوقها بالغشّ والخيانة والفجور لأنّ اللئيم الكفور لا يخدم السلطان ولا ينصح له إلّا عن فرق أو حاجة فإذا استغنى وذهبت الهيبة عاد إلى جوهره كذنب الكلب العَقد الذي يُربط ليستقيم فلا يزال مستقيمًا ما دام مربوطًا فإذا أُطلق عاد إلى انحنائه واعوجاجه.

٥٧،٤ واعلم أيّها الملك أنّه من لم يقبل من نصحائه ما يُنقل إليه[2] ممّا ينصحون له فيه لم يُحمد عن رأيه كالمريض الذي يدع ما ينعت له الطبيب فيعمد إلى ما تشتهيه نفسه.

وحقّ على موازر السلطان أن يبلغ الحقيقات له على ما ينفعه ويزينه والكفّ له عمّا يضرّه ويشينه. وخير الإخوان أقلّهم مصانعة في النصيحة وخير الأعمال أحلاها عاقبة وخير الثناء ما كان على أفواه الأخيار وخير السلطان ما لم يخالطه بطر وخير النساء الموافقة للبعل وأغنى الأغنياء من لم يكن للحرص أسيرًا وخير الأصدقاء من لم يخاصم وخير الأخلاق أعونها على الورع ثمّ قد قيل لو أنّ امرءًا قد توسّد النار وافترش الحيّات كان أحقّ لأن يهنئه[3] النوم منه[4] إذا أحسّ من صاحبه بعداوة

---

١ كذا ل٢؛ الأصل: العاجر. ٢ يُنقل إليه: ل٢: يثقل عليه. ٣ كذا پ٣٤٦٦؛ الأصل: يهيبه. ٤ كذا پ٣٤٧٥؛ الأصل: علمها.

for a solution!" So she played dead and floated on the water, belly up. The fisherman took her and, assuming she was dead, set her down on the ground between the pond and the river. She then jumped into the river and escaped. As for the feckless fish, she swam back and forth and was caught.

"I understand what you're saying," said the lion, "but I can't believe the ox would deceive me and wish to harm me after I've treated him so well. Why would he, when he has experienced no mistreatment at my hands?" 4.56

"But that," said Dimnah, "is the very thing driving him to it! Seeing as you've never mistreated him, and have favored him in every way and raised him to every rank, the only rank left for him to covet is yours! A low, incompetent person remains a useful counselor until he rises to a rank he doesn't deserve, but as soon he reaches it, he becomes dissatisfied; his loyalty turns into duplicity and his benevolence into treachery and harm, and he uses duplicity, treachery, and disobedience to seek an even higher rank. Such a low, ungrateful person serves the ruler and is loyal to him only out of fear or need; as soon as he feels himself secure and loses his fear, he reverts to his original nature—like a dog's curly tail that has been tied straight: as long as it is tied, it stays straight, but once released it goes back to being bent and crooked.

"Your Majesty, remember that anyone who doesn't accept the advice of his loyal advisers will regret his decision. He will be like a patient who abandons his doctor's prescription and follows his own appetites instead. A minister's duty is to inform the ruler of the facts, to benefit him and increase his renown, and to abstain from anything that would harm or disgrace him. The best brother flatters least when giving advice, the best deed has the most pleasing consequences, the best praise comes from the mouths of the righteous, the best governance is not mingled with arrogance, the best wife agrees with her husband, the richest of the wealthy aren't held prisoner by greed, the best friend never quarrels, and the best character traits promote the fear of God. They also say that a man who lays his head to rest on fire and lies on a bed of snakes is more likely to enjoy a sound sleep than someone who senses that his companion harbors enmity against him day and night. 4.57

يريد بها نفسه ويغدو عليه بها ويروح وأعجز الملوك آخَذهم بالهوينا وأقلّهم نظرًا في مستقبل الأمور وأشبههم بالفيل المغتلم الذي لا يلتفت على شيء فإن حزبه[1] أمر تهاون به وإن أضيع الأمور غضب الملك بقرابته.

قال الأسد غلطت في القول وغلظ قول الناصح يُحتمل ولكنّ شنزبة لو كان لي عدوًّا كما تقول لم يستطع لي ضرًّا وكيف يستطيع ذلك منّي وهو آكل عشب وأنا آكل لحم وإنّما هو لي طعام وليس عليّ منه خوف وليس لي إلى الغدر به سبيل بعد الأمان الذي جعلت له وبعد إكرامي إيّاه وثنائي عليه عند الجند فإنّي إن غيّرت ذلك وبدّلته جهّلت على نفسي وغدرت. ٥٨،٤

قال دمنة لا تغترّ بقولك هذا هو لي طعام وليس عليّ منه خوف فإنّ شنزبة إن هو لم يستطعك بنفسه احتال لك من قبل غيره وكان يقال إن أضافك ضيف ساعة وأنت لا تعرف أخلاقه فلا تأمنه أن يصل إليك منه سبب شرّ كما أصاب القملة.

قال الأسد وما أصاب القملة.

قال دمنة زعموا أنّ قملة لزمت فراش رجل من الأشراف زمانًا فكانت تصيب من دمه وهو نائم وتدبّ عليه دبيبًا رفيقًا فسلمت بذلك حتّى استضافها برغوث ذات ليلة فقالت القملة للبرغوث بت عندنا هذه الليلة في دم طيّب وعلى فراش ليّن. فأقام البرغوث عندها حتّى إذا أوى الرجل إلى فراشه وثب عليه البرغوث فلذعه لذعة شديدة استيقظ الرجل من نومه فأمر بفراشه أن يُنظر فيه فنظروا فيه وقد فُقد البرغوث وذهب فلم يجدوا إلّا قملة فقتلوها. ٥٩،٤

وإنّما ضربت لك هذا المثل ليعلم الملك أنّ صاحب الشرّ لا يُسلم من شرّه وإن هو ضعف عن ذلك جاء بسببه فإن كنت لا تخاف شنزبة خفت غيره من جندك الذين قد حملهم شنزبة على عداوتك وجرّأهم عليك مع أنّي قد عرفت أنّه لا بدّ من مناظرتك ولا يكل أمرك إلى غيره.[2] ٦٠،٤

---

١ كذا ع؛ الأصل: أحزنه. ٢ مع أنّي . . . غيره: الأصل: مع انى لو قد عرف لا ريد مناظرتك ولا نكل امرك الى غيرك.

The weakest king is the most remiss and least attentive to his affairs; the one who, like an elephant in rut, pays no attention to anything. He makes light of anything unexpected, and if an affair goes awry, he vents his wrath on his companions."

"You've spoken harshly," said the lion, "yet harsh words from a sincere 4.58
adviser must be borne. But even if Shanzabah were my enemy, as you say, he couldn't harm me. How could he, a grass eater, harm me, a meat eater? For me, he's nothing more than food! I'm not afraid of him. What's more, how can I betray him when I've given him a promise of safety, honored him, and praised him in front of all my troops? If I begin to behave differently, I make myself look like a fool and break my own promise."

"Don't delude yourself," replied Dimnah, "by saying that he's nothing more than food for you and that you do not fear him. Even if Shanzabah can do nothing to you on his own, he'll use others to scheme against you. They say that if a guest of unproven character asks you for an hour's hospitality, beware lest evil befall you because of him, as happened to the louse."

"What happened to it?" asked the lion.

The Louse and the Flea

And Dimnah told the following tale: A louse, they say, lived for a time in 4.59
a nobleman's bed. She would sip his blood while he slept and would crawl over him so gently that she escaped notice. One night, a flea asked to be her guest and the louse agreed: "Spend the night with us. You'll enjoy tasty blood and a soft bed." So he did. But when the man got into bed, the flea gave him such a vigorous bite that it woke him up. The man ordered that the bed be thoroughly checked. During the search, the flea got away, but they found the louse and killed her.

"I've told this story to show Your Majesty that one can never be safe from 4.60
a troublemaker; even if he's too weak to do anything himself, disaster may come about because of him. Although you don't fear Shanzabah, I worry about those in your army whom he has incited to hostility and emboldened against you. Still, I know that he himself will inevitably clash with you and will entrust the affair to no one else."

فوقع في نفس الأسد قول دمنة فقال ماذا ترى.

قال دمنة إنّ صاحب الضرس المأكول لا يزال صاحبه منه في أذى وألم حتّى يفارقه والطعام الذي غثيت منه النفس فالراحة في قذفه والعدوّ المخوف دواؤه فقده.

قال الأسد قد تركتني بشكّ فأنا أكره مجاورة شنزبة إيّاي فإنّي مرسل إليه وذاكر ما وقع في نفسي من أمره ثمّ آمره باللحاق حيث أحبّ.

٦١،٤ فكره ذلك دمنة وعرف إن كلّم شنزبة وسمع منه جوابه وعذره عرف باطل ما أتاه به واطّلع على كذبه ولم يخف عليه أمره فقال دمنة للأسد أمّا إرسالك إلى شنزبة ومذاكرتك ما كان من ذنبه فلا أراه حزماً فلينظر الملك في ذلك فإنّه لا يزال لك الخيار ما دام شنزبة لا يشعر أنّ أمره قد وصل إليك فإن هو شعر بذلك خفت أن يعاجلك بالمكابرة وإن قاتلك قاتلك مستعدّاً وإن فارقك فارقك فراقاً له عليك فضل وعليك منه عار مع أنّ ذوي الرأي من الملوك لا يعلنون عقوبة من لم يعلن ذنبه ولكنّ لكلّ ذنب عندهم عقوبة لذنب السرّ عقوبة السرّ[1] ولذنب العلانية عقوبة العلانية.

٦٢،٤ قال الأسد إنّ الملك إذا عاقب أحداً وأهانه عن ظنّ يظنّه من غير استيقان بجرمه فنفسه عاقب وإيّاها أهان.

قال دمنة أما الآن[2] فلا يدخلنّ عليك شنزبة إلّا وأنت مستعدّ لئلّا يصيبنّ منك غرّة فإنّي لا أحسبك[3] لو قد نظرت إليه حين يدخل عليك إلّا ستعرف أنّه قد همّ بعظيمة ومن علامة ذلك أن ترى لونه متغيّراً وترى أوصاله ترتعد وتراه يلتفت يميناً وشمالاً وتراه يهزّ قرنيه كفعل الذي يهمّ بالنطح.[4]

قال الأسد سأكون منه على حذر ولئن أنا رأيت منه حين يدخل هذه العلامات التي ذكرت فما في أمره شكّ.

٦٣،٤ فلمّا فرغ دمنة من تحميل الأسد على الثور وعرف أنّه قد أوقع في نفسه ما كان يلتمس وأنّ الأسد سيحذر الثور ويتهيّأ له أراد إتيان شنزبة ليغريه بالأسد وأحبّ

---

١ كذا ش، پ٣٤٦٦، پ٣٤٧٥؛ ساقطة من الأصل. ٢ كذا پ٣٤٧٥؛ الأصل: لا. ٣ لا أحسبك: كذا ل٢؛ الأصل: لأحسبك. ٤ كذا ل٢؛ الأصل: النطح.

Dimnah's words made a deep impression on the lion. "What do you advise?" he asked.

"A rotten tooth," replied Dimnah, "causes pain until it is pulled. The way to get relief from a food that makes you nauseous is to throw it up. The remedy for an enemy you fear is to get rid of him."

"You've given me doubts—I don't want Shanzabah living anywhere near me. I'll send him a message about how I feel and command him to go elsewhere."

Dimnah wasn't pleased. He knew that if the lion spoke with Shanzabah 4.61
and heard his defense, he would realize that there was no substance to the matter; that Dimnah had been lying, and his scheme would be exposed. So Dimnah said to the lion, "I don't think it wise to send Shanzabah a message and bring up his offense. Consider the matter, Your Majesty. You have the advantage as long as Shanzabah has no idea that you've received word of his actions. If he senses that you have, I'm afraid he'll immediately try to get the better of you. If he fights you, he'll fight well prepared; if he leaves you, he'll leave in a way that shows his superiority and that brings you shame. Furthermore, prudent kings do not inflict public punishment on those whose offense has not become public. Every crime has its punishment: secret punishment for a secret crime, public punishment for a public crime."

"A king who punishes or humiliates someone on suspicion," said the lion, 4.62
"without being certain about the crime, punishes and humiliates no one but himself."

"In that case," replied Dimnah, "let Shanzabah come into your presence only when you're ready. Don't let him catch you off guard. If you look at him when he arrives, I'm sure you'll see that he's planning to do something terrible. Look for these signs: see if his color changes and his muscles twitch; see if he looks right and left, waving his horns as if preparing to gore."

"I'll be on the alert," said the lion. "If I see the signs you've mentioned when he enters, there'll be no doubt about what he intends."

Once Dimnah had incited the lion against the ox and was satisfied that he 4.63
had put the thoughts he wanted into his mind, so that the lion would be alert and ready for the ox, he wanted to go to Shanzabah to incite him against the

أن يكون ذلك بأمر الأسد لئلّا يبلغه ذلك عن غيره فيتّهمه فقال للأسد ألا آتي شنزبة فأنظر إلى حاله وأستمع من كلامه لعلّي أطّلع على بعض ما في نفسه. فأذن له الأسد في ذلك.

٦٤،٤ فانطلق حتّى دخل على شنزبة متشبّهاً بالمكتئب الحزين فلمّا رآه رحّب به وقال له لم أرك منذ أيّام فما حبسك. أسلام.[١]

فقال دمنة ومتى كان من أهل السلام من لا يملك نفسه وإنّما أمره بيد غيره ممّن لا يُوثق به ومن هو لا ينفكّ على خطر وخوف حتّى ما يأمن من ساعة على دمه.

٦٥،٤ قال شنزبة وما الذي حدث.

قال دمنة حدث ما قُدّر فمن ذا الذي يغالب القدر ومن ذا الذي يبلغ في الدنيا جسيماً فلم يثبر ولم يبطر ومن ذا الذي يتّبع الهوى ولم يعطب ومن ذا الذي يأتي النساء فلم يُفتن ومن ذا الذي طلب إلى اللئام فلم يهن ومن ذا الذي خالط الأشرار فيسلم ولم يندم ومن ذا صحب السلطان فدام له منهم الإحسان. لقد صدق القائل الذي قال إنّما مثل السلاطين في قلّة وفائهم لمن صحبهم وسخاء أنفسهم عن من فقدوا من قرابتهم إلّا كمثل البغيّ والمكتب[٢] كلّما ذهب واحد جاء آخر.

قال شنزبة أسمع لك كلاماً أخاف أن يكون قد رابك من الأسد ريب.

قال دمنة لقد رابني منه شيء ولكن ليس من أمر نفسي.

٦٦،٤ قال شنزبة ففيمن وبمن.

قال دمنة قد علمت[٣] حقّك عليّ وودّ[٤] ما بيني وبينك وما كنت جعلت لك من ذمّتي أيّام أرسلني إليك الأسد فلم أجد بدّاً من حفظك وإطلاعك على ما أطّلع عليه ممّا أخاف عليك فيه.

قال شنزبة وما ذلك.

قال دمنة حدّثني الخبير الصدوق أنّ الأسد قال لبعض أصحابه قد أعجبني سمن هذا الثور وليست بي حاجة إليه ولا أرى إلّا أكله ونطعم أصحابي لحمه. فلمّا بلغني

١ كذا ش؛ الأصل: السلام. ٢ الأصل: والمكتب. ٣ كذا ش، پ٣٤٧٥؛ الأصل: علم. ٤ كذا ش، ع؛ الأصل: ذمام.

lion. But he wanted this done by the lion's command; he did not want the lion to learn about the meeting from someone else and become suspicious. So he said to the lion, "Why don't I go and see Shanzabah and listen to what he's saying? Maybe I can learn some of what he has in mind." The lion gave his permission.

Dimnah set off. He appeared before Shanzabah, pretending to be sad and 4.64
dejected. Shanzabah welcomed him as soon as saw him: "I haven't seen you for days! What's kept you away? Is everything all right?"

"How can everything be all right," replied Dimnah, "when you're not your own master; when your fate lies in the hands of a person who can't be trusted and of whom you're in such constant fear and danger that not a moment goes by without you fearing for your life?"

"What has happened?" asked Shanzabah. 4.65

"What was fated to happen has happened—and who can fight fate? Can anyone attain greatness in this world without being destroyed or becoming insolent? Can anyone follow desire without coming to a bad end? Can anyone keep company with women without being seduced? Can anyone beg from churls without being humiliated? Can anyone consort with evildoers and escape safely without regret? Can anyone serve a ruler and remain in his good graces? How right the one who said that rulers, in their scant loyalty to companions and abandonment of those they no longer need, are like a whore with her customers: when one leaves, another takes his place!"

Shanzabah responded, "Your words make me fear that something has filled you with misgivings about the lion."

"Something has indeed filled me with misgivings, but it doesn't concern me personally," said Dimnah.

"Who then?" asked Shanzabah. 4.66

"You know the claim you have on me," said Dimnah, "and the affection between us, and the promise of protection I gave you when the lion sent me to you. So now I must protect you and tell you what I've learned that makes me fear for you."

"What is it?" asked Shanzabah.

"A reliable source has informed me that the lion said to one of his companions, 'I like how fat this ox has become. Since I don't need him, I think

مقالته هذه عرفت[1] كفره ولؤم عهده فأقبلت إليك لأعلمك بذلك وأقضي الذي لك عليّ من الحقّ فتحتال في أمرك بلطف ورفق.

٦٧،٤ فلمّا سمع الثور كلام دمنة وتذكّرما بينهما وما جعل له من العهد والميثاق فكّر في أمر الأسد فظنّ أنّ دمنة قد صدقه ورأى أمر الأسد شبيهاً بما قال فأهمّه ذلك وقال لدمنة ما كان ينبغي للأسد أن يغدر بي ولم أذنب إليه ولا إلى أحد من جنده ذنباً قطّ وما أظنّه إلّا قد حُمل عليّ بالكذب وشُبّه عليه أمري فإنّ الأسد قد صحبه قوم سوء وجرّب منهم أموراً هي تصدّق عنده ما بلغه عن غيرهم فإنّ صحبة الأشرار ربّما أورثت صاحبها سوء ظنّ بالأخيار وحملته تجربته على خطإ ظنّة كخطإ البطّة التي[2] زعموا أنّها رأت في الماء ضوء كوكب فظنّته سمكة فحاولته أن تصيده فلمّا جرّبت ذلك مراراً عرفت أنّه ليس بشيء فرأت مساء الغد من ذلك اليوم سمكة فظنّت أنّها مثل الذي رأت قبلها فلم تطلب صيدها.

٦٨،٤ فإن كان الأسد بلغه[3] عنّي كذباً وصدّق به لما جرّب واختبر من غيري فبالحرى وإن كان لم يبلغه عنّي إلّا خيراً ثمّ أرادني سوءاً عن غير علّة[4] فذلك أعجب العجب وقد كان يقال إنّ العجب أن يطلب الرجل مرضاة صاحبه فلا يرضى وأعجب من ذلك أن يطلب رضاه فيسخط. فإذا كانت الموجدة عن علّة كان الرضى مرجوّاً وإذا كانت عن غير علّة انقطع الرجاء من الرضى لأنّ العلّة إذا كانت الموجدة في ورودها كان الرضى في صدورها فالعلّة لها وقوع[5] وذهاب توجد أحياناً والباطل قائم[6] موجود لا يقعد على حال.

٦٩،٤ وقد نظرت فلا أعلم لي فيما بيني وبين الأسد جرماً ولئن كان فما هو إلّا صغير فلعمري ما يستطيع أحد أطال صحبة صاحب أن يتحفّظ في كلّ شيء ويحترس حتّى لا يكون منه فارطة صغيرة ولا كبيرة يكرهها صاحبه ولكنّ الرجل ذا العقل والوفاء إذا سقط صاحبه بشيء أو أذنب نظر في ذنبه وسقطته وفي قدر مبلغها وخطرها

---

١ كذا ل٢؛ ساقطة من الأصل. ٢ كذا ل٢؛ ساقطة من الأصل. ٣ كذا ل٢؛ الأصل: بلغ. ٤ كذا ل٢؛ الأصل: علم.
٥ كذا ر؛ الأصل: رجوع. ٦ كذا ر؛ الأصل: قديم.

I'll eat him and we can feed his meat to my companions.' As soon as I heard this, I realized his ingratitude and wickedness. I've come to inform you and do my duty by you, so that you can devise a subtle and clever plan for yourself."

When the ox heard these words, he recalled the solemn promise Dimnah had once made to him. Thinking about the lion and believing that Dimnah had given a true account of his intentions, he became worried. "It isn't right for the lion to act so treacherously when I've never offended him or any of his troops. Lies must have turned him against me and made him suspicious. The lion has bad companions, and they've made him believe what has been reported to him about others. Bad company often makes you suspicious of good people; it leads you to make the same mistake as the duck who, they say, saw the reflection of a star in the water and, thinking it a fish, tried to catch it. After repeated tries, she realized that it was nothing. The next evening, she saw a fish there, but didn't try to catch it, thinking it was like the previous occasions. 4.67

The Duck Who Mistook the Reflection of a Star for a Fish

"It is understandable if the lion has believed the lies he has been fed about me because of his prior experience with others. But it is utterly amazing if he has received only good reports about me and wishes me ill for no reason. They say that it is strange when you seek to please your companion and he isn't pleased, but even stranger when you seek to please him and he becomes angry. Reconciliation can be hoped for when anger occurs for a cause; but there is no hope for reconciliation when it occurs without a cause. If anger is occasioned by the occurrence of a cause, then reconciliation can be hoped for when the cause ceases. Causes come and go, and exist for a while, but what is gratuitous lasts and never ceases. 4.68

"When I reflect on the matter, I can find no offense I've caused the lion, and if there was one it must have been small. By God, if you associate with a companion for a long time, you can never be so cautious as to avoid inadvertently doing something, small or great, that will displease him. A reasonable person ponders the magnitude and seriousness of an offence or mistake; 4.69

وعمداً كان ذلك منه أو خطأ وهل في الصفح عنه أمر يخاف ضرره أو يشينه أم لا ثمّ لا يؤاخذ صاحبه بشيء يجد إلى الصفح عنه[1] سبيلاً.

٧٠،٤ فإن كان الأسد يعدّ عليّ ذلك جرماً فلا أعلم ذلك إلّا أنّي ربّما خالفت عليه في بعض رأيه نظراً ونصيحة منّي إليه فعسى أن يكون أنزل ذلك منّي على الجرأة عليه والمخالفة له ويقول ما جرّأ شنزبة على أن يقول نعم إذا قلت لا ولا إذا قلت نعم.[2] ولا أجدني في هذا مخصوصاً لأنّي لم أخالفه في شيء إلّا فيما قد تدبّرت من عاقبته الرشد والمنفعة والزين[3] ولم أجاهره بشيء من ذلك قطّ على رؤوس جنده وعند أصحابه بل كنت أخلو به وأكلّمه بكلام الهائب المجلّل الموقّر وعرفت أنّه من التمس الرخص من الإخوان عند المشاورة ومن الأطبّاء عند المرض ومن الفقهاء عند الشبهة فقد أخطأ منافع الرأي.

٧١،٤ وإن لم يكن في هذا فعسى أن يكون في بعض سكرات السلطان فإنّه من سكرات السلطان أن يرضى عمّن يستوجب السخط ويسخط عمّن يستوجب الرضى من غير سبب معلوم ولذلك يقول القائل قد خاطر من لجّ البحر وأشدّ منه مخاطرة صاحب السلطان فإنّ مصاحب السلطان وإن هو صحبهم بالوفاء والاستقامة والمودّة والنصيحة خليق أن يعثر فلا ينتعش وإن يُنعش فبعد إشفاء على الهلكة.

٧٢،٤ وإن لم يكن هذه فلعلّ بعض ما أُعطيته من الفضل حصل لي به الهلاك فإنّ الشجرة الحسنة الكبيرة الكثيرة الحمل ربّما كان فسادها من حملها وطيب ثمرها وبال عليها والطاووس ربّما صار ذنبه الذي هو[4] جلّ حسنه وجماله وبالاً عليه حتّى إذا احتاج إلى الخفّة والنجاة ممّن يطلبه أثقله عن ذلك ذنبه والفرس الجواد القويّ ربّما أهلكه ذلك فاقتُعد واستُعمل وأُتعب لفضل ما عنده حتّى يهلك والرجل ذو المروءة ربّما كان فضله سبب هلاكه لكثرة ما يحسده ويبغي عليه من أهل الشرّ لأنّ من

---

١ أمر يخاف . . . إلى الصفح عنه: كذا ر؛ ساقطة من الأصل. ٢ نعم: الأصل: نعم قال لا. ٣ كذا ر؛ الأصل: والدن.
٤ كذا ش؛ ساقطة من الأصل.

he considers whether it was intentional or accidental, and whether pardoning it may incur some harm or shame. He will not hold anything against his companion that he can possibly forgive.

"If the lion thinks I've committed an offense, I don't know what it could be, other than opposing him in some of his ideas, out of consideration and in the form of sincere advice. Perhaps he takes it as insolence or disobedience when he says no and I say yes, or when he says yes and I say no. But I don't think I should be faulted for that. I disagreed with him only when by doing so I could foresee success, benefit, and renown for him. I never spoke to him about such matters openly in the presence of his soldiers or before his companions; I met him privately and spoke to him as a respectful servant obedient to his master. I know that to seek to be indulged by comrades when asking for advice, or by doctors when one is sick, or by scholars over an obscure point of religion, is to fail to benefit from their advice. 4.70

"If it isn't this, perhaps it's the sort of thing rulers do in moments of intoxication. Sometimes, in such moments, they favor those who deserve their anger and become angry with those who deserve their favor—all for no discernible reason. As has been said: To sail the sea is to run a risk, but to be a ruler's companion is to run an even greater risk. Though you attend on him with loyalty, uprightness, affection, and good counsel, you're still liable to stumble and fall, or to be lifted only when you're on the verge of destruction. 4.71

"If it isn't this, perhaps some excellence of mine has been my downfall. A heavily laden tree may be ruined because of its load, and the sweetness of its fruit may become its undoing. A peacock's tail—his pride and glory—may be his undoing as it weighs him down when he needs to escape his pursuers. A sturdy steed may be ridden so hard and become so worn out that he perishes. A virtuous man's excellence may cause his downfall because so many rogues envy him and seek to do him harm. Those who lack excellence are more numerous than those who possess it; the wicked 4.72

لا مروءة له أكثر من أهل المروءة وأنّ الأشرار أكثر من الأخيار بكلّ مكان فإذا عادوه كابروه وأوشكوا أن يهلكوه.

٧٣،٤ فإن لم يكن هذه فهو إذاً القدر الذي لا يُدفع فإنّ القدر هو الذي يسلب الأسد قوّته وشدّته فيدخله التابوت وهو الذي يحمل الضعيف على ظهر الفيل وهو الذي يسلّط الحوّاء على الحيّة ذات الحمة فينزع حمتها فيلعب بها وهو الذي يعجز الأريب ويحزم العاجز[1] ويثبّط الشهم ويشهم الثَبِط[2] ويوسع على المقتّر ويقتّر على الموسع ويشجّع الجبان ويجبّن الشجاع وتجري المقادير على أسباب ومعاريض وعلل وعليها قُدّرت مجاريها.

٧٤،٤ قال دمنة إنّ إرادة الأسد بك ليس لشيء ممّا ذكرت من تحميل الأشرار ولا سكر السلطان ولا غير ذلك ولكن لغدره وجوره وأنّه جبّار غدّار أوّل طعمه حلاوة وآخره مرارة بل آخره سمّ مميت.

قال شنزبة قد طعمت الحلاوة فاستلذذتها فأراني قد انتهيت إلى الذي فيه الموت ولا أظنّ مقامي عند الأسد برأي هو آكل لحم وأنا آكل عشب فقبحاً للحرص وقبحاً للأمل فهما أوقعاني في هذه الورطة وحبساني عن مذاهبي احتباس النحل على ورق اللينوفر إذا وجدت ريح اللينوفر استلذّتها وأغفلت عن حينها الذي ينبغي أن تطير فيه قبل أن ينضمّ ورقه وتلجّج فيه فتموت. ومن لم يرض من الدنيا بالكفاف واستعبده الحرص وطمحت عيناه إلى ما فوق ذلك ولم ينظر فيما يُتخوّف أمامه كان عاقبته عاقبة الذباب الذي لا يرضى بالشجر والرياحين حتّى يطلب الماء الذي يسيل من أصل أذن الفيل المغتلم فيضربه الفيل بأذنه فيهلكه ومن بذل نصيحته واجتهاده لمن لا شكر له فإنّما مثله مثل من بذر بذره في السباخ ومن أشار على المعجب أو من شاور الأصمّ.

٧٥،٤ قال دمنة دع عنك هذا الكلام واحتل لنفسك.

قال شنزبة بأيّ شيء أحتال لنفسي إن أراد الأسد قتلي. فما أعرفني بأخلاق الأسد ورأيه وأعلمني أنه لو لم يردني إلّا الخير ثمّ أراد أصحابه لمكرهم وفجورهم هلاكي

---

١ يُعجز . . . العاجز: كذا ش؛ الأصل: بحر الارنب ويحرم الحازم الماقور. ٢ كذا ش؛ الأصل: النشط.

everywhere outnumber the good and soon destroy a good man if they turn against him.

“If it’s not this, then it is fate, which cannot be repelled. Fate strips the lion of his strength and vigor, and puts him in a cage. Fate mounts the weakling on the elephant’s back, and gives the charmer mastery over the snake, extracting its venom, and playing with it as he pleases. Fate renders the resourceful inept and the inept resourceful. Fate frustrates the bold and emboldens the timid; it enriches the poor and impoverishes the wealthy; it instills courage into the coward and makes cowards of the courageous. Predetermined events take place in accordance with the means, occasions, and causes by which their courses have been determined.” 4.73

“The lion’s designs on you are not due to any of the reasons you’ve mentioned,” replied Dimnah, “such as incitement by villains, the intoxication of power, or anything of the sort. Rather, they are due to his treachery and injustice. He’s a treacherous tyrant: one’s first taste of him is sweet, one’s last taste bitter—a lethal poison.” 4.74

“Yes,” said Shanzabah, “I tasted the sweetness and found it delicious, but now I see that I’ve reached the lethal part. I don’t think my staying with the lion was a good idea, he being an eater of meat, I an eater of grass. A plague on greed and expectation! They’ve made me fall into this quagmire and kept me from going my way—like a bee on a lotus flower: delighted by the scent, she becomes oblivious to when she needs to fly away, before the lotus closes its petals, so she is caught and dies. A slave to greed, who isn’t satisfied with what is sufficient for this life, but sets his eyes on excess and fails to see the perils lying before him, is like a fly that isn’t content with trees and herbs, but seeks the liquid that flows from the ears of an elephant in rut, and the elephant kills it with a flap of his ear. To offer advice to an ungrateful person is like sowing seeds in brackish ground: the advice is offered to a self-satisfied know-it-all; or it’s like engaging a deaf man in debate.”

“Enough talk!” said Dimnah. “Do something to save your life.” 4.75

“How can I save myself if the lion wants to kill me?” said Shanzabah. “I know his character and how he thinks. I also know that even if he only wished me well, his wicked companions, with their guile, would prevail if they incited him against me and wanted me to perish at his hands. When

عنده وإغراءه بي قدروا على ذلك فإنّ المكرة الظلمة إذا اجتمعوا على البريء الصحيح كانوا خلقاء أن يهلكوه وإن كانوا ضعفاء وكان قويّاً كما أهلك الذئب والغراب وابن آوى الجمل حين اجتمعوا عليه بالمكر والخديعة.

قال دمنة وكيف كان ذلك.

٧٦،٤ قال شنزبة زعموا أنّ أسداً كان في أجمة مجاوراً لطريق من طرق الناس وكان له أصحاب ثلاثة ذئب وابن آوى وغراب وأنّ تجّاراً مرّوا في ذلك الطريق من طرق الناس فتخلّف منهم جمل لهم فدخل الأجمة حتّى انتهى إلى الأسد فسأله الأسد عن أمره وقال له من أين أقبلت. فأخبره بشأنه. قال فماذا تريد. قال ما أمرني به الملك. قال له إن أردت صحبتي فاصحبني في الخصب والأمن والسعة.

٧٧،٤ فأقام الجمل مع الأسد حتّى إذا كان ذات يوم توجّه الأسد في طلب الصيد فلقي فيلاً مغتلماً فقاتله قتالاً شديداً وانقلب الأسد مقبلاً تسيل دماؤه ممّا جرحه الفيل بنابه ووقع مريضاً لا يستطيع الصيد فلبث الذئب وابن آوى والغراب أيّاماً لا يجدون ما يعيشون به من فضول الأسد فأصابهم جوع وهزال فعرف الأسد ذلك فيهم فقال لهم لقد جُهدتم واحتجتم إلى ما تأكلون. قالوا ما تهمّنا أنفسنا ونحن نرى بالملك ما نرى فليتنا نجد للملك بعض ما يصلحه. قال الأسد ما أشكّ في نصحكم ولكن إن استطعتم فانتشروا وابتغوا لعلّكم تجدون قريباً صيداً فتؤذنوني لعلّي أكسبكم ونفسي رزقاً.

٧٨،٤ فخرج الذئب وابن آوى والغراب من عند الأسد وتنحّوا ناحية وائتمروا بينهم فقالوا ما لنا ولهذا الجمل الآكل[١] العشب الذي ليس شأنه شأننا ولا دأبه دأبنا ألا نزيّن للأسد أن يأكله ويطعمنا منه.

قال ابن آوى هذا ما لا نستطيع ذكره للأسد فإنّه قد أمّن الجمل وجعل له ذمّة.

قال الغراب أقيما مكانكما ودعاني والأسد.

٧٩،٤ فانطلق الغراب إلى الأسد فلمّا رآه قال له ما شأنك هل أحسستم شيئاً.

١ كذا ل٢؛ الأصل: آكل.

crafty villains unite against an innocent blameless person, they are likely to destroy him, even if they are weak and he is strong—just as the wolf, the crow, and the jackal destroyed the camel when they turned their wiles and deceptions against him."

"And how did they do that?" asked Dimnah.

So Shanzabah told the following tale: Once, they say, there lived a lion in a forest beside a well-traveled road. He had three companions: a wolf, a jackal, and a crow. One day, when some merchants were passing along the road, one of their camels lagged behind and wandered into the forest and encountered the lion. "Where have you come from?" asked the lion, and the camel told him his story. "What do you want?" asked the lion. "Whatever Your Majesty commands," replied the camel, and the lion said, "If you wish to become my companion, do so and enjoy abundance, safety, and comfort." 4.76

How the Wolf, the Crow, and the Jackal Destroyed the Camel

The camel lived with the lion until, one day, the lion went out hunting and encountered an elephant in rut. They fought fiercely. Wounded by the elephant's tusk, the lion returned bleeding and fell sick, unable to hunt. The wolf, the jackal, and the crow became emaciated with hunger because they could not enjoy the lion's leftovers on which they usually dined. The lion, who realized what was happening, said, "You are suffering and need something to eat," and they replied, "When we see the king's condition, we do not worry for ourselves. If only we could find the king something to restore his health!" The lion said, "I don't doubt your loyalty. If you can, spread out and search. Perhaps you'll find some game nearby. Let me know, so I can provide us all with sustenance." 4.77

The wolf, the crow, and the jackal left the lion and went aside to confer. "What do we have in common with this grass eater, this camel?" they asked. "His nature isn't like ours, nor are his habits. Why don't we convince the lion to eat him and feed us some of the meat?" 4.78

To which the jackal replied, "We can't propose this to the lion, because he has promised the camel safety and granted him protection."

"Stay here," said the crow, "and let *me* deal with the lion."

The crow went to the lion. "Well?" asked the lion on seeing him. "Have you spotted anything?" 4.79

قال الغراب إنّما يجد من به ابتغاء ويبصر من به بصر فأمّا نحن فقد ذهب عنّا المشي والبصر لما أصابنا من الجوع ولكنّا نظرنا في أمر اتّفق عليه رأينا فإن وافقنا الملك فنحن مخصبون.

قال الأسد وما ذلك.

قال الغراب هذا الجمل الآكل[1] العشب المتمرّغ بيننا في غير صنعة.

٨٠،٤ فغضب الأسد وقال أفّ لك ما أخطأ مقالتك وأعجز رأيك وأبعدك من الوفاء والرحمة. ما كنت حقيقاً أن تجترئ على استقبالي بهذه المقولة. ألم تعلم أنّي قد أمّنت الجمل وأنّي قد جعلت له ذمّتي وموثقي وعهدي أولم يبلغك أنّه لن يتصدّق المتصدّق[2] بصدقة وإن عظمت هي أعظم[3] أجراً من أن يجير نفساً خائفة أو يحقن دماً وقد أجرت الجمل ولست غادراً به.

قال الغراب إنّي لأعرف ما قال الملك ولكنّ النفس الواحدة يُفتدى بها أهل البيت وأهل البيت يُفتدى بها القبيلة والقبيلة يُفتدى بها أهل المصر وإنّ أهل المصر فدى للملك وقد نزلت بالملك وبنا الحاجة والنازلة وأنا جاعل للملك منه مخرجاً فلا يتكلّف الملك غدراً إن يكن ذلك من الجمل ولا يأمر به أحد ولكنّا محتالون حيلة فيها وفاء للملك في ذمّته وظفرنا بحاجتنا. فسكت الأسد.

٨١،٤ وانصرف الغراب حين رأى إقرار الأسد فأتى أصحابه وقال كلّمت الأسد حتّى أقرّ بكذا وكذا فكيف الحيلة للجمل إذا أبى الأسد أن يلي قتله أو يأمر أصحابه به.

قال[4] له صاحباه برفقك الذي نرجوه في ذلك.

قال الغراب أرى أن نجتمع نحن والجمل فنذكر حال الأسد وما أصابه من الجهد والجوع ونقول لقد كان إلينا محسناً ولنا مكرماً فإن لم يرمنّا اليوم حين[5] نزل به ما[6] نزل اهتماماً بأمره وحرصاً على صلاحه أنزل ذلك منّا كفراً ولؤماً ولكن تعالوا نتقدّم إلى الأسد فلنذكر له حسن بلائه عندنا وأنّا لو قدرنا على فائدة نأتيه بها لم ندّخرها عنه

---

١ كذا ش، ع؛ الأصل: آكل. ٢ كذا ر؛ ساقطة من الأصل. ٣ كذا ش؛ ساقطة من الأصل. ٤ كذا ش، ع؛ الأصل: قالا. ٥ كذا ر، پ٣٤٦٦؛ الأصل: حتّى. ٦ الأصل: ممّا.

"You can't find if you can't seek," replied the crow, "and you can't see if you don't have sight. We're so hungry that we can hardly walk or see. We do, however, have a proposal on which we're all agreed. If Your Majesty approves, we shall all have much to eat."

"And what is it?" asked the lion.

"This grass-eating camel," the crow answered, "who lazes about among us with nothing to do!"

This made the lion angry. "Shame on you! What a sinful thing to say! 4.80
What a terrible idea! What happened to loyalty and mercy? How dare you confront me with such a proposal! Don't you know that I solemnly promised the camel safety and protection? Haven't you heard that a benefactor can bestow no gift, however great, more meritorious than to extend protection to a fearful soul and save its life? I have granted the camel my protection; I will not betray him."

The crow said, "I understand what Your Majesty is saying, but a single life is sacrificed to save a family, a family to save a tribe, a tribe to save a city's inhabitants, and a city's inhabitants to ransom a king. Now that need and disaster have descended on both the king and us, I will give the king a way out. Your Majesty will not be personally responsible for any betrayal of the camel, nor for commanding it. We will devise a way for the king to keep his promise and for us to obtain what we need." The lion kept silent.

Interpreting this as a sign of agreement, the crow returned to his friends. 4.81
"I talked to the lion until he agreed to some such thing. But how do we deal with the camel if the lion refuses to kill him himself or to order his companions to do so?"

"We'll rely on your skill in the matter," replied his friends.

"Here is my plan," said the crow. "We meet with the camel. We mention the lion's hunger and exhaustion. We say, 'He's given us everything we need and been generous to us. If in his day of need he doesn't see how worried we are about him and how concerned for his welfare, he'll take it as ingratitude and baseness on our part. Let's go before the lion and speak of the favors he's bestowed on us; let us describe how, if we can acquire anything that will be

فإن لم نقدر على ذلك فأنفسنا له مبذولة ثمّ ليعرض عليه كلّ واحد منّا نفسه وليقل كلني أيّها الملك ولا تمت جوعاً فإذا قال ذلك قائل أجابه الآخرون وردّوا عليه[1] بشيء يكون لنا فيه عذر[2] فنسلم جميعاً ونكون قد قضينا ذمام الأسد ويرضى الأسد عنّا.

ففعلوا ذلك وواطأهم الجمل على رأيهم.[3]

٨٢،٤ وتقدّموا إلى الأسد فبدأ الغراب فقال إنّك أيّها الملك قد احتجت إلى ما يقيمك فإنّه قد أصابك جهد ونحن أحقّاء بأن نقي بأنفسنا نفسك لبلائك عندنا فإنّا كنّا بك نعيش وبك يعيش من بقي منّا وإن هلكت فليس لأحد منّا بعدك بقاء ولا في الحياة خير.

فأجابه الذئب وابن آوى مبادرين اسكت عنّا فما خير في إسلامك نفسك وليس فيك شبع للملك.

قال ابن آوى لكن أنا سيشبع منّي الملك.

قال الذئب والغراب أنت منتن الريح قذر الجوف.

قال الذئب لكنّي لست كذلك فليأكلني الملك.

قال الغراب وابن آوى من أراد قتل نفسه فليأكل لحم الذئب فإنّه يأخذه من أكله الخناق.

٨٣،٤ فظنّ الجمل أنّه إذا عرض مثل ذلك من نفسه التمسوا له مثل عذرهم فيسلم ويرضى الأسد عليه فقال فيّ للملك شبع وبطوني طيّبة ولحمي مريء.

قال الذئب وابن آوى والغراب صدقت وكرمت وقلت ما نعرف. فوثبوا عليه ومزّقوه.

٨٤،٤ قال شنزبة وإنّما ضربت لك هذا المثل في الأسد وأصحابه لعلمي بأنّهم إذا اجتمعوا في هلاكي لم أقدر على الامتناع منهم ولو كان رأي الأسد في أمري غير ما كان عليه إلى اليوم[4] فإنّه قد قيل إنّ خير السلطان من أشبه النسور حوله الجيف

١ ثمّ ليعرض . . . وردّوا عليه: كذا ش؛ ساقطة من الأصل. ٢ الأصل: عذرًا. ٣ وواطأهم...رأيهم: كذا ر؛ ساقطة من الأصل. ٤ ولو . . . اليوم: الأصل: ولكن ان راى الاسد فى امرى على ما كان هو عليه الى اليوم.

of use to him, we will bring it to him, holding nothing back; and how, if we fail, our very lives are his to dispose of. Let's each of us offer himself, saying, "Eat me, Your Majesty! Don't die of hunger!" When we say this, the others will respond with a reason to reject the offer, and so we shall all be safe. In this way, we shall have fulfilled our duty to the lion and he will be pleased with us.'"

They met with the camel, and he agreed to their plan.

When they came before the lion, the crow spoke first: "Your Majesty, you 4.82
need something to sustain you in your distress, so it behooves us to offer up our lives in order to preserve yours. After all, it is through you that we have lived and through you, we hope, that our offspring may live. If you perish, none of us will survive and our lives won't be worth living."

"Shut up," replied the wolf and the jackal. "How will offering your life do any good, when there isn't enough in you to satisfy the king's hunger?"

"But I will satisfy the king!" said the jackal.

"Your breath is putrid and your belly is filthy," said the wolf and the crow.

"I'm not like that!" said the wolf. "Let the king eat me!"

"Anyone looking to commit suicide should eat wolf meat. He'll choke to death on it!" said the crow and the jackal.

The camel thought that if he made the same offer, they would find him an 4.83
excuse, just as they had done for themselves; he would be safe and the lion would be pleased. So he said, "There is enough in me to satisfy the king's hunger; my innards are tasty and my flesh is wholesome."

"Well spoken!" said the wolf, the crow, and the jackal. "How noble! You've said what we know to be true!"—and they pounced on him and tore him to pieces.

Shanzabah said, "I've told you this parable with reference to the lion 4.84
and his companions because I know that if they unite to destroy me I couldn't protect myself, even if the lion's opinion of me were not what it has been until now. The best rulers, it is said, are those who are like vultures surrounded by carrion, not those who are like carrion surrounded by

لا من أشبه الجيفة حولها النسور. ولو[1] أنّ الأسد لم يكن في نفسه إلّا الخير والرحمة لم يلبث من الأقاويل إذا كثرت عليه أن يذهب ذلك كلّه عنه حتّى يستبدل به الشراسة والغلظة. ألا ترى أنّ الماء ألين من القول وأنّ الحجر أشدّ من القلب فالماء إذا كثر انحداره على الحجر لم يلبث أن يثلم منه.

قال دمنة فماذا ترى أن تصنع. ٨٥،٤

قال شنزبة ما أرى إلّا أن أجاهده القتال فإنّه ليس للمصلّي في صلاة الدهر ولا[2] للمتصدّق في صدقته ولا للورع في ورعه مثل أجر المجاهد نفسه بنفسه ساعتين من النهار إن كان محقًّا فإنّه[3] من جاهد عن نفسه ودافع عنها من أراد ظلمها كان أجره عظيمًا وذكره رفيعًا إن قُتل فالجنّة وإن قتل فالأجر والظفر.

قال دمنة ليس ينبغي لأحد أن يخاطر بنفسه وهو يستطيع حياتها فإن هلك كان قد أضاع نفسه وإن ظفر كان من قبل القضاء ولكنّ ذا العقل جاعل القتال آخر الحيل ومقدّم قبل ذلك ما استطاع من الرفق والتمحّل ولا أرى لك هذا ولا ينبغي القتال مع الأعداء إلّا بعد ذهاب الحيل وانقطاعها فإنّ معاجلة[4] القتال قبل الإعذار أشر وبطر وخفّة وبالجزاء إن بدأ منه صاحبه مع أنّه إن قتل عدوّه على تلك الحال عُدّ جاهلًا وإن قُتل أثم ورجع عليه عقوبة ذلك في معاده وقد قيل لا تحقرنّ العدوّ الضعيف المهين لا سيّما إذا كان ذا حيلة فكيف الأسد مع جرأته وشدّته على أنّي قد علمت أنّ من احتقر عدوّه لضعفه أصابه ما أصاب وكيل البحر من الطيطوى.

قال شنزبة وكيف كان ذلك.

قال دمنة زعموا أنّ طيرًا من طيور الماء يدعى طيطوى كان عشّه على ساحل البحر ٨٦،٤
مع زوجته فلمّا كان أيّام تفريخهما قالت الأنثى للذكر إنّه قد آن لي أن أبيض فالتمس لي مكانًا حريزًا أبيض فيه فإنّي أخاف البحر إن أدار أدّ الماء أن يذهب بفراخنا.

فقال الذكر بيضي مكانك فإنّ الماء والعشب منّا قريب ومكاننا هذا أرفق بنا.

١ كذا ل٢؛ الأصل: ولولا. ٢ كذا ل٢؛ الأصل: و. ٣ فإنّه: الأصل: فانه لس. ٤ كذا ر؛ الأصل: محاله.

vultures.[24] Even if the lion's heart harbored nothing but benevolence and mercy, much malicious talk would soon erase those feelings and replace them with cruelty and harshness. Water, you know, is softer than speech, and rock harder than the heart, but if water drips long enough on rock, it soon makes its mark."

"What do you intend to do?" asked Dimnah. 4.85

"I see no way but to fight him," said Shanzabah. "You can devote your whole life to prayer, almsgiving, and asceticism, and still not obtain the reward obtained in a mere two hours by a just fighter defending his life. Whoever fights to defend his life from someone who would wrongfully deprive him of it achieves great reward and great renown: if he is slain, he achieves Paradise; if he slays, he achieves reward and victory."

"No one should risk his life unnecessarily," replied Dimnah. "If you perish, you've thrown your life away, and if you're victorious, it is due to the workings of fate. The wise man makes fighting his last resort, preferring skill and cunning whenever possible. I don't think you're right. You should fight your enemies only after exhausting every other strategy. Hastening to fight before it is warranted is overconfidence, rashness, and light-headedness; you should fight only in response to an opponent who makes the first move. Otherwise, if you kill your enemy you will be thought to have acted rashly, and if you are killed you will have sinned and earned punishment in the afterlife. It has been said: Don't disparage a lowly, weak opponent, especially a crafty one—let alone the lion, with all his boldness and strength! I have learned that to disparage an enemy for his weakness is to suffer the fate of the Sea's Custodian at the hands of the shorebird Ṭīṭawā."[25]

"And what was his fate?" asked Shanzabah.

The Shorebird Ṭīṭawā and the Sea

And Dimnah told the following tale: They say that a shorebird, the kind called Ṭīṭawā, had his nest by the sea with his mate. When it came time for them to raise their brood, the female said to the male, "It's time for me to lay eggs. Find me a safe place—I am fearful of the Sea. If he comes with the full force of his water, he'll sweep away our chicks." 4.86

"Why not right here?" replied the male. "We have water and reeds nearby; our home here is very comfortable."

قالت الأنثى يا غافل لتحسن نظرك فيما تقول فأنا على ذعر من مكاننا هذا لأنّ البحر إذا مدّ ذهب بفراخنا.

قال الذكر لا أظنّ البحر يجهل علينا لما يخاف من الاجتزاء.

قالت الأنثى ما أشدّ بغيك في هذه المقالة أما تستحي من إيعادك البحر أما تعرف نفسك في تهدّدك إيّاه. حقّاً ما يقال إنّه ليس شيء أشدّ على الرجل من عرفانه نفسه فاسمع منّي وانتقل من هذا المكان.

فأبى الذكر أن يطاوعها فلمّا أكثرت عليه ولم يسمع منها قالت إنّ من لا يسمع قول النصحاء خليق أن يصيبه ما أصاب السلحفاة حين لم تقبل قول نصحائها.[1]

قال الذكر وكيف كان ذلك.

قالت الأنثى زعموا أنّ عيناً كان فيها بطّتان وسلحفاة وكان بينهم[2] للجوار إلف ٨٧،٤
ومصادقة فنقص في بعض الأزمنة ماء تلك العين نقصاً فاحشاً فلمّا رأى البطّتان نقصان الماء قالتا ينبغي لنا ترك هذه العين والتحوّل عنها.

فودّعتا السلحفاة وقالتا عليك السلام فإنّا ذاهبتان.

قالت السلحفاة إنّما يشتدّ نقصان الماء على مثلي الذي لا يقدر أن يعيش إلّا بالماء فأمّا أنتما تعيشان حيث توجّهتما فاحتالا لي واذهبا بي معكما.

قالتا لا نقدر أن نذهب بك معنا إلّا أن تشرطي لنا إن حملناك في الهواء ورآنا الناس فذكروك[3] وصاحوا بك ألّا أجبتهم.

ففعلت ذلك وشرطت لهما أنّها[4] لا تجيب أحداً فقالت كيف السبيل إلى حملي.

قالتا تقضمين على وسط عود ونأخذ نحن بطرفيه ونستعلي بك في الهواء.

فرضيت بذلك فحملتاها واستعلتا بها فلمّا رآهما الناس تنادوا وقالوا انظروا إلى العجب سلحفاة بين بطّتين في الهواء.

فلمّا سمعت السلحفاة مقالتهم غاظها ذلك فقالت فقأ الله أعينكم. فلمّا فتحت فاها للمنطق وقعت إلى الأرض فماتت.

---

١ الأصل: نصحائه. ٢ كذا ش، پ٣٤٧٥؛ الأصل: سهما. ٣ كذا ش، ع: الأصل: فدكرون. ٤ الأصل: انهما.

"Fool, consider what you're saying! I'm afraid of this place—if the Sea rises, he'll carry off our chicks."

"I doubt the Sea would ever act so recklessly against us, because of the punishment he fears," replied the male.

"What boastful words!" said the female. "Aren't you ashamed of threatening the Sea? Have you so little knowledge of who you are to threaten him? How true what they say—nothing is harder than self-knowledge. Mark my words and move away from this place."

But the male refused to obey her. She repeated her request many times, but still he wouldn't listen. Then she said, "Those who disregard good advice are likely to suffer the fate of the turtle when she didn't accept the advice of her friends."

"And what was her fate?" he asked.

And the female told the following tale: They say that a pond was home to two ducks and a turtle. Being neighbors, they had become fast friends. One season, the water in the pond sank dangerously low. When the ducks saw the water recede, they said, "We'd better leave this pond and move elsewhere." 4.87 *The Ducks and the Turtle*

They said goodbye to the turtle: "Farewell! We're leaving."

And the turtle said, "Drought is an especially great hardship for a poor creature like me who can only live in water. You, however, can live wherever you go. Please find a way to take me with you."

"We'll take you with us on one condition," they replied. "Promise that if we carry you up into the air and people see you, talk about you, and shout at you, you won't answer."

The turtle promised not to reply to anyone. "But how," she asked, "will you carry me?"

"Bite onto the middle of a stick," they said, "and we'll take hold of the ends and lift you into the air."

The turtle agreed, and off they flew. When people saw them, they cried out, "Look at that marvel! A turtle in the air, between two ducks!"

When the turtle heard their words, she became angry and said, "May God poke out your eyes!" As soon as she opened her mouth and spoke, she fell to the ground and died.

٨٨،٤ قال الطيطوى الذكر سمعت مقالتك لا تخافي البحر. ففرّخت الأنثى مكانها.

فلمّا سمع ذلك وكيل البحر أحبّ أن يعرف كنه الذي يقدر عليه الطيطوى الذكر من الاحتراز وما حيلته في ذلك فأمهله حتّى إذا مدّ البحر ذهب بفراخ الطيطوى مع عشّهنّ فقالت الأنثى لمّا افتقدت فراخها إنّي كنت عرفت في بدء أمري أنّ هذا كائن وأنّه[1] سيرجع علينا ضرّ قلّة معرفتك بنفسك فانظر إلى ما أصابنا.

قال الذكر وأنا قد قلت في أوّل الأمر وأقول في آخره إن جهل علينا البحر أخذت منه بثأري فسترين صنعي[2] في ذلك واجتزائي.

٨٩،٤ فذهب إلى أصحابه فشكى إليهم ما لقي من البحر وقال إنّكم إخواني وأصحابي وثقاتي وأعواني في طلب ثأري فأعينوني واحتالوا لي فإنّه عسى أن ينزل بكم ما نزل بي اليوم.

فقالوا إنّا أعوانك على ما تستعين بنا ولكن ما عسى أن نقدر عليه من البحر.

قال الطيطوى اجتمعوا بنا سائر الطير فنشكو إليهم ما لقينا من البحر ونقول إنّكنّ طير مثلنا فأعينونا فإنّ الذي نزل بنا اليوم عسى أن ينزل بكنّ غداً.

٩٠،٤ فجمع الطيطوى الذكر جميع الطيور في مكان وشكى إليهنّ ما لقي من البحر فقال الطير نحن أعوانك فما عسى أن نقدر نعمل في البحر.

قال الطيطوى إنّا معشر الطير نسير إلى باب العنقاء بالمغرب فلا نزال نصيح وننادي بأعلى أصواتنا حتّى ترانا فتجتزي لنا من البحر.

٩١،٤ ففعلن ذلك فأجابهنّ العنقاء فقال ما الذي جمعكنّ ولِمَ تدعونني. فشكون إليه أمر البحر وقلن إنّك سيّدنا والملك الذي يقتعدك[3] أقوى من وكيل[4] البحر وقد جئناك فانطلق إليه ليعيننا[5] على البحر.

ففعل العنقاء وذهب إلى الذي اقتعده فسأله قتال البحر فلمّا عرف البحر ضعفه عند قوّة ذلك الملك الذي اقتعد العنقاء عجّل ردّ فراخ الطيطوى وترك مكان الطيطوى.

---

١ كذا ش، پ٣٤٧٥؛ ساقطة من الأصل. ٢ كذا ل٢؛ الأصل: صعمى. ٣ كذا پ٣٤٧٥، ش، ع؛ الأصل: نعقد اتك.
٤ كذا ع، پ٣٤٧٥؛ الأصل: ملك. ٥ الأصل: لتعيننا.

The male Ṭīṭawā said, "I hear what you're saying, but you needn't be afraid of the Sea." So the female hatched her chicks where they were. 4.88

Now, when the Sea's Custodian heard of this, he wanted to determine the extent of the male Ṭīṭawā's ability to protect himself and how he would manage to do it, so he waited until the tide rose, and carried off the Ṭīṭawā's chicks, along with the nest. Bereft of her chicks, the female said to the male, "I knew from the start that this would happen and that your lack of self-knowledge would cause us harm. Just look at what's happened to us!"

"I said to you at the beginning, and I say it to you now," replied the male, "that if the Sea behaved foolishly toward us, I would take revenge. You'll see what I'm going to do and how I'm going to get even."

He went to his comrades and complained about how he had been treated 4.89
by the Sea: "You are my brothers, comrades I trust to help me seek redress. Assist me. Devise a plan for me. What happened to me today might also happen to you."

"We'll help you to get what you seek," they replied, "but what can we do to the Sea?"

The Ṭīṭawā said, "Let's assemble all the birds and complain to them about how the Sea has treated us. We'll say to them, 'You are birds like us. Help us, because what has happened to us today might happen to you tomorrow.'"

So the male Ṭīṭawā assembled all the birds in one place and complained 4.90
to them about how he had been treated by the Sea. "We're ready to help you," they said, "but what can we do to the Sea?"

"We birds will go as one to the palace of the Phoenix of the West," said the Ṭīṭawā. "We'll cry and cry as loudly as we can, and call out to her until she sees us and forces the Sea to make amends!"[26]

That is what they did, and the Phoenix responded to them with a ques- 4.91
tion: "What has brought you together, and why do you summon me?" They complained to her about the Sea. "You are our leader," they said, "and the king who rides mounted upon you is stronger than the Custodian of the Sea. Go and ask him to help us against the Sea!"

And the Phoenix did so. She went to the king who rides her and asked him to fight the Sea. When the Sea realized his weakness compared with the strength of the king who rides the Phoenix, he immediately returned the Ṭīṭawā's chicks and never again touched the Ṭīṭawā's home.

٩٢،٤ وإنّما قلت هذه الأحدوثة لأنّه لا ينبغي لك قتال الأسد ولا أرى لك ذلك.

قال شنزبة ما أنا بمقاتل الأسد ولا ناصب له العداوة سرًّا ولا علانية ولا بمتغيّر عن أحسن ما كنت عليه حتّى يبدو لي ما كنت أتخوّف.

فكره دمنة قوله لا أتغيّر للأسد عن حالي وظنّ أنّ الأسد إن لم ير من شنزبة العلامات التي ذكرها له اتّهمه فقال انطلق فستعرف حين تنظر إلى الأسد ما يريبك.

قال شنزبة فكيف أعرف ذلك منه.

فقال دمنة إن الأسد حين ينظر إليك ينتصب مقعياً نحوك رافعاً صدره مسدّدًا نظره نحوك صارًّا أذنيه فاغرًا فاه يضرب بذنبه الأرض فاعلم أنّه يريد قتلك.

قال شنزبة لئن رأيت من الأسد هذه العلامات فما فيما تقول من شكّ.

٩٣،٤ ثمّ إنّ دمنة لمّا فرغ من تحميل الأسد على الثور والثور على الأسد توجّه إلى كليلة فلمّا التقيا قال كليلة إلى[1] أين بلغ عملك الذي كنت فيه.

قال دمنة قد تقارب الفراغ على ما أحبّ فلا تشكّنّ في ذلك ولا تظننّ أنّ للإخاء بين الأخوين تماسكاً[2] إذا احتال لقطع ما بينهما ذو الحيلة والرفق قطعهما قطعَ الماءِ الحجرُ.

٩٤،٤ وانطلق كليلة ودمنة جميعاً ليحضرا[3] الأسد فوافقا شنزبة قد دخل على الأسد فلمّا رآه الأسد مقبلاً انتصب مقعياً وصرّ أذنيه وفغر فاه وضرب الأرض بذنبه فلم يشكّ الثور إلّا أنّه يريد قتله فقال في نفسه ما صاحب السلطان فيما لا يأمن[4] بوادره وتغيّر ما في نفسه عليه لما[5] يرقّي إليه أهل البغي والكذب إلّا كصاحب الحيّة التي يجاورها في مبيته ومقيله فلا يدري متى تهيج به وكمجاور الأسد في عرينه وكالسابح في الماء الذي فيه التمساح فلا يدري متى يساوره. وفكّر في هذا وهو يتهيّأ لقتال الأسد إن هو أراده.

---

١ كذا ر؛ ساقطة من الأصل. ٢ أنّ للإخاء . . . تماسكًا: كذا ر؛ الأصل: ان المتحاس الاخوين. ٣ كذا ش؛ الأصل: ليحصر. ٤ الأصل: يومن. ٥ الأصل: ما.

"I've told you this story because it wouldn't be good for you to fight the lion, and I don't think you should do it." 4.92

"I won't fight the lion," said Shanzabah, "or make any hostile moves, either secretly or openly. I'll be on my best behavior toward him, unchanged in any respect, unless there is an obvious threat to me."

Dimnah was displeased when Shanzabah said that he wouldn't change his behavior toward the lion. He thought he would fall under suspicion if the lion didn't see in Shanzabah any of the signs he had described, so he said, "Go! As soon as you look at the lion, you'll see things that will make you uneasy."

"How will I know?" asked Shanzabah.

"If when the lion looks at you," said Dimnah, "he sits up on his haunches, raises his chest, stares at you, pricks up his ears, opens his mouth wide, and beats the ground with his tail, you can be sure he intends to kill you."

"If I see these signs in him, what you're saying will be beyond a doubt," replied Shanzabah.

Dimnah went to Kalīlah as soon as he was done turning the lion against the ox, and the ox against the lion. "How has your project progressed?" Kalīlah asked. 4.93

"It's about to turn out just as I wish," Dimnah replied. "No doubt about it! Don't imagine that the brotherhood between friends can hold. When a clever schemer uses his wiles to separate them, he can slice them apart just as a stone slices through water."

Kalīlah and Dimnah went together to visit the lion. Shanzabah entered just as they arrived. When the lion saw him coming, he sat up on his haunches, pricked up his ears, opened his mouth wide, and beat the ground with his tail. The ox, certain that the lion intended to kill him, said to himself, "A ruler's companion is never safe from the shifts in his master's moods and the changes in his attitude due to the influence of malicious liars. He is like a man who shares his bed with a snake, not knowing when it will attack him, or one who lives with a lion in his den, or one who swims in a lake with crocodiles—he doesn't know when he will be attacked." Such were his thoughts as he prepared to fight the lion, should the lion so desire. 4.94

فلمّا نظر الأسد إلى حال الثور والعلامات التي ذكرها له دمنة لم يشكّ إلّا أنه جاء ٩٥،٤
لقتاله فواثبه ونشب[١] بينهما القتال فاشتدّ قتال الأسد والثور حتّى طال[٢] وسالت
بينهما الدماء جميعاً.

فلمّا رأى كليلة الأسد قد بلغ من الثور ما بلغ وسالت منه الدماء قال لدمنة انظر إلى حيلتك أيّها الفسل ما أنكدها وأسوأ عاقبتها.

قال دمنة وما سوء عاقبتها.

قال كليلة فضيحة الأسد وهلاك الثور وتفرّق كلمة الجند مع ما استبان لي من ٩٦،٤
خرقك فيما ادّعيت الرفق. أوما تعلم أنّ أخرق الخرق ما كلّف صاحبه القتال وهو يجد إلى غير ذلك سبيلاً أوليس الرجل ربّما أمكنته فرصة في القتال فتركها مخافة التعرّض للمخاطرة والنكبة ورجاء أن يقدر على حاجته بغير ذلك. وإذا كان وزير السلطان من يأمره بالمحاربة فيما يقدر على حاجته بالمسالمة فهو له أشدّ عداوة من عداوة المعادي بعداوته وكما أنّ اللسان تدركه الزمانة من نهكة الفؤاد وكذلك النجدة تدركها الزمانة من خطإ الرأي فإنّ النجدة والرأي إذا فقد أحدهما صاحبه لم يكن للآخر غناء عند المحاربة ولكن للرأي على النجدة الفضل فإنّ أموراً كثيرة يجزيها الرأي دون البأس ولا يجزي البأس شيئاً يستغنى به عن الرأي. ومن أراد المكر ولم يعرف وجوه الأمر الذي يأتيه فيه كان عمله كعملك وقد كان عملك ببغيك وعجبك.

ولم أزل منذ رأيت شرهك وسمعت كلامك أتوقّى داهية ومعرّة تجلبها عليّ[٣] وعلى نفسك فإنّ ذا العقل يبدأ بالنظر في الأمور والأعمال قبل ملابستها فما رجا منها أن يتمّ على ما يريد أقدم عليه وما خاف ألّا يتمّ انصرف عنه ولم يتلبّس به.

ولم يمنعني من نهيك في بدء أمرك وتوقيفك على عيوبك إلّا أنّه قد كان أمراً[٤] ٩٧،٤
لم أستطع إظهاره وابتغاء الشهود والأعوان عليك فيه وعرفت أنّ قولي لا يزيدك خيراً ولا يردّك عن شهوة فأمّا الآن حين استبان لي عجز رأيك وخرقك ورأيت ثمرة عملك وسوء عاقبة أمرك فسأخبرك عن نفسك وأقفك على عيوبك. من ذلك

١ الأصل: وسبب. ٢ كذا ر؛ الأصل: طالت. ٣ كذا ر؛ الأصل: علك. ٤ كذا ش؛ الأصل: امر.

As soon as the lion saw how the ox was behaving and perceived all the signs mentioned by Dimnah, he was certain that the ox had come to fight him. So he pounced on him and a fight ensued. The lion and the ox fought long and hard, until both were covered in blood. 4.95

When Kalīlah saw the lion bleeding and understood what he had endured from the ox, he said to Dimnah, "You wretch, look at your clever scheme now! How despicable! What an evil outcome!"

"And what evil outcome do you see?" asked Dimnah.

Kalīlah replied, "The lion's disgrace, the ox's destruction, and the sowing of discord in the army—to say nothing of your evident clumsiness in matters where you claimed to have skill. Don't you know that the worst foolishness is that which leads to unnecessary fighting? Don't those in a position to fight often avoid it, in fear of danger or defeat, hoping to attain their objective by other means? A minister who orders war when the objective can be achieved peacefully is more harmful to his ruler than an enemy. Just as the tongue can be crippled by a disorder of the heart,[27] so can courage be crippled by misjudgment. Courage and judgment need each other: alone, without their comrade, they are useless in battle. But good judgment is superior to courage, as there are many matters in which good judgment will serve without might, whereas might alone can achieve nothing in the absence of good judgment. Someone who wants to use cunning, but doesn't know every detail of a matter he embarks on, will act as you have in your insolence and conceit. 4.96

"Ever since I saw your greed and heard your talk, I have been expecting you to bring disaster and disgrace on us both. A wise man begins by reflecting on matters and actions before embarking on them: he proceeds with those he hopes will work out as he wishes and avoids becoming embroiled in those he fears will not.

"The only thing that prevented me from restraining you from the start and acquainting you with your faults was that it was something I couldn't make public for want of witnesses and supporters. Also, I knew that my words wouldn't make you a better person or turn you away from your desires. Now, however, I will tell you about yourself and acquaint you with your faults, for your misjudgment and clumsiness have become clear to me and I have seen 4.97

أنك[١] تحسن الكلام ولا تحسن العمل وقد قيل إنّه ليس شيء أهلك للسلطان من كلّ صاحب يحسن القول فلا يحسن العمل وإنّما غرّ الأسد منك أنّك تحسن الكلام وأهلكه أنّك لم تحسن العمل ولا خير في القول إلّا مع العمل ولا في المنظر إلّا مع المخبر ولا في المال إلّا مع الجود ولا في الصديق إلّا مع الوفاء ولا في العفّة إلّا مع الورع ولا في الصدقة إلّا مع النيّة ولا في الحياة إلّا مع الصحّة والأمن والسرور.

٩٨،٤ وقد سوّطت[٢] أمرًا لا يداويه إلّا العاقل الرفيق كالمريض الذي يجتمع عليه فساد المرّة والريح والدم والبلغم فلا يستطيع دواءه إلّا الطبيب الرفيق. واعلم أنّ الأدب يذهب عن العاقل السكر ويزيد الأحمق سكرًا كما أنّ النهار يزيد كلّ ذي بصر بصرًا ويزيد الخفّاش سوء بصر وعمى. وذو العقل لا تبطره منزلة أصابها ولا شرف بلغه وإن عظم كالجبل الذي لا يتزلزل وإن اشتدّت الريح.

٩٩،٤ وقد أذكر في أمرك شيئًا كنت سمعته يقال في السلطان أنّه إذا كان صالحًا وكان وزراؤه وزراء سوء امتنع خيره من الناس فلم يجترئ[٣] عليه أحد ولم يدن منه وإنّ مثله في ذلك مثل الماء الصافي الطيّب الذي فيه التمساح فلا يستطيع الرجل وإن كان سابحًا وكان إلى الماء محتاجًا أن يدخله. وإنّما حلية الملوك وزينتهم قرابتهم أن يكثروا ويصلحوا وإنّك أردت أن لا يدنو من الأسد واحد غيرك ولا يكون لأحد عنده منزلة سواك وإنّما السلطان بأصحابه كالبحر بأمواجه. ومن الخرق والحمق التماس الرجل الإخوان بغير الوفاء والأجر بالرياء ومودّة النساء بالغلظة ونفع نفسه بضرّ الناس والعلم والأدب والفضل بالدعة والخفض. ولكن ما يغني هذه المقالة عنك وما[٤] مبلغ هذه العظة وتأديبي إيّاك وأنا أعلم أنّ الأمر في ذلك كما قال الرجل لطائر حيث قال له لا تلتمس تقويم ما لا يستقيم ولا تعالج تأديب من لا يتأدّب.

قال دمنة وكيف كان ذلك.

١٠٠،٤ قال كليلة زعموا أنّ جماعة من القرود كانوا في جبل من الجبال فرأين في ليلة باردة يراعة في الليل كالنار فظنّوا أنها شرارة فجمعن حطبًا فوضعنه عليها وجعلن ينفخن

---

١ كذا ر؛ الأصل: انك لا. ٢ كذا ع؛ الأصل: سرطت. ٣ ل٢: يجتري؛ الأصل: يجرى. ٤ كذا ر؛ ساقطة من الأصل.

their evil consequences. You are good at talking, but bad at action. Nothing, they say, is more dangerous to a ruler than a companion who is good at talking, but bad at action. Your fine words beguiled the lion, but your ineptitude caused his downfall. Words without deeds; theory without experience; wealth without generosity; friendship without loyalty; abstinence without piety; almsgiving without good intentions; and life without health, safety, and happiness—there is no good in any of these.

"You have stirred up an affair that only the wise and skillful can remedy— 4.98
just as only a skilled physician can cure a patient who suffers from corruption of the bile, the wind, the blood, and the phlegm all at the same time. Learning sobers the wise, but intoxicates the fool—just as daylight sharpens the sight of every creature that can see, but dulls the sight of a bat. A wise man is not puffed up by office or honor, however great: he is like a mountain, unshaken even in a gale.

"Your case reminds me of something I've heard: They say that a ruler's 4.99
goodness will be inaccessible if he is good but his ministers are evil, as no one will dare approach him. He will be like a pool of pure water harboring a crocodile: you can't enter it, even if you can swim or need water. A numerous and prosperous entourage is a king's crowning glory, but you have desired that only you, and no one else, should have access to the lion. You wanted no one else to enjoy any standing with him, whereas the ruler and his companions are like the sea and its waves. How stupid and foolish it is to seek friends by means of disloyalty, seek reward by means of hypocrisy, seek a woman's love by means of boorishness, seek one's own benefit by means of harm to others, or seek knowledge and virtue by means of sloth and indolence. But what's the use of all this preaching and instruction? I know that it's just as when the man once said to the bird, 'Don't try to put straight what cannot be straightened, or instruct those who will not be instructed!'"

"And how was that?" asked Dimnah.

The Monkey, the Firefly, and the Bird

And Kalīlah told the following tale: Once, they say, a band of monkeys 4.100
who lived on a mountain saw a firefly on a cold night.[28] Thinking it was a spark, they collected firewood, piled it on her, and began blowing on it with their mouths and fanning it with their hands. A bird sitting in a nearby tree

بأفواههنّ وأيديهم وقريب منهنّ شجرة عليها طائر فجعل يناديهنّ وينهاهنّ ويقول لا تتعبن فإنّ الذي ترين ليس بنار. فلم ينتهين فلمّا طال ذلك نزل من الشجرة ليدنو من القردة فيخبرها ومرّ به رجل فقال له أيّها الطائر لا تلتمس تقويم ما لا يستقيم ولا تأديب من لا يتأدّب فإنّ الحجر الذي لا يُقدر على قطعه بالفأس لا تجرّب به السيوف والعود الذي لا ينحني لا يعالج انحناؤه ومن عالج ما لا يستقيم ندم. فأبى الطائر أن يطيعه وتقدّم إلى القردة[1] فأخذه قرد فضرب به الأرض فقتله.

فهذا مثلك في قلّة الانتفاع بالأدب والموعظة ثمّ إنّك مع ذلك قد غلب عليك ١٠١،٤
الخبث والفخر وهما خلّتا سوء والخبث شرّهما عاقبة ومثل ذلك ما كان من أمر الخبّ شريك المغفّل.

قال دمنة وكيف كان ذلك.

قال كليلة زعموا أنّ خبًا ومغفّلًا اشتركا في تجارة فبينما هما يمشيان في طريق من ١٠٢،٤
الطرق إذ تخلّف المغفّل عن صاحبه تخلّفًا فوجد بدرة فيها مائة ألف دينار فأخذها وأخبر الخبّ بها وبدا لهما أن يرجعا إلى أرضهما.

حتّى إذا دنوَا من مكانهما قعدا لاقتسام الدنانير فقال المغفّل للخبّ خذ نصفها وأعطني نصفها. فكان الخبّ قد وطّن نفسه على أن يذهب بها كلّها فقال[2] لا نقتسمها فإنّ الشركة والتفاوض أقرب إلى المخالطة والصفاء ولكن خذ منها بعضها وأنا آخذ مثل ذلك وندفن البقيّة مكانًا حريزًا فإذا احتجنا إلى البقيّة جئنا جميعًا وأخذنا حاجتنا.

قال المغفّل فافعل. فأخذا من تلك الدنانير شيئًا يسيرًا ودفنا ما سوى ذلك في أصل شجرة من عظام الدوح ثمّ إنّ الخبّ خالفه إلى الشجرة فأخذ الدنانير كلّها وسوّى الأرض كما كانت.

ثمّ قال الخبّ للمغفّل بعد ذلك بأيّام إنّا قد احتجنا إلى النفقة أفلا ننطلق إلى ١٠٣،٤
الدنانير فنأخذ منها نفقة. فانطلقا جميعًا فلمّا احتفرا المكان لم يجدا شيئًا فأقبل الخبّ على شعره نتفًا وعلى صدره ضربًا وصاح وقال لا يثقنّ أحد بأخ ولا يغترّنّ بصاحب.

١ كذا ر؛ الأصل: القرد. ٢ قد وطّن...فقال: كذا ر؛ ساقطة من الأصل.

called to them, "Don't tire yourselves out! What you saw isn't fire." But they wouldn't be deterred. Losing patience, the bird flew down to come closer to the monkeys and set them straight. A man who happened to be passing said, "Bird, don't try to set straight what cannot be straightened or instruct those who cannot be instructed! You don't test a sword on a rock that can't be split with an ax, and you don't try to bend brittle wood. To labor over what cannot be straightened is to regret it." But the bird refused to heed him. He approached the monkeys, and one of them grabbed him, dashed him on the ground, and killed him.

"This is exactly the way you are when it comes to how little you benefit 4.101
from instruction and admonition. Furthermore, deceitfulness and boasting are the keynotes of your character: both are bad, though deceitfulness entails worse consequences. This is illustrated by what happened to the swindler who was the simpleton's partner."

"And what happened to him?" asked Dimnah.

And Kalīlah told the following tale: Once, they say, a swindler and a sim- 4.102
pleton became business partners. While they were walking on the road, the simpleton lagged behind and found a purse containing a hundred thousand dinars. He picked it up and told the swindler about it. They decided to head back home.

The Swindler and His Partner the Simpleton

Close to town, they sat down to divide the money. "You take half, and give me half," the simpleton said to the swindler. But the swindler, intent on taking it all, said, "Let's not divide it: partnership and joint ownership are more conducive to familiarity and friendship. You take some, I'll take the same amount, and we'll bury the rest somewhere safe. When we need the rest, we'll come back together and get what we need."

"Fine," said the simpleton. So they took some of the money and buried the rest by the root of an imposing tree. Afterward, the swindler, unbeknownst to the simpleton, came back to the tree, made off with all the money, and leveled the ground over the spot.

A few days later, the swindler said to the simpleton, "We need to pay 4.103
some expenses. Why don't we go and get some more of the money?" So they set out together. They dug up the spot, but found nothing. The swindler began tearing his hair and beating his breast, and cried out, "Let no man

أخالفتَ إلى الدنانير فأخذتها. فجعل المغفّل يمتعض ويلتعن ولا يزداد الخبّ إلّا شدّة عليه في القول ويقول فمن أخذها غيرك وهل يشعر بها سوانا.

١٠٤،٤ فتعلّق بالمغفّل وقاده إلى القاضي فاقتصّا القصّة وزعم أنّ المغفّل هو الذي أخذ الدنانير.

فقال له القاضي هل لك من بيّنة.

قال الخبّ نعم تشهد لي الشجرة التي كانت الدنانير مدفونة في أصلها.

فأنكر القاضي قوله وتعجّب من استشهاده الشجرة فأمر بتسليمه إلى أن يكفل بنفسه وقال ائتوني غداً حتّى أطّلع طِلع[١] ما ادّعى من شهادة الشجرة.

١٠٥،٤ فانصرف الخبّ إلى بيته فقصّ على أبيه القصّة وقال يا أبت إنّي لم أستشهد الشجرة إلّا لأمر كنت قد رأيت فيه واتّكلت عليك فيما ادّعيت فيه فإن أنت طاوعتني فقد أحرزنا تلك الدنانير وكسبنا من المغفّل مثلها.

قال أبو الخبّ وما ذلك الأمر الذي تأمرني به.

قال الخبّ إنّي كنت احتفرت لتلك الدنانير تحت شجرة عظيمة جوفاء من عظام الدوح في جوفها مدخل رجل لا يُرى وإنّي أحبّ أن تذهب الليلة فتدخل في ذلك المكان فإذا جاء القاضي غداً فسأل الشجرة عن شهادتها تكلّمت من جوفها وقلت المغفّل هو الذي أخذ الدنانير.

قال أبو الخبّ يا بنيّ إنّه ربّ متمحّل قد أوقعه تمحّله في ورطة فأنا أخاف أن يكون تمحّلك كتمحّل العلجوم.

قال الخبّ وكيف كان ذلك.

١٠٦،٤ قال أبو الخبّ زعموا أنّ علجوماً جاورته حيّة فكان إذا أفرخ العلجوم ذهبت الحيّة إلى عشّه فأكلت فروخه وكان العلجوم وافقه مكانه ذلك فلم يستطع تركه وحزن لما أصاب من الحيّة ففطن لما به سرطان فدنا وسأله ما يحزنك. فأخبره بما لقي من الحيّة. قال السرطان أفلا أدلّك على أمر تنتقم به من الحيّة.

---

١ كذا ر؛ ساقطة من الأصل.

trust his brother or be fooled by his companion! Did you come back and take the money?" The simpleton became angry and swore he hadn't, but this only made the swindler more incensed. "Who else could have taken it?" he asked. "Does anyone else know about it?"

The swindler grabbed the simpleton and hauled him before the judge, 4.104
and they told their story. The swindler claimed that the simpleton was the one who had taken the money.

"Have you any evidence?" asked the judge.

"Yes," said the swindler. "The tree where the money was buried will testify for me!"

The judge, incredulous and amazed at the idea of calling a tree to testify, ordered that the swindler place himself in the custody of a bondsman,[29] and said to the bondsman, "Bring him to me tomorrow, so I can learn the truth about his claim that the tree will testify."

The swindler then returned home and told his father the story. "Father," 4.105
he said, "I called the tree as a witness because I have a plan. I'm relying on you: if you do as I say, we keep the money we have and we win as much again from the simpleton."[30]

"What do you want me to do?" asked his father.

"I buried the money," the swindler said, "at the foot of an imposing tree with a hollow a man can enter and hide in without being seen. I'd like you to go tonight and get inside the tree. Tomorrow, when the judge comes and asks the tree to testify, speak from inside the hollow, saying, 'The simpleton is the one who took the money.'"

"Son," said the swindler's father, "many a clever man has been undone by his own cunning. I'm afraid your cleverness will be like the heron's."[31]

"And how did his cleverness undo him?" he asked.

The Heron, the Snake, and the Mongoose

The swindler's father told the following tale: Once, they say, a heron had 4.106
a snake for a neighbor. Whenever the heron had young to raise, the snake would go to the nest and eat them. The place suited the heron well, so he couldn't just leave it, but he was saddened by what the snake was doing to him. A crab, surmising what he was feeling, approached the heron and asked what was making him so sad. The heron told him what the snake had done and the crab said, "Shall I show you how you can take revenge on the snake?"

قال وما ذلك.

فأومأ السرطان إلى جحر قبالته فقال أترى ذلك الجحر إنّ فيه ابن عرس وهو عدوّ للحيّات فاجمع سمكاً كثيراً ثمّ ضع منه شيئاً عند جحر ابن عرس وانظم ما سوى ذلك نظماً فيما بين جحر ابن عرس وجحر الحيّة فيقتلها.

ففعل العلجوم ذلك وانتهى ابن عرس إلى الحيّة فقتلها ثمّ جعل يرجع إلى ذلك المكان للعادة يلتمس السمك فلم يجد شيئاً فلم يزل يلتمس حتّى وقع على عشّ العلجوم لقرب مكانه وجواره من جحر الحيّة فأكل العلجوم وفراخه.

١٠٧،٤ وإنّما ضربت لك هذا المثل لتعلم أنّ من لم يتثبّت في الحيل أوقعته حيلته في أشدّ ممّا احتال لغيره.[١]

قال الخبّ قد سمعت هذا المثل فلا تهابنّ هذا الأمر فإنّه أيسر ممّا تظنّ.[٢]

فتابع الشيخ ابنه فانطلق إلى الشجرة فدخل في جوفها وغدا القاضي بالخبّ والمغفّل إلى الشجرة فسألها هل عندك من شهادة.

فأجابه الشيخ إنّ المغفّل هو الذي أخذ الدنانير.

فاشتدّ عجب القاضي واستنكره وجعل ينظر ويتفطّن وطاف بالشجرة فبصر بذلك الجوف فلم ير شيئاً لأنّ الرجل كان قد ارتفع عن المكان الذي تناله العين فأمر القاضي بحطب فجُمع ثمّ ألهب فيه ناراً ودخّن في ذلك الجوف فتصبّر أبو الخبّ ساعة ثمّ أصابه الجهد فصاح فنادى واستغاث فأمر به القاضي فأُخرج بعد ما أشفى على الموت وعاقب الخبّ وغرّمه الدنانير فانقلب بأبيه على ظهره ميتاً.

١٠٨،٤ وإنّما ضربت لك هذا المثل لتعلم أنّ المكر والخديعة ربّما كان صاحبها هو المغبون وأنت يا دمنة جامع للخبث والعجز وكان الذي اجتنيت من ثمرة فعلك ما ترى مع ما أنّك لعلّك لست بناجٍ منه وكذلك عاقبة من كان مثلك فيما بغى فإنّك ذو لسانين وذو وجهين وذو لونين وقد قيل إنّما عذوبة ماء الأنهار ما لم ينته إلى البحر ولم يخالطه وأنّه لا تزال العشيرة في سعادة مستقيماً أمرها مجتمعاً

---

١ في ... غيره: كذا ر؛ ساقطة من الأصل. ٢ كذا ر؛ الأصل: يطن.

"How?" asked the heron.

The crab pointed to a burrow in front of him. "See that burrow? There is a mongoose in it, an enemy of snakes.[32] Gather lots of fish; put some of them by the mongoose's burrow and line up the rest between the mongoose's burrow and the snake's den. The mongoose will then kill the snake."

The heron did this, and the mongoose followed the fish to the snake and killed it. But then, out of habit, the mongoose came back, searching for more fish. When he didn't find any, he kept searching until he stumbled upon the heron's nearby nest, and devoured both the heron and his young.

"I've told you this story to show that if you aren't careful you risk landing 4.107
yourself in worse trouble than you planned to inflict on the other person."

"I hear what you're saying," said the swindler, "but don't be afraid! It's easier than you imagine."

So the old man, following his son's wishes, went to the tree, and got inside. The next morning, the judge, the swindler, and the simpleton came to the tree. The judge asked it, "Do you have any testimony?"

"Yes," replied the old man. "The simpleton took the money."

Amazed and incredulous, the judge began looking hard and trying to figure it out. He walked around the tree and noticed the hollow, but saw nothing because the man was too high up inside to be seen. So he ordered that firewood be gathered and lit, so as to fill the hollow with smoke. The swindler's father held out for a time, but finally, overcome, he cried out for help. On the judge's order, he was pulled out—just as he was dying. The swindler was punished, forfeited the money, and went home carrying his dead father on his back.

Kalīlah said, "I've told you this story to show you that someone who 4.108
practices cunning and deception is often himself the loser. You, Dimnah, combine deceit and incompetence. Now you've seen the consequences of your deeds, and you're unlikely to come out unscathed. Such is the end of people who act as wrongfully as you have. You are two-tongued, two-faced, and duplicitous. River water, they say, is sweet until it reaches the sea and mixes with it; a family lives in happiness, prosperity, and unity until a wicked man sows discord among them; and friends remain friends until

شملها[١] ما لم ينشأ فيها ناشئ سوء ولا تزال المودّة ثابتة بين أهلها ما لم يداخلها ذو لسانين فإنّ ذا اللسانين ليس شيء أشبه منه بالحيّة إلّا هو لأنّ الحيّة ذات لسانين وهو يجري من لسانيه[٢] سمّ كسمّها ولم أزل لذلك السمّ من لسانك خائفاً مشفقاً من أن يعديني بشرّ كارهاً لقربك ذاكراً لموعظة العقلاء في اجتناب أهل الفجور وإن كانوا ذوي قرابة وصحبة فإنّ ذلك من الأصحاب والإخوان إنّما هو كالحيّة يربّيها صاحبها ويمسحها ثمّ لا يكون له منها ولا يجد منها إلّا اللدغ.

٤،١٠٩ وكان يقال الزم ذا العقل والكرم واسترسل إليه وإيّاك وفراقه ولا عليك أن تصحب ذا العقل وإن كان غير محمود الخليقة ولكن احترس من سيّء أخلاقه[٣] وانتفع بعقله ولا تدع مواصلة الكريم وإن لم يُحمد عقله ولكن انتفع بكرمه وانفعه بعقلك وفرّ الفرار كلّه من اللئيم الأحمق. فأنا بالفرار منك والاجتناب لك جدير وكيف يرجو عندك اليوم إخوانك وفاء وكرماً مع ما رأيتك قد صنعت بملكك الذي كرّمك وشرّفك ما صنعت بل مثلك في ذلك كما قال التاجر إنّ أرضاً يأكل جرذها مائة منّ من حديد يوشك فيها أن تختطف بزاتها الفيلة.

قال دمنة وكيف ذلك.

٤،١١٠ قال كليلة زعموا أنّه كان بأرض كذا تاجر قد تلف ماله فأراد التوجّه لوجه من الوجوه ابتغاء الرزق فكان معه مرزبة وزنها مائة منّ من حديد واستودعها رجلاً من معارفه وانطلق لوجهه فرجع بعد حين والتمس حديده من صاحبه فوجده قد باعه واستنفقه[٤] صاحبه وقال له كنت وضعت حديدك في ناحية البيت فأكله الجرذان.

فقال التاجر لقد كان يبلغني عن الجرذان أنّه ليس شيء أقطع للحديد من أسنانها وما أهون المرزئة فالحمد لله على صلاحك.

٤،١١١ ففرح الرجل بما سمع من التاجر وقال أقم عندي اليوم.

---

١ مستقيماً . . . شملها: الأصل: مستقيم أمرها مجتمع شملها. ٢ الأصل: لسانيها. ٣ كذا ر؛ الأصل: الحلق. ٤ باعه و: كذا ر؛ ساقطة من الأصل.

a two-tongued person comes between them. Nothing is more like a snake than a two-tongued man. A snake has two tongues, and what drips from them is venom, just like yours. I've always been afraid of the venom of your tongue, fearful that it would infect me with evil; I've been reluctant to be near you, mindful of the warning of the wise: Keep away from dissolute people though they be your own kin or companions. Such a companion or friend is like a snake: its owner raises it and treats it with kindness, but all he gets from it is a bite.

"They also say: Cleave to the intelligent and generous man, cultivate his 4.109
company, and don't part from him. There is no harm in associating with an intelligent man, even if his character leaves something to be desired: guard yourself from his vices, but benefit from his intelligence. Likewise, do not spurn the generous man, even if his intelligence leaves something to be desired: benefit from his generosity and help him with your intelligence. But shun completely the man who is both low-minded and foolish. Thus, it is right for me to shun and avoid you. How can your friends expect loyalty and generosity, now that I've seen what you have done to your king, who was generous to you and raised you to honor? In this respect, what the merchant said applies to you: 'In a land where rats can eat a hundredweight of iron, there is nothing preposterous about hawks carrying off elephants!'"

"And how does that saying apply to me?" asked Dimnah.

The Mice Who Ate a Hundredweight of Iron

And Kalīlah told the following tale: In a certain land, they say, lived a 4.110
merchant who, having exhausted his wealth, decided to travel abroad to seek his livelihood. He had in his possession an iron rod weighing a hundred *mann*,[33] which he left with an acquaintance for safekeeping, then set out. After a while he returned and asked for the rod, but the acquaintance, who he discovered had sold the iron and spent the proceeds, said to him, "I put your rod to one side in the house but the rats ate it up."

"Indeed," said the merchant, "I've heard that nothing cuts iron better than rats' teeth. A small loss! Thank God you're well."

Delighted by the merchant's reaction, the acquaintance said, "Come stay 4.111
with me today."

فخرج التاجر من عنده وقد وعده أن يرجع إليه فحمل لصاحبه ذلك ابناً صغيراً فخبّأه وانصرف إلى الرجل ففقد أبو الغلام ابنه فقال له هل رأيت ابني.

فقال التاجر لقد رأيت حين دنوت منكم بازياً اختطف غلاماً فعسى أن يكون ابنك.

فضجّ الرجل وصاح فقال من رأى أو سمع أنّ البزاة تختطف الغلمان.

فقال التاجر أما إنّ أرضاً يأكل جرذها مائة منّ حديد فليس بنكير أن تختطف بزاتها الفيلة.

قال الرجل فأنا أكلت الحديد وسحتاً أكلت فاردد عليّ ابني وخذ حديدك.

١١٢،٤ وإنّما ضربت لك هذا المثل لتعلم أنّك إذا غدرت بملكك ذي البلاء الحسن عندك فلا شكّ في غدرك بمن سواه وقد علمت أنّك ليس للمودّة عندك موضع فإنّه لا شيء أضيع من مودّة تُمنح[1] من لا وفاء له أو بلاء حسن يُصطنع به عند من لا شكر له وأدب صالح يُؤدَّب به من لا يستمع ولا ينتفع به أو سرّ[2] يُستودع من لا حصافة[3] له ولست في طمع من تغيير طبعك لأنّي قد عرفت أنّ شجرة المرار لو طُليت بالعسل والسمن لا تثمر إلّا مرّاً وقد خفت صحبتك على رأيي وأخلاقي فإنّ صحبة الأخيار تورث الخير وصحبة الأشرار تورث الشرّ كالريح إذا مرّت على النتن احتملت نتناً وإذا مرّت على الطيب احتملت طيباً وقد عرفت ثقل كلامي عليك فإنّه لم تزل الناس يستثقل جهلاؤهم عقلاءهم ولؤماؤهم كرماءهم وذو العوج يقيمه منهم مستقيمهم وسفهاؤهم[4] يردّهم[5] حلماؤهم ولم يزل يعادي وينتقص كلّ لئيم من الرجال كريماً وكلّ فسل حازماً وكلّ مبغض محبّاً وكلّ بخيل جواداً وكلّ طالح صالحاً.

١١٣،٤ فانتهى كليلة بهذا الكلام وقد فرغ الأسد من الثور ففكّر بعد ما قتله وسكن عنه الغضب فقال لقد كان ذا عقل ورأي وخلق ولا أدري لعلّه كان بريئاً مبغيّاً عليه. فحزن وندم.

---

[1] كذا ر؛ ساقطة من الأصل. [2] كذا ش، ع؛ الأصل: اسر. [3] كذا ش؛ الأصل: حصاضه. [4] كذا ع؛ الأصل: وسفاوهم. [5] الأصل: رده.

The merchant left, promising to come back. But he carried off his friend's young son, hid him, and then returned. The boy's father missed his son and asked him, "Have you seen my son?"

"As I was approaching your house," replied the merchant, "I saw a hawk carry off a young boy. Perhaps it was your son."

"Who has ever seen or heard of hawks carrying off young boys?" the man cried out.

"Surely," replied the merchant, "in a land where rats can eat a hundred *mann* of iron, there is nothing preposterous about hawks carrying off elephants!"

And the acquaintance said, "It was I who 'ate up' your iron—I consumed what wasn't lawful for me to take. Give me back my son, and take your iron."

Kalīlah said, "I've told you this story to demonstrate that if you can betray 4.112
your king, who has shown you such favor, you're sure to betray others. I see that love means nothing to you. Nothing is more wasted than love bestowed on someone who knows no loyalty, than favors bestowed on someone who knows no gratitude, than instruction given to someone who won't listen or benefit from it, or than a secret entrusted to someone who knows no discretion. I have no illusions about changing your nature: I know that a bitter tree can be smeared with honey and butter but will still produce bitter fruit. I fear the effect your company might have on my judgment and character; for the company of the good bestows goodness, while the company of the evil bestows evil. It is like the wind: if it wafts over something rotten, it spreads a stench; and if it wafts over something fragrant, it spreads a fragrance. I know how heavy my words will seem to you, but the foolish always make light of the wise, and the base make light of the noble. The crooked must be set straight by the upright, and impulsive fools brought back to their senses by the thoughtful. The low-minded never cease from attacking and denigrating the noble, the spineless from attacking the resolute, the rancorous from attacking the affectionate, the miserly from attacking the generous, and the vicious from attacking the righteous."

Kalīlah's words reached this point just as the lion finished dealing with the 4.113
ox. After he had killed the ox and his anger had subsided, the lion thought to himself, "He was a creature of intelligence, good judgment, and character. For all I know, he may have been an innocent victim of injustice." And he became filled with sadness and regret.

وبصر به دمنة فترك محاورة[1] كليلة ودنا من الأسد فقال لقد أظفر الله يدك ومكّنك من عدوّك فماذا يحزنك أيّها الملك.

قال لقد أسفت على عقل شنزبة ورحمته لخلقه.

١١٤،٤ فقال لا ترحمه فإنّ العاقل لا يرحم من يخافه وإنّ الحازم ربّما أبغض الرجل وكرهه ثمّ تكارم عليه وقرّبه وولّاه لما يعلم عنده من الغناء والفضل كالرجل المتكاره[2] على الدواء الشنيع الكريه رجاء منفعته وربّما أحبّ الإنسان الرجل وعزّ عليه فأقصاه ونحّاه وأهلكه مخافة ضرّه كفعل الرجل تلدغه حيّة على إصبعه فيقطعها ويرمي بها مخافة أن ينتشر سمّها في بدنه كلّه فيقتله.

فأقرّ الأسد لقوله ثمّ إنّ الأسد فحص عن أمر الثور وأمر دمنة وبغيه عليه فاستبان له الأمر فقتل دمنة شرّ قتلة.

١١٥،٤ ثمّ قال الفيلسوف للملك فكان في صنع دمنة على صغر سنّه وضعفه وهو من أرذل السباع وأحقرها بالأسد والثور ما فرق بينهما وخرجا عن مودّتهما وأكبّ كلّ واحد منهما على صاحبه حتّى تضاغنا وتنافرا العجب العجيب لذي الألباب والنهى. ومن الصواب الحذر لأهل النميمة والخديعة والدحس والحسد والبطر فيما يزوّرون من خديعتهم ومكرهم وسعايتهم وذوو الحجى أحقّاء أن يتّقوا كذب أولئك وإفكهم ويبحثوا عن صنعتهم ويفحصوا عن هذه الأشياء منهم ثمّ لا يأخذوا بشيء من أقاويلهم إلّا عن تثبّت ورضى وأن يرفضوا كلّ من عُرف ذلك منه فإنّ الرأي والحزم في الاتّقاء والاقتداء بأهل السعـادة.

انقـضى باب الأسـد والثور.

---

١ كذا ل٢؛ الأصل: محاولة. ٢ كذا ع، ي (٨٢)؛ الأصل: المتكره.

When Dimnah noticed the lion's mood, he stopped talking to Kalīlah and approached the lion. "Now that God has given you the upper hand and enabled you to defeat your enemy, what is making you sad?"

"I grieve over the loss of Shanzabah's intelligence," replied the lion, "and I feel pity for him because of his good character."

"Don't feel pity for him," said Dimnah. "A wise man shows no mercy to someone he fears. Someone who is prudent sometimes takes a dislike and forms an aversion to a man, but then, albeit reluctantly, treats him generously, draws him close, and appoints him to office because he knows the man's usefulness and merit—just as you force yourself to swallow a loathsome medicine because of its benefit. And sometimes you like a man and esteem him, but then you banish him, cast him aside, and destroy him, fearing harm from him—just as someone whose finger has been bitten by a snake will cut it off and throw it away for fear that the poison may spread throughout his body and kill him." 4.114

The lion acknowledged the truth of his words. Later, however, he investigated the matter of the ox and how Dimnah had wronged him. Everything became clear to him, and he put Dimnah to a most horrible death.

Then the philosopher said to the king, "There are marvels for intelligent people in this story of how Dimnah, young and weak as he was and among the most contemptible and despised of beasts, managed to separate the lion and the ox, so that they abandoned their friendship, each turning against the other and becoming filled with rancor and aversion. One learns to beware of slanderers, deceivers, sowers of discord, enviers, and insolent men, and to guard against their falsities, deceits, trickeries, and calumnies. Those with intelligence must guard against the fabrications and lies of such people. They should scrutinize their actions and accept their words only after proper investigation, and they should reject all people they know to be of this sort. Sound judgment and prudence lie in caution and in emulating people who are pleasing to God."[34] 4.115

Here ends the Chapter of the Lion and the Ox.[35]

باب الابتحاث[١] عن أمر دمنة

١،٥ قال الملك للعالم قد سمعت حديثك عن الواشي المحتال الماهر بالخلابة كيف أفسد النفس بالشبهة حتّى أزال المودّة وأدخل مكانها العداوة فحدّثني ما كان من معذرة دمنة للأسد وجنوده حتّى راجع الأسد رأيه في أمر الثور وأدخل التهمة على دمنة وأمر به أن يُقتل شرّ قتلة وكيف اطّلع على عدوّه وما كان حجّته التي أدلى بها.

٢،٥ قال الفيلسوف وجدنا في الأحاديث أنّ الأسد لمّا قتل الثور ندم على معاجلته إيّاه وذكر حرمته وصحبته وكان يطيل مسامرة أصحابه ليقطع عن نفسه بحديثهم بعض ما دخله من الحزن والكآبة فكان من قرابة الأسد نمر كان من أكرم أصحابه عليه وأخصّهم عنده[٢] منزلة وأطولهم به خلوة في الليل والنهار[٣] وأنّه أمسى ذات ليلة عند الأسد بعد قتل الثور وانصرف ممسياً إلى منزله فمرّ على مسكن كليلة ودمنة وكانا مترافقين في بيت واحد فسمع كليلة موبّخًا لدمنة فيما كان منه من الغدر والمكر مذكّرًا له نهيه إيّاه وعصيان دمنة له فسمع النمر كلامهما كلّه.

٣،٥ وكان ممّا قال كليلة لدمنة قد ركبت أمرًا عظيمًا قبيحًا ودخلت من الغدر مدخلاً ضيّقًا وخنت الأسد خيانة عظيمة توشك عواقبها أن تصرعك وينكشف أمرك فلا يبقى لك من السباع عاذر ولا ناصر بل يجتمع عليك كلمتهم بالهلاك والقتل ولا أرى مقارنتك ولا مشاركتك رأيًا.

قال دمنة قد وقع من الأمر ما لا مردّ له فدع أيّها الأخ تضييق الأمور عليّ وعلى نفسك واعمل في تغييب ما قرّ في نفس الأسد منه ولعمري ما أنا للرأي[٤] فيما سلف منّي بحامد ولكنّ الحرص والحسد حملاني على ما صنعت.

---

١ الأصل: الانبحاث. ٢ وأخصّهم عنده: كذا ش؛ الأصل: واحصه عندهم. ٣ والنهار: الأصل: والنهار النمر.
٤ الأصل: الراى.

The Investigation of Dimnah

The king said to the philosopher,[36] "I've listened to your account of how a crafty slanderer skilled at deception sowed so much unwarranted suspicion that he destroyed a friendship and replaced it with hostility. Now tell me how Dimnah defended his behavior to the lion and his entourage, and how the lion eventually changed his mind regarding the ox, became suspicious of Dimnah, and commanded that he be put to a most horrible death. Tell me how the lion learned about his enemy and what defense the latter offered." 5.1

The philosopher replied: The accounts tell us that after killing the ox, the lion regretted his haste. He remembered the ox's companionship and inviolability as a guest, and, to dispel some of his sadness and grief, he spent long evenings conversing with his companions. The lion's entourage included a leopard who, as one of the lion's most esteemed and distinguished companions, enjoyed access to the lion by day and by night. One evening after the ox's death, the leopard kept the lion company late into the night, before heading home. When he passed by the home of Kalīlah and Dimnah—they lived together in the same house—he overheard Kalīlah rebuking Dimnah for his treachery and deceit. Kalīlah was reminding Dimnah of how he had tried to restrain him and how Dimnah had rejected his advice. The leopard overheard the whole conversation. 5.2

Among other things, Kalīlah said, "You've done a terrible thing, an ugly thing, an appalling act of faithlessness. The consequences of your dreadful betrayal of the lion will soon bring about your downfall. When everything comes out, not one animal will defend your conduct or come to your aid. They will unite one and all to destroy you. For my part, I no longer want to associate with you or be your partner." 5.3

"What's done can't be undone," replied Dimnah. "Brother, don't cause the two of us any more grief. Try to dispel the effect the affair has had on the lion's mood. Rest assured, I'm not going to praise what I did: greed and envy drove me to it."

فلمّا سمع النمر ذلك من كلامهما انصرف فدخل على أمّ الأسد وأخذ عليها العهود والمواثيق أن لا تفشي بشيء من ذلك فجعلت له ذلك فأخبرها بما سمع من كليلة وإقرار دمنة فلمّا أصبحت دخلت على الأسد فوجدته مكتئباً حزيناً لما قد فرط منه في أمر الثور. ٤،٥

فقالت ما يحزنك.

فقال يحزنني قتل الثور وتذكّرت صحبته ومواظبته كانت معي وما كنت أستمتع به من رأيه وأسكن إليه من مشورته ونصيحته.

قالت له إنّ أقنع ما شهد على امرئ نفسه وهذا من قولك دليل على أنّ قلبك شاهد بأنّك قد أقدمت على الثور بغير علم ولا وضح يقين بذلك واعلم أنّ رأس الخطأ العجلة فلو كنت حين بلغك عن الثور ما بلغك كففت نفسك وملكت سورة غضبك ثمّ عرضت ما بلغك عنه على قلبك بحفظ نظر لاكتفيت بقلبك دليلاً على صدق ما أتاك عنه وكذبه لأنّ القلوب تتكافأ فيما بينهما فقس أمرك وأمر الثور بموقع أمره كان بنفسك[١] في حياته وموقعه اليوم بعد موته.[٢]

قال الأسد لقد أكثرت التفكّر في ذلك وحرصت على التجنّي[٣] على[٤] الثور بعد قتلي إيّاه وعلى أن أغضب به ذنباً واحداً فيما بيني وبينه أقوّي به تهمتي إيّاه فما يزداد تهمتي إيّاه ولا يزداد ظنّي به في ترداذي إلّا حسناً ولست أتذكّر منه شراسة خلق أقول حملته على أنّه حسدني ولا بغضاً أتّهمه في طلب مغالبتي ولا أتذكّر منّي إليه[٥] سبباً أرى أنّه دعاه إلى مغالبتي وإنّي لأحبّ أن أفحص عن أمره وأبالغ في الفحص عن شأنه وإن كنت أعرف أنّ ذلك غير مصلح ما فرط منّي في أمره ولكنّي أحبّ أن أعرف موقفي الذي أنا عليه فيما صنعت من الخطأ والصواب فأخبريني هل سمعت شيئاً. ٥،٥

قالت أمّ الأسد بلغني أمر استكتمته ولولا ما قالت العلماء ممّا في إذاعة السرّ من العيب لذكرته لك.

---

١ الأصل: بنفسك. ٢ اليوم . . . موته: كذا ش؛ ساقطة من الأصل. ٣ كذا ش؛ الأصل: التجنّي. ٤ كذا ش؛ الأصل: عن. ٥ منّي إليه: كذا ش؛ الأصل: منه الىّ.

After hearing their words, the leopard went back and paid a visit to the lion's mother. After making her promise to reveal nothing, he told her what he had heard Kalīlah say and what Dimnah had confessed. The next morning, the lion's mother went to visit the lion. She found him sad and dejected over his thoughtless treatment of the ox. 5.4

"What is making you sad?" she asked.

"The death of the ox," he replied. "I keep thinking of his companionship and devotion, and how I benefited from his opinions and trusted his counsel and advice."

"A man's conscience is the most convincing witness against him," she said. "As your words indicate, your own heart testifies that you attacked the ox before you knew the truth about the matter. Haste is the root of error. When you received the report about the ox, had you restrained yourself, controlled your temper, and compared the report carefully with what you felt in your heart, your heart would have provided sufficient evidence regarding the report's truth or falsity. Hearts reflect each other; therefore, judge how things stood between you and the ox during his lifetime by what you feel about him now after his death."

"Since killing the ox," the lion said, "I've thought and thought, trying to discover even one offense of his that ever excited my anger to confirm my suspicions; but the more I think, the better my opinion of him becomes. I can't recall any viciousness in his character that might have led to his envying me, or any hatred that might have caused him to try to overthrow me, and I see nothing on my part that might have provoked him. I want to investigate the case thoroughly, although I know it won't undo my thoughtlessness; I want to know where I stand regarding the right or wrong of what I did. Tell me, have you heard anything?" 5.5

"I've been told something that I've been asked to conceal," replied the lion's mother. "I would tell you, were it not for what the sages have said about the shamefulness of revealing secrets."

٦،٥ قال الأسد إنّ لأقوال العلماء وجوهاً كثيرة ومعاني مختلفة وأحوالاً يتصرّف فيها لذوي العقول العمل ببعضها في حال والترك للعمل بها في حال وقد قالت العلماء الكتمان على أهل الريبة والتغييب عنهم شعبة من الريبة وسبيل من الإساءة. ولا أدري لعلّ الذي طرح إليك ذلك إنّما أراد بذكره لك إخراج نفسه من الحجّة عليه فيه فانصري على ما يلزمك من ذلك فقد برئ إليك وخلع بإعلامه إيّاك الأمر من عنقه وقلّده في عنقك فاخلعيه أنت أيضاً من عنقك وبيّنيه لي لنعمل فيه الذي ينبغي لنا أن نعمل في مثله.

٧،٥ قالت أمّ الأسد قد عرفت صواب ما قلت ولكنّي أعرف ما يدخل عليّ في كشف السرّ وحمله إليك وأنّه يجتمع عليّ في ذلك خطآن منهما مقت المسرّ إليّ[1] وإنزاله أمري على الخيانة والسخف ومنهما أنّ غيره لا يثق بي في سرّ بعدها.

قال الأسد إنّي لأعرف ما تقولين وما أحبّ أن أطلب المخرج من الخطأ بإدخالك فيه غدراً فإذا رأيت أن لا تخبريني باسم المسرّ إليك وتفسير ما أسرّ فأخبريني بجملة الأمر.

فأخبرته أمّه بجميع ذلك الحديث ثمّ قالت لست أجهل قول العلماء في تعظيم[2] الفضل في العفو عن أهل الجرائم[3] لكنّ الفضل في ذلك إنّما[4] هو فيما[5] دون خيانة العامّة وخيانة الملوك فيما يقع بين الشيئين ويحتجّ به السفهاء عند ما يكون من أعمالهم السيّئة وإنّ من فساد العامّة ترك عقوبة مستوجبي العقوبة فلا تدع هذا الخائن المفسد هذا يعيش فوق ما عاش.

٨،٥ فدعا الأسد بوجوه أصحابه فأُدخلوا عليه ثمّ دعا بدمنة فلمّا قام بين يديه رأى من حاله وعرف من[6] حال جلسائه ما أيقن له بالشرّ فالتفت إلى بعض من يليه فقال له قولاً خفيّاً هل حدث حدث يحزن الملك أو حدث أمر جمعكم له كما أرى.

---

١ الأصل: اياى. ٢ تعظيم: الأصل: تعظيم من. ٣ في العفو...الجرائم: كذا ش، ع؛ ساقطة من الأصل. ٤ كذا ش، ع؛ الأصل: ربما. ٥ كذا ش، ع؛ الأصل: فى. ٦ ساقطة من الأصل.

“The sayings of the sages are ambiguous and can be taken in many ways,” responded the lion. “In some circumstances the reasonable thing is to act on them; in other circumstances to refrain from doing so. The sages have said that covering up and hiding the doings of suspicious people is in itself suspicious, a kind of wrongdoing. Perhaps your informant acquitted himself of a responsibility by passing on the information; therefore, you too should help him by doing what is incumbent on you. He acquitted himself of his obligation to you by informing you; he removed the burden from his neck and put it around yours. Therefore, you too should remove it from your neck by explaining it to me, so we can do what we ought to do in a case like this.” 5.6

The lion's mother said, “I know that what you say is true, but I also know that revealing the secret and burdening you with it would harm me in two ways. First, the person who told me the secret would hate me: he would take it as a betrayal of trust and ascribe it to weakness of character. Second, no one else would trust me with a secret after that.” 5.7

“I understand,” said the lion. “I don't want to look for a way out of my mistake by involving you in a betrayal of trust. If you're unwilling to divulge the informant's name and the details of what he told you, tell me about it in general terms.”

She told him all about the conversation. Then she said, “I know very well that the sages have exalted the virtue of pardoning offenders, but that applies only to offenses less serious than the betrayal of the whole community or the betrayal of kings. Fools plead with this saying to excuse their evil deeds. But failing to punish those who deserve punishment will corrupt the entire community. Do not, therefore, allow this traitor, this sower of corruption, to live.”

The lion summoned his main companions, who were ushered into his presence. Then he summoned Dimnah. Dimnah stood before him and saw from the demeanor of the lion and his companions that something was wrong. Turning to someone next to him, he asked quietly, “Has anything happened to make the king so sad? Has he summoned this gathering because something has happened?” 5.8

فسمعته أمّ الأسد فقالت نعم حزن الملك تركه إيّاك حيًّا بعد الذي رأى من غشّك له وإغرائك إيّاه بأهل نصيحته وليس ينبغي له أن يستبقيك طرفة عين.

قال دمنة ماذا أحدث من أمري.

قالت أمّ الملك استبان للملك صنعك به وتحميلك إيّاه بكذبك على شنزبة.

٩،٥ قال دمنة ما أرى الأوّل ترك للآخر مقالاً في شيء من معاريض الأمور فإنّه كان يقال إنّ أشدّ الناس اجتهادًا في توقّي شرور الناس أجدر أن يصيبه الشرّ. ولا يكون للملك ولا لجنوده المثل السوء وقد علمت أنّ ذلك إنّما قيل في صحبة الأشرار وأنّه من صحبهم وهو يعلم علمهم[١] لم ينجّه من شرّهم توقّيه إيّاه ولذلك انقطعت النسّاك بأنفسها فاختارت الوحدة على مخالطة الناس وآثرت العمل لله عزّ وجلّ على العمل لخلقه لأنّه لا يجزي بالخير خيرًا إلّا الله فأمّا أكثر أهل الدنيا فإنّهم لا يعملون بالعدل ولا يجزون كلّ واحد بعملهم بل عامّة ما ينبغي أن يعاقبوا به الفجّار يصيبون به الأبرار وما أحد أحقّ بإصابة الصواب من الملك الذي لا يصانع أحدًا[٢] لحاجة ولا يعاقبه لتخوّفه منه.

١٠،٥ فإنّ أحقّ ما عظمت رغبة الملوك فيه في محاسن الصواب مكافأة أهل البلاء الحسن وما بلاء أبين حسنًا من[٣] نصيحتي ولقد علم الملك وعلم جميع من حضر أنّه لم يكن بيني وبين شنزبة أمر أضطغن[٤] عليه له حقدًا أو بغيته[٥] له غائلة وما كان لي بذلك ضرّ ولا نفع[٦] ولكن نصحت الملك فيه وأعلمته على ما اطّلعت عليه من أمره وكان الشاهد عليه ما أبصر الملك من مصداق ما ذكرت له من أمره وكان أفصل فيه رأيًا وأشدّ عزمًا وقد عرفت أنّه قد تخوّف مثلها منّي[٧] غير واحد من أهل الغشّ والعداوة للملك فنصبوا لي العداوة وأجمعوا على طلب هلاكي وما كنت أرجو أن يكون جزائي على النصيحة وحسن البلاء حزن الملك على تركه إيّاي حيًّا.

١ علمهم: الأصل: علمهم ثم. ٢ كذا ش؛ الأصل: احد. ٣ بلاء . . . من: كذا ش؛ الأصل: لا كن حسنا احق.
٤ كذا ش؛ الأصل: ادخل. ٥ الأصل: نعشه. ٦ ضرّ . . . نفع: الأصل: ضرا ولا نفعًا. ٧ كذا ش، ع؛ الأصل: من.

The lion's mother heard him. "What saddens the king is that he left you alive after seeing how you deceived him and incited him against his loyal adviser. He shouldn't allow you to remain alive a moment longer."

"What has changed his attitude toward me?" asked Dimnah.

"Your machinations," the king's mother answered. "Now he clearly sees how your lies incited him against Shanzabah."

"I think," said Dimnah, "that the first speaker has left nothing for anyone 5.9
else to say about the ironies of fate. As the saying goes, he who tries hardest to fend off the evils that men do is most likely to become the victim of evil. May this saying not apply to the king and his soldiers! I know the saying was only about associating with evil men: that no amount of wariness will save from their evil someone who knowingly associates with them. That is why ascetics have sequestered themselves and chosen solitude instead of human company, electing to work for God rather than for His creatures, for only God rewards good with good. Most people in this world don't act justly or reward each person as he deserves; indeed, they often inflict on the innocent punishment befitting sinners. But who is more likely to hit the mark than a king who flatters no one out of need and punishes no one out of fear?

"The virtue to which kings should most aspire is to reward those who do 5.10
good service; and what service has been more conspicuously good than my advice? The king, and everyone here, knows there was nothing between me and Shanzabah to cause me to hold a grudge against him or seek his ruin. I had nothing to gain or lose. I advised the king and let him know what I had learned about Shanzabah. In the end, what he saw with his own eyes confirmed what I told him, and as a result he became more decisive and resolute in his judgment. I know that more than one scheming enemy of the king is afraid of me for the same reason, and so they've become my foes and have decided to destroy me. I never expected that the king's sorrow at letting me live would be my reward for sincere advice and good service."

١١،٥ فلمّا سمع الأسد قوله أمر به إلى القاضي وقال لقاضيه افتش عن أمره فإنّي لا أحبّ أن أحكم على محسن ولا مسيء إلّا بظاهر من وجود الحقّ والعدل.

قال القاضي أيّها الملك إنّه لا شيء أكشف للعمى وأوضح للشبهة وأشدّ استخراجاً لغامضات الأشياء من الاجتهاد والمبالغة في الفحص والكشف.

١٢،٥ قال دمنة ولست حقيقاً أيّها الملك بالعجلة في قتلي بقول لائم[1] بل يبحث الملك على هذا الأمر فإنّه كلّما ازداد في شأني نظرًا ازداد ببراءتي ونصيحتي يقيناً وقد علمت أيّها الملك أنّ النار يكون مسكنها الشجر والحجر ثمّ لا تُخرج ولا يُوصَل إلى منافعها إلّا بالعمل والطلب ولو كنت مجرماً لتخوّفت التكشّف عن أمري ولما[2] أصبحت ببراءتي عالمًا أرجو أن يستخرج الفحص صحّة أمري وكذلك كلّ شيء طابت ريحه فالتثوير يزيده فوحاً وظهوراً ولو كنت عرفت لنفسي ذنباً لوجدت في الأرض مذهباً ولما لزمت باب الملك أنتظر ثواب عمل وأسأله الفحص إن كان في شكّ من أمري أن يأمر بالنظر فيه ويوتي ذلك أميناً مسلماً لا يأخذه في الحقّ لومة لائم ليس بصاحب هوادة ولا حيف فقد كانت لي منزلة أُنافَس عليها ويُؤمَر إليه أن يكشف ويرفع إليه في كلّ يوم ما يضح له من أمري وما أدلي به من حجّتي فليرى الملك في ذلك رأيه ويقيس بعض أمري ببعض ولا يعجّل في أمري بتشبيه أهل البغي والعداوة فإنّه إن لم يفعل ذلك واستحلّ منّي ما لا يحلّ فإنّه لا وزير لي ولا ملجأ إلّا الذي يعلم سرائر عباده وخفيّات ضمائرهم وقد قالت العلماء إنّه من صدّق بما ينبغي أن يشكّ فيه وكذّب بما ينبغي أن يصدّق به أصابه ما أصاب المرأة التي بذلت نفسها لعبدها حتّى فضحها للاشتباه عليها.

قال الأسد وكيف كان ذلك.

١٣،٥ قال دمنة زعموا أنّه كان بمدينة كذا تاجر وكان له امرأة لها حظّ وجمال وكان إلى جنب بيتها مصوّر ماهر وكان لامرأة التاجر إلفاً فقالت له إن استطعت أن

[1] الأصل: الام. [2] الأصل: ولا.

When the lion heard Dimnah's words, he ordered him taken to the judge. 5.11
"Investigate his case. I don't want to judge the right or wrong of any action without clearly establishing the truth and justice of it."

"Your Majesty," said the judge, "nothing can dispel blindness, clarify doubt, and uncover obscurities better than a rigorous, thorough investigation."

And Dimnah added, "Your Majesty shouldn't hasten to kill me on the 5.12
word of a slanderer. Let him investigate the matter. The more he considers my case, the more certain he will be of my innocence and loyalty. As Your Majesty knows, fire dwells in trees and rocks; only through labor and effort can it be brought out and put to use. If I were a criminal, I would be as fearful of exposure as, knowing my innocence, I am now hopeful that the investigation will bring out the truth, just as perfumes diffuse their sweetness more widely when stirred. I would have found somewhere else to go if I were conscious of any crime or guilt; I wouldn't have stayed at the king's gate waiting for a reward. If he is in any doubt about me, I ask him to investigate. Let him entrust the matter to someone God-fearing and trustworthy, someone not swayed by slander, neither lenient nor arbitrary, for I held a position that others envied. Instruct that person to investigate and submit a daily report on what he finds out about my case and on the evidence I present. Let the king exercise his judgment, compare one part of the testimony with the other, and not hasten to act on the basis of dubious claims made by malicious and hostile people. If he doesn't do this and instead countenances something unlawful, then I have no helper or refuge but the One who knows the hidden thoughts and hearts of His servants. As the sages have said: If you believe what deserves to be doubted, and reject what deserves to be believed, you risk suffering the fate of the woman who in her confusion gave herself to her servant, who subsequently disgraced her."

"And what was her fate?" asked the lion.

And Dimnah told the following tale: They say that in a certain city there 5.13
lived a merchant whose wife was endowed with both beauty and wealth. Next door lived a skilled painter who was the wife's lover. She said to him, "It would make things easier for us if you could devise something to alert me

The Wife and Her Lover the Painter

تحتال بصناعة أطّلع بها على مجيئك إذا جئتني بالليل من غير نداء ولا رمي ولا شيء يُرتاب به كان ذلك أرفق بي وبك.

قال المصوّر عندي من الحيل في ذلك الذي يسرّك عندي ملاءة مصوّرة بتهاويل الصور وشبهاً بالبياض يقق وشبهاً بالسواد حالك تتألّق ائتلاقاً فبياضها يدعوك في الليلة الظلماء بضوئه وسوادها يبدو لك في الليلة المقمرة وأنا ألبسها إذا أردت إتيانك فإذا رأيت ذلك فاعلمي أنّي صاحبك فأتيني من غير أن أدعوك.

١٤٫٥ فكان إذا أتى المرأة لبس تلك الملاءة فعلمت المرأة مكانه ففرحت بذلك وتعجّبت منه وكان يأتيها إذا أرادها ففطن عبد التاجر لذلك فلمّا كان بعد ذلك بأيّام وكان العبد لأمة المصوّر خليلاً طلب إلى أمة المصوّر أن تعطيه الملاءة المصوّرة ليريها صديقاً له ويسرع ردّها فأعطته الملاءة فلبسها وأتى سيّدته على نحو ما كان يأتيها المصوّر فلمّا رأت لم ترتب بشيء من شأنه وحسبته خليلها فبذلت نفسها له وقضى منها حاجته ورجع العبد بالملاءة إلى الأمة[1] فوضعتها موضعها.

١٥٫٥ وكان المصوّر عن[2] بيته غائباً فلمّا مضى من الليل هدأة رجع المصوّر إلى بيته فلبس الملاءة فأتى المرأة فلمّا رأت الملاءة دنت منه فقالت ما شأنك أسرعت الرجعة وقد قضيت حاجتك. فلمّا سمع المصوّر ذلك خبثت نفسه ورجع نحو منزله ودعا وليدته[3] فتوعّدها بالضرب حتّى أخبرته بالأمر على وجهه فأحرق المصوّر الملاءة.

١٦٫٥ وإنّما ضربت لك هذا المثل لتعلم أنّ التشبيه كذب وأنت أيّها الملك والحمد لله الفاضل الرأي العظيم الحلم والعالم بالأمور وقد رأى الملك من تشبيههم ما قد استبان من عداوة الثور حتّى استحلّ بذلك قتله وإنّ ذلك جدير أن يمنعه من الإقدام على قتلي مع علمه لنصيحتي له وحفظي له من وزرائه إلى ما قد علم الملك من منزلتي في نفسي من خشانة الحال وصغر الحظّ وأنّي لا أقدر على رفع نفسي عن نسبة العبوديّة ولا أطمع فيما يسمو إليه من فوقي وأنا وإن كنت عند الملك صغير الحظّ أجد من عدله نصيباً أعرف أنّ الملك معطينيه من نفسه في حياتي وبعد موتي يهون عليّ

١ كذا ش، ع؛ الأصل: أمه. ٢ كذا ش؛ الأصل: في. ٣ كذا ش، ع؛ الأصل: والدته.

to your arrival when you come at night, without calling out, throwing something, or arousing suspicion."

"I have just the thing," said the painter, "a coat painted with fantastic images, some white as heart of palm and some jet black, brightly gleaming. Its whiteness will summon you on a dark night, and its blackness will stand out on a moonlit night. I'll wear it when I want to come to you. When you see it, know that it's your special friend and come to me without any summons."

He wore the coat whenever he came to visit the woman; she knew he 5.14
was there, admired his skill and delighted in it, and he could visit whenever he wanted. One of the merchant's servants realized what was happening. A few days later, the servant—who happened to be the painter's maidservant's lover—asked the maidservant to lend him the painted coat to show a friend of his, after which he would return it immediately. She gave it to him, and he put it on and visited the merchant's wife in the painter's guise. When she saw him, she had no idea it wasn't her lover and gave herself to him. He satisfied his lust and returned the coat to the maidservant, who put it back in its place.

The painter had been away, but he came home later that night, donned 5.15
the coat, and went to visit the woman. When she saw the coat, she came to him. "Why," she asked, "have you returned so soon after satisfying your desire?" The painter returned home in disgust, summoned his maidservant, and threatened to beat her, whereupon she told him the whole story. So the painter burned the coat.

Dimnah said, "I've told you this story to show you that sowing confusion 5.16
is as bad as lying. Your Majesty—praise God—is unsurpassed in judgment, great in forbearance, and experienced in affairs. Despite the confusion that's being sown, you saw clear evidence of the ox's hostility and this justified killing him. This should prevent Your Majesty from putting me to death, for you know how sincerely I advised you and protected you from your ministers. Furthermore, Your Majesty knows how I regard my harsh life and meager fortune. You know that I cannot raise my rank above that of a servant and that I don't aspire to what those above me aspire. Though I may be insignificant in the king's eyes, I hope to be granted a portion of his justice in my lifetime and after my death. Death is of little importance to me. I would

الموت وأحبّه إن قد علمت أنّ الملك يطمئنّ ويفرح ويسكن إذا قتلني فإنّ العلماء قالوا من أصاب خطيئة وإثماً ثمّ أسلم نفسه للقتل فدفع بها عن الصالحين عفي عنه يوم القيامة ونجا من الشرّ الدائم في الآخرة. وينبغي للحقير مثلي من عبيد الملك الموسوم بالعبوديّة أن يسلم نفسه فيما يصلح للملك العظيم التقيّ مثلك ثمّ وجب عليه أن يختار عاجل عقوبة الدنيا على آجل عقوبة الآخرة.

١٧،٥ فقال بعض من حضر الملك من جنوده أيها الملك إنّ دمنة ليس يقول ما يقول تعظيماً للملك ولا توقيراً له ولكنّه يريد أن يدفع عن نفسه ما قد نزل به من عاقبة سوء عمله.

قال دمنة من يحفظ نفسي إن أضعتها ومن يرفعها إن وضعتها هل لي نفس غيرها فأدفع عنها الردى. ولن يصون رهطه من لم يصن نفسه. أوما علمت أنّه ليس على المرء في التماس العذر لنفسه من غيره عار. لقد ظفرت منك بما لم تملكه من الحسد والشرّ والبغضاء والعداوة فمثلك لا يصلح أن يكون بباب الملك أو يعرفه بل ولا ينبغي أن يكون مع دوابّه أيضاً.

١٨،٥ قالت أمّ الأسد[1] لدمنة ما الذي سلف من خيانتك ومكرك ودحسك بأعجب منّي ممّا أسمع من موعظتك وضربك الأمثال لمن تكلّم فيك.

قال دمنة هذا موضع العظة إن قُبلت وموضع الأمثال إن سُمعت.

قالت أمّ الأسد أيّها الغادر الفاجر إنّ فيما قدّمت يداك لشاغلاً لك لو عقلت عن ضرب الأمثال.

قال دمنة إنّما الغادر الذي يؤتى[2] بالنصيحة ويُمكَّن من عدوّه ثمّ لا يشكر ذلك ولا يسرّه والذي يؤمّن عدوّه فإذا استمكن منه قتله بغير ذنب والذي يعادي من كشف له عداوة أعدائه.

١٩،٥ قالت أمّ الأسد شيطانك أيّها الفاجر الغادر ترجو أن ينفعك للمكابرة بالكذب.

قال دمنة إنّ الكذوب من كافأ بالإحسان الإساءة وبالخير الشرّ وبالأمن الخوف فأمّا أنا فقد أنجزت الوعد ووفيت بالعهد.

---

١ قالت أمّ الأسد: كذا ش، ع؛ الأصل: قال الملك. ٢ كذا ع؛ الأصل: لا ماتى.

even welcome it if I knew that the king would find comfort, joy, and relief after killing me. The sages have said that a sinner who delivers himself up to death to protect the righteous will be pardoned on the Day of Judgment and escape everlasting suffering in the hereafter. Someone as contemptible as I, marked with the stigma of servitude, ought to give up his life for the benefit of a great, God-fearing king like you. He ought to prefer punishment in this world to punishment in the hereafter."

One of the king's attendants said, "Your Majesty, Dimnah isn't speaking 5.17
out of reverence or respect for the king, but to escape the consequences of his mischief."

Dimnah replied, "Who will preserve my soul if I neglect it? Who will raise it up if I demean it? Have I any other soul to protect from perdition? Someone who doesn't protect his own life will never protect the lives of his kin. Don't you know there is nothing shameful in seeking to vindicate oneself? I've become the victim of your uncontrolled envy, evil, hatred, and hostility. Someone like you isn't fit to stand at the king's gate, let alone to know him. You shouldn't even keep company with his riding animals."

The lion's mother said to Dimnah, "I'm amazed less by your previous 5.18
faithlessness, deception, and corruption than I am by your preaching and reciting parables to those speaking about you."

"This," replied Dimnah, "is the place for preaching, if people would only accept it, and for parables, if people would only heed them."

"Sinful traitor," replied the lion's mother. "If you had any intelligence, you'd be too concerned about what you've laid up for yourself to busy yourself reciting parables."

"A traitor," replied Dimnah, "is someone who is given advice that enables him to triumph over his enemy and then shows no gratitude or joy; a traitor is someone who promises his enemy safety, but kills him though he has committed no misdeed when he gets his hands on him; and is someone who turns against the very person who revealed his enemies' hostility."

The lion's mother said, "Sinful traitor, you expect your devil to help you 5.19
argue with lies."

"A liar," replied Dimnah, "is someone who repays benevolence with malice, good with evil, and trust with fear. As for me, I've kept my promise and honored my oath."

قالت أمّ الأسد ما وعدك الذي أنجزت وعهدك الذي به وفيت.

قال دمنة الملك يعلم أنّي لو كنت كاذباً لم أقل هذه المقالة عنده عن انتحال من انتحل عنده.

٢٠،٥ فلمّا رأت أمّ الأسد أنّ الأسد لكلام دمنة غير رادّ عليه شيئاً ممّا يقول ارتابت وظنّت أنّ الأسد يغترّ ببعض ما يقول دمنة في براءته وعذره ارتابت فقالت إنّ الصمت عن احتجاج الخصم لشبيه بالإقرار بحقيقة ما يقول ولذلك قالت العلماء أقرّ صامت فخرجت.

وأمر الأسد بدمنة أن يُرفع إلى القاضي بالاستيثاق منه والفحص عن شأنه.

٢١،٥ ثمّ إنّ أمّ الأسد عادت إلى الأسد فقالت إنّي لم أزل أسمع بمكر دمنة ودحسه منذ زمان فحقّق ذلك عندي ما سمعت من إفكه وافتعاله المعاذير وكثرة مخارجه من غير صدق قول ولا وضح عذر فإنّك إن أمكنته من الكلام دفعك عن نفسه بمشتبه الحجج الكاذبة وفي قتله لك ولجنودك راحة عظيمة فعاجل بقتله ولا تأخذك فيه هوادة ولا توقّفك[1] في قتله شبهة.

قال الأسد لأمّه إنّ من شأن بطانة الملك وقرابتهم تنافس المنازل بينهم ودخول الحسد والبغي من بعضهم على بعض في ذلك ثمّ ذو الرأي والنبالة منهم خاصّة هم المبتلون بذلك وقد علمت أنّ مكان دمنة يثقل على غير واحد من أصحابي وأهلي فلست أدري لعلّ الذي أرى وأسمع من إجماعهم عليه لبعض ذلك فأنا أكره العجلة في أمره فإنّ العلق الصالح لا ينبغي أن يُستهلك إلّا في حجّة وفيما العذر واضح فيه لمن استهلكه.

ثمّ إنّ القاضي أمر بدمنة إلى السجن فغلّظ عليه الوثاق.

٢٢،٥ فدخل كليلة له رقّة وأدركه منه ذمام لقديم الإخاء وطول الصحبة وصافي المودّة التي كانت بينهما فانطلق إليه مستخفياً حتّى لقيه في السجن فبكى حين نظر إليه

[1] كذا ش؛ الأصل: بوقعك.

"And what," asked the lion's mother, "is this promise you've kept and oath you've honored?"

"The king knows that if I were a liar I wouldn't have spoken these words in his presence about the imposters in his entourage," replied Dimnah.

The lion's mother saw that the lion hadn't replied to any of Dimnah's 5.20
arguments, so she began worrying that he might be swayed by some of his excuses and protestations of innocence. She gave voice to her misgivings: "Silence in the face of an opponent's arguments is like conceding the truth of his words. As the sages have said, to keep silent is to agree." And she left.

The lion commanded that Dimnah be made to post bond and be brought before the judge for investigation of his case.

Later, the lion's mother returned to the lion and said, "I've been hear- 5.21
ing for a long time about Dimnah's deceit and corruption. Now his prolific lies, trumped-up excuses, and specious evasions have only confirmed this in my mind. If you give him a chance to speak, he will defend himself with lies and confusing arguments. Killing him will be a great relief to you and your soldiers. Kill him immediately! Don't be swayed by leniency or halted by doubt."

"Courtiers," replied the lion to his mother, "often compete among themselves for positions; envy and malice often develop among them, directed especially at judicious and intelligent colleagues. I know that Dimnah's position vexed more than one of my soldiers and my household. That might be the reason they're uniting against him, as I can well see and hear. So I don't want to act hastily in his case. A precious resource should be consumed only for a good reason and when one is clearly justified in doing so."

The judge ordered that Dimnah be sent to prison, and he was heavily shackled.

Because of their long companionship and close friendship, Kalīlah felt 5.22
pity and a sense of responsibility, so he went to visit Dimnah secretly in prison. When he saw Dimnah's distress and wretched state, he wept. "Your condition," he said, "makes admonition unnecessary. But I must remind

وإلى ما هو فيه من الضيق والغمّ ثمّ قال له إنّ ما أنت فيه لكافيك من العظة ولكن لا بدّ من إذكارك قضائي حقّك في النصيحة لك والتقدمة إليك فإنّ لكلّ مقالة موضعاً ولو كنتُ قصّرت في موعظتك حيث احتجتَ إلى ذلك منّي في حال العافية كنتُ اليوم شريكك[1] في الذنب ولكنّ الإعجاب دخل منك مدخلاً فهو الذي رابك وغلبك وقد كنت أضرب[2] لك قول العلماء إنّ المحتال يموت قبل أجله مثلاً وليس قولهم يموت قبل أجله بانقطاع الحياة ولكن بدخول أشياء تفسد الحياة عليه كنحو ما أنت فيه ممّا الموت أروح منه.

٢٣،٥ قال دمنة لم تزل منذ عرفتك تقول بالحقّ جهدك وقد كنت بحقّ إخائي مؤدّياً تعظني وتنصحني ولكنّ شره النفس والحرص على طلب المنزلة أرداني ومنعني الانتفاع بنصحك لي كالمريض المولّع بالطعام[3] الذي يعرف مضرّته له فيدع معرفته انقياداً لشهوته وقد عرفت أنّي زرعت البلاء لنفسي ولا ينبت إلّا بإبّانه وزمانه وإن تُقدَم في زرعه فهذا أوان نبت ما زرعته لنفسي وممّا يزيد هذا البلاء عليّ شدّة تخوّفي إيّاك أن تُتّهم في أمري لما كان بيني وبينك فلعلّك أن تأتيك عقوبة أن تعترف[4] ببعض ما كنت أطلعتك عليه من أمري فيدخل عليّ في ذلك موتتان أحدهما ما يصل إليك فلا تُتّهم على البعداء فكيف لمن كانت منزلته منك منزلتي.

٢٤،٥ قال كليلة قد عرفت ما قلت وقد قالت العلماء إنّ الأجساد لا تصبر على العذاب ولا تمتنع[5] من القول عند ذلك بكلّ ما دُفع به عنها من حقّ أو باطل وإنّي لأرى لك إذ أُنزلت بهذا الحال أن تتوب من ذنبك وتعترف بما كان منك فتخرج نفسك من تبعة الآخرة بالتوبة ممّا صنعت فإنّك لا محالة هالك فلا تجمع على نفسك هلاك العاجل والآجل.

فقال دمنة قد نصحت وأصبت وأنا ناظر فيما ذكرت ثمّ مجازيك في ذلك.

وانصرف كليلة مغموماً مكروباً خائفاً فمضى على وجهه هائماً.

---

[1] كذا ش؛ الأصل: شربك. [2] كذا ش، پ٣٤٦٦؛ الأصل: احترت. [3] المولّع بالطعام: كذا ش؛ الأصل: المولم بالعطام.
[4] أن تعترف: كذا ش؛ الأصل: وان اعرف. [5] كذا ش؛ الأصل: تسمع.

you of how I carried out my duty to give you advice and direction, for every utterance has its place. Had I failed to reprimand you when you needed it while all was going well, I would share your guilt today. But conceit took hold of you: it overcame you and confounded your judgment. I often cited the sages' maxim: 'The crafty man dies before his time.' By 'dies before his time,' they didn't mean that his life would end, but that he would suffer the things that ruin life, such as your present troubles, from which death would be a relief."

Dimnah said, "From our first acquaintance, you've always taken pains to 5.23
speak the truth. Fulfilling your brotherly obligation, you reproved me and advised me, but greed and ambition ruined me and kept me from taking your advice. I was like a sick man who craves food that he knows will harm him, but disregards that knowledge and surrenders to his appetite. I knew that I had sowed the seeds of trouble for myself and that, no matter how long ago they were planted, they would sprout in time—and the time has come for them to sprout. What torments me even more is my fear for you: that, because of our relationship, you might be suspected in my case and even tortured to make you confess anything I told you about my project. For me, that would be like dying twice, the harsh treatment you would receive being a kind of dying, for no one would doubt the truth of your words about others who have no ties to you, let alone about someone as close to you as I am."

"I understand what you're saying," said Kalīlah. "The wise have said 5.24
that our bodies can't bear pain and won't hesitate to say anything, true or false, to avoid it. But I think you should repent of your sin and confess your wrongdoing, since you've been brought to this state. By repenting, you'll free yourself from the consequences in the hereafter. You're going to perish in any case. Don't add perdition in the hereafter to perdition in the here and now."

"You've given sound advice," answered Dimnah. "I'll ponder it and repay you for it."

Filled with grief, distress, and fear, Kalīlah wandered away aimlessly.

وكان في ناحية السجن سبع محبوس وكان ما تراجع كليلة ودمنة بينهما من القول يسمعه فحفظ ذلك وسكت عليه.

٢٥،٥ وبلغ دمنة هروب كليلة فبكى طويلاً أسفاً عليه وحزن على فراقه وقال ما أصنع الآن بالحياة وقد فارقني الأخ الصالح والصديق الناصح كليلة. ما أرى ما قيل إلّا حقًّا إنّ الإنسان إذا ابتلي فأدبر بخته وسفل بعد ارتفاع توجّه إليه الشرّ وعاوده[1] الهمّ واكتنفه الغمّ والحزن وتراكم عليه الأشياء من كلّ جهة تطلبه المقادير وإن تحرّز منها وليس يغايب منها حتّى تصيبه ويقع كما وقعت في مخلسي هذا وقد فارقت أترابي وفارقني أحبّتي وفُجعت بأخي ونزل بي في عنفوان شبابي ونبغة حداثتي ورونق شبيبتي وغاب منّي أخي وصفيّي كليلة حزيناً كئيباً.

٢٦،٥ ثمّ إنّ أمّ الأسد ذكرت دمنة وغدره بالأسد وقالت إنّ استبقاء الفجّار يعدل قتل الأبرار وإنّ من استبقى فاجراً أشركه في فجوره أو برًّا أشركه في أعمال برّه.

فأمر الأسد القاضي بالنظر في أمر دمنة والمسألة عنه وأن لا يؤخّر ذلك وأن يرفع إليه ما يلحق دمنة من حجّة وما يدلي به من مخرج له فنصبه للناس وأعلم العامّة ما أمر به الملك في أمر دمنة من تفحّص عنه والاستبراء لما عند الخاصّة والعامّة من علم ما كان منه والمسألة لدمنة مع ذلك عن عذر إن كان له ليحكم في ذلك بالعدل ولا يأخذ فيه بغرّة الملك ولا قهر سلطان دون امتحان حقيقة الحكم وبلوغ علّة الإعذار.

٢٧،٥ قال القاضي من كان منكم يعلم من أمر دمنة علماً فلينطق[2] به لثلاث خصال منهنّ الإعانة على العدل والقيام بحجج الحقّ على أهلها واقعة حيث وقعت ومنها ومواقع الأحكام من نكال أهل الأحداث وعظة أهل البراءة والتحصين للأمور من ذرّيّة أهل الفساد ومنها الراحة من أهل المغالّة والغشّ وقطع أسباب موذياتهم على الخاصّة والعامّة.

---

[1] الأصل: وبعاوده. [2] الأصل: فسطق.

Nearby in the prison was another animal, who heard everything that had passed between Kalīlah and Dimnah. He committed it to memory, but kept it to himself.

When Dimnah learned of Kalīlah's flight, he wept for a long time in sorrow for him and in sadness at his departure. "What use is life to me, now that Kalīlah, my good brother and loyal friend, has left me? I see how true the saying is: When Fortune turns against someone in his afflictions and he sinks as low as once he was high, evil attacks him from every side; sadness and grief encompass him, and he is crushed by woes wherever he looks. Fate pursues him, however much he may guard himself against it. No sooner does one misfortune depart than another strikes, and he falls, just as I have fallen victim to this blow. I have lost my comrades, my friends have abandoned me, and now I grieve for the loss of my brother. Misfortune has descended on me in the prime of life, in my days of vigor and the freshness of youth. Kalīlah, my brother and best friend, has departed from me in sadness and sorrow." 5.25

The lion's mother again brought up Dimnah and his betrayal of the lion. "Sparing sinners," she said, "is as bad as killing the innocent. Whoever spares a sinner's life becomes a partner in his sinfulness; whoever spares an innocent's life becomes a partner in his good deeds." 5.26

So the lion commanded the judge to investigate Dimnah's case without delay. He was to submit a report of every argument Dimnah used and every exculpation he presented. The judge put Dimnah on the stand in front of the dignitaries, and he informed the common people of the king's orders to investigate Dimnah's case; to seek out any knowledge that anyone, high or low, had of his actions; to ask Dimnah for his defense, if he had any; and to pass a just judgment. Dimnah would not be allowed to deceive the king or prevent the ruler from reaching a true judgment and obtaining whatever was necessary to vindicate it.

The judge addressed the court: "Let any of you who knows anything about Dimnah's case speak—and that for three reasons: first, to uphold justice and to provide true evidence, however it may fall; second, to enable verdicts to be pronounced that punish offenders, encourage the righteous, and protect the state from evildoers and the offspring of evildoers; and third, to free us from people of malice and deception and to prevent them from harming nobles and commoners alike." 5.27

فلمّا قضى قوله ذلك سكت جميع من حضر ولم ينطق أحد منهم بشيء لأنّهم لم يعلموا من أمره علماً واضحاً يتكلّموا به وكرهوا القول بالظنون.

٢٨،٥ فلمّا رأى دمنة سكوتهم تكلّم وقال إنّي لو كنت مجرماً سُررت بسكوتكم[١] عن القول في أمري ولكنّي بريء قد علمتم ذلك أو لم تعلموا لي جرماً لأنّ كلّ من لا يُعلم له جرم فلا سبيل عليه فهو بريء إذاً[٢] لا بدّ من أن تقولوا فيّ بعلمكم وليعلم مع ذلك من عسى أن يقول في أمري أنّ لكلّ قول عاقبة عاجلة وآجلة وأنّ قوله في أمري حكم في إحياء نفسي أو موتها فمن عرّضني للعطب بغير علم أو قال في أمري بالظنّ أصاب من عاقبة قوله ما أصاب الطبيب الذي انتحل من علم ما لم يعلم.

قال القاضي وكيف كان ذلك.

٢٩،٥ قال دمنة كان في بعض المدائن طبيب له رفق وعلم وكان مع ذلك ذا حظّ ممّا يجري على يديه من مقادير العافية فيما يعالج به الناس من طبّه وأدويته فكبر ذلك الطبيب وذهب بصره وإنّ رجلاً سفيهاً ادّعى علم الطبّ في تلك المدينة فاشتاع ذلك من أمره في الناس وكان لملك تلك الناحية بنت فزوّجها ابن أخ له فحملت فعرض لها بعض ما يعرض للحوامل من الأوجاع فبعث الملك إلى الطبيب الأعمى فلمّا جاءه سأل أهل الجارية[٣] عن وجعها فأعلموه فوصف لهم دواء معروفاً وسمّاه لهم فأمر الملك أن يخلطه له في ذلك فقال لست أبصر فأجمع الأخلاط على معرفتي ولا أثق بجمع غيري منها. وإنّ السفيه المدّعي علم الطبّ أتاهم وأخبرهم أنّه بأخلاط ذلك الدواء وصنعته عالم فأمر الملك بإدخاله الخزانة ليأخذ من أخلاط ذلك الدواء ما يحتاج إليه فلمّا دخل عُرضت عليه أخلاط الأدوية واعتسف السفيه بتكلّفه فأخذ منها شيئاً بغير علم ولا معرفة على الظنّ والشبهة فكان ممّا أخذ صرّة فيها سمّ قاتل فخلطه فيما خلط ثمّ سقى الجارية فلم تلبث ساعة حتّى ماتت فدعا الملك به فسقاه من الدواء الذي خلطه فمات من ساعته.

١ كذا ش؛ الأصل: بسكوبهم. ٢ الأصل: اذ. ٣ أهل الجارية: الأصل: الحاريه اهلها.

Everyone remained silent. No one said a word, for they knew nothing certain about the case and were reluctant to give voice to suspicions.

When Dimnah saw their silence, he spoke up: "If I were a criminal, I would welcome your silence. But I am innocent. Either you know it, or you know of no offense on my part—and anyone not known to have committed an offense cannot be called to account and is innocent. Therefore, you must say about me what you know. But anyone who speaks should realize that words have consequences, whether immediate or delayed. What he says about me will determine whether I live or die. Anyone who without knowledge condemns me to destruction or speaks about me merely on the basis of suspicion will suffer the fate of the physician who pretended to know something about which he really knew nothing." **5.28**

"And what was his fate?" asked the judge.

5.29 *The Quack Physician Who Claimed Knowledge*

Dimnah told the following tale: In a certain city there lived a learned physician who prospered because of the providential cures that occurred at his hands through his treatments and drugs. In time, this physician grew old and lost his sight. In the same city lived a fool who claimed to know the science of medicine and whose reputation spread among the people. The king of that city had a daughter whom he married to a nephew. She became pregnant and began to feel some of the pains that women experience in pregnancy, so the king sent for the blind physician. He arrived and questioned the young woman's family about her pains. They told him, and he prescribed a well-known medicine, which he named. However, when the king commanded him to compound some of it, he said, "Because I can't see, I can't gather the ingredients as I know they should be, and I don't trust anyone else to gather them." Then the quack came and told them that he was familiar with the medicine's ingredients and their preparation. The king ordered that he be admitted to the storeroom to take what he needed. When the ingredients for medicines were presented to him, he proceeded arbitrarily according to his pretentions, and chose ingredients with neither knowledge nor experience, merely using guesswork and conjecture. One of the things he chose was a bag of deadly poison. He mixed it in with the ingredients and gave it to the young woman to drink. She died within the hour. The king summoned the quack and made him drink some of the medicine he had prepared. He died on the spot.

٣٠.٥ فتكلّم بعض من حضر وقال اسمعوا أيّها العلماء والأشراف مقالتي وفكّروا فيها بأحلامكم ومبلغ عقولكم وجهد رأيكم فإنّ العلماء قد قالوا في باب الصالحين يُعرفون بذلك وقد نعتوه وكتبوه وكشفوه وأنتم معشر الأحبار بحسن صنع الله إليكم ونعمته عليكم فيما أكمل لكم من العقل تعرفون الصالحين بسيماهم وتكتفون بالشيء اليسير من ذلك وإنّ أحقّ من لم يسأل عنه العامّة ولم يشكل على الخاصّة أمره لهذا الخبيث الذي ظهرت فيه علامات الشرّ وشامات الفجور[1] قد مضى رأي العلماء فيها.

٣١.٥ قال القاضي وما تلك العلامات والشامات فإنّك[2] تعرف أمرها أكثر ممّا نعرف.

قال المتكلّم وجدنا في كتب العلماء أنّه من كان علاماته أن تكون عينه اليسرى أصغر من عينه اليمنى وكان مع ذلك كثير اختلاج العين مائل الأنف إلى شقّه الأيمن متباعد ما بين الحاجبين وكانت منابت شعر جسده ثلاثًا ثلاثًا وإذا مشى كان أكثر نظرًا إلى الأرض وإذا مشى أدار رأسه حتّى يصير وجهه خلفه فذلك مستجمع للغدر والبغي على الصالحين وهذه العلامات كلّها في دمنة.

٣٢.٥ فلمّا أمضى فيه قوله قال دمنة إنّ حكم الله على خلقه عدل لا جور فيه وصواب لا خطأ فيه ولو كانت هذه العلامات التي ذكرتها يصاب بها وبأشباهها وجه العدل لما احتاج ولاة أهل الحقّ وحكّامهم معها إلى البيّنات والحجج ولما كان لأحد في الإحسان حمد ولا كان عليه في إساءة ذمّ لأنّه[3] ليس أحد يستطيع أن يغيّر شيئًا ممّا به من العلامات التي بها يعمل ولما كان جزاء أهل الإحسان ولا جزاء أهل الفجور إلّا على العلامات. ولو كنت عملت[4] هذا الذي لُطّخت به بالعلامات التي أعوذ بالله منها لكان تلك العلامات التي ألزم منها الله لا أستطيع التى الزمتنيها وقذفتني بها لا أستطيع امتناعًا. وممّا يدلّ على قلّة علمك بالأحكام ومواقعها أنّ الذي ذكرت لو كان كذلك لم[5] يوجب عليّ شيئًا لأنّ العلامات تُخلق مع صاحبها حين يُخلق وتولد معه حين يولد وليس لفعالها وقت في أيّ يوم تكون أو في أيّ عمر ومتى[6] ينبغي

---

١ كذا ش؛ ساقطة من الأصل. ٢ الأصل: فانا. ٣ الأصل: لبن. ٤ كذا ش؛ الأصل: علمت. ٥ كذا ش؛ ساقطة من الأصل. ٦ كذا ش؛ الأصل: وما.

At that point someone spoke up: "Scholars and nobles, hearken to my words and ponder them with your understanding, your fullest intelligence, and your most diligent judgment. Scholars have said that the righteous can be known by means of certain things which they have described, written down, and revealed. Thanks to God's kindness and favor toward you in perfecting your intelligence, you learned men know the righteous by their distinguishing features and need no more than the merest indications. This wretch, on whom are visible the signs of evil and marks of sinfulness spelled out by the sages, is someone whose wickedness is beyond question for ordinary people and whose case is unequivocal for the elite." 5.30

"What are those marks and signs?" asked the judge. "You know more about them than we do." 5.31

And the speaker explained:[37] "They are as we read in scholarly books: Anyone whose left eye is smaller than his right, whose eye blinks constantly, whose nose bends to the right, who has a wide space between his eyebrows, whose body hairs grow in threes, who looks mostly at the ground as he walks and repeatedly looks back—in such a person treachery and wrongful conduct toward the righteous coalesce. All these signs are present in Dimnah."

Dimnah responded: "God's judgment upon His creatures is just and contains no injustice; it is true and contains no error. Rulers and judges who seek the truth would need no further evidence or argument if justice could be attained by means of such signs as you have mentioned. No one could be praised for doing good or blamed for doing evil, for no one could change any of the signs that determine his actions. Benefactors could be rewarded, and malefactors punished, merely on the basis of these signs. And if—God protect me!—I did what I am being slandered for based on these signs, then it was those signs that God decreed; there was no way I could have resisted what you have attributed to me and accused me of doing. Another indication of your ignorance of how to pass judgment is that, if what you said were true, my mere possession of these signs would entail no legal consequences for me; for such signs are created with their possessor at the moment of his creation, and born with him at the moment of his birth. Their operations have 5.32

الحكم أن يقع على أهلها وما حال من لم يبلغ العقل إذا كانت به العلامات التي ذكرت فهذا الدليل لأهل العقل على سفهك وجهلك ولكنّك سمعت شيئاً لم تعرف موضعه فتكلّمت به في غير حينه ولست بأعلم وأفقه ممّن حضر ولا بأولاهم بالمنطق ولكنّك تكلّمت فأخطأت فمثلك مثل رجل قال لامرأته استري عورتك ثمّ التمسي بتستير عورة غيرك.

قال القاضي وكيف كان ذلك.

٣٣٫٥ قال دمنة كانت مدينة[١] تدعى بردجرد فأغار عليها العدوّ فقتل فيها وسبى وانطلق بمن سبى إلى بلادهم فأصاب رجل منهم في قسمة السبي حرّاثاً وامرأتين له فكان صاحبهم ذلك يضيّق عليهم في الطعام والشراب والكسوة فانطلق الحرّاث ذات يوم يحتطب ومعه امرأتاه عريانتان فأصابت إحداهما خرقة بالية في الصحراء فأخذتها فغطت بها عورتها وقالت الأخرى لزوجها ألا تنظر إلى هذه الفاعلة التي تمشي عريانة. فقال لها زوجها ويلك ألا تنظرين أنت إلى نفسك فإنّ جسمك عارٍ كلّه وأنت تطعنين على التي قد غطت عورتها وتعيّبينها بهذا وإليك العجب.

فلمّا سمع من حضر من حسن مراجعة دمنة لمن قال فيه شيئاً ورأوا قوّته على الحجج كفّوا عن القول في أمره فأمر القاضي بصرفه إلى السجن.

٣٤٫٥ فلمّا كان من الغد من ذلك اليوم دخل القاضي على الأسد في طائفة من وجوه من كان حضر مجلسه بالأمس فرفع إليه كتاباً فيه ما قال دمنة في معاذيره فقبض الأسد ذلك الكتاب وأمرهم بالانصراف عنه وأرسل إلى أمّه فقرأ عليها ذلك فشقّ عليها ما رأت من الأسد وعطفه على دمنة وقالت إن أنا غلظت لك أيّها الملك فلا تغضب.

قال الأسد افعلي وانعمي وقولي ما أحببت.

قالت ما أراك تعرف ما يضرّك ممّا ينفعك وإنّي لأحسب دمنة في طول تصريفك النظر في أمره سيهيّج عليك ما لا تقعد له ولا تقوم. ثمّ جرجت عنه غضبانة.

١ كذا ر؛ الأصل: بمدينة.

no fixed date: no day or age at which they come into force or when judgment should be passed on those who possess them. And what about those who possess these signs but haven't reached the age of reason? This proves to intelligent people that you are an ignorant fool. You've heard something whose import you didn't understand, and you've applied it wrongly. You are no more learned or intelligent than those present, nor the most qualified to speak. You've spoken in error. What the man said to his wife applies to you: 'First cover your own nakedness, then ask others to cover theirs.'"

"And how did that happen?" asked the judge.

Dimnah told the following tale: A city called Burdjird was attacked by 5.33
an enemy that killed some of its inhabitants and led others away as captives. *The Plowman and His Two Wives*
As his share of the spoils, one of the victors received a plowman and his two wives. As their master, he gave them little to eat and drink and little to wear. One day, the plowman and his naked wives went out to gather firewood. One of the wives found an old rag in the field and covered her private parts. The other wife said to her husband, "Look at that hussy walking around naked!" And her husband replied, "A plague on you! Look at yourself! You are completely naked, yet you find fault and speak evil of someone who has covered her own nakedness. Unbelievable!"

Everyone fell silent when they heard how well Dimnah had replied to his accuser and saw the strength of his arguments. The judge ordered him returned to prison.

The next morning, the judge went before the lion with a group of dig- 5.34
nitaries who had been present at the trial. The judge submitted a written account of the arguments that Dimnah had presented in his defense. The lion took the document and ordered them to leave. He then sent for his mother and read the document to her. Distressed to see that the lion was sympathetic to Dimnah, she said, "Don't be angry if I speak bluntly."

"Go ahead," replied the lion. "Say what you want to say."

"I don't think you can distinguish what harms you from what benefits you," she said. "By dragging things out so long, Dimnah is going to stir up so much discord that you won't be able to contain it." And with these words she left in anger.

٣٥،٥ فلمّا كان من الغد بعث القاضي إلى دمنة فوقّفه للعامّة فلم يقولوا شيئاً فقال له القاضي إنّه وإن سكت من حضر فلم يقولوا فيك شيئاً فإنّ[1] ظنونهم قد اجتمعت على أنّك مجرم فلم أر لك خيراً في الحياة بين ظهراني من يراك بعد استقرار تهمتك في قلوبهم ولا أرى لك شيئاً خيراً لك من أن تقرّ بذنبك فتخرج نفسك من تبعة الآخرة بالتوبة يعود لك أحسن القول من العامّة لخصلتين إحداهما قوّتك على المخارج والأخرى فإنّ الموت فيما يزين خير من الحياة فيما يشين.

٣٦،٥ قال دمنة مجيباً له إنّ صالحي القضاة لا تقضي بظنّة ولا بظنون الخاصّة والعامّة لمعرفتهم بأنّ الظنّ لا يغني من الحقّ شيئاً فإن ظننتم جميعاً أنّي صاحب جرم فيما فعلت فإنّي أعلم بنفسي منكم وعلمي بنفسي يقين لا شكّ فيه وإنّما قبح أمري في أنفسكم ظنّكم بي أنّي سعيت بغيري فما عذري عندكم إن سعيت بنفسي كاذباً عليها فأسلمتها للقتل على معرفة منّي ببراءتها. فنفسي أعظم النفوس عليّ حرمة[2] وأوجبها عليّ حقّاً ولو فعلت ذلك بأدناكم وأقصاكم لم يسعني ذلك في ديني ولم يحسن في رأيي وخلقي فكفّ عن هذه المقالة فإنّها إن كانت منك نصيحة فقد أخطأت موضعها وإن كانت خديعة فليس الخداع ولا المكر من أخلاق الصالحين. وأعلم أنّ قولك الصواب ويخطأها أهل الباطل والأدغال فأنا خائف عليك مقالتك هذه أعظم الوزر فإنّك لم تزل في أنفس الجند والملك فاضلاً في رأيك عادلاً في حكمك فتغيّر ذلك منك في أمري. وأمرك أمر القضاة وما يحقّ عليهم من الكفّ عن سقيط الناس واستدراجهم وانصرفت إلى العمل بالظنون بي التي تختلف بها الحالات والأمور. أما بلغك ما قالت العلماء من أنّه من ادّعى علم ما لم يعلم وقال ما لم يره وشهد عليه أصابه ما أصاب البازيار القاذف لمولاته التي زعم أنّه رآها مع رجل تفجر وتعمل ما لا ينبغي.

قال القاضي وكيف كان ذلك.

---

١ كذا ش؛ الأصل: وان. ٢ الأصل: جرمه.

5.35 The next morning, the judge sent for Dimnah and made him stand before the full assembly. When no one ventured to say anything, the judge himself addressed Dimnah: "Although everyone here has kept silent and said nothing against you, they all suspect you are a criminal. Now that the charge against you has taken root in their hearts, I see no good for you in a life lived among those who think this way about you. I think it would be best for you to admit your guilt and through repentance save yourself from the consequences in the hereafter. You would thereby earn universal praise for two reasons: for your ability to find ways to escape, and because death in a state of grace is better than life in a state of disgrace."

5.36 Dimnah answered: "Righteous judges don't pass judgment on the basis of their own suspicions or the suspicions of others, be they dignitaries or commoners. They know that suspicion is no substitute for the truth. Even if you all suspect that I acted culpably, I know myself better than you, and my knowledge of myself is certain and is free of doubts. It is your suspicion that I slandered someone else that disgraces me in your minds. How then could I plead my own defense if I falsely slandered my own self and handed myself over to death in spite of knowing about my innocence? No life is more sacred to me than my own and no one else has a stronger claim on me. If I had done this to any of you, near or far, it would have accorded with neither my religion nor my mind and character. Therefore, refrain from speaking as you did. If you said it sincerely, it was misguided; if you said it with ulterior motives, deception and guile have no place in the character of the righteous. I know the truth of your words, but mischievous liars will construe them wrongly. I fear that your words will become a heavy burden for you. With the soldiers and the king, you've always enjoyed a reputation for good judgment and just decisions, but that has changed in my case. You've always acted in accordance with a judge's obligation to refrain from people's errors and deceptions, yet in my case you've turned to acting on suspicions at complete variance with the facts. Haven't you heard what the sages said—that someone who claims to know what he doesn't know and attests to what he has never seen will suffer the fate of the falconer who slandered his master's wife, alleging that he had seen her fornicating with a man and doing what ought not to be done?"

"And what was his fate?" asked the judge.

٣٧،٥ قال دمنة زعموا أنّه كان بمدينة كذا رجل مذكور وكان له امرأة ذات عقل وحسب وحسن وعفاف وكان للرجل بازيار ماهر بسياسة البزاة ومعالجتها كريم على مولاه وكان قد راود امرأة سيّده فأبت عليه فحرص على سبّها وكان يكثر في ذلك الأقاويل فاستُخفّ بقوله فلمّا رأى أنّه لا يبلغ بشيء من ذلك ما أراد من فضيحتها اضطغن عليها وأجمع الحيلة في هتكها واغتدى في طلب الصيد فأصاب فرخي ببّغاء فربّاهما وفرّق بينهما وعلّم أحدهما قذفاً لمولاته وهو إنّي رأيت البوّاب مضاجعاً مولاتي على فراش سيّدي. ولقّن الآخر أن يقول أمّا أنا فلا أقول شيئاً. فأدّب الفرخين بذلك وحذقا به في ستّة أشهر وبلغا ما أراد وكانت لغة الفرخين بلسان البلخيّ فذهب بهما إلى مولاه ووضعهما بين يديه فصاحا فأعجبه حلاوة أصواتهما عن غير معرفة بما يقولان لأنّهما عُلّما ذلك بلسان البلخيّة ولم يكن ذلك بلسان سيّد العبد ولا لسان أهل بلده فقبضهما من البازيار وألطفه وأتحفه لإعجابه بهما وأمر امرأته بالاحتفاظ بهما والتعاهد لأمرهما ففعلت ذلك.

٣٨،٥ فلمّا كان بعد ذلك قدم على الرجل نفر من عظماء أهل بلخ فأدخلهم منزله وقرّب إليهم طعاماً كان قد تنوّق فيه ثمّ أتاهم بما يُتحف به الأضياف من الشراب وغيره فلمّا أخذوا مجلسهم للشراب أمر المرزبان بأن يؤتى بالببّغاءين فلمّا وُضعا بين يديه صاحا بما كانا عُلّما فعرف الضيفان ما قالا ونظر بعضهم إلى بعض ونكّسوا رؤوسهم استحياء.

ثمّ إنّ بعضهم قال للمرزبان هل تعرف ما يقولان.

قال لا غير أنّ صوتهما معجب.

فقالا لذلك الرجل لكنّا نعرف ما يقولان.

فاستحيا القوم من ذلك فألحّ عليهم حتّى قال بعضهم إنّ أحدهم يقول إنّي رأيت البوّاب مضاجعاً مولاتي على فراش سيّدي. والآخر يقول أمّا أنا فلست بقائل شيئاً. فمن شأننا[١] أيها المرزبان أنّا لا نطعم في بيت تُعمل فيه زنية.

---

١ الأصل: شئننا.

5.37 *The Wife, the Falconer, and the Parrots*

And Dimnah told the following tale: They say that in a certain city there lived a distinguished man whose wife was of noble descent, beautiful, intelligent, and chaste. The man had a falconer whom he valued for his skill in training and handling hawks. The falconer had made advances to his master's wife but had been rebuffed, so he decided to defame her. He spread many rumors, none of which were taken seriously. When he saw the failure of his attempts to expose her to scandal, he devised a malicious stratagem to disgrace her. He went out hunting one morning and trapped two fledgling parrots, which he raised separately. He taught one of them to slander his master's wife by saying, "I saw the doorkeeper lie with my mistress on my master's bed." He taught the other to say, "As for me, I won't say anything!" The fledglings, after six months' training, had mastered what he wanted them to say—they said it in the language of Balkh. He then set them before his master and they cried out. His master liked the sweetness of their voices, although he didn't understand what they were saying, as they had been taught to speak the language of Balkh, which was the language neither of the master nor of his compatriots. He took the birds from the falconer, whom he rewarded with gifts, delighted as he was, and ordered his wife to keep the birds and care for them, which she did.

5.38 Sometime later, he invited visiting dignitaries from Balkh to his home, served them fine food, and gave them wine and such other items as one offers one's guests. When they took their places to drink, the man, who was a military governor, ordered the parrots to be brought. They were set before him and cried out the phrases they had been taught. The guests, who understood what they said, looked at each another and hung their heads in embarrassment.

"Do you know what the parrots are saying?" asked one of them.

"No," he replied, "but I like their voices."

"We know what they are saying," the guests said.

The guests were embarrassed, but their host insisted they tell him. Finally, a guest told him, "One is saying, 'I saw the doorkeeper lie with my mistress on my master's bed.' The other is saying, 'As for me, I won't say anything!' It's not our custom, Governor, to eat in a house where there is fornication."

فلمّا انقضت مقالتهم أُفظع المرزبان فلمّا سمع البازيار مقالة القوم قال وأنا على مثل ما شهد به الببّغاءان شاهد.

٣٩.٥ فلمّا اتّفق ذلك من القول أمر المرزبان بقتل امرأته.

فقالت المرأة إنّ قتلك إيّاي على غير فحص عسى أن يورثك ما هو أشدّ من ذلك فافحص وسل الببّغاءين عمّا سوى ذلك من الكلام بهذا اللسان فإن كانا يحسنان غير هاتين الكلمتين فأنت على رأس أمرك وإن لم يكونا يحسنان غير هاتين الكلمتين فاعلم أنت ومن حضر أنّ هذا الشيء على تلقين الختّال المساور لي على هذه السوأة.

٤٠.٥ فطلب المرزبان إليهم فسألوا الببّغاءين فلم يحسنا بذلك اللفظ أن ينطقا غير تلك[1] الكلمتين فدعا المرزبان البازيار فأقبل واثقاً بنفسه على غير هيئة المريب ولا المذنب فدخل على يده باز فنادته مولاته من وراء الستر أيّها العدوّ أنت رأيتني على الزنية التي علّمت الببّغاءين.

فقال أمّا إذا سُئلت فقد قلت الذي رأيت.

فوثب البازي الذي على يده فتناول بمخلبيه حدقتي البازيار فانتزعهما.

فقالت مولاته إنّ هذا الذي أصابك أجزاك الله على شهادتك ما لم تره.

وإنّما ضربت لك هذا المثل لتزداد علماً بوخامة عاقبة الشهادة بالكذب في الدنيا والآخرة.

٤١.٥ قال القاضي إنّ الحاكم العادل ينبغي له أن يعرف عمل المحسنين ليجزي المحسنين بإحسانهم والمسيئين بإساءتهم فإذا هو قد أحسن إلى الفريقين جميعاً فازداد المحسنون حرصاً على الإحسان والمسيئون اجتناباً للذنوب. والذي أرى لك ويحك يا دمنة أن تنظر في أمرك وفي الذي غشاك ووقعت فيه من الإثم فتتوب منه وتعترف بالحقّ فقد قيل إنّ الذي يدان بالذنب بعد الصدّ منه والاعتراف به خير من المصرّ على ذنبه وأحسن حالاً من الجاحد له. وأنت ميّت لا محالة وإن عفي

[1] كذا الأصل.

The governor was shocked to hear the guests' words. The falconer, who heard what they were saying, said, "I, too, testify to what the parrots testified."

Since the accounts agreed, the governor ordered that his wife be executed. 5.39
To this, the wife said, "Putting me to death without an investigation is likely to cause you even greater trouble. Look into the matter. Ask the parrots to say something else in this language. If they can say anything other than these two sentences, go ahead and do as you intend. If, on the other hand, that is all they can say, everyone here, including you, should know that they were trained by the deceiver who tried to seduce me to commit such a shameful deed."

The governor asked the visitors to question the parrots, and it turned out 5.40
that they couldn't say anything but those two sentences in that language. The governor summoned the falconer, who entered confidently with a hawk on his arm, not at all like someone guilty or under suspicion. The wife called out from behind the curtain, "You villain! Did you see me do the foul deed you taught the parrots to describe?"

"I was asked," he replied, "and I said what I saw."

The hawk then leapt from his arm, grabbed his eyes with its talons, and tore them out.

"This," said the wife, "is God's punishment for bearing witness to something you didn't see."

Dimnah said, "I've told this story to impress on you the bitter consequences of false testimony in this world and the next."

The judge said, "A just judge needs to know the actions of those who do 5.41
good in order to requite them for their deeds, and the actions of those who do evil to requite them for their misdeeds. If he deals correctly with both, those who do good will be more eager to do good and those who do evil will be more inclined to avoid evil. Alas, Dimnah, I think you had better consider the dire situation you are in and the sin you have fallen into. Repent, and confess the truth. As has been said: Better someone who turns away from his sin, admits it, and confesses than someone who persists in his sin or denies it.

عنك فإنّ الذي يصيبك من بعد المضض جزاء لجرمك فتصبر عليه خير لك من أن تُعذّب في جهنّم التي لا رحمة فيها ولا راحة ولا انقطاع لعذابها.

٤٢،٥ قال دمنة قلت أيّها الحاكم قول الأتقياء البررة وصدقت في مقالك ولكنّ في كتب الدين أيضاً أنّ السعيد من استطاع أن لا يعمل بجسمه عملاً يضرّ بروحه فقد قالت العلماء أيضاً إنّ العاقل من أضرّ بجسمه وتمسّك بروحه. وليس ينبغي أيضاً أن يقال لأحد بشيء يكرهه إذا لم يكن له أهلاً. وإنّي لم أر لفرقي من الآخرة مهيناً لجسمي ممسكاً بروحي. ولم أقل كلمة كذب قطّ على أحد فيها مضرّة ولا أذى ولا يستطيع أحد أن يقدم بنظرة عليّ فيها. فكيف أكون تعاطيت هذا الذنب الذي هو أعظم الذنوب ووُجد بأقوال الرسل لا تكذب على أحد ولا تفتري عليه فكيف يفتري الإنسان على نفسه ويقول لما لم يفعل قد فعلته وقد قالت العلماء إنّ الذي تحمله مخافة شديدة أو جهالة على أن[١] يلزم نفسه عملاً لم تعمله فإنّه[٢] لم يسيء إلى نفسه ولا جاعله ذلك في الآخرة مع قتلة أنفسهم. وإنّي بريء ممّا لُطّخت به فإن قُتلت بهذا القذف فإنّ ذلك غير ضائري لما ألقاه في معادي من جزيل الثواب.

٤٣،٥ فكتب القاضي ذلك كلّه من قول دمنة ثمّ دفعه إلى الأسد فنظر فيه ودعا أمّه وعرضه عليها فقالت حين تدبّرت كلام دمنة أيّها الملك لقد صار اهتمامي بأن يحتال عليك دمنة بمكره ودهائه حتّى يقتلك أو ينقص عليك أمرك أعظم من اهتمامي بما سلف من ذنبه إليك من الغشّ لك والسعاية بوزيرك وضيفك حتّى قتلته بغير ذنب.

فوقع قولها في نفسه فقال لها أخبريني عن الذي أخبرك عن دمنة بما أخبر فيكون حجّة لي في قتله.

فقالت إنّي لأكره إفشاء شيء استكتمته ولا يهنأني سروري بقتل دمنة إذا تذكّرت أنّي استظهرت عليه بركوب ما نهت عنه العلماء من كشف الأسرار ولكنّي طالبة إلى الذي استودعنيه أن يحلّلني من ذكره أو يقوم بإعلامك ما سمع.

---

١ أن: الأصل: ان لا. ٢ الأصل: فاني.

You will inevitably die someday, even if pardoned. Better the pains you suffer and endure as punishment for your crime than the torments of Hell, where there is no mercy, no rest, and no end to the torment."

Dimnah said, "Your Honor has spoken the truth in words befitting the righteous and God-fearing. But we also read in the scriptures: Blessed is he who is able to avoid performing with his body actions that harm his spirit. The scholars say that a wise man disregards harm to his body, but holds fast to his spirit. They also say that it is unseemly for loathsome words to be addressed to the undeserving. I despise the body and hold fast to the spirit, so I don't think I need fear the hereafter. Never have I lied in order to harm or insult anyone, and no one has ever seen me do so. How can I commit this gravest of sins, when we read in the scriptures of God's messengers: 'Do not lie or utter falsehoods'? How can a man lie about himself and say he did something he never did? The sages have said: When you are moved by intense fear or folly to ascribe to yourself a deed you did not do, you do not wrong your soul, nor do you place yourself in the hereafter among those who kill themselves.[38] I am innocent of the charges against me. If I am put to death as a result of this slander, it will do me no harm, because of the great reward I shall receive in the hereafter." 5.42

The judge wrote down everything Dimnah said and delivered it to the lion. The lion examined the report, then summoned his mother and showed it to her. After considering Dimnah's words, she said, "Your Majesty, now I'm worried more by the prospect that Dimnah, through his deceit and cleverness, may contrive to kill you or drive you from power than by his past guilt in deceiving you and slandering your minister and guest, so that you killed him, even though he was guiltless." 5.43

Her words made a deep impression on him. "Tell me who gave you the information about Dimnah, so that I can use it as evidence for putting him to death."[39]

"I am reluctant to reveal something I've been asked to conceal," she replied. "My joy over Dimnah's death will give me no pleasure if I remember that I played a part in it by revealing secrets, something the sages have forbidden. However, I will ask the person who entrusted the information to me to allow me to name him or to inform you himself about what he heard."

٤٤،٥ ثمّ انصرفت فأرسلت إلى النمر وذكرت له ما يحقّ عليه من تزيين الأسد ويلزمه من حسن معاملته ومعاونته على الحقّ وإخراج نفسه من الشهادة التي لا يكتمها مثله مع ما يحقّ عليهما من نصرة المظلوم وتثبيت حجّة أهل الحقّ في الحياة والممات فإنّ العلماء قد قالت من كتم حجّة ميّت أخطأ حجّته يوم القيامة. فلم تزل به حتّى قام فشهد على دمنة بما سمع من إقراره فيما كان من توبيخ كليلة إيّاه بدخوله بين الأسد والثور.

٤٥،٥ فلمّا شهد النمر على دمنة بما سمع منه أرسل السبع المسجون الذي سمع قول كليلة لدمنة ليلة دخل عليه في السجن وما كان من إقرار دمنة إنّ عندي شهادة فأخرجوه فشهد على دمنة بما سمع من قوله وإقراره فيما كان من توبيخ كليلة إيّاه بدخوله بين الأسد والثور بالنميمة والكذب.

فقال الأسد ما منعكما أن تقوما بشهادتكما وقد علمتما أمرنا بالتفتيش عن حال دمنة.

٤٦،٥ فقال كلّ واحد منهما منعنا من ذلك أنّ شهادة الواحد منّا كانت لا توجب حكمًا وكلّ واحد منّا كان بشهادة صاحبه جاهلاً وكرهنا القول في غير شيء لا يقوم به حكم.

فرضي الأسد مقالتهما وأمر بدمنة فقُتل شرّ قتلة.

انتهى باب الابتحاث[1] عن شأن دمنة وكلّ ذلك يكون عواقب البغي ومواقع أمور الحسد والكذب.

---

١ الأصل: الانحاث.

She left and sent a message to the leopard. She reminded him of his responsibility to enhance the lion's prestige and of his duty to treat him well and guide him to the truth by delivering testimony that should not be concealed by someone like him. Both of them had a duty to side with the victim of injustice and exonerate a righteous person in life and in death. As the sages had said: Whoever conceals a dead man's vindication will fail to vindicate himself on the Day of Resurrection. Finally, after much persuasion, the leopard stood up and testified to what he had heard: that Dimnah, faced with Kalīlah's rebuke, had acknowledged coming between the lion and the ox. 5.44

After the leopard testified to what he had heard Dimnah say, the prisoner who had heard Kalīlah admonishing Dimnah on the night of his prison visit and Dimnah's admission sent a message that he had testimony to give. They brought him out of prison, and he testified to what he had heard: that Dimnah, confronted with Kalīlah's rebuke, had acknowledged using slander and falsehood to come between the lion and the ox. 5.45

"What," asked the lion, "kept the two of you from testifying when you knew we had ordered an investigation into Dimnah's case?"

Each answered, "The testimony of a single witness wouldn't have brought about a conviction. Neither of us knew of the other's testimony, so we were reluctant to speak to no avail." 5.46

The lion was satisfied with their answer. On his orders, Dimnah was put to a most horrible death.

Here ends the Chapter on the Investigation of Dimnah. Such are the consequences of wrongdoing and the effects of envy and lying.

باب الحمامة المطوّقة

وهو مثل إخوان الصفاء كيف بدء مواقع
تواصلهم واستماع بعضهم لبعض

قال الملك للعالم قد سمعت مثل الرجلين المتحابين كيف يقطع ما بينهما الكذوب المحتال ويحملهما على العداوة فاضرب لي مثل إخوان الصفاء كيف يكون بدء تواصلهم واستماع بعضهم لبعض. ١،٦

قال العالم إنّ العاقل لا يعدل بصالحي الإخوان شيئاً من الأشياء لأنّ الإخوان هم الأعوان على الخير والمؤاسون عند النوائب ومن أمثال ذلك مثل الحمامة المطوّقة والغراب والظبي والسلحفاة.

قال الملك وكيف كان ذلك.

قال الفيلسوف زعموا أنّه كان بأرض سيناند[١] قريب من مدينة ماروزود مكان كثير الصيد يتصيّد فيه الصيّادون وكان في ذلك المكان شجرة عظيمة كثيرة الغصون ملتفّة الأوراق وكان فيها وكر غراب فبينما الغراب ذات يوم على الشجرة إذ بصر برجل من الصيّادين قبيح المنظر سيّء الحال عليه أطمار وعلى عاتقه شرك وفي يده عصا مقبل نحو الشجرة فذعر منه الغراب وقال لقد جاء هذا الرجل إلى المكان لأمر فما أدري ألحيني أم لحين غيري ولكنّي ثابت مكاني ناظر ما يصنع. ٢،٦

ثمّ نصب الصيّاد شركه ونثر فيه حبّاً وكمن في مكمن قريباً منه فلم يلبث إلّا قليلاً حتّى مرّ به حمامة كان يقال لها المطوّقة كانت سيّدة حمام كثيرة فهنّ معها فلمّا أبصرت المطوّقة الحبّ ولم تنظر الشرك انقضّت هي وحمامها جميعاً فوقعن في الشرك وأقبل الصيّاد إليهنّ مسرعاً فرحاً بهنّ واضطربت كلّ حمامة على حالها تعالج لنفسها ٣،٦

---

١ كذا في الأصل.

The Ring Dove

A parable about the circumstances that initiate friendships between sincere brethren and how each benefits by following the other's advice.

The king said to the philosopher, "Now that I've heard a parable about how a crafty liar can drive friends apart and incite them to become enemies, tell me one about how friendships between sincere brethren begin and how each benefits by following the other's advice." 6.1

"A wise man values nothing more than good friends," replied the philosopher. "Friends help us achieve good things and they console us in times of adversity. The story of the ring dove, the crow, the gazelle, and the turtle is an example of this."

"And what was their story?" asked the king.

The philosopher told the following tale: They say that in the Deccan, near the city of Mārūzūd, was a place abounding in game, where hunters would come to hunt. A crow nested there, in a great tree with many branches dense with leaves. One day, as he sat, he became frightened as he spied a hunter approaching, foul-faced, ill-tempered, and shabbily dressed, with a net on his back and a stick in his hand. "This man," he said to himself, "has come for a reason—whether it's to destroy me or someone else, I don't know, but I'll stay put and see what he does." 6.2

The hunter set up his net, scattered grain, and hid nearby. Soon a ring dove flew by, a leader of many doves, who accompanied her. She saw the grain, but not the net, and, along with the other doves, swooped down and landed under the net. The hunter rushed up, delighted to have caught 6.3

المخرج فقالت المطوّقة لهنّ لا تتخاذلن[١] في المعالجة ولا تكوننّ نفس واحدة منكنّ هي أهمّ لها من نفس صاحبتها ولكن هلمّ تعاونّ جميعاً نقتلع الشبكة.

فتعاونّ فاقتلعنها وطرن بها فسرن علوة في السماء فاتّبعهنّ الصيّاد رجاء أن لا يتجاوزن إلّا قريباً حتّى يثقلهنّ الشبك فيقعن.

وقال الغراب وقد رأى ما رأى لأتّبعهنّ فلأنظرنّ إلى ما يصير أمرهنّ وأمر الصيّاد.

٤،٦ فنظرت المطوّقة فرأت الصيّاد يتبعهنّ غير منقطع الرجاء منهنّ فقالت لصواحبها هذا الصيّاد جاء في طلبكنّ فإن أمتنّ في الفضاء لم تخفين عليه ولكن توجّهن إلى العمران والحضر فإنّه لا يلبث أن يخفى عليه مذهبكنّ فينصرف آئساً منكنّ ومع ذلك فإنّ قريب من الريف مكاناً[٢] أنا به عارفة[٣] فيه جحر جرذ وهو صديق لي فلو قد انتهينا إليه قطع عنّا هذا الشبك وأفلتنا منه.

فتوجّهن حيث أمرتهنّ المطوّقة فخفين على الصيّاد وانصرف آئساً منهنّ. ولم ينصرف الغراب إرادة أن ينظر هل لهنّ حيلة يحتلنها للخروج من الشبكة فيتعلّمها فتكون له عدّة لنازلة إن نزلت به.

٥،٦ فلمّا انتهت بهنّ المطوّقة إلى مكان الجرذ أمرتهنّ بالوقوع فوقعن فوجدت حوالي جحر الجرذ مائة نفق أعدّها للمخاوف فنادته المطوّقة باسمه وكان اسمه زيرك فأجابها الجرذ من جحره وقال من أنت.

قالت أنا خليلتك المطوّقة.

فأقبل إليها سعياً فلمّا رآها في الشبك قال ما أوقعك في هذه الورطة وأنت من الأكياس.

قالت المطوّقة ألم تعلم أنّه ليس شيء من الخير والشرّ إلّا وهو مقدّر على من يصيبه بأيّامه وأوقاته وعلله ومدّته وقدر ما هو نصيبه في قلّته وكثرته فالمقادير التي أوقعتني حيث ترى. فقالت إنّي أوضحت إلى الحبّ وأعميت بصري عن الشبكة فلجت

---

١ الأصل: تخادلن. ٢ فإنّ . . . مكاناً: الأصل: فانا قربا من الريف مكان. ٣ الأصل: عارف.

them. Each dove fluttered about separately, straining to free herself, but the ring dove said, "Stay true to one another! Don't focus more on your own life than on your companion's. Let's work together and perhaps we can lift this net."

So they worked together, lifted the net, and carried it high into the air. The hunter followed, hoping that the net would weigh them down and that they would land before they could go very far.

The crow, who saw what was happening, said to himself, "I'll follow them to see how their run-in with the hunter ends."

The ring dove looked back and saw that the hunter was following, still 6.4
hoping to capture them, and she said to her companions, "The hunter, I see, is pursuing us. If we stay out in the open, we'll remain in his sight; let's head for the orchards and trees. He'll soon lose track of us and give up. I know a place by the fields where a rat has his den. He's a friend of mine. If we can get to him, he'll cut through the net and we'll be free."

So they headed for the place the ring dove had mentioned. When they disappeared from the hunter's sight, he gave up and went away. The crow, for his part, did not head back; he wanted to see whether the doves could manage to extricate themselves from the net, to learn how to do it himself and be prepared should a similar calamity ever befall him.

When the ring dove and her companions reached the rat's home, she 6.5
ordered the doves to land, which they did. She discovered a hundred holes around the rat's den that he had prepared as a precaution. The ring dove called out his name, Zīrak, and he answered from his den: "Who's there?"

"Your friend, the ring dove."

He hurried out, and when he saw her in the net, he asked, "You're so quick-witted; how did you get into this predicament?"

The ring dove said, "Don't you know that everything, both good and evil, that befalls us is determined by destiny—the day, the season, the cause, the duration, and the magnitude? Destiny cast me into this predicament: it made

فيها كما ترى أنا وصواحبي وليس أمري وقلّة امتناعي من القدر بعجب فقد لا يمتنع من القدر من هو أقوى منّي وأعظم أمرًا وقد تنكسف الشمس والقمر إذا انتهيا إلى ميقات قضاء ذلك عليهما وقد تصاب الحيتان في لجج البحار التي لا سبيل إلى السباحة فيها ويُستنزل الطير من الهواء فالسبب الذي يدرك به العاجز حاجته هو الذي يحول بين الحازم وطلبته.

٦،٦ ثمّ إنّ الجرذ أخذ في تقريض العقد[١] التي كانت فيها المطوّقة فقالت المطوّقة ابدأ بعقد صواحبي ثمّ أقبل على عقدي. وأعادت ذلك مرارًا على الجرذ كلّ ذلك لا يلتفت الجرذ إلى قولها فلمّا أكثرت عليه قال لها كأنّك ليست لك حاجة في نفسك ولا ترين لها حقًّا.

قالت المطوّقة لا تلمني على ما طلبت إليك فإنّه لم يحملني على ذلك إلّا أنّي تكلّفت لجماعة هذا الحمام بالرئاسة وحقّ ذلك عليّ عظيم وقد أدّين إليّ حقّي في الطاعة والنصيحة والمعونة وبذلك نجّانا الله من صاحب الشرك وإنّي خفت إن أنت بدأت بقطع عقدتي أن تملّ وتكسل عن بعض ما يبقى من عقدهنّ وعرفت إن بدأت بهنّ وكنت أنا الأخيرة لم ترض وإن أدركك الفتور والملل أن تترك معالجة قطع وثاقي عنّي.

قال الجرذ هذا ما يزيد أهل المودّة لك والرغبة فيك رغبة وودًّا لك. ثمّ أخذ الجرذ في تقريض الشبكة حتّى أتى على آخرها فانطلقت المطوّقة وحمامها راجعات إلى مكانهنّ.

٧،٦ فلمّا رأى الغراب صنع الجرذ وتخليصه الحمام رغب في مصادقة الجرذ وقال في نفسه ما أنا من مثل ما أصابهنّ[٢] بآمن ولا أنا عن الجرذ ومودّته بغنًى. فدنا من جحر[٣] الجرذ وناداه باسمه.

فأجابه الجرذ من أنت.

قال أنا غراب كان من أمري كيت وكيت وإنّي لمّا رأيت من وفائك لأصدقائك وما نفع الله بك الحمام ما رأيت رغبت في مخالطتك ومخاللتك فجئتك لذلك.

---

١ أخذ . . . العقد: كذا ش، ع؛ الأصل: أخد ى نعض تمريض العقد. ٢ كذا ر؛ الأصل: اصاب. ٣ جحر الجرذ: كذا ش؛ الأصل: الحرد.

me see the grain clearly and blinded me to the net. My companions and I plunged into it, as you can see. There is nothing amazing about my inability to protect myself from destiny: things stronger and greater than I can't escape their destiny. When it is decreed, the sun and the moon are eclipsed, fish are caught in the depths of the sea, and birds are brought down from the air. The very means that enable the weakling to reach his objective can block the resolute man from his goal."

The rat began to gnaw at the knots that entangled the ring dove, but she 6.6
said, "Begin with the knots ensnaring my companions; then attend to mine." She repeated this several times, but he paid no attention to what she said. Finally, after many such urgings, he said, "You seem to have no concern for your own life and not to recognize the claim it has on you."

"Don't chide me for my request," replied the ring dove. "I have a great responsibility as leader of this flock. They've fulfilled their duty of obedience, counsel, and assistance, and by that means God has delivered us from the hunter's snares. If you begin by cutting my bonds, I'm afraid you'll tire and neglect some of the others' bonds. But I know that if you start with them and leave me till last, you won't allow yourself, no matter how tired and weary, to stop cutting away my bonds."

"That," said the rat, "is what makes those who love you and desire your friendship love you and desire your friendship even more." He gnawed at the net until he was done, and the ring dove and her flock flew back home.

When the crow saw how the rat had freed the doves, he was keen to 6.7
become the rat's friend. He said to himself, "What happened to them might happen to me, and I might need the rat and his friendship." So he approached the rat's den and called him by name.

"Who are you?" came the reply.

"A crow," he said, introducing himself. "When I saw your loyalty to your friends and how through you God helped the doves, I became eager to spend time in your company and become friends. That's why I'm here."

قال الجرذ ليس بيني وبينك سبيل تواصل وإنّما ينبغي للعاقل أن يطلب ما إليه سبيل كيلا يُعدّ جاهلاً كرجل أراد أن يجري السفن في البرّ والعجل في البحر على الماء. وكيف يكون بيني وبينك سبيل التواصل وإنّما أنا طعام وأنت آكل.

٨،٦ قال الغراب اعتبر بعقلك أنّ أكلي إيّاك إن كنت لي طعاماً لا يغني عنّي شيئاً وأنّ بقاءك ومودّتك لي به أنس وأمن ما بقيت ولست حقيقاً إذا جئت أطلب مودّتك أن ترجعني خائباً فإنّه قد ظهر لي حسن خلقك وإن كنت لا تلتمس[١] ظهور ذلك منك فإنّ ذا الفضل[٢] لا يخفى فضله وإن هو أخفى ذلك كلّه جهده كالمسك الذي يُخبأ ويُكتم ولا يمتنع بذلك ريحه من الأرج والفوح فلا تغيّرنّ عليك خلقك ولا تمنعني ودّك وملاطفتك.

٩،٦ قال الجرذ إنّ أشدّ عداوة عداوة الجوهر وعداوة الجوهر عداوتان منهما عداوة متجازية[٣] كعداوة الفيل والأسد فإنّه ربّما قتل الفيل الأسد وربّما قتل الأسد الفيل ومنهما عداوة ضرّها من أحد الجانبين على الآخر كعداوة ما بيني وبينك فإنّ العداوة بيننا ليست لضرّ منّا عليكم ولكنّ لضرّ علينا منكم ولكن ليس بين عداوة الجوهر صلح إلّا ريثما يعود إلى العداوة وليس صلح العدوّ موثوقاً به ولا مسكوناً إليه فإنّ الماء وإن سُخّن فأطيل إسخانه فليس يمنعه ذلك من إطفاء النار إذا صُبّ عليها وإنّما صاحب العدوّ المصالح كصاحب الحيّة يحملها في كفّه ولا ينبغي للعاقل أن يستأنس بالعدوّ الأريب على كلّ حال.

١٠،٦ قال الغراب قد فهمت ما تقول وأنت حقيق أن تأخذ عقلك وتعرف فضل مقالتي ولا تصعّب الأمر فيما بيني وبينك بقولك ليس إلى التواصل فيما بيننا سبيل فإنّ أهل العقل يبتغون إلى كلّ معروف وصلة ذريعة وسبيلاً والمودّة بين الصالحين بطيء انقطاعها سريع اتّصالها ومثل ذلك مثل الكوز من الذهب الذي هو بطيء الانكسار هيّن الإصلاح والإعادة له إن أصابه كسر أو ثلم والمودّة بين الأشرار سريع انقطاعها بطيء اتّصالها كالكوز من الفخار يكسره أدنى عتب ثمّ لا وصل له أبداً

١ كذا ر؛ الأصل: ألتمس. ٢ كذا ر؛ الأصل: العقل. ٣ الأصل: متحاربه.

"Friendship between us? Not a chance! Someone with his wits about him should seek only what he can obtain, otherwise he'll be considered as foolish as a man who wants to make ships sail on dry land, or carts travel on the sea. How can there be friendship between us when I'm the dinner and you're the diner?"

"Consider it rationally," said the crow. "Though you are my food, eating 6.8
you will hardly benefit me, whereas your life and friendship will bring me joy and safety as long as I live. Now that I've come to seek your friendship, I don't deserve to be sent away disappointed, for your fine character is obvious, though you weren't trying to display it. It is easier to hide musk, whose scent diffuses no matter how much you try to hide it and seal it up, than it is to conceal an intelligent person's excellence, try as he may to conceal it. Do not act out of character and deprive me of your friendship and kindness."

"The strongest enmity is that which is innate," responded the rat. "It is of 6.9
two kinds. In some cases, the hostility works both ways, as with the elephant and the lion; sometimes the elephant kills the lion, and sometimes the lion kills the elephant. In other cases, only one of the parties harms the other—as is the case between me and you. Our hostility isn't due to any harm we've done to you; it's due to the harm you've done to us. Truces between innate enemies eventually revert to hostility. No truce with an innate enemy can be trusted or depended on. Heat water as long as you wish; it will still put out fire. A person who tries to befriend his enemy is like someone who carries a snake in the palm of his hand. No intelligent person should ever try to socialize with a clever enemy."

"I understand what you're saying," said the crow, "but you ought to follow 6.10
your intelligence, recognize the merit of my words, and not make matters difficult between us by saying that there's no way for us to become friends. Intelligent people will find ways and means to a good act. Affection between the good is quick to be cemented, slow to be broken. It is like a golden cup: slow to break, but easy to restore and mend if broken. Affection between the wicked, however, is quick to be severed and slow to be rejoined, like a clay

وذو الكرم يودّ الكريم على لقاء مرّة واحدة ومعرفة يوم واللئيم لا يصل أحداً إلّا عن رغبة أو رهبة وأنت كريم وأنا إلى ودّك محتاج وأنا لازم بابك وغير ذائق طعاماً ولا شراباً حتّى تؤاخيني.

قال الجرذ قد قبلت إخاءك فإني لم أردد ذا حاجة قطّ عن حاجته[١] وإنّما ابتدأتك بما ابتدأتك به للإعذار إلى نفسي فإن أنت غدرت لم تقل وجدت الجرذ ضعيف الرأي سريع الانخداع. ثمّ خرج فقام عند جحره. ١١،٦

فقال له الغراب ما يمنعك من الانبساط إليّ والاستئناس بي أفي نفسك ريبة بعد.

قال الجرذ إنّ أهل الدنيا يتعاطون أمرين يتواصلون عليهما ذات النفس وذات اليد فأمّا المتبادلون ذات النفس فهم الأصفياء المتخالصون وأمّا المتبادلون ذات اليد فهم المتعاونون الذين يسمح بعضهم بالانتفاع ببعض ومن كان إنّما يصنع المعروف التماس الجزاء واكتساباً لمنافع الدنيا فإنّما مثله فيما يأخذ ويعطي مثل الصيّاد وإلقائه الحبّ للطير لا يريد به نفع الطير ولكن نفع نفسه والردّ عليها فتبادل ذات النفس أفضل من تعاطي ذات اليد وقد وثقت بذات نفسك ومنحتك مثل ذلك من نفسي وليس يمنعني من الخروج إليك والانبساط عليك سوء ظنّ بك ولكن قد عرفت أنّ لك أصحاباً جوهرهم كجوهرك وليس رأيهم في أمري كرأيك فأخاف أن يراني معك بعضهم فيهلكني. ١٢،٦

قال الغراب من علامة الصديق أن يكون لصديق صديقه صديقاً ولعدوّ صديقه عدوّاً فإنّه ليس لي بصاحب ولا صديق من لم يكن لك محبّاً وفيك راغباً وقطيعة من كان على غير رأيي فيك هيّن فإنّ زارع الريحان إذا نبت في ريحانه شيء يفسده اقتلعه.

ثمّ إنّ الجرذ أقبل إلى الغراب فتصادقا واستأنس كلّ واحد منهما بصاحبه حتّى إذا مرّت بهما أيّام قال الغراب للجرذ إنّ جحرك قريب من طرق الناس فأخشى ١٣،٦

١ وأنا لازم . . . حاجته: كذا ش؛ ساقطة من الأصل.

cup broken by the slightest defect, never again to be put back together. After one meeting and a day's acquaintance, the noble love the noble; when the base form attachments it is from fear or desire. You are noble and I need your friendship. I will stay by your door and touch neither food nor drink until you become my brother."

"I agree to become your brother," answered the rat, "as I've never turned 6.11
a needy person away from what he needs. I spoke to you as I did in order to leave myself an excuse, so that if you betray me, you won't be able to say, 'I found the rat weak in judgment and easily deceived.'" The rat came out, but remained by the entrance to his burrow.

The crow said to him, "What's keeping you from relaxing and enjoying my company? Are you still uneasy?"

"People in this world base their relationships on two sorts of things," said 6.12
the rat. "Some relationships are based on feelings in the heart; other relationships are based on material goods. Those who share what resides in the heart are pure friends who regard each other with sincere affection. Those who exchange material goods are those who cooperate for an advantage and seek to profit from one another. Those who do good deeds only to gain a reward and acquire worldly benefits are like a hunter who scatters grain for the birds, not for their benefit, but for his own. The sharing of what resides in the heart is better than the exchange of material goods. I know how you feel toward me in your heart, and I feel the same toward you. No personal misgivings are preventing me from coming out and enjoying your company; however, I know you have companions whose nature is like yours, but whose view of me is different. One of them, I fear, might see me with you and kill me."

The crow answered, "The mark of a true friend is that he is a friend of his friend's friend, and an enemy of his friend's enemy. Those who neither love you nor wish you well are not companions or friends of mine. It will be easy for me to break with those who think otherwise about you. The farmer pulls out the weeds when they grow among his plants."

So the rat approached the crow. They shook hands, became friends, and 6.13
enjoyed each other's company. After a few days had passed, the crow said

أن يرميني بعض السفهاء فيأخذني وقد أعرف مكاناً مخصباً من السمك ذا عزلة ولي فيه صديق من السلاحف أنا واجد عنده مأكل فأريد الانطلاق إليها فأعشعش[1] معها آمناً.

قال الجرذ أفلا أنطلق معك فإنّي لمكاني هذا كاره.

قال الغراب وما تكره من مكانك.

قال الجرذ إنّ لي أخباراً وقصصاً سأقصّها عليك لو قد انتهينا إلى المكان الذي تريد.

١٤،٦ فأخذ الغراب بذنب الجرذ فطار به حتّى بلغ حيث أراد فلمّا قربا من العين التي فيها[2] السلحفاة ورأت[3] السلحفاة غراباً معه جرذ ذُعرت منه ولم تعلم أنّه صاحبها فغاصت في الماء فوضع الغراب الجرذ على الأرض ووقع على شجرة ونادى السلحفاة باسمها فعرفت صوته فخرجت إليه فرحّبت به وسألته من أين أقبل فأخبرها الغراب بقصّته من لدن رأى الصيّاد إلى أن انتهى إليها مع الجرذ.

فلمّا سمعت السلحفاة شأن الجرذ تعجّبت من عقله ووفائه ورحّبت به وقالت ما ساقك إلى هذه الأرض.

قال الغراب للجرذ أرأيت الأخبار والقصص التي زعمت أنّك تحدّثني بها فاقصصها عليّ الآن مع ما سألتك السلحفاة فإنّ السلحفاة منك بمثل منزلتي.

١٥،٦ فابتدأ الجرذ وقال كان أوّل منزل نزلته بمدينة ماروزود في بيت رجل من النسّاك ولم يكن للناسك عيال وكان يؤتى كلّ يوم بسلّة من طعام فيتعشّى منها ثمّ يعلّقها بما فيها من بقيّة الطعام فكنت أرصد الناسك حتّى يخرج فإذا خرج وثبت إلى السلّة فلم أدع فيها طعاماً إلّا أكلته ورميت به إلى أصحابي وجهد الناسك مراراً أن يعلّق تلك السلّة معلّقاً لا أناله فلم يقدر على ذلك ثمّ إنّ رجلاً استضاف الناسك ذات ليلة فتعشّيا جميعاً فلمّا فرغا أخذا في الحديث فقال الناسك للضيف من أيّ أرض أنت وإلى أيّ أرض توجّهت الآن. وكان الرجل الضيف قد جال الدنيا

[1] الأصل: فاعسعش. [2] العين التي فيها: كذا ع، پ٣٤٧٥؛ الأصل: العن الدى فيه. [3] كذا ش، ع؛ الأصل: فرأى.

to the rat, "Your den is close to roads frequented by people. I'm afraid some fool will shoot at me and take me. I know of a secluded place with plenty of fish. I have a friend there, a turtle. I'll find things to eat there. I'd like to go and live with her in safety."

"Why don't I come with you?" said the rat. "I don't like my home here."

"What don't you like about it?" asked the crow.

"I'll tell you some stories when we reach our destination," replied the rat.

So the crow picked up the rat by the tail and flew off with him to the 6.14
pond where the turtle lived. The turtle became frightened when she saw a crow approach carrying a rat; not realizing that it was her friend, she dove into the water. The crow put the rat down, perched on a tree, and called the turtle by name. Recognizing the crow's voice, she swam to the surface, greeted him, and asked where he had come from. The crow told her the whole story, from the time he first saw the hunter right up to the point of his arrival with the rat.

When the turtle heard the story of the rat, she marveled at his intelligence and loyalty,[40] and welcomed him. "What brings you to this land?" she asked.

At this point, the crow asked the rat, "What about the stories you said you were going to tell me? Tell them now, and answer the turtle's question, for the turtle, as my friend, is now your friend too."

The Rat's Story

The rat told the following tale: "My first home was in the city of Mārūzūd, 6.15
in the house of an ascetic who had no family.[41] Every day he would be given a basket of food; he would eat from it and then hang up the basket with any leftover food in it. I would watch for the ascetic to go out, and when he did, I would jump up into the basket, and, between what I ate and what I threw down for my fellow rats, there would be nothing left. The ascetic tried again and again to hang the basket out of my reach, but to no avail. Then one night a guest arrived at the ascetic's house. They struck up a conversation after they had eaten dinner together. The ascetic asked the guest what country he was from and where he was heading. The guest, it turned

ورأى العجائب وجعل الناسك في خلال الحديث يصفّق بيديه أحياناً لينفّر الجرذان عن السلّة فغضب الضيف وهو لا يعلم ما له فيما يلقى من الجرذان فقال أحدّثك وتصفّق كأنّك تهزأ بحديثي فما أردت إلى مسألتي.

١٦،٦ فاعتذر الناسك إلى الضيف وقال إنّي قد دبقت إلى حديثك ولكنّي صفّقت لتنفر جرذان قد شقّت عليّ وليس أضع[1] بالبيت طعاماً إلّا أكلنه.

قال الضيف أجرذ واحد أم أكثر.

قال الناسك جرذان البيت كثيرة وفيها جرذ هو الذي أثّر عليّ فلا أستطيع له حيلة.

قال الضيف ما هذا من شأن الجرذ إلّا لأمر وإنّك لتذكّرني قول الرجل الذي قال لامرء ما[2] باعت هذه المرأة سمسمها مقشوراً بغير مقشور إلّا لأمر.

قال الناسك وكيف كان ذلك.

١٧،٦ قال الضيف للناسك نزلت مرّة من المرّات على رجل من مدينة كذا فتعشّينا جميعاً ثمّ فرش لي وانقلب الرجل إلى فراشه وصاحبته وبيني وبينهما خصّ من قصب فسمعت الرجل وامرأته يتكلّمان في آخر الليل فسمعت كلامهما فإذا الرجل يقول أريد أن[3] أدعو غداً رهطاً ليأكلوا عندنا.

فقالت امرأته كيف تدعو الناس إلى طعامك وليس في بيتك فضل عن قوت عيالك وأنت رجل لا تبقي شيئاً ولا تدّخره.

فقال الرجل لا تندمي على شيء أنفقناه وأطعمناه فإنّ الجمع والادّخار ربّما كانت[4] عاقبته على صاحبه وخيمة كعاقبة الذئب.

قالت المرأة كيف كان ذلك.

١٨،٦ قال الرجل خرج رجل من القنّاص غادياً بقوسه وسهامه يبتغي القنص فما تجاوز بعيداً حتّى رمى ظبياً فأقصده فحمله راجعاً به إلى أهله فعرض له في طريقه خنزير فحمل الخنزير على الرجل حين نظر إليه فوضع الرجل الظبي وبرى للخنزير سهماً فرماه رمية

١ كذا ر؛ الأصل: أصنع. ٢ لامرء ما: كذا ل٢؛ الأصل: لامرأته ما. ٣ كذا ش، ع؛ ساقطة من الأصل. ٤ الأصل: كان.

out, had traveled the world and seen many wonders. In the course of the guest's account, the ascetic kept clapping his hands from time to time to drive away the rats. This angered the guest. 'I'm talking to you,' he said, 'and you clap your hands as if making fun of what I'm saying! Why did you ever ask me your question?'

"The ascetic apologized. 'I was intent on your words, but was clapping to drive away the rats. They are a torment and eat any food I leave in the room.' 6.16

"'Is it one rat or many?' asked the guest.

"'Many,' said the ascetic, 'but one of them has left me at my wits' end!'

"'There must be a reason for this,' said the guest. 'You remind me of what the man in the story said: "There must a reason why this woman has traded husked for unhusked sesame."'

"'And why did he say that?' asked the ascetic.

The Woman Who Traded Husked for Unhusked Sesame

"The guest told the following tale: 'Once I lodged with a man in a certain city. After dinner, he made up a bed for me and went off to bed with his wife. We were separated by a reed screen. Late that night, I heard the man and his wife talking and I listened to what they were saying. "Tomorrow," said the man, "I want to invite some people to eat with us." 6.17

"'"How can you invite people to dinner," asked the wife, "when you can hardly feed your own family? You're a man who never has enough to keep any surplus!"

"'The man said, "Don't regret what we spend on feeding others. People who hoard often suffer the same unsavory fate as the wolf."

"'"And what happened to him?" asked the woman.

The Hunter, the Boar, the Gazelle, and the Wolf

"'Her husband told her the story of a hunter who went out one morning with his bow and arrows in search of game. He hadn't gone far before he shot and killed a gazelle. He picked it up to take it back to his family. On the way, a boar crossed his path and charged when it saw him. The hunter put down the gazelle, sharpened an arrow, and shot the boar, the arrow piercing its testicles. But the boar overtook the man and gored him with its tusks, sending the bow flying—and both fell down dead. A wolf came by, and when he 6.18

نفذت خصيتيه وأدرك الخنزير الرجل فضربه بنابه ضربة أطارت القوس عن يده ووقعا جميعاً فأتى عليهما ذئب عابر فلمّا رأى الرجل والخنزير والظبي وثق بالخصب في نفسه وقال ينبغي أن أدّخر ما استطعت فإنّه لا يُعدّ حازماً من فرط في الجمع والادّخار وأنا جاعل ما وجدت ذخراً وكنزاً ومكتفٍ يومي هذا بوتر القوس. فدنا من القوس ليأكل وترها فلمّا قطع الوتر اضطربت القوس فأصاب وترها المقتل من حلق الذئب فمات مكانه.

وإنّما ضربت لك هذا المثل لتعلمي أنّ الحرص على الجمع وخيم العاقبة. ١٩،٦

قالت المرأة نعم ما قلت وعندنا من الأرزّ والسمسم ما فيه طعام لستّة رهط أو سبعة فأنا غادية[1] إلى صنعة الطعام فادع من أحببت عند الغداء.

فلمّا أصبحت المرأة أخذت السمسم وقشرته ثمّ بسطته في الشمس ليجفّ وقالت لغلام زوجها اطرد عن هذا السمسم الطير والكلاب. وتفرّغت المرأة لبعض صنعتها فغفل[2] الغلام ودبّ كلب إلى ذلك السمسم فجعل يأكل منه فبصرت به المرأة فقذّرته وكرهت أن تصنع منه طعاماً فانطلقت به إلى السوق وأخذت مقايضة سمسماً مقشوراً بسمسم غير مقشور مثلاً بمثل وأنا في السوق وأرى ما تصنع فسمعت رجلاً يقول ما أعطت هذه المرأة سمسمها مقشوراً بغير مقشور إلّا لأمر.

وكذلك قولي في الجرذ الذي تذكر أنّه يثب إلى السلّة حيث وضعتها إنّه لشيء ما ٢٠،٦ قوي على ما شكوته منه دون صواحبه فالتمس لي فأساً لعلّي أحتفر جحره وأنظر هل أجد له ذخيرة تشدّ ظهره أو شيئاً أطّلع به على شأنه.

فاستعار الناسك فأساً من بعض جيرانه فأتى بها[3] الضيف وأنا حينئذ في جحر غيري أسمع كلامهما وكان في جحري ألف دينار ولم أدر من وضعها وكنت أفترشها وأفرح بها وتشدّ من ظهري وإنّ الضيف احتفر حتّى انتهى إلى الدنانير فأخذها وقال للناسك هذه كانت تقوّي ظهر ذلك الجرذ على الوثوب بحيث كان يثب

---

[1] كذا ع؛ الأصل: غادي. [2] كذا ش، ع؛ الأصل: ففعل. [3] كذا ش؛ الأصل: به.

saw the man, the boar, and the gazelle, saw promise for a life of abundance. "I should store whatever I can," he said. "It's an improvident person who fails to store things away! I'll treat what I've found as a hoard for the future; today I'll be satisfied with just this bowstring." So he approached the bow to eat its string, but when he snapped it the bow sprang back and dealt his throat a mortal blow. He died on the spot.

"'The husband said, "I've told you this story to bring home to you the 6.19
unhealthy consequences of excessive thrift."

"'"You're right," said the wife. "We have enough rice and sesame to feed six or seven people. I'll start cooking tomorrow morning. Invite anyone you like for lunch."

"'The next morning, the woman took the sesame, husked it, and spread it in the sun to dry. She told her husband's apprentice to keep the birds and dogs away from the sesame; then she went off to see to her cooking. The apprentice paid no attention, and a dog crept up and began to eat. The woman saw this, and, considering the sesame unclean, was loath to cook it for food. So she took it to market and exchanged it for an equal amount of unhusked sesame. I was in the market watching what she was doing, and I heard someone say, "There must be a reason why this woman has traded husked for unhusked sesame!"

"'I say the same about this rat who you say jumps into the basket wher- 6.20
ever you put it. There must be a reason why he alone among his companions is strong enough to do what you're complaining of. Get me a pickax. If I dig up his burrow, I might find a stash of something that gives him strength or discover what's so special about him.'

"So the ascetic borrowed a pickax from one of his neighbors and brought it to the guest. Meanwhile, I was in someone else's burrow listening to what they were saying. In my burrow there were a thousand dinars—I don't know who put them there—and I used them as my bed. They made me very happy and gave me strength. The guest dug down to the coins and took them. 'These,' he said to the ascetic, 'are what gave that rat strength to jump so

لأنّ المال يزيد في القوّة والرأي وسترى أنّ الجرذ لا يقدر بعد اليوم على مثل[١] ما كان يقوى عليه فيما خلا.

٢١،٦ فسمعت قول الضيف وعرفت في نفسي الانكسار وأحسست بنقصان القوّة فانقلبت من جحري إلى جحر غيري فأصبحت ورأيت انحطاط منزلتي في أنفس الجرذان وقلّة توقّرمنهنّ لي. ما كنت عوّدتهنّ من الوثوب إلى السلّة تعجّزت عن ذلك فزهدن فيّ وقلن بينهنّ هلك هذا آخر الدهر وليوشكنّ أن يحتاج إلى أن يعوّله بعضكنّ. فرفضنني بأجمعهنّ ولحقن بعدوّ كان لي وعيّبنني وانتقصنني عند كلّ من ذكرني عنده فقلت في نفسي ما أرى التبع والأعوان والأهل والصديق والإخوان إلّا مع المال ولا الرأي والقوّة إلّا بالمال ووجدت من لا مال له إذا أراد تناول الأمر قعد به الفقر عمّا يسمو إليه فانقطع عن بلوغ غايته كما[٢] ينقطع ماء الأمطار الصيف في الأودية فلا يصل إلى بحر ولا نهر بل يبقى مكانه حتّى تنشّفه الأرض لأنّه لا مادّة له يبلغ بها نهايته.

٢٢،٦ ووجدت من لا مال له لا عقل له ولا دنيا له ولا آخرة. ومن لا مال له لا دنيا له لأنّ الرجل إذا أصابته الحاجة رفضه إخوانه وهان على ذوي قرابته وربّما اضطرّته المعيشة وما يحتاج إليه لنفسه وعياله إلى ما يغرّر فيه بدينه فعسى أن يهلك آخرته فإذا هو قد خسر الدنيا والآخرة.

فلا شيء أشدّ من الفقر فإنّ الشجرة النابتة في السباخ المأكولة من كلّ جانب أمثل حالاً من الفقير المحتاج إلى ما في أيدي الناس فالفقر رأس كلّ بلاء وداعٍ[٣] إلى صاحبه مقت الناس وهو مع ذلك مسلبة للعقل والمروءة ومذهبة للعلم والأدب ومظنّة للتهمة ومقطعة للحياء ومجمعة للبلاء ومن نزل به الفقر والفاقة لم يجد لترك الحياء وتضييعه بدًّا ومن انقطع حياؤه ذهب سَرْوُهُ ومن ذهب سروه[٤] مُقت ومن مُقت أوذي ومن أوذي حزن ومن حزن فقد عقله واستحال ذهنه واستُنكر

---

١ بعد... مثل: الأصل: على مثله بعد اليوم. ٢ الأصل: وكما. ٣ الأصل: وداعى. ٤ سَرْوُهُ... سروه: كذا ع؛ الأصل: سروره... سروره.

high. Money increases strength and intelligence. You'll see that the rat will no longer have the strength to do what he used to do.'

“When I heard the guest's words, I felt my spirit break and my strength 6.21
drain away. I moved to another burrow. The next morning, I noticed that the rats showed me less respect and deference. They had grown accustomed to me jumping up into the basket, but now that I could no longer do it, they abandoned me and said among themselves, 'He's finished forever! Soon he'll need one of you to take care of him.' They all rejected me and went over to one of my enemies. They began finding fault with me and disparaging me whenever I was mentioned. So I said to myself: 'I see that only money can guarantee followers, helpers, kinfolk, and friends. Only money can guarantee intelligence and strength.' Poverty, I learned, holds back from their aspirations the penniless who want to undertake a task, and so they fail to reach their goal. They are like water from summer rain that remains in the stream bed: it reaches neither the sea nor the river; it just stays put until it dries up in the ground because it has no strength to reach its goal.

“I discovered that the penniless have no intelligence: they have nothing 6.22
in this world or the next. Without money, a man has nothing in this world: when poverty strikes, his brothers spurn him and his kin despise him. The need to support himself and his family often forces him to seek sustenance in ways that endanger his soul, so he loses both this world and the next.

“Nothing is worse than poverty. A tree growing in a salt marsh, eaten away on all sides, is better off than a pauper dependent on others. Poverty is the source of every woe: its victim is despised and despoiled of intelligence and manliness; it banishes learning and good manners, brings suspicion in its train, deprives you of a sense of shame, and unites every woe. A man is forced to cast shame to the winds when poverty and destitution descend on him. He who loses his shame loses his dignity; he who loses his dignity is despised; he who is despised is insulted; he who is insulted grieves; and he who grieves loses his intellect: his mind is affected, and his memory and understanding become faulty. When a person is afflicted in intelligence,

حفظه وفهمه ومن أصيب في عقله وفهمه وحفظه كان أكثر قوله وعمله فيما يكون عليه لا له.

٢٣،٦ ووجدت الرجل إذا افتقر اتّهمه من كان له مؤتمناً وأساء به الظنّ من كان ظنّه به حسناً فإن أذنب غيره ظُنّ به وكان للتهمة موضعاً. وليس خصلة تكون للغنيّ مدحاً إلّا وهي للفقير عيباً فإن كان شجاعاً سمّي أهوج وإن كان جواداً سمّي مفسداً وإن كان حليماً سمّي ضعيفاً وإن كان وقوراً سمّي بليداً وإن كان لسناً سمّي مهذاراً وإن كان صموتاً سمّي غبيّاً فالموت أهون من الفاقة التي تضطرّ صاحبها إلى مسألة الناس ثمّ لا سيّما مسألة الأشحّاء اللؤماء فإنّ الكريم لو كُلّف أن يدخل يده في فم التنّين فيخرج سمّاً ثمّ يبتلعه كان ينبغي أن يكون ذلك أخفّ عليه من مسألة اللئيم البخيل. وقد قيل من ابتلي بمرض في جسده لا يفارقه أو[١] بفراق الأحبّة والإخوان أو بالغربة حيث لا يعرف مبيتاً ولا مقيلاً ولا يرجو إياباً أو بفاقة تضطرّ إلى المسألة فالحياة له موت والموت له راحة. وربّما كره الرجل المسألة وبه الحاجة فحمله على الخيانة والغصب وهما شرّ من التي رغب عنها فإنّه كان يقال الخرس خير من البيان بالكذب والعيّ خير من العاهر والفاقة خير من الشبع من الحرام.

٢٤،٦ وقد كنت رأيت الضيف حين أخرج الدنانير من جحري قاسمها الناسك فجعل الناسك نصيبه في خريطة فوضعها من الليل عند رأسه ونام فطمعت في أن أصيب منها شيئاً أدّخره فيردّ عليّ بعض قوّتي وأراجع به بعض إخواني فانطلقت والناسك نائم حتّى إذا كنت عند رأس الناسك وجدت الضيف مستيقظاً فتناول قضيباً فضربني به ضربة فسعيت حتّى دخلت جحري فلمّا سكن عنّي الوجع هاجني الشره والحرص وغلباني على عقلي فخرجت بمثل طمعي الأوّل أدبّ حتّى دنوت والضيف يرصدني فعاودني بضربة على رأسي أثقلتني فتحاملت حتّى دخلت جحري فسقطت مغشيّاً عليّ وخلص إليّ من الوجع ما بغّض إليّ المال وذكره حتّى إنّي اليوم أسمع ذكر المال فيدخلني من ذكره رعب.

١ كذا ش، ع، پ٣٤٦٦؛ الأصل: إلّا.

memory, and understanding, he does himself more harm than good by speaking and acting.

"When a man falls into poverty, I've learned, he is viewed with suspicion 6.23
by those who used to trust him; those who thought well of him think ill of him; offences committed by others are attributed to him, and he becomes the object of suspicion. Every trait deemed praiseworthy in a rich man is accounted a blemish in a poor one: if brave, he is called reckless; if generous, a spendthrift; if forbearing, weak; if dignified, dull; if articulate, garrulous; if taciturn, stupid. Death is easier to bear than poverty, which forces its victim to beg—especially if he must beg from those who are mean and miserly. It would be less onerous for a noble-minded man to be tasked with thrusting his hand into a dragon's mouth, extracting its poison, and swallowing it than to beg from a miserly scoundrel. They say that life is death and death a relief for the chronically ill, for those separated from loved ones and friends, for exiles in a foreign land without shelter by night or rest by day and with no hope of return, and for paupers forced to beg. Loath to beg, a poor man may be driven to treachery and robbery, which are worse than the poverty he tries to escape. Better, they say, to be mute than to be an eloquent liar, to be impotent than to be a lecher, to be poor than to live a life of ease from ill-gotten gains.

"After the guest had taken the coins from my burrow, I saw him divide 6.24
them with the ascetic, who put his share into a sack, which he placed by his head at night, and go to sleep. Eager to get some of them for myself, to restore some of my strength and to regain some of my friends, I came out while the ascetic was asleep and approached his head, but the guest was awake; he picked up a stick and dealt me a blow that sent me running back to my burrow. When my pain subsided, greed and covetousness overcame my reason, so out I came again, hopeful as before, and advanced. But the guest was on the lookout and hit my head again and dazed me. I dragged myself back into the burrow and fainted. So severe was my pain that it made me hate money so much that today the mere mention of it frightens me.

٦،٢٥ فرأيت البلايا في الدنيا إنّما يسوقها إلى أهلها الحرص والطمع يستفزّه فرأيت الحال مختلفة بأهل الشحّ والسخاء اختلافاً شديداً متفاوتاً ووجدت ركوب الأهوال والأخطار وتجشّم الأسفار البعيدة أهون على السخيّ من بسط اليد إلى قبض المال من الحريص الشحيح ووجدت الرضى والقناعة[١] هما[٢] جماع الغنى وقد قالت العلماء لا عقل كالتدبير ولا ورع كالكفّ ولا حسب كحسن الخلق ولا غنى كالرضى وأحقّ ما صُبر عليه ما ليس إلى تغييره سبيل. وقد كان يقال أفضل البرّ الرحمة ورأس المودّة الاسترسال ورأس العقل المعرفة بما لا يكون ممّا كان وطيب النفس حسن الانصراف عمّا لا سبيل إليه. فصار أمري أن قنعت ورضيت وانتقلت من بيت الناسك إلى البرّيّة.

٦،٢٦ وكان لي صديق من الحمام فساق إليّ بصداقته صداقة هذا الغراب ثمّ ذكر لي الغراب ما بينك وبينه من المودّة وأخبرني أنّه يريد أن يأتيك فأحببت أن آتيك معه وكرهت الوحدة فإنّه ليس شيء من سرور الدنيا يعدل صحبة الإخوان ولا غمّ من غموم الدنيا يعدل فقد الإخوان. وقد جرّبت فعرفت أنّه لا ينبغي للملتمس أن يلتمس من الدنيا فوق الكفاف والذي يدفع به عن نفسه الحاجة وذلك يسير إنّما هو المطعم والمأوى وأدنى الرياش وإذا أعين بسعة اليد في سخاء النفس. ولو أنّ رجلاً وُهبت له الدنيا بحذافيرها لم يخلص إليه من منفعتها إلّا القليل الذي يدفع به عن نفسه الحاجة فأمّا سوى ذلك ففي مواضعه ليس له منه إلّا مثل ما لغيره[٣] من حظّ العين فأقبلت مع الغراب على هذا وأنا لك أخ وكذلك فلتكن[٤] منزلتي في نفسك.

٦،٢٧ فلمّا فرغ الجرذ من كلمته هذه أجابته السلحفاة بكلام رقيق لطيف فقالت سمعت مقالتك فما أحسنها إلّا أنّي رأيتك بالمحزون تذكر بقايا بعض أمور كان في نفسك منها ومن اغترابك فينا شيء فلا يكوننّ ذلك من رأيك واعلم أنّ حسن القول لا يتمّ إلّا بحسن العمل فإنّ المريض وإن علم دواء مرضه لم ينتفع بعلمه ما لم يتداو به.

---

١ الأصل، ع: والقنوع. ٢ كذا ع؛ الأصل: هو. ٣ إلّا مثل ما لغيره: الأصل: إلّا مثل الغبرة. ٤ كذا ر؛ ساقطة من الأصل.

"People's troubles in this world, I saw, stem from inordinate desire incited by greed. I perceived the great difference between the covetous and the generous. I learned that it is easier for a self-respecting man to brave terrors and dangers and undertake long journeys than to stretch out his hand to receive money from a covetous miser. I realized that satisfaction and contentment are true wealth. As the sages have said: There is no intelligence like good management,[42] no piety like abstinence, no lineage as distinguished as a good character, and no wealth like contentment. What cannot be altered is best endured. As has been said: Mercy is the best part of piety, love begins with openness, intelligence begins with knowledge of what can and cannot be, and contentment means to willingly relinquish the unattainable. In the end, I found satisfaction and contentment, and moved from the ascetic's house to the countryside. 6.25

"I had a friend, a dove, who through her friendship led me to the friendship of this crow. The crow told me about his friendship with you and that he wanted to visit you, and I wanted to accompany him. I didn't want to be alone, for no joy in this world can compare to the companionship of friends, nor any sorrow compare to their loss. Experience has taught me not to ask more of this world than what suffices to ward off need and suffering—and that isn't much: food, shelter, and simple clothing, accompanied by openness of hand and generosity of spirit. If a man were given the world and all it contains, he would benefit only from the few things by which he keeps needs at bay; of all other things elsewhere he would have only what others have—namely, what the eye can see. This being so, I have come with the crow. I will be your friend. May my place in your soul be like his." 6.26

When the rat finished talking, the turtle answered him gently and kindly: "I understand what you are saying, and they are very fine words. Yet you seem saddened, saying that certain things still trouble you and that you have come to live among us as a stranger. You mustn't think that way. Know that good words find their completion only in action. Even if a sick man knows the remedy for his disease, his knowledge won't benefit him if he doesn't take the cure. Benefit from your intelligence and put your knowledge into 6.27

فانتفع بعقلك واستعمل علمك ولا تحزن لقلّة المال فإنّ المرء ذا المروءة يُكرَم على غير مال كالأسد يُهاب وإن كان رابضاً[١] والغنيّ الذي لا مروءة له يُهان وإن كان كثيرًا ماله كالكلب الذي يهون على الناس أمره وإن طوّق وحُلّي وكُلّل. ولا تكبرنّ عليك غربتك فإنّ العاقل لا غربة عليه وإن اغترب فإنّ معه ما يكتفي به كالأسد الذي لا يتقلّب إلّا ومعه قوّته التي يعيش بها حيثما توجّه. ولتحسن عدّتك وتعاهدك نفسك بما تكون به للخير أهلاً فإنّك إذا فعلت ذلك أتاك الخير يطلبك كما يطلب الماء الأخدود وطير الماء الماء.

٢٨،٦ وإنّما جُعل الفضل للبصير الحازم المعدّ فأمّا الكسلان المتردّد المواكل فإنّ الفضل قلّما يصحبه كما لا تطيب[٢] المرأة الشابّة نفساً بصحبة الهرم ولا يحزنك أن تقول كنت ذا مال فأصبحت معدماً فإنّ المال وسائر متاع الدنيا سريع إقباله إذا أقبل وشيك ذهابه إذا ذهب كالكرة التي هي سريع ارتفاعها سريع وقوعها وقد قالت الحكماء في أشياء لا ثبات[٣] لها ولا بقاء كظلّ الغمام وخلّة الأشرار وعشق النساء وثناء الكاذب والمال الحرام. وليس يفرح العاقل بكثرة المال ولا يحزنه قلّته ولكنّ ماله الذي يفرح به هو عقله وما قدّم من صالح الأعمال والعاقل واثق بأنّه لا يُسلب خيرًا قدّمه ولا يؤاخَذ بشيء لم يعمله. والعاقل حقيق أن لا يغفل عن آخرته والتزوّد لها فإنّ الموت لا يأتيه إلّا بغتة ليس بينه وبين أحد وقت معلوم. وقد أعرف أنك لما أُعطيت من فضل المعرفة عن موعظتي غنيّ بما ينفعك بصير بجميع الأسباب ولكن رأيت أن أقضي الذي يحقّ لك عليّ وأن أزيّن لك صالح الأخلاق فإنّك أخونا وكلّ ما كان قبلنا مبذول لك.

٢٩،٦ فلمّا سمع الغراب حسن مقالة السلحفاة للجرذ وإلطافها إيّاه سرّه ذلك وقال لها سررتني وأنعمت وأنت جديرة[٤] أن تسرّي نفسك بما سُررت لك فإنّ أحقّ الناس شدّة بالسرور وطيب النفس وحسن الثناء من لا يزال رحله من إخوانه وأصدقائه

١ كذا ر؛ الأصل: مربضًا. ٢ كذا ع؛ الأصل، ش: تطلب. ٣ كذا ر؛ الأصل: ثبت. ٤ كذا ش، ع؛ الأصل: جدير.

practice. Don't grieve over your lack of wealth. A man of valor is honored without wealth, just as a lion is feared even when at rest. A rich man without valor is scorned despite his wealth, as a dog is scorned even if he wears a jeweled collar. Don't worry about being in a strange land. No land is foreign to a person of intelligence; even if he goes to a strange land, he has enough to sustain him, like the lion who takes his strength with him wherever he goes. Take care to provide your soul with whatever will make it worthy of good things; if you do, good things will come looking for you, as water seeks a hollow and as waterfowl seek water.

"Excellence is the lot of those who are perceptive, resolute, and pre- 6.28
pared; it rarely keeps company with those who are lazy, vacillating, and listless—just as a young woman finds no delight in the company of an old man. Don't grieve yourself by saying, 'Once I was wealthy and now I've become poor.' Wealth and all the goods of this world come swiftly when they come, and depart swiftly when they depart—like a ball, swift to rise and swift to fall. As the sages have said: Things that lack stability and permanence are like the shadows cast by clouds, the friendship of evil men, the love of women, a liar's praise, and ill-gotten wealth. The wise man doesn't rejoice over an abundance of wealth or grieve over its loss; his intelligence and the good works he has performed constitute his wealth. He trusts that his deeds cannot be wrested from him and that he will not be held accountable for what he hasn't done. The wise man mustn't neglect to make provision for the afterlife, for death comes unexpectedly, at a time that none can know. I know that thanks to your knowledge you don't need my counsel and that you understand what will bring you benefit, but I felt I had an obligation to exhort you to act wisely, for you are our brother and all that we have is at your disposal."

The crow was delighted to hear the turtle's kind and eloquent response to 6.29
the rat. "You've made me rejoice," he said, "and done me a great favor. You should be as pleased with yourself as I am. The person visited constantly by righteous brethren and friends, surrounded by a throng of comrades whom he gladdens and who gladden him, attentive to them and to their needs,

من الصالحين موطوءاً[١] ولا يزال عنده منهم جماعة يسرّونه ويُسرّون به يعنى بأمورهم ويتكلّف ما ينفعهم ويحوطهم من ورائهم فإنّ الكريم إذا عثر لم ينتعش إلّا بالكرام كالفيل الذي إن وحل لم يستخرجه من الوحل إلّا الفيلة ولا يرى العاقل معروفاً صنعه وإن كثر كثيراً وإن هو خاطر بنفسه وعرّضها في وجوه المعروف للمتالف لم ير ذلك عتباً لمعرفته أنّه خاطر فانياً بباقٍ واشترى عظيماً بصغير وأغبط الناس من استجيد[٢] وسئل ما عنده ورُغب في ما لديه ولا يُعدّ غنيّاً من لا يشارك في غنائه ولا يُعدّ عائشاً من كان عيشه في بغضة وسوء ثناء ولا يعدّ الغرم غرماً إذا ساق غنماً ولا الغنم غنماً إذا أعقب غرماً.[٣]

٣٠،٦ فبينما السلحفاة والغراب والجرذ في كلامهم إذ أقبل نحوهم ظبي يسعى ففزع الغراب والجرذ والسلحفاة فوثبت السلحفاة في الماء ودخل الجرذ الجحر[٤] وطار الغراب فوقع على الشجرة وانتهى الظبي إلى الماء فشرب قليلاً ثمّ قام مذعوراً يلتفت ثمّ إنّ الغراب حلّق في السماء لينظر هل يرى للظبي طالباً فنظر كلّ ناحية فلم ير شيئاً فنادى السلحفاة فخرجت من الماء ونادى الجرذ وقال اخرج فإنّه ليس قريباً منّي شيء تخاف منه فاجتمع الغراب والجرذ والسلحفاة في مكانهم وقالت السلحفاة للظبي حين رأته ينظر إلى الماء ولا يشرب اشرب إن كان بك عطش ولا تخف فلا بأس عليك. فدنا الظبي منهنّ فرحّبت به السلحفاة وحيّته وقالت ما أمرك ومن أين أقبلت وما وراءك.

٣١،٦ قال الظبي كنت أكون في هذه الصحارى فلم تزل الرماة تطردني من مكان إلى مكان حتّى رأيت شبحاً[٥] له هيئة القنّاص فخفت أن يكون قانصاً فأقبلت خائفاً.

قال الغراب لا تخف فإنّا لم نر فيما حولنا قانصاً فيما مضى ونحن باذلون لك مودّتنا ومكاننا والمرعى منه قريب فاسكن واطمئنّ فلا بأس عليك.

---

١ كذا ر؛ الأصل: موطيًا. ٢ ش، ع: مستجيرًا. ٣ غرمًا: الأصل: عرما ادا ساق عما ولا العم عما إذا أعقب عرمًا.
٤ الجحر: الأصل: الجحر فصار مصورا معهم. ٥ كذا ر؛ الأصل: سحا.

deserves great joy, contentment, and praise. When a noble person stumbles, he rights himself only with the help of the noble—just as an elephant that sinks into the mud can only be pulled out by other elephants. The wise man doesn't make much ado about any favor he has done, no matter how great. He sees nothing blameworthy in risking his life and exposing it to danger in doing good, for he knows that he has risked what is transitory in order to gain what is lasting, and that he has purchased something great at the price of something small. The most fortunate are those whose generosity is appealed to, from whom alms are requested, and whose help is sought. Only those who share their wealth can be considered rich. To live your life as an object of hatred and opprobrium cannot be said to be a life. Expense that brings profit in its wake is no expense at all, and profit that brings loss in its wake is no profit at all."

While the turtle, the crow, and the rat were speaking, a gazelle came running toward them. The crow, the rat, and the turtle took fright: the turtle jumped into the water, the rat ran into his burrow, and the crow flew up into a tree. The gazelle came to the water, drank a little, and stood looking around fearfully. The crow circled in the air to see whether he could spot anyone pursuing the gazelle; he looked in every direction, but saw nothing. So he called to the turtle, who came out of the water, and called to the rat, "Come out; there is nothing nearby to fear." The crow, the rat, and the turtle rejoined each other. When the turtle saw the gazelle looking at the water but not drinking, she said to him, "Drink if you're thirsty. Don't be afraid; there is nothing for you to fear." The gazelle approached them, and the turtle, having welcomed him, asked, "What happened to you? Where have you come from, and where are you heading?" 6.30

The Gazelle's Story

The gazelle said, "I've been living in these plains, but archers kept chasing me from one place to another. Today I saw a shape that looked like a hunter. Afraid that it might be one, I came here out of fear." 6.31

"Don't be afraid," said the crow. "We've never seen a hunter here. We offer you our friendship and a place to live. The meadow is nearby. Stay and put yourself at ease. No harm will befall you."

فرغب الظبي في صحبتهنّ فأقام معهنّ فكان قريباً منهنّ عريش من الشجر فكنّ يأتين ذلك العريش كلّ يوم ويستمتعون بظلّه ويتذاكرن فيه الأمور وما يتلذّذن من الأحاديث والفكاهات الحسنة.

٦،٣٢ ثمّ إنّ الغراب والجرذ والسلحفاة وافين العريش ذات يوم وغاب عنهنّ الظبي فتوقّفن ساعة فلمّا أبطأ عليهنّ أشفقن أن يكون أصابه عنت وقال الجرذ والسلحفاة للغراب ألا تحلّق في السماء فتنظر هل ترى الظبي في شيء ممّا يلينا. فحلّق الغراب فنظر فإذا هو بالظبي في الحبائل فانقضّ سريعاً فأخبر الجرذ والسلحفاة.

ثمّ أقبل الغراب والسلحفاة فقالا للجرذ[1] إنّ هذا الأمر الذي نزل بالظبي لا يرجى له غير الله ولا نعرف سبب خلاصه إلّا بك وعلى يديك فأغث أخانا. فأجابهما الجرذ إلى ذلك وسعى سريعاً فلمّا انتهى إلى الظبي قال له يا أخي كيف وقعت في هذه الورطة وأنت من الأكياس.

قال الظبي وهل يغني الكيس مع المقادير المغيّبة شيئاً.

٦،٣٣ فبينما هما في محاورتهما إذ وافتهما السلحفاة فلمّا أبصرها الظبي قال لها ما أصبت في مجيئك لأنّ القانص إذا انتهى إلينا وقد فرغ الجرذ من قطع الحبال سبقتُه خطواً وللجرذ معاقل من الجحرة والغراب يطير وأنت ثقيلة لا سعي لك فأنا عليك خائف.

قالت السلحفاة لا يعدّ من العيش من كان في فراق الأحبّة فإنّ من المعونة على تسلية الهمّ وسكون النفس عندما تعمّ البلوى لقاء الأخ أخاه وإفضاء كلّ واحد منهما بذات نفسه إلى صاحبه وإذا فُرق بين الأليف وإلفه فقد سُلب فؤاده وحُرم سروره وغشي بصره.

فبينما الظبي والسلحفاة من كلامهما إذ طلع القانص ووافق ذلك فراغ الجرذ من قطع الحبالة عن الظبي فأحضر[2] الظبي وطار الغراب ودخل الجرذ الجحر وانتهى

١ كذا ش، ع؛ ساقطة من الأصل. ٢ الأصل: فاخطر.

The gazelle accepted their friendship and stayed with them. Every day, they went to a thicket to enjoy the shade, talk about events, and exchange pleasantries.

One day, the crow, the rat, and the turtle came to the thicket, but the 6.32
gazelle was missing. They waited for a while, and when he failed to appear, they became afraid that he had met with harm. The rat and the turtle said to the crow, "Why don't you fly up and see whether you can spot the gazelle nearby." The crow flew up and looked around, and saw the gazelle caught in a snare. He swooped down and told the rat and the turtle.

The crow and the turtle said to the rat, "God help us! You're the only means to save him we can think of. Help our brother!" So the rat set out in haste. When he reached the gazelle, he said, "Brother, you're so quick-witted; how did you fall into such a plight?"

The gazelle replied, "Is quick wit of any use against events that proceed in accordance with God's hidden decrees?"

The turtle arrived while the two were talking. When the gazelle saw her, 6.33
he said, "You shouldn't have come! If the hunter turns up when the rat finishes cutting the ropes, I can outrun him; the rat can retreat to one of his burrows, and the crow can fly; but you are heavy and can't run. I'm afraid for you."

"A life of separation from one's friends is no life at all," said the turtle. "Anxiety is dispelled and the mind becomes calm when brother meets brother in time of trouble and each shares his thoughts with the other, but the heart aches, joy is banished, and the eyes are dimmed when friend is separated from friend."

While the gazelle and the turtle were speaking, the hunter came into view, just as the rat finished cutting the ropes. The gazelle ran off, the crow flew away, and the rat went into its burrow. When the hunter arrived and

القانص إلى حباله فوجدها قد قُطعت فقام متعجّبًا وناظرًا فيما حوله فلم يرَ شيئًا غير السلحفاة فربطها.

فاشتدّ حزنهنّ لذلك فقال الجرذ ما أرى تجاوزنا من البلاء عقبة إلّا[1] صرنا ٣٤،٦
في أخرى لقد صدق القائل الذي يقول لا يزال الرجل مستمرًّا مستقيمًا ما لم يعثر فإذا عثر مرّة واحدة في أرض ذات أحجار لجّ به العثار وإن مشى في جدد. وما كان جدّي الذي فرق بيني وبين أهلي ومالي وبلدي ووطني ليرضى حتّى يفرق بيني وبين ما كنت أعيش فيه من صحبة السلحفاة خير الأصدقاء التي لم تكن خلّتها لالتماس مكافأة ولكن كانت خلّة الكرم والعقل والوفاء خلّة هي أفضل من مودّة الوالد لولده خلّة[2] لا يزيلها إلّا الموت. ويح لهذا الجسد الموكّل به الآفات الذي لا يزال في تصرّف وتقلّب لا يدوم له شيء ولا يثبت معه كما لا يدوم للطالع من النجوم طلوعه ولا لآفلها أفوله لكنّها في تصرّف وتقلّب لميقات ومستقرّ على إطلاق العليم ولا يزال الطالع من النجوم إلى أفول والآفل إلى طلوع والمشرق مغربًا والمغرب مشرقًا إلى الوقت المعلوم. ومن أمثالي فيما فُجعت به مثل الرجل يكون به الجرح فيقبل إلى برء ثمّ تصيبه عليه ضربة فيجتمع عليه ألمان أحدهما ألم الضربة والآخر انتقاض الجرح عليه كذلك من خفّت كلومه بلقاء إخوانه ثمّ فقدهم.[3]

قال الظبي والغراب للجرذ إنّ كلامنا وكلامك وإن كان بليغًا وحزننا وحزنك وإن ٣٥،٦
كان شديدًا غير مغنٍ عن صديقتنا السلحفاة شيئًا فدع هذا وأقبل على التماس المخرج للسلحفاة.[4] فإنّه كان يقال إنّما يُختبر ذو البأس عند اللقاء وذو الأمانة عند الأخذ والإعطاء والأهل والولد عند الفاقة والإخوان عند النوائب.

قال الجرذ أرى من الحيلة أن تذهب أيّها الظبي حتّى تكون صدرًا من طريق القانص فتربض كأنّك جريح أو كسير ويقع الغراب عليك كأنّه يأكل منك وأتبع أنا القانص فأكون قريبًا منه فإنّي أرجو لو قد نظر إليك القانص استخفّ بالسلحفاة

١ كذا ر؛ ساقطة من الأصل. ٢ كذا ش؛ الأصل: جنّه. ٣ كذلك . . . فقدهم: كذا ش، پ٣٤٦٦؛ الأصل: لانّ من حفت كلومه من فقد اصحابه بلماه فقدهم كان دلك الطبى. ٤ شيئًا . . . السلحفاة: كذا ر؛ ساقطة من الأصل.

found his ropes cut, he stood looking around in amazement. Seeing nothing but the turtle, he tied her up.

They all became very sad at the sight. The rat said, "Barely do we cross 6.34
one mountain of troubles before another looms. How true the saying, 'You walk straight ahead as long as you don't stumble, but stumble even once on rocky ground and you'll keep stumbling even when walking on level ground.' Not satisfied with separating me from family, wealth, home, and country, Fate has separated me from the companionship of the turtle, the best of friends, whose friendship asked for nothing in return, but was a friendship of generosity, intelligence, and loyalty; a friendship better than the love of parent for child; a friendship only death could end. Woe to this body prone to afflictions, constantly in a state of change and alteration, in which nothing is permanent or stable—just as a rising star must set, or a setting star must rise, undergoing change and alteration according to an appointed time and resting place set by the All-knowing.[43] The star that has risen sets, and the star that has set rises; the star in the east travels to the west, and the star in the west travels to the east until the appointed time.[44] The pain I feel now is like the pain of someone whose wound has begun to heal, but then his wound is struck a blow and he feels a double pain: the pain of the blow and the pain of the reopened wound. That is how a person feels whose wounds have been soothed by the companionship of brothers whom he then loses."

The crow and the gazelle said to the rat, "Our words and yours, however 6.35
well spoken, and our sorrow and yours, however intense, won't help the turtle. Enough! Try to find a way out for the turtle. They say that a soldier is tested only in combat; a trustee only in financial matters; family and children only when one is in need; and friends only in times of misfortune."

The rat replied, "I think we can manage it if you, gazelle, go lie down in the middle of the hunter's path, as if you were wounded or your leg broken. The crow will land on you, as if to feed on you. I'll follow the hunter and stay close to him. If the hunter sees you, I bet he'll scorn the turtle and turn

وأقبل إليك فإذا فعل ذلك ودنا إليك فتنفّس عنه متظالعاً كيلا ينقطع طمعه عنك فأمكنه أحياناً حتّى يدنو منك ومدّ به أحياناً كذلك فإنّي أرجو أن تزايله فلا ينصرف القانص إلّا وقد فرغت من قطع رباط السلحفاة ونجوت بها.

٣٦،٦ ففعل ذلك الظبي والغراب كما أمرهما الجرذ وفعل القانص كما ظنّ به الجرذ ولم ينصرف إلّا وقد قطع الجرذ رباط السلحفاة ونجوا جميعاً.

فلمّا وجد القانص الحبل[١] مقطوعاً ولم ير فيما هنالك شيئاً وقبل ذلك فيما أبصر ظبياً متظالعاً تارة وميتّاً تارة وأبصر الغراب واقعاً كأنّه يأكل وليس يأكل استوحش مكانه وارتاب لما رأى وقال إنّ هذه الأرض لأرض جنّ أو سحرة. فانصرف مذعوراً مولّياً لا يلتفت إلى شيء ولا يلوي عليه فاجتمع الظبي والغراب والسلحفاة والجرذ راجعات إلى عريشهنّ آمـنات.

١ كذا ش؛ ساقطة من الأصل.

his attention to you. As soon as he approaches, run from him, pretending to limp, so that he keeps hoping to catch you. Let him get close from time to time; then lead him on as far as you can and elude him. I bet that before the hunter returns I'll have cut the turtle's rope and rescued her."

The gazelle and the crow did as the rat said, and the hunter behaved just as 6.36
the rat thought he would. By the time he returned, the rat had cut the turtle's ropes and both had escaped.

When the hunter found the rope cut and nothing there, having previously seen a gazelle that seemed to be limping or dead by turns, and a crow perched on top of it as if to eat but not eating—he found the place uncanny and the sights made him uneasy. "This," he said, "must be a land of jinn or enchanters!" and he fled in terror, not stopping or turning aside to look at anything. The gazelle, the crow, the turtle, and the rat safely returned together to their thicket.

باب الغربان والبوم

وهو مثل العدوّ الذي لا يُوثَق به وإن أظهر النصيحة والصحبة والجود في العلانية

١،٧ قال الملك قد سمعت مثل الإخوان المتصافين المتحابين المتعاونين فاضرب لي مثل المغترّ بالعدوّ المبدي التضرّع والملق يريد به الخديعة والمكر بعدوّه وما يصيبه من اغتراره.

قال الفيلسوف من اغترّ بالعدوّ الأريب المعروف بالعداوة أصابه ما أصاب البوم من الغربان.

قال الملك وكيف كان ذلك.

٢،٧ قال العالم زعموا أنه كان في جبل من الجبال شجرة عظيمة من الدوح وكان فيها وكر ألف غراب عليها ملك منها وكان في ذلك الجبل أيضاً مكان فيه ألف بومة عليها ملك منها فخرج ملك البوم ذات ليلة[١] لعداوة قديمة بين الغربان والبوم فأغار على الغربان بمن معه فقتل منهم كثيراً وجرح كثيراً فلمّا أصبح ملك الغربان جمع الغربان فقال قد رأيتم ما لقيتم من بنات[٢] البوم وكم أصبح فيكم من قتيل وجريح وكسير ومنتوف الريش والجناح والذنب وأشدّ من ذلك في نفسي ضرّاً عليكم علمهنّ بمكانكم وجرأتهنّ عليكنّ وضراوتهنّ بكم ولا أظنّهنّ إلّا غاديات لمثلها وغير مقلعات عنكم فانظروا في أموركم في مهل.

٣،٧ وكان فيهم خمسة غربان معترَفين لهم بفضيلة الرأي وكمال العقل ونقد النظر وحسن التدبير وكان الملك لا يكاد يخرج من مشورتهم. قال الملك لأحدهم ما رأيك في هذا الأمر.

---

١ كذا ل٢؛ الأصل: يوم. ٢ الأصل: ساب.

The Crows and the Owls

A parable showing that even if your enemy assumes a façade of sincerity, friendship, and generosity, he should not be trusted.

The king said, "Now that I have heard a parable about true friends who love and help each other, tell me one about somebody misled by an enemy who assumed a façade of humility and flattery with the intention to deceive and beguile. Tell me what befell him because of his heedlessness." 7.1

And the philosopher said, "Anyone deceived by a clever enemy whose hostile intentions are well known will suffer the fate the owls suffered at the hands of the crows."

"And what was their fate?" asked the king.

The philosopher told the following tale: On a mountain, so they say, there stood an enormous banyan tree[45] that harbored the nests of a thousand crows ruled by a king. A thousand owls also lived on the mountain; they, too, were ruled by a king. One night, because of the long-standing enmity between owls and crows, the owl king and his followers made a sortie against the crows, killing and wounding many. The next morning, the king of the crows called a meeting of his followers. "See what you've suffered because of the owls! Many have been slain and many wounded; many have lost feathers from their heads, their wings, and their tails. What's worse, I think, is that the owls know where you live; they're bold and savage. I fear they'll return and won't leave you alone. So consider carefully what you want to do." 7.2

Five crows were recognized for their superior judgment, mature intelligence, penetrating insight, and skill at managing affairs. The king rarely disregarded their advice. He turned to one and asked, "What is your opinion on this matter?" 7.3

قال الأوّل رأي قد سبق إليه العلماء قالوا ليس للعدوّ الحنق الذي لا يطاق إلّا الهرب منه.

٤،٧ ثمّ قال للثاني فما رأيك.

فقال أمّا ما أشار به صاحبي من الهرب فلا أرى أن نخلو عن[١] أوطاننا ولا ان نذلّ لعدوّنا عند أوّل نكبة أصابتنا ولكنّا نجمع أمرنا ونستعدّ لعدوّنا ونحترس من الغرّة ونذكي العيون والطلائع فإذا أقبل إلينا عدوّنا لقينا مستعدّين فقاتلناهم قتالاً غير مستسلم ولا متوغّل ولكن تلقى أطرافهم أطرافنا ونتحرّز منهم وندافعهم الأيّام حتّى نصيب منهم فرصة وإلّا كان الهرب بعد الإعذار.

٥،٧ قال الملك للثالث ما رأيك في ذلك.

قال لا أرى ما قالاه ولكن أرى أن نذكي العيون والطلائع بيننا وبين عدوّنا وننظر هل يريد عدوّنا صلحاً أو يقبل منّا فدية ونتجسّس الأخبار فإن رأينا من ذلك أمراً متقارباً سمحاً لا شطط فيه لم نكره أن نصالحهنّ على خراج نؤدّيه إليهنّ فندفع عن أنفسنا بأسهنّ ونأمن ونطمئنّ في وطننا فإنّ من الرأي للملوك إذا اشتدّت شوكة عدوّهم فخافوا على البلاد والرعيّة أن يجعلوا الأموال جُنّة للبلاد والرعيّة.

٦،٧ قال الملك للرابع ما رأيك فيما ذكر صاحبك من طلب الصلح.

قال لا أراه رأياً بل[٢] ترك أوطاننا والاضطرار إلى الغربة عن بلادنا خير من وضع أحسابنا والخضوع للعدوّ الذي دوننا مع أنّي أعرف أنّا لو عرضنا الصلح لعظّموه علينا ولم يرضوه إلّا باشتطاط وقد يقال قارب عدوّك بعض المقاربة تنل منه حاجتك ولا تقاربه كلّ المقاربة فتذلّ نفسك وترعب جندك فيجترئ عليك عدوّك. ومثل ذلك مثل الخشبة المنصوبة في الشمس إن كان ميلها قليلاً ازداد ظلّها طولاً وإن جاوزت الحدّ في إمالتها قصر ظلّها. وليس عدوّنا يرضى منّا باليسير والرأي لنا الصبر والمحاربة.

٧،٧ قال الملك للخامس ما ترى القتال أم الصلح أم الجلاء.

---

١ كذا ل٢؛ ساقطة من الأصل. ٢ لا أراه . . . بل: كذا ل٢؛ الأصل: لا ارا رايا.

The first crow said, "My view accords with the scholarly consensus: The only way to deal with a bitter enemy against whom you are powerless is to flee."

The king asked the second crow, "What is your opinion?" 7.4

"As to my colleague's advice to flee," he replied, "I don't think we should abandon our homes or submit to our enemy at the first stroke of disaster. We should pull ourselves together, prepare to fight, and make sure we aren't caught off guard again, keeping a sharp lookout and sending out scouts. If our enemy advances, we meet them, ready to fight, but without submitting or rushing into the thick of the battle, allowing our contingents to engage theirs. We should prepare, but delay any fighting until an opportunity presents itself. If this doesn't work, then flight is justified."

The king asked the third crow, "And your opinion?" 7.5

"I don't agree with what they've said," he answered. "I would have you keep a sharp lookout and send out scouts to discover whether the enemy wants a truce or will accept a ransom. We should gather intelligence: if we detect a readiness to accept a generous but not excessive compromise, we shouldn't be averse to making peace with them by paying a tribute. That way we can keep violence at bay and live safely in our homes. It's good policy for kings to use money to protect their realms and peoples when they fear the enemy is strong."

The king asked the fourth crow, "What do you think of your colleague's 7.6
idea of seeking a truce?"

"I don't think it's a good idea," he replied. "Better to leave our homes and be driven into exile than to dishonor ourselves by submitting to an inferior enemy. Besides, I know they'll make exorbitant demands if we sue for peace. They say: Concede an inch to your enemy and you'll get what you want; concede everything, and you'll humiliate yourself, demoralize your army, and embolden your enemy. It is like a stick set up in the sun: bend it a little and its shadow lengthens; bend it beyond a certain point and its shadow shortens. Our enemy won't be satisfied with small concessions: our best course is to fight resolutely."

The king asked the fifth crow, "What do you think: battle, truce, or 7.7
withdrawal?"

قال أمّا القتال فلا سبيل إلى قتال من لا نقوى به وقد كان يقال من لم يعرف قدر نفسه وقدر عدوّه وقاتل من لا قوّة له به فعلى نفسه جهل. مع أنّ العاقل لا يستضعف عدوًّا فإنّ من فعل ذلك اغترّ ومن اغترّ عطب وأنا شديد الهيبة للبوم وإن أضربن عن قتالنا وقد كنت مستوحشاً منهنّ قبل إيقاعهم بنا فإنّ الحازم لا يأمن عدوّه على حال خوفاً لمواثبته إن قرب ولمعاودته[1] ومبادهته إن بعد ولكمونه إن تكشّف ولاستطراده إن ولّى ولمكره إن رآه وحيداً فأحزم القوم وأكيسهم من كره القتال ما وجد عنه سبيلاً لأنّ القتال إنّما النفقة من الأنفس وسائر المرزئة النفقة فيها من الأموال والقول والعمل فلا يكوننّ قتال البوم من رأيكم فإنّه من راكل الفيل راكل الحَيْن والبلاء.

٨،٧ قال الملك فإن كرهت القتال فماذا ترى.

قال أيّها الملك تأتمر وتنظر[2] فإنّ الملك المؤامر المشاور يصيب من مؤامرة النصحاء ذوي العقول من الظفر ما لا يصيبه بالجنود الكثيرة والملك الحازم يزداد برأي الوزراء الحزمة رأياً وحزماً كما يزداد البحر بموادّه من الأنهار. فليس يخفى على الحازم قدر أمره وأمر عدوّه وموضع فرصته ومكيدته ولا ينفكّ يعرض الأمور على نفسه أمرًا أمرًا ويروّي في التقديم والتأخير وفي[3] الأعوان الذين يعتمد عليهم فيها فمن لم يكن له رأي ولم يكن له من أهل الرأي والعقل وزراء يقبل منهم ويعمل برأيهم لم يلبث وإن ساقت الأقدار إليه حظًّا أن تفجأه مقادير[4] السوء بفساد ذلك فإنّ أقسام الخير لم توجّه على الحسب ولا على الجمال ولكنّها وُجّهت للعاقل المستمتع بذوي العقول من نصحائه وأنت أيّها الملك كذلك.

٩،٧ وقد استشرتني في أمر جوابك منّي في بعضه علانية وفي بعضه سرًّا فأمّا العلانية فإنّي كما كرهت القتال فكذلك أكره الخضوع بالخراج والرضى بذلّ القهر فإنّ[5] العاقل الكريم يختار الموت صابرًا محافظاً على الحياة حزيناً ذليلاً وأرى أن لا يؤخر[6] هذا

---

١ كذا ر؛ الأصل: معاوته. ٢ تأتمر وتنظر: الأصل: ياتمر وسطر. ٣ الأصل: ى. ٤ كذا پ٣٤٦٦؛ الأصل: معادير.
٥ كذا ش، ع، ر؛ الأصل: وان. ٦ الأصل: يوخر.

"We cannot fight an enemy that we cannot match in strength," he replied. "They say that if you don't know your capacity and your enemy's capacity and you go ahead and engage a foe you cannot overpower, you foolishly harm only yourself. A wise person doesn't underestimate an enemy; if he does so he lets himself be deceived, and the person who lets himself be deceived is vulnerable. I'm very fearful of the owls even if they don't attack us—I feared them even before they attacked us. A prudent person never trusts his enemy. If the enemy is near, he fears an assault; if the enemy is far off, he fears his sudden return; if the enemy shows himself in the open, he fears an ambush; if the enemy retreats, he fears he may wheel back to attack; and if the enemy is on his own, he fears his cunning. As long as he can find another way, the astute man avoids fighting. Fighting costs lives; other misfortunes only cost money, words, and labor. Don't resolve to fight the owls: anyone who gets into a kicking match with an elephant kicks with death and disaster."

"If we're not to fight," said the king, "what do you suggest?" 7.8

"Confer and consider," he replied. "By conferring with wise advisers, kings achieve victories beyond the means of a great army. By consulting the views of prudent minsters, kings augment their own judgment and prudence, just as the rivers that flow into the sea augment its waters. The prudent man knows his own capacity as well as his enemy's. He knows the opportune moment and the right time for deception. He reviews matters one by one; he considers which deserve priority and which can be postponed; he determines which subordinates he can rely on. Anyone who lacks such judiciousness and cannot heed the advice of wise ministers will soon find himself on the losing side, even if fate has granted him good fortune. For fortune doesn't bestow favor on renown or beauty; it bestows it on the wise who heed their wise advisers. And you are such a person, my king.

"Regarding the matter on which you've sought my advice, I will respond 7.9
partly in public and partly in private. I can state publicly that just as I do not advise fighting, I do not advise stooping to pay tribute or to accept the humiliation of subjection. It is wise and noble to choose death with honor over a life of sorrow and humiliation. And I think we should consider the matter immediately, without hindrance or indifference. What I wish to

الأمر ولا يدخل عليك فيه تثبّط وتهاون.[1] فأمّا السرّ منه فليكن مستورًا فإنّه كان يقال إنّما يصيب الملوك الظفر بالحزم والحزم بإجالة الرأي والرأي بتكرير النظر وتحصين الأسرار. ومن حصّن سرّه فله من تحصينه خلّتان إمّا ظفر بما يريد وإمّا سلامة من العيب والضرّ إن أخطأه الظفر.

ولا بدّ لصاحب السرّ من مستشار مؤتمن يفضي إليه سرّه ويعاونه على النظر فيه فإنّ المستشير وإن كان أفضل من المستشار رأيه فإنّه يزداد برأيه رأيًا كما تزداد النار بالودك ضوءًا. وعلى المستشار موافقة المستشير[2] على صواب ما يرى والرفق به مع ذلك في تبصيره خطأ ما أتاه به وتغليبًا للرأي فيما تلكّأ فيه وأشكل عليهما حتّى يستقيم لهما رأيهما بتعاونهما فإن لم يكن المستشار كذلك فهو على المستشير مع عدوّه كالرجل الذي يرقي الشيطان ليرسله على الإنسان فإذا لم يحكم الرقية كان به فلبس وإيّاه يأخذ إلّا أن يدفع الله. وإذا كان الملك محصّنًا للأسرار متخيّرًا لصالح الوزراء مهيبًا في أنفس العامّة بعيدًا[3] من أن يعلم الناس ما في نفسه لا يضيع ذو بلاء ولا يسلم منه ذو جرم مقدّرًا بما ينفق وما يقتر كان خليقًا أن لا يُسلب صالح ما أوتي. وللأسرار منازل فمن السرّ ما يدخل فيه رهط ومنه ما يدخل فيه رجلان ومنه ما يستعان فيه بقوم ولا أرى لهذا السرّ في مقدار منزلته أن يشترك فيه إلّا لسانان وأربع آذان.

١٠،٧ فنهض الملك من ساعته فخلا به فسأله فكان ما سأله عنه أن قال هل تعلم بدء عداوة ما بيننا وبين البوم.

قال نعم أيّها الملك كلمة تكلّم بها غراب.

قال الملك وكيف كان ذلك.

١١،٧ قال زعموا أنّ جماعة الطير لم يكن لها في بعض الأزمنة ملك وأنّها اجتمعت على بومة لتملّكها فبينما هي في جمعها إذ رُفع لهنّ غراب فقال بعضهنّ انتظرن هذا الغراب

١ تثبّط وتهاون: الأصل: شطأ وتهاونا. ٢ وعلى المستشار موافقة المستشير: كذا ر؛ الأصل: وعلى المستشر موافقه المستشار. ٣ كذا ش، ر؛ ساقطة من الأصل.

impart in secret will remain confidential. Kings, it has been said, obtain victories only through prudent management of their affairs; prudent management depends on weighing opinions; and sound opinions depend on repeated examination and well-guarded secrets. He who guards his secret benefits in two ways: either he gains his objective, or, if he fails, he avoids shame and harm.

"If you have a secret project, you need a trustworthy counselor you can apprise, and who can help you make decisions. Even if the person seeking advice is superior in judgment to the person whose advice is sought, the latter's judgment will increase his judiciousness, just as adding grease to a fire makes it brighter. A counselor should agree with his patron in what he thinks correct, but be gentle when enlightening the patron about any error he might have made—that way, the correct opinion gains prominence when there is hesitation and uncertainty. By cooperating in this way, they will arrive at the correct opinion. A counselor who is not like this is on the side of his patron's enemies. This is like a man who utters a spell and sends a demon against someone: if he utters the spell incorrectly, the demon in his confusion may seize the reciter of the spell, unless God repels it. A king is unlikely to lose the good fortune he has been given if he guards his secrets, chooses his ministers well, is feared by the common people, takes care not to let his innermost thoughts be known, lets no good service go unrewarded, leaves no criminal unpunished, and is moderate in his expenditures, neither a miser nor a spendthrift. Secrets differ in degree: some can be shared with kin and some with two men, while others require the cooperation of many people. Given the importance of this secret, I think that four ears and two tongues, no more, should be privy to it."

The king rose immediately to address him in private. One of his questions was: "Do you know how the enmity between us and the owls began?" 7.10

How the Enmity between Crows and Owls Began

"Yes, Your Majesty," he replied. "It was something a crow said."

"And how did that happen?" asked the king.

The crow told the following tale: Once upon a time, they say, the community of birds had no king. They had decided to make an owl their king, but during their assembly a crow appeared. "Let's wait for this crow," said 7.11

نستشيره في هذا الأمر. فلمّا انتهى الغراب إليهنّ استشرنه فقال الغراب لو أنّ جميع أصناف الطير بادت وفُقد الطاووس والكركيّ والحمام والبطّ لكان أن[1] تعشن بغير ملك أكرم لكنّ من أن تملّكن البومة أقبح الطير منظرًا وأشرّها مخبرًا وأقلّها عقلاً وأشدّها غضباً وأبعدها رحمة مع ما بها من الزمانة الظاهرة والعشاء بالنهار وأشدّ من ذلك سفهها وسوء أخلاقها إلّا أن تملّكنها وتدبّرن الأمور دونها برأيكنّ وعقولكنّ كما فعلت الأرنب التي زعمت أنّ القمر ملكها ثمّ عملت برأيها.

قال الطير[2] وكيف كان ذلك.

قال الغراب زعموا أنّ أرضاً من أرض الفيلة تتابعت عليها السنون فقلّ بها الماء ١٢،٧
وغارت عيونها وأصاب الفيلة بها عطش شديد فشكون ذلك إلى ملكهنّ فأرسل الملك رسله وروّاده[3] في طلب الماء في كلّ جهة فرجع إليه بعضهم فأخبره أنّه وجد بمكان كذا وكذا عيناً تسمّى القمريّة كثيرة الماء فتوجّه ملك الفيلة بمن معه إلى تلك الأرض فكانت العين بمكان فيه[4] أرانب فلمّا انتهت الفيلة إلى هنالك وطئت أرانب كثيرة في جحرتها ومجاثمها فهلكت طائفة منها فاجتمعت الأرانب إلى ملكها فقلن قد علمت ما أصابنا من هذه الفيلة فاحتل[5] لنا فإنّهنّ إن رجعن علينا لورودهنّ قتلننا بأجمعنا.

فقال الملك ليحضرني كلّ ذي رأي منكنّ.

فتقدّم خُزَز منها[6] يقال له فيروز وكان الملك يفضّل رأيه وأدبه فقال إن رأى الملك أن يبعثني إلى الفيلة ويبعث معي أميناً يرى ويسمع ما أقول وأصنع ثمّ يخبر به الملك فليفعل.

قال الملك أنت أميني أرضى رأيك وأصدّق قولك فانطلق إلى الفيلة وأبلغ عنّي ما أحببت واعمل برأيك واعلم أنّ برأي الرسول وأدبه به ما يُعتبر عقل المرسِل وعليك بالرفق واللين والتؤدة فإنّ الرسول إذا رفق ليّن القلب وإذا خرف ضيّق الصدر.

---

١ الأصل: لكنّ. ٢ كذا ر؛ الأصل: الملك. ٣ كذا ع؛ الأصل: ووزراوه. ٤ الأصل: فيها. ٥ كذا ل٢؛ الأصل: فاحسن. ٦ خُزَز منها: كذا ش، ع؛ الأصل: حزم لها.

one of them, "and ask his opinion about this." The crow arrived, and, when asked his opinion, he replied, "Even if all the other birds perished, and there were no longer any peacocks, cranes, ducks, and doves, it would be more honorable for you to live without a king than to make an owl your king—the ugliest, worst-natured, most irascible, least intelligent, and least merciful of birds—not to mention their midday laziness and daytime blindness. Their stupidity and bad character are the worst—unless, that is, you intend to crown him king, but manage affairs as you yourselves see fit, as did the rabbit who claimed that the moon was her king, then acted according to her own judgment."

"What do you mean?" asked the birds.

And the crow told the following tale: They say that a land where elephants lived experienced several years of drought. Water became scarce and the springs dried up. In their thirst, the elephants complained to their king, who sent out messengers and scouts in every direction to search for water. One of them returned and said that in another land he had found a spring full of water, called the Spring of the Moon. The king and his retinue set out for the land. It happened that the spring was located in a place full of rabbits, and the elephants trampled many of them to death in their burrows. The rabbits assembled before their king and said, "See what these elephants have done! Devise something for us, because if they come back to their waterhole, they'll kill us all." **7.12** *The Rabbit Who Claimed the Moon Was Her King*

And the king said, "If anyone has a plan, let him bring it."

A young buck named Fayrūz—whose good judgment and courtly manner had already impressed the king—stepped forward. "If it please the king, send me to the elephants, along with someone the king trusts, to see and hear everything I say and do, and to report back to the king."

"You are someone I trust," said the king. "I am satisfied with your judgment and will hold your words to be true. Go to the elephants and in my name deliver any message you please. Do as you see fit, but remember that the sender's intelligence is judged by the messenger's judgment and behavior. Be gentle, agreeable, and calm; a gentle messenger softens the heart, but a rough one hardens it."

فانطلق الأرنب في ليلة القمر فيها[1] طالع حتّى إذا انتهى إلى الفيلة فكره أن يدنو ١٣،٧
منهنّ مخافة أن يطأنه الفيلة فيقتلنه فأشرف على سنن من الأرض ثمّ نادى ملك الفيلة فأجابه فقال أرسلني إليك القمر والرسول مبلغ وغير ملوم وإن غلظت مقالته.

قال ملك الفيلة فما الرسالة.

قال الخزز[2] يقول لك القمر إنّه من عرف فضل قوّته على الضعفاء فغرّه ذلك من قوّة الأقوياء كانت قوّته حَيْنًا له وإنّك قد عرفت فضل قوّتك على الدوابّ فغرّك ذلك منك[3] فعمدت إلى عين لي تسمّى باسمي فشربت من مائها وكدّرتها وقذّرتها بفيلتك وإنّي أتقدّم إليك وأنذرك أن تعود فأتلف نفسك وإن كنت في شكّ من رسالتي فهلمّ إلى العين الساعة فإنّي موافيك بما لا تقدر عليه.

فعجب ملك الفيلة من قول الخزز[4] ثمّ انطلق معه إلى العين فلمّا أشرف عليها رأى فيها خيال القمر.

فقال له الخزز[5] خذ بمشفرك من الماء فاغسل وجهك واسجد للقمر.

فأدخل ملك الفيلة مشفره في الماء فخُيّل إليه أنّ خيال القمر الذي أبصره يرتعد فقال الفيل ما شأن القمر يرتعد أتُرى واجدًا عليّ.

قال نعم.

فسجد الفيل للخيال واعتذر إليه ممّا صنع وشرط أن لا يعود إلى تلك العين ولا شيء من فيلته.

فقال الغراب وإنّ مع ما ذكرت لكم من شأن البوم أنّ من طباعها الخبّ والخديعة ١٤،٧
وشرّ الملوك الخبّ المخادع ومن ابتلي بالسلطان الغدّار والمحكّم المخادع أصابه ما أصاب الصفرد والأرنب اللذين تحاكما إلى السنّور الصوّام القوّام.

قال الطير وكيف كان ذلك.

قال الغراب كان لي جار من الصفارد في جحر قريب من الشجرة التي كان فيها ١٥،٧
وكري وكان يكثر التقاؤنا وتواصلنا ثمّ إنّي طلبته وفقدته وطالت غيبته ولم أدر

١ كذا ل٢؛ الأصل: فيه. ٢ الأصل: الحزم. ٣ ر: منّي. ٤ الأصل: الحرم. ٥ الأصل: الحرم.

The rabbit set out just as the moon was rising. When he came to the elephants, he didn't wish to get too close, lest they trample him to death, so he went to a spot overlooking the path and called to the king of the elephants, who answered. The rabbit then said, "The moon has sent me to you. Though the message be harsh, the messenger who delivers it is blameless." 7.13

"What is the message?" asked the king of the elephants.

"The moon says, 'Someone who, knowing himself to be stronger than the weak, imagines himself to be stronger than the strong, will be undone by his own strength. You know that your strength is superior to that of other animals, and this has deluded you with respect to me. You have gone to my spring, which bears my name; you have drunk from it, muddying it and polluting it with your elephants. I command you and warn you: Don't do this again or I will destroy you. If you have any doubt about my message, go to the spring right away, and I will accost you in a way that will leave no doubt.'"

Amazed at the rabbit's words, the king of the elephants set off with him to the spring. He looked into it and saw the moon's reflection.

"Take some water in your trunk," Fayrūz said, "wash your face, and bow down before the moon in worship."

When the king of the elephants put his trunk into the water, it seemed to him that the moon's reflection was trembling. "Why is the moon trembling?" he asked. "Could he be angry with me?"

"He is," replied Fayrūz.

So the elephant bowed down to the reflection, apologized for what he had done, and promised that neither he nor any of his elephants would ever return to that spring.

The crow said, "In addition to what I've told you about owls, deceit and guile are part of their nature. A deceitful, guileful king is the worst king of all. Those afflicted with a treacherous ruler or a deceitful judge will suffer the fate of the partridge[46] and the rabbit who took their dispute for arbitration to a cat who fasted and prayed." 7.14

"And what was their fate?" asked the birds.

The Partridge, the Rabbit, and the Pious Cat

The crow told the following tale: Once I had as neighbor a partridge who lived in a burrow near the tree where I had my nest. He and I were fond of each other and met often. One day I looked for him and couldn't find him. 7.15

أين غاب فجاءت أرنب إلى مستقرّ الصفرد لتسكنه فكرهت أن أخاصمها[١] إذ غاب الصفرد فطالت غيبته وظننت أنّه قد هلك[٢] فلبثت[٣] الأرنب في ذلك زمانًا ثمّ إنّ الصفرد رجع إلى مكانه فوجد الأرنب هنالك فقال لها هذا المنزل لي فاخرجي.

فقالت الأرنب المسكن في يدي وأنت مدّعٍ[٤] فإن كان لك حقّ فعليك بالسلطان.

قال[٥] الصفرد لي البيّنة على ذلك.

قالت الأرنب اطلب القاضي قبل البيّنة.

قال[٦] الصفرد إنّ قريب منّا على شاطئ نهر كذا سنّورًا مقعدًا يصوم الدهر لا يفطر ويصلّي الليل والنهار ولا يؤذي أحدًا ولا يسفك دمًا وقد اجتزأ بالحشيش فإن أحببت تحاكمنا إليه ورضينا به.

قالت الأرنب ما أرضاني به إن كان كما وصفته.

١٦،٧ فانطلقا إليه فتبعتهما لأنظر ذلك السنّور المتعبّد وكيف قضاؤه بينهما فلمّا نظر السنّور من بعيد إلى الصفرد والأرنب انتصب قائمًا على رجليه يصلّي فأقبلا حتّى إذا كانا منه قريبًا وهما هائبان له مجلّان عارفان لفضله طلبا إليه أن يقضي بينهما فانصرف إليهما وأمرهما أن يقصّا عليه قصّتهما ففعلا. قال السنّور قد أدركني الكبر وثقلت أذناي فلا أكاد أسمع فادنوَا منّي وأعيدا قصّتكما. فدنوَا منه.

١٧،٧ فقال أنا أبادئكما بالنصيحة قبل القضيّة آمركما بتقوى الله وأن لا تطلبا إلّا الحقّ فإنّ طالب الحقّ هو الذي يفلح وإن قضي عليه وطالب الباطل مخصوم وإن قضي له وليس لصاحب الدنيا من دنياه شيء ولا له فيها مال ولا صديق أفضل من عمل صالح[٧] قدّمه فذو العقل حقيق أن يكون شغله في طلب ما يبقى ويعود عليه نفعه غدًا ويترك ما سوى ذلك.[٨]

فلم يزل يقصّ عليهما ويزدادان به أنسًا ومنه دنوًّا حتّى وثب عليهما جميعًا فضمّهما إليه فقتلهما.

---

١ الأصل: اخاصمه. ٢ أنه . . . هلك: الأصل: أنها قد هلكت. ٣ الأصل: فلث. ٤ كذا ر؛ الأصل: مدعى.
٥ الأصل: فالب. ٦ الأصل: فالب. ٧ كذا ل٢؛ ساقطة من الأصل. ٨ ويترك . . . ذلك: الأصل: ان ترك ذلك.

His absence dragged on, and I had no idea where he had gone. Meanwhile, a rabbit came to live in the partridge's home. I wasn't inclined to quarrel with him, because the partridge had been away so long that I thought he must have perished. The rabbit lived there for a time, but then the partridge returned and, finding the rabbit there, said, "This is my home. Get out!"

"I have possession," replied the rabbit. "You allege otherwise. If you have a valid claim, bring proof."

"I have clear evidence," said the partridge.

"First find a judge," said the rabbit. "Then we'll see about the evidence."

"By the riverbank near us," said the partridge, "lives a cat who is an invalid. He fasts endlessly, prays night and day, harms no one, spills no blood, and is content to live on grass. If you like, we can go to him for arbitration and abide by his decision."

"That's fine with me, if he is as you describe!" replied the rabbit.

So off they went, and I followed them to have a look at this pious cat and 7.16
to see how he would arbitrate between them. When the cat saw the partridge and the rabbit approaching in the distance, he stood up on his hind legs to pray. When they got close to him—making sure to be cautious and respectful, and to acknowledge his merit—they asked him if he would arbitrate. He asked them to tell their story, which they did, and then he said, "Old age has overtaken me; my ears have become so dull I can hardly hear. Come closer and repeat your story." So they did.

"Before pronouncing judgment, I'll start by giving you some good 7.17
advice," he said. "I charge you to fear God and seek nothing but the truth: the seeker of truth prospers, even if the judgment goes against him; but the seeker of falsehood loses, even if the judgment goes in his favor. The only things an inhabitant of this world takes with him from his earthly existence are neither money nor friends, but the good works he has done. A wise man should seek what endures and will bring him benefit tomorrow, and abandon everything else."

As he talked, they became more and more at ease with him and came closer and closer, until finally he pounced, grabbed them, and killed them both.

قال الغراب في حديثه أيضاً إنّ البوم يجمع معه سائر العيوب وما وصفت لكم من المكر والخبّ[١] والخديعة فلا يكوننّ تمليك البوم من رأيكنّ.

١٨،٧ فصدرت الطير عن رأي الغراب ولم تملّك البوم.

فقال البوم الذي كان أُختير للملك للغراب لقد وترتني أعظم الترة فلا أدري هل كان سلف إليك منّي سوء استحققت به هذا منك فإن يكن كان كذلك وإلّا فاعلم أنّ الفؤوس يُقطع بها الشجر فتنبت وتعود والسيف يُقطع به اللحم والعظم فيندمل بعد ويلتئم واللسان لا يندمل جرحه ولا يلتئم ما قُطع به وأنّ النصل من الحديد يغيب في الجوف فيُنزع وأشباه النصال من القول إذا وصلت إلى القلب لم تُنتزع ولم تُستخرج ولكلّ حريق مطفئ فمطفئ النار الماء ومطفئ السمّ الدواء ومطفئ الحزن الصبر ونار الحقد لا تخبو وإنّكم معشر الغربان غرستم فيما بيننا وبينكم غرس العداوة جري الليالي الغوابر.

فقضى البوم هذه المقالة وانصرف مغضباً موتوراً.

١٩،٧ وندم الغراب على ما فرط منه وقال في نفسه خرقت فيما كان من قولي وجنيت العداوة على نفسي وقومي ولم أكن أحقّ الطير بهذه المقالة ولا أعناها بأمر ملكها ولا أظنّ كثيراً من الطير إلّا وقد رأى مثل[٢] رأيي وعلم مثل علمي من البوم فمنعها من الكلام بمثل ما تكلّمت به اتّقاء ما لم أتقِ والنظر فيما لم أنظر من حذار العواقب ولا سيّما إذا كان الكلام مواجهة فإنّ المواجهة تورث الحقد والضغينة وإن كان القائل له واثقاً بقوّته وسعته وفضله لم يحمله ذلك على التعرّض للعداوة. وليس من سفهي إلّا إقدامي على التكلّم في الأمر الجسيم قبل أن أرى فيه وقبل أن أستشير الأولياء من النصحاء فإنّه من لم يستشر النصيح العاقل ولم يعمل برأيه مع ذلك بتكرار النظر والرويّة لم يُسرّ بمواقع رأيه فما كان أغناني[٣] عمّا اكتسبت في يومي هذا وما وقعت فيه من الهمّ. فعاتب الغراب نفسه طويلاً.

---

١ والخبّ: الأصل: والخب اى معناه انه محتال. ٢ مثل: الأصل: مثله مثل. ٣ كذا ل٢؛ الأصل: عناى.

The crow said, “To everything else I’ve described, the owl adds deceit, guile, and cunning. Therefore, you mustn’t make the owl your king.”

The birds followed the crow’s advice and didn’t make the owl king. 7.18

And the owl who had been chosen to be king said to the crow, “You’ve done me a terrible injury. I don’t know whether I did you some wrong in the past for which I might deserve this treatment from you. If that is the case, then so be it. If not, know that a tree felled by an ax will sprout again; flesh and bone cut by a sword will heal and mend, but wounds made by the tongue never heal. An arrowhead that sinks into the body can be pulled out, but arrow-sharp words that pierce the heart can never be pulled out. Everything that burns can be extinguished by something: fire by water, poison by an antidote, and sorrow by patience; but the fire of hatred never dies. You crows have planted a tree of enmity between us that will last for all time.”

With these words, the owl left in a fury, thirsting for revenge.

The crow regretted his rashness. “It was stupid of me to say things that 7.19
brought enmity on me and my people. I was neither the bird best qualified to speak about the subject, nor the one who had the biggest stake in the matter of the kingship. Many others may have thought what I thought and known what I knew, but, unlike me, they refrained from speaking, out of caution and consideration of the consequences. This is especially true when one speaks to someone face-to-face, as confrontation leaves a legacy of hatred and rancor. Even if as a speaker you are confident of your strength, ability, and virtue, you shouldn’t let it lead you to expose yourself to enmity. My foolishness lay in venturing to speak on a weighty matter before giving it due consideration and before consulting those entitled to give advice. Failure to consult a wise counselor and act on his opinion, after thorough examination and reflection, guarantees unhappiness with the results. I little needed what I’ve acquired today and the distress I find myself in!” The crow chided himself at great length.

فهذا ما كان من علّة العداوة[1] بيننا وبين البوم.

٢٠،٧ قال الملك[2] لقد فهمت كلامك وما ذكرته فأخبرني بما نحن أحوج إليه اليوم من بدء عداوة الغربان والبوم.

قال الغراب أمّا القتال فقد كنت فرغت إليك من رأيي فيه وكراهتي للقتال ولكن أرجو أن ييسّر الله من الخير ما فيه فرج قريب فربّ قوم قد احتالوا برأيهم للأمر العظيم حتّى ظفروا منه بحاجتهم وما كانوا ليقدروا عليه بالمكابرة كالقوم الذين مكروا بالناسك حتّى ذهبوا بعريضه.

قال الملك وكيف كان ذلك.

٢١،٧ قال الغراب زعموا أنّ ناسكًا اشترى عريضًا ضخمًا سمينًا يجعله قربانًا فانطلق به يقوده وبصر به نفر مكرة فائتمروا بينهم ليخدعوه عنه فقال له أحدهم أيّها الناسك ما هذا الكلب الذي معك. ثمّ عرض له الثاني أتريد الصيد بهذا الكلب. ثمّ لقيه الثالث فقال إنّ لباسك للباس ناسك وقودك للكلب ليس من عمل الناسك. فلمّا سمع الناسك ما سمع داخله شكّ واتّهم نفسه في أمر العريض وقال لعلّ الذي باعني سحرني. فخلّى عن العريض فأخذه النفر فاقتسموه فيما بينهم.

وإنّما ضربت لك هذا المثل لما رجوت من درك حاجتنا بالرفق والحيلة فأنا لديّ أن يتغضّب الملك على رؤوس الأجناد فيأمرني فأُضرب وأُخرج عنه وأُلطخ بالدماء ويُنتف ريشي وذنبي وأُطرح في أصل الشجرة ويذهب الملك مع جنده إلى مكان كذا ويكون فيه حتّى آتيه ببيان ما يكون من أمري وأمر البوم.

ففعل الملك بالغراب ذلك ومضى مع غربانه إلى المكان الذي وصف له.

٢٢،٧ ثمّ إنّ البوم جاءت من ليلتهم فلم يجدوا الغربان هنالك ولم تفطن للغراب المطروح في أصل الشجرة وأشفق الغراب أن ينصرفن قبل أن يرينه فيكون تعذيبه نفسه باطلًا فجعل يئنّ ويهمش حتّى سمع البوم صوته فلمّا رأينه أخبرن به ملكهنّ فعمد[3] نحوه

١ الأصل: العلة والعداوة. ٢ كذا ل٢؛ ساقطة من الأصل. ٣ كذا ر؛ الأصل: فعمدن.

"This, to answer your question, was the reason for the enmity between the owls and us."

7.20 "Now I understand," said the king. "But tell me something more pertinent to today than the origin of the hatred between crows and owls."

And the crow said, "I've already told you what I think about fighting. You know how much I dislike it. But I hope God will set in motion some good that will bring swift relief. Those in dire straits have often achieved through cunning what they could never have achieved in a contest of strength—like the men who tricked the ascetic and made off with his goat."

"And how did they do that?" asked the king.

7.21

The Sly Fellows Who Tricked the Ascetic Out of His Kid

The crow told the following tale: An ascetic, they say, once bought a large, fat kid to offer as a sacrifice, and set off with it. Some sly fellows saw him and conspired to trick him out of it. One of them approached and asked, "Sir, what is this dog you have there?" The second then approached and asked, "Sir, do you intend to hunt with this dog?" Then the third approached and said, "You may be dressed as an ascetic, but walking with a dog isn't the sort of thing ascetics do." After hearing these remarks, the ascetic had doubts and became suspicious about the kid. "Perhaps," he said, "the vendor cast a spell on me." He promptly released the kid, and the men took it and divided it among themselves.

"I've told you this story because I think we, too, can attain our end through skill and cunning. Here's what I think: The king should fly into a rage in the presence of his soldiers and order that I be beaten, expelled from his presence, and cast down at the foot of the tree, all bloody, feathers and tail plucked out. The king should then leave with his soldiers, go to a place I'll specify, and remain there until I report back on how matters play out between me and the owls."

The king had this done to the crow and went with his crows to the specified place.

7.22 The owls came that very night. They didn't find any crows, and didn't notice the crow lying at the foot of the tree. Fearing they might leave before seeing him and that his self-imposed torments might have been to no avail,

في بومات يسألنه عن الغربان فلمّا دنا منه أمر بومة أن تسأله فقالت من أنت وأين الغربان.

فقال الغراب أنا فلان فأمّا ما تسأل من أمر الغربان فقد ترى من حالي ما يدلّك أنّي لست من مواضع أسرار الغربان.

فقال ملك البوم هذا وزير ملك الغربان وصاحب سرّه ورأيه ومشورته. سلوه بأيّ ذنب صُنع به ما أرى.

فقال الغراب سفه رأيي صنع بي ما ترى هذا.

قال ملك البوم وما كان سفه رأيك.

٢٣،٧ قال الغراب لمّا كان من إيقاعكنّ بنا ما كان استشارنا ملكنا فقال أيّها الغربان ما رأيكنّ وما ترين فيما حلّ بنا. وكنت من الأمر عنده بمكان فقلت أرى أنّه لا طاقة لنا بقتال البوم لأنّهنّ أشدّ منّا بطشاً وأجرأ منّا قلوباً ولكنّ الرأي إن أخذنا التماس الصلح وعرض الجزية فإن قُبل ذلك منّا وإلّا فالهرب في البلاد. وقلت لهنّ فيما قلت إنّ قتالكنّ اليوم شرّ لكنّ وخير لهنّ والصلح أفضل ما هنالك. وأمرتهنّ بالخضوع وضربت لهنّ الأمثال في ذلك وقلت إنّ العدوّ الشديد لا يُردّ بأسه وغضبه بمثل الخضوع ألا ترون أنّ الحشيش إنّما يسلم من الريح العاصف بلينه وامتياله مع الريح حيث مالت. فغضبت الغربان من قولي وزعمن أنهنّ يردن القتال واتّهمنني وقلن غششتنا وملت علينا. فرددن رأيي ونصيحتي وعذّبنني بأنواع العذاب.

فلمّا سمع ملك البوم قوله قال لأحد وزرائه ما ترى في هذا الغراب.

٢٤،٧ قال الوزير ليس لك في أمره نظر إلّا معاجلة القتل فإنّ[1] هذا أفضل عدّة الغربان وفي قتله لنا فتح عظيم في الراحة من رأيه ومكيدته وفقده على الغربان شديد وقد يقال من استمكن من الأمر الجسيم فأضاعه كان خليقاً أن لا يناله بعد ومن التمس فرصة عمله فأمكنته فأخّر العمل فيها كان جديراً أن يفوته العمل ولا ترجع إليه

[1] كذا ش، ع، پ٣٤٦٦؛ الأصل: وان.

he began moaning and groaning until the owls heard him. When they saw him, they told their king, who approached, surrounded by owls, to question him about the crows. The king commanded an owl to ask him who he was and where the crows were.

The crow stated his name and then said, "You ask about the crows—I think you can see from my state that I am not privy to their secrets."

The king of the owls said, "This is the crow king's minister, confidant, and adviser. Ask him for what offense he has been treated in this way."

"The foolishness of my advice did this to me."

"Foolishness? How so?" asked the king.

The crow said, "After your attack, our king asked for advice. 'Crows!' 7.23
he said, 'what do you think we should do?' As I was well-regarded by the king, I said, 'I don't think we can fight the owls: they're stronger than we are, and bolder. I think we should sue for peace and offer to pay tribute. If they agree, well and good; if not, we should flee the country.' I told them, among other things, 'Fighting the owls now would be worse for you and better for them. A truce is the best option.' I told them to submit, and drew an analogy. 'Nothing,' I said, 'repels a powerful enemy's strength and fury better than submission. Don't you see that the grass is safe from the gale because it is flexible and bends whichever way the wind turns?' They were enraged by my words and insisted they wanted to fight. They accused me of disloyalty and of turning against them. They rejected my advice and subjected me to every sort of abuse."

When the king of the owls heard the crow's words, he asked one of his 7.24
ministers, "What's your opinion regarding this crow?"

"No two ways about it! Put him to death immediately. He's the crows' principal resource. Killing him earns us a great victory, as we will have deprived them of his expertise and cunning. His loss will be a blow to the crows. They say that when you hold the advantage at a critical moment and let it slip, you get no second chance; and that when you seek an opportunity to act, but neglect it when you get it, you're likely to lose the opportunity and never regain it. To catch your enemy weak and helpless and fail to get

الفرصة ومن وجد عدوّه ضائعاً معوزاً فلم يسترح منه أصابته الندامة حين[1] يقوى عدوّه ويستعدّ له فلا يقدر عليه.

٢٥،٧ قال ملك البوم لآخر من وزرائه ما رأيك في هذا الغراب.

قال أرى ألّا تقتله فإنّ العدوّ الذليل الذي لا شوكة له أهل أن يُرحم ويُصفح عنه والمستجير الخائف أهل أن يؤمَّن[2] ويجار مع أنّ الرجل ربّما عطّفه على عدوّه الأمر اليسير كالتاجر الذي عطّف السارق عليه امرأته بما لم يتعمّده.

قال ملك البوم وكيف كان ذلك.

٢٦،٧ قال الوزير زعموا أنّ رجلاً كان كثير المال كبير السنّ مفرطاً وكانت له امرأة ذات جمال وشباب وكان لها محبّاً وعاشقاً وكانت له مبغضة لا تمكّنه من التزامها ولا من كثير من حاجته منها وكان التاجر يعرفها بذلك ولا يزيده علمه بحالها إلّا حبّاً لها وأنّ سارقاً أتى بيت التاجر ليلة فوافق التاجر نائماً والمرأة مستيقظة فذُعرت من السارق والتزمت زوجها فاستيقظ التاجر بالتزامها إيّاه فقال من أين كانت النعمة عليّ. فلمّا بصر بالسارق ناداه فقال أيّها الرجل أنت في حلّ من مالي ومتاعي ولك الفضل عليّ بعطفك هذه عليّ حتّى عانقتني.

٢٧،٧ ثم إنّ الملك البوم سأل الثالث من وزرائه عن رأيه في الغراب.

فقال أرى أن تبقيه وتحسن إليه فإنّه خليق أن يناصحك فإنّ ذا العقل يرى معاداة بعض أعدائه بعضاً من حسن الظفر[3] في اشتغال بعضهم ببعض واختلافهم مثل الذي كان في اختلاف الشيطان واللصّ حتّى نجا الناسك.

قال الملك وكيف كان ذلك.

٢٨،٧ قال الوزير زعموا أنّ ناسكاً أصاب بقرة حلوباً فأقبل بها يقودها إلى منزله وتبعه لصّ يريد أن يسرقها وصحب اللصّ شيطان في صورة إنسان. فقال اللصّ للشيطان من أنت. قال أنا شيطان[4] أريد أن أتبع هذا الناسك فإذا نام أخذته.

---

١ كذا ش، ع، پ٣٤٦٦؛ الأصل: حتى. ٢ كذا ر؛ الأصل: يوبس. ٣ كذا ش، ع، پ٣٤٦٦، پ٣٤٧٥؛ الأصل: الطن.
٤ كذا ش، ع، پ٣٤٧٥؛ الأصل: الشيطان.

rid of him is to regret it when the enemy grows strong, readies himself, and becomes invincible."

The owl king then asked another of his ministers, "What's your opinion regarding this crow?" 7.25

"I think you shouldn't kill him. A humiliated enemy with no fight left in him deserves mercy and forgiveness; a frightened asylum seeker deserves safety and protection. Furthermore, a trivial matter will sometimes bring a person to show affection for his enemy—as happened when the thief inadvertently caused the merchant's wife to show affection for her husband."

"And how did that happen?" asked the king.

The Thief Who Caused the Merchant's Wife to Embrace Her Husband

The minister told the following tale: Once, they say, there was a man 7.26
who was rich, old, and exceedingly passionate. He had a beautiful young wife with whom he was head over heels in love, but she detested him and wouldn't allow him to embrace her and satisfy his desires. The merchant knew how she felt, but this made him love her all the more. One night, a thief came to the merchant's house and found the merchant asleep and the wife awake. Frightened by the thief, she threw her arms around her husband. The embrace aroused the merchant, who exclaimed, "Whence comes this bliss?" When he saw the thief, he called out to him, "Man, feel free to take all the money and belongings you want. You deserve my thanks for getting this woman to embrace me."

The king then asked the third minister for his opinion about the crow. 7.27

"I think you should spare him and treat him well, as he is likely to give you good advice. A wise man considers it a victory when his enemies fall out among themselves and are busy quarreling among themselves. This is exactly what happened when the ascetic escaped because the thief and the demon quarreled."

"And how did that happen?" asked the king.

The Ascetic Who Escaped When the Thief and the Demon Quarreled

The minister told the following tale: Once, they say, an ascetic set out to 7.28
take to his home a milch cow he had been given. A thief, intent on stealing it, followed him, joined in turn by a demon in human form. "Who are you?" asked the thief. "A demon," came the reply. "I intend to follow this ascetic, and when he falls asleep, I'll take him." "For my part," said the thief, "I intend

قال اللصّ إنّي لصّ أريد أن أتبعه إلى منزله لعلّي أسرق بقرته. فاصطحبا يتبعان الناسك فلمّا انتهى إلى منزله ممسياً دخل بيته وأدخل البقرة بيتاً فلمّا نام الناسك أشفق اللصّ إن بدأ الشيطان بأخذ الناسك قبل أن يسرق البقرة أن يصيح الناسك فتجتمع الناس عليه فلا يقدر على البقرة فقال اللصّ للشيطان أنظرني حتّى أخرج بالبقرة ثمّ عليك بالرجل. فأشفق الشيطان إن بدأ اللصّ بالبقرة أن يشعر به الناسك فيستيقظ ويستيقظ أهله فلا يقدر على شيء منه فقال[1] الشيطان بل أنظرني حتّى[2] آخذ الناسك ثمّ عليك بالبقرة. فأبى كلّ واحد منهما على صاحبه فلم يزالا في اختلافهما حتّى نادى اللصّ الناسك أيّها الرجل استيقظ فهذا الشيطان يريد أن يأخذك. وناداه الشيطان فقال استيقظ أيّها الناسك فإنّ هذا اللصّ يريد أن يأخذ بقرتك. فاستيقظ الناسك وأهله وجيرانه وهرب اللصّ والشيطان.

٢٩،٧ فلمّا فرغ الثالث من كلامه هذا قال الأوّل الذي أشار بقتل الغراب أراكم خدعكم هذا الغراب برفقه ومكره وتضرّعه فأنتم تريدون تضييع رأيكم والتغرير بجسيم من الأمر. مهلاً لا تفعلوا وانظروا نظر ذوي الألباب الذين يعزمون على أمورهم وأمور عدوّهم على الصواب ولا يغرّهم لين كلام عدوّهم ولا تلقيهم خصومة عن رأيهم ولا تكونوا كالعجزة الذين تلين قلوبهم لعدوّهم عند أدنى ملق وتضرّع ولا تكونوا بما تسمعون أشدّ تصديقاً منكم[3] بما تعقلون كالنجّار الذي كذّب بما رأى وعلم وصدّق بما سمع فاغترّ وانخدع.

٣٠،٧ قال الملك وكيف كان ذلك.

قال الوزير زعموا أنّ نجّاراً كانت له امرأة يحبّها وكان قد علقها رجل فاطّلع على ذلك بعض أهل النجّار فأطلعوه على خبر امرأته فأحبّ النجّار ان يستيقن ذلك فقال لامرأته إنّي ذاهب إلى قرية كذا وهي منّا على ثلاثة فراسخ لعمل بعض الأمراء وماكث هناك أيّاماً فأعدّي لي زاداً. ففعلت فخرج النجّار وقال احتفظي بيتك وأوثقي بابك حتّى أرجع إليك.

١ كذا ل٢؛ الأصل: قال. ٢ كذا ل٢؛ ساقطة من الأصل. ٣ كذا ش، ع؛ ساقطة من الأصل.

to follow him home and steal his cow." So together they followed the ascetic. When he arrived home that evening, he went into his room and put the cow in another room. When the ascetic went to bed, the thief feared that if the demon took the ascetic first, before he could steal the cow, the ascetic would scream; people would come running, and he wouldn't be able to steal the cow. So he said to the demon, "Wait until I make off with the cow; then do as you please with the man." The demon, for his part, feared that if the thief stole the cow first, the ascetic might hear him, wake up, and rouse the family, and he wouldn't be able to do anything. So he said to the thief, "Wait until I take the ascetic; then do as you please with the cow." Each refused to yield to the other, and they kept arguing until the thief shouted to the ascetic, "Get up, man! This demon wants to take you!" The demon, for his part, shouted, "Get up, ascetic! This thief wants to take your cow!" The ascetic, his family, and his neighbors all woke up, and the thief and demon fled.

When the third minister finished speaking, the first owl, who had advised killing the crow, said, "I think this crow has deceived you with his graciousness, cunning, and entreaties. You're about to throw caution to the winds and expose yourselves to great danger. Be careful! Don't do it! Consider the matter intelligently, like those who decide correctly about their own and their enemies' affairs, like those who aren't deceived by an enemy's smooth words and abandon good sense because of an argument. Don't be like weaklings whose hearts soften toward their enemies at the slightest flattery and entreaty. Don't give more credence to what you hear than to what you know. Don't be like the carpenter who disbelieved what he saw and knew, but believed what he heard, and so was beguiled and deceived." 7.29

"How was he deceived?" asked the king.

The Carpenter Who Disbelieved His Own Eyes

The minister told the following tale: A carpenter, they say, had a wife whom he loved. Another man fell in love with her, and some of the carpenter's kin found out and told him. The carpenter, wanting to know for sure, said to his wife, "I'm going to a village a few miles away to do some work for a prince. I'll be there for a few days, so pack me some food." The wife did so and the carpenter left, saying, "Stay in the house and keep your door locked until I return." 7.30

٣١٫٧ فلمّا فصل من عندها أرسلت إلى خليلها بأنّ النجّار قد غاب لحاجة له وهو ماكث عنّا أيّاماً. فأتاها وقد خالف النجّار فدخل البيت من مدخل خفيّ حتّى اندسّ تحت السرير الذي عليه فراشه وفراش امرأته. فلمّا جاء خليلها أكلت معه وشربت ثمّ اضطجعا على السرير فكانا كذلك ليلتهما فلمّا كان آخر الليل غلب النجّار النوم وخرجت رجله من تحت السرير فأبصرت المرأة رجله فعرفته وأيقنت بالسوء فسألت خليلها أن ارفع صوتك واسألني هل أنا أحبّ إليك أم زوجك. فسألها خليلها كما أمرته فردّت عليه يا خليلي ما اضطرّك إلى هذه المسألة ألست[1] تعلم أنّا معشر النساء إنّما نخالل الرجال لقضاء الشهوة ولا نلتفت في ذلك إلى أحسابهم ولا إلى أخلاقهم فإذا قضينا شهوتنا صاروا عندنا كغيرهم من الرجال الأبعدين وأمّا الزوج فإنّما هو كالأب والأمّ فلحا الله امرأة لا يكون زوجها عندها كعدل نفسها لأنّ سعيه وكدّه لها وإنّي لا أسمعك تذكره مرّة أخرى.

٣٢٫٧ فلمّا سمع النجّار مقالة امرأته رقّ لها وأخذه لها رحمة وعبرة ووثق منها بالمودّة ولم يبرح مكانه حتّى أصبح وأيقن أنّ الرجل قد ذهب ثمّ خرج فوجد امرأته متناومة فظنّها نائمة فقعد عندها يذبّ على وجهها ثمّ إنّ المرأة التوت كأنّها انتبهت فقال بأبي أنت وأمّي يا حبيبتي كأنّك بتّ ساهرة ولم تزالي منذ الليلة في تعب مع ذلك الخبيث ولولا أنّي كرهت مساءتك لشاتمته ولكنّي أمسكت عن ذلك لما أعرف من إلفك إيّاه.

٣٣٫٧ وإنّما ضربت لكم هذا المثل لئلاّ تكونوا كذلك النجّار المائق الذي كذّب بعلمه وما أبصرت عيناه وصدّق بما سمع من الغدر ومن كذب امرأته فلا[2] تصدّق الغراب بمقالته واعلموا أنّ العدوّ إذا لم يستطع ضرّ عدوّه بالمباعدة التمس ضرّه بالمقاربة والمناصحة إذا كان ذا أدب. ولم أخف الغربان قطّ خوفي إيّاهم حتّى رأيت هذا الغراب وسمعت مقالته.[3]

---

١ كذا ش، ع، پ٣٤٦٦؛ الأصل: لست. ٢ كذا ش، ع، پ٣٤٦٦، پ٣٤٧٥؛ الأصل: ولا. ٣ مقالته: الأصل: مقالته والقول محدوا برابى فاكم ان ركتم رأى واصعتموه وسدتم منه باالحرم وما كت دكركم به.

As soon as he was gone, she sent her lover a message: "The carpenter has left on business and will be away for a few days." The carpenter, however, came back surreptitiously, entered the house through a hidden entrance, and concealed himself under the bed on which he and his wife slept. When the lover arrived, the wife wined and dined him; then they got into bed and spent the night together. Toward the end of the night, the carpenter, overcome by sleep, stretched out his leg from under the bed. The wife saw it, and, recognizing him, knew it would mean trouble for her. So she said to her lover, "Raise your voice, and ask me, 'Whom do you love more: me or your husband?'" The man did so, and she answered, "Lover, why must you ask? Don't you know that we women take lovers only to satisfy our lust? We pay no attention to their achievements or character or anything else about them. As soon as we satisfy our lust, they become just like any other man out there. But a husband!—he is like one's own mother and father. God confound any woman who doesn't value the husband who toils and labors for her as much as her own soul! Never mention him again!" 7.31

The carpenter, moved by his wife's words, was overcome with compassion and tears. He was certain that his wife loved him. He stayed put until morning and when he was sure that his wife's lover had left, he came out from under the bed. His wife pretended to be asleep. Thinking she was sleeping, he sat beside her, fanning her face. When she stirred as if to wake, he said, "My precious, dear to me as my mother and father! You were up all night, tired out by that tedious man. I didn't want to upset you, otherwise I'd have reviled him. I desisted because of what I know about your affection for him." 7.32

"I've told you this story because I don't want you to be like the foolish carpenter who didn't believe what he saw with his own eyes but believed his wife's deceitful and lying words. Don't believe what the crow says. Remember that an enemy who can inflict no harm from a distance, often, if he is a smooth talker, tries to do it by drawing near and giving advice. I've never feared the crows as much as I do now, having seen this crow and heard his words." 7.33

فلم يلتفت ملك البوم إليه ولا إلى مقالته وما أشار به وأمر الغراب إلى منزله بأن يُكرَم واستوصى به خيراً.

٣٤،٧ فقال الوزير الذي كان أشار بقتله إن لم تقتلوا هذا الغراب فلتكن منزلته عندكم منزلة العدوّ المخوف واحترسوا منه فإنّه ذو إرب ومكر ولا أراه جاء إلى هاهنا إلّا لما يصلحه ويفسدنا.

فلم يرفع الملك لقوله رأساً ولم يمنعه ذلك من إكرام الغراب والإحسان إليه وجعل الغراب إذا دخل على الملك يكلّمه كلاماً رفيقاً فازداد له رقّة وبه لطفاً وإليه استئناساً واسترسالاً وله تصديقاً وانتصاحاً.[١]

٣٥،٧ ثمّ إنّه قال يوماً عند جماعة البوم وفيهنّ البومة التي كانت تشير بقتله ليبلّغ بعضكنّ عنّي الملك أنّ الغربان وترني بترة عظيمة بما عذّبني وتركني وركبن منّي عظيماً ولن يستريح قلبي أو أدرك فيهنّ نيلي وإنّي نظرت في ذلك فلم أجدني أستطيع ذلك وأنا غراب وقد بلغني عن بعض أهل العلم أنّ من طابت نفسه عن نفسها فأحرقها بالنار فقد قرّب إلى الله أعظم القربان وأنّه لا يدعو بعد ذلك بدعوة إلّا استجيب له فإن رأى الملك أن يأذن لي فأحرق نفسي وأدعو ربّي باستجابة ذلك بإهلاك الغربان لما يكون فيه شفاء لصدري ودرك لنيلي ولأن يحوّلني في صورة بومة لأصول على الغربان معكنّ.

٣٦،٧ قالت البومة التي كانت تشير بقتله ما أشبّهك في حسن ما تبدي وسوء ما تواري إلّا بالخمرة الطيّبة الريح الحسنة اللون المنتقع فيها السمّ. أرأيت لو أحرقناك بالنار لكان جوهرك الخبيث وطباعك السوء يحترقان معك. ما هما إلّا دائران معك حيث درت وزائلان حيث زلت وما كنت أرى لك دعوة عند ذلك لو عرفت أنّها مستجابة إلّا بهلاك البوم ولما كنت في ثبوتك على جوهرك وطباعك السوء إلّا كالفأرة التي عُرض لها من الأزواج الأفضل فالأفضل من الشمس والسحاب والريح والجبل فتركت ذلك وكرهته واختارت جرذاً فنكحته.

١ الأصل: وانصاحا.

But the king of the owls disregarded his advice and commanded that the crow be taken to his home, honored, and treated well.

The minister who had advised execution said, "If you don't kill this crow, at least treat him as an enemy to be feared and guarded against. He's cunning and deceitful. I think he's come here with a plan to do harm to us and to benefit himself." 7.34

But the king paid no heed, and the minister failed to stop him from treating the crow with honor and favor. The crow spoke courteously to the king when in his presence, and the king became more and more gracious, friendly, at ease, and credulously reliant on his advice.

One day, in the midst of the owls' assembly—with the owl who had advised execution present—the crow said, "One of you should tell the king on my behalf that the crows did me a great wrong by tormenting me and abandoning me. Tell him that my heart will never rest until I work my will on them. Tell him I've given much thought to the matter, and I see that it will not be possible as long as I remain a crow. I've heard on the authority of a learned man that anyone who willingly renounces his life and immolates himself in fire will have made such a magnificent sacrifice to God that any prayer he subsequently makes will be granted. Therefore, if the king permits, I will immolate myself and pray to the Lord to destroy the crows, thereby quenching my thirst for vengeance and achieving my objective, and I will pray to be turned into an owl, so I can join in your attack on the crows." 7.35

The owl who had advised execution said, "Like sweet-smelling, fine-colored wine in which poison has been dissolved, you appear to be good, but conceal evil. Do you think your vile nature and evil character will be consumed if we burn you in fire? No, they will accompany you wherever you go. If you know that your prayers will be answered, you will, I think, pray only for the destruction of the owls. You will remain true to your evil nature and character, like the lady mouse who was offered better and better husbands—the sun, the cloud, the wind, and the mountain—but scorned them all and chose to marry a rat." 7.36

قيل له وكيف كان ذلك.

٣٧،٧ قالت البومة زعموا أنّ ناسكًا عابدًا كان من أفضل أهل زمانه مستجاب الدعوة فبينما[١] هو قاعد على شاطئ نهر إذ مرّت به حدأة في رجلها فأرة فسقطت من رجلها قريبًا من الناسك فرحمها الناسك فأخذها ولفّها في ردائه وأراد أن يذهب بها إلى منزله ثمّ خاف أن يشقّ عليه وعلى أهله تربيتها فدعا الله أن يحوّلها جارية ليهون عليهم تربيتها فاستجيب له وتحوّلت جارية حسناء فانطلق بها الناسك إلى امرأته وقال لها اصنعي بهذه صنيعك بولدي. ففعلت المرأة.

٣٨،٧ وكانت عندهم على ذلك حتّى بلغت فلمّا أدركت خيّرها الأزواج وقال لها قد بلغت التزويج. وقال لها إنّ الأسعد من الرجال من لم تحيض امرأة ببيته وأنا أبتغي أن أفعل بك فعل الآباء بأولادهم فانظري ما تريدين من الأزواج فأعلميني به فإنّي فاعل الذي تأمرينني به.

قالت الجارية أريد زوجًا قويًّا شديدًا منيعًا.

قال الناسك ما أظنّ شيئًا أقوى من الشمس. فقال للشمس إنّ هذه الجارية جميلة وهي عندي بمنزلة الولد وقد زوّجتك بها فإنّها طلبت زوجًا قويًّا شديدًا منيعًا.

فقالت الشمس أنا شديدة ولكنّ السحاب أشدّ منّي فإنّه يغطّي شعاعي.

٣٩،٧ فقال الناسك للسحاب إنّ هذه الجارية تريد منّي البعولة التي ليس شيء أشدّ منه فتزوّجها. فقال السحاب أنا شديد ولكنّ الريح أشدّ منّي فإنّها تقبل بي وتدبر.

فقال الناسك للريح مثل ما قال للسحاب فقالت الريح أنا شديدة ولكنّ الجبل أشدّ منّي فإنّي لا أستطيع تحريكه.

فقال الناسك للجبل مثل ما قال للريح فقال الجبل أنا شديد ولكنّ الجرذ أشدّ منّي فإنّه ينقب فيّ الأنقاب ويدخل من حيث شاء ولا أستطيع له شيئًا.

٤٠،٧ فقال الناسك للجرذ إنّ هذه الجارية تريد منّي البعولة ما هو أشدّ خلق الله.

---

١ كذا ش؛ الأصل: سما.

"How did that come about?" they asked.

The owl told the following tale: Once, they say, there was a pious ascetic, one of the most distinguished of his time, whose prayers were always answered. While he was sitting by a riverbank, a kite flew by with a mouse in its foot, and it fell from the bird's claws and landed near him. Out of compassion, he picked it up and wrapped it in his cloak. He wanted to take it home, but concerned that raising it would be a burden on his family, he prayed to God to turn it into a young woman easy for them to raise. His prayer was answered, and the mouse turned into a beautiful maiden. He took her home and said to his wife, "Treat her as you would our own child," which she did. 7.37

The Lady Mouse and Her Choice of Husbands

The maiden lived with them until she came of age, at which time the ascetic gave her a choice of husbands. "You're of a marriageable age now," he said, and added, "The man in whose house a woman has not menstruated is most fortunate.[47] I wish to treat you as a father would his own child. Think about what you want in a husband; tell me, and I will do as you command." 7.38

"I want a husband who is strong, powerful, and invincible."

"I do not think," he said, "that there is anything stronger than the sun." And to the sun he said, "This beautiful maiden has been like a child to me. She has asked for a husband who is strong, powerful, and invincible—I give her to you in marriage."

And the sun replied, "I am powerful, but the cloud is more powerful, for he can block my rays."

So the ascetic said to the cloud, "This maiden has asked for a husband more powerful than anything else." And the cloud replied, "I am powerful, but the wind, which drives me this way and that, is more powerful." 7.39

The ascetic put the same proposal to the wind. And the wind replied, "I am powerful, but the mountain is more powerful, because I cannot move it."

The ascetic repeated his words to the mountain and the mountain replied, "I am powerful, but the rat is more powerful, because he bores into me and enters where he will, and I can do nothing to stop him."

So the ascetic said to the rat, "This maiden has asked for a husband who is the most powerful of God's creatures." 7.40

فقال الجرذ كيف أتزوّجها وجحري ضيّق وأنا صغير الجسم وهي عظيمة[1] فلا تستطيع الدخول معي في جحري.

فدعا الناسك ربّه عن طلب الجارية وأمرها حتّى جعلها فأرة فتزوّجها الجرذ.

فهذا مثلك أيّها الخادع.

٤١،٧ فلم يلتفت الملك وأصحابه إلى قوله وأمر بإكرام الغراب وإتحافه وإنعامه له والطافه ففُعل ذلك ولم يزدد عليهنّ إلّا كرامة حتّى استأنس بهنّ واستأنسن به ونبت جناحه وذنبه وريشه وسمن واشتدّ وصلح وعلم كلّ ما أراد أن يعلم من عورة البوم واطّلع على عدّتهنّ وسرّهنّ واستفطن جميع أمورهنّ واطّلع على ما أحبّ أن يطّلع عليه من أمرهنّ ثمّ إنّه راغ روغة فتحلّق حتّى لحق بالغربان فلمّا انتهى إليهنّ سلّم على الملك فرحّب به وقال ما وراءك.

قال الذي يسرّك أبشر بظفرك وهلاك البوم.

قال وكيف ذلك.

قال قد فرغت ممّا حاولت وإنّما بقي ما قبلك.

قال ملك الغربان نحن مستعدّون نتطلّع أمرك.

٤٢،٧ فقال الغراب إنّ جماعة البوم بمكان كذا وكذا وهنّ يجتمعن بالنهار في نقب جبل هنالك وقد علمت قريباً من ذلك الجبل مكاناً فيه حطب كثير يابس فليحمل كلّ غراب ما استطاع من ذلك الحطب إلى باب النقب الذي يجتمع فيه البوم بالنهار وقريب من ذلك الجبل قطيع غنم وأنا مصيب عند الراعي ناراً آتيكم بها فأطرحها على ذلك الحطب ثمّ تعاونّ ولا تفترن ضرباً بأجنحتكنّ ترويحاً ونفخاً للنار حتّى يضطرم الحطب فإذا صنعتم ذلك فما خرج من البوم احترق وما بقي في النقب قتله الدخان.

ففعلن ذلك كما أمرهنّ فأهلكن البوم[2] جميعاً ورجع ملك الغربان ومن معه قد سلمن وظفرن بحاجتهنّ من البوم.

---

١ الأصل: عظيم. ٢ فأهلكن البوم: كذا ش، د؛ الأصل: فهلكن البوم.

"How can I marry her," replied the rat, "when my burrow is so narrow? I am small and she is large and won't fit in there with me."

So at the maiden's request, the ascetic prayed to the Lord, who turned her back into a mouse, and she was married to the rat.

"Your case, deceiver, is just like hers."

Neither the king nor his companions heeded his words. The king ordered 7.41
that the crow be honored, shown favor, given gifts, and treated courteously, which was done. As he grew in esteem, they all came to be on friendly terms. His wing feathers, tail, and plumage grew back and he became plump, strong, and healthy. He learned everything about the owls' vulnerabilities. He kept himself informed about their numbers and secrets and collected information about their affairs. Having learned all he wanted, he sneaked off and flew back to the crows. When he arrived, he greeted the king, who welcomed him and asked for a report.

"Good news! Rejoice in your victory and the owls' destruction."

"How so?"

"I've accomplished everything I wanted; the rest is up to you."

"We're ready and await your orders," replied the king.

"The owls," said the crow, "live in this location"—he named it. "By day 7.42
they gather in a cave in a mountain there. I know of a place near the mountain where there is an abundance of dry wood. Each crow should carry as much wood as he can to the mouth of the cave where the owls roost during the day. There's also a flock of sheep near the mountain; I'll get fire from the shepherd, bring it to you, and drop it on the wood. Work together, flap your wings vigorously, and fan the fire until the wood blazes up. The owls who come out of the cave will be consumed by the fire and those who stay in the cave will be killed by the smoke."

And that is what they did. All the owls perished. The king and those with him returned safe and victorious.

ثمّ إنّ ملك الغربان قال لذلك الغراب الذي عمل في هلاك البوم ما عمل كيف صبرت على صحبة البوم طول ما صبرت ولا صبر للأخيار على صحبة الأشرار وقد يقال إنّ الصالحين يرون أنّ دخول النار أهون من المكث مع الأشرار. ٤٣.٧

قال الغراب أيّها الملك إنّ ذلك لكذلك ولكنّ الرجل العاقل إذا أتاه الأمر الفظيع الذي يخاف منه الجائحة على نفسه وقومه لم يجزع من شدّة تصبّر نفسه عليها إذا كان يرجو أن يعقبه صبره روحاً وعافية ولم يجد لذلك شيئاً ولم يكرم نفسه عن الخضوع لمن هو دونه على أن يبلغ حاجته فيغتبط بغبّ أمره واصطباره.

قال الملك للغراب أخبرني عن عقول البوم. ٤٤.٧

قال لم أجد فيهنّ عاقلاً ولم تكن لهنّ أخلاق إلّا للبومة التي كانت تحثّهنّ على قتلي فكنّ أضعف رأياً أن يصدّقن قوله[١] ويعرفن فضل رأيه وينظرن في أمري ويذكرن أنّي قد كنت ذا منزلة في الغربان وأنّي أُعَدّ من ذوي الرأي فيتخوّفن مكري وحيلتي. فأخبرهنّ الحازم الناصح المطّلع على ما في نفسي برأيه وأشار عليهنّ بالنصح لهنّ فرددن رأيه ونصيحته فلا كفاهنّ عقلهنّ ولا من ذوي العقل قبلن ولا أسرارهنّ حصّنّها دوني ولا حذرنني وكان يقال ينبغي للملك أن يحصّن من ذوي التهم أسراره وأموره فلا يدنو من مواضع أسراره وأموره[٢] وكتبه ولا من الماء والحوض الذي يُعَدّ لغسله ولا من[٣] فرشه ودثاره ولا من كسوته ولا من مراكبه ولا من سلاحه ولا من طعامه ولا من شرابه ولا من دهنه وطيبه ولا من رياحينه إلّا من لا يتّهمه.[٤]

قال ملك الغربان إنّما هلك ملك[٥] البوم وأصحابه بالبغي وضعف رأي الوزراء. ٤٥.٧

قال الغراب صدقت أيّها الملك إنّه قلّ ما ظفر أحد يبغي. ومن ذا الذي بلغ جسيماً[٦] من الأمر فلم يبطر ومن ذا الذي أكثر من الطعام فلم يسقم ومن ذا الذي حرص فلم يفتضح ومن ذا الذي وثق بمشاورة وزراء السوء والأشرار فلم يقع في المهالك وكان يقال لا يطمعنّ ذو الكبر في الثناء الحسن ولا الخبّ في كثرة الصديق ولا السيّء

---

١ كذا الأصل. ٢ فلا يدنو . . . وأموره: كذا ش؛ ساقطة من الأصل. ٣ كذا ش؛ ساقطة من الأصل. ٤ يتّهمه: الأصل: يتّهمه لكن لا يتهم احدا في النطر في مواضع اسراره. ٥ كذا ل٢؛ ساقطة من الأصل. ٦ الأصل: حسيم.

Afterward, the king asked the crow who had brought about the owls' 7.43
destruction, "How could you tolerate the company of owls so long, when the good cannot bear to keep company with evildoers? The good, so they say, would rather plunge into fire than live with evildoers."

"True, Your Majesty," replied the crow, "but a wise man doesn't fall to pieces when confronted with a disaster that threatens to destroy him and his people. He forces himself to be patient, in the hope that patience will bring relief and safety in its wake. He doesn't grieve at all or think himself above submitting to inferiors, provided that he can attain his objective and rejoice over the fruits of his action and patience."

"Tell me about the owls' intelligence." 7.44

"I encountered no owl of any intelligence or worth except the one who pressed for my execution," replied the crow. "Their judgment was too weak to believe him and recognize the merit of his opinion—to recall that I had been a crow of some standing and respected for my judgment, and that they ought to fear deception or trickery at my hands. He cautioned them about what I might have in mind. He gave them good advice, but they rejected it; their own intelligence wasn't adequate, and they wouldn't accept the advice of those whose intelligence was. They didn't fear me or keep secrets from me. A king, so it has been said, should keep his secrets and affairs from all who are suspect; only persons above suspicion should be allowed near where he keeps his secrets, plans, and letters; near the basin where he bathes, near his bed, blankets, and clothing; near his mounts and weapons, his food and drink, or his oils, perfumes, and herbs."

The king said, "It was pride and his ministers' bad judgment that killed 7.45
the owl king."

"You're right," said the crow. "Rarely do the proud win a victory. Has eminence ever been attained without insolence ensuing? Can we eat to excess without falling ill? Can we covet without suffering disgrace? Can we trust the counsel of rogues and evil ministers without falling into peril? It has been

الأدب[١] في الشرف ولا[٢] الشحيح في البرّ ولا الحريص في قلّة الذنوب ولا الملك المختال المتهاون بالأمر الصعب وقلّة مشاورة الوزراء في ثبات ملكه وصلاح رعيّته.

قال ملك الغربان لقد احتملت مشقّة شديدة في خضوعك للبوم وتضرّعك ٤٦،٧
إليهنّ.

قال الغراب قلت حقّاً لقد شقّ عليّ ولكن تصبّرت عليه للذي رأيت فيه من الفرج فإنّه قد قيل إنّ الرجل العاقل لو حمل عدوّه على عنقه لم يشقّ عليه للذي يعلم أنّه يصيبه بعد ذلك من الفرج ومن احتمل مشقّة يرجو فيها منفعة صبر على ذلك كما صبر الأسود على حمل الضفدع على ظهره.

قال الملك وكيف كان ذلك.

قال الغراب زعموا أنّ أسود كبر وهزل وضعف وذهبت قوّته فلم يستطع صيداً ٤٧،٧
ولم يقدر على طعام فقال في نفسه إنّي لا أستطيع الطوفان لابتغاء المعيشة إلّا بالحيلة والرفق. فبينما هو ذات يوم يلتمس شيئاً يعيّشه إذ انتهى إلى عين كثيرة الضفادع قد كان يأتيه ويصيد من ضفادعها فرمى بنفسه قريباً من العين مظهراً الكآبة والحزن.

فقال له بعض الضفادع يا أسود ما لي أراك حزيناً.

قال ومن أحقّ بطول الحزن منّي وأنا أكثر معيشتي ممّا كنت أصيب من الضفادع فابتُليت ببلاء حُرمت الضفادع حتّى لو التقمت بعضها لم أقدر على إساغته.

فانطلق الضفدع إلى ملك الضفادع وبشّره بما سمع من الأسود. قال ملك ٤٨،٧
الضفادع للأسود كيف كان ذلك.

قال سعيت في إثر ضفدع[٣] منذ أيّام لآخذه فاضطررته إلى بيت فدخل ودخلت على إثره فإذا هو بيت مظلم من بيوت النسّاك وفي البيت ابن للناسك فأصبت إصبعه وظننت أنّه الضفدع فلدغته فمات فخرجت هارباً وسعى الناسك في طلبي ودعا عليّ ولعنني وقال إن كان الأسود قتل ابني ظلماً متعدّياً فأنزل به الذلّ والهوان

---

١ السيّء الأدب: كذا ش، ع، پ٣٤٦٦، ي (١٤٧)؛ الأصل: شى مثل الادب. ٢ كذا ش، ع، ي (١٤٧)؛ ساقطة من الأصل. ٣ إثر ضفدع: كذا ر؛ الأصل: امر الصفدع.

said: A proud man should not expect honest praise; a deceiver should not expect many friends; a churl should not expect honor; a miser should not expect charity; a covetous man should not expect to have few sins; and a haughty, negligent king who rarely consults his ministers should not expect his reign to last or his people to prosper."

"It must have been distressing," said the king, "to humble yourself before 7.46
the owls."

"Yes, it was," said the crow, "but I bore it patiently because I expected a good outcome. As has been said: When certain of a good outcome, a wise man must not be too proud to carry his enemy on his shoulder. Those who hope for benefit bear hardship patiently—just as the cobra patiently carried the frog on his back."

"How did that come about?" asked the king.

The Cobra Who Stooped to Carry the King of the Frogs

And the crow told the following tale: A cobra, they say, grew so old and 7.47
feeble that he could no longer hunt and feed himself. So he said to himself, "Only by employing cunning and skill will I be able to find sustenance." One day, as he was out looking for some food, he happened upon a pool filled with many frogs, which he once used to catch. He lay down there, looking sad and dejected.

"Snake, why are you so sad?" asked one of the frogs.

"Who is more entitled to be sad than I?" he replied. "I used to live almost entirely on the frogs I caught, but now I'm in trouble. Frogs are off limits for me—I couldn't swallow one even if I had it in my mouth."

The frog went to his king and told him this good news. The king asked the 7.48
cobra how this had come about.

The cobra said, "A few nights ago I was chasing after a frog. I drove him to a house. In he went, and in I went after him. The house, which was dark, belonged to a holy man whose son was in the house. I felt the boy's toe and, taking it for the frog, I bit it, and the boy died. I fled, with the holy man in pursuit, cursing me: 'If this snake has slain my son unjustly and wrongfully,

واجعله مركبًا لملك الضفادع لا يستطيع أخذ شيء منها إلّا ما تصدّق به عليه ملك الضفادع. فأقبلت إليك لتركبني بذلك راضياً.

فرغب ملك الضفادع في ركوب الأسود ورأى ذلك شرفًا وفخرًا ومكرمة فركبه أيّاماً ثمّ قال له الأسود قد علمت أيّها الملك أنّي ملعون محروم فاجعل لي رزقًا أعيش به.

قال الملك لعمري ما لك بدّ وأنت مركبي من رزق يقيمك. فأمر له بضفدعتين كلّ يوم تؤخذان له وتُدفعان إليه فعاش بذلك ما عاش ونفعه خضوعه للعدوّ الذليل.

فكذلك كان صبري على ما صبرت عليه التماس ما نلت من النفع العظيم الذي اجتمع لنا فيه بوار[1] العدوّ والأمن منه.

٤٩،٧ قال الملك إنّي وجدت صرعة اللين والرفق أسرع وأشدّ استئصالاً للعدوّ من صرعة المكابرة فإنّ النار لا تزيد بحرّها إذا أصابت الشجرة على أن تحرق ما فوق الأرض منها إلّا بقوّة شديدة والماء بلينه وبرده يستأصل ما تحت الأرض منها وكان يقال أربعة أشياء لا يُستقلّ منها القليل النار والمرض والعدوّ والدَّيْن.

٥٠،٧ قال الغراب كلّ ما كان منّي في ذلك فمن رأي الملك وأدبه وسعادة جدّه فإنّه كان يقال إذا طلب اثنان أمرًا ظفر به أفضلهما مروءة فإن اعتدلا في المروءة فأشدّهما عزماً فإن استويا في العزم فأفضلهما أعواناً فإن استويا في ذلك فأسعدهما جدّاً. وكان يقال من غالب الملك الحازم الأريب المصنوع له الذي لا تبطره السرّاء ولا تدهشه الضرّاء فإنّ حَيْنه يحدوه إلى نفسه[2] ثمّ لا سيّما إذا كان مثلك أيّها الملك العالم بالأمور العارف بمواضع الشدّة واللين والغضب والرضى والمعاجلة[3] والأناة الناظر في يومه وغده وعواقب أعماله وكلّ ذلك صائر إلى موضع القضاء.

٥١،٧ قال ملك الغربان للغراب بل برأيك وعقلك ونصيحتك ويُمن نفسك كان ذلك فإنّ رأي الرجل الحازم أبلغ في هلاك العدوّ الكبير الشديد البأس من الجنود

---

١ كذا ل٢؛ الأصل: تباور. ٢ فإنّ. . . نفسه: پ٣٤٦٦: فهو حادي الحين إلى نفسه؛ الأصل: فان حنده يحمدونه.
٣ الأصل: المعالحه.

send down shame and humiliation upon him and make him a mount for the king of the frogs, able to catch only those the king gives him as charity.' As a result, I've come to you willingly so that you can ride me."

The king of the frogs was eager to ride the cobra—he considered it an honor that would bring him glory and prestige. After he had ridden the cobra for a few days, the cobra said to him, "Your Majesty knows that I've been cursed and placed under a ban; please give me some food to live on."

The king of the frogs said, "I swear that as long as you are my mount, you must have something to live on!" He ordered that every day two frogs be seized and given to the cobra. Thus the cobra lived out his life, and benefited by demeaning himself before a contemptible enemy.

"Similarly, I too patiently endured what I had to in order to obtain a great benefit for us: our safety and the enemy's destruction."

The king said, "I see now that a downfall effected through gentleness and 7.49
skill eradicates the enemy more thoroughly than one effected through open conflict. For all its heat and fury, when fire attacks a tree, it burns only the part above the ground; but water, for all its gentleness and coolness, uproots the part under the ground. They say that four things should not be taken lightly even in small doses: fire, disease, enemies, and debt."

The crow said, "Everything I did was a result of Your Majesty's judgment, 7.50
discipline, and good fortune. If two men seek a thing, they say, the more valiant of the two will win it; if they are equal in valor, the more determined; if they are equal in determination, the one with better helpers; and if they are equal in that respect, the one who is more fortunate. They also say that to try to get the better of a resolute, intelligent, fortunate king—one whom prosperity doesn't make overconfident and adversity doesn't dismay—is to invite your own death. All the more so when the king is like Your Majesty: knowledgeable about affairs, knowing the right time for severity or softness, anger or contentment, haste or deliberateness; a ruler who ponders today, tomorrow, and the consequences of his deeds—all of which leads to proper judgment."

The king of the crows said, "Not so! It was due to your judgment, intelli- 7.51
gence, and advice, and at the risk of your life. One resolute man's good judgment can destroy a powerful enemy more effectively than many soldiers. But

الكثيرة. ومن أعجب الأمور إليّ طول لبثك بين أظهر البوم تسمع الغيظ ولم تسقط بينهم بكلمة.

قال الغراب لم أزل متمسّكًا بأدبك أيّها الملك أصحب القريب والبعيد بالرفق واللين والمتابعة والمؤاتاة.

٥٢.٧ قال الملك وجدتك صاحب العمل ووجدت غيرك من الوزراء أصحاب الأقاويل ليست لها عاقبة وكذلك أصحاب الكلام وقد منّ الله بك علينا منّة عظيمة لم نكن قبلها نجد لذّة الطعام والنوم فإنّه كان يقال لا يجد السقيم لذّة الطعام والنوم حتّى يبرأ ولا الرجل الشديد الحرص[١] الذي قد أطمعه السلطان في عمل أو مال حتّى ينجز ذلك ولا الرجل الذي قد ألحّ عليه عدوّه فهو يخافه صباحه ومساءه حتّى يستريح منه وكان يقال من أقلع همّه عنه أراح قلبه ومن وضع الحمل الثقيل أراح متنه[٢] ومن أمن من عدوّه ثلج قلبه.

قال الغراب أسأل الله الذي أهلك عدوّك أن يمتّعك بسلطانك ويجعل ذلك في صلاح رعيّتك ويشركهم في قرّة العين بملكك.

قال الملك إذا لم يكن في مملكته قرّة عيون رعيّته فمثله مثل زنمة[٣] العنز التي يمصّها الجدي فلا يصادف فيها خيرًا.

٥٣.٧ قال الملك أخبرني أيّها الوزير الصالح كيف كان سيرة ملك البوم في جنوده.

قال الغراب كان سيرته سيرة بطر وأشر وفخر وخيلاء وعجز وضعف رأي وكلّ أصحابه ووزرائه شبهاء به إلّا البومة التي أشارت عليهم بقتلي.

قال الملك وما الذي رأيت منه ممّا[٤] كان دلّك على عقله.

قال الغراب خلّتان منهما رأيه كان في معاجلة قتلي والأخرى أنّه لم يكتم صاحبه نصيحته وإن استقلّها[٥] وكلامه كلام لا عنف فيه ولا خرق ولكن كلام رفق ولين حتّى ربّما لو أخبره بعيبه فلم يغضبه إنّما يضرب الأمثال ويحدّث عن عيب غيره

---

١ الشديد الحرص: الأصل: الشديد الحريص. ٢ كذا ش، پ٣٤٦٦، ي (١٢٥)؛ الأصل: منه نفسه. ٣ كذا ش، پ٣٤٦٦، ي (١٤٨)؛ الأصل: نذره. ٤ كذا ع؛ الأصل: ما. ٥ ع: استثقلها.

what amazes me most is how you were able to stay among the owls so long, listening to their furor, without uttering a word."

"I always followed Your Majesty's own practice of associating with everyone, high or low, with courtesy, gentleness, acquiescence, and complaisance," responded the crow.

"I see now that you are a master of action," said the king. "My other min- 7.52
isters are masters of fruitless words, for that is how the masters of talk are. We derived no pleasure from eating or sleeping before God gave you to us as a great blessing. A sick man, they say, finds no pleasure in sleep or food until he recovers his health; a greedy man promised office or wealth by his ruler finds no pleasure until the promise is fulfilled; and a man beset by an enemy whom he fears night and day finds no pleasure until he is rid of him. They say that the heart finds rest when worry departs; the back finds rest when a heavy load is removed; and the heart fills with joy when one becomes safe from one's enemy."

"I ask God, who has destroyed your enemy, to grant you enjoyment of your sovereignty," said the crow. "May He cause it to be for the benefit of your subjects and give them a share in the happiness of your reign."

And the king said, "If a king's subjects derive no joy from his reign, he is like a nanny goat's wattle, which the kid sucks, thinking it a teat, but gets no good out of it."

The king then asked, "Tell me, good minister, how did the king of the 7.53
owls behave toward his soldiers?"

"With arrogance, insolence, boastfulness, conceit, incompetence, and poor judgment. All his companions and ministers were like him, except the one who advised them to kill me."

"What indications of intelligence did you see in him?" the king asked.

"Two things: first, his opinion that I should be executed on the spot; second, that he didn't keep his advice hidden even if it was made light of by his master. Furthermore, he spoke politely and gently, without harshness or roughness, so that he often apprised the king of a shortcoming without angering him. He would cite parables and speak of others' shortcomings,

فيعرف منه الملك عيب نفسه ولا يجد إلى الغضب عليه سبيلاً وكان فيما سمعته يقول للملك لا ينبغي للملك أن يغفل عن أمر ملكه فإنّه أمر جسيم لا يظفر به إلّا القليل من الناس ولا يستقيم إلّا بالحـزم.

تمّت حكاية الغربان والبوم

so that the king might recognize his own through theirs, yet find no way to become angry with him. This is one of the things I heard him say to the king: 'A king must not become negligent about his authority, for it is a momentous matter that few obtain and that prospers only through sound judgment.'"

Here ends the Story of the Crows and the Owls.

باب السلحفاة والقرد

وهو مثل من[1] يعمل في اكتساب الشيء
فإذا اكتسبه لم يحسن اعتقاده

١،٨ قال الملك للفيلسوف قد سمعت حديثك عن أهل العداوة وكيف لا ينبغي أن يُغترّ بهم[2] ولا يُسكن إليهم وإن هم تضرّعوا وتودّدوا فاضرب لي مثل من يعمل في اكتساب الشيء فإذا اكتسبه لم يحسن اعتقاده وحفظه فذهب عنه ضياعاً ولا يبقى في يده إلّا الحسرة والندامة.

٢،٨ قال الفيلسوف زعموا أنّه كان في بعض سواحل البحر أرض فيها قردة عليها ملك منها وأنّ ملكها ذلك كبر وضعف وطمع في ملكه قرد من ذوي قرابته قد انطبع لأهل مملكته حتّى استمال أهواءهم فملّكوه وطردوا ذلك القرد عنهم فلحق بمكان من ساحل البحر فيه غيضة عظيمة ذات أخلاط من الشجر فتعلّق بشجرة من التين مشرفة على البحر فكان يأكل من تينها وكان ألف ظلّ تلك الشجرة سلحفاة يستظلّ بظلّها ويصيب ما يسقط من التين في الماء فبينا القرد يوماً يجتني التين إذ سقط منه تينة في الماء فأعجبه صوت وقعها في الماء فجعل يطرح من ذلك التين في الماء متلذّذاً بما يسمع من وقعه في الماء فجعل السلحفاة يأكل ولا يشكّ أنّ القرد إنّما يطرح التين من أجله فرغب في مؤاخاة القرد وكلّمه بكلام لطيف وأعلمه رغبته في مؤاخاته فأجابه القرد بمثل ذلك وسكن كلّ واحد منهما إلى صاحبه وسُرّ به واغتبط السلحفاة بجوار القرد ومؤاخاته واستغنى كلّ واحد منهما بصاحبه ومكانه عمّا وراءه من أهله وأصحابه.

١ من: ساقطة من الأصل. ٢ الأصل: لهم.

The Turtle and the Monkey

A parable about someone who works hard to acquire a thing, but having acquired it, doesn't know how to hold on to it.

The king said to the philosopher, "Now that I've heard you speak about people who harbor hostility, and how we should not be taken in by them or trust them, even if they entreat us and court our affection, tell me a parable about someone who works hard to acquire a thing, but having acquired it, doesn't know how to hold on to it, so that he loses it and has nothing but grief and regret to show for his efforts." 8.1

And the philosopher told the following tale: They say that by the shore of the sea there was a land full of monkeys ruled by a monkey king. Eventually the king became old and weak, and his throne was coveted by a kinsman who so ingratiated himself with the monkeys and won their affections that they made him king and banished his predecessor. The old king fled to a place by the seashore where there was a large grove full of all sorts of trees. He became fond of a fig tree overlooking the sea and would eat its figs. There was a turtle who liked to rest in the tree's shade and eat any figs that fell into the water. One day, while the monkey was picking figs, one fell from his hand, and he was so pleased by the sound it made as it fell into the water that he began throwing figs into the water, delighting in the sound. Convinced that the monkey was throwing them down for his sake, the turtle began to eat them. Eager, therefore, to make friends with the monkey, he addressed him politely and told him of his desire for friendship. The monkey agreed, and each came to trust the other and enjoy his company. The turtle rejoiced to have the monkey as neighbor and friend, and each devoted himself exclusively to the other, to the neglect of family and friends. 8.2

٨،٣ فطالت غيبة السلحفاة عن امرأته ولم يكن عوّدها ذلك فاشتدّ حزنها فشكت ما داخلها من همّ زوجها إلى صديقة لها.

فقالت لها صديقتها لا يخزنك[1] الله ولا يسوءك ولا تهتمّي بأمر زوجك فإنّه قد بلغني أنّه بمكان كذا وكذا قد جاور قردًا هنالك وصادقه وسكن إليه ورضي به خلفًا منك ومن غيرك من أهله وأحبابه فلا تحزني عليه ولكن هلمّي فلننظر الحيلة لهلكة القرد الذي جلب عليك الحرارة فإنّه لو قد هلك رجع إليك زوجك وإلى ما كنت تعهدين من المعاشرة واللطف.

٨،٤ فكان ما استقام رأيهما عليه من الحيلة أن تمارضت امرأة السلحفاة فأرسلت إلى زوجها رسولاً يعلمه بحالها وتسأله أن يأتيها حتّى ينظر إليها قبل الموت.

فلمّا أتى الرسول إلى السلحفاة استأذن القرد في الإحداث بأهله عهدًا فأذن له فقدم عليها فلمّا رآها أقبل يسائلها متلطّفًا بها في جميع القول فجعلت لا تردّ جوابًا وعندها صديقتها فلمّا رآها لا تكلّمه قال لصديقتها ما بالها لا تنطق.

قالت صديقتها وكيف تنطق المريض الذي أيقن أنّه ليس لمرضه إلّا دواء واحد لا يُقدَر عليه في البلاد التي هو بها.

فلمّا سمع السلحفاة مقالتها دخله حزن وهمّ فقال وما ذلك الدواء أخبريني به أطلبه بجهدي فإنّ دواءها لو كان في إخراج نفسي جدت بها لذلك.

فقالت صديقتها إنّا معشر النساء أعلم بما يصلح للنساء في أمراضهنّ من الأطبّاء لا سيّما أوجاع باطنة لا يعلمها إلّا النساء ووجعها هذا من أوجاع الأرحام ودواؤه معروف غير أنّه ليس بموجود.

قال السلحفاة ما هو.

قالت قرد تأكل من قلبه.

قال السلحفاة ومن أين أقدر على ذلك وكيف لنا به.

قالت صديقتها قد أعلمتك أنّه لا يُوصَل إلى دوائها فالرأي في شأنها الصبر.

---

١ يخزنك: الأصل: يحزنك.

The turtle stayed away so long and it was so out of character that his wife became sad and complained to a friend of hers of her anxiety about her husband. 8.3

"May God not bring you shame or cause you sadness," replied the friend. "Don't be grieved, and don't worry about your husband. I've heard that he is living as the neighbor of a monkey. He likes his new friend so much that the friend has replaced you and his other kinfolk and friends in his affections. Don't be sad, but let's devise a way to destroy the monkey who has brought you so much heartache. If the monkey perishes, your husband will come home and resume his intimacy and kindness."

They devised the following plan. The turtle's wife pretended to be sick and sent a messenger to inform her husband about her condition, asking him to come see her before her death. 8.4

When the messenger arrived, the turtle asked the monkey for permission to pay his family a visit, and the monkey agreed. When the turtle saw his wife's condition, he questioned her, speaking as gently as he could, but she didn't answer. The wife's friend was standing beside her, and the turtle, seeing that his wife would say nothing, asked the friend, "What's wrong? Why can't she say a word?"

"How can a sick person speak," replied the friend, "when she knows for certain that there is only one medicine for her illness, a medicine that can't be obtained here?"

The turtle was overcome by sadness and grief at these words. "Tell me what the medicine is and I'll gladly do everything to find it, even if I have to give up my life."

"We women are more knowledgeable than doctors about women's diseases, especially the internal pains that only women experience," replied the friend. "This pain involves her womb. The remedy for it is known; it just isn't available."

"What is it?" he asked.

"A monkey. She must eat some of its heart."

"Where can I find this?" asked the turtle. "How can we get it?"

"I've already told you the medicine isn't available. We have no choice but to endure patiently whatever happens to her."

٨،٥ فداخل السلحفاة همّ شديد ونظر في الحيلة لامرأته فلم يجد مطمعاً إلّا في صديقه فدعته نفسه إلى الاحتيال له فأمر نفسه وخاصمها وذكّرها حرمة القرد وما بينهما من المؤاخاة والمحافظة وخوّفها الغدر وعاقبته وتذكّر مع ذلك منزلة امرأته منه وحلاوتها في صدره ومنافعها له وفضلها في نفسها على النساء فجعل يمثل بين رأيه ثمّ قال الغدر عند الله عظيم وفي أخلاق الناس غير جميل وتركي امرأتي على ما أعرف من وجدي بها وأنّ نفسي معلّقة بنفسها شديد. فأطال النظر في ذلك وغلب عليه الهوى فمال به في امرأته على الوفاء لصديقه فأجمع رأيه وأمره على قتل القرد ثمّ قال الرأي في قتله أن أحتال بحمله إلى الجزيرة التي فيها منزلتي فإذا انتهينا إلى ما هنالك فلا طعام له ولا شراب ولا شيء يتعلّق به ممّا فيه معاش فلم يلبث أن يهلك جوعاً وعطشاً فإذا مات أخذت قلبه فأطعمته امرأتي.

٨،٦ فلمّا أجمع السلحفاة على ذلك واستحكم له رأيه في نفسه انصرف إلى القرد وقد كان استبطأه واستوحش لغيبته فلمّا وصل فرح به وسكن إليه وسأله عن أهله وولده فأخبره عنهم خبراً فقال لم ينفعني مع شوقي إليك شيء كنت فيه من السرور بالأهل والولد وما كنت أتذكّره فيتغيّر له حالي من وحدتك وانقطاعك عن الأهل والولد فلم أصبر حتّى انصرفت إليك فأنا أحبّ أن تصلني وتكرمني بأن تنطلق معي وتنظر إلى أهلي وينظرون إليك ويعرفون منزلتي منك وتقرّ أعينهنّ بالمؤاخاة بيني وبينك وتصيب من طعامنا وشرابنا فإنّي أحبّ مكافأتك أنّي وصلت إليها من برّ جزاء لما أوليتني من نفسك مذ جاورتني.

٨،٧ قال القرد لا تعدّنّ ذلك منّي عليك فضلاً فإنّي قد أصبحت أرى لك عندي أكثر ممّا ترى لي عندك فإنّي إليك أحوج منك إليّ لأنّي انقطعت عن مملكتي وأهلي ووطني وإخواني ومعارفي فصرت وحيداً طريداً فلولا أنّ الله منّ عليّ بأنسي منك ومؤاخاتك لهلكت غمّاً ووحشة ففضلك عليّ أعظم وأجسم ممّا عسيت أن أذكر

The turtle was consumed with grief. He considered what he could do for his wife, but his only hope lay with his friend. He was tempted to trick the monkey and in this way obtain what was needed, but he rebuked himself for thinking this and reminded himself of the sacred bond of brotherhood and protection that existed between them, warning himself of the consequences of treachery. At the same time, he remembered how much his wife meant to him, the sweetness she brought to his heart, her helpfulness to him, and her superiority over other women. He began to weigh the two things. Treachery was a grievous sin in the eyes of God and unseemly by the standards of morality, but he could hardly abandon his wife, given his strong attachment to her. He pondered the matter for a long time. Finally, passion won the day and inclined him toward his wife and against loyalty to his friend, and he decided to kill the monkey. He reasoned that the way to do it was to work out how to transport him to the island where the turtle's home was located. "When we get there, he'll have no food or drink to nourish him; soon enough he'll perish of hunger and thirst, and when he dies I'll take his heart and give it to my wife to eat." 8.5

Having settled on this plan, the turtle went back to the monkey, who missed him and was eagerly awaiting his return. The monkey, joyful and relieved to see him back, asked after the turtle's family and children. The turtle filled him in, adding, "Because I longed for you so much, I got nothing from the joy of seeing my family and children. Everything was spoiled as soon as I remembered that you were alone and cut off from your own family and children. I could hardly wait to get back to you. Now I want you to strengthen our bond of friendship and honor me by accompanying me to see my family. They will see you, learn the place you hold in my heart, and rejoice in our brotherhood, and you will partake of our food and drink. I wish to repay you for the kindness you've bestowed on me since becoming my neighbor." 8.6

The monkey said, "You mustn't think that I deserve any credit for what I did for you. I've come to believe that I owe you more than you owe me. I needed you more than you needed me. Cut off from my kingdom, my 8.7

فإن كان أحبّ إليك أن أزور معك أهلك وولدك فعلت ذلك. وكيف[1] لي بقطع اللجّة التي ترى.

قال السلحفاة أحملك على ظهري حتّى أعبر بك إلى الجزيرة التي نحن فيها وفيها شجر كثير من صنوف الفواكه وظلّ ظليل وأمن من كلّ ما يُخاف وإنّ ممّا يزداد به اللطف ما بين الإخوان استرسال بعضهم إلى بعض والنظر إلى الحشم والأهل والمؤاكلة ولم يجرِ من ذلك بيني وبينك شيء.

٨،٨ فلم يزل يشوّقه إلى ما هنالك حتّى تابعه فحمله السلحفاة على ظهره ثمّ ولج به البحر قاصداً نحو أهله فلمّا مرّ بمكان غير غمر قام به ثمّ ذكر ما بينه وبين القرد من المؤاخاة وما قد أجمع عليه من الغدر به فداخله من ذلك ضيق نفس وخصومة لها وكان ممّا خاصم به نفسه أن قال إنّ الأمر الذي هممت به أمر كبير وغدر وما النساء بأهل بأن يُركب من أجلهنّ الغدر واللؤم لأنّه لا يُوثَق منهنّ بحسن عهد ولا يُعتمد منهنّ على وفاء وقد قيل إنّه يُستدلّ على جودة الذهب الأحمر بالإحماء في النار وعلى قوّة الدوابّ بتثقيل الحمل وعلى أهل الأمانة بالأخذ والإعطاء ولا يُستدلّ على أقصى علوم النساء بشيء من الأشياء.

٩،٨ وجعل السلحفاة يناظر نفسه في ذلك فاستراب القرد ممّا رأى منه فقال ما لي أراك مغتمّاً حزيناً لعلّي قد شققت[2] عليك.

قال وما الذي أنكرت عليّ.

قال القرد أراك تحدّث نفسك.

قال السلحفاة صدقت وذلك أنّي ذكرت أنّ زيارتك إيّاي أهلي وأنّ امرأتي مريضة فلعلّ ذلك يقصّر بكثير ممّا أحبّ أن ترى من كرامتنا إيّاك وإلطافنا لك.

قال القرد إنّ الذي قد أيقنت به من حرصك على كرامتي يكفيك مؤنة التكليف فيما بيني وبينك.

---

١ الأصل: كف. ٢ كذا پ٣٤٦٦؛ الأصل: اسقف.

family, my homeland, my friends, and my acquaintances, I had become a solitary outcast. If God hadn't granted me your companionship and friendship, I should have perished of grief and loneliness. Therefore, you deserve more than I can ever recount. However, if you would like me to visit your family and children with you, I'll come. But how can I cross this stretch of water?"

"I'll carry you on my back," said the turtle, "until we reach the island where I live. It is free from danger, with shady groves and many kinds of fruit trees. Affection increases when friends are at ease with each other, visit each other's acquaintances and family, and share food, and this hasn't happened between us yet."

The monkey finally gave in to his exhortations. The turtle had the monkey 8.8
mount his back, and set out on the sea toward his family. At one point, he stopped at a place that wasn't too deep and remembered the brotherhood that existed between them and thought of the treachery he had decided to commit. He felt deeply troubled and inwardly was very torn. He debated with himself, saying, "I am about to commit a terrible act of treachery. Women don't deserve to have people commit treachery and villainy for their sake. They're not to be trusted or relied on to keep a promise. Gold, they say, is tested by fire; an animal's strength is tested by a heavy load; a merchant's honesty is tested in transactions; but no test whatsoever yields thorough knowledge about women."

The monkey noticed that the turtle was debating with himself and became 8.9
uneasy. "Why do you seem worried and sad? Am I burdening you?"

"What have I done to make you feel this way?" asked the turtle.

"I see you're deep in thought," said the monkey.

"You're right," said the turtle. "I recalled that you are coming to visit my family while my wife is ill, which is going to curtail our kindness and hospitality considerably."

"What I've already experienced of your eagerness to show me kindness makes it unnecessary for you to go to any more trouble."

فمضى السلحفاة بالقرد ساعة ثمّ وقف يحدّث نفسه فقال فيما حدّثها به كيف لي بترك امرأتي على ما أرى بها من الحال أم كيف لي بالغدر بصاحبي. ثمّ قال عاذرًا نفسه من خطأ الرأي إنّه قد كان يقال إذا لم تصل إلى عظيم الأجر إلّا بيسير من الإثم فالرأي اكتساب عظيم الأجر بيسير الإثم. وكان الذي رأى من جليل الأجر الاحتيال لمصالح امرأته بما وصل إليه والذي رأى من يسير الإثم قتل القرد.

١٠،٨ فبينما هو في فكر من ذلك بضرب الأمثال لنفسه إذ تفكّر القرد في أمره فاستراب وساء به ظنًّا ثمّ قال لنفسه قد قالت العلماء إذا دخلت قلب صديق من صديقه ريبة فليأخذ بالحزم في الحفظ برفق فإن كان ذلك الذي ظنّ كما ظنّ ظفر بالسلامة وإن كان على غير ذلك ظفر بالحزم ولم يضرّه ولا صديقه أخذه لأمره بالحزم.

ثمّ قال القرد للسلحفاة ما لي أراك تكثر حديث نفسك.

قال السلحفاة تذكّرت مرض المرأة وحالها ومكانها منّي فداخلني من ذلك حديث نفسي.

فقال القرد قد أحزنني ما داخلك من أمرها وكثر عليّ ممّا أرى بك من الغمّ فلننظر لما فيه منفعتها فإنّي لست أرى معتزلًا لشيء نزل لك.

قال السلحفاة قد نظرت في ذلك ووصف الأطبّاء الدواء الذي لا يشفيها غيره.

قال القرد وما هو ذلك.

قال السلحفاة قلب قرد.

١١،٨ فلمّا سمع القرد ذلك أيقن الشرّ وقال في نفسه هذا ما صنع بي شره نفسي وغلبت شهوتي على رأيي ولست بأوّل من اغتيل بالشهوة والحرص وقد قيل يعيش القانع الراضي آمنًا مطمئنًّا مستريحًا وذو الحرص والشره يعيش ما عاش في تعب ونصب وخوف. والرأي على كلّ حال الاستعانة بالله وطلب الحيلة. فقال القرد إنّ العلماء قد قالت ليبذل ذو المال ماله في ثلاثة مواضع في الصدقة إن أراد الآخرة وفي مصانعة السلطان إن أراد المنزلة في الدنيا وفي النساء إن أراد رخاء العيش.

The turtle carried the monkey a bit farther. Then he stopped again to debate with himself. "How can I leave my wife in her present state? But how can I betray my friend?" Then, to absolve himself from a wrong decision, he told himself, "They say that if you can obtain a great reward only by means of a slight sin, then the right thing to do is to obtain the reward by means of the sin." The great reward he would obtain, so he thought, would be his wife's recovery; the slight sin, so he thought, would be to kill the monkey.

While the turtle was pondering these things and citing maxims to him- 8.10
self, the monkey, too, was pondering his situation. Full of misgivings and suspicions, he said to himself, "The sages say that you should use prudence and skill to protect yourself against misgivings about a friend who finds his way into your heart. If your suspicion is true, you achieve safety; if not, you practice prudence, which harms neither you nor your friend."

"Still so lost in thought?" the monkey asked the turtle.

"I became lost in thought when I remembered my wife's illness and the place she holds in my heart."

"Your anxiety about her saddens me," said the monkey. "And your grief troubles me. Let's find a way to help her. Anything that troubles you troubles me."

"Actually," said the turtle, "I've looked into it. The physicians have prescribed the only medicine that will heal her."

"And what is it?" asked the monkey.

"A monkey's heart," replied the turtle.

The monkey realized this spelled disaster. "This is what greed has done 8.11
to me," he said to himself. "Desire overcame my better judgment—and I'm not the first to be undone by desire and greed. They say that to be satisfied and content is to live a secure life, restful and at ease; but to be covetous and greedy is to live a life of weariness, fatigue, and fear. In any case, the only thing to be done is to seek help from God and to use my own cunning." So he said to the turtle, "The sages have said that those with means should spend it on three things: charity, if they desire a heavenly reward; service to their ruler, if they desire honor in this world; and women, if they desire a life of comfort.

وقد عرفت موضع هذه المرأة من قلبك وليس ينبغي أن أؤخّر ما احتجت إليه في صلاحها وقد عرفت هذا الوجع الذي ذكرت وقد أصاب واصف الدواء الصفة وذلك أنّ نساءنا ربّما أصاب بعضهنّ هذا الوجع فأعطاها بعضنا قلبه فصحّت ثمّ لا يضرّنا ذلك شيئاً إلّا ضرّاً نحتمله لفضل ما في ذلك من منافع نسائنا. ولو كنت ذكرت لي مثل هذا لحملت معي قلبي ثمّ لم أدّخره عنك فيما فيه صلاح امرأتك ولا سيّما وقد بلغت من السنين ما لا حاجة لي إلى القلب بقيّة عمري وقد أصبحت مع ذلك بمنزل ما شيء أشدّ عليّ من صحبة قلبي لكثرة ما يسكن فيه من الهمّ ويعرض فيه من الأحزان وإنّي كنت لحريصاً على فراقه غير أنّي كرهت ذلك لطول صحبته إلّا في حقّ لازم ووجه معروف لأنّه إذا فارقني انقطع عنّي أكثر الهمّ والأحزان.

١٢،٨ فطمع السلحفاة فيما ذكر القرد وقال يا خليلي وأين قلبك.

قال خلّفته ورائي في المنزل.

قال السلحفاة ولِمَ خلّفته.

قال القرد إنّما كان ذلك سنّة فينا معشر القرود إذا توجّه بعضنا لأمر يريد أن يتمّ له فيه السرور لم يخرج معه قلبه لإنّ القلب يجتمع فيه من الفكر والهموم ما يكدّر كلّ صفو وينغّص كلّ عيش وسرور فأحببت في مخرجي هذا أن أستكمل سروري وقرّة عيني فخلّفت قلبي وكرهت صحبته فلمّا ذكرت لي ما ذكرت من مرض امرأتك والذي بها كرهت أن ترى[١] امرأتك أنّ كرامتك عليّ وأنّي قصّرت عن بذل قلبي لك وعساها مع ذلك أن تظنّ إنّما خلّفت قلبي ضنانة عنك وعنها فإنّ النساء أضعف شيء رأياً وأوهنه عقلاً فانصرف بنا لنحمله إليها.

١٣،٨ فلمّا سمع السلحفاة ذلك اطمأنّت نفسه ووثق بالنجح بالحاجة فانصرف بالقرد[٢] مسرعاً حتّى انتهى به إلى الساحل فوثب القرد إلى الأرض وسعى هارباً إلى الشجرة فرقيها[٣] ومكث مكانه فلمّا أبطأ على السلحفاة استحثّه.

١ الأصل: والذي بها...أن ترى. ٢ الأصل: القرد. ٣ الأصل: فرقاها.

"I know the place this woman holds in your heart. It isn't right for me to withhold what you need for her health, and I recognize the pain she's experiencing. Whoever prescribed the medicine did so correctly: the same pain sometimes affects our womenfolk, and one of us gives up his heart and she recovers. Our loss is small, and we tolerate it on account of the benefit it brings to our womenfolk. I would have brought my heart along if you'd mentioned this to me. I wouldn't withhold anything that would benefit your wife, especially since I've reached the age when I no longer need a heart for the rest of my life. I'm at the stage when nothing is more troublesome than my heart's companionship—it's where so many worries and sorrows dwell. I've been eager to part with it, but because of our long companionship, I was loath to do so except out of duty or as a favor. In any case, if it leaves me, most of my worries and sorrows will cease."

His hopes raised by the monkey's words, the turtle said, "Friend, where 8.12
is your heart?"

"I left it at home."

"And why did you do that?" asked the turtle.

"It has always been the custom among us monkey folk. We don't take our hearts with us when we go somewhere we expect to experience unbridled joy, because the cares and worries that have accumulated in our hearts would disturb us and cloud our happiness. Therefore, when I set out, wanting my joy and pleasure to be complete, I didn't want my heart to accompany me, so I left it behind. Now that you've mentioned your wife's illness and her sorry state, however, I don't want her to think I failed to offer you my heart despite my debt of gratitude to you. She might even think I left my heart behind on purpose, begrudging it to you and her—women's minds have weak judgment. Let's go back to get it and bring it to her."

When the turtle heard this, his mind was set at ease and he became con- 8.13
fident that he would obtain what he needed. He immediately turned back. When they reached the shore, the monkey jumped onto land, ran to the tree, climbed up, and stayed there. After a while, when the monkey hadn't returned, the turtle urged him to hurry.

فضحك القرد وقال قد عرفناك فلا تظنّ أنّي كالحمار الذي قال الثعلب للأسد لم يكن له قلب ولا أذنان.[١]

قال السلحفاة وكيف كان ذلك.

١٤،٨ قال القرد زعموا أنّه كان في بعض الآجام أسد أصابه جرب شديد فجهده ونهكه وأذهب قوّته حتّى عجز عن الصيد وكان ثعلب منقطع إليه يعيش من فضوله.

قال له الثعلب أما لدائك هذا دواء.

قال الأسد بلى دواؤه ما لا سبيل إليه وإن كان يسيرًا.

قال الثعلب وما هو.

قال الأسد هو قلب حمار وأذناه.

قال الثعلب ما هذا من الدواء الذي لا ينبغي أن يكون لك لا سبيل إليه.

١٥،٨ قال الأسد قد أصابني من الجرب ما ترى فذهب عنّي شعري وفقدت جمالي وأنا أستحيي أن أخرج من الأجمة فيراني بعض من أحتشم منه من أكفائي.

قال الثعلب أمّا إذا كرهت الخروج لما بك فإنّي آتيك بحمار فأمكّنك منه في أجمتك.

قال الأسد وكيف ذلك ومن أين.

قال الثعلب إنّ قريبًا منّا موضع فيه ماء كثير قد ألفه قصّار للثياب ومعه حمار يحمل عليه ثيابه فإذا انتهى إلى العين التي عندها يقصّر ثيابه وضع[٢] عن الحمار حمله وخلّى عنه يرعى في مرج دون العين فإنّي آتيه . . . [٣] آتيك به وأرى لك مع ذلك أن لا تأكل منه غير ما فيه شفاؤك من قلبه وأذنيه وأن تجعل بقيّته قربانًا.

قال الأسد نعم.

١٦،٨ فانطلق الثعلب إلى الحمار فلاطفه وكلّمه ثمّ قال له ما لي أراك مهزولًا.

قال الحمار هزالي من هذا القصّار الذي ترى فهو يجهدني بالعمل ويجفوني العلف.

قال له الثعلب فلِمَ تقيم على الشرّ وأنت تجد عنه مرحلًا ومذهبًا.

١ كذا ل٢؛ الأصل: أذن. ٢ كذا ل٢؛ في الأصل خلل طوله كلمة. ٣ في الأصل خلل طوله كلمة أو كلمتان أوّله: محاد . . . .

The monkey replied, laughing, "I know you. Don't think I'm like the donkey who the fox told the lion had no heart and no ears."

"What do you mean by that?" asked the turtle.

The monkey told the following tale: They say that in a jungle there lived a lion who came down with a bad case of mange. It wearied and weakened him, and so sapped his strength that he could no longer hunt. A fox, his devoted companion, lived with him and used to eat the lion's leftovers. 8.14

The Donkey Who Had No Heart and No Ears

"Isn't there any medicine for this disease?" asked the fox.

"Yes," replied the lion. "But the medicine, simple as it is, can't be obtained."

"What is it?"

"A donkey's heart and ears."

"Surely it shouldn't be difficult for you to obtain this kind of medicine!" exclaimed the fox.

"You can see how I suffer from the mange," said the lion. "My hair is gone, 8.15
I've lost my beauty, and I'm ashamed to leave the jungle and be seen by any of my colleagues."

"Well," said the fox, "I'll get you a donkey and bring him to you right here in your jungle if you're reluctant to go out because of your condition."

"How will you do it? Where will you get him?" asked the lion.

"There is a place with lots of water nearby. A fuller goes there frequently and his donkey carries the laundry. When he reaches the spring where he washes the clothes, he unloads the donkey and frees it to graze in the meadow by the spring. I'll go there . . .[48] and bring you the donkey. But I think you should eat only what is needed for your recovery—the heart and the ears. The rest you should offer as a sacrifice."

"Very good!" said the lion.

The fox went to the donkey and spoke to him very politely. Then he asked, 8.16
"Why are you so thin?"

"This fuller—you see him over there—works me to death and feeds me coarse fodder," replied the donkey.

"Why do you stand for such mistreatment, when you can just leave?" asked the fox.

قال الحمار ومن لي بذلك أين أذهب وكيف أنفلت من أيدي الناس.

قال الثعلب إنّك إن أطعتني ذهبت بك إلى مكان كثير العشب والماء ليس فيه أحد من الناس وقد كنت دُللت عليه منذ أيّام فيه[1] دابّة بها من الضرّ أشدّ ممّا بك فهي هنالك في أخصب الخصب قد امتلأت وصلحت فلو رأيتها أنكرت لما بها من السمن وحسن الحال.

فلمّا سمع الحمار إلى ذكر الدابّة وإلى ما وصف له الثعلب من طيب الماء والمرعى اهتاج لذلك وقال انطلق بي إلى حيث شئت فإنّي وإن لم أصب في صحبتك إلّا مصادقتك فإنّ لي في ذلك رغبة.

١٧،٨ فانطلق به الثعلب حتّى هجم به على الأسد فوثب عليه فضربه ضربة ضعيفة وعجز عن ضبطه لما كان بلغه من الجهد والضعف فانفلت الحمار منصاعاً نحو المكان الذي كان فيه وبقي الثعلب ينظر الى الأسد متعجّباً من سوء حاله ثمّ قال يا سيّدي ما هذا الضعف وما[2] الذي صنعت. إن كنت تركت الحمار عمداً فلِمَ عنّيتني في طلبه وإن كنت لم تضبطه فقد لقيت من الشقوة والبلاء أن يكون سيّدي قد عجز عن حمار مهزول قد دبر.

١٨،٨ فلمّا سمع الأسد ذلك شقّ عليه وقال في نفسه إن قلت تركته عمداً أقررت على نفسي بالمكر وإن[3] قلت تركته ضعفاً أقررت بالعجز. فأقبل الأسد على الثعلب وقال ليس كلّ ما تأتي الملوك في أمورهم ينبغي للرعيّة أن تتكلّف علمه. للملوك من فضيلة الرأي والنظر فيما نقص عنه أبصار من هو دونهم من السوقة والعامّة فاكفف عن المسألة عمّا لا يسأل مثلك وارجع إلى الحمار والطف به عسى أن تردّه إليّ فإنّك إن فعلت عرفت صدق نصيحتك وفضلك على جميع نظرائك من جندي.

قال الثعلب لقد جرّب منّي الحمار الغدر وإنّي على ذلك لعائد إليه ومحتال له ما استطعت.

---

١ فيه: ساقطة من الأصل. ٢ وما: ساقطة من الأصل. ٣ الأصل: و.

"Who will help me?" replied the donkey. "Where can I go? How can I escape from men?"

"If you'll do as I say," said the fox, "I'll take you to a place with lots of grass and water and no people. I found my way there a few days ago. There is an animal there who has suffered even more grievously than you, but now she's living in utter luxury. She has put on weight and recovered her health. If you saw her, you wouldn't believe how fat and well off she is."[49]

The donkey became excited at the story of the animal and the fox's description of the good pasture. "Take me wherever you wish," he said. "I'm eager to go, even if by accompanying you I gain nothing but your friendship."

The fox brought him, much to his surprise, face to face with the lion. 8.17
The lion attacked the donkey and struck a light blow, but was so weak and exhausted that he was unable to hold onto him, and the donkey fled as fast as he could back to where he had come from. The fox was left looking at the lion in amazement at his wretched condition. "Master," he asked, "what is this weakness? What have you done? Why did you put me to the trouble of finding the donkey if you meant to let go of him? If it was because you couldn't hold on to him, then I'm in real trouble, if my master can't hold on to an emaciated donkey with sores on its back."

The lion was very uncomfortable. "If I say I let him go intentionally," he 8.18
said to himself, "I admit my deceitfulness; if I say I let him go from weakness, I admit my impotence." He turned to the fox and said, "Subjects shouldn't trouble themselves trying to comprehend everything kings do in their affairs. Kings have a level of judgment and understanding not attained by subjects and commoners. Stop asking questions that shouldn't be asked by someone like you. Go back to the donkey, flatter him, and bring him back. If you do, I will extol your loyalty and superiority to all your colleagues in my entourage."

"The donkey has known treachery at my hands," said the fox. "But I'll go back and do my best to trick him."

فرجع الثعلب إلى الحمار فلمّا رآه الحمار قال له ما الذي صنعت بي. ١٩،٨

قال الثعلب صنعت بك خيرًا ولكن إنّما الذنب لإفراط الغلمة وإنّ الذي وثب عليك الدابّة التي كنت اخبرتك بها ولكنّك فزعت من غير فزع وإنّ الدابّة لمّا رأتك وثبت عليك وصنعت بك ما رأيت لفرط فرحها بك وحرصها عليك فلو أنّك أقررتها ساعة صارت تحتك.

فلمّا سمع الحمار كلامه هاجت به الغلمة ولم يكن الحمار رأى أسدًا فيما خلا ليعرفه فلم يزل الثعلب يخدعه ويشبّه عليه حتّى صدّقه واطمأنّ إليه وإلى قوله ثمّ انصرف معه فلمّا نظر إليه الأسد ختله حتّي وثب عليه مستمسكًا منه فقتله.

ثمّ قال الأسد للثعلب احفظه حتّى أنطلق فأغتسل ثمّ آكل منه قلبه وأذنيه فإنّه كذلك ما وُصف لي أن أصنع.

فانطلق الأسد ليغتسل فعمد الثعلب إلى أذني الحمار وقلبه فأكلهما. ٢٠،٨

فلمّا رجع الأسد لم ير للحمار أذنًا ولا قلبًا فسأل الثعلب عن ذلك.

فقال له الثعلب أوما شعرت أنّ هذا الحمار لم يكن له قلب ولا أذن لو كان له قلب يعقل به وأذن يسمع بها لم يصدّقني مع ما اختبر من غدري ولم يكن ليرجع إليك بعد الذي عاين منك.

قال القرد للسلحفاة إنّما ضربت لك هذا المثل لأنّك خدعتني بالمكر والحيلة فجزيتك بمثل خديعتك لتعلم أنّي لست كذلك[١] الحمار الذي زعم الثعلب أنّه لم يكن له قلب ولا أذن وقد قالت العلماء إنّ كلّ آفة يشبهها شيء من الأشياء فإنّه لا يقوى عليها إلّا عمل الذي يشبهها من خير أو شرّ. ٢١،٨

قال السلحفاة صدقت وقد قيل إنّ ذا العقل يقلّ من الكلام ويبالغ في العمل ويعترف بالزلّة[٢] إذا كانت منه ويتبيّن الأمور قبل الإقدام عليها ويستقيل عثرة عقله بعقله[٣] كالرجل الذي يعثر بالأرض وينتعش بها وينهض. وأنا بما سلف منّي إليك ٢٢،٨

١ كذا ر؛ الأصل: دلك. ٢ كذا ر؛ الأصل: فى الزله. ٣ ويستقيل . . . بعقله: كذا ر؛ الأصل: وستقيل عثرته وعلته.

The fox returned to the donkey, who immediately said, "What have you done to me?" 8.19

"I was only trying to look out for you," replied the fox. "The problem was an excess of lust. The animal that jumped onto you was indeed the one I told you about. You panicked when there was nothing to fear. When she saw you, she was so overcome by joy and desire that she jumped on you and did what she did. Had you waited a moment, she would have become your wife."

The donkey's lust was inflamed by the fox's story. He had never seen a lion before. The fox continued to deceive and mislead him until he believed him. At that point, trusting the fox and his words, the donkey returned with him. When the lion saw him, he approached stealthily, pounced on him, clung to him, and killed him.

The lion said to the fox, "Guard the body while I go wash. Then I'll eat its heart and ears, as prescribed."

The lion went off to wash himself, and the fox helped himself to the don- 8.20
key's ears and heart and ate them.

When the lion returned, seeing no ears and no heart, he asked the fox for an explanation.

"Didn't you sense that this donkey had no heart or ears? Had he a heart with which to understand and ears with which to hear, he wouldn't have come back to you after what he'd experienced."

"I've told you this story," said the monkey to the turtle, "because you 8.21
tricked me with deceit and cunning, and now I've paid you back in kind, to show you that I'm not like the donkey the fox claimed had no heart or ears. As the scholars put it: Every evil has a counterpart, good or bad, by which alone it can be overcome."

The turtle said, "You're right. As they say, a wise man is sparing of words, 8.22
unsparing of deeds; he acknowledges a mistake when he makes one; he ascertains the facts before embarking on anything; and by his intelligence he seeks to undo any lapse of his intelligence—like a man who stumbles on the ground, but uses the ground to right himself and stand up. I confess my

معترف ولك بالذنب مقرّ وأنّ الحجّة لا تقرّبني من غدر ولا تخرجني من إساءة. وقد أحببت أن أعلمك معرفتي بإساءتي وإن كنت عارفًا بأنّك[1] غير عائد إلى مثل الذي كنت لي عليه من المؤاخاة لما اختبرت منّي من الغدر فنفسي[2] جلبت عليّ الحرارة ومثل هواي قطع عنّي مثلك من الأصدقاء.

---

[1] عارفًا بأنّك: الأصل: عارفا فا نانك. [2] الأصل: فمسى فنفسى.

deed and acknowledge my guilt, though my plea cannot undo my treachery or excuse my wrongdoing. I want you to know that I recognize my wrongdoing, though I know that because of my treachery you aren't going to resume our former friendship. This pain has been brought upon me by my own soul, and I have lost a friend because of my own evil inclination."

باب الناسك وابن عرس

وهو مثل من يعمل العمل بغير الرويّة والنظر
والبيان وكيف يكون عاقبة أمره

١،٩ قال الملك للعالم قد علمت هذا المثل وقد صدقت وأصبت فاضرب لي مثل العجل في أمره والعامل بغير رويّة وتثبّت.

قال العالم إنّه من لم يستقبل الأمور بالأناة والتثبّت وعمل بغير حسن النظر كان مثله مثل الناسك الذي قتل ابن عرس بغير ذنب وصار عاقبة أمره حسرة وندامة.

قال الملك وكيف كان ذلك.

٢،٩ قال العالم زعموا أنّ ناسكاً من النسّاك كانت له امرأة وكان لها محبّاً فمكثت عنده زماناً طويلاً لا تحمل ثمّ حملت بعد إياس منه ومنها فاشتدّ سروره فأكثر ذكرما يؤمّل في ولده منها وقال لها أبشري فإنّك تلدين غلاماً إن شاء الله تعالى فأسمّيه اسماً حسناً ثمّ أؤدّبه أحسن الأدب وأعلّمه وجوه العلم فيكون لنا عقباً صالحاً وأنا متقدّم في التماس الأظآر[١] له.

٣،٩ قالت المرأة دع عنك ذكرما لا يحسن بمثلك ذكره ولا تتكلّمنّ فيما لا تدري كيف هو كائن. ما يدريك ألد أم لا ألد وما ألد إن ولدت وكيف يكون المولود[٢] من ذا الذي يعلم ما في الأرحام إلّا الله سبحانه وما علّمك بأنّه يسلم إن ولدت فدع عنك أيّها الرجل هذا القول فإنّه من قال فيما لا يدري هل يكون أم لا مثل مقالتك كان خليقاً أن يصير أمره إلى ما صار إليه أمر الناسك الذي انصبّ سمنه وعسله على رأسه.

قال الناسك لامرأته وكيف كان ذلك.

١ كذا ر؛ الأصل: الأوطار. ٢ ألد . . . المولود: كذا ر؛ الأصل: ألد ام لا ألد ان ولدت ام كف يكون المولود.

The Holy Man and the Mongoose

A parable about the consequences of acting without deliberation, reflection, or clarity.

The king said to the philosopher, "I have listened to a parable that was truly spoken and hit the mark! Now tell me one about a man who acts too quickly, without reflecting or ascertaining the facts." 9.1

The philosopher said, "Anyone who does not ascertain the facts and approach his affairs with calm deliberation, but instead acts without careful reflection, will suffer the fate of the holy man who, to his grief and regret, killed the innocent mongoose."

"What was his fate?" asked the king.

And the philosopher told the following tale: Once, they say, a holy man 9.2
had a wife whom he loved. She lived with him a long time without conceiving. Then, much to his joy, just when they had given up hope, she became pregnant, and he took to recounting his hopes for the child. "Rejoice," he said, "for you're going to give birth to a boy, God willing. I'll choose a beautiful name, give him the finest upbringing, and teach him all sorts of subjects, and we shall have a righteous legacy. I'll set out at once to find nurses for him."

"Stop going on about things you know nothing about and that you have 9.3
no business talking about," replied the wife. "How do you know whether I'll give birth or not, what sex the child will be if I give birth, and how the child will turn out? Who except God—glory to Him—knows what is in the womb?[50] How do you know that I'll give birth to a healthy child? Stop chattering like this. You're likely to suffer the fate of the holy man who spilled his butter and honey on his own head if you speak about outcomes you know nothing about."

"And what was his fate?" he asked.

٩،٤ قالت المرأة زعموا أنّ ناسكاً كان له رزق من طعام وأدم من عند تاجر يبيع السمن والعسل وكان يأتيه في كلّ يوم من السمن والعسل[١] بشيء معلوم فيأكل منه حاجته ويرفع ما يبقى فيجعله في جرّة ويعلّقه في وتد في ناحية بيته حتّى امتلأت الجرّة من السمن والعسل فلمّا كان ذات يوم وهو مضطجع على فراشه تحت الجرّة إذ تحدّث فقال لو أنّي قد بعت ما اجتمع في هذه الجرّة من السمن بعته بعشرة دراهم فاشتريت بها خمس شياه فيحملن ثمّ يلدن لخمسة أشهر بطناً فلا يلبث أن يصير غنماً كثيرة عظيمة إذا ولدت أولادها معها. ثمّ حزر[٢] على هذا النحو خمس سنين فوجد ذلك أكثر من أربعمائة شاة ثمّ قال أنا أبيعها وأشتري بها مائة من البقر بكلّ أربعة أعنز ثوراً او بقرة فأصيب بذراً فأزرع على الثيران وأنتفع ببطون الإناث وألبانها فلا يأتي عليّ خمس سنين إلّا وقد كثر معي مالاً ورياشاً ومتاعاً فإذا فرغت من ذلك تزوّجت امرأة حسناء ذات حسب وجمال فإذا دخلت بها أحبلتها فتلد منّي غلاماً سويّاً فأسمّيه اسماً وأؤدّبه وأعلّمه علماً كثيراً فإن عصاني في الأدب رفعت عصاي هذه فضربت بها رأسه. وفي يده عصا فرفع العصا يشير بها فأصاب طرف العصا الجرّة فانكسرت وانصبّ السمن والعسل على رأس الناسك.

٩،٥ قالت وإنّما ضربت لك هذا المثل لكي لا تعجل بذكر ما لا ينبغي ذكره وما لا تدري أيكون أم لا يكون.

فلمّا سمع الناسك هذا المثل من امرأته سكت.

٩،٦ ثمّ لم تلبث المرأة أن نفست فولدت غلاماً فاشتدّ فرح الناسك به فلمّا مضت أيّام نفاسها وأرادت المرأة الطهر لزوجها قالت إنّي أريد أن[٣] أتطهّر فاقعد عند الصبيّ فاحفظه حتّى أرجع إليك. فجلس الناسك عند الصبيّ يحفظه وخرجت المرأة لحاجتها ولم يلبث إلّا قليلاً حتّى جاء رسول الملك يدعوه فاستحثّه فلم يستطع التخلّف ولم يكن في البيت أحد يحفظ الصبيّ وكان له ابن عرس داجن عنده وكان لهم نافعاً في أمور كثيرة فتركه الناسك عند الصبيّ وأغلق عليهما الباب وانطلق مع الرسول.

١ كذا ش، ع؛ ساقطة من الأصل. ٢ الأصل: احرز. ٣ ساقطة من الأصل.

The wife told him the following tale: A holy man, they say, used to receive an allowance of food from a butter and honey merchant every day; he would eat what he needed and store the rest in a jar he hung on a peg in the corner of his room. Eventually the jar was full of butter and honey. One day, while he was lying on his bed underneath the jar, he said to himself, "If I sell the butter in this jar, I can make ten dirhams, and use that to buy five female goats. They'll become pregnant, and after five months each will give birth; when their kids give birth in turn, they'll be a large flock." He calculated five years on this basis and reckoned that it would come to more than four hundred goats. "Then I'll sell them and use the money to buy a hundred head of cattle, an ox or a cow for every four goats. I'll get seeds, use the oxen to plow, and profit from the cows' milk and from their calves. Within five years I'll have lots of money, produce, and property. Then I'll marry a beautiful woman from a good family; I'll lie with her and get her pregnant, and she'll give birth to a strapping young lad. I'll choose a name for him, educate him, and teach him many subjects; if he becomes disobedient, I'll raise this stick of mine and beat him on the head." Whereupon he lifted the stick in his hand and waved it. The stick struck the jar and broke it, and the butter and honey poured down over the man's head. 9.4

The Holy Man and His Jar of Butter

"I've told you this parable," said the wife, "to keep you from rushing to talk about things you shouldn't talk about and which you don't know will happen or not." 9.5

The holy man learned a lesson from his wife's parable and thereafter kept silent on the subject.

It wasn't long before the woman gave birth to a son, and his father was overjoyed. When the days of her confinement were over, the woman wanted to become available for her husband, so she said, "I am going to do my ablutions. Sit by the child and take care of him until I come back."[51] The wife left and the husband sat by the boy, to care for him, while his wife was busy. Before long, a messenger from the king arrived, summoning the holy man and urging him to make haste. There was no one else in the house to care for the boy, but he could hardly refuse. He did, however, have a tame mongoose that had proven useful on many occasions; so he left it with the boy, locked them in the room, and departed with the messenger. 9.6

٧،٩ فلمّا خرج أقبلت حيّة سوداء من جحر في البيت حتّى دنت من الصبيّ فوثب عليها ابن عرس فقتلها وقطّعها قطعاً ولم يلبث ربّ البيت أن رجع ففتح الباب فاستقبله ابن عرس مختضباً بدم فلمّا أبصره الناسك سُلب عقله وظنّه قتل الصبيّ فلم يتوأّد[١] في أمره ولم يتردّد حتّي يعلم تصديق ما ظنّه من ذلك ولكن عجل على ابن عرس فقتله. فدنا من الصبيّ فوجده حيّاً ووجد حيّة سوداء مقطّعة عند الصبيّ قطعاً فجعل يضرب صدره ووجهه حزناً وأسفاً على ما صنع وقال ليت هذا الصبيّ لم يُولَد ولم يجرِ على يديّ ما جرى من الغدر ولم أفعل فعل من لا يشكر الحسنة ولا يكافئ بها.

٨،٩ فلمّا رجعت المرأة ورأت زوجها يصنع ما يصنع قالت ما يبكيك وما شأن الأسود وابن عرس مقتولين.[٢]

فأخبرها الخبر فقالت هذه ثمرة العجلة.

١ الأصل: يتأيد. ٢ كذا ر؛ الأصل: مقتولا.

After he had gone, a cobra came out of its hole and approached the boy. 9.7
The mongoose pounced on it, killed it, and tore it to pieces. The holy man
returned soon after. When he opened the door, the mongoose, stained with
blood, came to greet him. When the holy man saw this, he lost his mind and
thought the mongoose had killed the boy. He rushed at the mongoose and
killed it without pausing to think or confirm his suspicions. Then he went
over to the boy, whom he found alive, with a snake torn to pieces beside
him. He beat his breast and face in grief over his deed. "If only this boy had
never been born! If only I'd never committed such an act of betrayal! If only
I hadn't behaved with such a display of ingratitude and without rewarding a
favor!"

When the wife returned and saw how her husband was behaving, she 9.8
asked, "Why are you crying? Why are the snake and the mongoose both
dead?"

He told her what had happened and she said, "This is the fruit of haste."

باب السنّور والجرذ

وهو مثل رجل كثر عدوّه واحترس من كلّ جانب فأشفق على نفسه وأيقن بالهلاك والتمس المخرج من ذلك بموالاة بعض العدوّ ومصالحته فسلم ممّا يتخوّف ووفى لمن صالح.

١٠،١ قال الملك للعالم قد سمعت مثل من يجهل في الأمور ويعمل بغير التثبّت فاضرب لي مثل الرجل الذي كثر أعداؤه فاكتنفوه من كلّ جانب فأشرف على الهلاك والتمس المخرج منه بموالاة بعض ذلك العدوّ[1] ومسالمته فسلم ممّا تخوّف ووفى لمن صالح فأخبرني عن الصلح كيف يُلتمس.

١٠،٢ قال العالم إنّ العداوة والولاية ليس كلّها تدوم وكثير من المودّة يتحوّل بغضاء وكثير من البغضاء يتحوّل[2] مودّة عن حوادث الأمور والعلل وذو الرأي يحدث لكلّ حديث من ذلك رأيه من طمع فيما قبل العدوّ ويأس ممّا عند الصديق ولا تمنع ذا العقل عداوة كانت في نفسه لعدوّه من مقاربته والتماس ما عنده إذا طمع منه في دفع مخوف أو جرّ مرغوب ولا يعبأ مع ذلك بإحداث الرأي في المواصلة والموادعة فمن أبصر الرأي في ذلك وأخذ فيه بالحزم ظفر بحاجته. ومن المثل في ذلك مثل السنّور والجرذ اللذين اصطلحا حين كان ذلك الرأي لهما وكان في صلحهما خلاصهما من الورطة الشديدة التي كانا تورّطا فيها.

قال الملك وكيف كان ذلك.

١٠،٣ قال العالم زعموا أنّه كان بأرض كذا وكذا شجرة تسمّى النيرود[3] وكان في أصلها جحر جرذ يسمّى أفريدون وكان قريباً من ذلك المكان جحر سنّور يسمّى روميّ وكان ناس من

---

١ بعض ذلك العدوّ: كذا پ٣٤٧٥؛ الأصل: بعض ذلك الأعداء. ٢ يتحوّل ... يتحول: كذا ل٢؛ الأصل: يحول ... يحول. ٣ الأصل: السرود.

The Cat and the Rat

A parable about someone beset by foes on every side, who fears for his life and is certain that he is about to perish, but finds a way to avoid disaster by befriending and making peace with one of his foes, and then keeps his promise to the foe he made peace with.[52]

The king said to the philosopher, "Now that I've listened to your parable about rushing into action without ascertaining the facts, tell me one about someone surrounded by many enemies, who, on the brink of death, finds a way to avoid disaster by befriending and making peace with one of his foes, and then keeps his promise to the foe he made peace with. Tell me about truces and the circumstances when one should seek them." 10.1

The philosopher said, "Not all enmities and friendships endure. Affection sometimes turns into hatred, and hatred into affection, in response to changes in circumstances and conditions. The wise man plans for every contingency: sometimes he seeks help from an enemy; sometimes he despairs of receiving it from a friend. Antagonism should not prevent a wise man from approaching an enemy for help when he hopes to avert danger or attain an objective; under such circumstances he will have no qualms about changing his mind regarding rapprochement or mutual separation. If we understand this clearly and act on it prudently, we can achieve our ends. The story of the cat and the rat will serve as an example: they concluded a truce when it was to their advantage, and it saved them from the terrible predicament into which each of them had fallen." 10.2

"And how did that happen?" said the king.

The philosopher told the following tale: In a certain country, they say, at the foot of a banyan tree lay the den of a rat named Afrīdūn; nearby was the den of a cat named Rūmī. Hunters often came to the tree in search of game. 10.3

الصيّادين قد اعتادوا تلك الشجرة لطلب الصيد فنصب الصيّاد حبائله ذات ليلة فيما هنالك فوقع فيها[1] السنّور. وخرج الجرذ يدبّ ويطلب بعض ما يصلحه وهو مع ذلك ينظر ويلتفت ويحذر فبينما هو يمشي إذ رأى السنّور متقنَّصاً في الحبائل ففرح بذلك ثمّ التفت الجرذ خلفه فنظر ابن عرس قد كمن له ثمّ رفع رأسه نحو الشجرة فإذا هو ببومة على الشجرة ترصده فخاف إن انصرف إلى جحره أن يثب عليه ابن عرس وإن ذهب يميناً أو شمالاً أن تختطفه البومة وإن تقدّم فالسنّور أمامه فقال الجرذ عند ذلك اكتنفتني وتظاهرت عليّ أمور نغّصت عليّ سروري بما أُلقي على السنّور ولا أرى مفزعاً إلّا إلى الله تعالى وأن أعمل بعقلي وحيلتي.

٤،١٠ فأوّل ذلك أن لا يكون شأني الدهش فيذهب عقلي شعاعاً فإنّ العاقل لا يتفرّق عليه رأيه ولا يعزب عنه عقله على حال وإنّما عقول[2] ذوي العقول كالبحر الذي لا يُدرَك غوره وليس البلاء ببالغ من ذي الرأي مجهود عقله[3] حتّى يهلكه ولا الرجاء ببالغ منه مبلغاً يبطره ويعمّي عليه أمره. ثمّ قال في نفسه لا أرى حيلة أمثل من التماس صلح السنّور وقد نزل به بلاء شديد وأنا أقدر بإذن الله تعالى على خلاصه ولعلّه لو قد سمع ما أريد أن أكلّمه به من صحيح الكلام الذي لا خداع فيه ولا مماكرة ولا تقريعاً أن يفهم عنّي ويعرف منفعة ما أصف له وأدعوه فلعلّه[4] يطمع في معونتي إيّاه في خلاصه فيصالحني فعسى أن يكون له ولي في ذلك صلاح وخلاص.

٥،١٠ ثم دنا من السنّور فقال له كيف حالك.

قال السنّور حالي ما تهوى من الضيق والضنك.

قال الجرذ لا كذب لقد كان قبل اليوم كنت وأنا يسرّني ما ساءك وأرى ما ضيّق عليك سعة ولكن قد شاركتك اليوم في البلاء فلست أرجو لنفسي خلاصاً إلّا بما فيه خلاصك فعطّفني ذلك عليك وستعرف في مقالتي صدقها وأنّه لا مخادعة فيها. انظر أترى مكان ابن عرس كامناً لي ومكان البومة مشرفاً وكلاهما لي ولك

١ كذا ر؛ الأصل: فه. ٢ كذا ر؛ ساقطة من الأصل. ٣ مجهود عقله: كذا ر؛ الأصل: مجهود محمله. ٤ الأصل: فلعل.

One night a hunter set up his snares and the cat fell into them. When the rat crept out to find something to eat, looking warily in every direction as he advanced, he saw the cat entangled in the snares and rejoiced at the sight. But then he looked back and saw a weasel lying in wait; he looked up, and there was an owl in the tree, watching him. He feared that the weasel would pounce on him if he turned back and that the owl would snatch him if he turned right or left, and the cat was directly in front of him if he went straight ahead. "I am surrounded by troubles," he said to himself, "all in league to spoil my joy over the cat's distress. I see no recourse for me but to rely on God, and to use my intelligence and ingenuity.

"First, I mustn't become confused or distraught, for a wise man doesn't 10.4
lose his composure and, whatever the circumstances, his intelligence never deserts him. Wise minds are like the sea, whose depths cannot be plumbed. Trouble cannot exhaust a wise man's intelligence and destroy him, nor is he so dominated by hope as to become reckless or blind." Then he thought, "The best strategy is to seek a truce with the cat. The cat is in deep trouble, but I may, God willing, be able to save him. If he hears me speak honest words, without guile, deceit, or reproach, he may appreciate what I propose; recognizing the benefit to be gained, he may desire my help in saving him and make peace with me for our mutual good."

So he approached the cat. "How are you?" he asked. 10.5

"In deep trouble," replied the cat, "just as you would wish."

"Truth be told," said the rat, "that's how it used to be: I was delighted if something upset you, and I welcomed it if it annoyed you. Today, however, I'm your companion in misfortune, and my only hope for salvation lies in what I hope will be your salvation, too. This has aroused in me sympathy for you. Rest assured that my words contain no lies or deceit. Look: do you see that weasel lying in wait for me, and that owl up above? They are enemies both to me and to you, but they fear you. I'll come over to you, cut your cords, and rescue you if you swear not to harm me and promise to protect

عدوّ غير أنّهما لك خائفان فإن أنت أمّنتني وحلفت وجعلت لي أن تمنعني ممّا تمنع به نفسك دنوت منك فقطعت حبائلك وخلّصتك ممّا أنت فيه. فثق بما أقول واطمئنّ إليه فإنّه ليس أحد أبعد من الخير إلّا اثنان منزلتهما واحدة وصفتهما مختلفة أحدهما من لا يثق بأحد والآخر من لا يثق به أحد. وإنّ لك عندي الوفاء بما جعلت لك من نفسي فاقبل منّي واسترسل إليّ ولا تؤخّر العمل فلعلّ الصيّاد يأتيك فتلقى ما تكره وأقع فيما لا أحبّ فإنّ العاقل لا يؤخّر عمله ولتطب نفسك ببقائي كما طابت نفسي ببقائك فإنّ كلّ واحد منّا تسبّب خلاصه بصاحبه بعون الله تعالى كما أنّ السفينة والركّاب في البحر تخرج السفينة بالركّاب وبهم تخرج السفينة وكلّ ذلك يأتي عليه مقادير بما هو آتٍ.

٦،١٠ فلمّا سمع السنّور مقال الجرذ عرف صدقه وسُرّ بذلك وقال للجرذ أنا على قولك فورًا لا أشكّ في صدقك عندي فيه فأنا قابل هذا الصلح الذي أرجو لنفسي ولك به الخلاص وسأشكر ذلك لك أيّام حياتي ومجازيك به أحسن الجزاء.

قال الجرذ فإذا دنوت منك فضمّني إليك والطف بي فإنّه إذا رأى ابن عرس والبومة منك ما يعرفان به صلحنا انصرفا عنّا وأقبلت على قرض حبائلك.

قال السنّور أفعل ذلك ونعمة.

فدنا منه الجرذ فالتزمه السنّور صالحه وسُرّ به فلمّا رأى ابن عرس والبومة ذلك يئسا وانصرفا خائبين.

٧،١٠ وأخذ الجرذ في قطع حبائل السنّور فاستبطأه السنّور في قطع الحبائل وقال ما لي أراك كأنّك لست تجدّ في قطع حبائلي فإن كنت لمّا ظفرت بحاجتك تغيّرت عمّا كنت عليه وتوانيت في حاجتي فما ذلك من فعل الصالحين ولا من أخلاق أهل الكرم ولا من صنع أهل الوفاء فقد كان لك في عاجل مودّتي من النفع والخلاص من الهلكة ما قد رأيت فأنت حقيق أن تكافئني بذلك وألّا تذكر سالف العداوة بيننا فإنّ الذي حدث بيني وبينك من الصلح حقيق[١] أن ينسيك ذلك مع ما في

---

١ كذا ع، پ٣٤٦٦؛ ساقطة من الأصل.

me as you would your own life. Trust what I say and rely on me, for no one is farther off the mark than two persons who, though of different character, are on equal footing: the person who trusts no one and the person whom no one trusts. Rest assured I'll keep my promise. Accept my offer and have confidence in me. And don't delay: the hunter may return and the outcome will be equally unpleasant for both of us. A wise person doesn't procrastinate. Take as much pleasure in my survival as I will take in yours. Each of us, with God's help, will be the cause of the other's salvation, like a ship and its crew: the ship brings the crew home, and the crew brings the ship home to port. All this comes to pass as ordained."[53]

The cat was delighted, recognized the truth of the rat's words, and replied 10.6
at once, "I agree with what you say, and I don't doubt your honesty. I agree to this truce, which I hope will save us both. I will thank you as long as I live, and will reward you well."

The rat said, "Embrace me gently when I approach. The weasel and the owl will go away when they see the evidence of our truce, and I'll start gnawing through your cords."

"With pleasure!" exclaimed the cat.

The rat approached, and the cat drew him close and made peace. The weasel and the owl left in disappointment and frustration.

The rat began to bite through the cords. The cat, thinking he was work- 10.7
ing too slowly, said, "I don't think you're serious about cutting my bonds. If you've changed your mind now that you've gotten what you need and have become indifferent to what I need, that's not how generous, noble, and loyal people behave. My prompt display of affection benefited you by saving you from destruction, as you saw. You ought to reciprocate and not brood over our former hostility. What has happened between us should make you forget all about it. Think also of the merits of loyalty and the evil consequences of treachery. A noble person is ever grateful, never malicious: a single favor makes him forget many insults. The swiftest punishment, they say,

الوفاء من الفضل والأجر وما في الغدر من سوء العاقبة فإنّ الكريم لا يكون إلّا شكورًا غير حقود تنسيه الخلّة الواحدة ممّا يسرّه الخلال الكثيرة ممّا ساء. وأعجل العقاب عقاب الغدر والأيمان الكاذبة ومن إذا تُضرّع إليه وسئل[1] العفو لم يرحم ولم يعفُ ولم يغفر.

٨.١٠ قال الجرذ إنّ الصديق صديقان طائع ومضطرّ وكلاهما يلتمس المنافع ويحترس من[2] المضارّ. فأمّا الطائع فيُسترسل إليه ويُعمل له[3] على كلّ حال وأمّا المضطرّ فإنّ له حالة يُسترسل إليه فيها وأخرى أن يُحترس منه فيها. فلا يزال العاقل يرتهن بعض حاجته منه ببعض ما يتّقي[4] ويخاف. وليس عامّة التواصل بين المتواصلين إلّا لطلب عاجل النفع وما هو له. وأنا وافٍ لك فيما جعلت لك ومحترس منك مع ذلك من حيث أخافك أن يصيبني منك مثل ما نحن فيه ممّا ألجأني إلى مصالحتك وألجأك إليّ. فثق بذلك فإنّ لكلّ عمل حينًا يُعمَل فيه ولا يُجاوَز به حينه فأنا قاطع حبائلك لحين القطع وتارك منها عقدة أرتهنك بها فلا أقطعها إلّا في الساعة التي أعرف أنّك تشتغل بنفسك فيها عنّي وذلك عند مقابلة الصيّاد.

٩.١٠ فقطع الجرذ الحبائل إلّا عقدة واحدة ثمّ لزم مكانه تكرّمًا ووفاءً حتّى إذا أصبحا أقبل الصيّاد من بعيد فلمّا رآه السنّور[5] استسلم للموت وقال الجرذ[6] هذا الوقت الذي أخّرت له قطع السلك.[7] فأخذ الجرذ في قطع السلك فلم يدن الصيّاد منهما حتّى قطعه على سوء ظنّ من السنّور ودهش وخوف من الهلكة فلمّا فلت السنّور أقبل لا يلتفت إلى شيء عدوًا الى الشجرة وصعدها وانجحر الجرذ وأخذ الصيّاد حبائله مقطّعة وانصرف خائبًا.

١٠.١٠ ثمّ إنّ الجرذ خرج بعد ذلك من جحره فرأى السنّور من بعيد فكره الدنوّ منه وناداه السنّور فقال أيّها الصديق الذي بلاؤه عندي حسن ما يمنعك من الدنوّ منّي فأجزيك بأحسن ما أوليتني. هلمّ إليّ ولا تقطع إخائي فإنّه من اتّخذ صديقًا

---

١ كذا ع، ش؛ الأصل: سأل. ٢ كذا ر؛ الأصل: عن. ٣ ويُعمل له: كذا ل٢؛ الأصل: ويعمل. ٤ الأصل: سقى. ٥ كذا پ٣٤٦٦؛ ساقطة من الأصل. ٦ كذا ش، ع، پ٣٤٦٦؛ ساقطة من الأصل. ٧ السلك: الأصل: السلك فلم تدن.

is the punishment of treachery and perjury, or of a merciless person who, entreated and begged for forgiveness, neither pardons nor forgives."

The rat said, "Friends are of two kinds: those who become friends freely and those who do so out of necessity. Each kind seeks benefits and protection from harm. One can feel at ease with someone who freely becomes a friend, and will accommodate that friend in any situation. Sometimes one can feel at ease with a friend acquired out of necessity, but sometimes one must be wary. The wise person always withholds the fulfillment of part of such a friend's needs as security against what he guards against and fears. Most people maintain relationships for the sake of immediate benefits. I will keep my promise, but will also be careful not to suffer at your hands the very thing that compelled me to seek a truce with you and compelled you to grant it to me. Be confident. Every action has its time and should not be undertaken at the wrong time. I'll cut your cords at the right time, but for now I'm leaving one knot as security: I'll cut it only when I know you're too preoccupied with saving your own life to think about me. That will be when the hunter approaches." 10.8

So the rat cut the cords, except for the last knot, and stayed by the cat, nobly fulfilling his promise. In the morning, the hunter approached from afar. The cat resigned himself to death. "This," said the rat, "is the time I was waiting for to cut the cord." And he began cutting the last cord. Before the hunter arrived, he was done cutting it—but the cat was all the while full of mistrust, apprehension, and mortal fear. When the cat escaped, he ran straight for the tree and climbed up it, and the rat dived into his hole. The hunter collected his mangled snares and left empty-handed. 10.9

Sometime later, the rat came out of his burrow. He saw the cat at a distance, but was reluctant to approach him. "Gallant friend," called the cat, "what is keeping you from coming near so that I can reward you for your good deed? Come! Don't break off our friendship! Anyone who makes a friend and fails to cultivate his friendship and affection loses friendship's fruits and benefits, and his companions despair of deriving any benefit from him. I must try to reward you. The favor you did me can never be forgotten. 10.10

ثمّ أضاع حفظه وصداقته وقرب مودّته حُرم ثمرة الإخاء ومنفعته ويئس من منفعة الإخوان ويدك عندي بيضاء لا تُنسى وأنا حقيق بالتماس مكافأتك فإنّك ما بقيت فلا تخافنّ منّي غدراً وإنّ ما قبلي لك مبذول. ثمّ حلف له على ذلك واجتهد في اليمين.

١١،١٠ فأجابه الجرذ فقال له إنّه ربّ صداقة باطنها عداوة وهي أشدّ ضرّاً من العداوة الظاهرة وإنّ الذي لا يحسن مداراة الخليل بعد العداوة ولا مصارمة العدوّ بعد الصداقة يجعل الخليل عدوّاً ويمكّن من نفسه العدوّ. والمظهر بلسانه من النصح خلاف ما يواري ضميره من الغشّ فهو أعدى عدوّ ولا سيّما إذا كانت عداوته جوهريّة فإنّه إنّما دعا إلى المخالّة والمصاحبة حاجة اضطرّته إلى عدوّه فمن لم يحترس من هذا كان كالراكب على ناب فيل مغتلم فينام. وإنّما سمّي الصديق صديقاً لما يرجى من منفعته والعدوّ عدوّاً لما يُخاف من ضرّه فالعاقل إذا رجا نفع العدوّ أظهر له الصداقة وإذا خاف ضرّ الصديق له أظهر له العداوة.

١٢،١٠ ألا ترى البهائم إنّما تتبعها أولادها رجاء غذائها[١] فإذا انقطع ذلك انصرفت عنها. وكما أنّ السحاب يفشو ساعة ويتقطّع أخرى ويمطر ساعة ويقلع أخرى كذلك العاقل يتلوّن على إخوانه بمتلوّنات الأمور على اختلاف حالات الأصحاب فينبسط تارة وينقبض أخرى ويسترسل ساعة ويحترس أخرى ويرضى تارة ويسخط أخرى ويتجلّد تارة ويستكين أخرى. وربّما قطع الصديق عن صديقه بعض الحوادث فلم يخف شرّه لأنّ أصل أمره لم يكن عداوة فأمّا من كان أصل أمره عداوة ثمّ أحدث صداقة لحاجة حملته على ذلك فإنّه إذا ذهب الأمر الذي حمله على ذلك تحوّل عداوة وصار إلى أصل أمره كالماء الذي يُسخّن بالنار فإذا رُفع عنها عاد بارداً.

١٣،١٠ فمن كانت عداوته جوهريّة فليس المصاحبة له برأي الأريب إلّا لحاجة إليه. ولا عدوّ أضرّ لي عداوة منك وقد اضطرّتني وإيّاك حاجة ونازل بلاء الجأني إلى المصالحة لينتفع بعضنا ببعض فقد ذهب الأمر الذي احتاج كلّ واحد منّا إلى

---

١ الأصل: عداوها.

As long as I live, fear no treachery from me. Everything I have will be given unsparingly." The cat solemnly swore to this.

"Many a friendship," replied the rat, "conceals hostility within and is even more dangerous than open hostility. If you're not skilled at soothing a friend's feelings after hostility or breaking up with an enemy after friendship, you'll make an enemy out of your friend and give your enemy power over you. The worst of enemies is the person who gives voice to fine words that are at odds with the deceit hidden in his heart, especially if the hostility is innate and the association and friendship were occasioned by necessity. To fail to be on guard against this is like riding on the tusk of a rutting elephant and falling asleep. Friends are called friends only because of the benefit we expect from them, and enemies are called enemies because of the harm we fear from them. If a wise man hopes to benefit from an enemy, he makes a show of friendship; and if he fears harm from a friend, he makes a show of hostility. 10.11

"Haven't you seen how young animals follow their mothers hoping for nourishment, and when that stops, they go on their way? The wise person changes his disposition in response to changing circumstances and the changing moods of his companions, just as clouds form one moment and disperse the next, shed rain one moment and withhold it the next. Sometimes he will be open, sometimes reserved; sometimes easygoing, sometimes cautious; sometimes pleased, sometimes angry; sometimes harsh, sometimes compliant. Sometimes friend is separated from friend by changes in circumstances, but the friend who has been separated from his friend will fear no evil, because there was no underlying hostility. But when hostility is the underlying reality, and friendship is occasioned by a need that drives the person to it, the relationship will turn into enmity and revert to its underlying reality as soon as the cause occasioning the friendship disappears—just as water heated on a fire becomes cold once taken off the fire. 10.12

"It isn't a good idea to associate with someone whose enmity is innate unless you need to. No enemy can be more harmful to me than you. Misfortune forced us to call a truce for our mutual benefit. I'm afraid that hostility will return now that we no longer have a reason to need each other. The weak person stands to gain nothing by remaining in the vicinity of a 10.13

صاحبه وأخاف أن تعود العداوة إذا ذهب ذلك الأمر. ولا خير للضعيف في قرب العدوّ القويّ ولا للذليل في قرب العدوّ[1] العزيز. ولا أعلم لك قبلي حاجة إلّا أن تريد أكلي ولا أظنّ بك إلّا شرّاً فيما تدعوني به إلى نفسك من لطيف المنطق. ولا أرى رأياً في الثقة بك وقد يقال إنّ الضعيف المحترس بإذن الله من العدوّ أقرب إلى السلامة من القويّ المغترّ بالضعيف من الأعداء. والعاقل يصانع عدوّه ويظهر ودّه ويريه من نفسه الاسترسال إليه إذا لم يجد من ذلك بدّاً ويعجّل الانصراف عنه إذا صار عنه غنيّاً. واعلم أنّ سريع الاسترسال لا يكاد يستقيل عثرته. والعاقل يفي لمن صالح بما جعل له ولا يثق لنفسه بمثل ذلك من أحد[2] وقد قالت العلماء إنّه ينبغي للعاقل أن يصالح العدوّ الجريء ويحمل التضرّع إليه في حسن الحاجة ويتجنّبه في حال الغنى عنه ولا يثق به. وكان يقال لا تؤثر على البعد من عدوّك شيئاً ما استطعت. ولا شيء من السلامة لي في نفسي ولك بالوفاء بعهدك أحزم من أن أباعد نفسي منك وكذلك لا أرى لك شيئاً أسلم لنفسك من التباعد من الصيّاد في السلامة وأنا أودّك من بعيد[3] ولا عليك أن تجازيني بمثل ذلك والجملة التي ينقطع عنها المنطق أنّه لا سبيل إلى اجتماعنا إلّا أن تنزل نازلة مثل الذي جمعني وإيّاك.

١ ولا للذليل . . . العدوّ: كذا ش، ع، پ٣٤٦٦، پ٣٤٧٥؛ ساقطة من الأصل. ٢ والعاقل . . . أحد: كذا ش، پ٣٤٧٥، ع؛ الأصل: اداكان سق من نفسه بالوفا ولا سق لها بمىل دلك. ٣ وأنا . . . بعيد: كذا ل٢؛ ساقطة من الأصل.

powerful enemy; the humble person stands to gain nothing by remaining in the vicinity of a proud foe. I know of no need you have for me, other than a desire to eat me. I think you harbor evil intentions toward me when you address me with such gentle words. I don't think it's a good idea for me to trust you. As the saying goes, the weakling who guards against his enemy is more likely, God willing, to remain safe than a powerful enemy taken in by a weak foe. A wise man flatters his enemy, feigns affection, and pretends to be at ease with him when he must, but gets away from him as fast as he can when he has no further need. If we're too quick to let down our guard, we can hardly beg pardon for our downfall. A wise man keeps his promise to the one with whom he has made a truce, but doesn't trust anyone to do the same to him. As scholars have said, a wise man should make peace with a bold enemy and abase himself to him when there is a need to do so, but should avoid him when he has no need for him and should not trust him. They also say that above all you should prefer to keep as far as possible from your enemy. When it comes to the safety of my life and your keeping your promise, the most prudent course is for me to keep my distance from you; similarly, I think the safest thing for you is to keep away from the hunter. I'll be your friend from a distance, and there is no need for you to reciprocate. When all is said and done, there is no way for us to meet, except in the case of a misfortune like the one that previously brought both of us together."

باب الملك والطائر فنزة[١]

وهو مثل أهل الترات والذحول والذي ينبغي لبعضهم من الاحتراس من بعض

١.١١ قال الملك للعالم قد سمعت مثل الرجل الذي اكتنفته أعداؤه فاستظهر ببعضهم وصالحه حتّى تخلّص ممّا خاف ووفى وسلم فاضرب لي مثل أهل الترات والذحول وما[٢] ينبغي لبعضهم من اتّقاء بعض.

٢.١١ قال العالم زعموا أنّ ملكًا من الملوك كان له طائر يسمّى فنزة[٣] وكان كيّسًا ناطقًا وكان معه فرخ له فأمر الملك بفنزة وفرخه فجُعلا عند امرأة له كانت سيّدة نسائه وأمرها بالاستيصاء به وبفرخه وأنّ امرأته تلك ولدت غلامًا فألف الفرخ الغلام فكانا يلعبان جميعًا وكان فنزة يذهب إلى الجبل في كلّ يوم فيأتي منه بثمرتين من فواكه الجبل لم يعرفهما أحد فيطعم إحداهما فرخه ويطعم الأخرى ابن الملك فأسرع ذلك في نباتهما وقوّتهما حتّى استبان ذلك فيهما فازداد فنزة على الملك كرامة حتّى إذا كان ذات يوم وفنزة غائب في الجبل وثب الفرخ في حجر ظئر الغلام فغضب من ذلك فأخذ الفرخ وضرب به الأرض فقتله.

٣.١١ فلمّا جاء فنزة ورأى[٤] فرخه مقتولًا حزن وصاح وقال قبحًا لصحبة الملوك الذين لا عهد لهم ولا وفاء وويح من ابتلي بصحبتهم فإنّه لا حريم لهم ولا حميم ولا ذمام لأحد عندهم ولا يحبّون أحدًا ولا يكرمون إلّا أن يكون بهم حاجة إليهم أو يطمعوا عندهم في غناء او يحتاجون إليه فيقرّبونه عند ذلك فإذا قضوا منهم حاجتهم فلا ودّ ولا إخاء الذين لا يجزون بحسن البلاء ولا يغفرون الذنب إنّما أمورهم فخر ورياء وسمعة يستصغرون ما يركبون من عظيم الذنوب ويستعظمون اليسير إذا خولف

---

١ الأصل: قتره. ٢ الأصل: وهل. ٣ كذا ش؛ الأصل: قبره. ٤ كذا ش، ع، پ٣٤٦٦؛ الأصل: راى.

The King and the Bird Finzah[54]

A parable about aggrieved parties who have reason to retaliate and how each should guard against the other.

The king said to the philosopher, “I have heard your parable about someone surrounded by enemies, who saved himself from peril, kept his promise, and remained safe by enlisting the help of and making a truce with one of his enemies. Now tell me a parable about aggrieved parties who have reason to retaliate against each other and how each should guard against the other.” 11.1

The philosopher told the following tale: Once, they say, there was a king who had a bird named Finzah. The bird was clever and could talk, and was the father of a chick. The king commanded that Finzah and his chick be kept in his principal wife’s apartment, and ordered her to care for them. Then this wife gave birth to a son. The chick became fond of the boy and they became playmates. Finzah went to the mountains every day and brought back two mysterious fruits; one he fed to his chick, and the other to the king’s son. This so hastened their growth and increased their strength that the king noticed it and honored Finzah even more. One day, while Finzah was away in the mountains, the chick hopped onto the lap of the boy’s nurse. The boy became angry, grabbed the chick, and dashed it to the ground, killing it. 11.2

When Finzah returned and saw his chick lying dead, he cried out in grief, “Fie on the companionship of kings, who know neither trustworthiness nor loyalty! Woe to anyone who has the misfortune to be their companion! They have no real friends, hold no one sacred, and love no one. They honor and cultivate only those whom they need or want to benefit from. But the moment their need is satisfied, it’s farewell to affection and friendship! They reward no good deed and forgive no sin. Their life is nothing but pomp, ostentation, and acclaim. They dismiss their own crimes as trivial, but treat the slightest opposition to their whims as a crime.” Then he said, “I will 11.3

فيه هواهم. ثمّ قال إنّه ينبغي لي أن أنتقم لفرخي من الكفور الغادر الذي لا رحمة له القاتل قرنه وصاحب ملاعبته ومؤاكلته. ثمّ وثب في وجه الغلام ففقأ عينيه برجليه ثمّ طار حتّى وقع على مكان مشرف حريز.

٤،١١ فبلغ ذلك الملك فجزع جزعًا وطمع في أن يحتال لفنزة حتّى يظفر به فركب بخيله ووقف حيث يسمعه الصوت فناداه وقال له إنّك آمن فأقبل إليّ.

فأبى فنزة ذلك وقال له اعلم أيّها الملك أنّ الغادر معاقب بغدره وأنّه وإن أخطأ عاجل العقوبة لم يخطئه آجلها حتّى إنّ عقوبته لتدرك الأعقاب وأعقاب[1] الأعقاب وإنّ ابنك غدر بابني فعجّلت له العقوبة.

قال له الملك لعمري لقد غدرناك فانتقمت منّا فليس لك قبلنا ولا لنا قبلك وتر مطلوب فارجع إلينا آمنًا.

٥،١١ قال فنزة لست راجعًا إليك وإنّ ذوي الرأي قد نهوا عن قرب الموتور وقالوا لا يزدك لطف الحقود بك ولينه بالكلام وتكرمته إيّاك إلّا وحشة منه وسوء ظنّ به فإنّك لا تجد للموتور الحقود أمانًا هو أوثق من الذعر ولا حرز أحرز منه من البعد عنه والاحتراس منه. وكان يقال إنّ العاقل إنّما يعدّ أبويه من الأصدقاء ويعدّ الإخوة رفقاء والأزواج من الألفاء والبنين ذكرًا والبنات خصمًا والأقارب غرماء ويعدّ نفسه فريدًا وحيدًا. فأنا اليوم الفريد الحزين قد تزوّدت من عندكم من الحزن حملًا ثقيلًا لا يحمله معي أحد وأنا ذاهب فعليك السلام.

٦،١١ قال الملك إنّك لو لم تكن اجتزيت منّا ما صنعنا بك ولو كان صنيعك بنا[2] عن غير ابتداء منّا بالغدر لكان الأمر كما ذكرت فأمّا إذ[3] كان بدء ذلك من قبلنا فما ذنبك وما الذي يمنعك من الثقة بنا فهلمّ فارجع.

قال فنزة إنّ للأحقاد في القلوب مواقع متمكّنة موجعة فالألسنة لا تصدق عن القلوب والقلب على القلب أعدل شهادة من[4] اللسان وقد علمت أنّ قلبي لا يشهد للسانك ولا قلبك للساني.

١ كذا ش، ع، پ٣٤٧٥، ي (٦٣): الأصل: اواعقاب. ٢ الأصل: منا. ٣ كذا ل٢؛ الأصل: إذا. ٤ أعدل...شاهدة من: كذا ي (١١٠)؛ الأصل: أعدل شاهد من.

avenge my chick's death on that ungrateful, merciless wretch who killed his comrade, the playmate who shared his meals." So saying, he jumped onto the boy's face and scratched out the boy's eyes with his feet; then he flew away and perched beyond anyone's reach.

The king was overcome with grief at the report of this and determined to 11.4
trick Finzah and trap him. So he rode forth and, halting where he could make his voice heard, called out, "You will be safe. Come to me!"

But Finzah refused and said, "King, traitors are punished for their treachery. Even if they escape immediate punishment, they won't escape it in the long run: punishment may even overtake their children and their children's children. Your son behaved treacherously to my son, and I exacted swift punishment."

"True, we did this to you," said the king. "But now that you've avenged yourself on us, you have no further grievance against us, nor we against you; so come back to us in safety."

"I won't come back," replied Finzah. "People who understand such things 11.5
have forbidden us to approach people with an injury to avenge. The more kindness, gentleness, and hospitality displayed by someone with a rancorous heart, they say, the more uneasy you should be; you'll find no better way of keeping safe from someone with a grievance than fear, distance, and caution. A wise man, they say, regards his parents merely as friends, his brothers merely as comrades, his wives merely as companions, his sons merely as a memorial, his daughters merely as liabilities, his relatives merely as rivals, and himself as solitary and alone. Today I am sad and solitary. Because of you I now shoulder a heavy burden of sorrow that I alone carry. I am leaving. Goodbye!"

The king said, "It would be as you say had you not repaid us for what we 11.6
did to you, and had you not reacted to our prior treachery. But since we acted first, what wrong have you done? What prevents you from trusting us? Come back!"

"Grudges hide in the heart and fester," replied Finzah. "Men's tongues don't speak the truth about their hearts. The testimony of the heart about the heart is truer than the testimony of the tongue. I know that my heart doesn't testify to the truth of your tongue, nor your heart to the truth of my tongue."

قال الملك ألست تعلم أنّ الضغائن والأحقاد تكون[١] بين كثير من الناس فمن كان منهم له عقل كان على إماتة الحقد أحرص منه على تربيته.

قال فنزة إنّ ذلك لكما ذكرت فليس ينبغي لذي الرأي أن يظنّ مع ذلك بالموتور الحقود أنّه ناسٍ ما وُتر به ولا مضرب عنه وذو الرأي يتخوّف المكر والحيل ويعلم أنّ كثيرًا من الأعداء لا يستطاع بالشدّة والمكابرة حتّى يصاد بالرفق والملاينة كما يصاد الفيل الوحشيّ بالفيل الداجن.

٧،١١ قال الملك إنّ الكريم لا يترك إلفه ولا يقطع إخوانه ولا يضيّع الحفاظ وإن هو خاف على نفسه حتّى إنّ هذا الخلق في أوضع الدوابّ منزلة وقد عرفنا أنّ ناسًا من السند يذبحون الكلاب ويأكلونها فيرى الكلب الذي قد ألفهم ذلك من صنيعهم فيمنعه إلفه إيّاهم من مفارقتهم.[٢]

٨،١١ قال فنزة إنّ الأحقاد مخوفة حيث كانت وأخوفها وأشدّها أمرًا ما كان في أنفس الملوك فإنّ الملوك يدينون بالانتقام ويرون الطلب بالوتر[٣] مكرمة وفخرًا ولا ينبغي للعاقل أن يغترّ بسكوت الحقود إذا سكتت فإنّما مثل الحقد في القلب ما لم يجد متحرّكًا مثل الجمر المكنون ما لم يجد حطبًا وليس ينفكّ الحقد من تطلّع إلى العلل كما تتطلّع النار للحطب فإذا وجد أدنى ريح استعر استعار النار والنار تطفئها بالماء والحقد لا يطفئه ماء ولا كلام ولا لين ولا رفق ولا تضرّع ولا خضوع ولا شيء دون تلف الأنفس[٤] مع أنّه ربّ واتر يطمع في مراجعة الموتور لما يرجو أن يقدر عليه من النفع له والدفع[٥] عنه وأنا أضعف من أن أقدر لك على ما يذهب ما في نفسك ولو كانت نفسك لي على ما تقول لكان[٦] ذلك عنّي مغيّبًا ولو رجعت إليك لم أزل في خوف ووحشة وسوء ظنّ ما اصطحبنا وليس فيما بيني وبينك إلّا الفراق وأنا أقرأ عليك السلام.

---

١ كذا ش، ع، پ٣٤٧٥؛ ساقطة من الأصل. ٢ فيرى . . . مفارقتهم: الأصل: فرى الكلب الدى الف دلك من صنيعهم لا بمنعه الفهم من مفاركهم. ٣ ويرون . . . بالوتر: كذا ش، ع، پ٣٤٦٦، ي (١١١)؛ الأصل: وراهم الاىصار ويرون ذلك الوتر. ٤ تلف الأنفس: كذا ع؛ الأصل: قلب النفس. ٥ كذا ش، ع؛ الأصل: والرفع. ٦ كذا پ٣٤٦٦؛ الأصل: ما كان.

"Surely you know," responded the king, "that although resentments and grudges exist between many people, a wise man is more eager to quell hatred than to nurture it."

"It is indeed as you say," replied Finzah. "Nonetheless, it's unwise to suppose that an injured party full of resentment will simply forget and turn away from his injury. A wise person fears deceit and cunning; he knows that many enemies who cannot be overcome by brute force are ensnared by gentleness and mildness, just as a wild elephant is ensnared by using a tame one."

The king said, "Even if he fears for his life, a man of noble character 11.7
doesn't leave his friend, abandon his brothers, or allow the memory of friendship to fade. We find this virtue in even the lowliest of animals. Some people in Sind are notorious for slaughtering dogs and eating them; even though a canine companion may see this, his friendship for them will keep him from leaving them."

Finzah said, "Hatreds are to be feared wherever they exist, but the stron- 11.8
gest hatreds are those that dwell in the minds of kings. Kings make a religion of revenge; they see vengeance as a noble deed worth boasting about. A wise man shouldn't be fooled when hatred is quiescent; as long as it finds nothing to stir it, hatred in the heart is like a hidden coal without wood to burn. Hatred constantly yearns for pretexts, just as fire yearns for wood; and it flares up in the slightest breeze. Water quenches fire, but no water, words, softness, gentleness, entreaty, or humility—nothing less than people's lives—can quench hatred. In spite of this, those who have caused injury, hoping for benefits or protection, are often eager for the aggrieved party's return. I, however, am too weak to do anything for you that will dispel your feelings. And even if you felt toward me as you say, it would be impossible for me to know; if I returned, I should live in fear, disquiet, and misgiving as long as we were together. Between me and you there can only be separation. I therefore bid you farewell."

قال الملك لو علمت أنّه لا يستطيع أحد لأحد ضرّاً ولا نفعاً ولا صغيراً ولا كبيراً إلّا بقدر مقدور كما أنّ خلق ما يُخلق وولاد ما يُولَد ليس منه إلى الخلائق شيء إلّا كذلك فناء ما يفنى وهلاك ما يهلك ليس للعباد منه شيء إلّا بقدر فليس لك فيما صنعت بابني ولا لابني[1] في هلاك فرخك ذنب إنّما ذلك بقدر مقدور وكنّا له علّلاً وأنا محتمل ما كان منك ولا سيّما إذ[2] كان ذنبنا إليك ابتداءً وكان مع ذلك أعظم من ذنبك إلينا. ٩،١١

قال فنزة إنّ أمر القضاء والقدر لكما ذكرت ولكن لا يمنع الحازم ذلك من توقّي المخاوف والاحتراس من المكاره. ولا ينبغي لمن عقل أن يعذر نفسه ممّا يأتي من المعاصي وقد خوّف الله وأمر ونهى ولكنّا نصدّق بالقدر ولا ندع مع[3] ذلك الأخذ بالحزم والاستعانة بالله عزّ وجلّ في الاحتراس ممّا نخاف. وقد تخبرني نفسي أنّك تكلّمني بكلام غير صحيح فإنّ لسانك يؤدّي عن نفسك غير ما فيها والأمر ما بيني وبينك غير صغير لأنّ ابنك قتل ابني وأنا فقأت عيني ابنك فأنت تريد أن تستشفي منّي بقتلي وتحاولني عن نفسي ونفسي تكره الموت وكان يقال الفاقة بلاء والحزن بلاء وقرب العدوّ بلاء وفراق الأحبّة بلاء والسقم بلاء والهرم[4] بلاء ورأس البلاء الموت. وليس أحد بأعلم بما في نفس الموجع الحرّان ممّن[5] قد ذاق مثل ما به فأنا بما في نفسك من أمري عالم لما عندي منه ولا خير لي في صحبتك فإنّك لا تذكر صنيعي بابنك ولا أذكر صنيع ابنك بفرخي إلّا أحدث ذلك لقلوبنا تغييراً. ١٠،١١

قال الملك إنّه لا خير فيمن لا يستطيع الإعراض عن ما في نفسه والتناسي له حتّى لا يذكر منه شيئاً. ١١،١١

قال فنزة إنّ الرجل الذي في باطن قدمه[6] قرحة إن هو حرص على خفّة من المشي فلا بدّ أن ينكأها والرجل الأرمد إذا استقبل الريح فقد تعرّض لأن يزداد رمده وكذلك الواتر إذا دنا من الموتور فقد عرّض قرحته لإنكائها. ومن الرأي للعاقل توقّي

---

١ كذا ل٢؛ الأصل نابى. ٢ الأصل: إذا. ٣ الأصل: من. ٤ كذا ع، پ٣٤٧٥؛ الأصل: والهم. ٥ كذا ش، ع، پ٣٤٧٥، ي (٦٧)؛ الأصل: الا من. ٦ كذا ش، ع، پ٣٤٧٥؛ الأصل: رجليه.

The king replied, "Know that no harm or benefit, great or small, can be done, except by preordained fate. Just as created beings do not decide the creation of what is created or the birth of what is born, so too the perishing of what perishes and the destruction of what is destroyed occur by fate, not by the decision of God's servants. Therefore, you bear no guilt for what you did to my son, nor does my son bear any guilt for the destruction of your offspring. It happened in accordance with preordained fate, and we were merely its conduits.[55] Since our offense happened first and was greater than your offense toward us, I will forgive what occurred through you." 11.9

Finzah then said, "The role of what is destined and preordained is as you have said, but that should not prevent a prudent person from taking precautions and protecting himself against what he fears. No wise person should excuse the sins he commits, when God has provided us with warnings, commandments, and prohibitions. We believe in destiny; nevertheless, we continue to act prudently and ask for God's help in protecting us from what we fear. My soul tells me that you aren't speaking the truth; the words on your tongue don't reflect what is in your heart. The matter between us is no small thing. Your son killed my son, and I scratched out your son's eyes, so now you want to avenge yourself by killing me. You're looking for a way to trick me out of my life, but my soul rejects death. Poverty, they say, is an affliction; so too are sorrow, the proximity of enemies, separation from loved ones, sickness, and old age; but death is the greatest affliction. No one knows what is in the heart of one who is in pain and distress better than someone who has tasted the same thing. I know how you feel about me in your heart because my heart shares the same feeling. No good can come to me through associating with you. The memory of what I did to your son, or of what your son did to mine, will cause our hearts to change." 11.10

"There is no goodness in a man who cannot turn aside from something in his heart and consign it to oblivion, so that he remembers nothing of it," said the king. 11.11

Finzah replied, "If we try to walk quickly with a blister on the sole of our foot, we're sure to burst it; if we face the wind with sore eyes, we will exacerbate the inflammation. Similarly, a person who has inflicted an injury that

المتالف وتقدير الأمور وقلّة الاتّكال على القوّة والحيلة وقلّة الاغترار بما لا يأمن منه فإنّه من اتّكل على قوّته حمله ذلك على أن يسلك الطريق المخوف فقد سعى في حتف نفسه ومن لا يكون طعامه وشرابه بقدر فحمّل نفسه من ذلك ما لا تحتمل ولا تطيق فربّما كان سبب هلاكه ومن عظّم لقمته فوق مقدارها فربّما غصّ بها فمات ومن اغترّ وضيّع الحذر فهو أعدى لنفسه من أعدائه. وليس على أحد النظر في القدر الذي لا يُدرى ما يأتيه منه وما يصرف عنه ولكنّ عليه العمل وتكلّف الأخذ بالحذق في رأيه والقوّة في علمه ومخاصمة نفسه في ذلك.

١٢،١١ والعاقل لا يخيف أحدًا[١] ما استطاع ولا يقيم على خوف وهو يجد مذهبًا وأنا كثير المذاهب أرجو أن لا أذهب إلّا أصبت ما يغنيني فإنّ خلالًا خمسًا من تزوّدهنّ بلّغته حيث يريد وآنسته في الغربة وكسّبته المعيشة والإخوان وهنّ كفّ الأذى وحسن الأدب ومجانبة الذنب وكرم الخلق والنبل في العمل فإذا خاف العاقل على نفسه طابت نفسه عن المال والأهل والولد والوطن لأنّه يرجو الخلف في ذلك كلّه ولا يرجو من النفس خلفًا وشرّ المال ما لا يُنفق منه وشرّ الأزواج التي لا تؤاتي بعلها وشرّ الولد العاصي وشرّ الإخوان الخاذل لأخيه عند النكبات وشرّ الملوك من يخافه البريء ولا يواظب على حفظ أهل مملكته وشرّ البلاد بلاد ليس فيها أمن ولا خصب ولا خصب لي عندك ولا طمأنينة لنفسي في جوارك. ثمّ ودّع الملك وطار ذاهبًا عنـه.

١ أحدًا: كذا ش، ع، پ٣٤٦٦، پ٣٤٧٥، ي (٦٩)؛ الأصل: نفسه أبدًا.

demands retaliation runs the risk of reopening the wound if he approaches the injured party. A wise man must be wary of dangers, assess the situation, place little reliance on strength and craftiness, and avoid being deceived by those he doesn't trust. Relying on your own strength can lead you to follow a dangerous path and speed you to your own destruction. He who bites off more than he can chew often chokes to death. The fool who abandons caution is his own worst enemy. No one should scrutinize Fate, for no one knows what it will bring or avert; we should act resolutely, proceed decisively in our affairs, and keep account of ourselves.

"A wise man, as much as he is able, strikes fear into no one, and, when he 11.12
can find some other place to go, doesn't stay where there is fear. I have many places to go, and hope to prosper wherever I turn. There are five things, if you equip yourself with them, that will assist you to your destination, will keep you company in foreign lands, and will gain you a livelihood and friends. They are: avoidance of injury, good manners, keeping clear of sin, generosity of character, and high-minded acts. When a wise man fears for his life, he willingly forgoes wealth, family, children, and homeland, as these can all be replaced, but he cannot expect to replace his life. The worst wealth is wealth spent badly, the worst wife is ungracious to her husband, the worst child is a rebellious one, the worst brother abandons his brother in distress, the worst king is feared by the innocent and does not devote himself to the good of his people, and the worst country is one where there is neither safety nor prosperity. I can have no prosperity and no peace of mind near you." So saying, he bade the king farewell and flew away.

باب الأسد وابن آوى

مثل الملوك فيما بينهم وبين قرابتهم في مراجعة من يراجعون منهم بعد عقوبة أو جفوة تكون بعد ذنب.

قال الملك قد سمعت مقالتك في العدوّ الموتور الذي لا يطمئنّ إليه عدوّه فاضرب ١،١٢
لي مثل الملوك وأعوانهم.

قال العالم لو كان لا يراجع من أصابته منهم جفوة أو عقوبة عن جرم اجترمه ٢،١٢
إذاً لأضرّ ذلك بالأمور والأعمال ولكنّ الملك حقيق أن ينظر من ابتلي بشيء من ذلك وما عنده[١] من الغناء والذي يرجوه منه من النفع فإن كان ممّا يستعان به ويُوثَق برأيه وأمانته كان الملك أحقّ بالحرص على مراجعته[٢] فإنّ الملك لا يستطيع إلّا بالوزراء والأعوان ولا ينتفع بالوزراء والأعوان إلّا بالمودّة والنصيحة ولا تنفع المودّة والنصيحة إلّا مع الرأي والعفاف. وأعمال الملوك كثيرة وما[٣] يحتاجون إليه من الأعوان والعمّال[٤] كثير ومن[٥] يجمع منهم ما يُحتاج إليه من النصيحة وإصابة الرأي والعفاف قليل.

وإنّما السبيل في ذلك والوجه الذي يستقيم به العمل أن يكون الملك عالماً بمن ٣،١٢
يريد الاستعانة به وبأموره عارفاً ما[٦] عند كلّ رجل منهم من الغناء والرأي وما فيه من العيوب فإذا استقرّ ذلك عنده عن علمه وعلم أهل بيته وجّه لكلّ عمل من يعرف أنّ عنده من الرأي والنجدة والأمانة ما يحتاج إليه فيه ويعلم مع ذلك أنّ ما فيه من عيب إن كان فيه لا يضرّ بذلك العمل[٧] ثمّ على الملك بعد ذلك[٨] بتعاهد عمّاله وبنقد

---

١ عنده: الأصل: عنده لسى. ٢ مراجعته: الأصل: مراحعته منه. ٣ الأصل: وما لا. ٤ كذا ر؛ الأصل: والعمل.
٥ كذا ر؛ الأصل: وما. ٦ كذا ش، ع؛ ساقطة من الأصل. ٧ العمل: الأصل: العمل ومن لم. ٨ ثمّ... بعد ذلك: كذا ع؛ ساقطة من الأصل.

The Lion and the Jackal[56]

A parable about relations between kings and their courtiers; about restoring one of them to favor after a punishment or an estrangement due to an offense.

The king said, "Now that I've heard you speak about an aggrieved enemy who is not to be trusted, tell me a parable about kings and their assistants." 12.1

The philosopher said, "Were a king never to restore to favor any assistant who, for some offense, suffered estrangement or punishment, both he and his affairs would be harmed. A king should consider the potential usefulness of the individual who has endured such treatment; the king should be eager to restore him to favor if he is someone he can look to for assistance and rely on for his trustworthiness and sound judgment. A kingdom can be ruled only by means of ministers and assistants; ministers and assistants are useful only on account of their love and loyalty; and love and loyalty are useless without sound judgment and moderation. Kings require many assistants and officials to oversee their numerous affairs, but few men combine the necessary qualities of loyalty, soundness of judgment, and moderation. 12.2

"Things will not go well for a king unless he truly knows those he calls on for assistance—knows each man's usefulness and judgment, as well as his shortcomings. When he finds this out directly or through others in his retinue, he will assign to every task someone he knows to possess the necessary judgment, energy, and trustworthiness, and whose shortcomings, if any, will not spoil it. Furthermore, a king must monitor his officials, so that no official's good deeds and no official's misdeeds remain hidden. No good official should be left unrewarded and no incompetent official or one guilty 12.3

أمورهم حتّى لا يخفى عليه إحسان محسن ولا إساءة مسيء ثمّ عليه بعد ذلك أن لا يترك محسناً بغير جزاء ولا يقرّ مسيئاً ولا عاجزاً على العجز والإساءة فإنّه إن ترك ذلك تهاون المحسن واجترأ المسيء وفسدت الأمور وساء أدب الرعيّة وضاعت الأعمال والمثل في ذلك مثل ابن آوى والأسد.

قال الملك وكيف كان ذلك.

٤،١٢ قال العالم زعموا أنّه كان في أرض الهند ابن آوى وكان يتألّه ويتعبّد ويكون مع بنات آوى وذئاب وثعالب ولا يصنع بصنعهنّ ولا يغدر كما يغدرن ولا يظلم كما يظلمن ولا يأكل لحماً فخاصمته تلك السباع فقلن ليس نرضى سيرتك ولا رأيك الذي أنت عليه مع أنّ تألّهك لا يغني عنك شيئاً وإنّما أنت كبعضنا وإن تألّهت لأنّك تصحبنا وتسعى معنا.

٥،١٢ قال ابن آوى صحبتي إيّاكنّ على الاضطرار لا تؤثّمني إذا لم أؤثّم نفسي فإنّ الآثام ليست من قبل الأماكن ولا من قبل الأصحاب ولكنّها من قبل القلوب والأعمال فإنّه لو كان صاحب المكان الصالح يكون كلّ عمل فيه صالحاً وصاحب المكان السوء يكون كلّ عمل فيه سيّئاً لكان إذاً من قتل النفوس في المساجد بغير حقّها لم يأثم ومن عمل أعمال البرّ في بيوت النيران أثم وإنّما أصحبكم ببدني ولست بصاحب لكم بقلبي وعملي فإنّي أعرف ثمرة الأعمال.

٦،١٢ ولم يزل ابن آوى على حالته تلك حتّى شُهر بالورع والنسك والتألّه وبلغ من العفاف والصدق والإنابة أحسن ما بلغه أحد من نظرائه في زمانه حتّى بلغ أسداً كان ملك السباع بتلك الناحية فأرسل إليه الأسد فكلّمه وفاتشه فرأى عقلاً وحسن منطق فدعا به بعد أيّام فقال له إنّ ملكي كبير وأعمالي كثيرة وأنا إلى الأعوان محتاج وقد بلغني عنك تبتّل وعفاف ثمّ قدمت عليّ فازددت فيك رغبة حين كلّمتك وسمعت حسن مراجعتك فأنا مقلّدك من عملي عملاً جسيماً ورافعك إلى منزلة شريفة وجاعلك من خاصّتي.

of misconduct should be allowed to persist in his misconduct and incompetence; otherwise, the good official will become negligent, the bad official will be emboldened, the people will become demoralized, and everything will go awry. The parable of the jackal and the lion illustrates this."

"How does it go?" asked the king.

The philosopher told the following tale: They say that in the land of India 12.4
there once lived a jackal. He was God-fearing and pious, and although he lived among jackals, wolves, and foxes, he didn't behave like them by acting treacherously, wronging others, or eating meat. The other animals argued with him: "We don't approve of your way of life or your views. Your pious devotions won't do you a bit of good. You may engage in acts of devotion, but you're no different from us, because you still associate with us and run with us."

The jackal said, "I associate with you out of necessity, and it doesn't make 12.5
me a sinner if I don't make myself a sinner. Sins don't derive from locations or companions, but from hearts and actions. If being in a holy place rendered our actions there righteous, or being in an evil place rendered our actions there evil, it would be no sin to commit wanton murder in a mosque, while it would be a sin to perform charitable deeds in a fire temple. I associate with you only through my body, not through my heart and actions, for I know the fruit of actions."

The jackal persevered, and became renowned for piety, asceticism, and 12.6
devotion, surpassing all his contemporaries in abstemiousness, honesty, and humility. Word of him reached a lion who was king of the beasts in that region. The lion sent for him, examined him extensively, and, impressed with his mind and eloquence, invited him a few days later to become his companion. "My kingdom is vast, my works many, and I need assistants. I've received reports of your devoutness and abstemiousness. I'm even more pleased now that I've met you in person and have talked with you and heard your excellent replies. I will appoint you to high office, raise you to the ranks of the nobility, and make you a member of my inner circle."

قال ابن آوى إنّ الملوك أحقّ باختيار الأعوان فيما يهتمّون به من أمورهم وأعمالهم ٧،١٢
وأحقّ من ذلك أن لا يكرهوا على أعمالهم أحداً فإنّ[١] المكره لا يستطيع المبالغة في العمل وإنّي أيّها الملك كاره للعمل وليست لي به خبرة ولا بعمل السلطان رفق وأنت ملك السباع عندك من أجناس السباع عدد كثير فيهم نبل وقوّة وبهم على العمل حرص ولهم به وبالسلطان رفق وإن استعملتهم أغنوا عنك واغتبطوا لأنفسهم بما أصابوا من ذلك.

قال الأسد دع عنك هذا فإنّي غير معفيك من العمل.

قال ابن آوى إنّما يستطيع عمل السلطان وصحبتهم رجلان لست بواحد منهما ٨،١٢
إمّا فاجر مصانع ينال حاجته بفجوره[٢] ويسلم بمصانعته وإمّا مغفّل مهين لا يحسده أحد فأمّا من أراد أن يصحب السلطان بالصدق والنصيحة والعفاف ولا يخلط ذلك بمصانعة فقلّ ما يستقيم له ذلك وقلّ ما يدوم له صحبتهم فإنّه يجتمع عليه عدوّ السلطان وصديقه فيبغي عليه بالعداوة والخبّ والحسد فأمّا صديق السلطان فينافسه في منزلته ويبغي عليه فيها وأمّا عدوّ السلطان فيضطغن عليه لنصيحته وغنائه فإذا اجتمع عليه هذان الصنفان كان تعرّض للهلاك[٣] ويدفع الله.

قال الأسد لا يكوننّ بغي أصحابي عليك وحسدهم لك ممّا يعرض في نفسك فإنّي كافيك ذلك وبالغ بك ما أنت أهله في المنزلة والإكرام.

قال ابن آوى إن كان الملك يريد بي الإحسان فليدعني أعيش في هذه البرّيّة آمناً ٩،١٢
من أن أُحسد قليل الهمّ راضياً بمعيشتي من الماء ونبت الأرض فإنّي قد علمت أنّ صاحب السلطان يصل إليه في ساعة واحدة من الخوف والأذى ما لا يصل إلى غيره بالغ أمره وأنّ قليل العيش في أمن وطمأنينة خير من كثيره في خوف ونصب.

قال الأسد قد سمعت مقالتك فلا تخف شيئاً ممّا أراك تخوّفه ولا بدّ فاعلمنّ من الاستعانة بك.

---

١ كذا ر؛ الأصل: وان. ٢ كذا ر؛ الأصل: بحوره. ٣ كذا ش، ع، پ٣٤٦٦؛ الأصل: هلاك.

The jackal replied, "Kings indeed should choose assistants for their works and affairs, but they shouldn't force anyone to serve, because a reluctant assistant will not devote his best efforts to the office. I don't want the job, Your Majesty. I have no experience or skill in statecraft. As king of the beasts, you have animals of every kind at your disposal, ones with nobility and strength, skillful and eager to serve. If you employ them, they will count themselves lucky and bring you benefit." 12.7

"Enough said!" replied the lion. "I will not excuse you from the job."

"Only two sorts of people can associate with rulers and do their bidding," replied the jackal, "and I'm neither. The two sorts are an unscrupulous flatterer who gets what he wants through scheming and ensures his own safety through flattery, and a pitiful fool whom no one envies. Rarely do things turn out well for the person who would associate with a ruler on terms of truthfulness, sincerity, and modesty, untinged by flattery, for the ruler's foes and friends will join forces against him in envy, enmity, and deceit. The ruler's friends will compete with him for rank and envy him for it; the ruler's enemies will hate him for his good advice and service to the ruler. When both groups join forces against him, he is likely to perish, God forbid." 12.8

"Don't worry about the malice and envy of my companions," replied the lion. "I will protect you and raise you to the honor and rank you deserve."

"If the king wishes to show me kindness," said the jackal, "let him allow me to dwell in this wilderness, safe from envy. I have few worries and live contentedly on water and plants. A ruler's companion, I know, experiences more fear and annoyance in one hour than others experience in a lifetime: a little sustenance enjoyed in peace and tranquility is better than a great deal of it accompanied by fear and distress." 12.9

"I hear what you're saying," said the lion, "but set aside your fears. I must have your assistance."

قال ابن آوى أمّا إذا أبى الملك إلّا ما أبى[١] فليجعل لي عهداً إن بغى عليّ أحد من أصحابه ممّن هو فوقي لخافني على منزلته ومن هو دوني ممّن ينازعني في منزلتي فذكر للملك ذاكر منهم بلسانه أولسان غيره بشيء يريد به تحميل الملك عليّ أن لا يعجل وأن ويتثبّت فيما رُفع إليه من أمري ويفحص عنه ثمّ يصنع ما أراه الله تعالى فإذا وثقت من الملك بذلك أعنته بنفسي وعملت له فيما ولّاني بنصيحة واجتهاد وحرص على أن لا أجعل على نفسي سبيلاً. ١٠،١٢

قال الأسد فإنّ ذلك لك عليّ.

فولّاه الأسد خزانته واختصّه دون أصحابه بالمنزلة والمشاورة والرأي وازداد به على الأيّام عجباً وزاده كرامة وثقل ذلك على من يطيف بالأسد من أصحابه وعمّاله وعادوه وحسدوه وائتمروا ليحملوا عليه الأسد ويهلكوه فلمّا أجمعوا على ذلك من كيدهم وسوء خيانتهم عمدوا ذات يوم إلى لحم كان الأسد استطابه واستطرفه فأمر الأسد بوضعه في موضع طعامه ليعود إليه فسرقوه ثمّ أرسلوا به إلى منزل ابن آوى فخبّأوه في منزله في مخبأ لا يطّلع عليه أحد فلمّا كان من الغد دعا الأسد بغدائه ففُقد ذلك اللحم والتمسه فلم يوجَد وغاب ابن آوى وحضر القوم الذين اجتمعوا ليكيدوه فلمّا رأوا الأسد قد اشتدّ في السؤال عن ذلك اللحم حتّى غضب نظر بعضهم إلى بعض ثمّ قال أحدهم قول[٢] المخبر الناصح إنّه لا بدّ لنا أن نخبر الملك عن علمنا فيما يضرّه وينفعه وإن شقّ ذلك على من شقّ عليه أنّه قد بلغني أنّ ابن آوى كان ذهب باللحم إلى منزله. ١١،١٢

قال آخر ما أراه شبيهاً أن يكون فعل ذلك ولكن افحصوا عن ذلك فإنّ معرفة الخلائق شديدة. ١٢،١٢

قال آخر أجل لعمري ما تكاد السرائر تُعرف ولكنّكم إن فحصتم عن هذا ووجدتم ذلك اللحم في منزل ابن آوى فكلّ شيء كان يُذكَر لنا من عيوبه وخيانته حقّ ثمّ نحن أولى أن نصدّق عليه كلّ ما كان يقال عليه.

---

١ كذا پ٣٤٦٦؛ الأصل: الا ما ابا. ٢ كذا ش، ع، پ٣٤٦٦؛ الأصل: قال.

"If the king insists," replied the jackal, "let him promise that should any of his companions try to harm me, be it a superior who fears for his station or a subordinate who wishes to wrest my station from me, and should one of them, be it with his own lips or through someone else, mention to the king something intended to turn the king against me, the king will not act hastily against me, but will investigate and examine what has been brought to his attention and then do what God shows him to be best. If the king guarantees this, I will assist him with my life, and work for him in whatever he delegates to me with honest advice and diligent effort, striving not to expose myself to blame." 12.10

"You have my promise," said the lion.

The lion put the jackal in charge of his storeroom and preferred him over his other companions for his advice and judgment. With every passing day, he became more pleased with the jackal and increased his honors, much to the annoyance of the lion's companions and officials. Hostile and envious, they plotted to turn the lion against the jackal and do away with him. With this treacherous plan in mind, one day they sneaked into the king's larder and stole some meat that the lion, finding it especially tasty, had commanded to be stored there for later enjoyment. Then they had it hidden out of sight in the jackal's house. The next morning, the meat was missing and nowhere to be found when the lion called for his breakfast. The jackal was absent, but the artful conspirators were in attendance. The lion asked about the meat again and again and became angry. They looked at one another, and, in the tone of a well-meaning informant, one of them said, "When we know something that will harm the king or benefit him, it is our duty to inform him, whomever else it may distress. The jackal, I have been told, took the meat home with him." 12.11

Another said, "I think it unlikely that he would do this, but you must look into it. Character, after all, is very difficult to know." 12.12

Another said, "Yes, by my life, secret thoughts are hard to know. If you do look into this and find the meat in the jackal's house, everything we've been told about his faults and treachery is true, and we should believe everything that has been said against him."

قال آخر ما ينبغي لأحد أن يغترّ بما يعلم في نفسه من المخاتلة فضلاً عن غيره فإنّه لا يسلم صاحبها ولا تخفى له.

قال آخر وكيف يسلم من خاتل السلطان أو كيف يخفى ذلك له ومخاتلة الأصحاب لا تكاد تخفى. ١٣،١٢

قال آخر لقد خبّرني مخبّر عن ابن آوى بأمر عظيم ما وقع في نفسي حتّى سمعت كلامكم.

قال آخر لكنّي لم يخف عليّ أمره وخبثه أوّل ما رأيته وقد قلت مراراً واستشهدت فلاناً أنّ هذا الخادع المتنسّك لن يفتّش إلّا عن خيانة فاحشة وذنب عظيم.

قال آخر لئن كان[1] هذا المتألّه المتخشّع الذي كان يرينا أنّ عمله الذي يلي[2] مصيبة له وبلاء قد خان هذه الخيانة فإنّ[3] ذلك لمن أعجب العجب.

قال آخر لئن وُجد هذا حقّاً ما هي بالخيانة فقط ولكن مع الخيانة كفر النعمة والجرأة على الذنوب. ١٤،١٢

وقال آخر إنّكم أهل العدل والفضل ولا أستطيع أن أكذّبكم ولكن سيبين صدق هذا من كذبه لو قد أرسل الملك إلى بيت ابن آوى ففُتّش.

وقال آخر إن كان لا بدّ من فتش منزله فليعجل فإنّ عيونه وجواسيسه مبثوثة بكلّ مكان.

قال آخر إنّي قد علمت أنّ ابن آوى لو فُتّش منزله واطّلع على خيانته لاحتال بخبّه ومكره حتّى يشبّه على الملك فيعذره.

فلمّا توالوا بهذا الكلام وأشباهه حتّى وقع ذلك في نفس الأسد فأمر بابن آوى فدعي فقال له ما صنعت باللحم الذي كنت أمرتك بالاحتفاظ به. ١٥،١٢

قال قد دفعته إلى فلان صاحب الطعام ليقرّبه إلى الملك.

فدعا صاحب الطعام وكان ممّن يتابع القوم على أمرهم فسأله الأسد عن ذلك.

فقال ما دفع إليّ شيئاً.

---

١ لئن كان: كذا ع؛ الأصل: لكن. ٢ كذا ش؛ الأصل: نرى. ٣ الأصل: وان.

Another said, "No one should fool himself about the deceit he knows to be in his own soul, let alone in the souls of others, for the deceiver is never safe, and his deceptions won't stay hidden."

Another said, "How can someone get away with deceiving the ruler? 12.13
How can it be hidden from him, when deceit among friends can scarcely be hidden?"

Another said, "I was told something terrible about the jackal, but it made no impression on me until I heard your words."

Another said, "His true nature and dishonesty were obvious as soon as I laid eyes on him. As I've said many times—and I have a witness—this imposter who pretends to be so religious would turn out to be guilty of foul treachery and a great crime."

Another said, "What a great surprise if this pious fraud who protests to us that his office is nothing but toil and affliction has committed this treachery!"

Another said, "If it turns out to be true, not only is it treachery, but also 12.14
ingratitude and criminal effrontery."

Another said, "You are honest, upstanding people and I can't accuse you of lying, but if the king sends someone to search the jackal's house the facts will become clear."

Another said, "If it must be, let his house be searched quickly, for he has spies and informers everywhere."

Another said, "If the jackal's house is searched and his treachery becomes known, I know he'll resort to deceit and trickery to raise doubts in the king's mind, so that he pardons him."

They sowed suspicion in the lion's mind with comments like these and 12.15
more. He summoned the jackal. "What did you do with the meat I ordered you to keep?"

"I gave it to the chef to serve to the king."

The king therefore summoned the chef—he was on the side of the jackal's enemies—and questioned him.

"He gave me nothing," said the chef.

فبعث الأسد أمناءه ليفتّشوا منزل ابن آوى فوجدوا ذلك اللحم في منزله فأتوا به الأسد.

١٦،١٢ فدنا من الأسد ذئب لم يتكلّم في شيء من تلك الأمور وكان يظهر أنّه من العدول الذين لا يتكلّمون إلّا فيما استبان لهم أنّه حقّ فقال للأسد أمّا إن اطّلع الملك من ابن آوى على هذه الخيانة فلا يعفونّ عنه فإنّه إن عفا عنه لم يعد أحد يطلع الملك على خيانة خائن ولا ذنب مذنب.

فأمر الأسد بابن آوى أن يُخرَج من عنده وأن يُحتفظ به.

فقال عند ذلك بعض جلساء الأسد إنّي لأعجب من رأي الملك ومعرفته بالأمور كيف يخفى عليه معرفة أمر هذا الخائن وخبّه ومخادعته.

وقال آخر وأعجب من ذلك أنّي لأراه أن يصفح عنه بعد ما ظهر منه.

وأرسل بعضهم رسولاً إلى ابن آوى يسأله عن عذره[1] فرجع برسالة كاذبة غضب منها الأسد فأمر بابن آوى أن يُقتل.

١٧،١٢ وبلغ ذلك أمّ الأسد فعرفت أنّ الأسد قد عجل في أمره فأرسلت إلى الذين أُمروا بقتله أن يؤخّروه[2] ودخلت على ابنها فقالت لأيّ ذنب أمرت بابن آوى أن يُقتل.

فأخبرها الأسد بالأمر.

فقالت عجلت يا بنيّ وإنّما يسلم العاقل من الندامة بترك العجلة وبالأناة والتثبّت فإنّ العجول لا يزال يجتني من عجلته ثمرة الندامة لضعف رأيه وقلّة نظره وليس أحد أحوج إلى التؤدة والتثبّت من الملوك فإنّ المرأة بزوجها والولد بوالده والمتعلّم بالمعلّم والجند بالقائد والناسك بأهل الدين والعامّة بالملوك والملوك بالتقوى والعقل والتثبّت. ورأس الحزم للملك معرفة أصحابه وإنزالهم منازلهم واتّهام[3] بعضهم على بعض فإنّه إن وجد بعضهم إلى هلاك بعضهم سبيلاً أو إلى تهجين بلاء المبلين وإحسان المحسنين والتغطية على إساءة المسيئين[4] كان ذلك إليه سريعاً موثراً.

١ كذا ش، ع؛ الأصل: غدره. ٢ كذا ش، ع، پ٣٤٦٦؛ الأصل: يجرحوا. ٣ كذا ش، ع؛ الأصل: وإقدام. ٤ كذا ش، ع؛ الأصل: المسى.

The lion then sent his agents to search the jackal's house, where they found the meat and brought it to the lion.

A wolf had said nothing about the case, and had made a pretense of being 12.16
the kind of reliable witness who would speak only about what he knew for certain to be true. He approached the lion and said, "Now that the king has discovered this treachery, he mustn't pardon the jackal; if he does, no one will ever inform the king about any treachery or crime."

The lion commanded that the jackal be taken away and kept under guard.

Thereupon one of the lion's companions said, "Given the king's judgment and experience, I'm amazed at how this traitor's deceitfulness and guile escaped his notice."

Another said, "Even more amazing: I think, despite the evidence against the jackal, he'll forgive him."

The lion sent one of his companions to ask the jackal to provide some justification of his deed. When the fellow brought back a false account, the lion became so angry that he ordered the jackal to be killed.

Word of these events reached the lion's mother. Realizing that the lion 12.17
had acted hastily, she sent word to those who had been ordered to kill the jackal to grant him a delay. Then she visited her son. "For what crime," she asked, "did you order the jackal to be killed?"

The lion told her what had happened.

"My son," she said, "you've acted in haste. Only by deliberateness, by avoidance of haste, and by ascertaining the facts can a wise man protect himself from regret. A hasty man will always taste regret as the fruit of bad judgment and shortsightedness. A king more than anyone needs calmness and deliberateness: a woman is kept safe by her husband; a child by its parents; a student by his teacher; an army by its general; an ascetic by religious scholars; the common folk by kings; and kings by piety, intelligence, and careful establishment of the facts. For a king, sound judgment begins with knowing his companions, appointing them to the right positions, and being aware of their intrigues. There are people who, if they can find a way, will not hesitate to destroy others, disparage the bravery of the brave and the good deeds of the righteous, and cover up the deeds of wrongdoers.

١٨،١٢ وقد كنت بلوت ابن آوى واختبرت أدبه ومروءته قبل استعانتك به وتفويضك إليه ثمّ لم تزل راضياً عنه تزيدك الأيّام إليه استنصاحاً وإليه استرسالاً وفيه رغبة ومع ذلك فقد أثنيت عليه عند جندك غير مرّة بأحسن الثناء ومدحته أعظم المدح فلم يكن جديرًا أن تأمر بقتله في يسير من اللحم فقدته وعسى أصحابك أن يكونوا ألزموه من ذنبه باطلاً لحسدهم[1] له وتعاونهم عليه. واعلم أنّ الملوك إذا وكّلوا على غيرهم ما ينبغي لهم مباشرته من أمورهم وألزموا أنفسهم مباشرة ما ينبغي لهم تفويضه إلى غيرهم من الكفاة[2] ضاعت أمورهم ودعوا الفساد إلى أنفسهم.

١٩،١٢ وربّما احتاجوا مع ذلك أن ينظروا من النظر في وجوه شتّى فإذا لم يكن نظرهم إلّا في بعض تلك الوجوه دون بعض لم يأمنوا خطأ النظر وزلل الرأي كصاحب الخمر التي إذا اشتراها صاحبها احتاج إلى اختبار لونها وطعمها وريحها فإن هو اقتصر على اختبار بعض ذلك دون بعض لم يأمن الغبن والخسران. وكالرجل يرى بين عينيه كالشعرة لمرض بعينه يسمّى السمادير فإذا نظر بعقله علم أنّها لو كانت شعرة رآها غيره ممّن ينظر إليه كما هو يراها. وكالبعوضة التي تُرى بالليل كأنّها نار فإذا قضى عليها الجاهل وحده حسبها نارًا فإذا أخذها ولمسها علم أنّه قد أخطأ في القضاء.

٢٠،١٢ وأنت أيّها الملك حقيق أن تنظر في أمر[3] ابن آوى نظر تثبّت فتعلم أنّه لا يخون فيه ولقد كنت ربّما أمرت له باللحم الكثير فيجعله في طعامك وطعام جندك فليس بخليق أن يسرق قليلاً من اللحم أمرته بالاحتفاظ به فافحص عن أمره فإنّه لم تزل عادة الأراذل حسد أهل الفضل والمروءة واستفناءهم[4] ولابن آوى مروءة وفضل فعسى أعداؤه من أصحابك تلطّفوا بوضع ذلك اللحم في منزله عن غير علم منه بذلك فإنّ الحدأة إذا أصابت البضعة من اللحم نافسها فيها كثير من الطير وكالكلب إذا كان في فيه العظم تعاون عليه كثير من الكلاب. فإذا لم ينظر أعداء ابن آوى من أصحابك لك فانظر لنفسك ولا تنقادنّ لهم فيما يدّعون إنّه يوصل الضرر إلى نفسك فإنّ أعظم

---

١ كذا ش، ع؛ الأصل: حسدهم. ٢ كذا ش، ع؛ الأصل: الكفايه. ٣ كذا ش، پ٣٤٧٥؛ الأصل: نظر. ٤ الأصل: واسفتابهم.

"You tested the jackal and examined his behavior and character before you made him your aide and placed your trust in him. You were always pleased with him; your approval, friendship, and desire for his company only increased with each passing day. You often praised him and commended him in front of your soldiers; he doesn't deserve to be put to death because a bit of meat has gone missing. Perhaps out of envy, and in collusion, his companions have falsely accused him of a crime. You can be sure that kings bring ruin on themselves when they entrust to others what they should carry out themselves or take on themselves what they should entrust to others. 12.18

"Kings need to consider an affair from many angles. If they consider only one aspect, they risk misunderstanding or misjudgment. It's like someone buying wine: he needs to test it for color, taste, and fragrance. If he tests for only one of these attributes, he risks being cheated and stands to lose. Or it's like the man who, because he has an eye disease, thinks he sees what appears to be a hair before his eyes: if he gave it some thought, he'd realize that if it really were a hair, others would see it too. Or it's like a firefly that at night looks like a fire: the ignorant man judges it only from its appearance, but when he touches it he realizes his mistake. 12.19

"Your Majesty should examine the jackal's case carefully and realize that he would not act treacherously. You've often put him in charge of large amounts of meat, and he has served it to you and your soldiers without fail. Is it likely, then, that he'd steal a small amount you ordered him to keep? Investigate the case. Worthless men will always envy men of worth and character, and try to destroy them. The jackal is brave and worthy. His enemies among your companions may have smuggled the meat into his house without his knowing. Many birds will jostle a kite when she finds a chunk of meat; many dogs will join forces against a dog with a bone in his mouth. If the jackal's enemies among your companions haven't considered your welfare, consider it yourself and don't succumb to their allegations. Indeed, it will cause you harm. For the two most harmful things, especially 12.20

الأشياء ضررًا على الناس عامّة وعلى الولاة خاصّة أمران أحدهما أن يُحرَموا صالح الأعوان والوزراء والإخوان[1] وأن يكون[2] أعوانهم ووزراؤهم غير ذوي[3] المروءة. ولم يزل غناء ابن آوى عندك عظيمًا يؤثر منفعتك على هواه ويشتري راحتك بنصبه ورضاك بسخط الأصحاب[4] لا يطوي عليك أمرًا ولا يكتمك سرًّا ولا يرى شيئًا بذله لك واحتمله لك عظيمًا وإن عظم ومن كان من الأصحاب هذه صيغته فإنّما منزلته منزلة الآباء والإخوان والأبناء.

فبينما أمّ الأسد في كلامها إذ دخل عليه بعض الذين مكروا بابن آوى فأخبر الأسد ٢١،١٢
ببراءته.

فلمّا أن علمت أمّ الأسد أنّ الأسد قد اطّلع على براءة ابن آوى وتعاون أصحابه عليه قالت له لا ترضينّ بذلك منهم ولا تدعنّ تشتيت ذات بينهم حتّى ينقطع عنك سفه السفيه وليمنعهم الملك عن اتّخاذهم الغيّ مركبًا وعودتهم للاجتماع على ضرّك وشينك ولا تغترّنّ[5] بسلطانك عليهم فيدعوك[6] ذلك إلى استصغار أمرهم والتهاون به فإنّ الحشيش الضعيف إذا جُمع وفُتل منه الحبل العظيم القويّ رُبط به الفيل المغتلم. وأعد لابن آوى منزلته منك وخاصّتك ولا يؤيّسنّك من مناصحته ما فرط منك إليه من الإساءة فإنّه ليس كلّ[7] من أسيء إليه[8] ينبغي أن يُتخوّف منه غشّه وعداوته ويُؤيَس من نصيحته ومودّته ولكنّه ينبغي أن يُنزل الناس في ذلك منازلهم على اختلاف ما بينهم فمنهم من إذا ظُفر بقطيعته كان الرأي أن يُغتنم ذلك منه ويُمتنع من معاودته ومنهم من لا ينبغي تركه بالانقطاع منه على حال. فمن عُرف بالشراسة ولؤم العهد وقلّة الوفاء والشكر والبعد من الورع والرحمة والجحود لثواب الآخرة وعقابها والعداوة للناس والحسد لهم وبإفراط الطمع والحرص والسرعة إلى سوء الظنّ والقطيعة والإبطاء عن المعاودة والمراجعة فالانقطاع عنه وعن صحبته

---

١ صالح . . . والإخوان: كذا ش، ع، پ٣٤٧٥؛ الأصل: صالح الاعمال والاعوان والوررا والاخوان. ٢ الأصل: نكونوا. ٣ غير ذوي: كذا ش، ع؛ الأصل: دوى. ٤ بسخط الأصحاب: كذا ل٢؛ الأصل: نسحطه حر الاصحاب. ٥ كذا ع، ش، پ٣٤٧٥؛ الأصل: والاعرار. ٦ كذا ش، ع، پ٣٤٧٥؛ الأصل: ولا ندعن. ٧ كذا ش، ع، ي(٨٦)؛ ساقطة من الأصل. ٨ كذا ش، ع، ي(٨٦)؛ ساقطة من الأصل.

to rulers, are, first, the want of good helpers, assistants, and friends, and, second, assistants and friends who aren't of good character. The jackal has always been very useful to you. He sets your interests above his desires; he procures your comfort at the cost of his own welfare, and your contentment at the cost of angering his colleagues; he conceals nothing and hides no secrets from you; and he considers no burden or exertion too great for your sake. A companion of such character should be as precious as one's parents, brothers, and children."

During the lion's mother's speech, one of the plotters came and informed 12.21
the lion of the jackal's innocence.

Once the lion's mother knew that the lion had learned of the jackal's innocence and of the conspiracy, she said to him, "Don't tolerate your companions' behavior. Break up their scheming, and put an end to their foolishness. Don't let them use deception as a vehicle. Don't let them regroup to bring you harm and disgrace. Don't let your own power tempt you to underestimate them and make light of them; for weak straw, gathered and braided, becomes a strong rope that can hold a full-grown elephant. Restore the jackal to his office and to your favor. Don't despair of receiving good advice from him on account of your rash mistreatment of him. One needn't fear treachery and enmity, nor despair of receiving good advice and affection from those who have suffered mistreatment. People should be treated according to the differences in their character. In some cases, when relations are severed, the breach should be final and irrevocable; in other cases, the person shouldn't be abandoned or cut off. The best policy is to sever relations and avoid contact with people known for wickedness and villainy; disloyalty and ingratitude; lack of piety and mercy; disbelief in the rewards and punishments of the hereafter; malice, envy, and excessive greed and ambition; swiftness to foster suspicions and break off relations; and slowness to reconsider and resume relations. However, we should eagerly seek the companionship of, and avoid any break with, people known for righteousness,

أحزم الرأي. ومن عُرف بالصلاح وكرم العهد والشكر والوفاء والمحبّة للناس والسلامة من الحسد والحقد والبعد من الأذى والاحتمال للإخوان والأصحاب وإن ثقلت عليه منهم المؤنة فهو حقيق أن يُغتنم صلته ويُمتنع من قطيعته.

فدعا الأسد عند ذلك ابن آوى واعتذر إليه وقال له إنّي رادّك إلى منزلتك التي كنت عليها منّي ومؤتمنك من أمري على ما ائتمنتك عليه قبل اليوم. ٢٢،١٢

قال ابن آوى أيّها الملك إنّ اتّخاذ الخليل المناصح القائل في منفعة خليله بما يعلم وإن ثقل ذلك عليه وإذا احتمل لخليله ما يسمع منه ممّا يكره وصبر عليه لعزيز المطلب فلا يشقّنّ على الملك إن قلت إنّي غير واثق به وأنّه لا ينبغي لي صحبته فإنّه من قد أصيب بعظيم من البلاء وهو غير مستحقّ له أو كان قد أزيل عن مرتبته وولايته أو كان قد سُلب ماله ظلماً أو كان مقرّبًا فأقصي من غير علّة أو كان قد استحقّ مع نظرائه ثوابًا فأثيبوا دونه وفُضّلوا عليه أو عقابًا فعفي عنهم دونه أو بُلغ ما لم يُبلغ منهم أو كان معروفًا بإفراط الحرص والشره أو كان يرى في منفعة السلطان ضرًّا أو يخاف منها ضرًّا فهو حقيق أن لا يسترسل إليهم ولا يثق بهم.

وقد ذُكرت اليوم بأنّي لم أزل عدوًّا للملك فليس ثبوتي على ما كنت عليه للملك من المودّة والنصيحة بمانع الملك من اتّهامي وسوء الظنّ بي والتخوّف لتغييري عن حالي لما سبق منه إليّ لا إلى ما أظهر له من مودّتي ونصيحتي مراقبة منّي له عن غير صدق نيّة منّي في ذلك. ولست مع ذلك آمنًا من عودة[١] أعدائي تحميل الملك عليّ بالكذب والباطل إشفاقًا من مكافأتي لهم وحرصًا عليّ أن لا أستحقّ[٢] عند الملك كذبهم فيما حملوه به عليّ فإذا فعلوا ذلك لم يحتاجوا في قبول الملك ذلك منهم إلى عون أقوى من هذه التهمة التي وقعت لي في نفسه. مع أنّ الملك لو كان رجع بالثقة بي وقلّة الاتّهام لي على ما كان عليه لكان ذلك مغبيًا ولما وجدت بدًّا من تخوّف تهمته بنصيحتي وسوء ظنّه بي وسرعته إلى تصديق أعدائي لما يحملونه[٣] على إلقائي ٢٣،١٢

١ كذا ش؛ ساقطة من الأصل. ٢ ش، پ٣٤٧٥: يستحقّ. ٣ الأصل: يحملوه.

honesty, gratitude, loyalty, and benevolence; people free from envy, malice, and offense; and people who bear unpleasantness from their companions and help them even when it is burdensome."

The lion summoned the jackal and apologized. "I restore you to office and entrust my affairs to you as in the past." 12.22

The jackal responded,"Your Majesty, a loyal friend who gives his friend advice he knows will be beneficial, though burdensome, and who patiently bears harsh words from his friend—such a friend is rare indeed. Therefore, Your Majesty, do not be offended if I tell you that I cannot trust you or be your companion. The ruler should neither befriend nor trust an individual who has suffered great affliction he doesn't deserve; or who has been stripped of rank and office; or whose property has been wrongly confiscated; or who once was a favorite and was then banished without cause; or who, along with his colleagues, deserved a reward, but saw them rewarded and promoted in his place; or who deserved to be punished alongside them, but they, rather than he, were pardoned; or who was mistreated, while they were not; or who has a reputation for excessive ambition and greed; or who sees harm in benefiting the ruler or fears harm to himself from it.

"Even today, I have been mentioned as still being an enemy of the king. 12.23
The fact that I remain, as always, the king's friend and loyal adviser will not prevent the king from harboring evil thoughts and suspicions. He will inevitably fear that my attitude has changed because of his action. He may fear that the affection and advice I give him are insincere. Also, I am afraid that my enemies will incite the king against me again by means of lies and falsehoods, fearing that I might requite them, eager that the lies they employed to turn the king against me not come to light. If they do try this, they will need no assistance greater than the suspicion that has already entered the king's mind. Even if the king restores his former trust and confidence in me, it would be impossible for me to know. Remembering his former haste, I would need to fear his suspicion of my advice, his evil opinion of me,

لما أتذكّره من عجلته إليّ فإذا كانت حال الملك في الثقة بي على ما وصفت فلينظر وجه ما يراني عليه من صحبته.

قال الأسد إنّي قد بلوت طبائعك وأخلاقك فمنزلتك في نفسي منزلة الكرماء الأخيار والكريم[1] تنسيه الخلّة الواحدة من الإحسان ألف خلّة من الإساءة واللئيم تنسيه الخلّة الواحدة من الإساءة ألف خلّة من الإحسان وإنّي واثق أنّه سينسيك ما سلف من إحساننا إليك هذا الذي فرط منّا في أمرك وقد عدنا بالثقة بك فعد للثقة بما قبلنا[2] فإنّه كائن لك في ذلك غبطة وسرور. ٢٤،١٢

فعاد ابن آوى إلى ما كان يلي فلم تزل الأيّام تزيده انتفاعاً واغتباطاً حتّى هلك.

انقضى باب الأسد والشعهر الصوّام

١ كذا ش، ع، پ٣٤٧٥؛ الأصل: الكرم. ٢ كذا ش؛ الأصل: قلنا.

and his readiness to believe my enemies' attacks on me. If I have correctly described how the king regards placing trust in me, let him consider how he thinks I feel about being his companion."

The lion replied, "I've tested your nature and character. In my mind you **12.24**
are among the noble and the good. One good deed makes a noble man forget a thousand bad ones, while one bad deed makes an ignoble man forget a thousand good ones. I trust that my former benevolence will make you forget what I so rashly did to you. My trust in you has been restored; now resume your trust in me. Doing this will bring you joy and happiness."

So the jackal resumed his management of the lion's affairs as before, and his devotion and happiness deepened right up to the time of his death.

Here ends the Chapter of the Lion and the Abstinent Jackal[57]

باب هَيلار ووزيره بَيلار

١،١٣ قال دبشلم لبيدبا الفيلسوف قد فهمت هذا المثل فأخبرني إن رأيت ما الذي إذا عمل به الملك كرم على أهل مملكته ورعيّته وثبّت ملكه وحفظ أرضه الحلم أم المروءة أم الجرأة أم الجود.

٢،١٣ قال الفيلسوف إنّ أفضل ما هو مدرك به ذلك الحلم والعقل لأنهما رأس الأمور وملاكها مع مشاورة اللبيب الرفيق العالم وأنفع ما يستنفع به الناس الحلم للملك خاصّة فإنّه لا شيء أعون منه ولا من صلاح المرء في معيشته من المرأة الصالحة الفاضلة المؤاتية فإنّ الرجل وإن كان شجاعاً رئيساً ثمّ لم يكن حليماً وكان مشاوره غير لبيب فإنّه يبهظه الأمر[١] اليسير حتّى يُرى فيه القبح والضعف لجهالته وخطأ رأي نصحائه وإن أصاب ظفراً ولقي رشداً لقدر ساقه إليه صارت عاقبة أمره إلى ندامة وإذا كان على خلاف ذلك من الفضل ومن قبل الوزير ثمّ أعانه القضاء أصاب الفلج على من خاصمه والغلبة لمن ناوأه والسرور لمن أحزنه كما زُعم لنا ممّا كان بين هيلار ملك الهند وإيراخت امرأته وبيلار صاحب سرّه ورأيه.

قال الملك وكيف كان ذلك.

٣،١٣ قال الفيلسوف ذكروا أنّ بيلار كان ناسكاً مجتهداً حسن الخلق ليّناً حليماً عالماً كاملاً فبينا الملك ذات ليلة نائم في غرفة له إذ رأى ثمانية أحلام يستيقظ عند كلّ حلم منها فلمّا أصبح دعا البرهميّين وهم النسّاك فقصّها عليهم وأمرهم أن يعبّروها فقالوا له قد رأيت أيّها الملك أمراً منكراً معجباً لم نسمع بمثله فيما مضى فإن أحببت أن ننطلق فنتفكّر فيه ستّة أيّام ونأتيك في اليوم السابع فنخبرك به ولعلّنا إن استطعنا أن ندفع ما تخوّف[٢] منه فعلنا.

---

١ كذا ل٢؛ ساقطة من الأصل. ٢ الأصل: بحوف.

King Haylār and His Minister Baylār

Dabshalim said to Baydabā the Philosopher, "Now that I've understood this parable, please tell me which quality a king must use in order to enjoy the respect of his officials and subjects, bolster his reign, and protect his land: judiciousness, virtue, boldness, or generosity?"[58] 13.1

The philosopher said, "Judiciousness and intelligence are the best means to these ends; along with consulting an intelligent, skillful, and learned adviser, they provide the cornerstone and foundation. In particular, a king's judiciousness is the quality most beneficial for the people. Nothing is more helpful, and nothing more conducive to a life well-lived, than a righteous, virtuous, well-disposed wife. If a man is a brave leader but lacks judiciousness, and if his adviser is unintelligent, his own ignorance and the mistakes of those he consults will cause the simplest affair to overwhelm him, and he will be regarded as disgraced and weak. Even if by some turn of fortune he wins victory or finds the right path, he will eventually come to grief. On the other hand, a king will achieve success over his rivals, victory over his opponents, and joy over those who grieve him if he and his minister possess these virtues and if he is favored by fortune. This is what happened, we have been told, in the case of King Haylār of India, his wife Īrākht, and his confidant and adviser Baylār." 13.2

"How did it happen?" asked the king.

The philosopher told the following tale: Baylār, they say, was a diligent, virtuous, gentle, judicious, learned, and respected holy man. One night the king, asleep in his bedroom, dreamt eight dreams, waking after each. In the morning he summoned the Brahmins—the holy men, that is—told them his dreams, and commanded them to interpret. "Your Majesty has dreamt something horrible and astounding," they said, "like nothing we've ever heard. With your permission, we will go and ponder the matter for six days and report back on the seventh. Hopefully we can do something to ward off what you fear." 13.3

قال الملك نعم واعملوا برأيكم فيما تعلمون أنّه يوافقني.

فقالوا نعم أيّها الملك.

٤،١٣ فخرجوا واجتمعوا وقالوا لم نجتمع منذ قتل منّا[١] اثني عشر ألفاً وقد استمكنّا منه إذ أفضى إلينا بسرّه وعرّفنا فرقه من رؤياه ولعلّنا ننتقم منه إن نحن أغلظنا[٢] له في القول فيحمله الخوف على أن يتابعنا على ما نريد فنأمره أن يدفع إلينا من يكرم عليه من أهله ووزرائه ونقول له إنّا قد نظرنا في كتبنا فلم نجده يصرف ما رأيت إلّا قتل من نسمّي لك فإن قال ومن تريدون قلنا إيراخت امرأتك وابنها جوير[٣] وابن أخيك وبيلار صاحب أمرك[٤] فإنّه ذو حيلة وعلم وكال[٥] كاتبك ولسانك وسيفك والفيل الأبيض الذي تقاتل عليه والفيلين العظيمين والفرس الذي تركب والنجيب الذي تسير عليه إلى كانزون الفقيه لنجعل دماءهم في آبزن ثمّ نقعدك فيه فإذا أردت أن تخرج منه اجتمعنا معشر البرهميّين من الآفاق الأربعة فرقيناك ومسحنا عنك الدم وغسلناك بالماء والدهن المطيّب ثمّ صيّرناك إلى مجلسك فيذهب الله عنك ما يريد[٦] ممّا رأيت فإن صبرت على هذا وطبت به نفساً خلصت ونجوت من البلاء العظيم الذي قد رهقك وأشرف عليك واستخلفت مكانهم مثلهم وإن أنت لم تفعل فإنّا نتخوّف أن يُسلب بهاؤك ويُنتزع ملكك وتهلك ويُستأصل عقبك.

٥،١٣ فلمّا أبرم البرهميّون ذلك من رأيهم واتّفقوا عليه أتوا الملك فقالوا له إنّا قد نظرنا في كتبنا ورسّخناها وفكّرنا في رؤياك وأعملنا العقول فيها ولسنا نقدر على أن نعلمك بما رأينا لك حتّى تحلّنا.

ففعل ذلك فقصّوا إليه الأمر على ما هيّأوا منه.

٦،١٣ فقال الموت خير من ما أسمع أبداً نقتل هذه النفوس التي هي عندي عدل نفسي وأحتمل الضرّة والوزر ولا بدّ من الموت على كلّ حال ولست آمن الدهر على ملكي هذا وإنّه سواء عليّ الهلاك وفراق الأحبّة.

---

١ كذا ل٢؛ ساقطة من الأصل. ٢ كذا ل٢؛ الأصل: علطنا. ٣ الأصل: حوىر. ٤ كذا ل٢؛ الأصل: أمرانك. ٥ كذا الأصل. ٦ الأصل: يريد.

"Very well," said the king. "Go and determine what is my best course of action."

"Very well, Your Majesty."

They convened once they had left. "We haven't met," they said, "since he killed twelve thousand of us. But now that he has revealed his secret and his anxiety about his dreams to us, we have him in our power and may be able to exact revenge. If we speak to him bluntly, fear may drive him to agree to what we want. We will command him to hand over his dearest family members and ministers. We will say to him, 'We have searched our books and found that the only way to avert what you have dreamt is to kill those we name.' If he asks who, we will say, 'Your wife Īrākht, her son Jawbar, your nephew, your resourceful and learned minister Baylār, and your secretary and spokesman Kāl; we also need your sword, your white battle elephant, both your mighty elephants, the horse you ride, the camel of noble breed on which you journey, and the jurist Kamānzūn. We will put their blood into a basin and sit you in it. When you are about to get out, we Brahmins will assemble from all four corners of the land, recite incantations over you, wipe off the blood, and wash you with water and fragrant oil. Then we will escort you to your throne room, and, of the things you have dreamt, God will avert whatever He wishes. If you bear this patiently and willingly, you will be saved and escape imminent disaster, and you will be able to replace what you have lost. If you do not, we fear that your glory will be stripped away and your kingdom wrested from you; you will perish and your posterity will be eradicated.'" 13.4

Having agreed on the plan as devised, the Brahmins went to the king and said, "We have examined our books thoroughly, pondered your dreams, and put our minds to work, but we can't tell you what we think unless you allow us to speak without fear of punishment." 13.5

He did so, and they told him what they had devised.

"Death is better than what I am hearing!" replied the king. "Never will I slay these souls who are my very life or take such a burden of distress and sin on myself. Death, in any case, is inevitable; my reign won't last forever. Separation from everybody I love is tantamount to death." 13.6

فقال البرهميّون إن أنت لم تغضب أخبرناك أنّ رأيك هذا مخطئ وأنّك لم تصب إذ أهنت نفسك وأكرمت عليها غيرك. أولست تعلم أنّ كلّ شيء خُلف منه[1] وأنّه لا يعدلها شيء وإن عظم خطره أو صغر فلعمري لئن فديتها بمن سمّيناه لك إنّه لأمثل وأخير فتبقى في ملكك وسلطانك ويفلح لك أمرك فانظر لها ودع ما سواها فإنّه لا شيء يعدلها.

٧،١٣ فلمّا رآهم أغلظوا له في القول واجترأوا عليه فيه دخل منزله ووقع لوجهه وجعل يتقلّب مهموماً محزوناً وفكّر في رأيه أيّ أمريه يركب الموت عياناً وهو ينظر إليه أو إعطاءهم ما سألوا ومكث بذلك أيّاماً وفشا الحديث في أرضه وقالوا لقد نزل بالملك أمر عظيم هو منه في كرب.

٨،١٣ فلمّا رأى بيلار الذي وقع فيه الملك من ذلك فكّر ونظر وكان فطناً عالماً مجرّباً فقال ما ينبغي أن أستقبل الملك بشيء دون أن يدعوني ولكنّي أنطلق إلى إيراخت امرأة الملك فأسألها عن ذلك.

٩،١٣ فأتاها فقال إنّي لا أعلم الملك ركب أمراً صغيراً ولا كبيراً منذ كنت معه إلّا بمشورتي فإنّي كنت صاحب سرّه ولم يكن يكتمني شيئاً وكان إذا أحزنه أمر مفظع عزّى نفسه واصطبر على ما نزل به منه وذكر لي ذلك فأسلّيه عنه بأرفق ما أقدر عليه وأراه مستخلياً بالبرهميّين منذ سبعة أيّام احتجب فيها عن الناس وأنا خائف أنّه قد أدخلهم على جلله[2] وأطلعهم على سرّه ولست آمنهم عليه فاذهبي إليه واسأليه عن حاله وما بلغه وما الذي ذكروا له ثمّ أعلميني ذلك فإنّي لا أستطيع أن أدخل عليه وإنّي لأحسبهم قد زيّنوا له أمراً قبيحاً وحملوه على قبيحة أو أغضبوه بشيء شبّهوا له فيه فإنّ من أخلاق الملك إذا هو اغتاظ لا يلتفت إلى أحد ولا يسأل عن شيء وكان سواء عنده الكبير من الأمور والصغير فلعلّ أن يحمله الغضب وقول أولئك الأثمة على إهراقة الدماء.

---

١ الأصل: منها. ٢ الأصل: حلله.

The Brahmins said, "Don't be angry if we tell you that you're wrong to value others' lives above your own. Don't you know that your life is irreplaceable and that nothing, great or small, can equal it? Better to ransom your life by sacrificing those we've named and retain your throne. Look to your own life. Nothing can equal it."

When the king saw how harshly and boldly they had spoken to him, 13.7
he entered his chamber and fell to the ground, tossing and turning in grief and despair, considering which course to follow: risk imminent death, or give them what they asked. He remained thus for some days, and news of it spread throughout the land. People said, "Something terrible must have happened to cause the king such grief."

Baylār became pensive when he saw the king's condition. Being percep- 13.8
tive, wise, and experienced, he told himself, "It isn't my place to confront the king about anything without being summoned, but I'll go to the king's wife Īrākht and ask her about it."

So he went to her and said, "I've never known the king to do anything, be 13.9
it small or great, without first consulting me. I've always been his confidant; he's never kept anything secret from me. He would console himself when distressed and bear it patiently; then he would mention it to me, and I would comfort him as gently as I could. But now I see that for the past seven days he has sequestered himself with the Brahmins and no one else can see him. I fear he's made them privy to something momentous, and I don't trust them with it. Go to him; ask how he is, what he has heard, and what they have told him. Then let me know, as I can't go before him. I think they've presented an evil action in a good light and have incited him to do something disgraceful, or have angered him with their dark pronouncements. I know that when angry, the king isn't in the habit of consulting anyone, be the matter small or great. His anger, combined with the words of those evildoers, could induce him to shed blood."

فقالت إيراخت امرأة الملك إنّه كان بيني وبين الملك بعض العتاب فلست داخلة ١٠،١٣
عليه على حالتي هذه.

فقال لا تنظري عند تقارب الأمر وما يُخاف من البلاء في هذا الأمر وفي مثل هذا العتاب ولا يخطرنّ[١] على بالك فإنّه ليس يقدر على الدخول عليه أحد غيرك فكثيرًا ما كنت أسمعه يقول إذا اشتدّ حزني ثمّ نظرت في وجه إيراخت ذهب حزني. فقومي أيّتها المرأة الصالحة فانطلقي إلى الملك ففرّجي عنه غمّه وحزنه وقولي ما تعلمين أنّه يصلحه ويجدي عليه[٢] وأعلميني ما يكون منك فإنّ لنا ولأهل مملكته في ذلك أعظم الفرج والراحة.

فقامت إيراخت فدخلت على الملك إيوانه وجلست عند رأسه ورفعت رأسه ١١،١٣
من الأرض وقالت ما لك أيّها الملك الكريم وما الذي سمعت من البرهميّين فأهمّك وأحزنك فإن كان أمر ينبغي فيه الحزن فأخبرني به لأن أحزن معك كما أفرح بفرحك فإنّ الملك إذا فرح فرحت لفرحه وإذا حزن كنت حقيقة بالحزن معه.

قال الملك أيّتها المرأة لا تزيديني حزنًا ولا تسأليني عن حزني هذا.

فقالت إيراخت وقد نزلت عندك منزلة من يجاب[٣] في مثل هذه المسألة بهذا ١٢،١٣
الجواب الذي أسمع أوما علمت أنّ أحمد الناس عند أهل الفضل رأيًا أحسنهم حيلة وأصبرهم إذا نزلت به نازلة وأشدّهم لنفسه تعزيّة وتجلّدًا وأظهرهم عزمًا وأشدّهم سكينة واستماعًا من أهل النصح حتّى ينجو من تلك النازلة أو يبلغ عند نفسه عذرها وعند أهل مملكته فيها فإنّ من قارف عظيم الذنوب يقدر بالحلم والعلم على مداواة ذنبه ذلك وإصلاحه حتّى يعود إلى الخير والعمل الصالح ويعود إلى الفرح والسرور وكذلك أنت أيّها الملك لست حقيقًا بالحزن والجزع وترك الأخذ بالرأي والحزم وإظهار العزيمة والصبر ولا أن تحزن أهل ودّك توجع قلوبهم وتفرح أعداءك وتقرّ أعينهم فإنّ العاقل لا يُعَدّ عاقلًا ولا حليمًا إن أحزن أهل ودّه وأقرّ أعين أعدائه.

١ الأصل: يحطرى. ٢ ويجدي عليه: الأصل: واىحدى عله. ٣ الأصل: يحاف.

13.10 Īrākht replied, "The king and I have had a falling out. I won't go before him under the present circumstances."

Baylār said, "At a time like this, when trouble is near, pay no heed to your disagreement. Banish it from your mind. No one but you can go before him. I've often heard him say, 'My deepest sadness vanishes when I look on Īrākht's face.' Go to the king, good lady. Dispel his grief and despair. Speak the words that you know will restore him to his proper state. Do us this favor, and keep us informed of what happens, for it will bring enormous relief to us and all of his kingdom."

13.11 Īrākht rose and went to the king. She sat down before him and lifted his head from the ground. "What is wrong, noble king? What have you learned from the Brahmins that troubles and saddens you? If it is something that must cause sadness, tell me and I will be sad with you, just as I rejoice when you are joyful. For when the king rejoices, I rejoice with him, and when he is sad, I ought to be sad too."

"Lady," replied the king, "do not make me sadder still. Do not ask about it."

13.12 "Have I sunk so low in your eyes," replied Īrākht, "that you answer me in this way? Don't you know what wise men have said: The person whose judgment most deserves praise is the one who is never at a loss, who bears misfortune patiently, is undismayed, and listens to his devoted advisers, so that by stratagem and acumen he escapes misfortune, doing his utmost for himself and his kingdom? Someone who yields to a great sin can, through judiciousness and intelligence, remedy and repair his sin, and return to goodness and righteous action in order that joy and happiness may return. Therefore, Your Majesty must not grieve and be dismayed, casting aside judgment and resolve as well as abandoning determination and patience. Don't bring heartache to those who love you while giving joy and comfort to your enemies. If you do, you will not be considered a man of intelligence or judiciousness."

١٣،١٣ قال الملك أيّتها المرأة الناصحة الشفيقة قد شفقت عليّ ولا خير لي ولا لك إن أخبرتك بحالي إنّي ميّت هالك أنا وابنك وأنت وسائر من أحبّ من الناس فإنّ البرهميّين أمروني بقتلك وقتل ابنك وسائر خاصّتي وأهل ودّي. فكيف أفرح إذا لم أرك أم كيف أُسَرّ إذا أنا قتلت جميع من أمرني البرهميّون بقتله وهل أحد يسمع مثل هذا فلا يعتريه الحزن.

١٤،١٣ فلمّا سمعت إيراخت ذلك منعها عقلها وحلمها أن تريه أنّها تجزع من ذلك أو يشقّ على نفسها منه شيء فقالت لا تحزن أيّها الملك السعيد أطال الله لك البقاء ودام لك السرور فنفسي فداؤك ولك من النساء العوض من يصلح لك وتقرّ به عينك ولك حوز فيه ستّة عشر ألف امرأة بما يصلحهنّ من المساكن وغيرها ولكنّي أطلب إليك خصلة يحملني على طلبها حبّي لك ونصيحتي إيّاك لا تثق بعد موتي بالبرهميّين ولا تستشرهم في شيء ولا تقتل أحدًا حتّى تتثبّت في أمره عشر مرّات لئلّا تندم فإنّك لا تستطيع أن تحيي من قتلت وقد قيل في الأحاديث إذا وجدت جوهرًا لا خير فيه فلا تلقه من يدك حتّى تستشير به من يعرف الجوهر.

١٥،١٣ وأنت أيّها الملك لا تعرف أعداءك واعلم أيّها الملك أنّ البرهميّين لا يحبّونك أبدًا وقد قتلت منهم قريبًا من اثني عشر ألفًا ولم يكن ينبغي لك أن تقصّ رؤياك عليهم ولا تقبل منهم قولهم فإنّهم يريدون أن يزيلوا الحقد الذي في أنفسهم بقتل الحكماء من عبيدك الذين هم أعوان صدق لك على ملكك والمرأة الكريمة عليك والولد الذي هو عدل نفسك وفرسك الذي هو مركبك والنجيب العظيم والفيلين اللذين تقاتل عليهما عدوّك وتضبط بهما ملكك فإذا قتلت هؤلاء وذهبت قوّة عبدك وقوّة ملكك ظفروا بك واجترأوا عليك وأخذوا منك بثأرهم وعملوا بحقدهم وسلبوك ملكك فعاد إليهم كما كان قبل ذلك.

١٦،١٣ ولكن ابعث أيّها الملك إلى كانزون العالم فهو عالم بالأمور كلّها ناقد بالبصيرة فيها فأطلعه على أمرك واستشره فيه فإنّه عالم دين صادق وهو أيضًا من أصل البرهميّين غير أنّه أفضلهم فقهًا وعلمًا ونسكًا وطلبًا لأجر الآخرة فإن أحببت فسله عمّا رأيت

"Loyal and kind lady," said the king, "how compassionate you are! But nothing good for either of us will come from my telling you about an affair that means death and destruction to me, you, your son, and everyone else I love. The Brahmins have commanded me to kill you, your son, my other courtiers, and the people I love. How can I rejoice if I can no longer set eyes on you? How can I be happy if I kill everyone the Brahmins have commanded me to? Is it possible to hear this without being overwhelmed with sadness?" 13.13

When Īrākht heard this, her intelligence and judiciousness prevented her from displaying any fear of death or concern for her own life. "Do not be sad, blessed king. May God lengthen your life and grant you lasting joy. I will sacrifice my life to save yours. You have other wives to delight you—your estate is home to sixteen thousand other women, all with fine palaces and lodgings. But I beg Your Majesty, grant me one thing that my love and loyalty lead me to request. When I am dead, make certain tenfold before you trust the Brahmins, seek their advice, or put anyone to death, lest you regret it, for you cannot revive someone you've killed. As they say, don't discard a stone you deem worthless before you consult an expert on gems. 13.14

"Your Majesty, you don't recognize your enemies. You can be certain that the Brahmins will never love you, given that you've killed nearly twelve thousand of them. You shouldn't have told them your dreams or accepted their advice. They want to vent the hatred in their hearts by killing your beloved wife, the son who is your second self, the wise officials who loyally administer your kingdom, the horse you ride, your camel of noble breed, and the two elephants on which you battle your foes and defend your kingdom. When you kill them, losing everything that delights your eyes and weakening your kingdom, they'll have you in their grip and will dare to exact vengeance. Driven by the hatred in their hearts, they'll wrest your kingdom from you, and it will revert to them as once it was. 13.15

"Send word, Your Majesty, to the sage Kamānzūn, who is learned in all things and has insight into all matters. Inform him of this, and ask his advice. He is an honest scholar of religion; though a Brahmin by descent, he excels them in understanding, learning, piety, and devout pursuit of the hereafter. 13.16

في منامك فإن هو قال[1] كما قالوا فافعل ما أمروك به وإن هو خالفهم فأنت أيّها الملك قادر على ما في أرضك بمعرفة ما أحببت.

فلمّا سمع الملك ذلك من قولها أعجبه فأمر بإسراج فرسه الكبير ثمّ ركبه فانطلق حينئذ إلى كانزون فلمّا انتهى إليه نزل عن فرسه ثمّ سجد له وحيّاه ونكس رأسه ومثل قائماً بين يديه. ١٧،١٣

فقال كانزون أيّها الملك ما لي أراك متغيّر اللون ممتلئاً حزناً وغمّاً ولا أرى عليك التاج ولا إكليل الملك.

قال الملك كنت ذات يوم نائماً على ظهر الإيوان فسمعت من الأرض ثمانية أصوات فاستيقظت ثمّ رقدت فرأيت أيضاً ثمانية أحلام فقصصتها على البرهميّين فأنا خائف حزين أخاف أن يصيبني أمر عظيم إمّا أن أُقتل في حرب وإمّا أن أُغصب ملكي وأُغلب عليه.

فقال كانزون نامت عينك أيّها الملك وقرّت لا يحزنك هذا الأمر ولا توجلنّ منه فإنّك لا تموت الآن ولا تُسلب ملكك ولا تصيب شيئاً من الآثام والشرور التي تخوّف فأمّا الأحلام الثمانية التي رأيت فإنّي مخبرك بتأويلها. أمّا السمكتان الحمراوان اللتان رأيتهما قامتا على أذنابهما فإنّه يأتيك رسول ملك هيمون بتاجين مكلّلين بالدرّ والياقوت قيمتهما[2] أربعة آلاف رطل من ذهب فيقوم بين يديك. وأمّا الإوزّتان اللتان رأيتهما طارتا من وراء ظهرك فوقعتا بين يديك فإنّه يأتيك من ملك بلخ فرسان ليس في الأرض مثلهما. وأمّا الحيّة التي رأيتها دبّت على رجلك اليسرى فإنّه يأتيك من ملك صنجين من يقوم بين يديك بسيف خالص من الحديد لا يوجَد مثله. وأمّا ما رأيت من تخضيب جسمك بالدم فإنّه يأتيك من ملك كاسرون من يقوم بين يديك بلباس يسمّى حلل الأرجوان تضيء في الظلمة. وأمّا ما رأيت من غسلك جسمك بالماء فإنّه يأتيك من ملك رزين من يقوم بين يديك بثياب كتّان من لبوس الملوك. وأمّا ما رأيت أنّك على جبل[3] أبيض فإنّه يأتيك من ملك كدفور من يقوم بين يديك ١٨،١٣

١ كذا پ٣٤٦٦؛ ساقطة من الأصل. ٢ كذا پ٣٤٦٦؛ الأصل: فهما. ٣ كذا ل٢؛ الأصل: حمل.

Ask him about your dreams. If his words agree with theirs, do as they have commanded; but if he disagrees with them, Your Majesty has power over everything in your lands to do whatever you wish."

The king was pleased by her words. He ordered his horse to be saddled, 13.17
and set out at once to see Kamānzūn. When he arrived, he dismounted, prostrated himself, greeted him, bowed his head, and stood before him.

"Your Majesty," asked Kamānzūn, "why do I see you so pale, filled with sadness and grief, wearing neither the crown nor the royal diadem?"

The king replied, "One day as I was sleeping in my chamber, I heard eight voices coming from the earth. I woke up, but then went back to sleep and dreamt eight dreams. I told them to the Brahmins. I am sad because I fear some disaster: either my death in battle or the conquest of my kingdom."

Kamānzūn said, "Rest assured, Your Majesty. Don't be sad or frightened. 13.18
You aren't going to die, your kingdom won't be lost, and none of the sins and evils you fear will occur. I will tell you the meaning of the eight dreams. The two red fish you saw standing on their tails signify that a messenger will arrive from the king of Haymūn and stand before you bearing two pearl- and ruby-encrusted crowns worth four thousand pounds of gold. The two geese you saw fly from behind you and land in front of you signify that you will receive from the king of Balkh two horses unmatched in all the world. The snake you saw crawl up your left leg signifies that someone sent by the king of Ṣanjīn will stand before you with a peerless sword of pure steel. The blood you saw staining your body signifies that someone sent by the king of Kāsrūn will stand before you with a wondrous garment: the Crimson Cloak, which glows in the dark. The dream of washing your body with water signifies that someone sent by the king of Razīn will stand before you with linen garments fit for a king. Your dream of being atop a white mountain signifies that someone sent from the king of Kadfūr will stand before you with a white elephant that no horse can outrun. Your dream of having something like fire on your head signifies that someone sent by King Dār will stand before you

بفيل أبيض لا تلحقه الخيل. وأمّا ما رأيت على رأسك شبيهاً بالنار فإنّه يأتيك من دار الملك من يقوم بين يديك بإكليل من ذهب مكلّل بالدرّ والياقوت. وأمّا الطير الذي رأيته فوق رأسك وضرب رأسك بمنقاره فلست مفسّرًا لك ذلك اليوم وليس بضارّك فلا توجلنّ منه ولكنّ فيه بعض الإعراض والسخط عمّن تحبّ. فأمّا هذه البرد والرسل فإنّهم يأتونك جميعاً إلى سبعة أيّام حتّى يقوموا بين يديك.

فلمّا سمع الملك ذلك سجد بين يدي كانزون ورجع إلى منزله فرحاً مسرورًا وقال إنّ كانزون لفاضل عالم وإنّي على ذلك لناظر فيما قال.

١٩.١٣ فلمّا كان اليوم الثامن لبس الملك ثياب زينته وقعد على سريره في أكبر مجالسه وأذن لعظماء أهل مملكته فدخلوا عليه وأخذوا مجالسهم فلم يلبثوا أن جاءته الهدايا التي أخبره عنها كانزون فوُضعت بين يديه.

فلمّا رأى الملك البرد والهدايا اشتدّ فرحه بذلك وقال لم أوفَّق حين قصصت رؤياي على البرهميّين فأمروني بما أمروني به فلولا أنّ الله رحمني وتداركني برأي إيراخت المباركة سيّدة النساء كنت قد هلكت وأهلكت وزلت عن ديني ودنياي ولذلك ينبغي لكلّ أحد أن يسمع من الأخلاء وذوي المودّة والنصيحة رأيهم ويقبل مشورتهم وإنّ إيراخت أشارت عليّ بحسن رأي فقبلته واغتبطت به فثبّت الله ملكي برأي الأخلاّء والنصحاء واستبان لي أيضاً علم كانزون وصدق قوله.

٢٠.١٣ ثمّ دعا الملك جوبر وبيلار وكال الكاتب فقال لهم إنّه لا ينبغي أن ندخل هذه الهدايا خزانتنا ولكنّي قاسمها بينكم بالذي وطّنتم عليه أنفسكم من الموت بسببي وبين إيراخت التي أشارت عليّ بالرأي الذي ثقفت منه بقاء ملكي والذي أصبحنا فيه من السرور والفرح.

قال بيلار أيّها الملك إنّه لا ينبغي للعبيد أن يُعجَبوا[١] لما كان منهم في ذلك. وأيّ عبد لا ينبغي له أن يسلم نفسه للموت فداء لسيّده المحسن إليه المنعم عليه المكرم له فإنّ الذي لا تطيب نفسه بالموت فداء لسيّده والأحبّة له فليس بكامل الحلم. ولا تعجبنّ

---

١ الأصل: نعحلوا.

with a tiara of gold encrusted with pearls and rubies. I won't interpret for you today the bird you saw above your head and that pecked your head with its beak. Don't be frightened; it won't harm you, but it involves some anger and estrangement from someone you love. All these messengers and couriers will stand before you seven days from now."

When the king heard this, he bowed before Kamānzūn and returned to his palace overjoyed. "Kamānzūn is a very wise man. I'll wait and see, as he said."

Seven days later, the king donned his robes and regalia, seated himself on 13.19
the throne in the main hall, and gave audience to the most distinguished men of the kingdom. It wasn't long before the gifts foretold by Kamānzūn arrived and were set before him.

The king rejoiced at the sight of the couriers and the gifts. "I made a mistake when I told my dreams to the Brahmins and they gave me their commands. If God in His mercy hadn't restrained me through the advice of Īrākht, the best and most blessed of women, I should have perished, caused death, and lost all I have in this world and the next. Everyone should heed the opinion and accept the advice of loving and loyal friends. Īrākht gave me good advice, and to my great joy I accepted it. Through the judgment of friends and sincere advisers, God has firmly established my kingdom. Kamānzūn's knowledge and the truth of his words have become clear to me."

The king then summoned Jawbar, Baylār, and his secretary Kāl. "It isn't 13.20
right for us to put these gifts into our treasuries. I will distribute them to you, because you were prepared to die for my sake, and to Īrākht, who gave me the advice that enabled me to preserve my kingdom and that has led to our present joy and gladness."

Baylār responded, "Servants have no right to pride themselves on what they have done. What servant wouldn't die to save the master who has honored and dignified him? Any servant unwilling to die to save his master

أيّها الملك أن يسلم عبد نفسه للموت مكان مليك قد شرّفه وأكرمه وفي بقائه بقاء النعمة عليه فأمّا هذه الهدايا العظيمة فلا ينبغي لنا معشر العبيد أن ندنو منها فأمّا جوبر الحبيب ولدك وإيراخت سيّده النساء فإنّهما أهل لذلك فليأخذا ما أعطيتهما.

٢١،١٣ فقال الملك قد شاع لنا في هذا الأمر ذكر عظيم وخير كثير فلا تحتشمنّ يا بيلار فخذ نصيبك منه فقرّ به عيناً.

فقال بيلار ليكن من ذلك ما أحبّ الملك السعيد ولكن إن رأى الملك أن يبدأ فيأخذ ما يريد فليفعل.

فأخذ الملك الفيل الأبيض وأعطى جوبر أحد الفرسين وأعطى بيلار السيف الخالص الحديد وأعطى كال الكاتب الفرس الآخر وبعث إلى كمانزون بالثياب الكتّان التي من لباس الملوك وأعطى التاجين ابن أخيه الكريم عليه وقال وأمّا الإكليل وسائر اللباس فإنّما يصلح للنساء فخذ يا بيلار الإكليل والثياب فاحملها واتبعني إلى مجلس النساء.

٢٢،١٣ فدعا الملك إيراخت وجورفنه[١] فجلستا بين يديه فقال لبيلار ضع الكسوة والإكليل بين يدي إيراخت لتأخذ أيّهما شاءت.

فلمّا رأت إيراخت أنّ كليهما معجب نظرت إلى بيلار بمؤخر عينها ليريها أيّهما أفضل فأراها بيلار الثياب وأشار عليها أن تأخذها فحانت من الملك لحظة فرأى لحظة بيلار فلمّا رأت إيراخت أنّ الملك قد أبصر لحظة بيلار إليها بعينه خافت عليه وعلى نفسها فتركت الذي أراها بيلار لئلّا يظنّ الملك أنّ ذلك لشيء بينهما فتركت الثياب وأخذت الإكليل فعاش بيلار بعد ذلك أربعين سنة كلّما دخل على الملك كسر عينه كيلا يظنّ الملك أنّه أرى[٢] ايراخت يومئذ شيئاً ولولا عقل إيراخت وعقل بيلار لم ينج واحد منهما من القتل.

٢٣،١٣ وكان الملك يكون عند إيراخت ليلة وليلة عند جورفنه وكان الملك من شأنه أن تهيّئ له المرأة التي يبيت عندها في ليلتها أرزاً بحلاوة فتطعمه إيّاه فأتى الملك

---

١ الأصل: وجودفنه. ٢ الأصل: راى.

and loved ones lacks understanding. Don't marvel, Your Majesty, that a servant should die in place of the master who has honored and dignified him, and in whose survival rests his continued welfare. It isn't fitting for us servants to touch these magnificent gifts, but your beloved son Jawbar and Īrākht, the best of women, are worthy of them. Let them have what you give them."

The king said, "Because of these events, our praise and renown have already spread far and wide. So don't be shy, Baylār! Take your share. Enjoy it!" 13.21

"As the king wishes," replied Baylār. "But, if it please the king, let him first take what he desires."

The king took the white elephant. He gave Jawbar one of the horses, Baylār the sword of pure steel, and his secretary Kāl the second horse; he sent the regal linen garments to Kamānzūn, and gave the two crowns to his beloved nephew. When it came to the tiara and other garments suitable for women, he said to Baylār, "Take the tiara and the robe, and follow me to the women's quarters."

The king summoned Īrākht and Gūlpanāh,[59] and the women sat before him. The king told Baylār, "Set the robe and tiara before Īrākht, and let her pick which one she wishes." 13.22

When Īrākht saw that both were breathtaking, she looked at Baylār out of the corner of her eye, to have him show her which was superior. Baylār directed her to the robe and signaled that she should pick that. It so happened that the king was watching and saw Baylār wink. Īrākht saw that the king had noticed, so she didn't touch what Baylār had indicated but instead took the tiara, fearing for her life and for Baylār's, lest the king suspect something was going on between them. Baylār lived another forty years and would always avert his glance in the king's presence, lest the king suspect him of having signaled to Īrākht that day. Had Īrākht and Baylār not been so astute, neither would have escaped death.

The king used to spend one night with Īrākht and one night with Gūlpanāh. The custom was that each wife would prepare a dish of sweetened rice on her night and serve it to the king. The king came to Īrākht on her night; she had 13.23

إيراخت في ليلتها وقد صنعت الأرزّ والإكليل على رأسها فقامت على رأسه بالصحفة فجعلت تطعمه منها فلمّا رأت جورفنه ذلك غارت على إيراخك فلبست تلك الكسوة ثمّ مرّت بين يدي الملك وكان ضوء تلك الثياب وبياضها كشعاع الشمس فأضاءت البيت وأضاءت جورفنه في تلك الثياب مثل الشمس فلمّا رأى ذلك الملك اشتاق إلى جورفنه وقال لإيراخت إن كنت لجاهلة حين أخذت الإكليل وتركت الكسوة التي ليس[1] في خزانتنا مثلها.

٢٤،١٣ فلمّا سمعت إيراخت قوله ومدحه جورفنه وتسفيهه رأيها داخلها الغيظ والغضب فضربت بالصحفة التي كانت على يدها رأس الملك فسال الأرزّ على رأسه فكان ذلك تصديق الحلم الثامن الذي كان[2] كمانزون قد فزع الملك بطرف منه ولم يبيّنه له.

فدعا الملك بيلار فقال ألا ترى إلى ملك العالم كيف[3] حقرته هذه المرأة وعملت به ما عملت فانطلق بها واضرب عنقها ولا ترحمها.

٢٥،١٣ فخرج بيلار بإيراخت من عند الملك وقال في نفسه ما أنا بقاتلها حتّى ينسلّ غضب الملك فإنّها امرأة عاقلة سعيدة ليس في النساء لها عدل في الحلم والعقل وليس الملك فيما يُظنّ بصابر عنها وقد خلّص الله بها ناساً من القتل والهلكة وعملت أعمالاً صالحة ورجاؤنا فيها عظيم ولست آمن أن يقول الملك أما[4] استطعت أن تؤخّر أمرها وتتأنّى في قتلها حتّى نراجعها. فلست قاتلها حتّى أنظر ما رأي الملك فيها فإن ندم على قتلها وحنّ إليها جئته بها وكنت قد عملت ثلاثة أعمال عظيمة أنجيت الحبيب إيراخت من القتل وسلّيت حزن الملك وافتخرت بذلك على الناس عامّة فإنّها بقيّة البرّ والأجر وإن هو لم يذكرها ولم يشتق إليها أمضيت فيها أمره.

٢٦،١٣ فانطلق بها بيلار سرّاً إلى منزله فوكّل بها رجلين من أمناء الملك الذين يلون نساءه وأمر أهله وأمرهما بحفظها وصيانتها وإكرامها حتّى ينظر كيف يكون آخر

١ ليس: كذا ر؛ الأصل: لسس. ٢ كذا ر؛ ساقطة من الأصل. ٣ كذا ل٢؛ ساقطة من الأصل. ٤ كذا ر؛ الأصل: ما.

the rice ready for him and stood before the king, wearing the tiara. She held out a platter and served him. When Gūlpanāh saw this, she became jealous, and she put on the robe and came before the king. The brilliant sheen of the robe was like the radiance of the sun, and the room lit up; Gūlpanāh herself was as dazzling as the sun. When the king saw this, he was filled with desire for her and said to Īrākht, "You were a fool to take the tiara and pass up such a peerless robe, unlike anything in our treasuries."

When Īrākht heard the king belittle her judgment and praise Gūlpanāh, 13.24
she was overcome with indignation and anger; she struck the king's head with the platter she held and the rice spilled over his head: this was the fulfillment of the eighth dream, part of which Kamānzūn had begun to tell the king, without explaining it further.

The king summoned Baylār. "Do you see what this woman has done and how she has insulted the king of the world! Take her away and cut off her head. Show her no mercy."

As Baylār was taking Īrākht away, he said to himself, "I won't put her to 13.25
death until the king's anger subsides. I think the king won't be able to bear her loss; she is so intelligent and well-favored, a woman of such judiciousness and intelligence. Thanks to her, God has rescued many people from death and destruction. She has done good deeds, and our hopes for her are great. I fear that the king will say, 'Couldn't you have delayed putting her to death until I reconsidered?' I won't kill her until I see how the king's view of her develops. If he regrets her death and misses her, I'll bring her to him alive, thereby accomplishing three good things: saving his beloved Īrākht, dispelling his sadness, and earning everyone's gratitude, as she is a woman of exceptional righteousness and piety. If he doesn't mention her or yearn for her, I'll carry out his command."

Baylār took her home secretly and placed her in the safekeeping of two 13.26
of the king's chamberlains who were in charge of his wives and household. He ordered them to care for her and show her every courtesy, until he'd

أمرها ثمّ خضّب بيلار سيفه بالدم ودخل على الملك كئيباً حزيناً فقال قد أمضيت أمرك في إيراخت.

فلم يلبث الملك إلّا قليلاً حتّى سكن غضبه وذكر جمال إيراخت ومكانها من نفسه والمنزل الذي كانت تحلّ منه فاشتدّ حزنه وجعل يعزّي نفسه ويتجلّد وهو يستحيي أن يسأل بيلار هل أمضى فيها أمره حقّاً أم لا وجعل يرجو لما يعرف من عقل بيلار وحلمه ورفق تدبيره وأناته أن لا يكون قتلها. ونظر بيلار بفضل عقله فقال لا تحزن أيّها الملك ولا تغتمّ فإنّه ليس في الحزن والهمّ فضل منفعة ولكنّهما يحلان الجسم ويفسدان العقل مع ما يدخل على أهل ودّ الملك أيضاً من الحزن فاصبر أيّها الملك ولا تحزن على ما لست بناظر إليه أبداً. وإن أحبّ الملك حدّثته بأحدوثة شبيهة بأمره هذا. ٢٧،١٣

قال الملك حدّثني بها.

قال بيلار زعموا أنّ حمامتين ذكراً وأنثى كبسا عشّهما برّاً وشعيراً فقال الذكر للأنثى أمّا ما وجدنا في الصحارى ما نعيش به فلا ينبغي لنا أن نأكل من كبسنا شيئاً فإذا جاء الشتاء ولم نصب في الصحارى شيئاً أقبلنا على ما جمعناه فأكلناه. فرضيت الأنثى بذلك وقالت نعم ما رأيت سنفعل ذلك إن شاء الله تعالى. وكان البرّ والشعير الذي وضعا في عشّهما ندياً. ٢٨،١٣

فانطلق الذكر إلى مكان كان يغيب فيه زماناً فلمّا كان الصيف يبس ذلك الحبّ فنقص ممّا كان عليه فلمّا رجع الذكر رأى الحبّ ناقصاً قال قد كنّا أجمعنا رأينا على أن لا نأكل ممّا قد كان كبسنا شيئاً فلِمَ أكلت منه.

فحلفت له الأنثى أنّها ما أكلت منه شيئاً فلم يصدّقها وجعل ينقرها حتّى قتلها فلمّا جاء الشتاء ووقعت الأمطار ندي الحبّ وامتلأ العشّ كما كان فلمّا رأى الذكر أنّ العشّ قد امتلأ علم أنّه قد ظلم وأساء وعجل في التهمة بالقضاء فاضطجع إلى جنبها ندامة على ما صنعه وقال كيف ينفعني العيش إذا طلبتك فلم أقدر عليك ٢٩،١٣

seen how things progressed. With his sword stained with blood, a downcast Baylār then came before the king, and said, "I have carried out your command concerning Īrākht."

The king's anger soon subsided. He remembered Īrākht's beauty, the place she held in his heart, and everything she had meant to him, and he became very sad. He tried to console himself and show strength. He was ashamed to ask Baylār whether he had really carried out the order, but he began to hope that he hadn't killed her, acquainted as he was with Baylār's intelligence, judiciousness, skillful management of affairs, and thoughtfulness. Baylār, by virtue of his intelligence, perceived this. "Don't be sad or grieve, Your Majesty," he said. "Grief and sorrow will only weaken your body and damage your mind and sadden your close friends. Be patient, Your Majesty, and do not grieve for something you will never behold. If Your Majesty wishes, I will tell you a story that resembles this case." 13.27

"Tell it to me!"

The Doves Who Filled Their Nest with Wheat and Barley

And Baylār told the following tale: Two doves—a male and a female—filled their nest with wheat and barley. The male said to his mate, "We shouldn't eat anything we've laid away as long as we can find enough in the fields to live on. We can eat what we've gathered when winter comes and we can find nothing in the fields." The female agreed. "What a good idea! That's what we'll do, God willing." The wheat and barley were moist when they put them into the nest. 13.28

The male flew off and was away for a time. The grain dried up and shrank when summer came. When he returned and saw the grain so diminished, he said, "We agreed to eat nothing we had laid away. Why did you eat some of it?"

The female swore she hadn't eaten a single grain, but he didn't believe her and pecked her to death. When the winter rains arrived, the grain became moist again and the nest filled up as before. When the male saw the nest full, he knew he had acted unjustly and had been too quick to accuse 13.29

وإذا فكّرت في أمرك فعلمت أنّي قد ظلمتك. فلم يذق طعاماً ولا شراباً حتّى مات إلى جانبها.

فمن كان عالماً حليماً علم أنّه لا ينبغي له أن يعجل بالعذاب والعقوبة ولا سيّما على من يخاف أنّه يندم على فراقه كما ندم ذلك الحمام الذكر.

٣٠،١٣ وقد سمعت أيضاً أنّ رجلاً كانت على ظهره كارة من عدس فدخل بين شجر يستظلّ فوضع كارته ثمّ نام فنزل قرد من شجرة فوق رأسه فأخذ ملء كفّه من ذلك العدس ثمّ صعد إلى الشجرة فسقطت من يده حبّة فطلبها فلم يجدها وانتثر العدس جميعه من يده.

وأنت أيضاً أيّها الملك عندك اثنا عشر ألف امرأة تدع أن تلهو بهنّ وتطلب ما لا تجد.

٣١،١٣ فلمّا سمع الملك كلام بيلار خشي أن يكون بيلار قد قتل إيراخت فقال لبيلار من سخطة واحدة كانت منّي فعلت ما أمرتك به في ساعة واحدة وتعلّقت بكلمة واحدة ولم تتثبّت في الأمر.

قال بيلار إنّي أعلم أنّ الذي قوله واحد لا يختلف عندي.

قال الملك ومن ذلك.

قال بيلار ذلك الله لا يتبدّل كلامه فما قال فحقّ وما صنع فعدل.

٣٢،١٣ قال الملك لقد اشتدّ حزني يا بيلار لقتل إيراخت.

قال بيلار اثنان ينبغي لهما أن يشتدّ حزنهما الذي يعمل الإثم في كلّ يوم والذي لا يعمل خيراً قطّ ففرحهما ونعيمهما في الدنيا قليل وندامتهما حين يعاينان الجزاء طويلة لا يستطاع إحصاؤها.

قال الملك إن كانت إيراخت حيّة لا أحزن على شيء بعدها أبداً.

قال بيلار اثنان لا ينبغي لهما أن يحزنا الذي لم يأثم قطّ والذي هو مجتهد في الله كلّ يوم.

٣٣،١٣ قال الملك ما أنا بناظر إلى أحد أكثر ممّا قد نظرت.

and pass judgment. He lay down beside her in remorse and said, "What good to me is life if I seek but cannot find you, and realize how I mistreated you whenever I think of you?" And he took neither food nor drink till he died by her side.

"Thus," said Baylār, "a judicious, intelligent man knows he shouldn't be quick to punish, especially someone he may regret losing, as the male dove did.

"I've heard, too, that a man carrying a sack of lentils entered a wood to 13.30
rest in the shade. Setting down his load, he went to sleep. A monkey came *The Monkey and the Lentils*
down from a tree above his head, took a handful of the lentils, and climbed back into the tree. A single lentil fell from the monkey's hand; as he searched for it fruitlessly, all the lentils scattered from his hand.

"Your Majesty, you have twelve thousand women, yet instead of diverting yourself with them, you seek what you'll never find. "

When the king heard these words, he feared that Baylār had indeed killed 13.31
Īrākht, and said to Baylār, "As a result of a single moment of anger on my part, did you execute my command immediately, fastening on one word, without further consideration?"

"I know of only one whose word is unvarying for me," replied Baylār.

"And who is that?" asked the king.

"God," replied Baylār, "whose word never changes. What He says is true and what He does is just."

The king said, "I am so very saddened by the death of Īrākht." 13.32

And Baylār responded, "Two kinds should feel sadness: those who sin every day and those who never do good—their joy and pleasure in this world are brief, and their regret, when they face the consequences, will be long and incalculable."

The king then said, "If Īrākht is alive, I will never be sad again."

And Baylār responded, "Two kinds should never feel sadness: those who never sin and those who strive for the sake of God every day."

The king then said, "I will never again look on anyone." 13.33

فقال بيلار اثنان لا يبصران أبدًا الأعمى والذي لا عقل له فإنّه كما أنّ[١] الأعمى لا يبصر العالم والسماء ونجومها وأرضها ولا يبصر البعيد من القريب ولا أمامه ولا ما خلفه كذلك من لا عقل له لا يعرف العالم من الجاهل ولا الحسن من القبيح ولا المحسن من المسيء له.

٣٤،١٣ قال الملك لو رأيت إيراخت لاشتدّ فرحي.

قال بيلار اثنان هما يريان البصير والعالم فكما أنّ البصير يبصر نور العالم وما فيه من الزيادة والنقصان والبعد والقرب فكذلك العالم يبصر البرّ والإثم ويعرف عمل الآخرة ويستبين له ومن كان معه هذا نجا به وهداه إلى صراط مستقيم.

قال الملك ما شبعت قطّ من نظر إيراخت.

قال له بيلار اثنان لا يشبعان أبدًا الذي لا همّ له إلّا جمع المال والذي يأكل ما يجد ويسأل عمّا لا يجد.

٣٥،١٣ قال الملك إنّه ينبغي لنا أن نتباعد منك يا بيلار فإنّ مثلك يُحذر يُتّقى.

قال بيلار إنّما ينبغي التباعد من اثنين الذي يقول لا برّ ولا إثم ولا ثواب ولا عقاب إلّا ما هو فيه والذي لا يستطيع صرف بصره عمّا ليس له ولا أذنه عن استماع السوء ولا فرجه عن نساء غيره ولا قلبه عمّا همّت به نفسه من الإثم والحرص وأشدّ من ذلك الندامة والخلود في عذاب النار.

٣٦،١٣ قال الملك صرت من إيراخت صفرًا.

قال بيلار ثلاثة كلّهم صفر اليدين النهر الذي ليس فيه ماء والبلاد التي ليس فيها ملك والمرأة التي ليس لها بعل.

قال الملك إنّك لتلقّن الجواب يا بيلار.

قال بيلار ثلاثة يلقّنون الجواب الملك الذي يعطي ويقسم من خزانته والمرأة التي تهيّأ لمن تهوى من ذوي الأحساب والرجل العالم الموفّق للخير وتعليم دين الله تعالى.

٣٧،١٣ قال الملك إنّه لتحزنني تعزيتك إيّاي.

---

١ كذا ل٢؛ ساقطة من الأصل.

And Baylār responded, "Two kinds never see: the blind man and the fool. Just as the blind man can't see the world, the sky, the stars, and the earth, and cannot tell near from far, and before from behind, the fool cannot tell the wise from the ignorant, the beautiful from the ugly, or someone who wishes him well from someone who would do him harm."

The king said, "What a joy it would be if I could see Īrākht!" 13.34

And Baylār responded, "Two kinds truly see: those blessed with sight and those who are wise. Just as someone who can see perceives the light of the world and all that waxes and wanes in it, both near and far, the wise man perceives righteousness and sinfulness; he sees clearly the works that are rewarded in the hereafter, which saves him and guides him to a straight path."

The king added, "I could never get enough of seeing Īrākht."

And Baylār responded, "Two kinds never get enough: those concerned only with amassing wealth and those who consume everything they find and seek what they will never find."

"We should keep clear of you, Baylār," said the king. "People like you are 13.35
to be feared and guarded against."

And Baylār responded, "There are two types one should keep clear of: those who say righteousness and sin, reward and punishment, exist in this world alone; and those who can't avert their eyes from what isn't theirs, stop their ears from listening to evil, keep their members away from other men's wives, or curb their hearts from the promptings of sin and greed. Both their remorse and their everlasting punishment in the fire of Hell will be great indeed."

"I am empty without Īrākht," said the king. 13.36

And Baylār responded, "Three things are truly empty: a river without water, a land without a king, and a woman without a husband."

"You are quick to respond, Baylār," said the king.

And Baylār responded, "Three are quick to respond: a king disbursing gifts from his treasury, a woman betrothed to a kinsman she loves, and a scholar able to do good deeds and teach God's religion."

The king said, "Your consolation is making me sad." 13.37

قال بيلار ثلاثة ينبغي لهم أن يحزنوا الذي فرسه سمين حسن المنظر سيّء المخبر والذي يكثر النفقة على الطعام ولا يستطيبه ولا يستطاب عنده فتذهب نفقته ضياعاً[١] والذي ينكح المرأة الحسيبة ذات الجمال ثمّ لا يقدر على إكرامها فلا تزال تشتمه وتؤذيه.

٣٨،١٣ قال الملك هلكت إيراخت ضيعة في غير حقّ.

قال بيلار ثلاثة يضيّعون في غير حقّ الحدّاد الذي يلبس الثياب البيض ولا يزال عند كيره جالساً والقصّار يلبس الخفّ الجديد وقدماه في الماء والرجل التاجر يتزوّج المرأة الشابّة الحسناء ثمّ لا يزال غائباً.

٣٩،١٣ قال الملك إنّك أهل أن تعذَّب أشدّ العذاب.

قال بيلار ثلاثة ينبغي لهم أن يعذَّبوا المجرم المذنب العظيم والمنتهك للمحارم الذي يزني بحرمة غيره والمتقدّم إلى مائدة لم يُدع إليها والذي يسأل أصدقاءه ما ليس عندهم فإذا أخبروه أنّه ليس عندهم لم يعذرهم وانتهك أعراضهم.

٤٠،١٣ قال الملك إنّه لينبغي لك أن تسفَّه.

قال بيلار ثلاثة ينبغي لهم أن يسفَّهوا النجّار الذي لا يزال ينحت الخشب فيملأ بيته من الحطب ويصير هو وزوجته وولده في الضيق والطبيب الذي يقطع بالموسى ولا يحسم فيقطع لحم الناس والغريب المقيم بين ظهراني عدوّه لا يريد الرجوع إلى أهله فيصير آخر أمره إلى الندامة.

٤١،١٣ قال الملك كان ينبغي لك أن تسكن حتّى يذهب غضبي.

قال بيلار ثلاثة ينبغي لهم أن يسكنوا الذي يرقى الجبل الطويل والذي يصيد السمك والذي يهمّ بالخطر العظيم.

٤٢،١٣ قال الملك ليتني قد رأيت إيراخت فإنّي قد اشتهيتها.

قال بيلار ثلاثة يتمنّون ما لا يجدون الفاجر الذي لا ورع له يريد إذا مات منزلة الأبرار ويرجو مثل ثوابهم والبخيل الذي يريد أن تكون روحه في الآخرة في منزلة

١ على طعام . . . ضياعًا: كذا پ٣٤٦٦؛ ساقطة من الأصل.

And Baylār responded, "There are three who should be sad: the owner of a fine horse that lacks spirit; the man who spends lavishly on food that pleases neither him nor his guests; and the husband of a beautiful wife of noble family whom he cannot maintain in proper style, so that he suffers from her constant slander."

"Īrākht has perished wrongfully and pointlessly," said the king. 13.38

And Baylār responded, "Three suffer pointless loss: the blacksmith who wears white when he sits by the bellows, the laundryman who puts on new shoes when his feet are in the water, and the merchant who marries a beautiful young wife and then is never home."

The king said, "You deserve to be punished severely." 13.39

And Baylār responded, "Three types deserve to be punished: the shameless evildoer who seduces other men's wives; the guest who attends a banquet uninvited; and the man who asks his friends for what they don't have, and, when they tell him they don't have it, accepts no excuses and blackens their reputation."

"You should be considered a fool," said the king. 13.40

And Baylār responded, "Three types should be considered fools: the carpenter who cuts timber until he fills his house with so much wood that he, his wife, and his children are left with no room; the doctor who wields his razor without cauterizing the wound and is so incompetent that he slices off people's flesh; and the stranger who lives among his foes but doesn't want to return home and regrets it in the end."

"You should have kept calm until my anger subsided," said the king. 13.41

And Baylār responded, "Three kinds should keep calm: those climbing a high mountain, those angling for fish, and those embarking on a dangerous enterprise."

"I wish I could see Īrākht," said the king. "I miss her." 13.42

And Baylār responded, "Three types wish for what they will never obtain: the godless sinner who would be numbered with the saints when he dies and receive their reward, the miser who wants his soul to dwell among the

السمحاء والعامد إلى إهراق الدماء وقتل الأبرار ويريد أن تكون روحه مع الأرواح ذي المخافة لله تعالى.

قال الملك أنا الذي أوجعت نفسي. ٤٣،١٣

قال بيلار ثلاثة هم أوجعوا أنفسهم الذي يأتي القتال ولا يتّقي فيُقتل والكثير المال الذي لا ولد له ولا أخ وإنّما تجارته في الربا والاستغلاء على الناس فربّما حسده بعضهم فقتله والشيخ الكبير ينكح المرأة الحسناء الجريئة على ما ركبته فلا تزال تتمنّى موته لتنكح رجلاً شاباً فهذا تكون هلكته على يديها.

قال الملك إنّي لحقير في عينك حتّى تجترئ في مثل هذه المقالة بين يديّ. ٤٤،١٣

قال بيلار ثلاثة هم يحقرون أربابهم الذي يهذي بالكلام ويقع فيما لا يُسأل عنه ويقول فيما لا يعلم فلا يزال يزري مليكه والمملوك الغنيّ وسيّده فقير فلا يعطي سيّده من ماله شيئاً والعبد يغلظ لسيّده في القول ويخاصمه ويستطيل عليه.

قال الملك أراك كأنّك تهزأ بي لما ترى من أسفي. ٤٥،١٣

قال بيلار ثلاثة ينبغي لهم أن يستهزأ بهم الذي يقول قد شهدت حروباً كثيرة فأكثرت القتل والسبي ولا يُرى في جسمه أثر شيء من القتال والذي يخبر أنّه عالم بالدين ناسك مجتهد وهو بادن[1] غليظ الرقبة أسمن من الأئمة الفجّار فهو حقيق أن يُسخر منه فإنّه من أجهد نفسه في طاعة الله ألفي منهوك الجسم قليل الطعم والمرأة العذراء التي لا تزال تسخر من ذات الزوج ولعلّها أن تكون حزينة.

قال الملك إنّك لمدلَّه. ٤٦،١٣

قال بيلار ثلاثة يشبهون المدلَّهين وكأنّهم يهذون مع الشياطين الحليم الذي يؤدّب الجاهل ولا يقبل منه ويماريه بجهله فهو في حاله تلك في غير عمل وآخر أمره في الندامة والذي يهيّج السفيه ويتحرّش به ويتعمّد أذاه والكذب عليه فيؤذي بذلك نفسه ومن سمع قوله ندم والذي يفضي بسرّه إلى من لم يجرّب من الأخلّاء ويدخله في الأمر العظيم ويثق[2] به ثقته بنفسه.[3]

١ كذا ع؛ الأصل: بادي. ٢ كذا ل٢؛ الأصل: ويوثق. ٣ كذا ل٢؛ الأصل: نفسه.

generous in the hereafter, and the man who sheds innocent blood and wants his soul to dwell with the souls of the God-fearing."

"I am someone who has brought pain on himself," said the king. 13.43

And Baylār responded, "Three types bring pain on themselves: those who go into battle without a shield and get killed; a rich man who is without children and brothers, who lives by usury and profiteering, and who in the end is killed by an envier; and an old man married to a beautiful but brazen woman who constantly hopes for his death in order to marry a younger man, and who perishes at her hands."

"I must be contemptible in your eyes," said the king, "when you dare to say such things in my presence." 13.44

And Baylār responded, "Three types show contempt for their masters: the jabberer who babbles on regardless of whether he has been asked or not, prattling about what he knows and doesn't know, thus dishonoring his owner; the rich servant of a poor master, who gives his master none of his wealth; and the servant who speaks rudely, quarrels, and argues arrogantly with his master."

"You seem to be mocking me for my sadness," said the king. 13.45

And Baylār responded, "Three kinds deserve to be mocked: those who say they have seen many campaigns, killed many foes, and captured many prisoners, though they have no battle scars on their bodies; those who claim to be scholars of religion and zealous ascetics, but who, obese and thick-necked, are fatter than a profligate sinner—they should be mocked, and their pretentions doubted, because all who exhaust themselves obeying God are emaciated and sparing in diet; and the virgin who derides a married woman, while she herself comes to a sorrowful end."

"You are out of your mind," said the king. 13.46

And Baylār responded, "Three types seem to be out of their minds, acting like persons raving with demons: the intelligent man who educates a fool—the fool is unteachable and in his ignorance argues with the teacher, who earns nothing but regret for his effort; a person who provokes a fool, who in exasperation takes to insulting him and spreading lies about him, and thereby injures himself; and a person who reveals his secret to a friend he hasn't tested, brings him in on an important affair, and trusts him as he would trust himself."

قال الملك أنا الذي جنيت المشقّة على نفسي. ٤٧،١٣

قال بيلار ثلاثة هم يجنون المشقّة على أنفسهم الذي يقاتل من يعلم أنّه أقوى منه وأشدّ بطشاً حتّى يُقتل أو يهرب والذي ينكص على عقبيه فربّما تردّى في جبّ أو وقع في مهواة فينكسر والذي يضرب في الأسفار البعيدة في غير حاجة ولا يصيب إلّا العناء والذي يقول لست أهاب القتال ولا أتّقيه ويغترّ غيره فإذا حضر القتال تلفّت يميناً وشمالاً يحتال للفرار.

قال الملك قد تصرّم ودّ ما بيني وبينك. ٤٨،١٣

قال بيلار ثلاثة لا يلبث ودّهم أن يتصرّم الخليل الذي لا يلقى خليله ولا يكاتبه ولا يراسله والمرأة التي إذا مات لها زوج عرم عليها التمست غيره والذي خلّته على الفجور لا تدوم بل تنقطع عند أوّل عثرة.

قال الملك قد عملت في قتل إيراخت عملاً يُستدلّ به على خفّة عقلك وحلمك. ٤٩،١٣

قال بيلار ثلاثة يعملون بجرأتهم ما تستبين به خفّة أحلامهم المستودع ماله من لا يثق به ثمّ يجعل من لا يعرف عدالته فيما بينه وبين خصمه والقليل العقل والحياء ثمّ يخبر أنّه عاقل مقاتل بصير باتّخاذ الأخدان وخدمة السلطان وتقدير البنيان وبجميع الأعمال الشاقّة وهو كاذب في جميع ما ذكر والذي يرفض دنياه ويذكر أنّه يعمل للآخرة ويكون عمله الذي يظهر لآخرته رياء وسمعة ولا دنيا أصاب ولا آخرة.

قال الملك إنّك لغير عاقل. ٥٠،١٣

قال بيلار ثلاثة لا ينبغي لهم أن يُعَدّوا من ذوي العقول الإسكاف الذي يجلس في المكان المرتفع فإذا تدحرجت شفرته أو شيء من أداته شغله طلبه عن كثير من عمله والخيّاط الذي يطيل خيطه فإذا انعقد شُغل بتخليصه عن كثير من عمله والذي يقصّ من أشعار الناس وهو يلتفت يميناً وشمالاً فيفسد أشعارهم فيُسخر منه وربّما أصيب بالعقوبة المؤذية.

قال الملك إنّك تريد أن تعلّم الناس كلّهم حتّى يمهروا وتريد أن تعلّمني أيضاً حتّى أكون ماهراً. ٥١،١٣

"I've brought trouble on myself," said the king. 13.47

And Baylār responded, "Three kinds bring trouble on themselves: those who fight an opponent they know to be stronger and more aggressive, and are either killed or run away and retreat, walking backward, likely to stumble into a well or fall into a pit and break a limb; those who go on a long voyage for no purpose and gain nothing but trouble; and those who say they have no fear of battle—they may deceive others, but when war comes, they look right and left to find a way to escape."

"Our friendship is at an end," said the king. 13.48

And Baylār responded, "There are three kinds whose affection is soon severed: the friend who doesn't visit, write, or send messengers to his friend; the woman whose abusive husband has died and seeks another; and those whose friendship, based on profligacy, doesn't last, but is severed at the least mishap."

"By killing Īrākht you've shown your lack of intelligence and good sense," 13.49
said the king.

And Baylār responded, "Three types by their rashness show their lack of intelligence and good sense: those who deposit money for safekeeping with someone untrustworthy and make a person of untested honesty a witness between themselves and an opponent; those devoid of intelligence and modesty who claim to be military men and to be intelligent, skilled at acquiring friends and serving rulers, designing buildings, and every difficult task, lying with every word; and those who claim to have renounced the things of this world and to be intent on the hereafter, but do so as part of a hypocritical search for celebrity—they profit neither in this world nor the next."

"You aren't being intelligent," said the king. 13.50

And Baylār responded, "Three types shouldn't be considered intelligent: the shoemaker who sits on a seat so high that if his knife or other tool falls, he is distracted from his work looking for it; the tailor who uses such a long thread that he is distracted from his work untangling its knots; and the barber who spoils a haircut by looking right and left, and thus earns a painful beating."

"You want to teach everybody, myself included, to be adept," said the 13.51
king.

قال بيلار ثلاثة يزعمون أنّهم قد مهروا ولم يمهروا وينبغي لهم أن يتعلّموا الذي يضرب بالصنج[1] والطبل ثمّ لا يوافق الأصوات واللحون والمصوّر الذي يزعم أنّه يحسن التصوير وهو لا يحسن خلط الأصباغ والذي يزعم أنّه ليس أحد أكمل علماً منه ولا أبصر بالكلام ولا مقدار ما ينبغي أن يتكلّم به.

٥٢،١٣ قال الملك لم تعمل بحقّ حين قتلت إيراخت.

قال بيلار أربعة يعملون بغير حقّ الذي لا يصدق لسانه والذي لا يصدّق قوله فعله والسريع في الأكل البطيء في العمل والحرث وخدمة من فوقه والذي يغضب من غير[2] أن يُجترم إليه والملك الذي يهمّ بالأمر العظيم من الجور فيركبه.

٥٣،١٣ قال الملك لو حسن نظرك لم تقتل إيراخت.

قال بيلار أربعة يحسن نظرهم الذي يصنع الطعام ويقدّمه إلى سيّده لحينه والذي يرضى بامرأته وحدها ولا يطلب شيئاً غيرها والملك الذي لا يقدم على الأمر الجسيم إلّا بمشاورة العلماء والرجل الذي يقهر غضبه ويكظم غيظه.

٥٤،١٣ قال الملك إنّي لخائف عليك يا بيلار.

قال بيلار أربعة يخافون ما لا ينبغي لهم أن يخافوه الطير الصغير الذي يكون في الشجر يرفع جناحه مخافة أن تسقط السماء عليه يقول إن سقطت حبستها بجناحي والكركيّ الذي يقوم على إحدى رجليه مخافة أن تخسف به الأرض إن وضع الأخرى والدويبة التي تأكل التراب تأكل يوماً وتصوم يوماً مخافة أن تموت جوعاً والخفّاش الذي يمنعه من الطيران بالنهار أنّه[3] يرى أنّه ليس على الأرض طائر أحسن منه فيخاف أن يصيده الناس فيتّخذوه لأنفسهم لحسنه.

٥٥،١٣ قال الملك أكنت نذرت نذراً لتقتلنّ إيراخت.

قال بيلار أربعة ينبغي لهم أن تُنذَر فيهم النذور أن يعاقَر الفرس الجواد الثمين الذي هو قعدة ربّه ومركبه والثور الذي يحرث عليه والمرأة العاقلة المحبّة لبعلها والعبد الجاهد الناصح في الخدمة الصدوق الهائب لسيّده.

[1] كذا ش، ع؛ الأصل: الوخ. [2] كذا پ٣٤٦٦؛ ساقطة من الأصل. [3] كذا ع، ش؛ ساقطة من الأصل.

And Baylār responded, "Three types prematurely claim to be adept, but have more to learn: someone who can play the harp and drums, but cannot keep time with the voices or the tunes; the painter who claims to be an adept draftsman, but cannot mix colors; and those who claim that they know better than anyone else but fail to speak clearly or know how much they ought to say."[60]

"You did not act correctly when you killed Īrākht," said the king. 13.52

And Baylār responded, "Four types do not act correctly: those whose tongues never speak the truth and whose actions do not match their words; those swift to eat, but slow to work, plow, or serve their superiors; those who become angry at no offense; and the king who rushes to carry out a grave injustice."

"Had you given the matter due consideration, you wouldn't have killed 13.53
Īrākht," said the king.

And Baylār responded, "Four types give matters due consideration: those who prepare food and serve it to their masters on time; those who are content with their own wives and seek no other; the king who embarks on an important affair only upon the advice of his scholars; and those who subdue their anger and suppress their wrath."

"I fear for you, Baylār," said the king.[61] 13.54

And Baylār responded, "Four fear needlessly: the little bird who dwells in the trees yet raises its wings for fear that the sky might fall on him, saying, 'If it falls, I'll hold it up with my wings'; the stork who stands on one leg, fearing that if he puts the other down, the earth will collapse under him; the earthworm who eats and fasts on alternate days for fear of starving to death; and the bat who won't fly by day because, fancying himself the world's most beautiful bird, he fears people will trap him and keep him for his beauty."

"Did you vow to put Īrākht to death?" said the king. 13.55

And Baylār responded, "One should vow to cling to four things: the prize steed that is its owner's mount; the ox with which you plow; the wise wife who loves her husband; and the industrious servant who is loyal, truthful, and respectful toward his master."

٥٦،١٣ قال الملك لا تطيب لك نفسي بعد قتلك إيراخت.

قال بيلار أربعة لا تطيب أنفسهم لأربعة العالم لا تطيب نفسه بمواصلة الجاهل والرغيب الشره لا تطيب نفسه بمواصلة الناسك الصوّام والأديب العاقل لا تطيب نفسه بمواصلة العدوّ الحنق والأنف الحميّ لا تطيب نفسه بمواصلة المهين له المستطيل عليه.

٥٧،١٣ قال الملك لا أقدر على مثل إيراخت في النساء أبدًا.

قال بيلار أربعة أشياء لا يكاد يُقدَر عليها المرأة الثيّب أن ترضى بزوج والمعوّد لسانه الكذب لا يقدر على النزوع عن ذلك والمعجب برأيه السيّئ الخلق لا يقدر أحد على معاشرته والأشر البطر لا يقدر على تغيير طباعه.

٥٨،١٣ قال الملك ليت هذا العلم كان قبل اليوم فأمّا اليوم فإنّه قليل النفع والغنى عنه اليوم.

قال بيلار أربعة أشياء ينبغي التقدّم في العلم لها والعمل بها الحرب ينبغي لأهل الشجاعة التقدّم فيها والعلم بها وتهيئ الآلة قبل ملابستها ومنافرتها وينبغي لصاحب المال أن يعدّ قاضياً عدلاً لا يجور ولا يحيف ولا يرتشي قبل منافرة خصمائه والرجل الكثير المال يريد اتّخاذ العبيد والضياع ينبغي أن يعدّ الثقات من الوكلاء والأعوان قبل اتّخاذ الضياع والرجل الذي يريد أن يدعو الملوك والأشراف إلى طعامه ينبغي له أن يعدّ قبل ذلك ما يحتاج إليه حتّى يستغني عن جمع ذلك بعد حضور من يدعو إلى طعامه لئلاّ يلزمه عنت ولا تقصير.

٥٩،١٣ قال الملك ولا البرّ تعرف يا بيلار ولا الإثم.

قال بيلار أربعة لا يفكّرون في برّ ولا إثم المريض الشديد المرض والخائف لسيّده أو للسلطان والمكابر لعدوّه المظلوم الجريء والمتعدّي الذي يروع من هو أفضل منه.

٦٠،١٣ قال الملك إنّك لمؤدّب يا بيلار.

قال بيلار أربعة لا يطاق تأديبهم الذي قد لهج بالظلم والفجور والأشر المعجب برأيه والمتعوّد السرقة والسريع الغضب البطيء الرضى.

٦١،١٣ قال الملك ما ينبغي لنا أن نثق بك يا بيلار.

"I will never take pleasure in your company now that you've killed Īrākht," said the king. 13.56

And Baylār responded, "Four take no pleasure in the company of four others: the scholar takes no pleasure in the company of the ignoramus, the glutton takes no pleasure in the company of the ascetic, the man of refinement takes no pleasure in the company of a resentful foe, and the proud man who tolerates no slight takes no pleasure in the company of an arrogant, disrespectful man."

"I shall never find another woman like Īrākht," said the king. 13.57

And Baylār responded, "Four things are nearly impossible to find: a woman of much experience who becomes satisfied with one man; a habitual liar who ceases to lie; a bad-tempered, conceited man whose company one can enjoy; and a proud, insolent man who manages to change his nature."

"I wish this knowledge had come earlier, for now it is useless and has come too late," said the king. 13.58

And Baylār responded, "Four things should be ascertained and acted on in advance: soldiers going into battle should obtain intelligence and prepare their gear before the fighting begins; a man of means, before contending with his opponents, should find an honest judge who doesn't swerve from the truth, act unjustly, or accept bribes; a man of wealth who intends to acquire slaves and estates should first find trustworthy agents and assistants before acquiring the estates; and a man who intends to invite kings and nobles to dinner should prepare what he needs in advance, lest, after they arrive, he run into difficulties or fall short."

"You know neither piety nor sin, Baylār," said the king. 13.59

And Baylār responded, "Four types pay piety and sin no heed: the gravely ill, those afraid of their master or ruler, bold men badly treated who contend with their enemy, and an assailant terrorizing someone better than he."

"You are imparting discipline, Baylār," said the king. 13.60

And Baylār responded, "Four types tolerate no discipline: the man addicted to wrongdoing and licentiousness; the insolent, conceited man; the habitual thief; and those quick to anger, slow to be pleased."

"We shouldn't trust you, Baylār," said the king. 13.61

قال بيلار أربعة لا ينبغي أن يثق بهم أحد الحيّة الماردة وكلّ سبع من الحيوان والأثمة الفجّار من الناس والمال لأنّه لا يؤمن انتقاله عن صاحبه والجسد الذي قد قضي عليه الموت لا يوثَق ببقائه وسلامته.

قال الملك لا يجوز لذي العقل أنّه يمزح مع من يملكه ولا مع المتّهم من نظرائه فضلاً عن سيّده. ٦٢،١٣

قال بيلار أربعة لا يمزحون ولا يُنطلق إليهم السلطان ذو الهيبة والمروءة والمقدرة واللبيب العاقل الرزين والسكران البطر والذي يرجى طَوْله وفضله.

قال الملك ما ينبغي لنا مخالطتك يا بيلار بعد قتلك إيراخت. ٦٣،١٣

قال بيلار خمسة أشياء لا يختلط واحد منها بصاحبه الليل والنهار والبرّ والفاجر والنور والظلمة والخير والشرّ والحرّ والبرد.

قال الملك لا ينبغي مواصلتك يا بيلار. ٦٤،١٣

قال بيلار خمسة لا ينبغي لهم أن يواصَلوا اللصّ الفاجر والخبّ الكذوب والبذيّ العجول وذو الكبر الحسود والسليط الحقود.

قال الملك إذا رأيت ستّة عشر ألف امرأة ليس فيهنّ إيراخت اشتدّ حزني يا بيلار. ٦٥،١٣

قال بيلار خمس من النساء ليس أحد بحقيق أن يحزن عليهنّ الورهاء الجريئة والجفيّة البذيّة والسفيهة الذميمة والرعناء التي لا حلم لها والمخالفة لزوجها المؤذية له.

قال الملك لم يصبني حزن قطّ كما أصابني لمكان إيراخت ورأيها يا بيلار. ٦٦،١٣

قال بيلار خمس من النساء ينبغي الحزن عليهنّ الكريمة الحسب ذات الشرف والبهاء والعفيفة الميمونة الحليمة والجميلة الجهيرة والراضية ببعلها الهيّنة المؤونة عليه.

قال الملك من يدلّني على إيراخت حيّة وله عندي من المال ما أحبّ. ٦٧،١٣

And Baylār responded, "Four things shouldn't be trusted: untamed snakes and predators; profligate sinners; wealth, which can never be trusted not to pass out of its owner's hands; and the body, whose survival and health one can never count on, condemned as it is to death."

The king said, "A wise man shouldn't jest with his servants or with colleagues he has doubts about, let alone with his master." 13.62

And Baylār responded, "There are four sorts one shouldn't jest with or speak to without reserve: an awe-inspiring, valiant, powerful ruler; a skillful, intelligent, dignified man; an insolent drunkard; and those from whom you hope to gain favor and benefit."

The king said, "We should no longer mingle with you, Baylār, after your killing of Īrākht." 13.63

And Baylār responded, "Five things do not mingle with each other: night and day, the pious and the dissolute, light and dark, good and evil, hot and cold."

"No one should share your companionship, Baylār," said the king. 13.64

And Baylār responded, "There are five sorts with whom one shouldn't share companionship: the dissolute thief, the lying cheat, the man quick to revile, the proud envier, and the wanton tyrant."

"I am very sad, Baylār," said the king, "when I see sixteen thousand women, without Īrākht among them." 13.65

And Baylār responded, "There are five women for whom no one should feel sad: a clumsy and audacious one; an impudent, foul-mouthed scold; a stupid, ugly woman; a frivolous and indiscrete one; and a disobedient woman who insults her husband."

"Never before," said the king, "have I felt such sadness as I now feel recalling Īrākht's superiority and judgment." 13.66

And Baylār responded, "There are five women for whose loss one should feel sad: a noble woman of distinguished lineage; a woman chaste, fortunate, and prudent; a woman beautiful and attractive to behold; a woman content with her husband; and a woman who is ready to assist her husband."

"Whoever guides me to the living Īrākht," said the king, "shall have all the money he desires." 13.67

قال بيلار خمسة المال أحبّ إليهم من أنفسهم الذي يقاتل بالأجرة والذي يحفر القناة والسرب بالأجر والتاجر الذي يركب البحر والرقّاء الذي يرسل الحيّة على نفسه لشيء يعطاه والذي يخاطر على شرب السمّ.

١٣،٦٨ قال الملك لا أرى لأملي في إيراخت ثمرة محمودة تعقد رجائي منها يا بيلار.

قال بيلار سبعة ليست لأعمالهم ثمرة محمودة الذي يعمل بغير نيّة محمودة ولا حصافة والذي يصنع معروفه عند من لا شكر له ولا وفاء والفظّ الغليظ الذي لا رحمة له والمرأة التي تزني وتلد ولد السوء وتغذوه والذي يأمن الخبّ الكفور والذي يسرع ملالة إخوانه والذي لا يعرف الله ولا أولياءه.

١٣،٦٩ قال الملك قد أثبتّ في نفسي عليك حقدًا بقتلك إيراخت.

قال بيلار ثمانية الحقد بينهم ثابت الذئب والشاة والسنّور والفأر والبازي والدّراج والبوم[١] والغراب والحيّة وابن عرس والبرّ والفاجر وذو المروءة ومن لا مروءة له والمكثر والمقلّ.

١٣،٧٠ قال الملك أما لك رحمة ترحمني يا بيلار.

قال بيلار ثمانية لا يستحقّون الرحمة من الناس الملك الحقود والعامل بحقده والرجل الهذر الذي يتكلّم بما لا ينفعه ويضرّ غيره واللصّ الذي يترقّب دخول الليل ليمكنه من السرق والذي يحمل الموتى بالأجر فيتعطّل لقلّة عمله والمرأة البذيّة الفاجرة والتارك سلوك الطريق الأعظم واختصاره الطرق الذي يعطب فيها والمحارب الذي يسعى في الأرض للفساد والذي يشرب السمّ للتجربة.

١٣،٧١ قال الملك امتنع النوم منّي حزنًا على إيراخت يا بيلار.

قال بيلار تسعة لا ينامون المريض الذي لا طبيب له والكثير المال الذي خاف على ماله ولا يثق عليه أحدًا والذي يهمّ بدم يسفكه والذي يتمنّى الشرّ للناس ويحتال لإدخال الضرّ عليهم والمحارب الذي يتخوّف البيات والذي يؤخذ بغرم مال وليس

[١] كذا ش، پ ٣٤٧٥؛ ساقطة من الأصل.

And Baylār responded, "Five sorts love money more than life: the mercenary who fights for pay; the man who earns his wage by digging canals and tunnels; the merchant who sails the seas; the snake charmer who, for a price, sets a snake loose on himself; and the man who risks his life by drinking poison for a wager."

"I see that my hopes for Īrākht will have no welcome outcome," said the king. 13.68

And Baylār responded, "There are seven types whose actions have no welcome outcome: those who act without commendable intention or sound judgment, those who bestow favors on a person devoid of gratitude and loyalty, the crude boor who knows no mercy, the adulterous woman who gives birth to a bastard and raises it, those who trust an ungrateful deceiver, those quick to weary their brothers, and those who recognize neither God nor His saints."

"By killing Īrākht," said the king, "you have planted in my heart implacable hatred for you." 13.69

And Baylār responded, "Eight there are between whom implacable hatred is fixed: the wolf and the lamb, the cat and the mouse, the goshawk and the francolin, the owl and the crow, the snake and the mongoose, the saint and the sinner, the valorous and the coward, the rich and the poor."

"Have you no sympathy for me, Baylār?" said the king. 13.70

And Baylār responded, "Eight types deserve no sympathy: the malicious king who acts on his malice; the babbler whose prattling does him no good and harms others; the thief who waits for nightfall so that he can steal; the pallbearer idle for lack of work; the foul, licentious woman; the traveler who leaves the highway to take a shortcut and perishes; the soldier who wreaks havoc in the land; and someone who drinks poison as an experiment."

"Sorrow for Īrākht keeps me from sleeping, Baylār," said the king. 13.71

And Baylār responded, "Nine types do not sleep: a sick man with no physician, an anxious rich man who trusts no one with his wealth, a man who intends to shed blood, a man who wishes people ill and devises ways to harm

عنده والذي يعشق المرأة ولا يصل إليها والذي يطّلع على فجور امرأته ويمسكها عنده والذي يباهَت بالكذب ويرمى ما لم يكن منه.

قال الملك لقد فارقتني إيراخت على كره مني لفراقها يا بيلار. ٧٢،١٣

قال بيلار يُكرَه من الأشياء تسعة حلول الكبر وذهاب الشباب والمرض الذي يسهر صاحبه ليله ويضجره نهاره والخوف والرغب اللذان يشغلون القلب والغضب الذي يضرّ بالجسد ويهجن بالعقل والحلم والهمّ والحزن اللذان يخلان الجسم ويهلكانه والموت الذي لا يبقي على أحد والحرّ والبرد اللذان يضرّان بالنبات[1] والجوع والعطش اللذان فيهما الهلكة والمشؤوم الذي يهلك على يديه بالقيام جماعة من الناس.

قال الملك أبقوّتك قتلت إيراخت. ٧٣،١٣

قال بيلار عشرة يشبهون على الناس أمورهم لما يدّعون فأمرهم على الناس مشتبه حتّى يُبلوا ويُختبروا المقاتل عند الحرب والعمل والقانع عند الحاجة وذو المروءة عند الغضب والتاجر عند البيع والشراء والصديق عند الشدائد والعالم عند الرأي والمشورة ومباشرة الأعمال وذو الدين والنسك عند الصبر على العبادة وذو الجود عند العطاء والأمانة عند الوديعة.

قال الملك إنّك لتكلّمني بكلام السخط يا بيلار. ٧٤،١٣

قال بيلار إنّما يتكلّم بكلام السخط عشرة الملك المترف والشيخ القلق والسفيه الذي لا أدب له والباذل نصحه للأخرق والمتكلّف للأعمال بغير رفق والذي يقضي بجهله فيردّ عليه قضاؤه والقاضي الذي يحكم بالجور للطمع والشحيح الذي يُلِحّ عليه في المسألة فيضيق عليه والذي يعطي فيكثر المنّ.

قال الملك قد عنّيتني وعنّيت نفسك يا بيلار. ٧٥،١٣

قال بيلار الذين يعنّون أنفسهم ويعنّون معهم غيرهم عشرة القليل العلم الذي يدّعي أكثر ممّا يحسن فتكثر عليه المسائل والفتيا يعنّيه من يسائله عمّا لا يحسن ويعنّي من

[1] كذا ر؛ الأصل: بالشاب.

them, a soldier who fears a night attack, a debtor who has no money, a man with no access to the woman he loves, a man who knows his wife is unfaithful but doesn't repudiate her, and someone slandered and wrongly accused of something he never did."

"Īrākht's departure was loathsome to me, Baylār," said the king. 13.72

And Baylār responded, "Nine things are loathsome: the onset of old age and the departure of youth; illness that brings with it sleepless nights and unquiet days; fear and greed that occupy the heart; anger that harms the body and degrades the mind; cares and sadness that emaciate and destroy the body; death, which spares no one; heat and cold that damage crops; hunger and thirst that bring perdition; and the ill-fated rebel at whose hands many perish."

"Did you slay Īrākht by your own hand?" said the king. 13.73

And Baylār responded, "There are ten types whose claims remain uncertain until they are tried and tested: the soldier by combat and action; the contented man by need; the gentleman by anger; the merchant by buying and selling; the friend by adversity; the scholar by his judgment, advice, and management of affairs; the pious ascetic by persistence in worship; the generous man by his gifts; and the trustee by keeping whatever is entrusted to his care."

"Baylār," said the king, "you are addressing me with harsh words." 13.74

And Baylār responded, "Ten types are addressed with harsh words: an insolent king; an excited old man; an uncultured fool; those who offer advice to bumblers; those who undertake works for which they have no skill; those who judge with ignorance, to their detriment; the judge whose unjust judgments are motivated by greed; the miser who loses his temper when pressed for alms; and the giver who gives in order to increase his recipient's obligation."

"You've wearied me," said the king, "and wearied yourself, Baylār." 13.75

And Baylār responded. "Ten types weary themselves and others, too. Those with little learning who lay claim to more than they know: they receive

يجيب لقلّة الإفهام له والجواب والذي يلي الأعمال الكثيرة من تحت يده والذي يلحّ على صاحبه في طلب ما لا يمكن من قبله فيعنّيه لشدّة الإلحاح عليه ويعنّي نفسه بكثرة الطلب والرجل الجاهل الذي يريد أن يحمل الناس على مثل رأيه ولا يتابعونه[١] فهو في عناء من إرادتهم على ما لا يمكن وهم في عناء منه والذي يخدم السلطان بلا فهم ولا علم به فهو في عناء من لائمة السلطان إيّاه والسلطان في عناء من قلّة فهمه والذي يتكلّف ما لا يحسن من الصناعات فيعنّى في العمل ويعنّي من يعمل له إذا لم يرعمله صحيحاً فيحوجه إلى إعادة ما عمل له والذي وُكل بتأديب البليد فالمؤدِّب والمؤدَّب في عناء والذي يضع سرّه عند امرأة لا تقوى على كتمان السرّ فإذا أفشت سرّه أدّبها فلم تقبل فكلّ واحد منهما في عناء من صاحبه وراعي الفرس البليد فكلّما تبلّد ضربه وكلّما ضربه ازداد بلادة فكلّ واحد منهما في عناء من صاحبه والمبتلى من الرعيّة بالسلطان الكذّاب المخلف فهو لا يجد بدّاً من الإلحاح في حاجته والآخر لا يألوه إطماعاً وترديداً وإخلافاً فكلّ واحد منهما من صاحبه في عناء.

قال الملك قد طوّلت عليّ فأوضح لي الأمركان عليّ أو لي يا بيلار. ٧٦،١٣

فسكت بيلار وعلم أنّ الملك قد اشتدّ حزنه على إيراخت واشتاق إليها فقال في نفسه أنا حقيق بإتيان الملك بهذه المرأة التي قد أحبّها هذا الحبّ وحرص على رؤيتها هذا الحرص وصبر على طول تصريفي إيّاه في أشياء كثيرة وإغلاظي له في القول عن عقوبتي.

ثمّ قال أيّها الملك أطال الله عمرك وأدام سلامتك وزادك حلماً وكرماً الآن أتكلّم بلساني كلمة وأقول إنّه ليس في الأرض ملك مثلك ولا شبيه لك ولا كان فيما مضى ولا يكون بعدك إذ لم يسلبك الغضب وأنا مع دقّة شأني وصغر خطري أقول لك ما أقول ولكن لم تزل عنك السكينة والوقار موسّعاً عليك في العلم والحلم ولين الكنف والجانب في سلطانك ولست تقول في الغضب والرضى ما لا ينبغي ولا تأمر به ولكنّك لين الكنف محبّ للسلامة فإن نزل بك من تصرّف حوادث الأيّام نقص

---

١ الأصل: سعابعونه.

many inquiries and provide many responses; the inquiries weary them, and they weary their respondents by their meager guidance. Those charged with many tasks. Those who importune a friend for the impossible, weary him by their insistence, and exhaust themselves by their persistence. The opinionated fool who would convert everybody to his opinion, which they do not agree with, and wearies himself and everybody else by his unsuccessful persuasion. Those devoid of understanding and knowledge who serve the ruler are wearied by the ruler's rebukes and weary the ruler by their lack of understanding. Those who contract to complete a job they're unskilled at and weary themselves with their labor and weary their employer, who must oblige them to redo the bungled job. Those charged with teaching a dunce weary both themselves and their pupils. Those who entrust their secret to a woman too weak to hide it, and who rebuke her vainly when she reveals it—each will be wearied by the other. The owner of a stupid horse, who beats it whenever it does something stupid, only increasing its stupidity, so that each is wearied by the other. The unfortunate subject who serves a mendacious ruler who breaks his promises wearies the ruler by his insistent requests, while the ruler keeps fanning his hopes, repeating his promises and disappointing them, so that each grows weary of the other."

"You've drawn the matter out at great length," said the king. "Now tell me 13.76
clearly, Baylār, whether it has turned out against me or for me."

Baylār fell silent. Realizing how sad the king was and how he longed to see Īrākht, he said to himself, "I ought to bring the king the woman he loves so deeply and yearns so much to see. He has patiently endured my lengthy exchanges with him and my blunt words without punishing me."

So he said, "May God grant Your Majesty long life, preserve you in health, and increase your judiciousness and nobility. I speak now in my own words. No king on earth is your equal or like you: there never has been and never will be. Anger has not overcome you; for despite my insignificance and unimportance, you remained calm and dignified while I spoke, abundant in your knowledge, judiciousness, and mildness—in the midst of your authority.

لبعض ما قسم الله تعالى لك من الكرامة أو رُزئت من أمورك ما يضطرّ إلى الأمر الشديد صبرت ولم تهلع فيه ولم تجزع منه ولكنّك تعزّي نفسك وتظهر منك القناعة والرضا بما كان من ذلك. ومن لم يكن من أصلكم وسار في ملكه بالبطر والسخف قمعتموه وأذللتموه وإن كان ممّن تقرّبون وتلطفون[1] فعمل في أموركم بالخيلاء والكبر أقصيتموه ونفيتموه عن أموركم فإذا فعلتم ذلك بهم وفارقوا[2] ما كانوا فيه من تكرمتهم فزعوا من ذلك وآلمهم ولم ينفعهم دواء الجرح ولم يغنِ عنهم شيئاً ولكنّهم يزدادون بالجرح حزناً وهمّاً وزيادة في مصيبتهم. فأمّا أنتم أيّها الملك فإنّكم لكرم أصلكم وشرف أخلاقكم ملكتم أنفسكم وصبرتم على ما سمعتم من عبدكم مع صغر أمره وخساسة شأنه فأشكرلك أيّها الملك إذ[3] لم تأمر بقتلي وها أنا ذا قائم بين يديك قد[4] فعلت ما فعلت بنصيحتي وحبّي إيّاكم فإن كانت قد دخلت في ذلك معصية فإنّ لكم الحجّة البالغة في ذلك بمعصيتي والسلطان على عقوبتي وقتلي.

٧٧،١٣ فلمّا سمع الملك مقالة بيلار علم إيراخت أمّ جوبرحيّة وأنّه لم يقدم على قتلها فاشتدّ فرحه وقال لبيلار إنّ الذي كان يمنعني من الغضب عليك ما أعرف من نصيحتك وصدق حديثك وكنت أرجو لمعرفتي بعلمك أن لا تكون قتلت إيراخت فإنّها وإن كانت أتت عظيماً وأغلظت لي في الفعل فإنّها لم تفعل ذلك لعداوة ولا طلب مضرّة لكنّها فعلت ذلك للغيرة وقد كان ينبغي لي أن أعرض عن ذلك وأحتامه. ولم أغضب لأنّي عرفت أنّ الذنب كان لي ولأنّي كنت مستيقناً أنك تعلم أنّه ما كان منّي لما أمرتك به من قتلها لعزيمة من أمري أو رأيي وقد ندمت على ما أمرتك به ولكنّك أردت يا بيلار تجريب عقلي وأن تجعله في شكّ وخفت مع ذلك أن أعاقبك في أمرها بالقتل ومعاذ الله أن يكون ذلك رأيي وأن أكون فاعلاً ذلك بك ولكنّي لك شاكر وقد اصطنعت عندي أفضل يد يجب عليّ شكرها فانطلق فأتني بإيراخت.

١ تقرّبون وتلطفون: كذا ل٢؛ الأصل: بقربون وبلطفون. ٢ كذا ل٢؛ الأصل: أو فارقوا. ٣ كذا ل٢؛ الأصل: اذا.
٤ كذا ل٢؛ الأصل: منذ.

Whether angry or pleased, you never say or command what should not be said or commanded; you remain gentle and peace-loving. If, with time's vicissitudes, you suffer loss of some of the benefits that God has bestowed on you, or a calamity forces you to suffer adversity, you bear it patiently. You do not become dismayed or paralyzed by grief, but console yourself and show contentment and acceptance of what has happened. You restrain and humble him who, not of your lineage, conducts himself with arrogance and pride in his domain. You dismiss and banish from your presence even those closest to you, those whom you regard with affection, if they manifest haughtiness and pride regarding your affairs. Severed from your favor, they grieve and become dismayed; their grief does not benefit them, but their sadness and concern grow, and thus their misfortune increases. Your Majesty has been restrained by noble lineage and great forbearance, and, for all my insignificance and unimportance, you have listened patiently to me. I am therefore grateful to Your Majesty for not commanding my death. I stand here before you, having done what I did out of devotion and love of Your Majesty. If this has involved disobedience, you have sufficient evidence and the power to punish me and to put me to death."

When the king heard Baylār's words, he knew that Īrākht, the mother 13.77
of Jawbar, was alive and that Baylār had not dared execute her. Overjoyed, he said to him, "I was kept from anger by what I knew of your sincerity and truthfulness. Knowing your wisdom, I hoped that you had not killed Īrākht; for even if she offended and behaved rudely, she acted out of jealousy, not hostility or malice. I should have overlooked it and accepted it. Also, I didn't become angry with you, for I knew the fault was mine. I was sure you would realize that my order to kill her was not my real intention and that I regretted it. But you wanted to test my mind and cause it to doubt. You feared I would punish you because of the command to kill her. But God forbid that I should think in that way or do that to you! Rather, I am grateful. You have done me a favor that deserves the greatest thanks. Go now, and bring Īrākht to me."

فخرج بيلار من عند الملك فرحاً مسروراً فأمر إيراخت أن تُهيّأ وتزيَّن ففُعل بها ذلك ثمّ انطلق بها مع الأمينين اللذين كان وكّلهما بها إلى الملك فلمّا رآها اشتدّ فرحه وقال لها اصنعي ما أحببت فلست أصرف هواك بعد هذا عن شيء. ٧٨،١٣

فقالت إيراخت دام ملكك إلى الأبد فإنّه لولا رأفتكم وسعة أحلامكم وأخلاقكم لم تندم على قتلي هذه الندامة فإنّك لو لم تذكرني إلى آخر الأبد كنت لذلك أهلاً[1] للذي فعلت وكان منّي وللذي استحققت به ما أمر به الملك من قتلي وبرأفتك أيضاً شكرت أيضاً لبيلار كفّه عن قتلي ولولا ثقته بسعة حلمك مع رأفته وعدله ووقاره لقد كان أنفذ فيّ ذلك الأمر فأهلكني.

فقال الملك لبيلار إنّك قد اصطنعت عندي ما أوجب به شكرك وما لم ير ملك من عبيده مثله ولم تصنع بي قطّ أمراً أعظم عندي من أنّك لم تقتل إيراخت أمّ جوير بل أحييتها بعد قتلي إيّاها فوهبتها لي اليوم ورددتها عليّ فلم أكن قطّ أرضى عليك منّي اليوم وقد سلّطتك على ملكي وعلى جميع رعيّتي وجعلتك خليفتي وملّكتك ما وراء بابي فاصنع ما أحببت. ٧٩،١٣

قال بيلار أنا عبدك أيّها الملك وإنّما حاجتي اليوم أن لا تعجل بمثل هذا الأمر العظيم الذي يُندم[2] على عاقبته وتكون ثمرة ذلك الهمّ والحزن لا سيّما في أمر هذه الملكة التي لا يوجد مثلها في الأرض وأن تتثبّت أيّها الملك وتتبيّن. ٨٠،١٣

قال الملك بحقّ قلت يا بيلار وقد قبلت قولك ولست عاملاً بعدها عملاً صغيراً ولا كبيراً فضلاً عن مثل هذا الأمر العظيم الذي سلف منّي إلّا بعد المؤامرة والنظر والتؤدة.

ثمّ إنّ الملك أعطى إيراخت تلك الثياب وأراضي كثيرة وسلّطها على جميع ملكه وأخدمها جورفنه وجميع نسائه وأعطى بيلار أموراً كثيرة ثمّ قام الملك إلى دار نسائه فرحاً مسروراً. ٨١،١٣

١ لذلك أهلاً: كذا ر؛ الأصل: كدلك. ٢ كذا ل٢؛ الأصل: ندم.

Baylār left the king, filled with joy and gladness. He commanded that Īrākht be made ready in all her finery, and escorted her to the king along with both of the retainers to whose care he had entrusted her. The king was overjoyed to see her. "Do whatever you please," he said. "Never again will I refuse you anything." 13.78

And Īrākht said, "May your reign last forever! How, but for your mercy and keen intellect, would you have felt such regret over my death? Had you forgotten me forever, I would have deserved it because of the offense for which the king ordered my death. In your mercy you have thanked Baylār for not killing me. Were it not for Baylār's trust in your great moderation, and for his mercy, justness, and calmness, he would have carried out the command and killed me."

"You have done me a favor that deserves gratitude," the king said to Baylār, 13.79
"something that no king has ever seen from his servants. Not killing Īrākht, Jawbar's mother, is the greatest favor you have ever done for me. I took her life and you brought her back to life, and now you have given her back to me. I have never been more pleased with you than I am today. I give you authority over my kingdom and all my subjects. I hereby make you my deputy, to rule over everything beyond the gate of my palace. Do as you please."

"I am Your Majesty's servant," replied Baylār. "All I ask today is that you 13.80
not act hastily in any matter of such importance—the consequences of which you might regret and which might bring grief and sorrow in their wake, particularly regarding this queen who has no equal on earth—and that first you investigate and ascertain the facts."

"You are right, Baylār," said the king. "I accept your advice. From now on I will do nothing, great or small, let alone something as momentous as this, without consultation and careful consideration."

The king gave Īrākht the robe, bestowed many estates on her, gave her 13.81
authority over his entire kingdom, and made Gūlpanāh and all his other wives her servants. He gave many gifts to Baylār, then went into his harem happy and joyful.

٨٢،١٣ ثمّ ائتمر الملك بعد ذلك هو وبيلار بقتل أولئك الأعداء الذين أرادوا هلاك الملك وحشمه ومملكته فقُتلوا جميعاً وأعانه عليهم عظماء أهل مملكته وحمد الملك الله تعالى وأثنى عليه وشكر لكانزون فعله لأنّ الله تعالى بعلمه خلّصه وامرأته وولده والوزير الصالح من الموت ببركته وبمنّه.

انقضى باب هيلار وبيلار وإيراخت أمّ جوبر

Later, the king consulted Baylār about executing the enemies who had sought to destroy him, his entourage, and his kingdom. With the help of the great men of the kingdom, they were all put to death. The king praised God and thanked Kamānzūn for what he had done; for God, by His blessing and favor, had saved the king, his wife, his children, and his righteous minister through Kamānzūn's wisdom. 13.82

Here ends the Chapter of Haylār, Baylār,
and Īrākht, the Mother of Jawbar.

باب السيّاح والصوّاغ

وهو باب اصطناع المعروف إلى غير أهله والثقة بالإخوان والأعوان

١٤،١ قال دبشلم لبيدبا الفيلسوف قد فهمت ما ذكرت في أمر من ينبغي للملوك اصطناعه ومراجعة من يراجعون فاضرب لي إن رأيت مثل من ينبغي له أن يصنع إليه المعروف ومن يحقّ له أن يوثَق به ويرجى عونه.

١٤،٢ قال الفيلسوف إنّ الملوك وغيرهم جدراء أن يأتوا الخير إلى أهله وأن يصلوا من كان عندهم شكر وحمد ولا ينظروا إلى أقاربهم وأهل خاصّتهم ولا إلى أشراف الناس وأغنيائهم وذي القوّة والرأي منهم دون غيرهم ولا يمتنعوا أن يصنعوا المعروف إلى أهل الضعف والجهد والضعة[1] وإنّ الرأي في ذلك أن يجرّبوا ويختبروا صغار الناس وعظماءهم في شكرهم وحفظهم الودّ وفي[2] غدرهم وقلّة وفائهم وشكرهم ثمّ يكون عملهم[3] في ذلك كلّه على قدر الذي يرون أو يبدو لهم فإنّ الطبيب الرفيق من لا يداوي المرضى بالمعاينة لهم فقط ولكنّه ينظر إلى البول ويجسّ العروق[4] ثمّ يكون العلاج على نحو المعرفة وقدرها. ويحقّ على المرء اللبيب إن وجد قوماً ذوي مهابة ووفاء وشكر ومن البهائم على مثل حالهم أن يحسن فيما بينه وبينهم فلعلّه يحتاج إليهم يوماً من الدهر فيكافونه فإنّ العاقل ربّما حذر الناس ولم يأمن على نفسه أحداً وأخذ ابن عرس فأدخله كمّه والطير فوضعه على يده وقد قيل ينبغي لذي العقل أن لا يحقر صغيراً ولا كبيراً من الناس ولا من البهائم ولكنّه جدير بأن يبلوهم ويختبرهم ويكون ما يصنع إليهم على قدر الذي يرى منهم وقد مضى في ذلك مثل ضربه بعض الحكماء.

---

١ كذا ش، پ٣٤٧٥؛ الأصل: الصعفه. ٢ كذا ع؛ الأصل: في. ٣ كذا ل٢؛ الأصل: علمهم. ٤ ويجسّ العروق: كذا ل٢؛ الأصل: ويحسن المعروف.

The Mendicant and the Goldsmith

A chapter about rendering favors to the undeserving and about trusting true friends and assistants.

Dabshalim said to Baydabā the Philosopher, "I understand what you've told me about a king's choosing to restore certain people to favor. Now tell me a parable about those to whom he should show favor, those who should be trusted and on whose help he can rely." 14.1

The philosopher said, "Kings and others should treat well those who deserve it and establish close ties with those who will return gratitude and praise. They shouldn't look only to their relatives and entourage or to the noble and wealthy who enjoy power and influence, nor should they refrain from showing favor to the weak, the distressed, and the humble. They should test and examine individuals great and small, to assess their gratitude and loyalty, or their ingratitude and disloyalty, and act according to what they discover. A skilled physician doesn't treat his patients merely by looking at them; he examines their urine, feels their pulse, and treats each patient according to what he knows about them. When a wise man finds people—and animals, too—endowed with dignity, loyalty, and gratitude, he should treat them well, for he may need them some day and they will repay his kindness. Sometimes an intelligent man is so cautious with people that he feels safe with no one, but he still puts a mongoose up his sleeve and keeps a bird on his hand. A man of intelligence, they say, should despise no one, great or small, human or animal; he should test them and show them favor according to what he sees in them. There is a parable about this told by one of the sages." 14.2

قال الملك وكيف كان ذلك.

٣،١٤ قال الفيلسوف زعموا أنّ ناساً انطلقوا إلى مغارة فحفروا فيها زبية للسباع فوقع فيها رجل صوّاغ وببر وحيّة وقرد فلم يقدر على الخروج منها واحد منهم فمرّ رجل سيّاح بالزبية فاطّلع فيها فلمّا رآهم فكّر في نفسه وقال ما أراني مقدّماً عملاً لآخرتي أفضل من خلاص هذا الإنسان من بين هؤلاء الأعداء. فأخذ حبلاً فأدلاه إليه فتعلّق به القرد لخفّته فأصعده ثمّ أعاده ثانية فتشبّث به الببر فأخرجه ثمّ أعاده الكرّة الثالثة فتعلّقت عليه الحيّة فاستنقذها فشكروا له صنيعه بهم وقالوا له لا تخرج هذا الرجل خاصّة فإنّه لا شكر له ولا حمد ولا وفاء. فلم يلتفت إلى قولهنّ وأدلى الحبل فأطلع الرجل.

٤،١٤ فقال له القرد وطني إلى جانب مدينة يقال لها برجوان.[١]

فقال الببر وأنا أيضاً في أجمة إلى جانبها.

وقالت الحيّة وأنا أيضاً في سورها فإن أتيتها يوماً من الدهر أو مررت بها فاحتجت إلينا فنوّه بنا حتّى نأتيك ونجازيك بما أوليتنا وأتيت إلينا.

وقال الصوّاغ وأنا أيضاً في المدينة. وقال له بعد أن شكره وأثنى عليه إنّك قد أوليتني معروفاً فأنا حقيق بحفظه فإن قضي لك أن تأتي المدينة فسل عنّي فإنّ منزلي بها ولعلّي أن أجازيك ببعض ما كان منك من الجميل إليّ.

٥،١٤ ومضى كلّ واحد منهم[٢] لوجهه فمكث السيّاح حيناً ثمّ عرضت له حاجة نحو تلك المدينة فسار إليها فلقيه القرد فسجد له وقبّل يديه ورجليه واعتذر إليه وقال إنّي لا أملك شيئاً ولكن اطمئنّ ساعة حتّى آتيك ببعض ما أصيب منه. فانطلق فلم يلبث إلّا يسيراً أن جاءه بفاكهة طيّبة فوضعها بين يديه فأكل منها.

ثمّ توجّه نحو المدينة فاستقبله الببر فسجد له وحيّاه وقال قد أوليتني معروفاً جسيماً فلا تبرح حتّى أرجع إليك. فلم يلبث أن ذهب إلى ابنة الملك فقتلها وأخذ حليها ثمّ أتاه به فدفعه إليه من غير أن يعلمه بشيء من أمره.

---

١ الأصل: برحوان. ٢ كذا ش، پ٣٤٧٥؛ الأصل: منهما.

"How does it go?" asked the king.

The philosopher related the following tale: Some men, they say, once went to a cave and dug a pit to catch wild animals. Into it fell a goldsmith, along with a tiger, a snake, and a monkey. None of them could get out. A mendicant[62] passed by and looked into the pit. When he saw them, he thought to himself, "I can think of no deed that will earn me more merit in the hereafter than rescuing this man from his enemies." So he took a rope and lowered it to the man. The monkey, being nimble, grabbed hold of it, so he pulled him out. Then he lowered it again; the tiger clung to it, and he pulled him out. He did it a third time; the snake wrapped herself around the rope, and he rescued her. They thanked him for his good deed, but said, "Don't help this man to get out, for he knows nothing about gratitude, praise, or loyalty." He disregarded their warning, lowered the rope, and pulled the man out. 14.3

The monkey said, "I live on a hill near a city called Barjawān." 14.4

The tiger said, "I live there too, in a forest near the city."

The snake said, "I live in the city wall. If you ever come to the city or pass by and happen to need us, let us know, so that we can come and reward you for your deed."

"I too live in that city," said the goldsmith. He thanked the mendicant, praised him, and added, "You've done me a great favor, which I must remember. If you ever happen to come to the city, inquire after me, for I have my home there. Hopefully, I can repay you somehow for your good deed."

Each then went his way. Sometime later, the mendicant needed to go to that city. The monkey met him, bowed to him, kissed his hands and feet, and said apologetically, "I own nothing, but rest here for a moment until I bring you some of my food." The monkey went off and brought back a ripe fruit and placed it before the mendicant, who ate it. 14.5

As the mendicant continued on his way to the city, the tiger came out to meet him. Bowing before him in greeting, he said, "You did me an enormous favor. Don't leave until I return." The tiger went off immediately, killed the king's daughter, and took her jewelry. He gave it to the mendicant, telling him nothing about where it came from.

فقال السيّاح هذه البهائم قد أولتني معروفاً هذا وصنعته بي فكيف لو قد انتهيت إلى الصوّاغ فإنّه إن كان معسراً لا شيء عنده فإنّه سيبيع لي هذا الحلي بثمنه فيعطيني بعضه ويأخذ بعضه.

ثمّ إنّ السيّاح دخل المدينة فأتى منزل الصوّاغ فرحّب به وأدخله منزله فلمّا ٦،١٤
أبصر بالحلي معه عرفه وقال له اطمئنّ حتّى آتيك بطعام تأكله فإنّي لست أرضى لك ممّا في البيت.

فانطلق الصوّاغ حتّى أتى باب الملك فأرسل إليه أنّ الرجل الذي قتل ابنتك وأخذ حليها قد أخذته وهو عندي محبوس.

فأرسل الملك إلى السيّاح فأخذه فلمّا رأى الحلي معه أمر به أن يعذَّب ويُتظاهر به في المدينة ثمّ يُضرَب عنقه. فلمّا فُعل ذلك به جعل يبكي ويستغيث ويقول بأعلى صوته لو أنّي أطعت الحيّة والقرد والببر فيما أمروني لم يصبني هذا البلاء.

فلمّا سمعت الحيّة هذه المقالة خرجت من جحرها فلمّا بصرت به اشتدّ عليها ٧،١٤
أمره وفكّرت في الاحتيال لخلاصه فانطلقت إلى ابن الملك مسرعة فلدغته فدعا له الملك أهل العلم والمعرفة فرقوه ليشفوه فلم يغنوا عنه شيئاً ونظروا في النجوم واحتالوا له حتّى تكلّم فقال إنّي لا أبرأ حتّى يأتيني هذا السائح فيمسحني بيده فإنّك أيّها الملك قد أمرت بقتله ظلماً وعدواناً.

فلمّا سمع الملك ذلك بعث إلى السائح فأُتي به فأمره أن يرقي ابنه.

فقال لست أحسن ما أمرتني به أيّها الملك.

فقال الملك إنّما دعوتك لتخبرني بقصّتك وحاجتك إلى هذه المدينة.

فقصّ عليه السيّاح قصّته وما كان من صنيعه إلى الصوّاغ والقرد والببر والحيّة والذي قلن له في أمر الصوّاغ وما حمله على إتيان مدينته ثمّ قال اللّهمّ إن كنت تعلم أنّي صادق فيما ذكرت فعجّل لابن الملك الشفاء وعافِه.

The mendicant said to himself, "Seeing that these animals have done me these favors, shouldn't I try to find the goldsmith? Even if he is poor and penniless, he can sell this jewelry for me, and we can share the proceeds."

The mendicant entered the city and came to the goldsmith's house, who 14.6
welcomed him and invited him in. The goldsmith recognized the jewelry the moment he saw it. "Make yourself at home," he said, "while I go and get you something to eat. I don't think what I have in the house is good enough for you."

The goldsmith then went to the palace and sent the king a message: "The man who killed your daughter and took her jewelry—I've got him. He's being held in my house."

The king sent someone to arrest the mendicant. When he saw the jewelry in the mendicant's possession, he commanded that he be tortured, paraded through the city, and beheaded. At this, the mendicant began to weep, imploring assistance, and crying aloud, "Had I obeyed the snake, the monkey, and the tiger, this misfortune would never have befallen me."

The snake heard these words and came out of her nest. When she saw 14.7
him, she was distressed by his plight and pondered how she might help effect his escape. She went to the king's son and bit him. The king summoned the learned men. They recited spells to heal him, to no avail. Then they consulted the stars and drew up various schemes. Finally the boy spoke up, saying, "I will not recover until this mendicant comes and strokes me with his hand, for Your Majesty has wrongly and unjustly commanded his death."[63]

When the king heard these words, he sent for the mendicant and commanded him to recite spells over his son.

The mendicant replied, "I'm unable to do what you've commanded."

The king said, "I require only that you tell me about yourself and why you came to this city."

So the mendicant told the king his story: the favor he had done for the goldsmith, the monkey, the tiger, and the snake; what they had told him about the goldsmith; and why he had come to the city. Then he prayed: "O God, if You know that I have spoken the truth, hasten to cure the king's son and restore his health."

فبرئ الغلام ممّا كان به وكشف الله عنه وأعطى الملك السيّاح مالاً ووصله وأحسن إليه وأمر بالصوّاغ فعوقب.

انقضى باب السـيّاح والصوّاغ.

So God delivered the boy from his malady and he recovered. The king rewarded the mendicant with gifts, and ordered that the goldsmith be punished.

Here ends the Chapter of the Mendicant and the Goldsmith.

باب ابن الملك وأصحابه

١،١٥ قال دبشلم لبيدبا الفيلسوف قد فهمت ما ذكرت وما يحقّ على الملك في التوخّي بمعروفه أهل الشكر والوفاء قربوا أو بعدوا فأخبرني ما بال الرجل السفيه يصيب الرفعة والشرف العظيم والرجل الحكيم اللبيب يلحقه البلاء والجهد والغرم الثقيل.

٢،١٥ قال الفيلسوف كما أنّ الرجل لا يبصر إلّا بعينيه ولا يسمع إلّا بأذنيه وكذلك العلم إنّما تمامه بالحلم والعقل والتثبّت غير أنّ القضاء والقدر يغلبان ذلك كلّه وإنّما يريدان أدنى علّة فيموّلان صاحبهما أو يهلكانه ومثل ذلك مثل ابن[١] الملك الذي رئي على باب مدينة يقال لها قطون جالساً ثمّ كتب عليه بعد أن تمّ أمره إنّ العقل والجمال والاجتهاد والقوّة وما سوى ذلك إنّما ملاكه القضاء والقدر.[٢]

قال الملك وكيف كان ذلك.

٣،١٥ قال الفيلسوف حديث ابن الملك وأصحابه زعموا أنّ أربعة نفر اصطحبوا أحدهم ابن ملك[٣] والثاني ابن تاجر والثالث ابن شريف والرابع ابن أكّار وكانوا محتاجين قد أصابهم ضرّ وجهد لا يملكون[٤] شيئاً إلّا ما عليهم من ثيابهم فبينما هم يمشون إذ قال ابن الملك إنّ أمر الدنيا كلّه بقدر.

قال ابن التاجر العقل أفضل من كلّ شيء.

قال ابن الشريف الجمال خير ممّا ذكرتم.

قال ابن الأكّار الاجتهاد أفضل من ذلك كلّه.

٤،١٥ ثمّ مضوا نحو مدينة يقال لها قطون فلمّا انتهوا إلى تلك المدينة قاموا في ناحية منها وقالوا لابن الأكّار انطلق فاطلب لنا باجتهادك طعاماً ليومنا هذا.[٥]

١ كذا ل٢؛ الأصل: راى. ٢ إنّما . . . والقدر: كذا ع؛ الأصل: فان هلاكه القدر. ٣ كذا ل٢؛ الأصل: الملك.
٤ كذا ل٢؛ الأصل: بلفون. ٥ طعامًا . . . هذا: كذا ل٢؛ الأصل: طعامنا يومنا هدا.

The King's Son and His Companions

Dabshalim said to Baydabā the Philosopher, "I understand what you have said about a king's bestowing favor only on those who know how to show gratitude and loyalty, wherever they may be, near or far. Now tell me why a simple fellow sometimes attains eminence and honor, and a wise and intelligent man suffers hardship, toil, and loss." 15.1

The philosopher said, "Just as sight requires eyes and hearing ears, knowledge, for its perfection, requires judiciousness, intelligence, and resolute conduct. But Destiny and Fortune overpower everything; they need only the slightest cause to enrich a person or destroy him. The Parable of the King's Son exemplifies this. He was seen sitting at the gate of the city of Qaṭūn, but after the turn in his fortunes, he inscribed on its gate: 'Intelligence, beauty, hard work, strength, and all else operate only in accordance with Destiny and Fortune.'" 15.2

"And what was his story?" asked the king.

The philosopher told the following tale: Four people, they say, became traveling companions: a king's son, a merchant's son, a nobleman's son, and a farmer's son. All had suffered hardship and distress, and owned only the clothes on their backs. As they walked, the king's son said, "All the affairs of this world are determined by Destiny." 15.3

The merchant's son said, "Intelligence is better than everything."

The nobleman's son said, "Beauty is better still."

The farmer's son said, "Hard work is best of all."

They traveled to a city called Qaṭūn. There they halted and said to the farmer's son, "Go, and through your hard work earn the food we need for today." 15.4

فانطلق يسأل عن عمل إذا عمله الرجل من غدوة إلى الليل كسب فيه ما يشبع أربعة نفر فقيل له ليس شيء بأعزّ من الحطب. وكان على رأس فرسخ منها فتوجّه إليه فحمل حزمة من حطب فباعه بنصف درهم ثمّ اشترى به ما يصلح أصحابه وكتب على باب المدينة اجتهاد يوم واحد يبلغ ثمنه نصف درهم وأتاهم بما اشترى فأصابوا منه.

٥،١٥ فلمّا أصبحوا قالوا لابن الشريف انطلق فاكسب لنا بجمالك بعض ما يرفق بنا.

فانطلق وتفكّر في نفسه وقال لست أحسن شيئاً من الأعمال وأستحيي أن أرجع إلى أصحابي بغير طعام. وهمّ أن يفارقهم فأسند ظهره إلى شجرة في المدينة من الغمّ فمرّت عليه امرأة لبعض عظماء المدينة فأعجبها جماله فأرسلت إليه جاريتها فانتهت به إليها فأمرت به فنُظّف ثمّ ظلّ معها يومه ذلك في نعمة وكرامة فلمّا كان عند المساء أجازته بخمسمائة دينار فتوجّه إلى أصحابه وكتب على باب المدينة جمال يوم واحد قيمته خمسمائة دينار.

٦،١٥ فلمّا أصبحوا قالوا لابن التاجر انطلق فاكسب بعقلك وتجارتك شيئاً.

فذهب فلم يبرح إلّا قليلاً حتّى أبصر سفينة عظيمة في البحر قد أرست إلى الشطّ غير بعيد من المدينة فخرج إليها ناس من التجّار ليبتاعوا ما فيها فساوموا أصحابها ثمّ قال بعضهم لبعض انصرفوا يومكم هذا حتّى نكسر عليهم متاعهم فيرخصونه علينا. ففعلوا فخالف إليها ابن التاجر فاشترى منهم ما كان فيها فخرج إليه تجّار المدينة فأربحوه مائة ألف دينار فتوجّه إلى أصحابه وكتب على باب المدينة عقل يوم واحد قيمته مائة ألف دينار فتمتّعوا بما أصابوا وأخصبوا منه.

٧،١٥ فلمّا أصبحوا في اليوم الرابع قالوا لابن الملك انطلق فاكتسب لنا شيئاً بقدرك.

فذهب حتّى أتى باب المدينة فجلس على دكّان عالية وقضي أنّ ملك المدينة هلك يومئذ ولم يترك ولداً ولا أخاً ولا ذا قرابة فمرّوا عليه بجنازة الملك وهو قاعد فسأله رجل منهم وقال له من أنت وما يقعدك على باب المدينة ولا يحزنك موت الملك. فلم يجبه بشيء فشتمه وطرده فلمّا مضوا رجع إلى مكانه فلمّا انصرفوا رآه

So he set out and asked what sort of labor, carried out from morning till night, would earn enough to feed four people. He was told, "Nothing is more valuable than firewood." So he went about a league from the city, where there was some firewood, gathered a bundle, sold it for half a dirham, and with the money bought enough to satisfy his companions. He wrote on the city gate: "One day's hard work is worth half a dirham." His companions ate the provisions he returned with.

The next morning they said to the nobleman's son, "Go, and use your beauty to earn something of benefit to us." 15.5

So he left, thinking to himself, "I'm no good at any kind of work, but I'm ashamed to return to my friends without any food." As he was about to abandon them in despair, he leaned against a tree in the city, and just then a dignitary's wife passed by and was struck by his beauty. She sent her slavegirl to bring him to her house and ordered that he be bathed, and he spent a day of pleasure and feasting with her. In the evening, she rewarded him with five hundred dinars. So he went back to his companions and wrote on the city gate: "One day's beauty is worth five hundred dinars."

The next morning, they said to the merchant's son, "Go, and earn something using your business acumen." 15.6

Off he went. Soon he saw a great ship anchored by the shore, not far from the city. Some merchants had gone out to buy its cargo. They had bargained with the owners, but after a while, they had told each another, "Let's leave for the rest of the day; we'll get them to sell their merchandise bit by bit and they'll lower the price for us." In their absence, the merchant's son bought the cargo. When the city merchants got word of this, they came to him and upped the price by one hundred thousand dinars. He returned to his friends and wrote on the city gate: "One day's intelligence is worth one hundred thousand dinars." He and his friends enjoyed their new prosperity.

On the morning of the fourth day, they said to the king's son, "Go, and earn something for us in accordance with your rank and destiny."[64] 15.7

At the city gate, he sat on a high bench. As fate would have it, the king of the city had died that very day, without issue, brothers, or kin. As the king's bier passed by, someone asked him, "Who are you, and why are sitting here unmoved by the king's death?" He made no answer, so the man chased him away with a curse. When they had gone, he returned to his place. On their return, the man who had treated him so brusquely saw him and

ذلك الرجل الذي صنع به ما صنع فقال ألم أنهك عن هذا المجلس. وتقدّم إليه فأخذه وحبسه.

٨،١٥ فلمّا اجتمعوا ليملّكوا عليهم رجلاً يختارونه قام الذي كان أمر[١] بالفتى الى السجن فحدّثهم بقصّته وقال إنّي أتخوّف أن يكون علينا عيناً لعدوّنا.

فبعثوا إليه فأتوا به فسألوه من هو وما أمره وما أقدمه أرضهم فقال أنا ابن اصطهر ملك أرض قرونا توفّي والدي فغلبني أخي على الملك وأنا أكبر منه فهربت منه حذرًا على نفسي حتّى انتهيت إليكم.

فلمّا سمعوا ذلك منه عرفه بعض من كان يغشى أرض أبيه منهم وأثنوا عليه خيرًا فملّكوه عليهم وقلّدوه أمرهم وكانت سنّتهم الطواف بمن يملّكونه عليهم ويقلّدونه أمورهم وحملوه على فيل وطافوا به المدينة فلمّا مرّ على باب المدينة بصر وإنّما رأى عليه ما[٢] كتب أصحابه فأمر فكُتب إنّ الاجتهاد والعقل والجمال وما أصاب المرء من خير أو شرّ بقضاء وقدر واعتبروا بما ساق الله لي من الخير والسعادة.

٩،١٥ ثمّ إنّ ابن الملك أتى مجلسه وقعد على سريره وأرسل إلى أصحابه فأتوه فموّلهم وأغناهم ثمّ جمع عمّاله وأهل الفضل والرأي من أهل مملكته فقال أمّا أصحابي فقد استيقنوا أنّ الذي رزقهم الله من الخير إنّما كان بقدر وكان عونهم عليه بعض ما ذكروا وأمّا أنا فإنّ الذي منحني الله وهيّأه لي لم يكن من الجمال والعقل والاجتهاد بل كان بقضاء وقدر وما كنت أظنّ إذ طردني أخي وأخافني أن أصيب هذه المنزلة ولا أن أكون بها لأنّي قد رأيت من أهل هذه الأرض من هو أفضل منّي جمالاً وحسناً[٣] وأنّ فيها من هو أزكى منّي رأيًا وأشدّ اجتهاداً فساقني القضاء والقدر إلى أن تغرّبت[٤] فملّكت بأمر الله تعالى وعلمه وقضائه وقدره وقد كنت راضياً أن أعيش بحال خشونة وشظف[٥] معيشة.

١ كذا ل٢؛ الأصل: اسر. ٢ كذا ش، ع؛ الأصل: من. ٣ كذا ل٢؛ الأصل: حسبا. ٤ الأصل: نعربت. ٥ كذا ش؛ الأصل: ووسط.

said, "Didn't I forbid you to sit here?" And he ordered that he be arrested and imprisoned.

When the people assembled to choose a new king, the man who had sent the young man to prison told them about him and said, "I'm afraid he's an enemy spy." 15.8

So they sent for him and asked him who he was, what he was up to, and what had brought him to their country. He replied, "I am the son of King Iṣṭahr of Qurūnā. When my father died, my brother seized the kingdom from me, though I am older than he. Fearing for my life, I fled and came to you."

At these words, the people who had visited that country recognized him and praised him. They made him their king and put him in charge of their affairs. As it was their custom to process through the city with whomever they made ruler, they mounted him on an elephant and processed around the city. When he passed by the city gate and saw what his friends had inscribed, he ordered the following inscription: "Hard work, intelligence, beauty, and the good and evil a man attains come by Destiny and Fortune. Learn this lesson from the prosperity and happiness God has brought me."

Then, as king, he went to his council chamber, seated himself on his throne, and sent for his companions. He gave them gifts and made them wealthy. He gathered his officials and the wise men of the kingdom and said, "My companions now know for certain that what prosperity God bestowed on them came only by Destiny and that the other things they referred to were merely ancillary. Whatever God granted and prepared for me did not come from beauty, intelligence, or hard work; it came by God's Decree and Destiny. I never imagined that I would attain this position when my brother forced me to flee in fear. I saw people in this country who surpassed me in beauty and grace, and I knew that it had people better in judgment and more diligent in their labors. Destiny and Fortune drove me into exile; then, by God's command and by His knowledge, decree, and predestination, I was made king, although I would have been content to live a life of hardship and austerity." 15.9

فقام سيّاح كان في جمعهم ذلك فقال أيّها الملك إنّك قد تكلّمت بحلم وعقل ١٠،١٥
ورأي لحسن ظنّنا بك ورجاؤنا فيك وعرفنا ما ذكرت وصدّقناك بما وصفت وعلمنا[١] أنّك قد كنت لما ساق الله إليك من ذلك أهلاً لفضل قسمه وتتابع نعمه عليك فإنّ أسعد الناس في الدنيا والآخرة وأولاهم بالسرور فيها من رزقه الله مثل ما رزقك وجعل عندهم مثلما جعل عندك وقد أرانا الله سبحانه الذي نحبّ إذ ملّكك علينا وقلّدك أمرنا فنحمد الله على ما أكرمك به من ذلك وامتنّ به علينا فيك.

ثمّ قام سيّاح آخر فحمد الله عزّ وجلّ وأثنى عليه ومجّده وذكر آلاءه وقال أيّها الملك ١١،١٥
إنّي كنت وأنا غلام قبل أن أكون سائحاً أخدم رجلاً من الأشراف وعظماء الناس فلمّا بدا لي أن أرفض الدنيا فارقته وقد كان أعطاني من أجرتي دينارين فأردت أن أتصدّق بأحدهما وأستبقي الآخر لأستنفقه فقلت ليس شيء أعظم أجراً من أن أشتري نفساً فأعتقها لوجه الله تعالى فأتيت السوق فوجدت رجلاً صيّاداً معه حمامتان فساومته بهما فأبى أن ينقصهما من دينارين فجهدت على أن يعطيني إيّاهما بدينار فأبى ذلك فقلت لعلّهما أن يكونا زوجين أو أخوين أخاف إن أعتقت أحدهما وفرقت بينهما أن يموت الآخر غمّاً. فابتعتهما منه بالثمن الذي أراد وأشفقت إن أنا أرسلتهما في أرض عامرة أن لا يستطيعا أن[٢] يطيرا ممّا لقيا من الهزال والجهد فذهبت بهما إلى أرض كثيرة الرعي فخلّيتهما هنالك وطارا حتّى وقعا على شجرة قريبة ثمّ انصرفت راجعاً فقال أحدهما للآخر لقد خلّصنا هذا السيّاح من البلاء الذي كنّا فيه وإنّا لخليقان أن نجازيه بحسن فعاله فينا. فقالا لي إنّك قد أتيت إلينا ما أنت أهل أن نشكرك به ونعرفه لك وإنّ في أصل هذه الشجرة جرّة فيها دنانير مملوءة فخذها. فأتيت الشجرة وأنا في شكّ ممّا قالا لي فلم أحفر إلّا قليلاً حتّى انتهيت إليها فاستخرجتها ودعوت الله لهما بالعافية وقلت لهما إذ كان علمكما على ما أرى وأنتما تطيران بين السماء والأرض وأخبرتماني بما تحت الأرض فكيف وقعتما في الورطة التي

١ كذا ل٢؛ الأصل: وعلى. ٢ الأصل: ان لا.

A mendicant stood up in the assembly and said, "Your Majesty has spoken with judiciousness, intelligence, and discernment. We think well of you and have great hopes for you. We recognize what you have said and acknowledge its truth. We know that you were worthy of what God sent you through the favor He apportioned to you and His continued grace toward you. The most fortunate people in this world and the next, those likeliest to enjoy happiness, are those whom God has sustained as He has sustained you and to whom He has granted what He has granted you. God has favored us by making you our king. We praise God for the gift He has given us in you." 15.10

Then another mendicant stood up. Having praised, extolled, and glorified God and recounted His bounties, he said, "Your Majesty, when I was young, I served a rich nobleman before becoming a mendicant. When I decided to abandon the world and left him, he gave me two dinars as my wage. I decided to give one away in charity and keep the other to spend. 'Nothing,' I said, 'will bring a greater reward than to buy a living soul with one dinar and set it free for the love of God.' So I went to the market and found a hunter who had two doves. Despite my haggling, he refused to sell them for less than two dinars. I tried as hard as I could to have him give me the two for one dinar, but he refused. I told myself, 'Perhaps they are mates or siblings. I fear that if I free one and separate them, the other will die of grief.' So I bought both at the price he had set. Then I worried that if I set them free in town, they might not be able to fly away because they were weak with exhaustion. I took them to a meadow, where I released them, and they flew off and perched in a nearby tree. As I turned to leave, one said to the other, 'This mendicant has rescued us from our distress; we should reward him for his deed.' Then they said to me, 'We must thank you and reward you for the favor you have done us. At the foot of this tree you will find a jar full of dinars. Take it.' I went to the tree, dubious about what they had said, but I didn't have to dig deep before I reached the jar. I pulled it out and called on God to grant them prosperity. Then I said to them, 'I see that your knowledge is such that while flying through the air you know enough to tell me what is under the earth. How then did you get into the 15.11

نجّيتكما منها. فقالا لي ألم تعلم أيّها العاقل أنّه إذا نزل القضاء أغشى البصر وأنّ القدر يغلب على كلّ شيء ولا يستطيع أحد أن يجاوزه أو يقصر منه.

١٢،١٥ ثمّ قال الفيلسوف للملك ليعرف أهل النظر في الأمر والعلم أنّ الأشياء كلّها بقضاء وقدر لا يجلب أحد إلى نفسه نجاحاً ولا يدفع عنها مكروهاً إلّا بقضاء وقدر فإنّ ذلك كلّه من الله تعالى وإنّ الله يفعل ما أراد ويمضي ما أحبّ فلتسكن إلى ذلك الأنفس ولتطمئنّ إليه القلوب فإنّ ذلك لمن ألهمه الله ووفّق له سعة وراحة.

انقضى باب ابن الملك وأصحابه.

predicament from which I rescued you?' They said, 'Wise man, don't you know that the sight is dimmed when Fortune descends? Fortune overcomes everything; no one can go beyond it or fall short of it.'"

The philosopher said to the king, "Let the learned men who speculate about matters acknowledge that all things come to pass through Destiny and Fortune, without which no one can attain any success or ward off any evil. All these things are from God, who does what He wishes and decrees what He likes. Let all souls trust and rest content in this, for this doctrine brings comfort and peace of mind to those whom God inspires and directs aright." 15.12

Here ends the Chapter of the King's Son and His Companions.

باب الإسوار واللبؤة والشعهر

وهو باب من يترك ضرّ غيره لضرّ أصابه
فينصرف لما يتّعظ من ضرّه عن ضرّ الناس.

١،١٦ قال الملك قد سمعت هذا المثل فاضرب لي إن رأيت مثل من يدع ضرّ غيره لضرّه.

٢،١٦ قال بيدبا الفيلسوف إنّه لا يقدم على مساورة الناس والاقتحام عليهم في شرّهم إلّا أهل الجهالة بسوء نظرهم في عواقب الدنيا والآخرة وقلّة علمهم بما يرجع عليهم منه ويلزمهم من تبعة ما اكتسبوا ما لا يحيط به القول. فإن رُزقوا جزاء ذلك في أوّل أفعالهم لم يصرف سوء الجزاء عنهم عواقب أمورهم بما يقصر به الكلام عنهم والوصف فيهم وكلّ ما هوآتٍ قريب. وربّما اتّعظ الجاهل من ضرّ يصيبه فيعرف في مبلغ ذلك الضرّ منه أن قد بلغ إلى غيره كما قد بلغ إليه فيردعه وينزع عنه وينصرف عن ظلم الناس وضرّهم فيدرك بذلك نفع ذلك في العاقبة. نظير ما سألتني عنه أيها الملك من الحديث مثل اللبؤة والشعهر.

قال دبشلم وكيف كان ذلك.

٣،١٦ قال بيدبا الفيلسوف زعموا أنّ لبؤة كانت في غيضة ومعها شبلان لها فخرجت ذات يوم من الغيضة تطلب صيداً وخلّفت شبليها في الغيضة فمرّ بهما إسوار فقتلهما وسلخ جلديهما واحتملهما وانصرف بهما إلى منزله.

فلمّا رجعت اللبؤة ورأت شبليها قد كُشط عنهما جلداهما ونُبذا بالعراء داخلها في ذلك أمر عظيم فظيع ورأت سخنة عين وغيظاً شديداً وداخلها همّ شديد طويل واضطربت وصاحت وجزعت وكان إلى جانبها شعهر مجاورها فلمّا سمع صوتها خرج إليها وقال ما بالك وما يبكيك وما هذا الجزع وما الذي نزل بك.

قالت شبلاي مرّ عليهما إسوار فقتلهما وسلخ جلديهما.

The Horseman, the Lioness, and the Jackal

About those who stop injuring others because of an injury they themselves have suffered, and, having learned a lesson from their own misfortune, turn away from injuring people.

The king said, "Now that I have heard this parable, please tell me one about someone who stops injuring others because he has been injured himself." 16.1

Baydabā the Philosopher said, "Only the ignorant, blind to the consequences in this world and the next, viciously assault other people. Little do they know the immeasurable repercussions in store for them as a result of their actions. Even if all goes well at first, the terrible requital for their deeds is inevitable. But sometimes an ignorant fellow learns a lesson from suffering an injury. Deterred by the realization that others have been similarly affected by the injuries he has inflicted on them, he desists from doing wrong; thus he benefits in the end from his misfortune. The Parable of the Lioness and the Jackal illustrates Your Majesty's inquiry." 16.2

"How does it go?" asked Dabshalim.

Baydabā the Philosopher related the following tale: Once, they say, a lioness lived in a thicket with her two cubs. One day she left her cubs behind and went in search of prey. Her cubs were killed by a horseman, who skinned them and made off with their pelts. 16.3

When the lioness returned, she was aghast at the sight of the skinned bodies of her cubs lying in the field. Weeping and raging and overcome by grief, she trembled and roared uncontrollably. Her neighbor, a jackal, heard her voice and came to her. "What's wrong?" he asked. "What is making you cry? Why such grief? What has happened?"

"My cubs! A horseman found them. He killed them and stripped their pelts."

قال الشعهر لا تحزني ولا تجزعي كلّ هذا الجزع وأنصفي من نفسك فإنّما بلغ منك هذا الإسوار في شبليك من العبط ما قد بلغت منه إلى غير واحد ممّن كان يجد بحبيبه ويعزّ عليه كوجدك بشبليك وحزنك عليهما فاصبري من غيرك كما صبر غيرك عليك فإنّه قد قيل كما تدين تدان وقد دنت فدين منك ولكلّ عمل ثمرة وثمرة العمل الثواب والعقاب على قدر العمل في القلّة والكثرة كالبذر إذا زرعه زارعه دفع إليه حصاده على قدر بذره. ٤،١٦

قالت اللبؤة قصّ لي ذلك من قولك وأوضحه. ٥،١٦

قال الشعهر عرّفيني كم أتى عليك من العمر.

قالت اللبؤة مائة سنة.

قال الشعهر فما كان الذي يقوتك وتستعينين به على معيشتك.

قالت اللبؤة كنت آكل لحوم الوحوش وأعيش بها.

قال الشعهر فمن كان يطعمك ذلك اللحم.

قالت اللبؤة نفسي كنت أصيد الوحوش فأقتلها ثمّ آكلها.

قال الشعهر أرأيت الوحوش التي كنت تأكلين هل كان لها آباء وأمّهات.

قالت اللبؤة بلى قد كان لها آباء وأمّهات.

فقال الشعهر فما بال تلك الآباء والأمّهات ليس لها من الضجر والخوف والحزن والجزع والصراخ كما نسمع لك. أما إنّه ما نزل بك ما نزل إلّا من سوء نظرك في العواقب وقلّة تفكّرك فيها وجهالتك بما يرجع إليك من ضرّها.

فلمّا سمعت اللبؤة ذلك من كلام الشعهر عرفت أنّ ذلك بما اكتسبت على نفسها من الجور والظلم واستيقنت أنّ من عمل بغير حقّ وعدل أُديل منه[١] فتركت صيد الوحوش وانصرفت عن أكل اللحم إلى أكل الثمار والتنسّك والعبادة. ٦،١٦

فرأى الشعهر ذلك وكان عيشه الثمار فلمّا رأى اللبؤة تأكل الثمار قال قد كنت أظنّ بقلّة الثمار عامنا وما افتقدت منها أنّ الشجر لا يحمل العام فلمّا أبصرتك تأكلينها وأنت ٧،١٦

١ أُديل منه: الأصل: أزيل منه.

"Don't be so sad," said the jackal, "and don't grieve so excessively. Judge your situation fairly. The distress this horseman has inflicted on you by killing your cubs was no more than what you have inflicted on many. They felt the same grief for their loved ones as you feel for your cubs. So bear patiently your suffering at others' hands, just as others have borne what they've suffered at yours. As the saying goes: As you do, so shall it be done to you. Every deed has an outcome. The outcome of a deed is a reward or punishment proportional to the deed's magnitude, great or small: when a farmer sows seed, it yields a harvest in proportion to what he has sown." 16.4

"Explain yourself," said the lioness. 16.5

"How old are you?" asked the jackal.

"One hundred."

"What has nourished and sustained you?"

"The flesh of wild animals."

"And who fed you that meat?" asked the jackal.

"I hunted the animals myself, and killed them and ate them."

"Tell me: did the animals you ate have fathers and mothers?"

"Of course they did."

And the jackal said, "Why don't these parents display the distress, fear, sadness, and clamor we hear from you? Your misfortune is the result of how little thought you gave to the consequences and how ignorant you were of the harm that would redound to you from the harm you inflicted on them."

The jackal's words made the lioness realize that what had happened was payment for the wrongdoing and injustice she had heaped upon herself. She understood that anyone who acts wrongly and unjustly will be repaid; so she gave up hunting, turned from meat to fruit, and began to live a life of asceticism and devotion. 16.6

The jackal, who lived on fruit, took note. When he saw the lioness eating fruit, he said, "Because fruit is in such short supply this year, I thought the trees hadn't produced enough. But then I saw you, a meat eater, eating fruit, abandoning the sustenance allotted to you by God and turning to the sustenance allotted to others, interfering with it and reducing it, and I realized 16.7

آكلة لحم وتركت رزقك وطعامك وما قسم الله تعالى لك وتحوّلك إلى رزق غيرك انتقصتيه ودخلت عليه علمت أنّ الشجر قد أثمر[1] كما كان يثمر وإنّما أتى النقصان لذلك من قبلك فويل للشجر وللثمار وويل لمن كان عيشه منها ما أسرع هلاكهم لما جُعل عليهم في أرزاقهم وغلبهم عليه من ليس له حقّ ولا نصيب.

فلمّا سمعت اللبؤة ذلك من كلام الشعهر تركت أكل الثمار.

٨،١٦ وإنّما ضربت لك هذا المثل لتعلم أنّ الجاهل ربّما كان[2] مصروفاً عن ضرّ الناس لضرّ يصيبه كاللبؤة التي انصرفت لما لقيت في شبليها حتّى تركت أكل اللحوم وتركت أكل الثمار لقول الشعهر وأقبلت على العبادة والتنسّك فالناس أحقّ بالنظر في ذلك من غيرهم فإنّه قد قيل ما لا ترضاه لنفسك فلا ترضه لغيرك ولا تُدِلّهُ إليه فإذا هو العدل والعدل رضا الله سبحانه وتعالى ورضى للناس.

انتهى باب اللبؤة والشعهر.

---

١ قد أثمر: كذا پ٣٤٦٦؛ الأصل: لم يثمر. ٢ الأصل: كان ضره.

that the trees had produced fruit as usual and that the shortage was your fault. Alas for the trees and their fruit! Alas for those who lived on them! How swiftly they will perish when their sustenance is wrested from them by one who has no right to a share of it!"

And when she heard the jackal's words, the lioness stopped eating fruit too.

Baydabā continued, "I have told you this parable to teach you that some- 16.8
times an ignorant fellow stops harming people because of a misfortune that has befallen him—like the lioness who, because she suffered for her cubs, abandoned meat; then, because of the jackal's words, abandoned fruit; and in the end ate grass in a life of devotion and asceticism. People should consider carefully how they deal with others. As has been said: Do not approve for others or inflict on them what you do not approve for yourself.[65] This is justice, and justice is pleasing to God and to men."

Here ends the Chapter of the Lioness and the Jackal.

باب الناسك وضيفه

١،١٧ قال دبشلم الملك لبيدبا الفيلسوف قد سمعت مقالتك فإذا رأيت أن تحدّثني عمّن يدع عمله الذي يشاكله ويليق به فيتعدّى ذلك إلى غيره من الأعمال فلا يدركه وينسى عمله الذي كان يحسنه فيصير حيران.

٢،١٧ قال بيدبا زعموا أنّه كان في أرض الكرخ[١] ناسك فأضافه ضيف يوماً من الأيّام فدعا الناسك لضيفه بتمر لطرفته عندهم فأكلا منه جميعاً فقال الضيف للناسك ما أحلى هذا التمر وأطيبه وليست أرضنا التي نسكنها بأرض نخل مع أنّه إذ لم يكن عندنا قد اكتفينا بغيره من الثمار فإنّه من يقدر على التين وغيره من الثمار فما حاجته إلى التمر مع وخامته وقلّة[٢] موافقته للجسد.

٣،١٧ فقال له الناسك إنّه لا يُعَدّ سعيداً من احتاج إلى ما لا يجد ولا يقدر على الصبر عنه فيرجع عليه من ثقل ذلك وغمّه ما يضرّ به. وأنت سعيد الجدّ إذ قنعت بما تجد وزهدت فيما لا تجد وصبرت نفسك عنه ورضيت بما تجد.

٤،١٧ وكان الناسك يتكلّم بلسان العبرانيّة فاستحسن الضيف كلامه وأعجبه فتكلّف أن يتعلّمه وعالج نفسه على ذلك أيّاماً فلم يحسنه.

فقال الناسك لضيفه ما أخلقك أن تقع فيما تركت من كلامك وتتكلّف من تعلّم[٣] كلام العبرانيّة ما وقع فيه الغراب مرّة.

قال الضيف وكيف كان ذلك.

٥،١٧ فقال الناسك زعموا أنّ غراباً رأى مرّة حجلة وهي تدرج فأعجبته مشيتها وطمع في تعلّمها وراض نفسه عليها ولم يقدر على إحكامها فانصرف إلى مشيته التي

---

١ كذا ر؛ الأصل: الكرح. ٢ كذا ر؛ الأصل: وفانه. ٣ الأصل: نعلم.

The Ascetic and His Guest

King Dabshalim said to Baydabā the Philosopher, "Now that I've listened to what you've said, would you tell me about a person who abandons the trade that suits him and is appropriate for him, then turns to another trade, but fails to master it, and, having forgotten his original trade, falls into confusion?" 17.1

And Baydabā related: A certain ascetic, they say, lived in the land of Karkh. One day a guest arrived, and the ascetic called for some dates to serve as a treat. "How sweet and delicious!" exclaimed the guest. "There aren't any palm trees where we live, but we have plenty of other kinds of fruit to enjoy. You don't need dates if you have figs and other fruits—and, incidentally, dates are hard to digest and unhealthy." 17.2

"Yes," replied the ascetic. "Someone can hardly be counted happy if he seeks what he can't get and can't bear to do without it. He will only hurt himself by becoming heavyhearted and sorrowful. You, on the other hand, are fortunate to be content with what you can obtain and to have renounced what you cannot, to have curbed your appetite for what you can't reach and to be satisfied with what you can." 17.3

The ascetic knew Hebrew, which the guest found beautiful. So he set out to learn it, applying himself to the task for days, but to no avail. 17.4

The ascetic said to the guest, "If you abandon your own language and burden yourself with learning Hebrew, you'll likely suffer the same fate as the raven."

"How so?" asked the guest.

And the ascetic told the following tale: A raven, so they say, once saw a partridge walking along with delicate steps. He liked its gait and wanted to learn it, so he practiced, but, unable to master it, went back to his old gait; however, he couldn't remember it, so he became confused and hesitant: 17.5

The Raven Who Tried to Learn to Walk Like a Partridge

كان عليها فإذا هو لا يحفظها فصار حيران متردّداً لم يدرك ما طلب ولم يحسن لما كان في يديه حفظاً.

٦،١٧ وإنّما ضربت لك هذا المثل لتعلم أنّك خليق إن تركت لسانك وتكلّفت علم ما لا يشاكلك من كلام العبرانيّة ألّا[١] تدركه وأن تنسى الذي كان في يدك من غيره فإنّه قد قيل يُعَدّ جاهلاً من طلب من الأمر ما لا يشبهه وليس من أهله ولم يدركه آباؤه ولا أحد من قبله ولا يُعرفون بمثله.

٧،١٧ ثمّ قال الفيلسوف للملك فالولاة في قلّة تعاهدهم الرعيّة في هذا وأشباهه ألوم وأسوأ تدبيراً لأنّ تنقّل الناس من بعض المنازل إلى بعض[٢] وتركهم منها ما قد لزموه وجرت المعايش فيه مضرّ بالملوك وفي التماس[٣] من أهل الطبقة السفلى مراتب أهل الطبقة العليا تضييع للحزم[٤] وانتشار من الأمر وفساد من الأدب ومنازعة من اللئيم للكريم ثمّ الأشياء في ذلك تجري على مثال حتّى تنتهي إلى الخطر الجسيم من مضرّة الملك.

انتهى باب الناسك والضيف.

٨،١٧ فلمّا انتهى المنطق بالملك والفيلسوف إلى باب الناسك والضيف سكت الملك فقال الفيلسوف أيّها الملك عشت ألف سنة وملكت الأقاليم السبعة وأُعطيت من كلّ شيء سبباً وبُلّغته[٥] في سرور منك برعيّتك وقرّة عين منهم بك ومساعدة من القضاء والقدر لك فإنّه قد كمل فيك الحلم والعلم وزكا منك العقل والحفظ[٦] وتمّ فيك البأس والجود واتّفق منك العقل والقول والنيّة فلا يوجد في رأيك نقص

١ كذا ش، ع؛ الأصل: لا. ٢ إلى بعض: كذا ش، ع، ي (١٥٠)؛ ساقطة من الأصل. ٣ وفي التماس: كذا پ٣٤٧١؛ الأصل: والتماس. ٤ كذا پ٣٤٧١؛ ساقطة من الأصل. ٥ كذا ل٢؛ الأصل: وبلغه. ٦ كذا ل٢؛ الأصل: وحفظ

he hadn't obtained what he sought, and in the process hadn't retained what he once had.

17.6 "I've told you this parable to demonstrate that if you abandon your own language and set out to learn Hebrew, which doesn't suit you, you're likely to fail and in the process forget the language you already know. It has been said: The person who seeks what doesn't suit him and is not appropriate for him, what his fathers and forefathers never attained and for which they had no reputation, must be judged ignorant."

17.7 Then the philosopher said to the king, "Today's rulers deserve to be reprimanded even more for mismanagement, given their lack of care for their subjects in this and similar matters. For kings suffer harm when people move from one position to another and abandon the position they occupied and that provided them with a livelihood. When people in the lower ranks seek to rise into the upper ranks, then comes loss of sound management, disorder in the state, degeneration of manners, and competition between people of low character and those of noble character. Events then take their course until, in the end, there is grave danger of harm to the king."

Here ends the Chapter of the Ascetic and the Guest.

17.8 When the conversation between the king and the philosopher reached the end of the Chapter of the Ascetic and the Guest, the king fell silent, and the philosopher said,"May Your Majesty live a thousand years and rule over the Seven Climes. May you be granted the means to succeed in all your endeavors, amid happiness on your part in your subjects and contentment on their part with you—with the help of the divine Decree and Providence. Your discretion and knowledge are complete, your intelligence and memory keen, and your courage and generosity perfect. Your intelligence, your words, and your intentions are in harmony. There is no deficiency in your judgment, no

ولا في قولك سقط ولا في فعلك عيب وجمعت القوّة واللين فلا توجد جبانًا عند اللقاء ولا ضيّق الصدر فيما ينوبك من الأشياء.

٩،١٧ وقد شرحت لك الأمور ولخّصت[١] لك جواب ما سألتني عنه منها واجتهدت لك في ذلك كلّه رأيي ونظري ومبلغ فطنتي التماسَ قضاء حقّك فاقضِ حقّي بحسن النيّة منك بإعمال فكرك وعقلك فيما وصفت لك. مع أنّه ليس الآمر بالخير بأسعد به من المطيع له فيه ولا الناصح بأولى بالنصيحة من المنصوح له بها[٢] * ولا المتعلّم بأسعد بالعلم ممّن يعلّمه فمن تدبّر هذا الكتاب بعقله وعمل فيه بإصابة رأي ثمّ فكّر فيه بأصالة رأي حسن كان قمنًا للمراتب[٣] العظام والأمور الجسام مع مساعدة القدر ووقته إذا حضر ولا يستغني امرؤ عن النظر فيه والتدبّر له.

١٠،١٧ والله يوفّقك أيّها الملك ويصلح منك ما كان فاسدًا ويسكن عن غرب حدّك ما كان حادًّا[٤] ويستتمّ الرحمة على روحك وأرواح آبائك[٥] الماضين معشر أهل بيت العقل والأدب والفضل.

١١،١٧ فأمر الملك عند ذلك بفتح أبواب خزائنه وأن يحكّم بيدبا الفيلسوف في أخذ ما أحبّ من الأموال من صنوف الدرّ والجوهر والذهب والفضّة وألّا يُمنع شيئًا من ذلك وأقطعه قطائع كثيرة ورفع درجته ومرتبته فوق الدرجات والمراتب التي تسمو إليها منية المتمنّي من نظرائه.

١٢،١٧ فهذا ما كان من أمر دبشلم الملك وبيدبا رأس الحكماء والفلاسفة.

تمّ الكتاب المنعوت بكتاب كليلة ودمنة.

---

١ كذا ل٢؛ الأصل: بحلصت. ٢ إلى هنا ينتني نصّ الأصل لفقد بعض الصفحات وأثبتنا بقيّة الباب من ل٢. ٣ كذا ش؛ ل٢: كمينًا للأجوبة. ٤ كذا ش؛ ل٢ حامد. ٥ وأرواح آبائك: كذا ش؛ ل٢: وآبائك.

error in your speech, and nothing blameworthy in your actions. You combine strength and gentleness; you are never timid in battle or discouraged by sudden adversity.

"I have explained matters to you and answered your questions in the best 17.9
possible way. To fulfill my duty to you, I have summoned my judgment, insight, and ingenuity; repay me now by a sincere intention to apply your mind and intelligence to what I have described. The person who obeys a wise command is no less fortunate than the person who gives it; the person who accepts good advice is no less fortunate than the person who imparts it;[66] and the person who learns is no less fortunate in his knowledge than the person who teaches. Whoever ponders this book with his intelligence, and acts on it according to his right judgment, and reflects on it with his sound judgment deserves an exalted position and, with the help of Providence, will be fit to deal with weighty matters when the time comes. No one can dispense with reflecting on this book and learning its lessons.

"May God grant Your Majesty success. May He correct whatever in you is 17.10
amiss, calming any sharpness in your temperament and bestowing the fullness of His mercy upon you and upon your forefathers, a house renowned for intellect, cultivation, and merit."

The king then commanded that the doors of his treasuries be opened and 17.11
that the philosopher Baydabā be allowed to take anything he wanted: pearls, jewels, gold, silver—nothing was to be denied him. The king bestowed many estates on him, and raised his rank and station above those aspired to by his peers.

This, then, is what took place between King Dabshalim and the chief sage 17.12
and philosopher Baydabā.

Here ends *The Book of Kalīlah and Dimnah.*

Notes

1 The reading and vocalization of the name are conjectural (see Justi, *Iranisches Namenbuch*, 74a). ʿAzzām's text conjectures Ādharhirbad.

2 Later in the chapter (§1.14 and §1.17) it is implied that Barzawayh brought back more than one book.

3 The Arabic has *mithqāls* (standard weights), a synonym for the gold dinar.

4 From here until "Buzurgmihr, you know Barzawayh's devotion to us" (§1.23), several pages in MS London Or. 4044 are lost. The translation is based on the text in MS London Or. 8751.

5 The gap in MS London Or. 4044 ends here.

6 One manuscript family (e.g., Paris 3466 and de Sacy's edition) adds, significantly, "and his journey to India in search of drugs and medicines, and how he learned their scripts and language."

7 This chapter is Ibn al-Muqaffaʿ's preface.

8 Literally "byways into which they could turn"—that is, ways to hint at doctrines whose explicit statement might imperil the speaker.

9 Correcting the manuscript's "six."

10 Another instance of an unelaborated list.

11 From information here and in the previous chapter, one can deduce that Barzawayh lived in the time of the Sasanian ruler Khosrow I Anūsharwān (r. AD 531–79).

12 In other versions, Barzawayh divides his education into two phases, the first beginning with his parents' sending him to learn to read and write, the second when he searched for a vocation and settled on medicine, based on his appreciation of its merits.

13 That is, for stringing into necklaces.

14 Wind is one of the elements or humors that constitute the body, according to some versions of the Indian tradition.See Nöldeke, *Burzoēs Einleitung zu dem Buche Kalīla wa-Dimna*, 22, 23n4.

15 Or. 4044 reads "two branches," but the copyist has added in the margin "the correct reading is a branch," although he has left the rest of the paragraph in the dual. The Indian sources of the parable point to a single branch or, at best, two branches or roots dangling

from a single tree. See Ernst Kuhn, "Der Mann im Brunnen, Geschichte eines indischen Gleichnisses."

16 Or "correcting what I could of my action."

17 Or "guidance to lead me aright, power over my soul, and aides to help me in my affairs."

18 The carpenter has apparently laid the second wedge aside, to be driven in upon his return, leaving only one wedge in the log.

19 That is, many people can seek the same place or rank, which are not the exclusive property of anyone.

20 The go-between's husband is a *ḥajjām*, a cupper or phlebotomist, but since these tasks were part of the barber's trade, we translate it as "barber."

21 The Arabic has *aswad*, a large black snake, and *ghurāb*, either crow or raven. The identifications "cobra" and "crow" are taken from the *Panchatantra.*

22 The Arabic has *makkāʾ*, usually a "lark," which does not fit the context. We translate "heron," following the *Panchatantra.*

23 The lion appears to expect a party of animals escorting his "lunch."

24 The comparison can be traced to the Sanskrit, although it has been distorted in transmission. See Schulthess, *Kalīla und Dimna*, 185n139. Edgerton's reconstruction of the *Panchatantra* (2:311) reads: "Better [a king who is like] a vulture, attended by *swans* that live contentedly in the water, than [a king who is like] a *swan*, attended by savage carrion-birds that eat flesh. A mean retinue destroys even a man of fine qualities, while even one lacking in virtue becomes virtuous if his followers are above meanness."

25 "Sea's Custodian" corresponds to Arabic *wakīl al-baḥr*, an agent, administrator, or custodian of someone else's affairs or property. The Old Syriac (ed. Schulthess, 36) reads *gnīzā d-yammā*, the genius or spirit of the sea, and this seems to be the meaning here. The bird's name (Arabic *ṭīṭawā*) reproduces Sanskrit *ṭiṭṭibha*, the jacana, a tropical bird that breeds on ponds. Indian folklore makes it proverbial for conceit and therefore likely to challenge the water spirit. See Wilson, *Essays Analytical, Critical and Philological on Subjects Connected with Sanskrit Literature*, 2:18–19.

26 Phoenix (*al-ʿAnqāʾ*): The Sanskrit identifies the chief of the birds as Garuḍa, the mount of the god Vishnu. The Syriac, presumably echoing the Persian, identified Garuḍa with the legendary Iranian bird Simorg. Arabic *al-ʿanqāʾ* can be grammatically masculine or feminine. Although Or. 4044 refers to it in the masculine, we translate it as feminine in order to distinguish the Phoenix from the "king" (originally the god Vishnu) who flies through the air mounted on her and exacts vengeance from the Sea's Custodian.

27 The heart was considered to be the seat of thought.

28 Or glowworm, as the Arabic *yarāʿah* can mean either.

29 That is, someone who would guarantee the plaintiff's future appearance in court, since an unsubstantiated accusation would render the plaintiff himself subject to punishment.

30 The implication is that the judge will rule that the simpleton must pay the swindler the hundred thousand dinars he is presumed to have taken.

31 The Arabic *ʿuljūm* has been translated "heron," as in the *Panchatantra*. (François de Blois, *Burzōy's Voyage to India*, 12n3, has argued that *ʿuljūm* derives ultimately from Greek *ἀλκυών*, "kingfisher.")

32 The Arabic has *ibn ʿirs*, weasel, but in the *Panchatantra* the animal is a mongoose, not a weasel, and the story hinges on the well-known ability of the mongoose to kill snakes because of its immunity to venom.

33 Either a rod used for breaking up clods (*mirzabbah*) or a blacksmith's hammer or mallet (*mirzabah*). One hundred *mann* is approximately two hundred pounds.

34 The Arabic is simply *ahl al-saʿādah* (people of prosperity, fortunateness, felicity), but the religious overtone needs to be preserved.

35 The colophons at the end of each chapter have been preserved as in the manuscript. Although they may have been inserted by the copyist, they sometimes do not agree exactly with the title of the chapter and sometimes add information.

36 The text of London Or. 4044 varies between calling Baydabā "philosopher" (*faylasūf*) and "scholar" (*ʿālim*). For convenience, we use "philosopher" throughout.

37 The unidentified speaker turns against Dimnah the very arguments from physiognomy that Dimnah had used to turn the lion against Shanzabah.

38 The text is corrupt; accordingly, the translation is conjectural.

39 The lion's request depends on the legal point that anonymous testimony cannot be admitted as evidence.

40 That is, loyalty to his dove friends in their distress.

41 That is, no dependents. The point is that he lived alone.

42 The saying could be interpreted as meaning that the best intelligence is the one that foresees the outcome of affairs, or it could be interpreted as meaning that the best intelligence is the kind that is applied to managing one's affairs properly.

43 This clause, unique to this redaction, is another example of the redactor's piety. Cf. Q Yā Sīn 36:38: «And the sun—it runs to a fixed resting-place; that is the ordaining of the All-mighty, the All-knowing.»

44 Another pious insertion unique to this redaction. The phrase echoes Q Ḥijr 15:38 and Ṣād 38:82, referring in each case to the Day of Judgment, at which time the stars will cease their regular rising and setting.

45 The Arabic *dawḥ* is any tree with spreading branches. The translation as "banyan" follows the *Panchatantra.*

46 Arabic *ṣifrid*, a bird of uncertain identity. We translate it as "partridge," following the *Panchatantra.*

47 This refers to a father's obligation to arrange a suitable marriage for his daughter, preferably even before she has reached puberty.

48 There is a lacuna one or two words in length due to damage of the manuscript.

49 Likely a female horse, donkey, or mule.

50 See Q Luqmān 31:34.

51 The episode hinges on the fact that the woman must perform certain ritual ablutions after childbirth before she can lie with her husband.

52 This chapter draws its story from the twelfth book of the *Mahābhārata.*

53 Again, this reference to things ordained to happen, presumably by God's decree, is characteristic of this redaction. The clause does not occur in the Old Syriac, and appears to be unique to this manuscript.

54 The story goes back to the twelfth book of the *Mahābhārata* (trans. Benfey, *Pantschatantra*, 1:561–73). The copyists of the London and Rabat manuscripts wrote the bird's name as *Fatrah.* The copyist of the Istanbul manuscript, the basis of ʿAzzām's edition, turned it into *qubbarah* (lark) by rearranging the diacritical dots. This edition and translation follow the most likely transcription, *Finzah*, as in the editions of de Sacy and Cheikho. This agrees with the Old Syriac *Panzōh*, which apparently goes back to Sanskrit *Pūjanī* (venerating).

55 Arabic *ʿilal* (plural of *ʿillah*), literally "occasions" or "causes."

56 This story goes back to the twelfth book of the *Mahābhārata.*

57 Unlike the heading, this closing remark characterizes the jackal as abstinent (*ṣawwām*).

58 Of judiciousness (*ḥilm*), Thomas Hefter writes that it is "the virtue of self-mastery and patient, rational behaviour, and . . . may also refer to the faculty of reason (*al-ʿaql*) itself. It is used most frequently to describe an individual's forbearance and control of anger when in a position of power, and this is often the context presumed in ethical discussions or praise." Hefter, "Ḥilm" in *EI3*.

59 Gūlpanāh is a conjectural reconstruction of the name of Īrākht's rival wife. It appears in the manuscript as Jūrfanah. See Schulthess, *Kalīla und Dimna*, 226, n. 508.

60 The text of the end of the sentence is problematic. The Old Syriac is quite different: "and doesn't know an unskilled man [*hedyōtā*, literally 'an idiot'] from a reasonable/eloquent one [*mlīlā*] and even how to talk [*da-nmallel*]."

61 A variant reads: "I am afraid *of* you, Baylār."

62 Literally "traveler" (*sayyāḥ*). The term had an extended meaning of pilgrim or mendicant.

63 MS London Or. 4044 omits any explanation of how the king's son knew that only the mendicant could cure him. In some other versions, the snake's sister, a jinni, out of compassion appears to the king's son in a dream and gives him this information.

64 The Arabic involves a pun. *Qadr* means both "rank" and "destiny."

65 This echoes a well-known hadith in both Muslim and al-Bukhārī: "None of you truly believes until he loves for his brother what he loves for himself."

66 One or more final folios of MS London Or. 4044 are missing. We base our translation of the remainder of the chapter on MS London Or. 8751.

Glossary

Anūsharwān the Sasanian monarch Khusraw I, surnamed Anūsharwān (or in Middle Persian Anōshagruwān, "of immortal soul"), reigned AD 531–79.

Balkh a major city of central Asia, located in present-day Afghanistan. The language of the inhabitants was Bactrian, an eastern Iranian language.

Barzawayh the physician sent by King Anūsharwān to India to obtain and translate Indian books. Barzawayh is an Arabicized form probably corresponding to Middle Persian Burzōē.

Baydabā (or Baydanā) the fictional chief philosopher whose conversations with King Dabshalim generate the parables of Kalīlah and Dimnah. The Old Syriac form can be read Bēdawāg or Bīdwāg. In the West, the name has often been given as Bidpai.

Burdjird an unidentified city.

Buzurgmihr the minister of Anūsharwān credited with composing Barzawayh's biography, and in some manuscripts the introductory chapter.

Dabshalim (or Dabshalīm) the fictional Indian king whose conversations with the chief philosopher Baydabā generate the parables of the book *Kalīlah and Dimnah*. The Old Syriac *d-b-sh-r-m*, possibly read Debsharām, might correspond to Sanskrit Dēvaśarman ("Beloved of the gods").

Deccan a plateau in south-central India.

Dimnah the name of one of the two jackals who are the protagonists of the first story. The Old Syriac transcription Damnag apparently derived from Sanskrit Damanaka ("Victor").

dinar (dīnār) a gold coin weighing about 4.25 grams. One dinar was worth about twenty dirhams.

dirham a silver coin usually equivalent to one twentieth of a dinar.

Kalīlah the name of one of the two jackals who are the protagonists of the first story. The Old Syriac transcription Kalīlag apparently derived through Middle Persian from the Sanskrit Karaṭaka—the meaning is unclear.

Kamānzūn a jurist who appears in Chapter 13 as a member of the court of King Haylār.

kohl (kuḥl) a dark cosmetic powder used as eye shadow or mascara. Traditionally, it is prepared by grinding the mineral stibnite (antimony trisulfide).

mann a measure of weight equivalent to two *raṭl*s, approximately two pounds.

Marw a major city on the Silk Road in Central Asia. Its ruins are located near the present city of Mary in Turkmenistan.

Mārūzūd this corresponds to Sanskrit Mihilārōpya or Mahilārōpya, a city in the Deccan, in south-central India.

Qūhistān Persian for "mountain country," designating various mountainous areas of the Iranian plateau. The province was noted for *qūhiyyah,* a fine linen weave.

Sind the region of the Indian subcontinent around the lower course of the Indus River. The area was conquered by the Arabs in 93/711, during the caliphate of al-Walīd ibn ʿAbd al-Malik.

Zoroastrianism the official religion of Sasanian Iran, based on the teachings of the prophet Zoroaster (Zarathustra).

Bibliography

Allen, Clifford G., ed. *L'ancienne version espagnole de Kalila et Digna*. Mâcon, France: Protat frères, 1906.

AnonymClassic. "Kalīla and Dimna: AnonymClassic." http://www.geschkult.fu-berlin.de/en/e/kalila-wa-dimna/index.html.

Arjomand, Said Amir. "'Abd Allah Ibn al-Muqaffa' and the 'Abbasid Revolution." *Iranian Studies* 27 (1994): 9–36.

Audebert, Claude. "La condition humaine d'après *Kalīla wa Dimna*." *Arabica* 46 (1999): 287–312.

Audebert, Claude. "La violence dans Kalîla wa-Dimna d'Ibn al-Muqaffa'." *Alif: Journal of Comparative Poetics* 13 (1993): 24–45.

Beeston, A. F. L. "The 'Alī ibn Shāh Preface to Kalīlah wa Dimnah." *Oriens* 7, no. 1 (1954): 81–84.

Benfey, Theodor. *Pantschatantra: Fünf Bücher indischer Fabeln, Märchen und Erzählungen*. 2 vols. Leipzig: F. A. Brockhaus, 1859.

Bickell, Gustav. *Kalilag und Damnag, alte syrische Übersetzung des indischen Fürstenspiegels*. Leipzig: F. A. Brockhaus, 1876.

Bosworth, C. E. "Ebn al-Moqaffa', Abū Moḥammad 'Abd-Allāh Rōzbeh." In *Encyclopaedia Iranica*. http://iranicaonline.org/articles/ebn-al-moqaffa.

Brockelmann, Carl. "Kalīla wa-Dimna." In *Encyclopaedia of Islam, Second Edition*. Brill Online.

Brunschvig, Robert. "'Abd." In *Encyclopaedia of Islam, Second Edition*. Brill Online.

Bürgel, Johann Christoph. "Language on Trial, Religion at Stake: Trial Scenes in Some Classical Arabic Texts and the Hermeneutic Problems Involved." In *Myths, Historical Archetypes and Symbolic Figures in Arabic Literature: Towards a New Hermeneutic Approach; Proceedings of the International Symposium in Beirut, June 25th – June 30th, 1996*, edited by Angelika Neuwirth, Birgit Embaló, Sebastian Günther, and Maher Jarrar, 189–204. Stuttgart: Franz Steiner Verlag, 1999. http://menadoc.bibliothek.uni-halle.de/inhouse/content/pageview/2073796.

De Blois, François. *Burzōy's Voyage to India and the Origin of the Book of Kalīlah wa Dimnah*. London: Royal Asiatic Society, 1990.

———. "Zindīḳ." In *Encyclopaedia of Islam, Second Edition*. Brill Online.

Dozy, R. P. A. *Supplément aux dictionnaires arabes*. 2 vols. Leiden, Netherlands: Brill, 1881. Reprinted Beirut, 1968.

Edgerton, Franklin. *The Panchatantra Reconstructed: An Attempt to Establish the Lost Original Sanskrit Text of the Most Famous of Indian Story-Collections on the Basis of the Principal Extant Versions*. 3 vols. New Haven, CT: American Oriental Society, 1924.

Enderwitz, Suzanne. "Al-Shuʿūbiyya." In *Encyclopaedia of Islam, Second Edition*. Brill Online.

Fahd, Toufic, and A. Rippin. "Shayṭān." In *Encyclopaedia of Islam, Second Edition*. Brill Online.

Gabrieli, Francesco. "Ibn al-Muḳaffaʿ." In *Encyclopaedia of Islam, Second Edition*. Brill Online.

Gimaret, Daniel. "Muʿtazila." In *Encyclopaedia of Islam, Second Edition*. Brill Online.

Gruendler, Beatrice. "Les versions de *Kalīla wa-Dimna*: Une transmission et une circulation mouvantes." In *Énoncés sapientiels et littérature exemplaire: Une intertextualité complexe*. Edited by Marie-Sol Ortola, 385–416. Nancy, France: Éditions Universitaires de Lorraine, 2013.

Gruendler, Beatrice, Jan J. van Ginkel, Rima Redwan, Khouloud Khalfallah, Isabel Toral, Johannes Stephan, Matthew L. Keegan, et al. "An Interim Report on the Editorial and Analytical Work of the AnonymClassic Project." *Medieval Worlds* 11 (2020): 241–79.

Guidi, Ignazio. *Studii sul testo arabo del Libro di Calila e Dimna*. Rome: Libreria Spithöver, 1873.

Hämeen-Anttila, Jaakko. "Adab (a) Arabic, Early Developments." In *Encyclopaedia of Islam, Three*. Brill Online.

———. *Khwadāynāmag: The Middle Persian Book of Kings*. Studies in Persian Cultural History 14. Leiden, Netherlands: Brill, 2018.

Hefter, Thomas. "Ḥilm." In *Encyclopaedia of Islam, Three*. Brill Online.

Hertel, Johannes. *Tantrākhyāyika: Die älteste Fassung des Pañcatantra*. 2 vols. Leipzig: B. G. Teubner, 1909.

Ibn Khallikān, Abū l-ʿAbbās Shams al-Dīn Aḥmad ibn Muḥammad. *Wafayāt al-aʿyān*. Edited by Iḥsān ʿAbbās. 8 vols. Beirut: Dār al-Thaqāfah, 1968–72.

Ibn al-Muqaffaʿ, ʿAbdallāh. *Calila et Dimna: Ou fables de Bidpai en Arabe*. Edited by Sylvestre de Sacy. Paris: Imprimerie Royale, 1816.

———. *Le livre de Kalila et Dimna*. Translated by André Miquel. Paris: C. Klincksieck, 1957.

———. *Kalila and Dimna, or, The Fables of Bidpai*. Translated by Wyndham Knatchbull. Oxford: W. Baxter for J. Parker, 1819.

———. *Kalilah and Dimnah: An English Version of Bidpai's Fables Based upon Ancient Arabic and Spanish Manuscripts*. Translated by Thomas Ballantine Irving. Newark, DE: Juan de la Cuesta, 1980.

———. *Kalīlah wa-Dimnah*. Edited by ʿAbd al-Wahhāb ʿAzzām. Cairo: Maṭbaʿat al-Maʿārif, 1941.

———. *La version arabe de Kalîlah et Dimnah*. Edited by Louis Cheikho. Beirut: Imprimerie Catholique, 1905.

Ibn al-Nadīm, Abū l-Faraj Muḥammad ibn Abī Yaʿqūb. *Kitāb al-Fihrist*. Translated by Bayard Dodge as *The Fihrist of al-Nadīm*. 2 vols. New York, NY: Columbia University Press, 1970.

Ibn Qutaybah. *The Excellence of the Arabs*. Edited by James E. Montgomery and Peter Webb, translated by Sarah Bowen Savant and Peter Webb. New York, NY: New York University Press, 2017.

Justi, Ferdinand. *Iranisches Namenbuch*. Marburg, Germany: N. G. Elwert, 1895.

Keegan, Matthew L. "'Elsewhere Lies Its Meaning': The Vagaries of *Kalīla and Dimna*'s Reception." *Poetica* 52 (2021): 13–40.

Keith-Falconer, I. G. N. *Kalīlah and Dimnah, or The Fables of Bidpai: An English Translation of the Later Syriac Version*. Cambridge, UK: Cambridge University Press, 1885. Reprinted Amsterdam: Philo Press, 1970.

Khalfallah, Khouloud. "Digital Reconstruction." http://www.geschkult.fu-berlin.de/en/e/kalila-wa-dimna/topics/Digital-Reconstruction.html.

Kristó-Nagy, István. *La pensée d'Ibn al-Muqaffaʿ: Un "agent double" dans le monde persan et arabe*. Studia Arabica 19. Versailles: Éditions de Paris, 2013.

———. "Wild Lions and Wise Jackals: Killing Kings and Clever Counsellors in Kalīla wa-Dimna." In *Prophets, Viziers and Philosophers: Wisdom and Authority in Early Arabic Literature*, edited by Emily J. Cottrell, 147–209. Groningen: Barkhuis & Groningen University Library, 2020.

Kuhn, Ernst. "Der Mann im Brunnen, Geschichte eines indischen Gleichnisses." In *Festgruss an Otto von Böhtlingk*, 68–76. Stuttgart: W. Kohlhammer, 1888.

Lane, Edward. *An Arabic-English Lexicon*. London: Williams and Norgate, 1863–93. Reprinted Beirut, 1968.

Latham, J. D. "Ibn al-Muqaffaʿ and Early ʿAbbasid Prose." In *ʿAbbasid Belles-Lettres*, edited by Julia Ashtiany, T. M. Johnstone, J. D. Latham, and R. B. Serjeant, 48–77. Cambridge, UK: Cambridge University Press, 1990.

Lowry, Joseph E. "The First Islamic Legal Theory: Ibn al-Muqaffaʿ on Interpretation, Authority, and the Structure of the Law." *The Journal of the American Oriental Society* 128, no. 1 (2008): 25–40.

Marlow, Louise. "Adab al-Mulūk: The Mirrors for Princes of Classical Islam." In *Encyclopedia of Mediterranean Humanism*, edited by Houari Touati. http://www.encyclopedie-humanisme.com/?Adab-al-Mulūk.

Marsham, Andrew, and Chase F. Robinson. "The Safe-Conduct for the Abbasid ʿAbd Allāh b. ʿAlī (d. 764)." *Bulletin of the School of Oriental and African Studies* 70, no. 2 (2007): 247–81.

Miskawayh, Abū ʿAlī Aḥmad ibn Muḥammad. *Al-Ḥikmah al-khālidah: Jāvīdān khirad.* Edited by ʿAbd al-Raḥmān Badawī. Cairo: Maktabat al-Nahḍah, 1952.

Nöldeke, Theodor. *Burzoēs Einleitung zu dem Buche Kalīla waDimna.* Strassbourg: Trübner, 1912.

———. "Zu Kalīla waDimna." *Zeitschrift der Deutschen Morgenländischen Gesellschaft* 59 (1905): 794–806.

Nöldeke, Theodor, ed. and trans. *Die Erzählung vom Mäusekönig und seinen Ministern.* Abhandlungen der Königlichen Gesellschaft der Wissenschaften zu Göttingen 25. Göttingen, Germany: Dieterich, 1879.

Al-Qāḍī, Wadād. "ʿAbd al-Ḥamīd al-Kātib." In *Encyclopaedia of Islam, Three.* Brill Online.

Riedel, Dagmar. "Kalila wa Demna i. Redactions and Circulation." In *Encyclopedia Iranica.* http://iranicaonline.org/articles/kalila-demna-i.

Rieu, Charles. *Supplement of the Catalogue of the Arabic Manuscripts in the British Museum.* London: Longmans, 1894.

Schiefner, Anton. *Mahâkâtjâjana und König Tshaṇḍa-Pradjota: Ein Cyclus buddhistischer Erzählungen.* Mémoires de l'Académie impériale des sciences de St.-Pétersbourg (series 7, vol. 22, no. 7). St. Petersburg: Académie des sciences, 1875.

Schulthess, Friedrich, ed. *Kalīla und Dimna: Syrisch und Deutsch.* Berlin: G. Reimer, 1911.

Shamma, Tarek. "Translating into the Empire: The Arabic Version of Kalila wa Dimna." *The Translator* 15 (2009): 65–86.

Sourdel, Dominique. "La biographie d'Ibn al-Muqaffaʿ d'après les sources anciennes." *Arabica* 1 (1954): 307–23.

Sprengling, Martin. "Kalîla Studies. I." *The American Journal of Semitic Languages and Literatures* 40, no. 2 (1924): 81–97.

Van Ruymbeke, Christine. "Kalila and Dimna as a Case Study: Ibn al-Muqaffaʿ's and Nasrullah Munshi's Translations." In *The Routledge Handbook of Arabic Translation.* Edited by Sameh Hanna, H. El-Farahaty, and A.-W. Khalifa. Abingdon, UK: Routledge, 2020.

Vishnusharman. *Five Discourses on Worldly Wisdom.* Translated by Patrick Olivelle. New York, NY: New York University Press, 2006.

Wensinck, A. J. "Bidpai." In *Encyclopaedia of Islam*. 1st ed. Brill Online.

Wilson, Horace Hayman. *Essays Analytical, Critical and Philological on Subjects Connected with Sanskrit Literature*. 3 vols. London: Trübner, 1864.

Wood, Ramsay. *Kalila and Dimna: Selected Fables of Bidpai, Retold*. London: Granada Books, 1982.

Wright, William, ed. *The Book of Kalīlah and Dimnah, Translated from Arabic into Syriac*. Oxford, UK: Clarendon Press, 1884.

Al-Yamanī, Abū ʿAbdallāh Muḥammad ibn Ḥusayn. *Kitāb Muḍāhāt amthāl kitāb Kalīlah wa-Dimnah bi-mā ashbahahā min ashʿār al-ʿArab*. Edited by Muḥammad Yūsuf Najm. Beirut: Dār al-Thaqāfah, 1961.

Al-Yaʿqūbī, Aḥmad ibn Abī Yaʿqūb. *Ibn-Wādhih Qui Dicitur Al-Jaʿqubī Historiae*. Edited by M. Th. Houtsma. 2 vols. Leiden, Netherlands: Brill, 1883. Translated as *The Works of Ibn Wāḍiḥ al-Yaʿqūbī*. Edited by Matthew S. Gordon, Chase F. Robinson, Everett K. Rowson, and Michael Fishbein. 3 vols. Leiden, Netherlands: Brill, 2018.

Yousefi, Najm al-Din. "Islam without Fuqahāʾ: Ibn al-Muqaffaʿ and His Perso-Islamic Solution to the Caliphate's Crisis of Legitimacy (70–142 AH/690–760 CE)." *Iranian Studies* 50:1 (2017): 9–44.

Zilio Grandi, Ida. "Ḥilm or 'Judiciousness': A Contribution to the Study of Islamic Ethics Based on the Traditional Sources." *Studia Islamica* 110 (2015): 81–100.

Further Reading

On the life and works of Ibn al-Muqaffaʿ, F. Gabrieli's article "Ibn al-Muḳaffaʿ" in the second edition of the *Encyclopaedia of Islam* is a good starting point. The latest work in Gabrieli's bibliography dates from 1966. C. E. Bosworth's 1997 article "Ebn al-Moqaffaʿ" in the *Encyclopedia Iranica* is a more recent general treatment. Dominique Sourdel's 1954 article "La biographie d'Ibn al-Muqaffaʿ d'après les sources anciennes" examines the sources for the author's biography. István Kristó-Nagy's *La pensée d'Ibn al-Muqaffaʿ* (2013) is a recent examination of Ibn al-Muqaffaʿ's oeuvre as a whole. Ibn al-Muqaffaʿ's treatment of Persian historical sources is discussed by Jaakko Hämeen-Anttila in Khwadāynāmag*: The Middle Persian Book of Kings* (2018).

The article "Kalīla wa-Dimna" by C. Brockelmann in the second edition of the *Encyclopaedia of Islam* deals specifically with *Kalīlah and Dimnah*; its bibliography ends in 1964. Brockelmann provides an introduction to the Arabic work and also traces in detail the work's subsequent adaptations into Arabic verse, later Syriac prose, Persian prose and verse, and into Western languages: Hebrew, Latin, medieval Spanish, and medieval Greek. Dagmar Riedel's 2010 article in the *Encyclopedia Iranica*, "Kalila wa Demna i. Redactions and Circulation," focuses in greater detail on the many New Persian adaptations of the work.

Readers interested in comparing the present translation, based on a single manuscript, with translations based on other versions of the text will find little in English at present. This deficiency is being remedied by AnonymClassic, a remarkable project underway in Germany. Professor Beatrice Gruendler and her team of scholars have identified about 140 manuscripts and have obtained copies of 95 to date. They are creating a digital library that will make it possible to employ sophisticated computer tools to make detailed comparisons of the versions. AnonymClassic intends to publish representative chapters of the text in parallel-text editions, with translations into English, to illustrate the changes the text underwent in the course of its transmission. The reader can form an idea of its scope by visiting the project's website: http://www.geschkult.fu-berlin.de/

en/e/kalila-wa-dimna. Especially valuable as an introduction to the project is the article by Beatrice Gruendler et al.: "An Interim Report on the Editorial and Analytical Work of the AnonymClassic Project" (2020).

A very different work, intended as a reworking made from several earlier translations (the author admits to knowing no Arabic), is *Kalila and Dimna: Selected Fables of Bidpai, Retold* by Ramsay Wood. It is a thoroughly enjoyable free retelling, much to be recommended for its liveliness.

The text of 'Azzām's edition, based on manuscript Aya Sofya 4095, was translated into French as *Le livre de Kalila et Dimna* (1957) by André Miquel and includes valuable notes. Cheikho's text formed the basis of T. B. Irving's *Kalilah and Dimnah: An English Version of Bidpai's Fables* (1980).

Readers interested in the Indian sources of *Kalīlah and Dimnah* can consult Franklin Edgerton's *The Panchatantra Reconstructed* (1927), whose second volume provides an English translation of the reconstructed Sanskrit text, or Patrick Olivelle's *Five Discourses on Worldly Wisdom* (2006). Although the Middle Persian text from which Ibn al-Muqaffa' produced his Arabic translation does not survive, a single manuscript of the older Syriac translation, which predates Ibn al-Muqaffa''s translation, did survive, and was carefully reedited and provided with a German translation and notes by Friedrich Schulthess, *Kalīla und Dimna: Syrisch und Deutsch* (1911). Schulthess's version is invaluable, as its notes frequently compare the Syriac text with the Arabic versions and with the early translations of the Arabic. It supersedes the earlier edition by G. Bickell (1876), which, however, contains a useful introduction by Theodor Benfey.

For most readers, the later Syriac version will be something of a curiosity: evidence of how *Kalīlah and Dimnah* was adapted by redactors for specific purposes—in this case, the interest of a writer intent on giving the work Christian resonances. It is available in the translation made by I. G. N. Keith-Falconer, *Kalīlah and Dimnah, or The Fables of Bidpai* (1885, reprinted 1970). Readers of Spanish will enjoy the medieval version (dated to 1251) in the edition published in 1906 by Clifford G. Allen as *L'ancienne version espagnole de Kalila et Digna* or in later editions published in Spain.

The additional preface to *Kalīla wa-Dimnah* by 'Alī ibn al-Shāh al-Fārisī (also known as Bahnūd ibn Saḥwān) was later added to many manuscripts and formed part of many editions of the Arabic text. A. J. Wensinck's article "Bidpai" in the first edition of the *Encyclopaedia of Islam* summarizes its content. A more recent discussion is A. F. L. Beeston's article "The 'Alī ibn Shāh Preface to Kalīlah wa Dimnah" (1954). The preface was edited and translated into German by T. Nöldeke, *Burzoēs Einleitung zu dem Buche Kalīla waDimna* (1912). In 1879, Nöldeke also edited and translated an additional chapter, "Die Erzählung vom Mäusekönig und seinen Ministern" ("The Story of the King of the Mice and His Ministers").

In addition to the works mentioned above, the following articles on various aspects of Kalīlah and Dimnah are of interest:

- Said Amir Arjomand, "'Abd Allah Ibn al-Muqaffa' and the 'Abbasid Revolution" (1994), places the author in his historical context, noting the connection between the discussion of human dignity in *Kalīlah and Dimnah* (see, for example, §3.25 of the present translation) and the invocation of "Abdalla the Saracen" (apparently Ibn al-Muqaffa') on the same subject at the beginning of the *Oration on the Dignity of Man* by the Renaissance humanist Pico della Mirandola.
- Najm al-Din Yousefi, "Islam without Fuqahā': Ibn al-Muqaffa' and His Perso-Islamic Solution to the Caliphate's Crisis of Legitimacy (70–142 AH/690–760 CE)," explores the intersection of Persian and Islamic ideas about legitimate rule in Ibn al-Muqaffa''s *Risālah fī l-ṣaḥābah* (*Epistle on the Caliph's Entourage*).
- Tarek Shamma, "Translating into the Empire: The Arabic Version of Kalila wa Dimna" (2009), explores the ways in which Ibn al-Muqaffa' "domesticated" the text in an Islamic context.
- Christine van Ruymbeke, "Kalila and Dimna as a Case Study: Ibn al-Muqaffa''s and Nasrullah Munshi's Translations," explores the ways in which Kalīlah and Dimnah "transcended the boundaries of time and culture and was able to adapt to new contexts, languages and cultures."
- Claude Audebert, "La violence dans Kalîla wa-Dimna d'Ibn al-Muqaffa'" (1993) and "La condition humaine d'après *Kalīla wa Dimna*" (1999), considers the ethical universe of the work.
- Johann Christoph Bürgel, in "Language on Trial, Religion at Stake: Trial Scenes in Some Classical Arabic Texts and the Hermeneutic Problems Involved" (1999), places the trial of Dimnah in the context of another trial scene in early Arabic literature, "Man and Animal before the King of Demons," in the collection of essays attributed to the Brethren of Purity (*Ikhwān al-Ṣafā'*).

- István Kristó-Nagy, "Wild Lions and Wise Jackals: Killing Kings and Clever Counsellors in Kalīla wa-Dimna" (2020) explores the image of rulers and their advisers in the book, especially in "The Lion and the Ox" and "The Owls and the Crows," but with some discussion of the theme as it appears in other chapters, with attention to how certain themes were expanded and adapted as the work traveled from its Indian sources.
- Matthew L. Keegan, "'Elsewhere Lies Its Meaning': The Vagaries of *Kalīla and Dimna*'s Reception" (2021), explores how interpreters reconfigured the book's generic affiliation, making it by turns "a Quranic competitor, a repository of proverbs, an allegory for the soul, a source of law, and a model for storytelling that imparts practical wisdom."

Index of Proper Names

About the NYU Abu Dhabi Institute

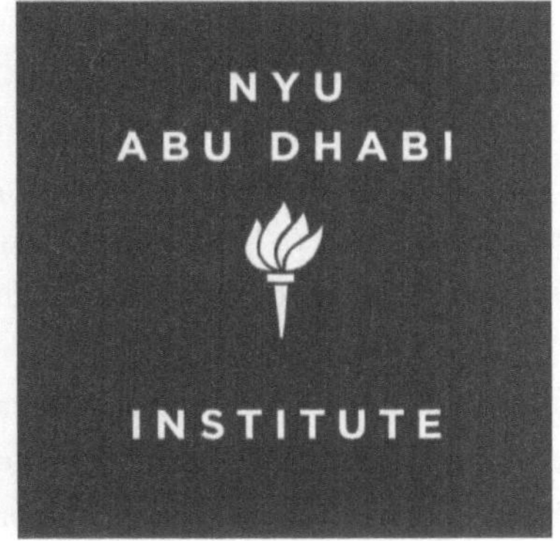

The Library of Arabic Literature is supported by a grant from the NYU Abu Dhabi Institute, a major hub of intellectual and creative activity and advanced research. The Institute hosts academic conferences, workshops, lectures, film series, performances, and other public programs directed both to audiences within the UAE and to the worldwide academic and research community. It is a center of the scholarly community for Abu Dhabi, bringing together faculty and researchers from institutions of higher learning throughout the region.

NYU Abu Dhabi, through the NYU Abu Dhabi Institute, is a world-class center of cutting-edge research, scholarship, and cultural activity. The Institute creates singular opportunities for leading researchers from across the arts, humanities, social sciences, sciences, engineering, and the professions to carry out creative scholarship and conduct research on issues of major disciplinary, multidisciplinary, and global significance.

About the Typefaces

The Arabic body text is set in DecoType Naskh, designed by Thomas Milo and Mirjam Somers, based on an analysis of five centuries of Ottoman manuscript practice. The exceptionally legible result is the first and only typeface in a style that fully implements the principles of script grammar (*qawāʿid al-khaṭṭ*).

The Arabic footnote text is set in DecoType Emiri, drawn by Mirjam Somers, based on the metal typeface in the naskh style that was cut for the 1924 Cairo edition of the Qur'an.

Both Arabic typefaces in this series are controlled by a dedicated font layout engine. ACE, the Arabic Calligraphic Engine, invented by Peter Somers, Thomas Milo, and Mirjam Somers of DecoType, first operational in 1985, pioneered the principle followed by later smart font layout technologies such as OpenType, which is used for all other typefaces in this series.

The Arabic text was set with WinSoft Tasmeem, a sophisticated user interface for DecoType ACE inside Adobe InDesign. Tasmeem was conceived and created by Thomas Milo (DecoType) and Pascal Rubini (WinSoft) in 2005.

The English text is set in Adobe Text, a new and versatile text typeface family designed by Robert Slimbach for Western (Latin, Greek, Cyrillic) typesetting. Its workhorse qualities make it perfect for a wide variety of applications, especially for longer passages of text where legibility and economy are important. Adobe Text bridges the gap between calligraphic Renaissance types of the 15th and 16th centuries and high-contrast Modern styles of the 18th century, taking many of its design cues from early post-Renaissance Baroque transitional types cut by designers such as Christoffel van Dijck, Nicolaus Kis, and William Caslon. While grounded in classical form, Adobe Text is also a statement of contemporary utilitarian design, well suited to a wide variety of print and on-screen applications.

Titles Published by the Library of Arabic Literature

For more details on individual titles, visit www.libraryofarabicliterature.org

Classical Arabic Literature: A Library of Arabic Literature Anthology
Selected and translated by Geert Jan van Gelder (**2012**)

A Treasury of Virtues: Sayings, Sermons, and Teachings of ʿAlī, by al-Qāḍī al-Quḍāʿī, with the **One Hundred Proverbs** attributed to al-Jāḥiẓ
Edited and translated by Tahera Qutbuddin (**2013**)

The Epistle on Legal Theory, by al-Shāfiʿī
Edited and translated by Joseph E. Lowry (**2013**)

Leg over Leg, by Aḥmad Fāris al-Shidyāq
Edited and translated by Humphrey Davies (**4 volumes; 2013–14**)

Virtues of the Imām Aḥmad ibn Ḥanbal, by Ibn al-Jawzī
Edited and translated by Michael Cooperson (**2 volumes; 2013–15**)

The Epistle of Forgiveness, by Abū l-ʿAlāʾ al-Maʿarrī
Edited and translated by Geert Jan van Gelder and Gregor Schoeler (**2 volumes; 2013–14**)

The Principles of Sufism, by ʿĀʾishah al-Bāʿūniyyah
Edited and translated by Th. Emil Homerin (**2014**)

The Expeditions: An Early Biography of Muḥammad, by Maʿmar ibn Rāshid
Edited and translated by Sean W. Anthony (**2014**)

Two Arabic Travel Books
Accounts of China and India, by Abū Zayd al-Sīrāfī
Edited and translated by Tim Mackintosh-Smith (**2014**)
Mission to the Volga, by Aḥmad ibn Faḍlān
Edited and translated by James Montgomery (**2014**)

Disagreements of the Jurists: A Manual of Islamic Legal Theory, by al-Qāḍī al-Nuʿmān
Edited and translated by Devin J. Stewart (2015)

Consorts of the Caliphs: Women and the Court of Baghdad, by Ibn al-Sāʿī
Edited by Shawkat M. Toorawa and translated by the Editors of the Library of Arabic Literature (2015)

What ʿĪsā ibn Hishām Told Us, by Muḥammad al-Muwayliḥī
Edited and translated by Roger Allen (**2 volumes; 2015**)

The Life and Times of Abū Tammām, by Abū Bakr Muḥammad ibn Yaḥyā al-Ṣūlī
Edited and translated by Beatrice Gruendler (2015)

The Sword of Ambition: Bureaucratic Rivalry in Medieval Egypt, by ʿUthmān ibn Ibrāhīm al-Nābulusī
Edited and translated by Luke Yarbrough (2016)

Brains Confounded by the Ode of Abū Shādūf Expounded, by Yūsuf al-Shirbīnī
Edited and translated by Humphrey Davies (**2 volumes; 2016**)

Light in the Heavens: Sayings of the Prophet Muḥammad, by al-Qāḍī al-Quḍāʿī
Edited and translated by Tahera Qutbuddin (2016)

Risible Rhymes, by Muḥammad ibn Maḥfūẓ al-Sanhūrī
Edited and translated by Humphrey Davies (2016)

A Hundred and One Nights
Edited and translated by Bruce Fudge (2016)

The Excellence of the Arabs, by Ibn Qutaybah
Edited by James E. Montgomery and Peter Webb
Translated by Sarah Bowen Savant and Peter Webb (2017)

Scents and Flavors: A Syrian Cookbook
Edited and translated by Charles Perry (2017)

Arabian Satire: Poetry from 18th-Century Najd, by Ḥmēdān al-Shwēʿir
Edited and translated by Marcel Kurpershoek (2017)

In Darfur: An Account of the Sultanate and Its People, by Muḥammad ibn ʿUmar al-Tūnisī
Edited and translated by Humphrey Davies (2 volumes; 2018)

War Songs, by ʿAntarah ibn Shaddād
Edited by James E. Montgomery
Translated by James E. Montgomery with Richard Sieburth (2018)

Arabian Romantic: Poems on Bedouin Life and Love, by ʿAbdallāh ibn Sbayyil
Edited and translated by Marcel Kurpershoek (2018)

Dīwān ʿAntarah ibn Shaddād: A Literary-Historical Study
By James E. Montgomery (2018)

Stories of Piety and Prayer: Deliverance Follows Adversity, by al-Muḥassin ibn ʿAlī al-Tanūkhī
Edited and translated by Julia Bray (2019)

The Philosopher Responds: An Intellectual Correspondence from the Tenth Century, by Abū Ḥayyān al-Tawḥīdī and Abū ʿAlī Miskawayh
Edited by Bilal Orfali and Maurice A. Pomerantz
Translated by Sophia Vasalou and James E. Montgomery (2 volumes; 2019)

Tajrīd sayf al-himmah li-stikhrāj mā fī dhimmat al-dhimmah: A Scholarly Edition of ʿUthmān ibn Ibrāhīm al-Nābulusī's Text
By Luke Yarbrough (2020)

The Discourses: Reflections on History, Sufism, Theology, and Literature—Volume One, by al-Ḥasan al-Yūsī
Edited and translated by Justin Stearns (2020)

Impostures, by al-Ḥarīrī
Translated by Michael Cooperson (2020)

Maqāmāt Abī Zayd al-Sarūjī, by al-Ḥarīrī
Edited by Michael Cooperson (2020)

The Yoga Sutras of Patañjali, by Abū Rayḥān al-Bīrūnī
Edited and translated by Mario Kozah (2020)

The Book of Charlatans, by Jamāl al-Dīn ʿAbd al-Raḥīm al-Jawbarī
Edited by Manuela Dengler
Translated by Humphrey Davies (2020)

A Physician on the Nile, by ʿAbd al-Laṭīf al-Baghdādī
Edited and translated by Tim Mackintosh-Smith (**2021**)

The Book of Travels, by Ḥannā Diyāb
Edited by Johannes Stephan
Translated by Elias Muhanna (**2 volumes; 2021**)

Kalīlah and Dimnah: Fables of Virtue and Vice, by Ibn al-Muqaffaʿ
Edited by Michael Fishbein
Translated by Michael Fishbein and James E. Montgomery (**2021**)

English-only Paperbacks

Leg over Leg, by Aḥmad Fāris al-Shidyāq (**2 volumes; 2015**)
The Expeditions: An Early Biography of Muḥammad, by Maʿmar ibn Rāshid (**2015**)
The Epistle on Legal Theory: A Translation of al-Shāfiʿī's *Risālah*, by al-Shāfiʿī (**2015**)
The Epistle of Forgiveness, by Abū l-ʿAlāʾ al-Maʿarrī (**2016**)
The Principles of Sufism, by ʿĀʾishah al-Bāʿūniyyah (**2016**)
A Treasury of Virtues: Sayings, Sermons, and Teachings of ʿAlī, by al-Qāḍī al-Quḍāʿī, with the **One Hundred Proverbs** attributed to al-Jāḥiẓ (**2016**)
The Life of Ibn Ḥanbal, by Ibn al-Jawzī (**2016**)
Mission to the Volga, by Ibn Faḍlān (**2017**)
Accounts of China and India, by Abū Zayd al-Sīrāfī (**2017**)
A Hundred and One Nights (**2017**)
Consorts of the Caliphs: Women and the Court of Baghdad, by Ibn al-Sāʿī (**2017**)
Disagreements of the Jurists: A Manual of Islamic Legal Theory, by al-Qāḍī al-Nuʿmān (**2017**)
What ʿĪsā ibn Hishām Told Us, by Muḥammad al-Muwayliḥī (**2018**)
War Songs, by ʿAntarah ibn Shaddād (**2018**)
The Life and Times of Abū Tammām, by Abū Bakr Muḥammad ibn Yaḥyā al-Ṣūlī (**2018**)
The Sword of Ambition, by ʿUthmān ibn Ibrāhīm al-Nābulusī (**2019**)
Brains Confounded by the Ode of Abū Shādūf Expounded: Volume One, by Yūsuf al-Shirbīnī (**2019**)

Brains Confounded by the Ode of Abū Shādūf Expounded: Volume Two, by Yūsuf al-Shirbīnī and **Risible Rhymes**, by Muḥammad ibn Maḥfūẓ al-Sanhūrī (2019)

The Excellence of the Arabs, by Ibn Qutaybah (2019)

Light in the Heavens: Sayings of the Prophet Muḥammad, by al-Qāḍī al-Quḍāʿī (2019)

Scents and Flavors: A Syrian Cookbook (2020)

Arabian Satire: Poetry from 18th-Century Najd, by Ḥmēdān al-Shwēʿir (2020)

In Darfur: An Account of the Sultanate and Its People, by Muḥammad al-Tūnisī (2020)

Arabian Romantic, by ʿAbdallāh ibn Sbayyil (2020)

The Philosopher Reponds, by Abū Ḥayyān al-Tawḥīdī and Abū ʿAlī Miskawayh (2021)

Impostures, by al-Ḥarīrī (2021)

The Discourses: Reflections on History, Sufism, Theology, and Literature—Volume One, by al-Ḥasan al-Yūsī (2021)

About the Editor–Translators

Michael Fishbein studied English literature at Columbia and at Yale University, and Arabic as a CASA fellow at the American University in Cairo. He obtained a Ph.D. in Arabic from the University of California at Los Angeles in 1988, and taught Arabic language and literature at that university until his retirement in 2007. Interested primarily in Arabic historical writings and narrative, he contributed to the 1994 translation of the works of the Egyptian historian al-Jabartī, translated Volumes VIII, XXI, and XXXI of the SUNY *History of al-Ṭabarī*, and contributed several sections to the Brill *Works of Ibn Wāḍiḥ al-Yaʿqūbī*. He lives in Los Angeles.

James E. Montgomery is Sir Thomas Adams's Professor of Arabic, Fellow of Trinity Hall at the University of Cambridge, and an Executive Editor of the Library of Arabic Literature. His latest publications are *Loss Sings*, a collaboration with the celebrated Scottish artist Alison Watt, and *Dīwān ʿAntarah ibn Shaddād: A Literary-Historical Study*.

www.ingramcontent.com/pod-product-compliance
Lightning Source LLC
Chambersburg PA
CBHW020302030826
48979CB00027B/1993/J

* 9 7 8 1 4 7 9 8 0 6 5 3 9 *